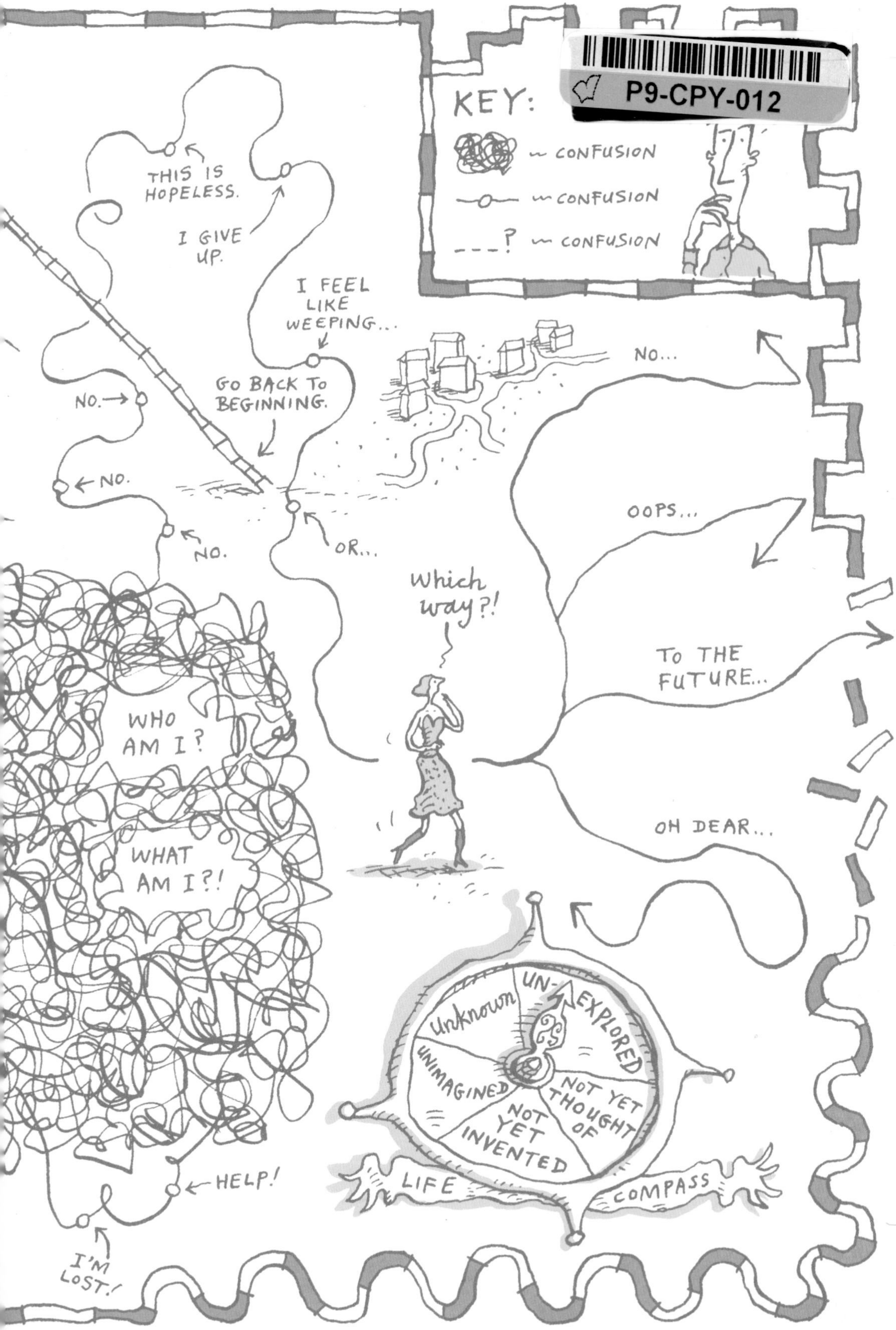
KEY:
~ CONFUSION
~ CONFUSION
~ CONFUSION
THIS IS HOPELESS.
I GIVE UP.
I FEEL LIKE WEEPING...
GO BACK TO BEGINNING.
NO.
NO.
NO.
OR...
NO...
OOPS...
Which way?!
TO THE FUTURE...
OH DEAR...
WHO AM I?
WHAT AM I?!
HELP!
I'M LOST!
Unknown
UN-EXPLORED
UNIMAGINED
NOT YET THOUGHT OF
NOT YET INVENTED
LIFE
COMPASS

DRAGMAN

DRAGMAN

a Novel

Steven Appleby

Watercolour by Nicola Sherring

Metropolitan Books
Henry Holt and Company   New York

Friday

The year – – – –
The place – – – – – –

5·37 am

IT IS ELEPHANT LIGHT, that strange, smoky time just before dawn when the burnt-black sky is shot through with gashes of vivid acid-yellow and green. 'Fools gather at elephant light,' goes the saying, and people repeat it without knowing what it means and without meaning anything by it. Elephant light is particularly beautiful over the sea, and this morning slashes of colour writhe across the sky, reflecting in the black, glistening mudflats of the estuary like neon. The flickering yellow and green is complemented perfectly by the twinkling blue lights of two police cars and an ambulance parked near a slipway.

Meanwhile, a few miles away a man drives south tapping his fingers to a hidden tune repeating inside his head. Perhaps he's the person who dialled 999. Or maybe he's the killer, slip-slipping calmly away from the scene of the crime … who knows? Only he.

Back at the estuary police officers stretch crime scene tape between boats pulled up onto the slipway while others gather round a body lying face down in the mud.

A woman, it appears, from the bra strap across her back and the matching panties pulled down to just above her knees. A police photographer takes pictures while an ambulance man consults the small device he has used to scan her body.

'Her soul is missing,' he says. 'Just like the others.'

And just like the others, when the photographer has finished and the ambulance crew turn her over it becomes clear, from the penis and the hairs on her chest, that she is, in fact, a he.

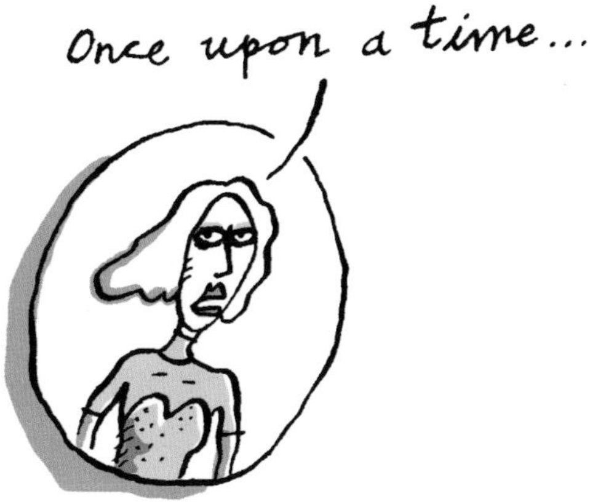
Once upon a time...

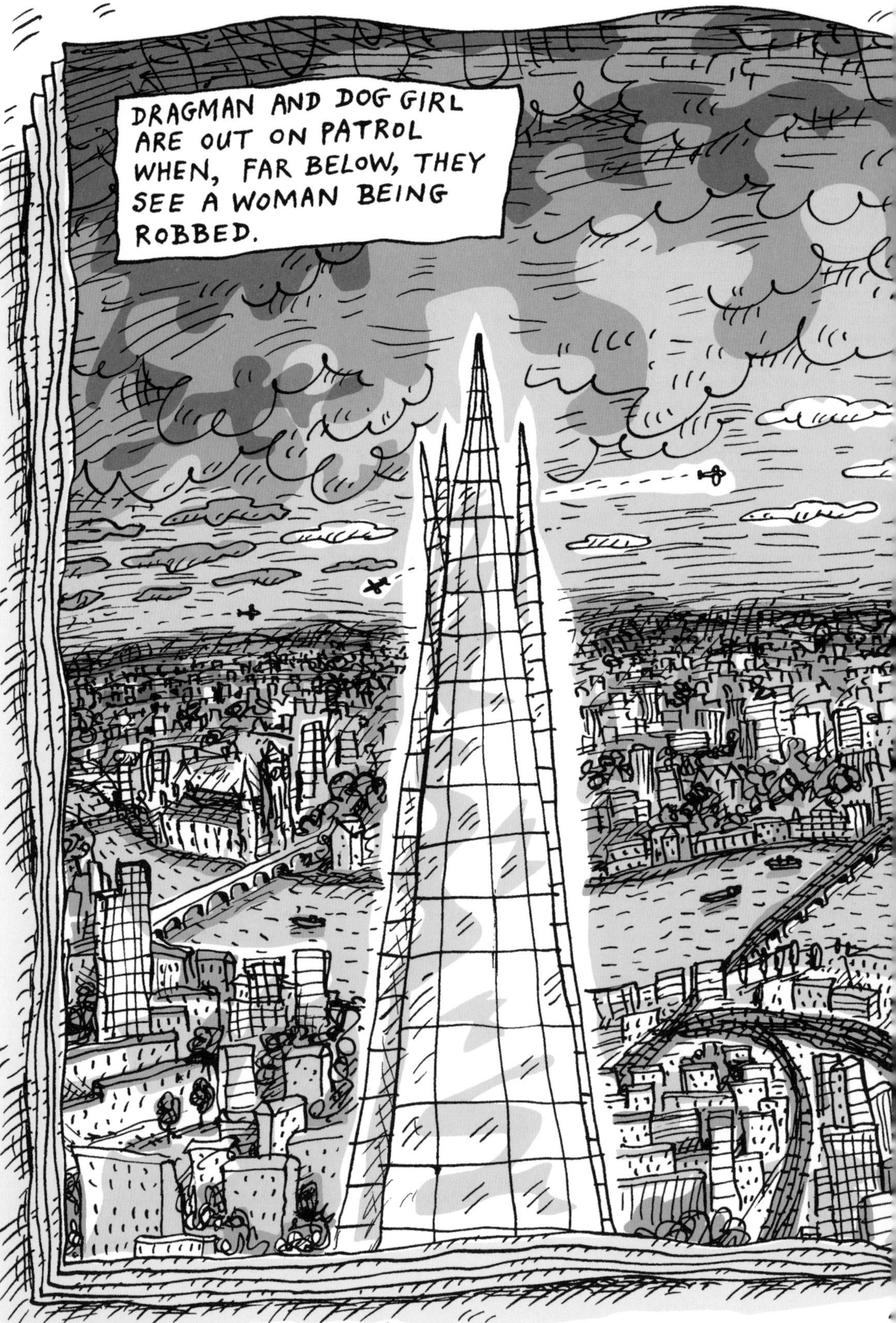
DRAGMAN AND DOG GIRL ARE OUT ON PATROL WHEN, FAR BELOW, THEY SEE A WOMAN BEING ROBBED.

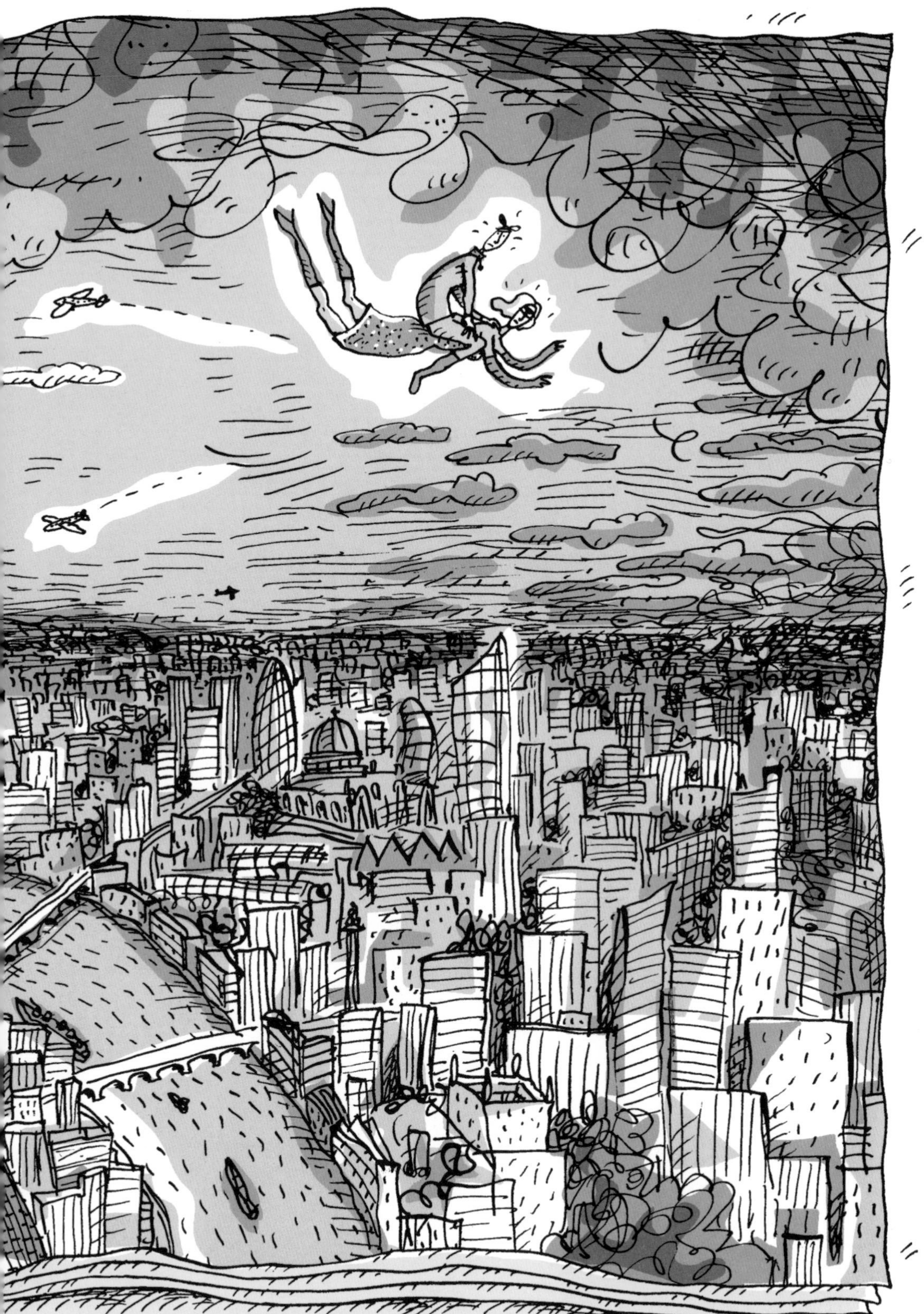

Unique archive copy of proposed Dragman comic book, issue 1. Never published.

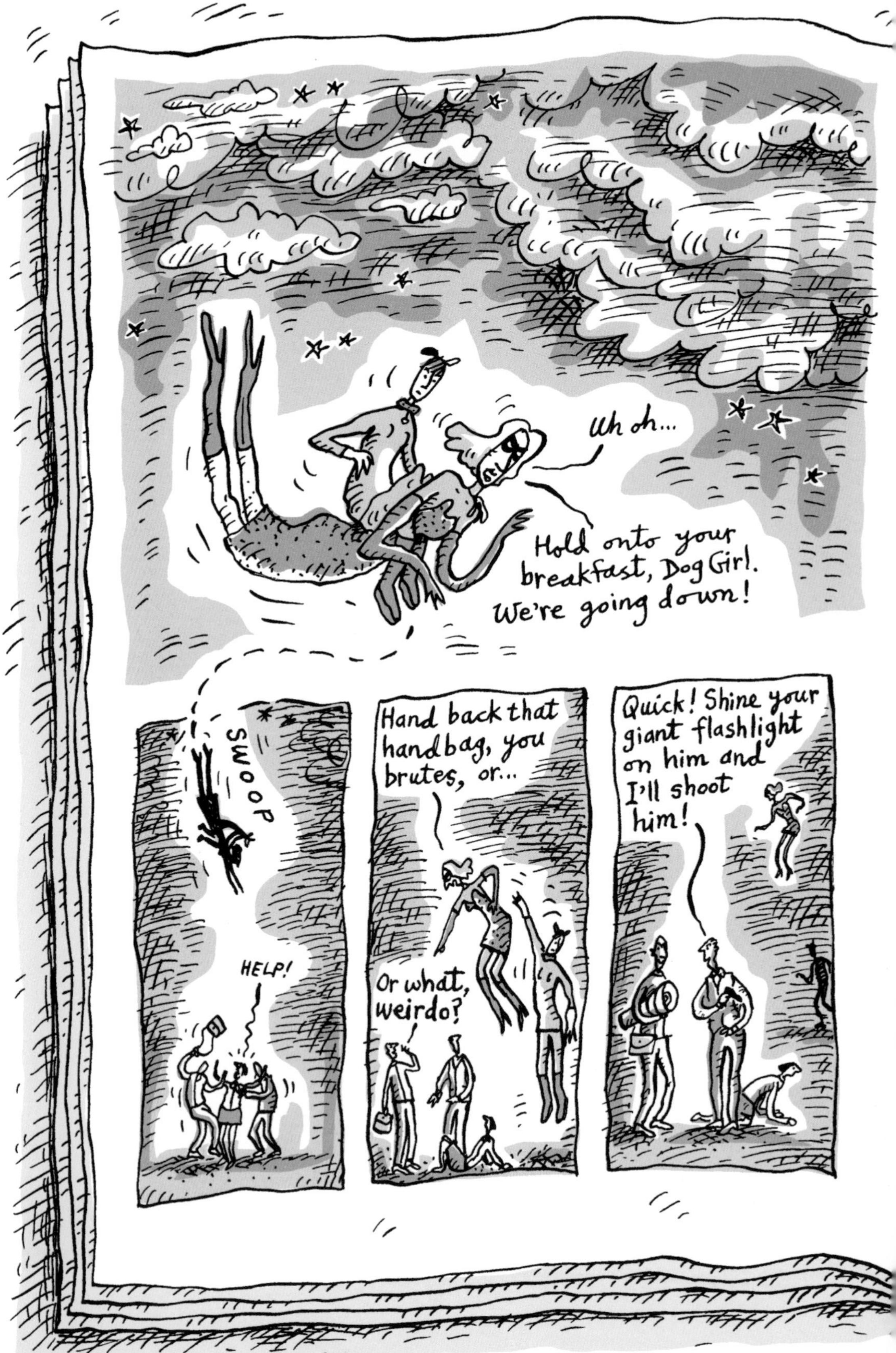
Uh oh...
Hold onto your breakfast, Dog Girl. We're going down!
SWOOP
HELP!
Hand back that handbag, you brutes, or...
Or what, weirdo?
Quick! Shine your giant flashlight on him and I'll shoot him!

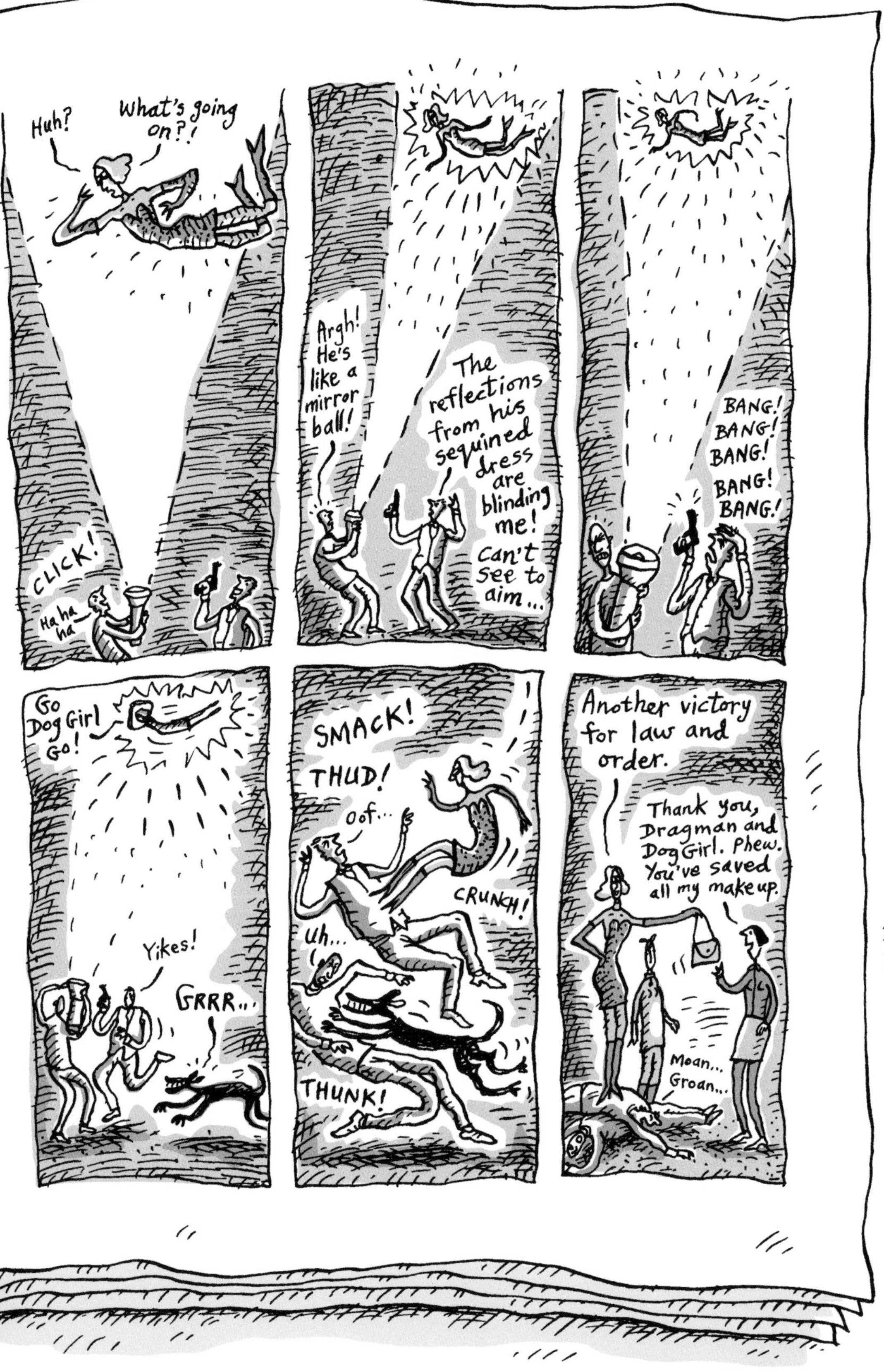
Huh?
What's going on?!
CLICK!
Ha ha ha
Argh! He's like a mirror ball!
The reflections from his sequined dress are blinding me!
Can't see to aim...
BANG! BANG! BANG!
BANG! BANG!
Go Dog Girl Go!
Yikes!
GRRR..
SMACK!
THUD!
Oof...
CRUNCH!
Uh...
THUNK!
Another victory for law and order.
Thank you, Dragman and Dog Girl. Phew. You've saved all my make up.
Moan... Groan...

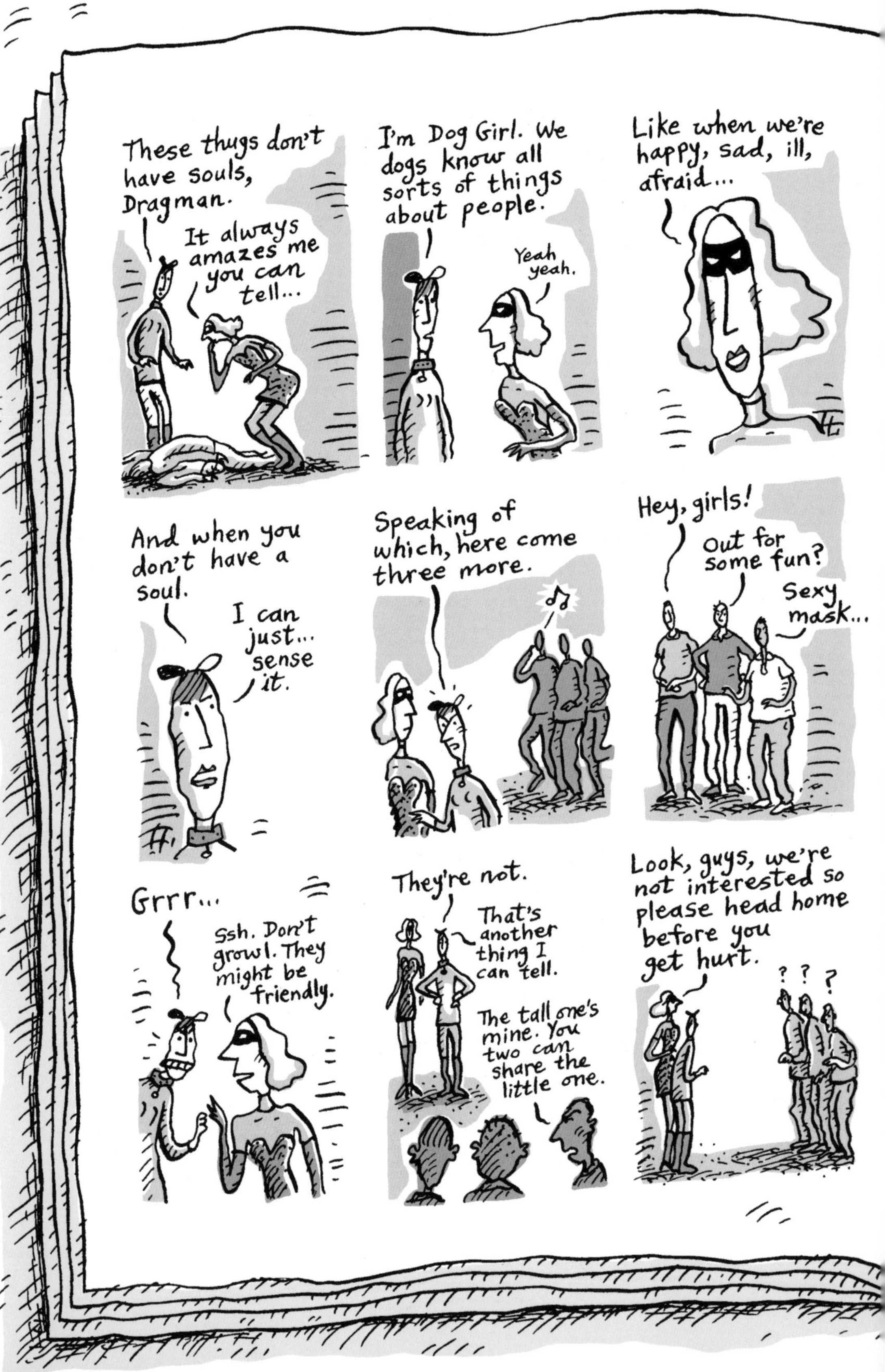
These thugs don't have souls, Dragman.
It always amazes me you can tell...
I'm Dog Girl. We dogs know all sorts of things about people.
Yeah yeah.
Like when we're happy, sad, ill, afraid...
And when you don't have a soul.
I can just... sense it.
Speaking of which, here come three more.
Hey, girls!
Out for some fun?
Sexy mask...
Grrr...
Ssh. Don't growl. They might be friendly.
They're not.
That's another thing I can tell.
The tall one's mine. You two can share the little one.
Look, guys, we're not interested so please head home before you get hurt.
? ? ?

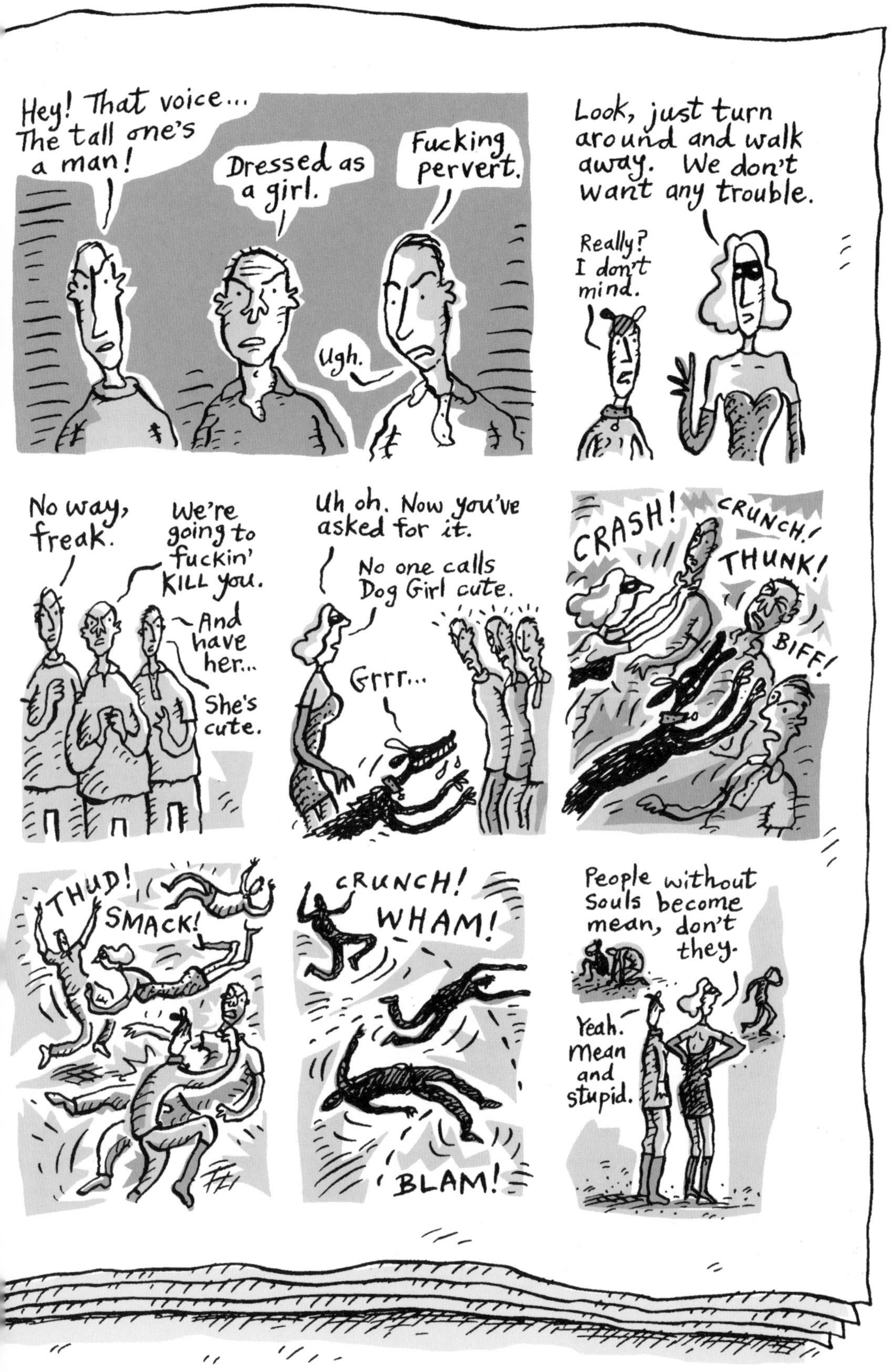

Hey! That voice... The tall one's a man!
Dressed as a girl.
Fucking pervert.
Ugh.
Look, just turn around and walk away. We don't want any trouble.
Really? I don't mind.
No way, freak.
We're going to fuckin' KILL you.
And have her...
She's cute.
Uh oh. Now you've asked for it.
No one calls Dog Girl cute.
Grrr...
CRASH!
CRUNCH!
THUNK!
BIFF!
THUD!
SMACK!
CRUNCH!
WHAM!
BLAM!
People without Souls become mean, don't they.
Yeah. Mean and stupid.

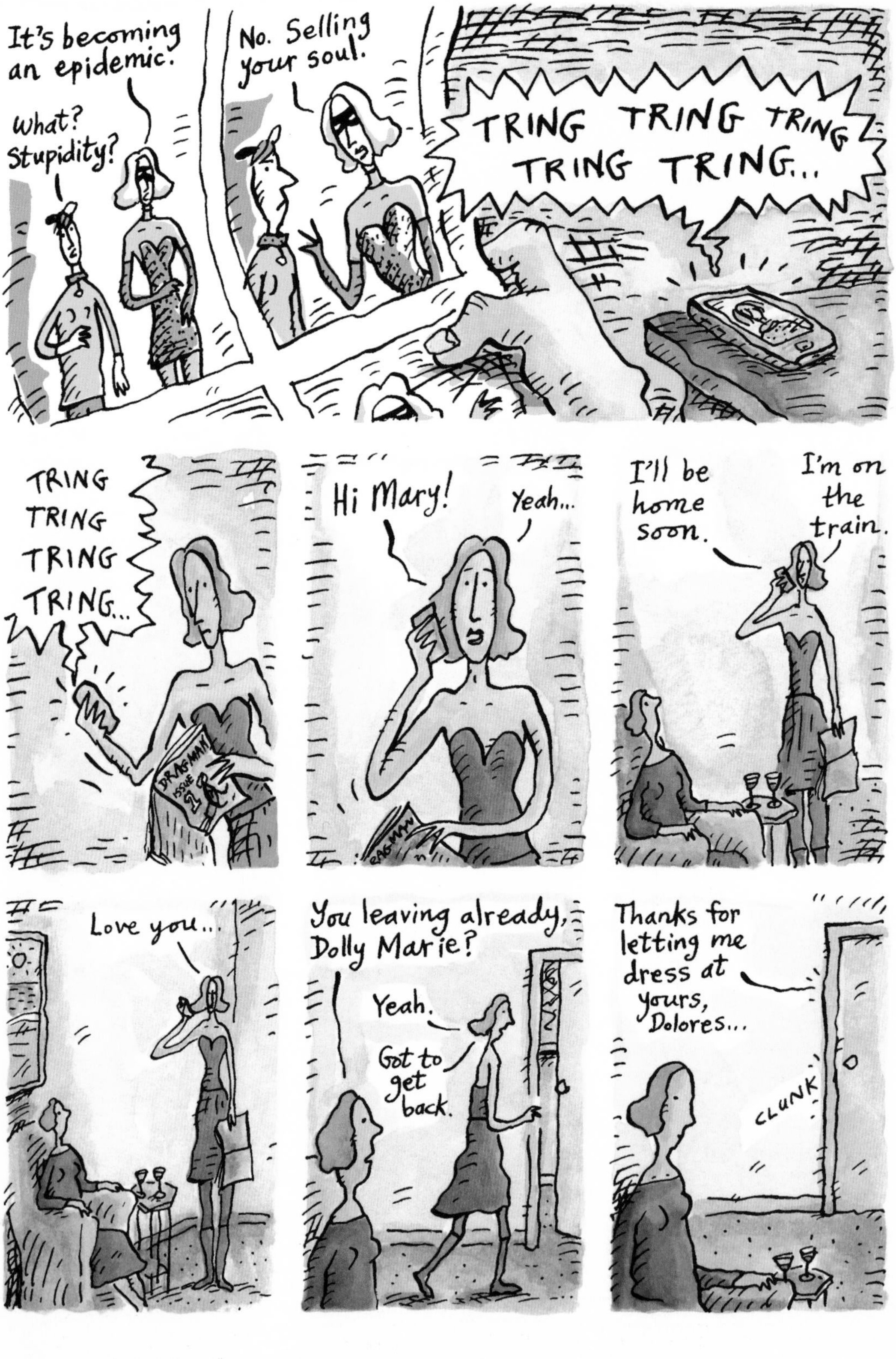

It's becoming an epidemic.
What? Stupidity?
No. Selling your soul.
TRING TRING TRING TRING TRING...
TRING TRING TRING TRING...
DRAGMAN ISSUE 2
Hi Mary!
Yeah...
I'll be home soon.
I'm on the train.
Love you...
You leaving already, Dolly Marie?
Yeah.
Got to get back.
Thanks for letting me dress at yours, Dolores...
CLUNK

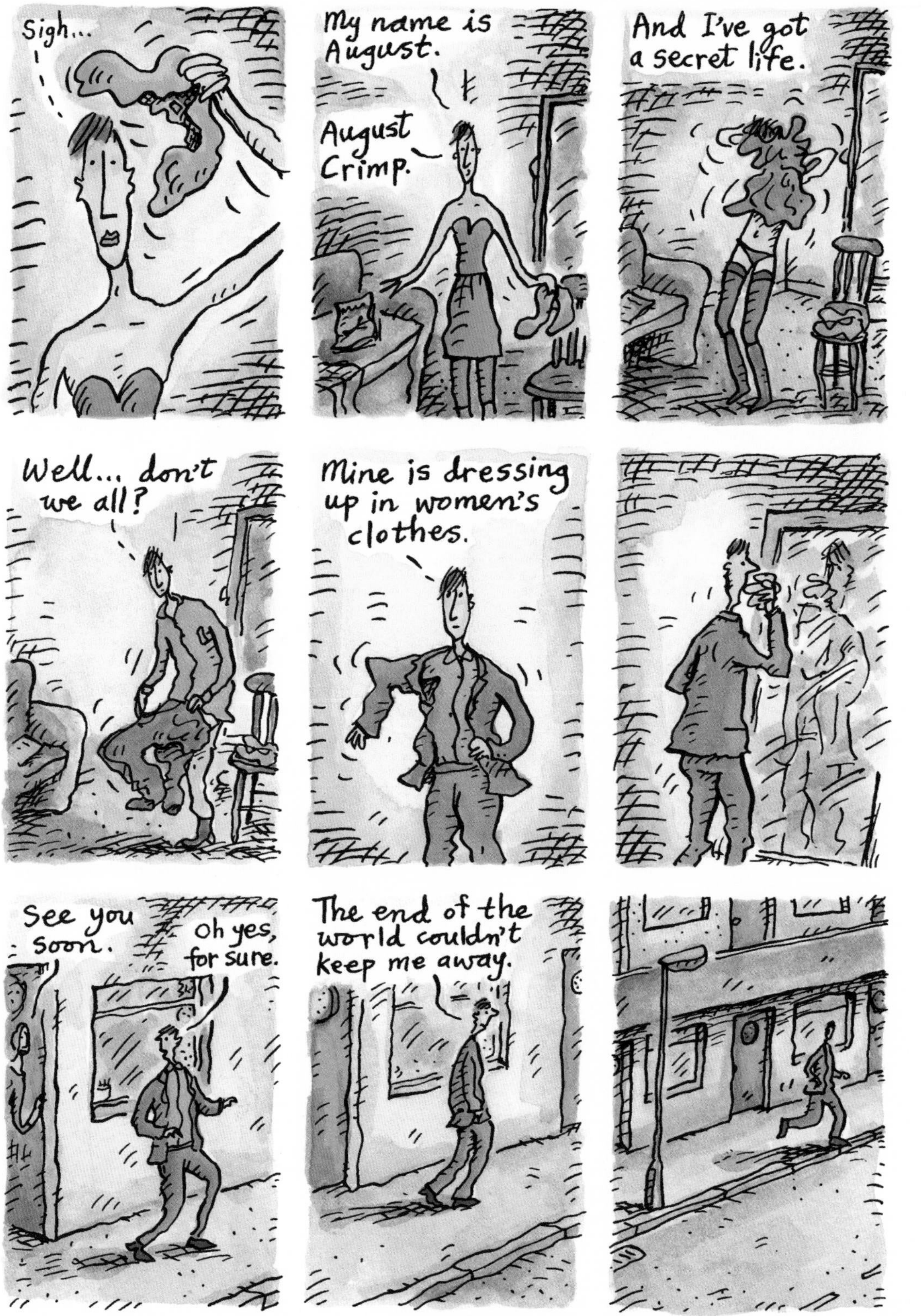
Sigh...
My name is August.
August Crimp.
And I've got a secret life.
Well... don't we all?
Mine is dressing up in women's clothes.
See you soon.
Oh yes, for sure.
The end of the world couldn't keep me away.

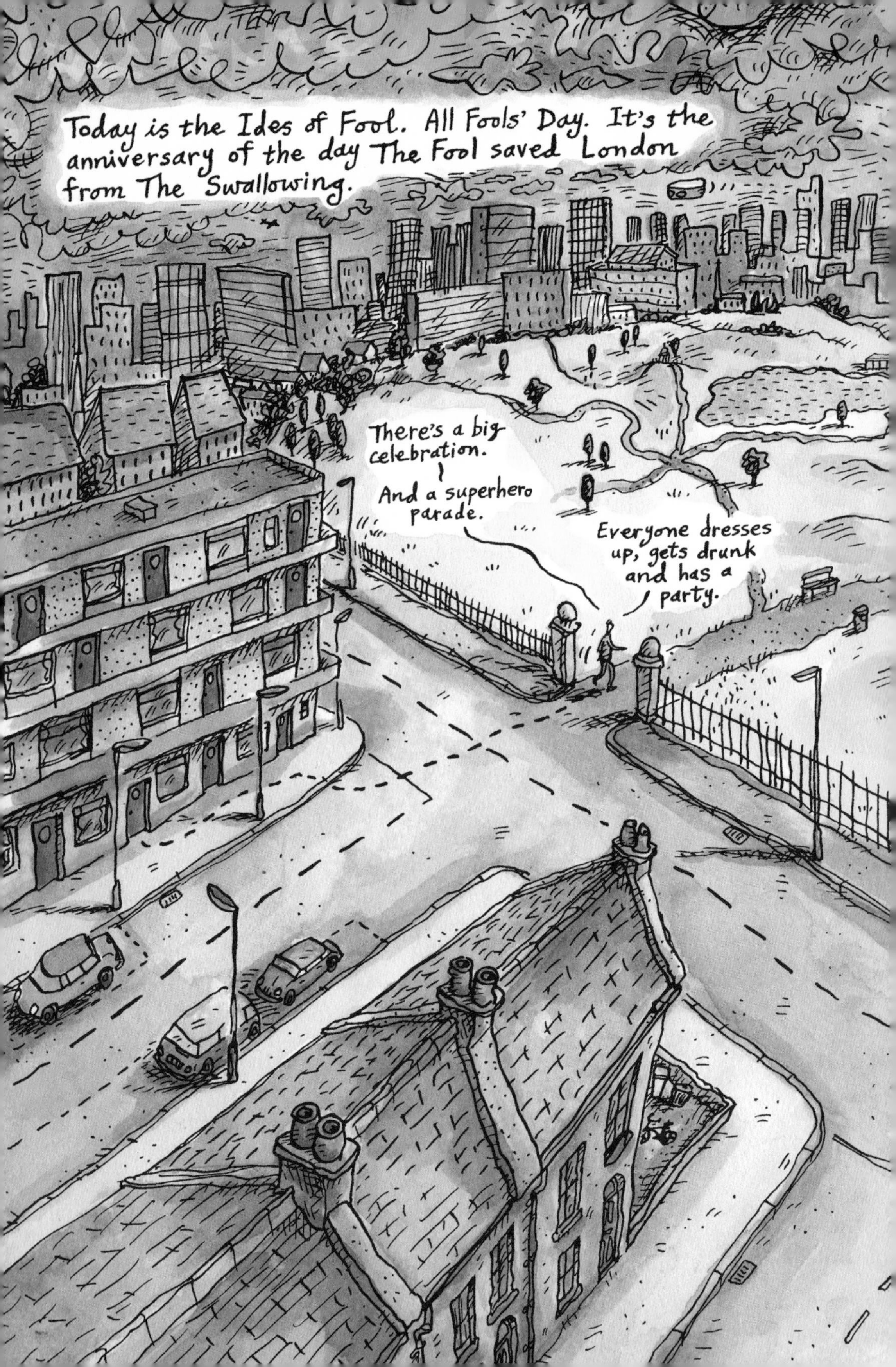
Today is the Ides of Fool. All Fools' Day. It's the anniversary of the day The Fool saved London from The Swallowing.
There's a big celebration.
And a superhero parade.
Everyone dresses up, gets drunk and has a party.

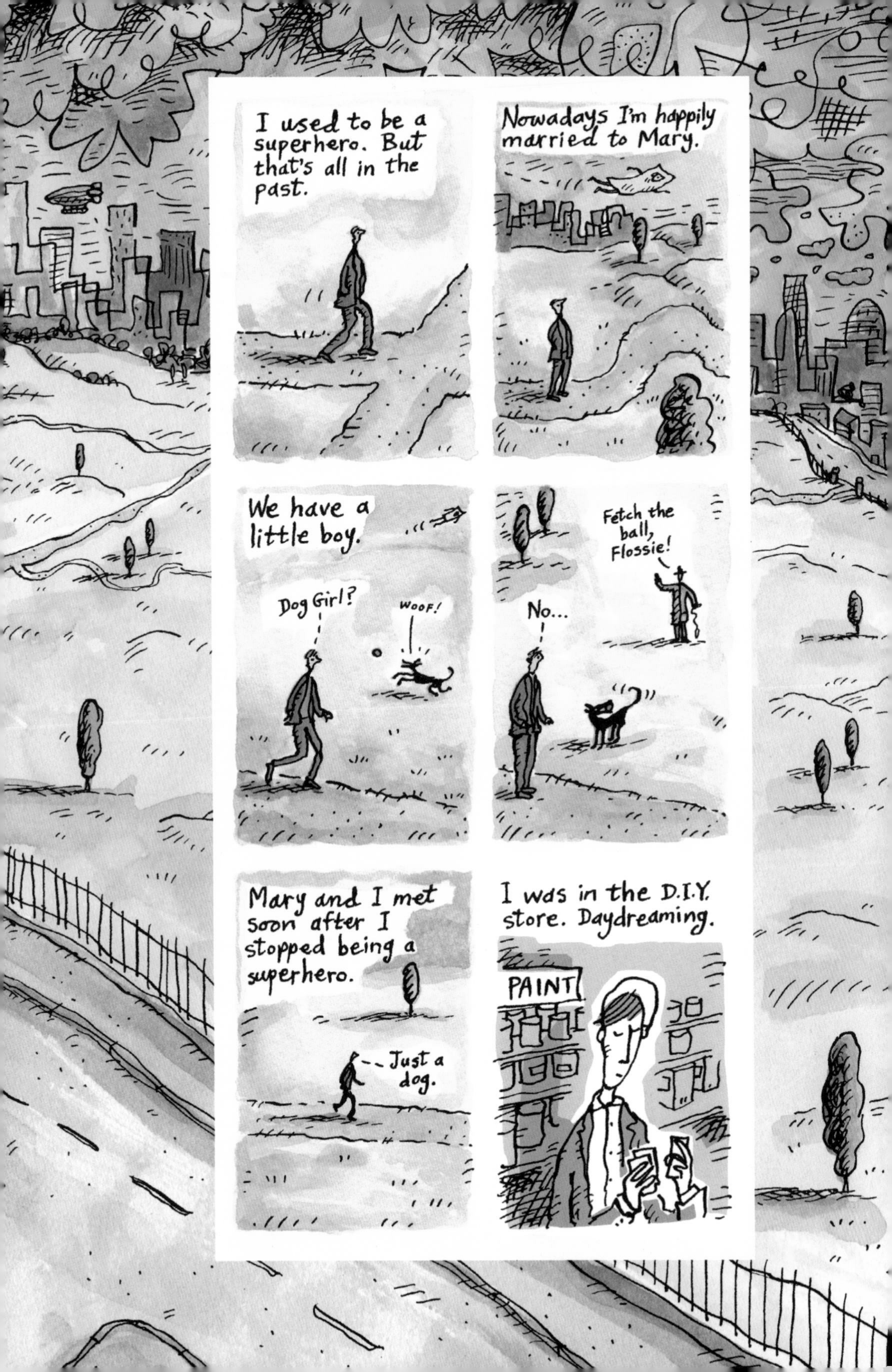
I used to be a superhero. But that's all in the past.
Nowadays I'm happily married to Mary.
We have a little boy.
Dog Girl?
WOOF!
Fetch the ball, Flossie!
No...
Mary and I met soon after I stopped being a superhero.
Just a dog.
I was in the D.I.Y. store. Daydreaming.
PAINT

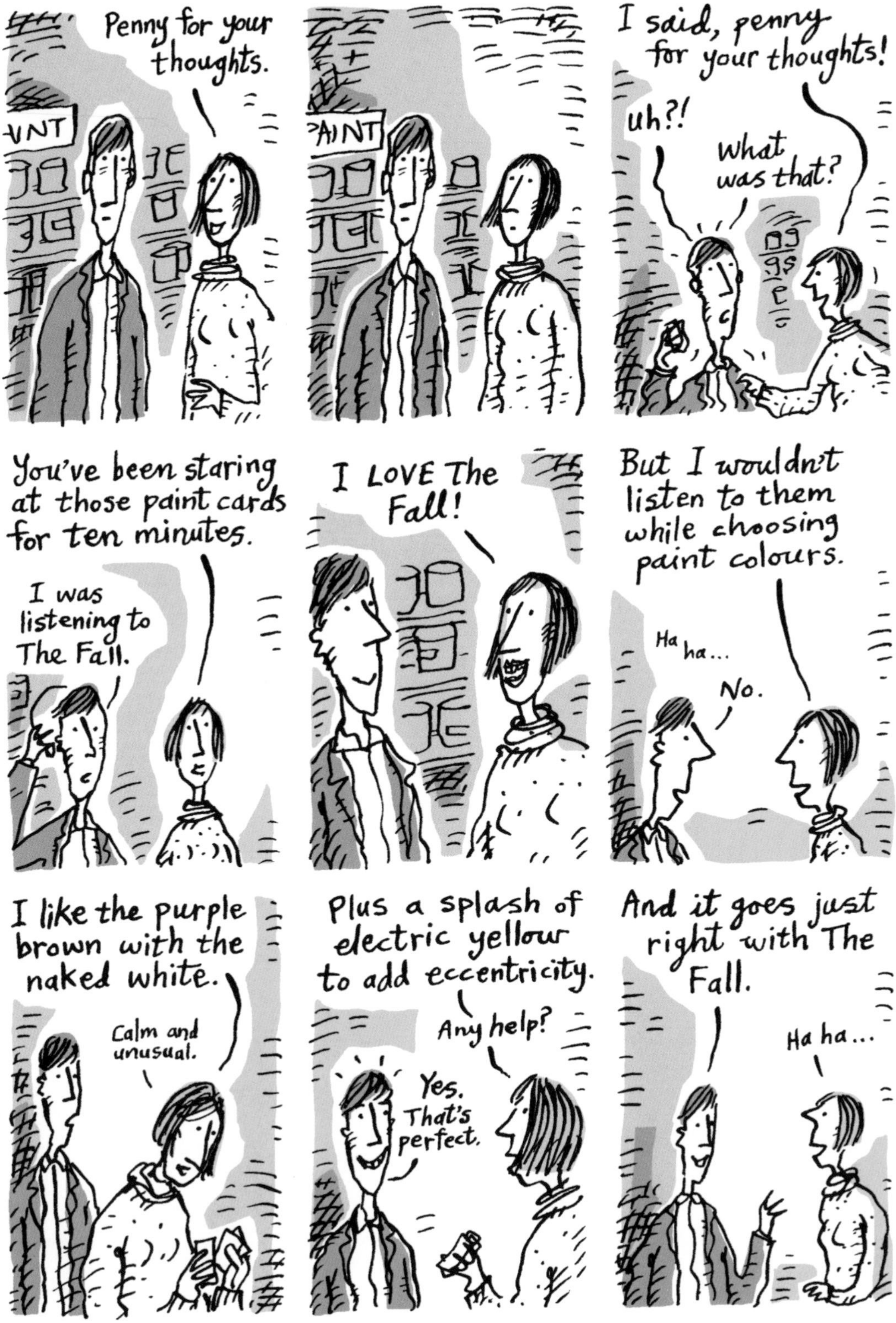

Penny for your thoughts.
I said, penny for your thoughts!
uh?!
What was that?
You've been staring at those paint cards for ten minutes.
I was listening to The Fall.
I LOVE The Fall!
But I wouldn't listen to them while choosing paint colours.
Ha ha...
No.
I like the purple brown with the naked white.
Calm and unusual.
Plus a splash of electric yellow to add eccentricity.
Any help?
Yes. That's perfect.
And it goes just right with The Fall.
Ha ha...

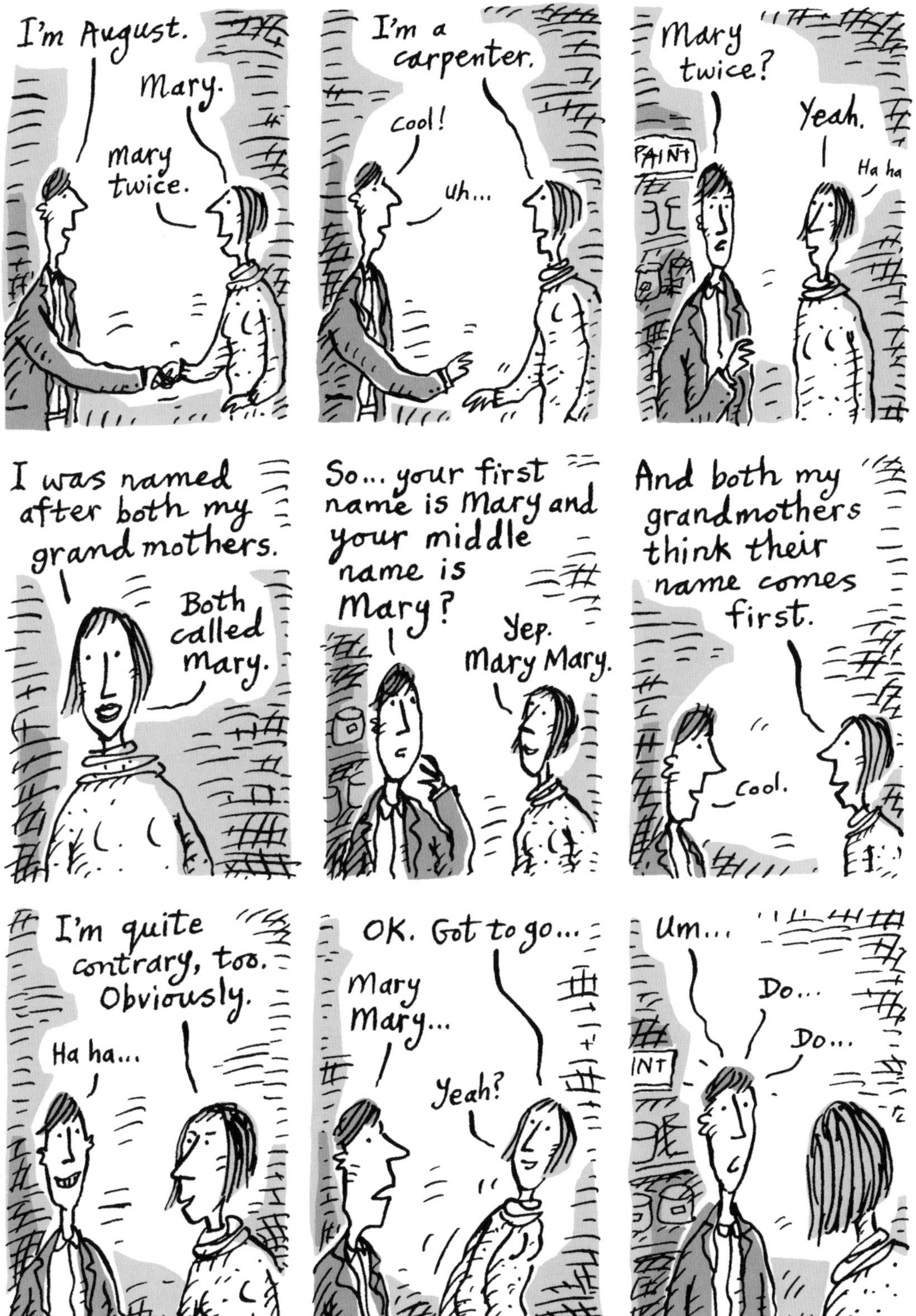
I'm August.
Mary.
Mary twice.
I'm a carpenter.
Cool!
Uh...
Mary twice?
Yeah.
Ha ha
PAINT
I was named after both my grandmothers.
Both called Mary.
So... your first name is Mary and your middle name is Mary?
Yep. Mary Mary.
And both my grandmothers think their name comes first.
Cool.
I'm quite contrary, too. Obviously.
Ha ha...
OK. Got to go...
Mary Mary...
Yeah?
Um...
Do...
Do...
INT

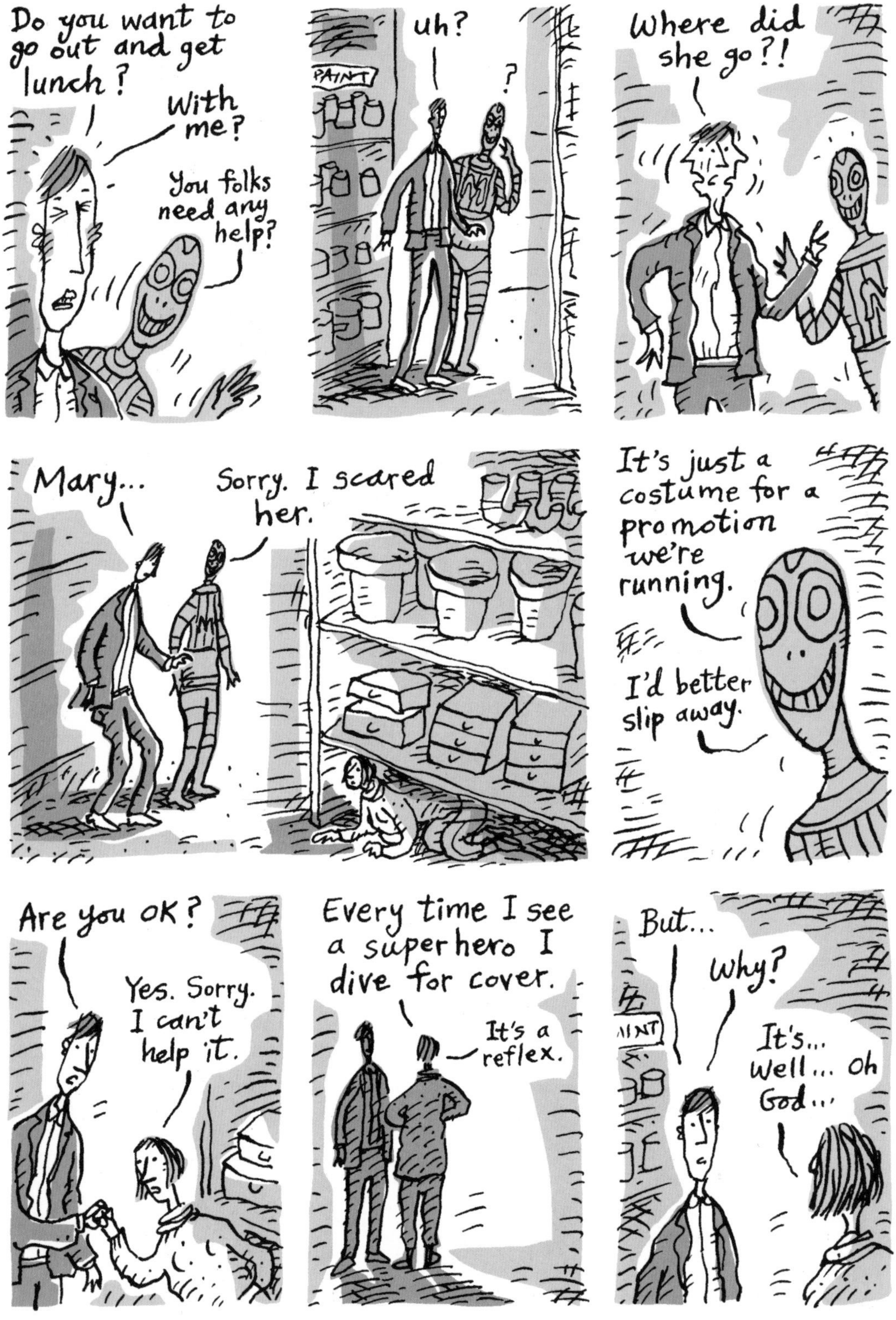
Do you want to go out and get lunch?
With me?
You folks need any help?
uh?
?
PAINT
Where did she go?!
Mary...
Sorry. I scared her.
It's just a costume for a promotion we're running.
I'd better slip away.
Are you OK?
Yes. Sorry. I can't help it.
Every time I see a superhero I dive for cover.
It's a reflex.
But...
Why?
It's... Well... Oh God...

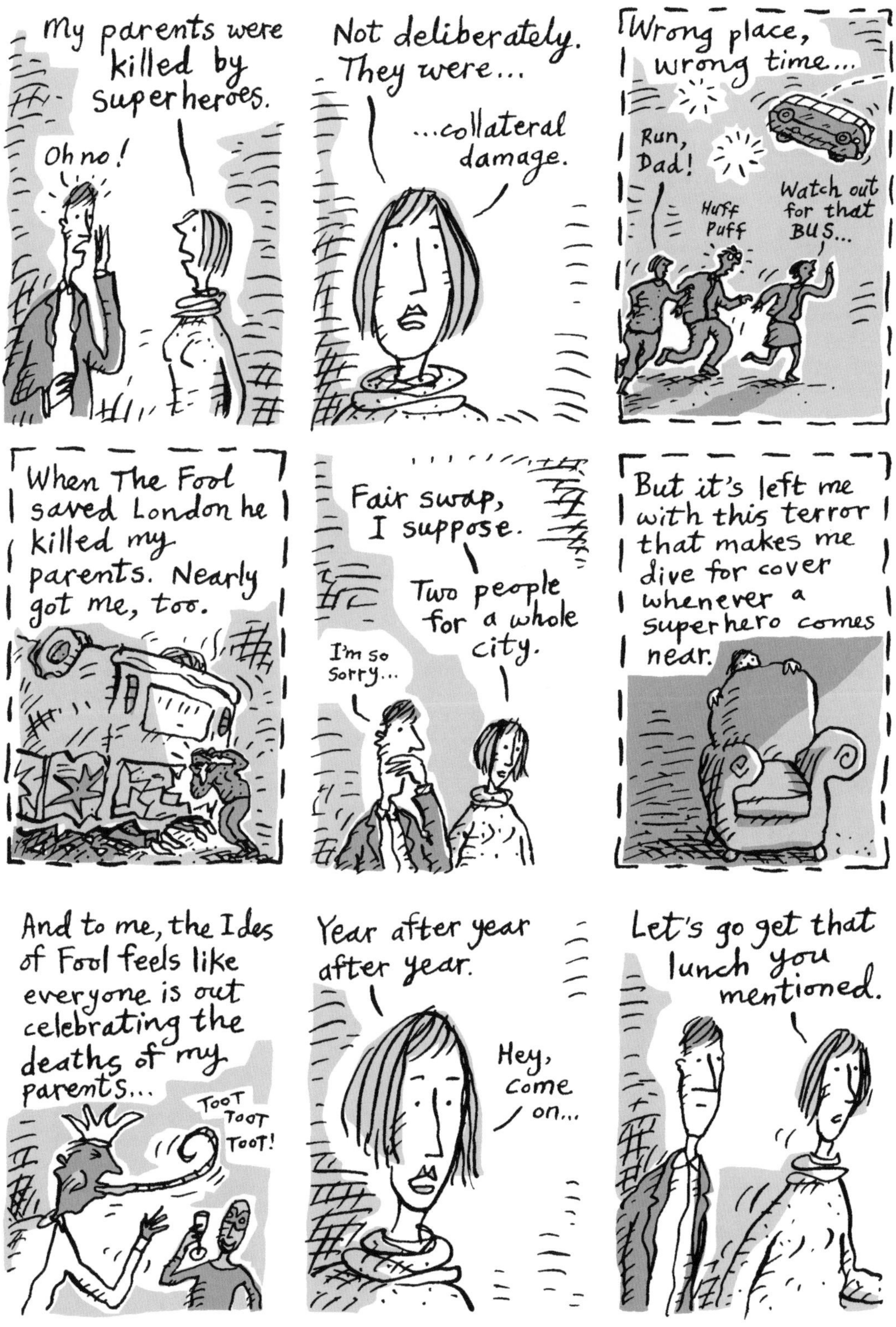
My parents were killed by superheroes.
Oh no!
Not deliberately. They were...
...collateral damage.
Wrong place, wrong time...
Run, Dad!
Huff Puff
Watch out for that BUS...
When The Fool saved London he killed my parents. Nearly got me, too.
Fair swap, I suppose.
Two people for a whole city.
I'm so sorry...
But it's left me with this terror that makes me dive for cover whenever a superhero comes near.
And to me, the Ides of Fool feels like everyone is out celebrating the deaths of my parents...
TOOT TOOT TOOT!
Year after year after year.
Hey, come on...
Let's go get that lunch you mentioned.

6·22 pm

THE TIDE IS IN and the police tape droops into the
water, rising and falling as a fresh breeze sweeps in off
the sea, rocking the boats on their moorings. Waves
slap-slop up and down the grooves in the concrete
slipway while far out in the estuary birds bob on the
surface in dotted flocks. High overhead an airliner
from Schiphol or Hamburg crosses the coastline and
heads up the Thames on the final stage of its journey
to City Airport. The plane reflects in a car windscreen
– a tiny flying machine crawling across a cloud-spotted
glass sky – while in the car a man with a ghost inside
him sits gazing out at the vast expanse of sea. But he's
not looking at the water, he's staring beneath it, at the
site where, last night, the dead trans-woman lay still
and silent in the mud. He can see her clearly in his
mind's eye despite the fact that the site has vanished
beneath the waves, because he is her killer and she is
the ghost, her soul seething and screaming with fury
within his cells.

He enjoys her shock and pain and anger and he
smiles, because she is doing the cellular equivalent of
pacing up and down exploring every wall and rattling
the door as she searches for a way out ... but there
isn't one.

After a few minutes the man with the ghost inside him starts the engine, turns the car and drives back in the direction whence he came. Back towards the yellow-green skies of London, shivering deliciously as the ghost wriggles and jiggles and giggles inside him, lighting up his cells with a billion little sparks like a huge city lights up in the dark.

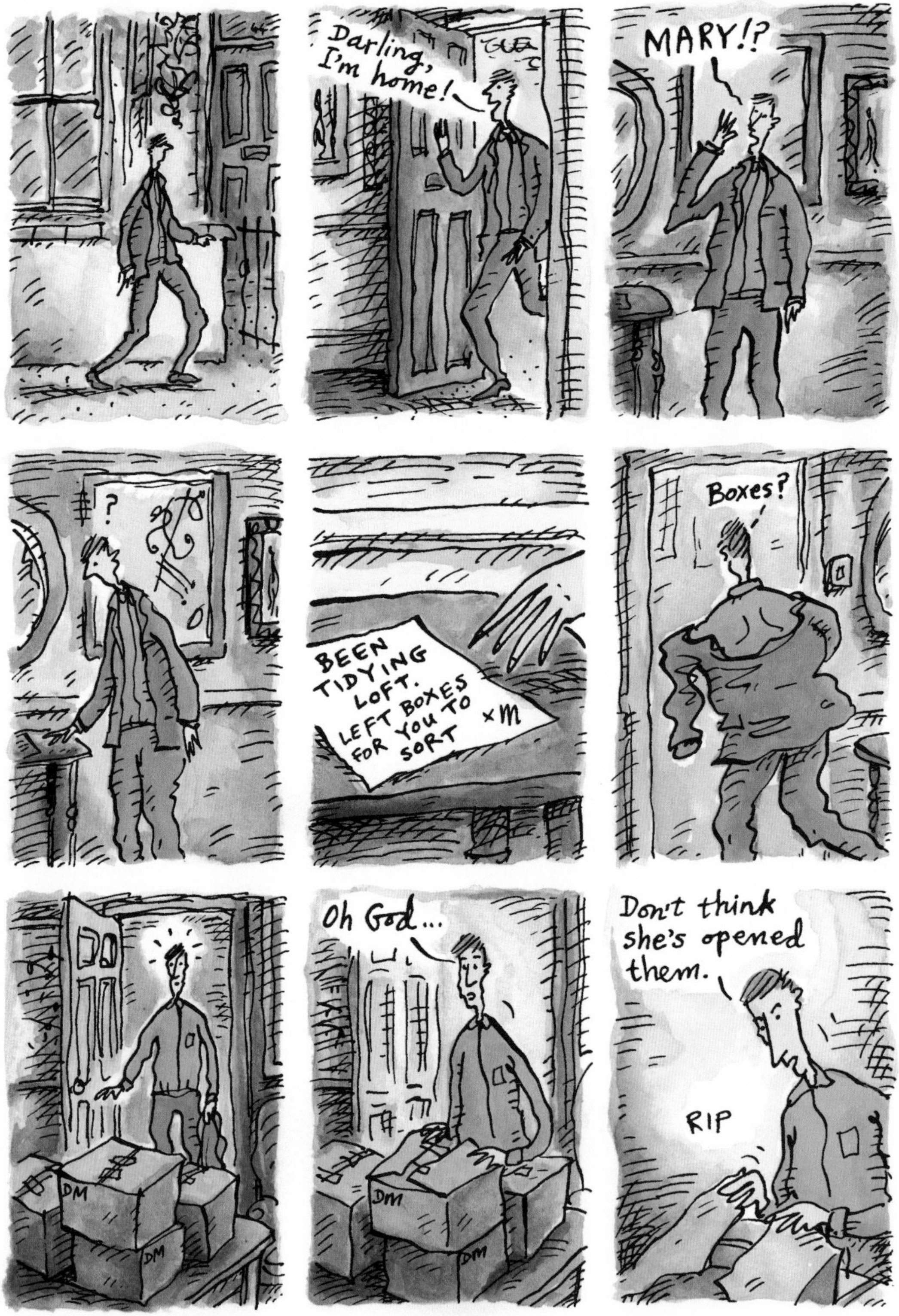
Darling, I'm home!
MARY!?
?
BEEN TIDYING LOFT. LEFT BOXES FOR YOU TO SORT ×M
Boxes?
DM
DM
Oh God...
DM
DM
Don't think she's opened them.
RIP

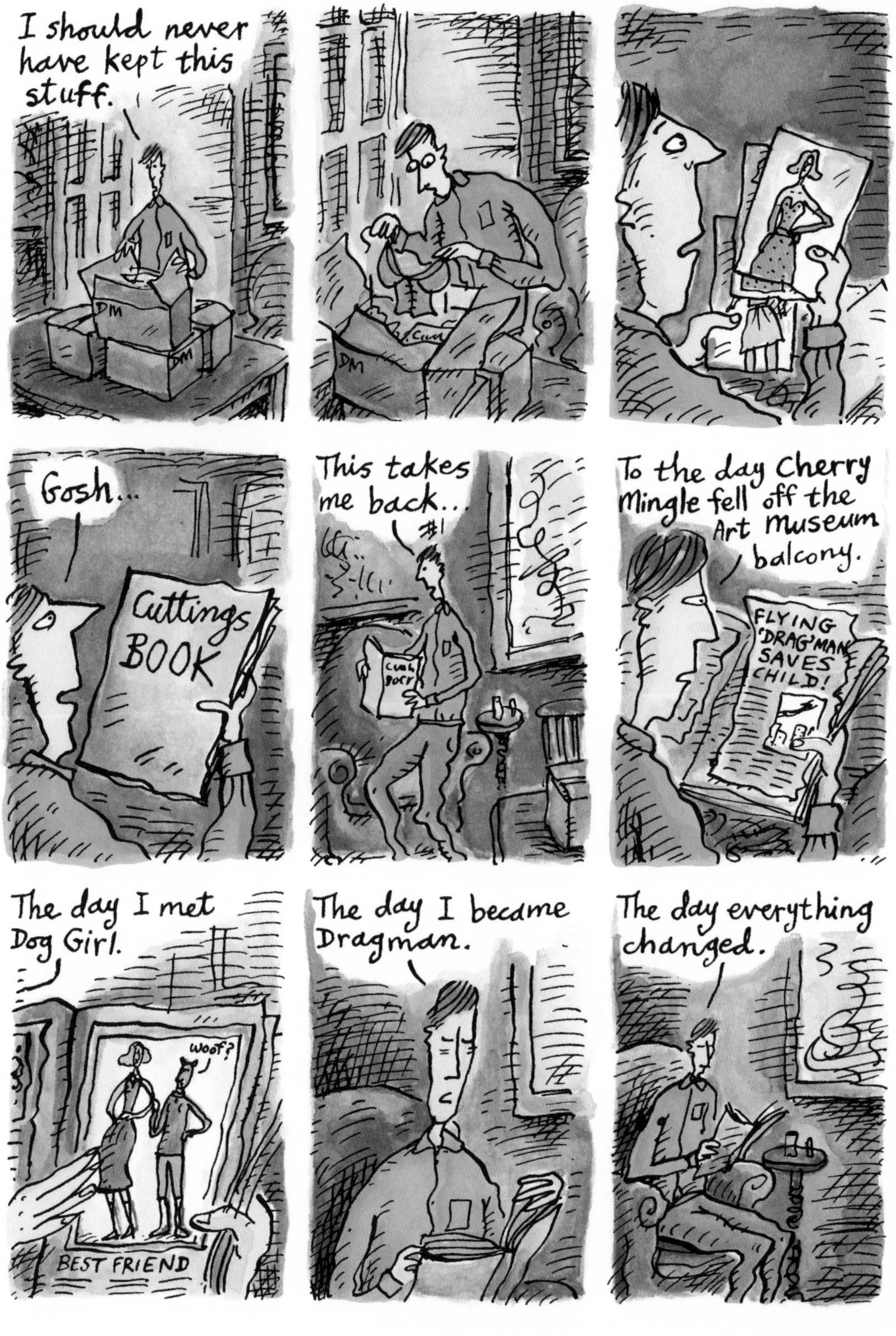
I should never have kept this stuff.
DM
DM
DM
Gosh...
Cuttings BOOK
This takes me back...
To the day Cherry Mingle fell off the Art museum balcony.
FLYING 'DRAG' MAN SAVES CHILD!
The day I met Dog Girl.
WOOF?
BEST FRIEND
The day I became Dragman.
The day everything changed.

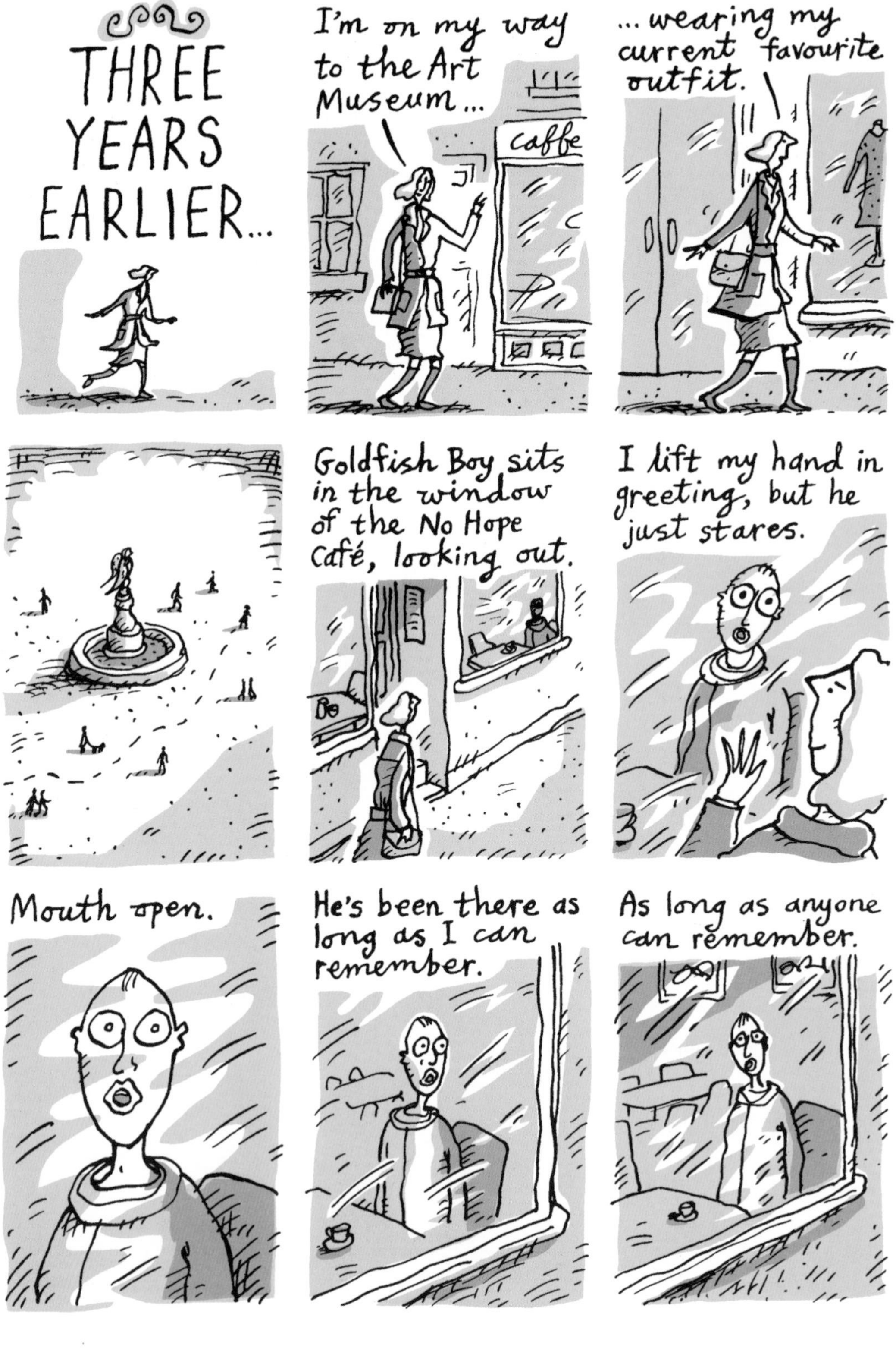
THREE YEARS EARLIER...
I'm on my way to the Art Museum...
caffe
...wearing my current favourite outfit.
Goldfish Boy sits in the window of the No Hope Café, looking out.
I lift my hand in greeting, but he just stares.
Mouth open.
He's been there as long as I can remember.
As long as anyone can remember.

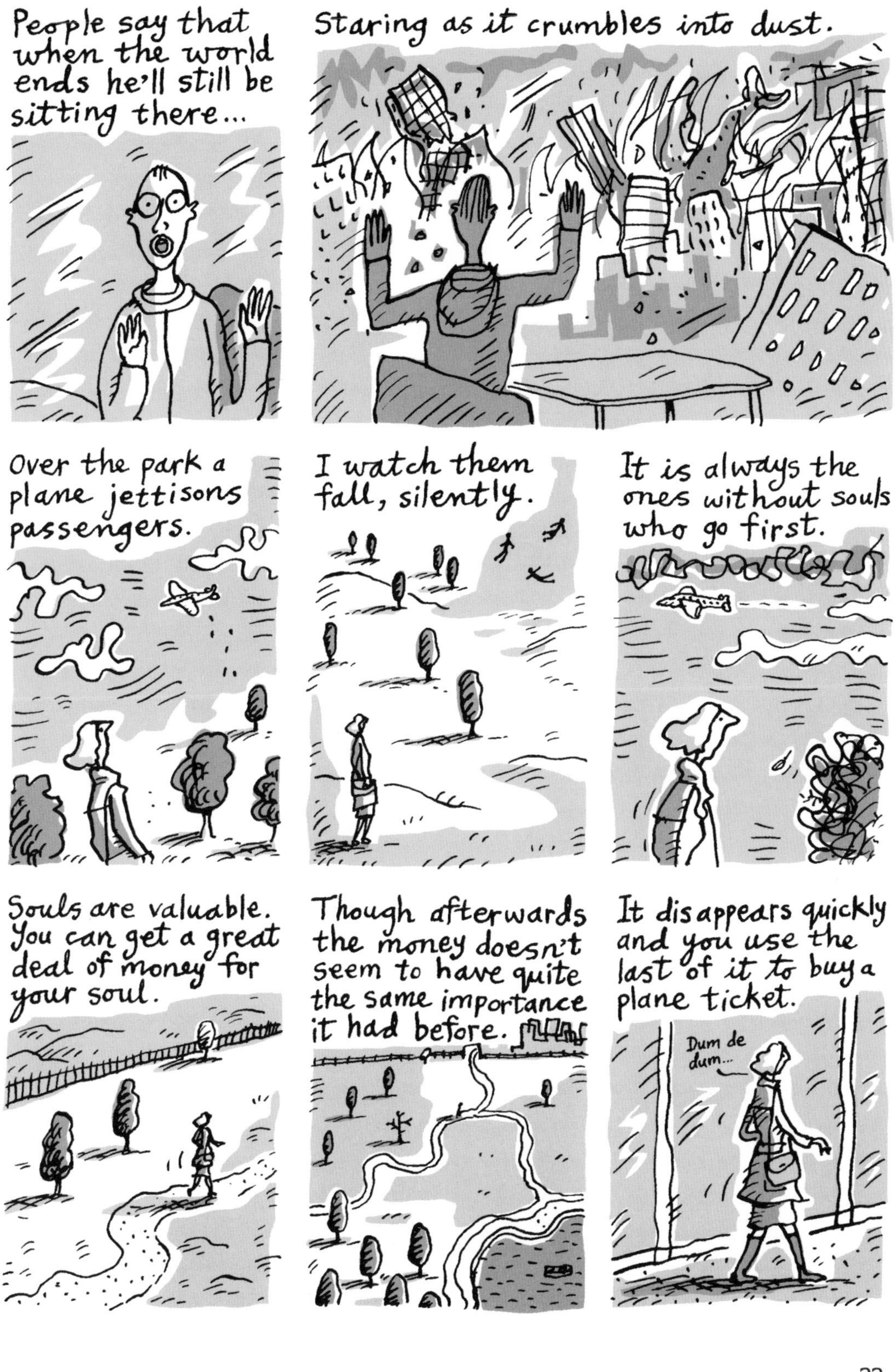
People say that when the world ends he'll still be sitting there...
Staring as it crumbles into dust.
Over the park a plane jettisons passengers.
I watch them fall, silently.
It is always the ones without souls who go first.
Souls are valuable. You can get a great deal of money for your soul.
Though afterwards the money doesn't seem to have quite the same importance it had before.
It disappears quickly and you use the last of it to buy a plane ticket.
Dum de dum...

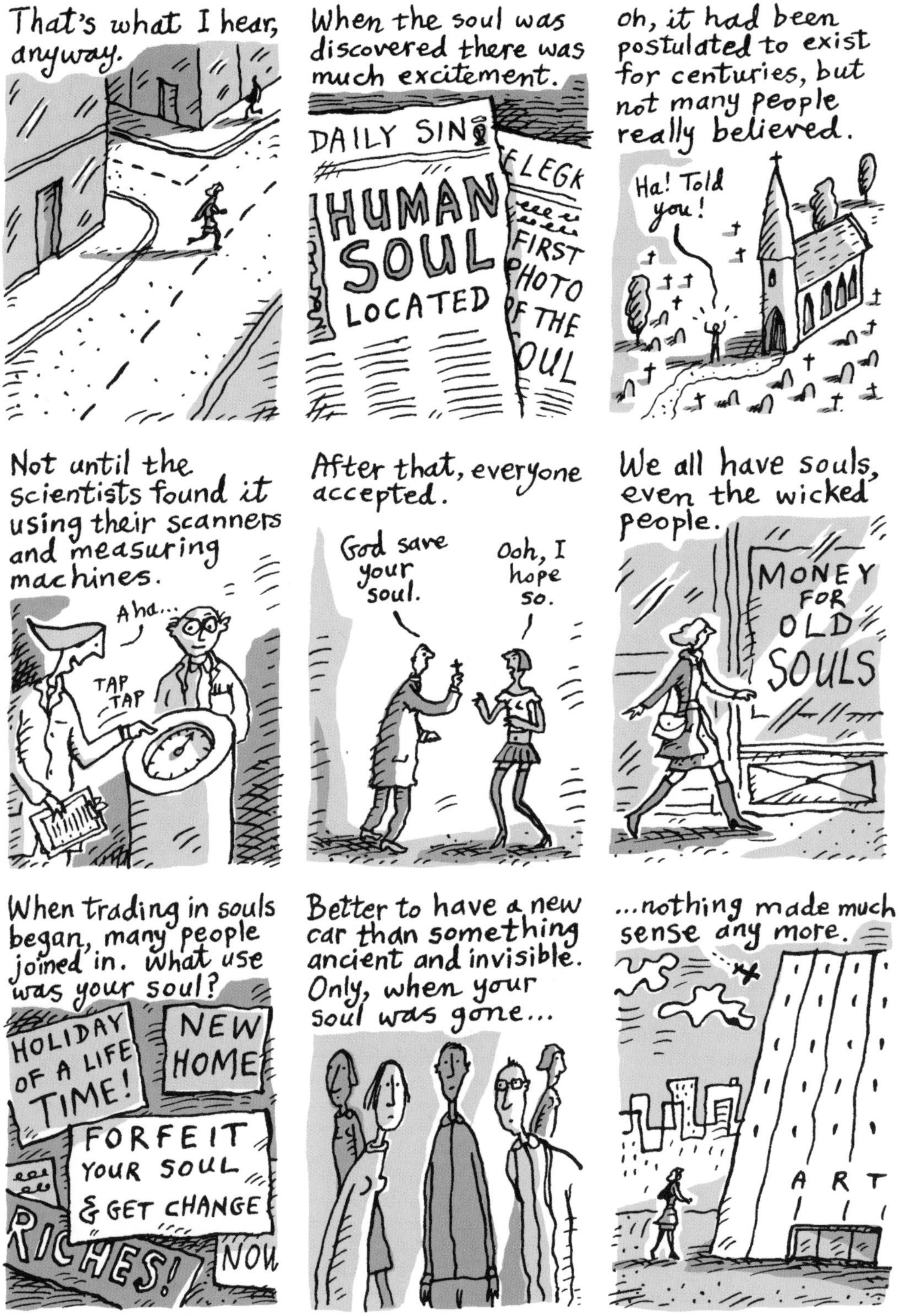
That's what I hear, anyway.
When the soul was discovered there was much excitement.
DAILY SIN
HUMAN SOUL LOCATED
FIRST
Oh, it had been postulated to exist for centuries, but not many people really believed.
Ha! Told you!
Not until the scientists found it using their scanners and measuring machines.
Aha...
TAP TAP
After that, everyone accepted.
God save your soul.
Ooh, I hope so.
We all have souls, even the wicked people.
MONEY FOR OLD SOULS
When trading in souls began, many people joined in. What use was your soul?
HOLIDAY OF A LIFE TIME!
NEW HOME
FORFEIT YOUR SOUL & GET CHANGE
RICHES!
NOW
Better to have a new car than something ancient and invisible. Only, when your soul was gone...
...nothing made much sense any more.
ART

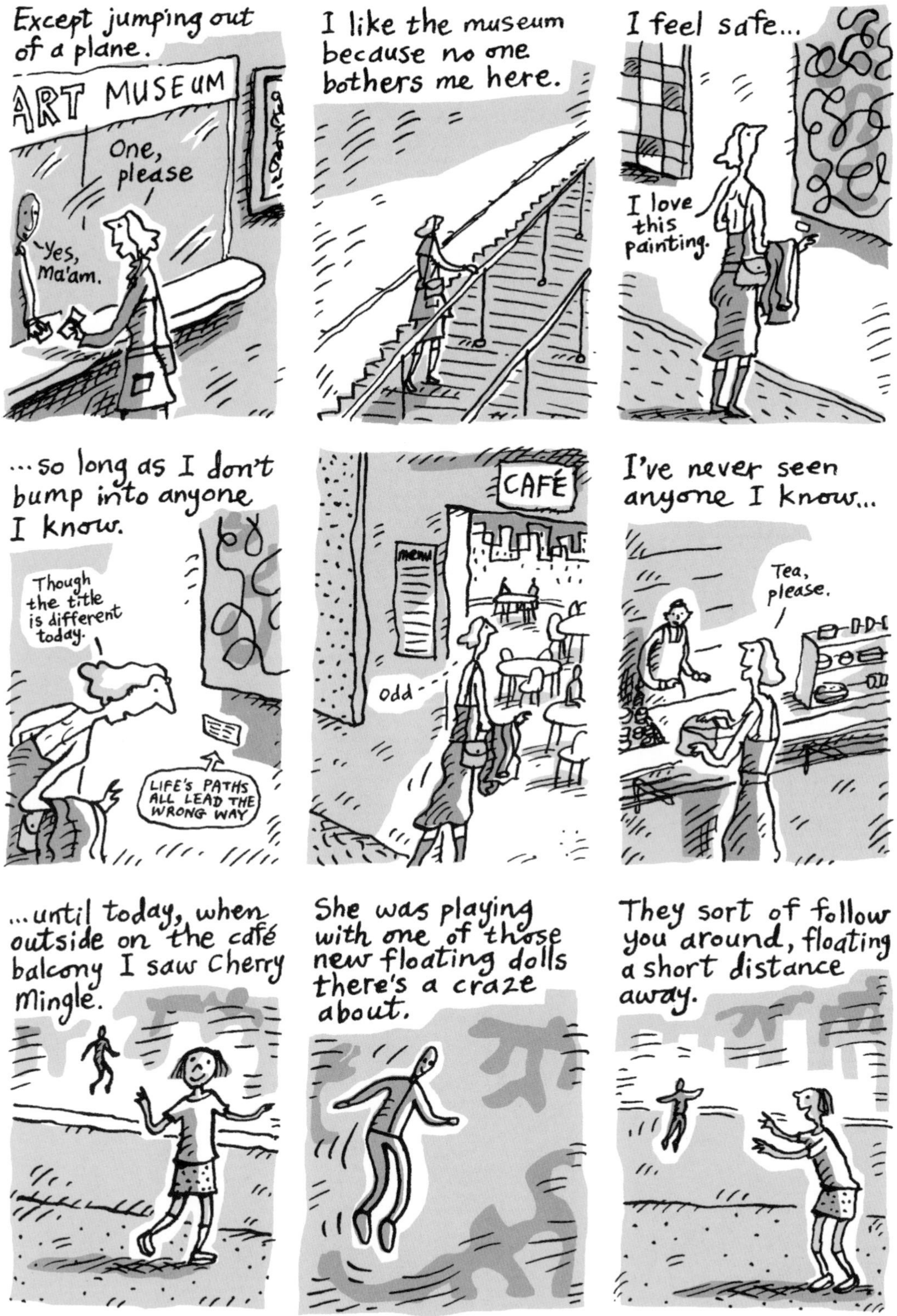

Except jumping out of a plane.
ART MUSEUM
One, please
Yes, ma'am.
I like the museum because no one bothers me here.
I feel safe...
I love this painting.
...so long as I don't bump into anyone I know.
Though the title is different today.
LIFE'S PATHS ALL LEAD THE WRONG WAY
CAFÉ
menu
odd
I've never seen anyone I know...
Tea, please.
...until today, when outside on the café balcony I saw Cherry Mingle.
She was playing with one of those new floating dolls there's a craze about.
They sort of follow you around, floating a short distance away.

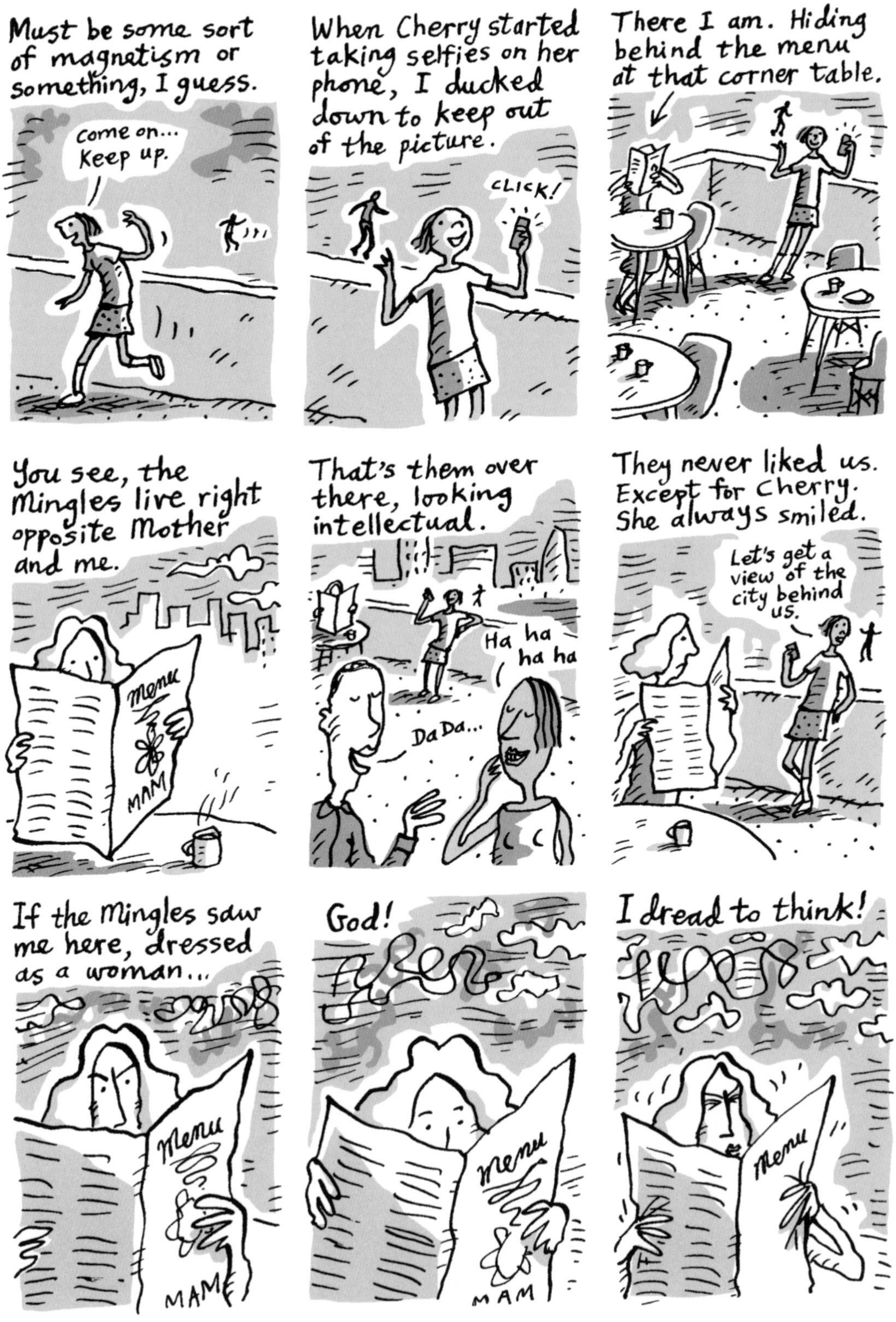
Must be some sort of magnetism or something, I guess.
Come on... Keep up.
When Cherry started taking selfies on her phone, I ducked down to keep out of the picture.
CLICK!
There I am. Hiding behind the menu at that corner table.
You see, the Mingles live right opposite Mother and me.
Menu
MAM
That's them over there, looking intellectual.
Ha ha ha ha
Da Da...
They never liked us. Except for Cherry. She always smiled.
Let's get a view of the city behind us.
If the Mingles saw me here, dressed as a woman...
Menu
MAM
God!
Menu
MAM
I dread to think!
Menu

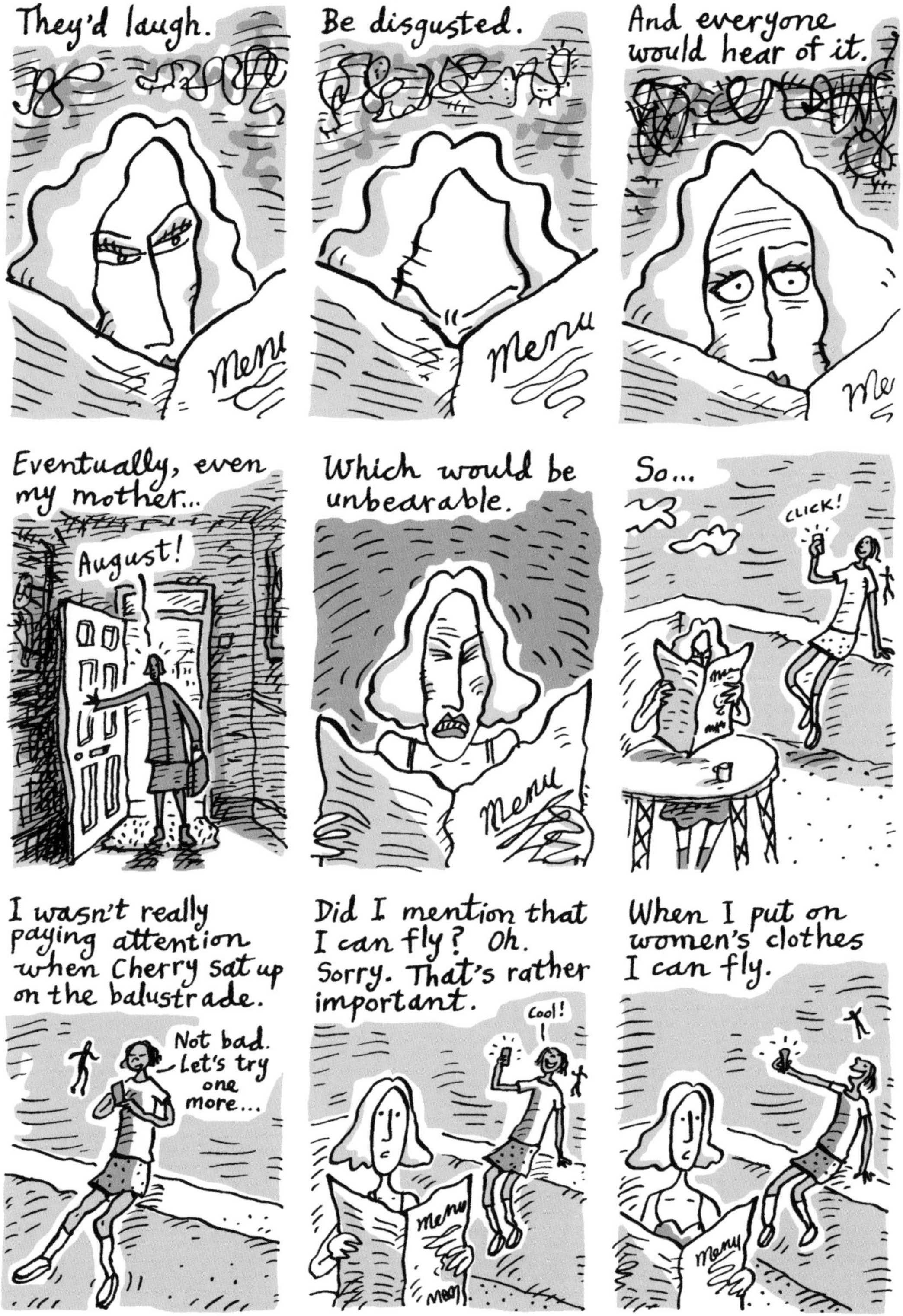

They'd laugh.
Menu
Be disgusted.
Menu
And everyone would hear of it.
Me
Eventually, even my mother...
August!
Which would be unbearable.
Menu
So...
CLICK!
I wasn't really paying attention when Cherry sat up on the balustrade.
Not bad. Let's try one more...
Did I mention that I can fly? Oh. Sorry. That's rather important.
Cool!
menu
When I put on women's clothes I can fly.
Menu

It just happens.

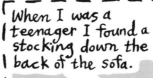

When I was a teenager I found a stocking down the back of the sofa.

The sofa was second hand so the stocking could have been down there for years.

Mother was out. Church, probably... She was always searching.

I was bored.

A typical sixteen year old.

Well...

I bet you were, too.

Anyway, I started poking about in the sofa...

Found the stocking...

And put it on. Instinctively. Without thinking.

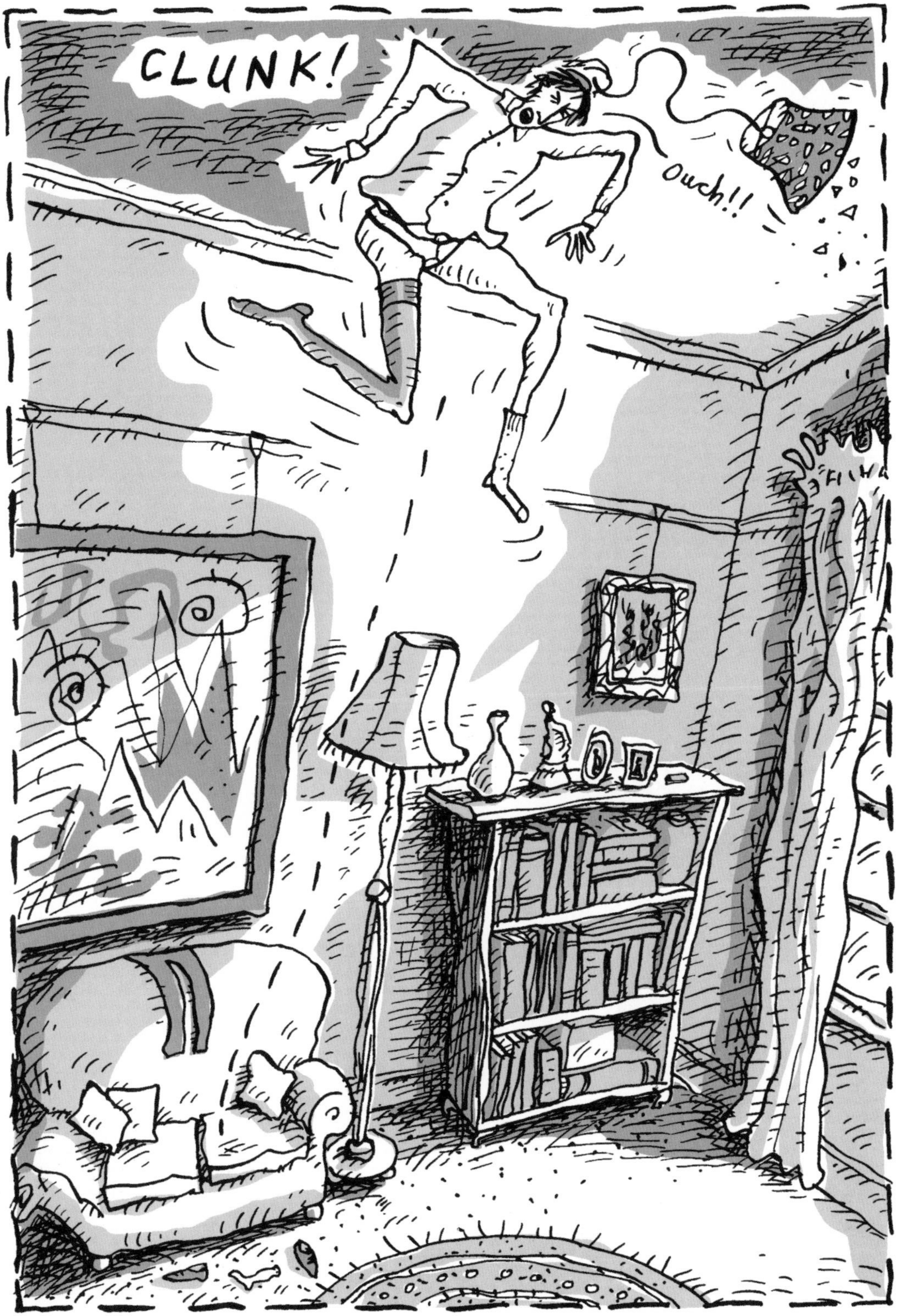
CLUNK!
Ouch!!

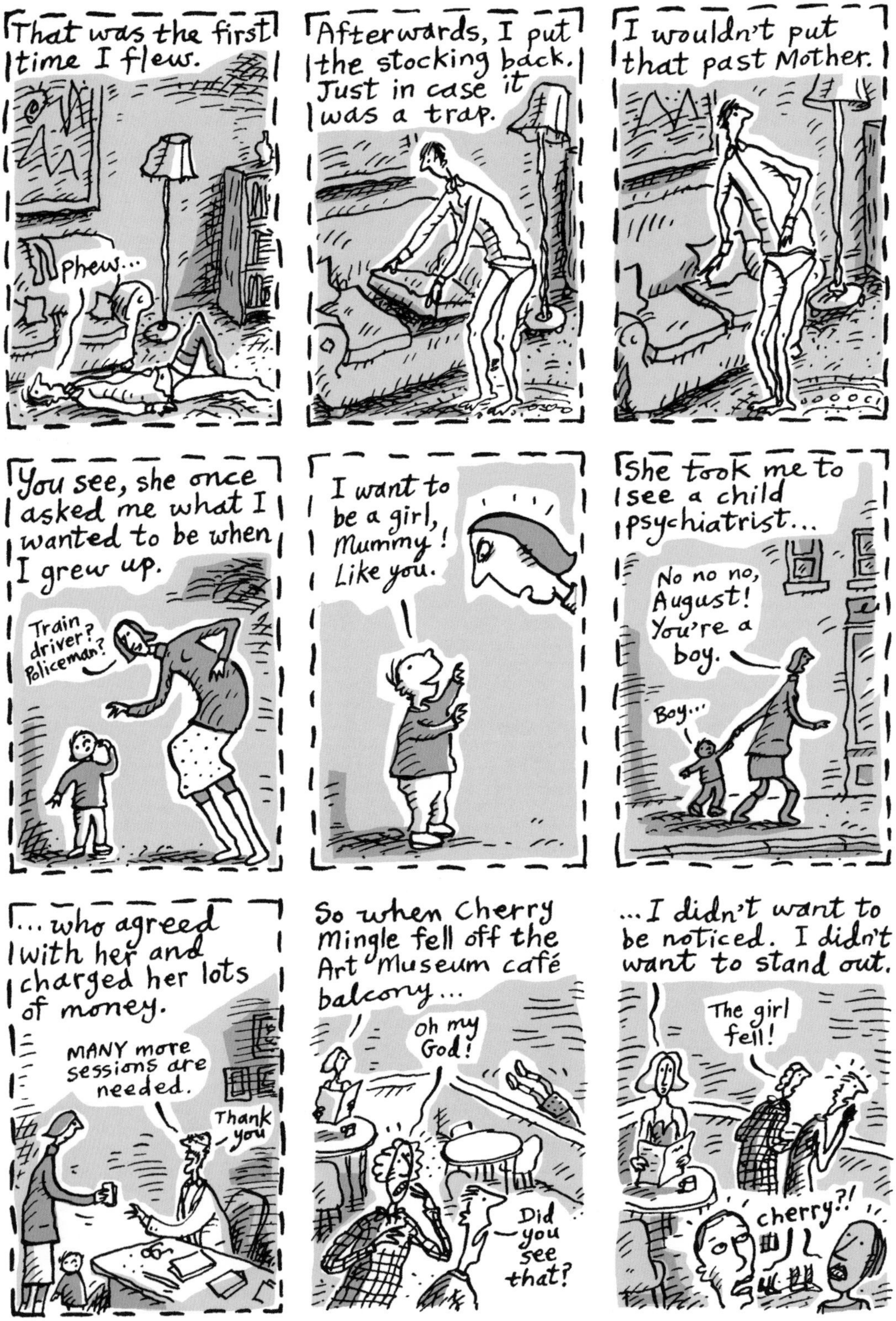
That was the first time I flew.
Phew...
Afterwards, I put the stocking back. Just in case it was a trap.
I wouldn't put that past Mother.
You see, she once asked me what I wanted to be when I grew up.
Train driver? Policeman?
I want to be a girl, Mummy! Like you.
She took me to see a child psychiatrist...
No no no, August! You're a boy.
Boy...
...who agreed with her and charged her lots of money.
MANY more sessions are needed.
Thank you
So when Cherry Mingle fell off the Art Museum café balcony...
Oh my God!
Did you see that?
...I didn't want to be noticed. I didn't want to stand out.
The girl fell!
Cherry?!

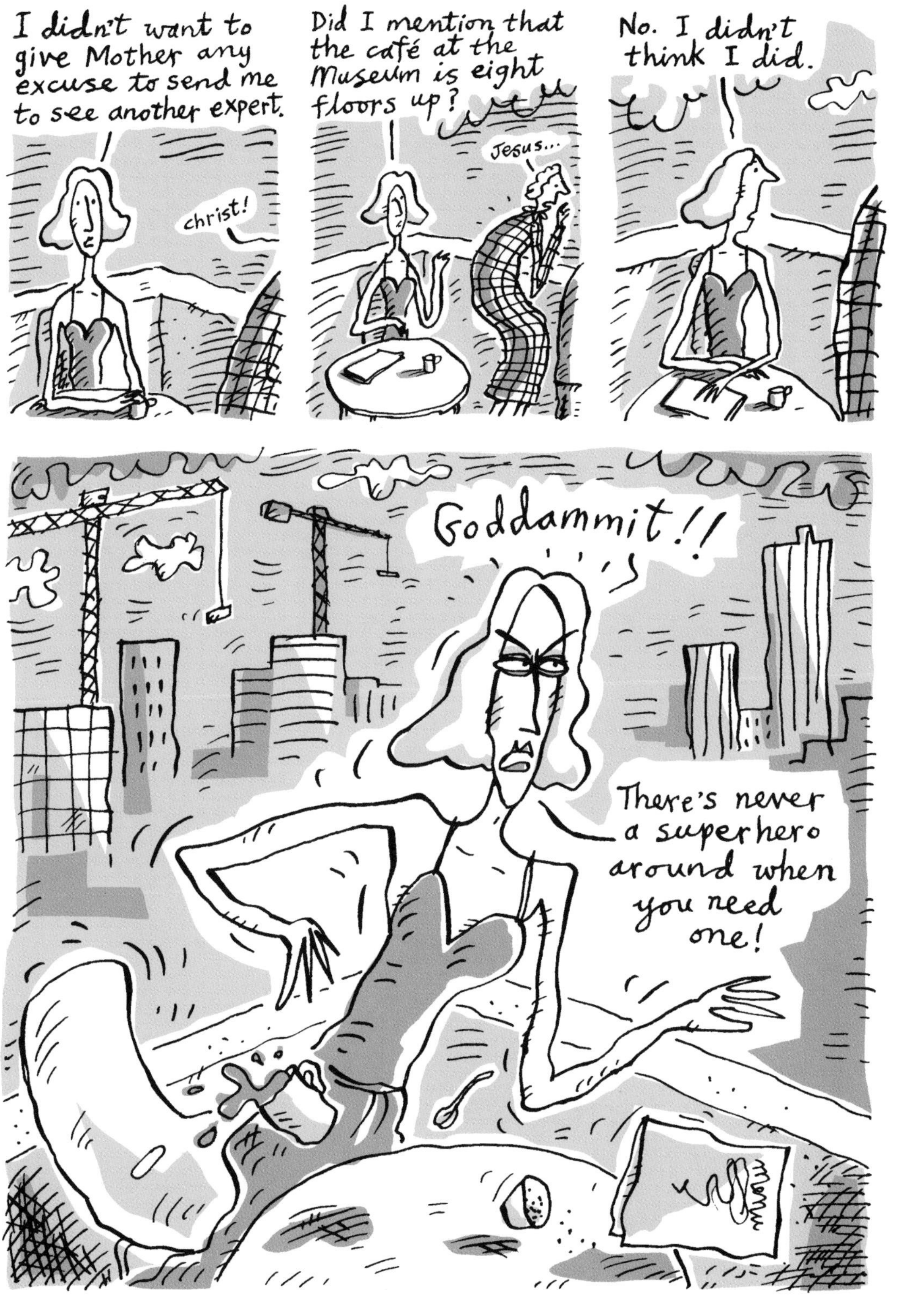
I didn't want to give Mother any excuse to send me to see another expert.
christ!
Did I mention that the café at the Museum is eight floors up?
Jesus...
No. I didn't think I did.
Goddammit!!
There's never a superhero around when you need one!
Menu

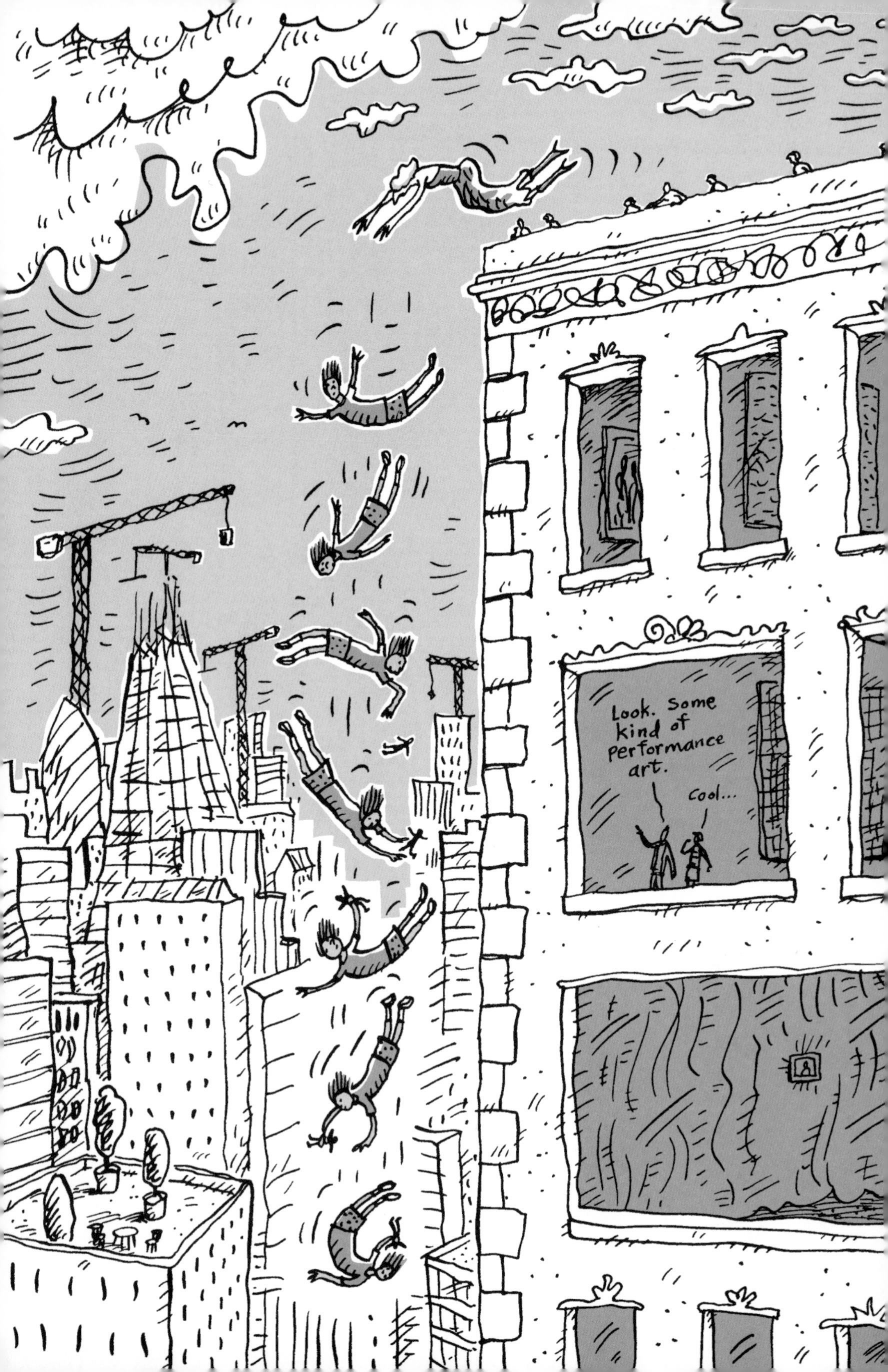
Look. Some kind of performance art.
Cool...

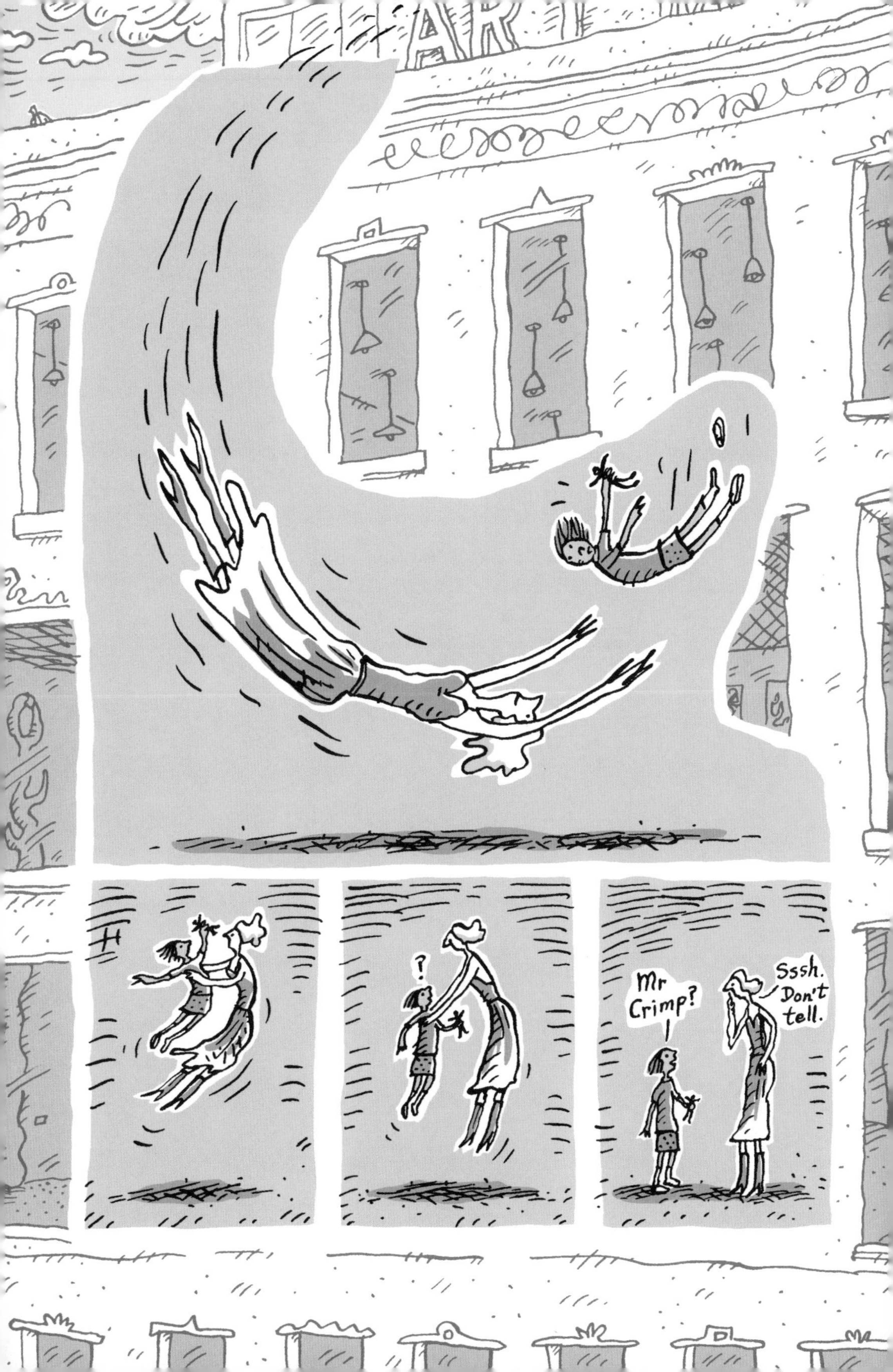
AR
?
Mr Crimp?
Sssh. Don't tell.

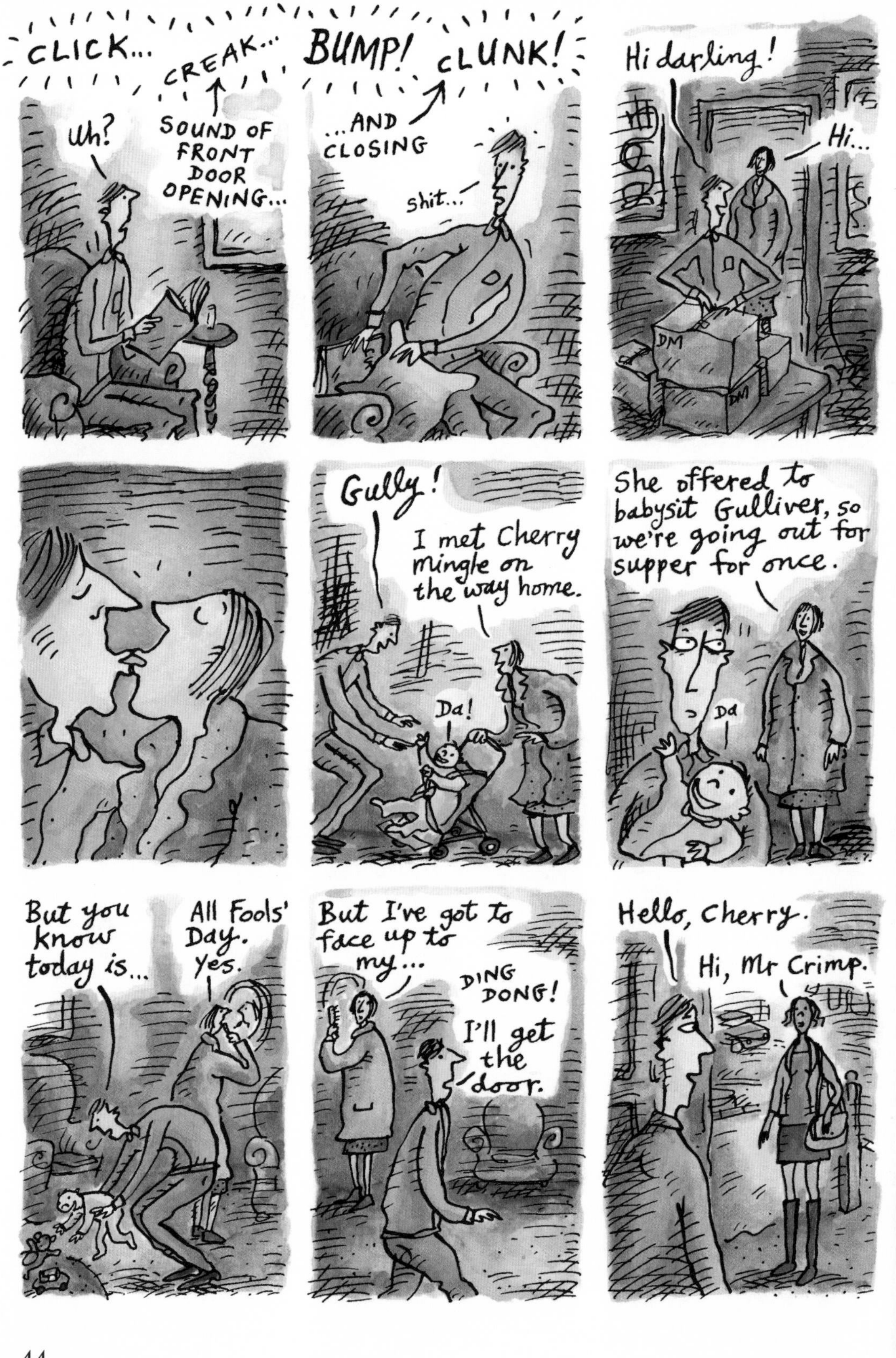
CLICK...
CREAK...
BUMP!
CLUNK!
Uh?
SOUND OF FRONT DOOR OPENING...
...AND CLOSING
shit...
Hi darling!
Hi...
Gully!
I met Cherry Mingle on the way home.
Da!
She offered to babysit Gulliver, so we're going out for supper for once.
Da
But you know today is...
All Fools' Day. Yes.
But I've got to face up to my...
DING DONG!
I'll get the door.
Hello, Cherry.
Hi, Mr Crimp.

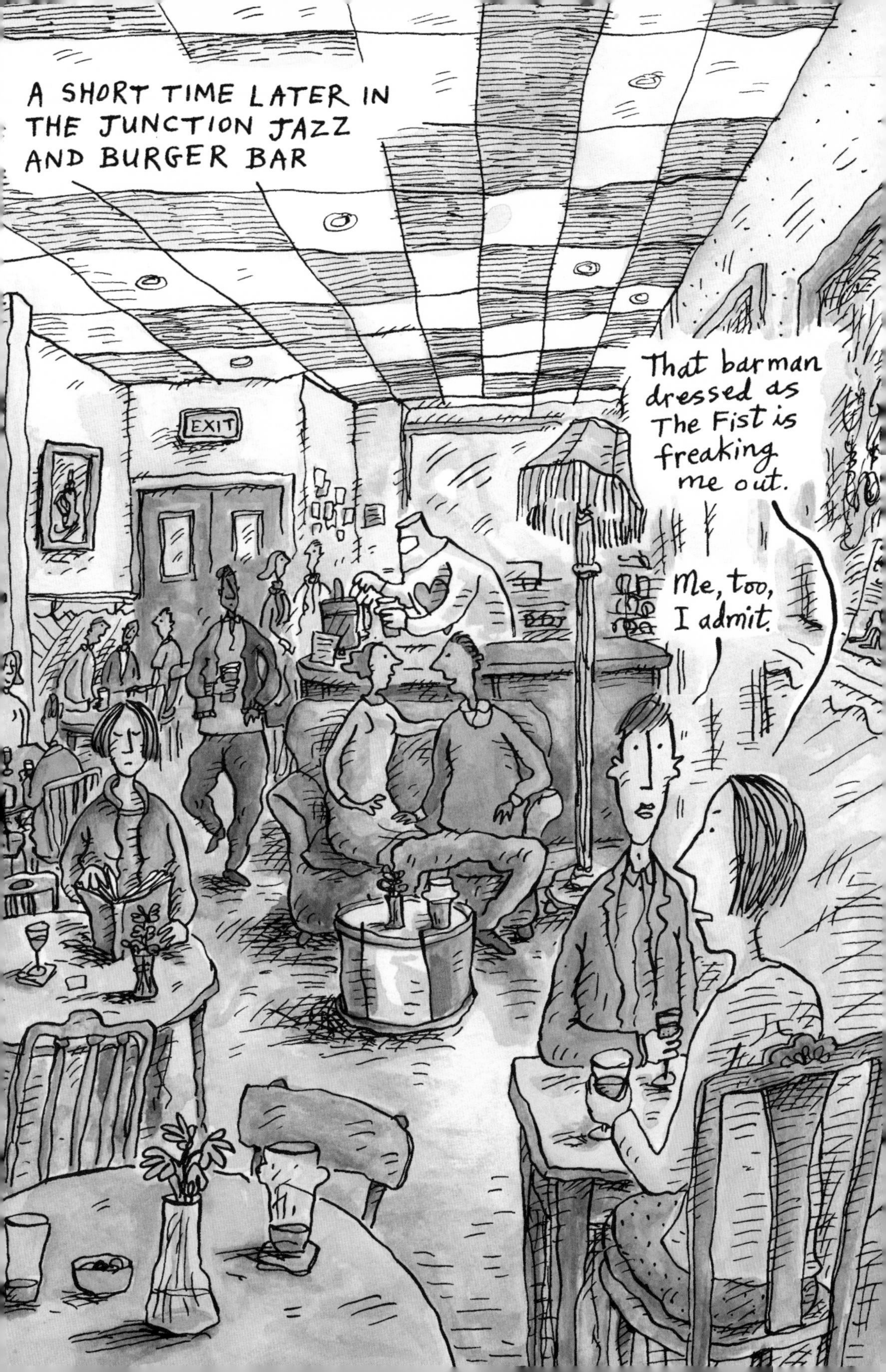
A SHORT TIME LATER IN THE JUNCTION JAZZ AND BURGER BAR
EXIT
That barman dressed as The Fist is freaking me out.
Me, too, I admit.

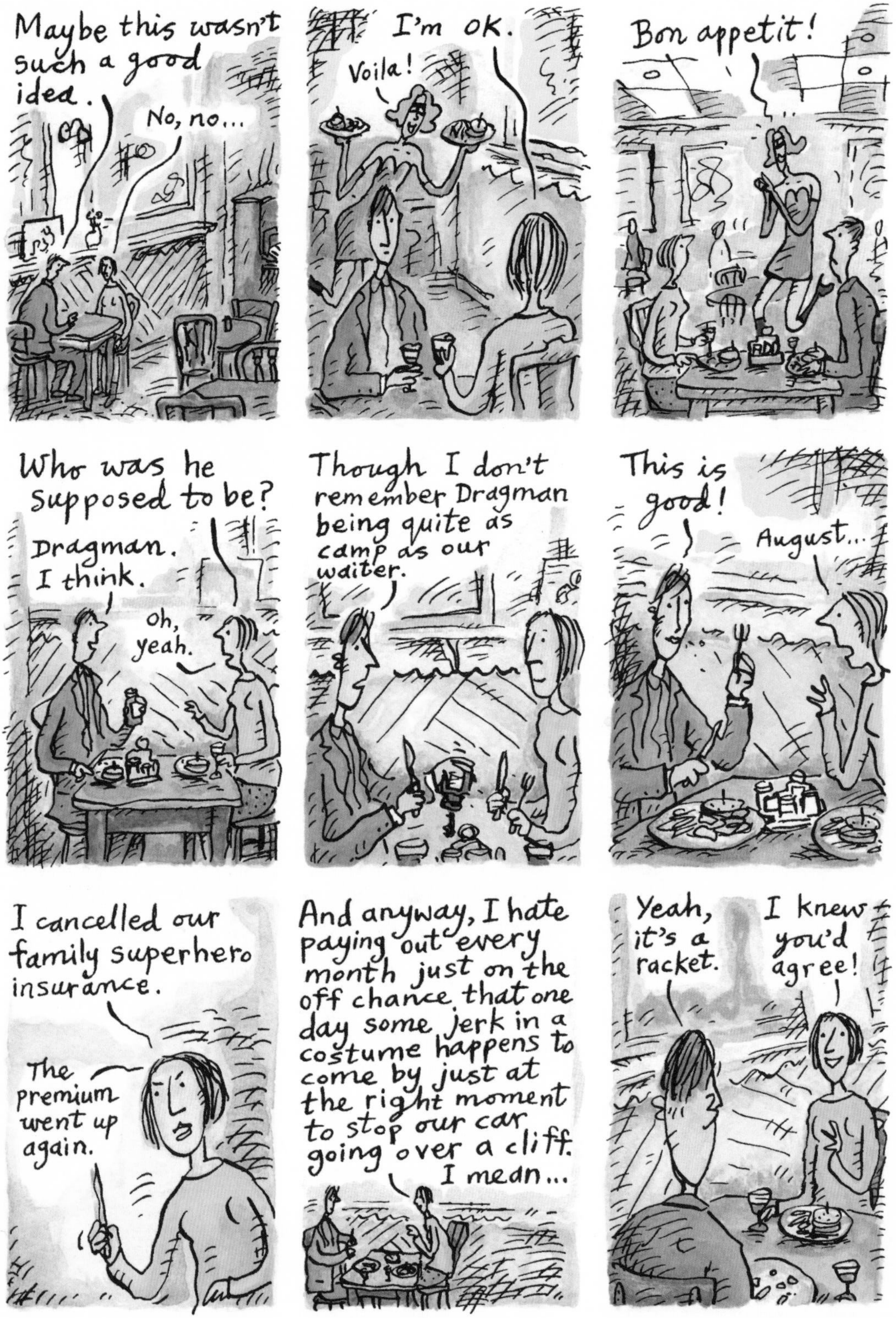
Maybe this wasn't such a good idea.
No, no...
I'm OK.
Voila!
Bon appetit!
Who was he supposed to be?
Dragman. I think.
Oh, yeah.
Though I don't remember Dragman being quite as camp as our waiter.
This is good!
August...
I cancelled our family superhero insurance.
The premium went up again.
And anyway, I hate paying out every month just on the off chance that one day some jerk in a costume happens to come by just at the right moment to stop our car going over a cliff. I mean...
Yeah, it's a racket.
I knew you'd agree!

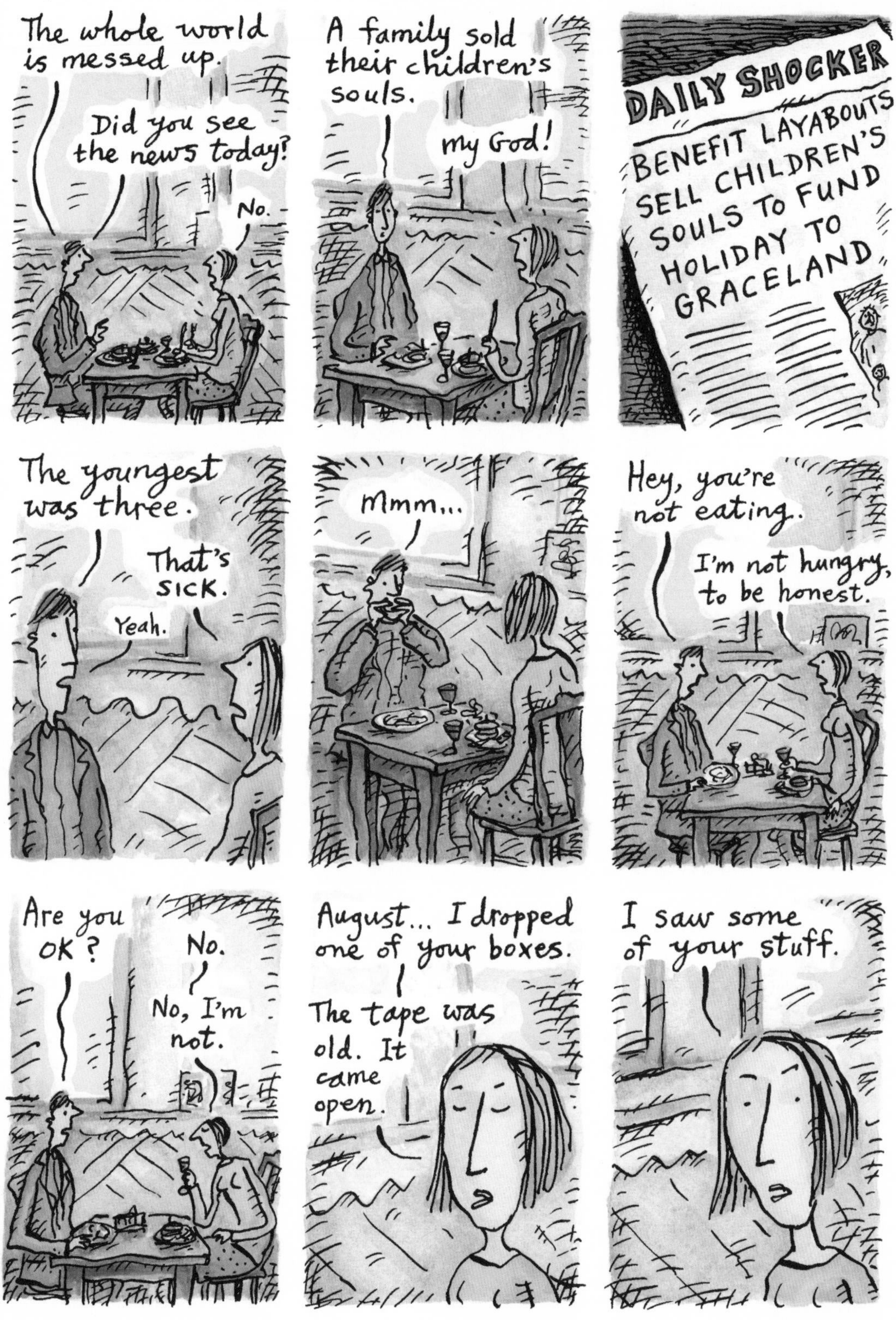
The whole world is messed up.
Did you see the news today?
No.
A family sold their children's souls.
my God!
DAILY SHOCKER
BENEFIT LAYABOUTS SELL CHILDREN'S SOULS TO FUND HOLIDAY TO GRACELAND
The youngest was three.
That's SICK.
Yeah.
Mmm...
Hey, you're not eating.
I'm not hungry, to be honest.
Are you OK?
No.
No, I'm not.
August... I dropped one of your boxes.
The tape was old. It came open.
I saw some of your stuff.

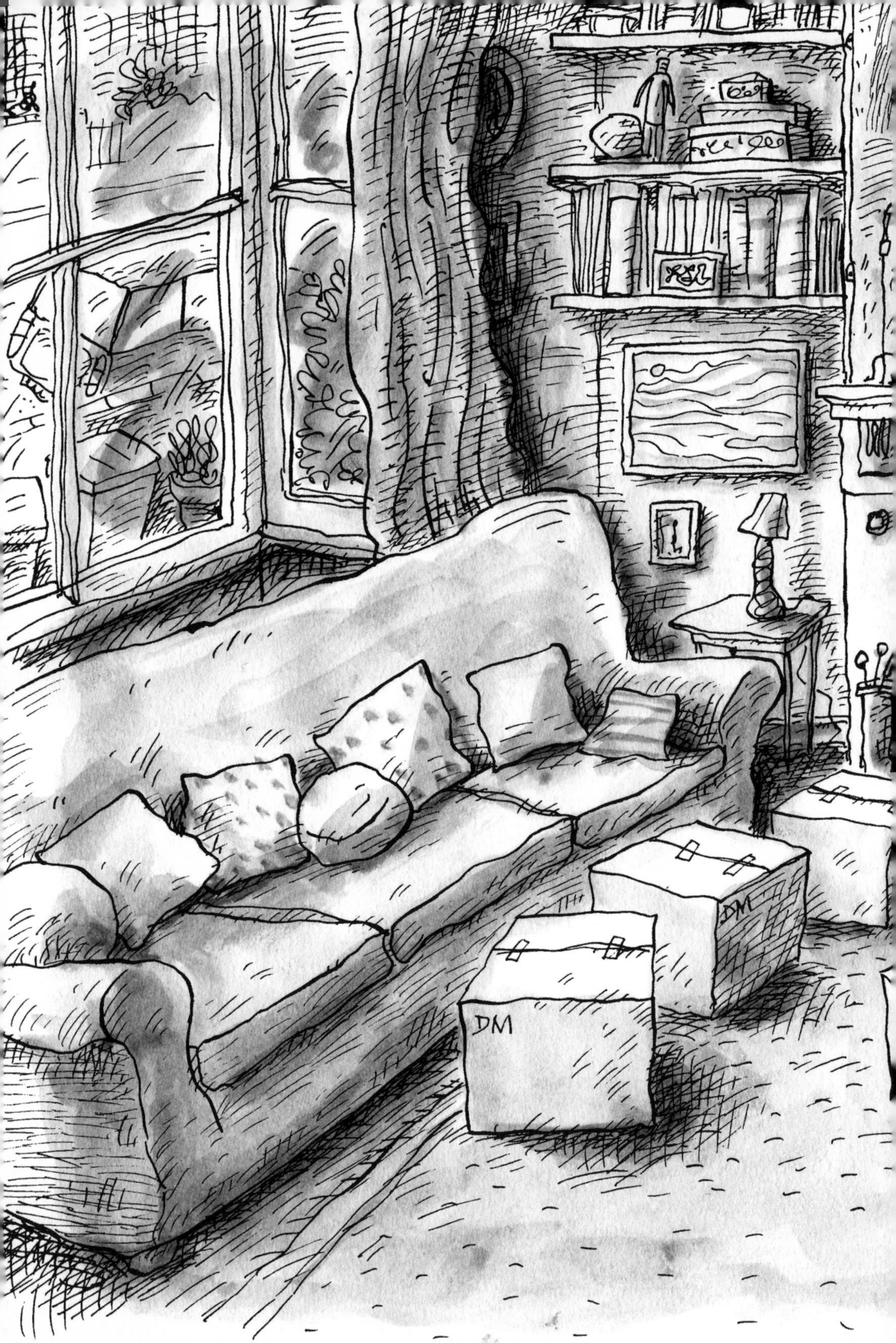
DM
DM

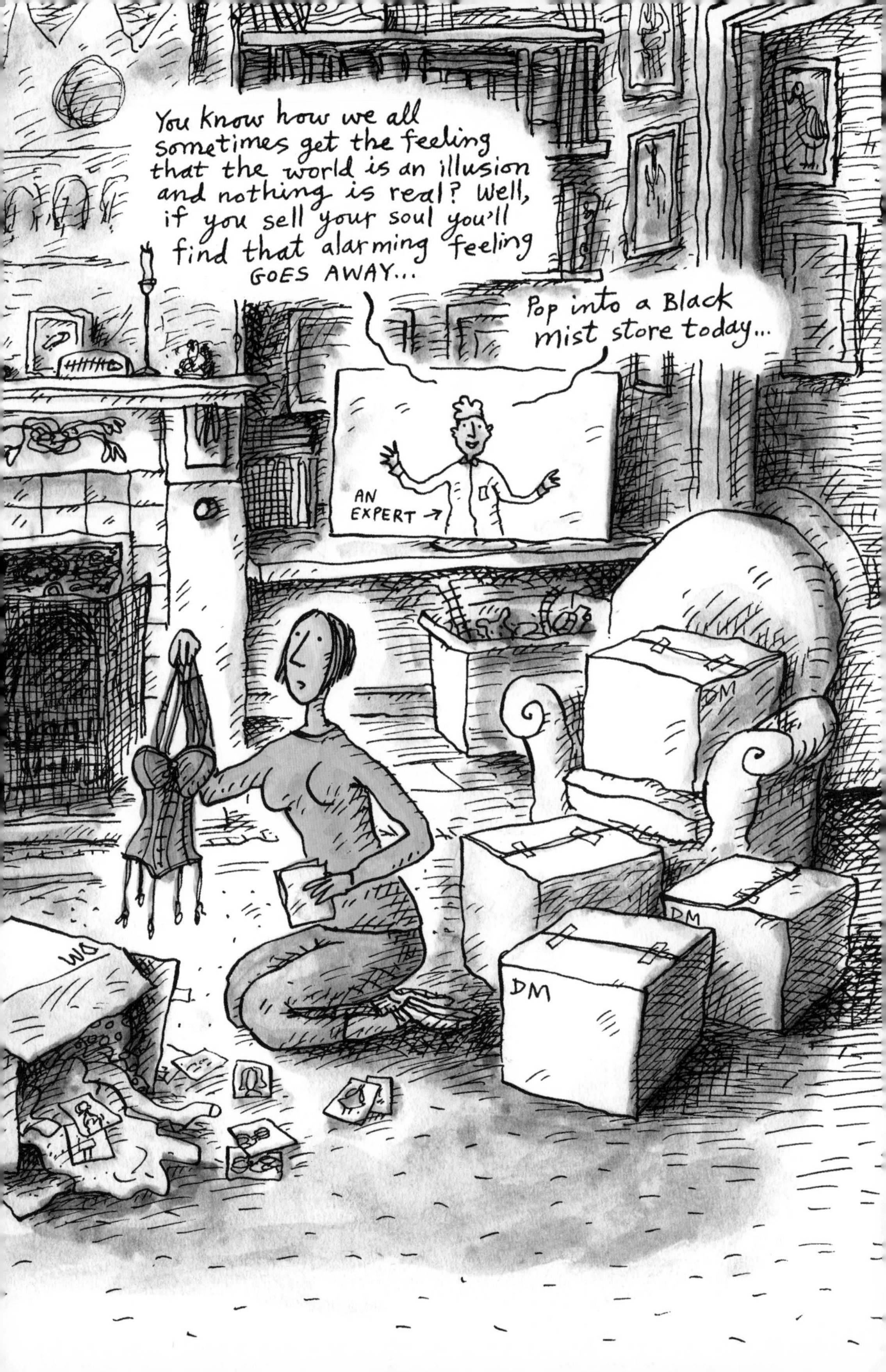
You know how we all sometimes get the feeling that the world is an illusion and nothing is real? Well, if you sell your soul you'll find that alarming feeling GOES AWAY...
Pop into a Black mist store today...
AN EXPERT →
DM
DM
DM
DM
WO

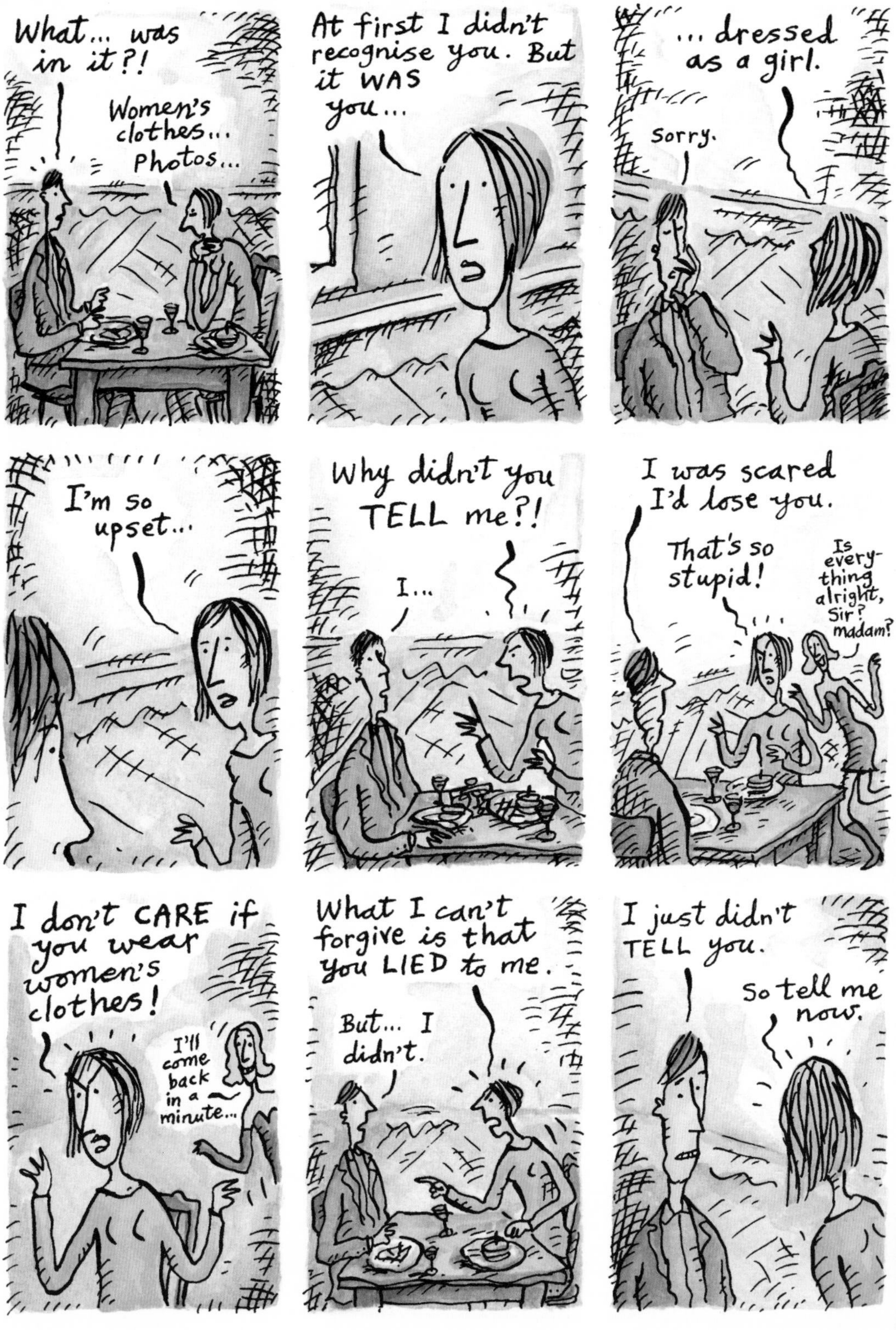
What... was in it?!
Women's clothes... Photos...
At first I didn't recognise you. But it WAS you...
...dressed as a girl.
Sorry.
I'm so upset...
Why didn't you TELL me?!
I...
I was scared I'd lose you.
That's so stupid!
Is everything alright, Sir? madam?
I don't CARE if you wear women's clothes!
I'll come back in a minute...
What I can't forgive is that you LIED to me.
But... I didn't.
I just didn't TELL you.
So tell me now.

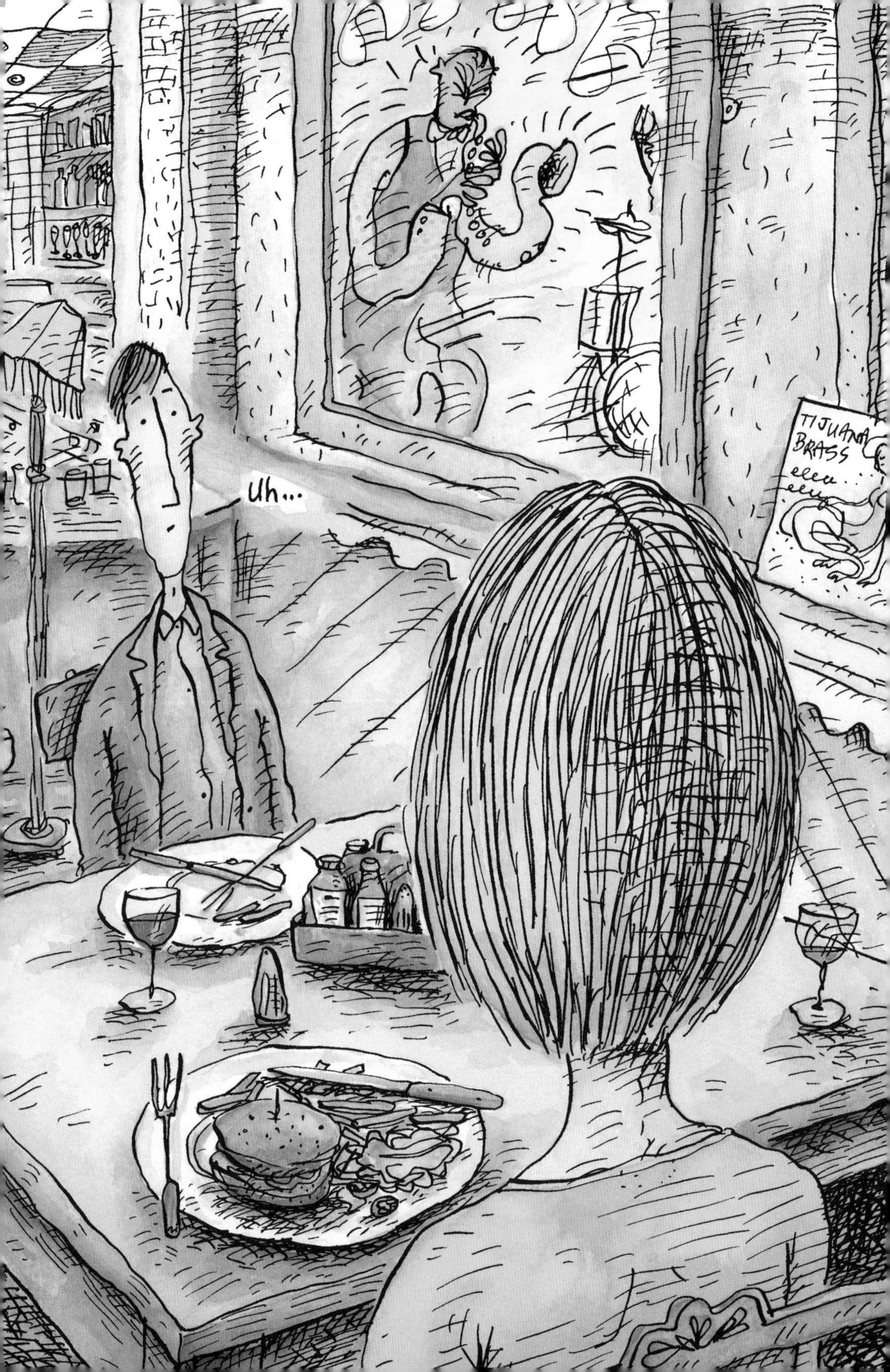

Uh...
TIJUANA BRASS

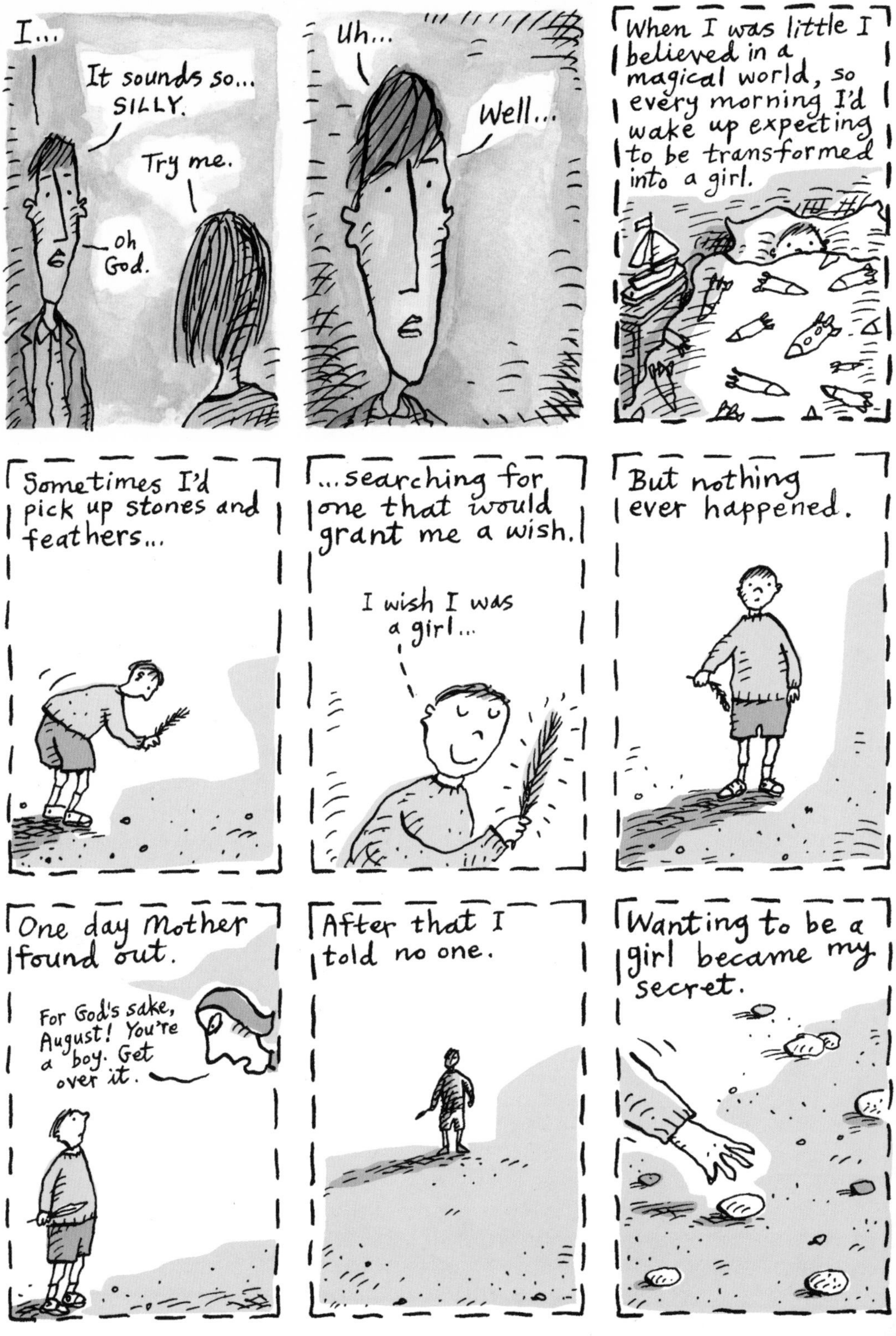
I...
It sounds so... SILLY.
Try me.
oh God.
Uh...
Well...
When I was little I believed in a magical world, so every morning I'd wake up expecting to be transformed into a girl.
Sometimes I'd pick up stones and feathers...
...searching for one that would grant me a wish.
I wish I was a girl...
But nothing ever happened.
One day Mother found out.
For God's sake, August! You're a boy. Get over it.
After that I told no one.
Wanting to be a girl became my secret.

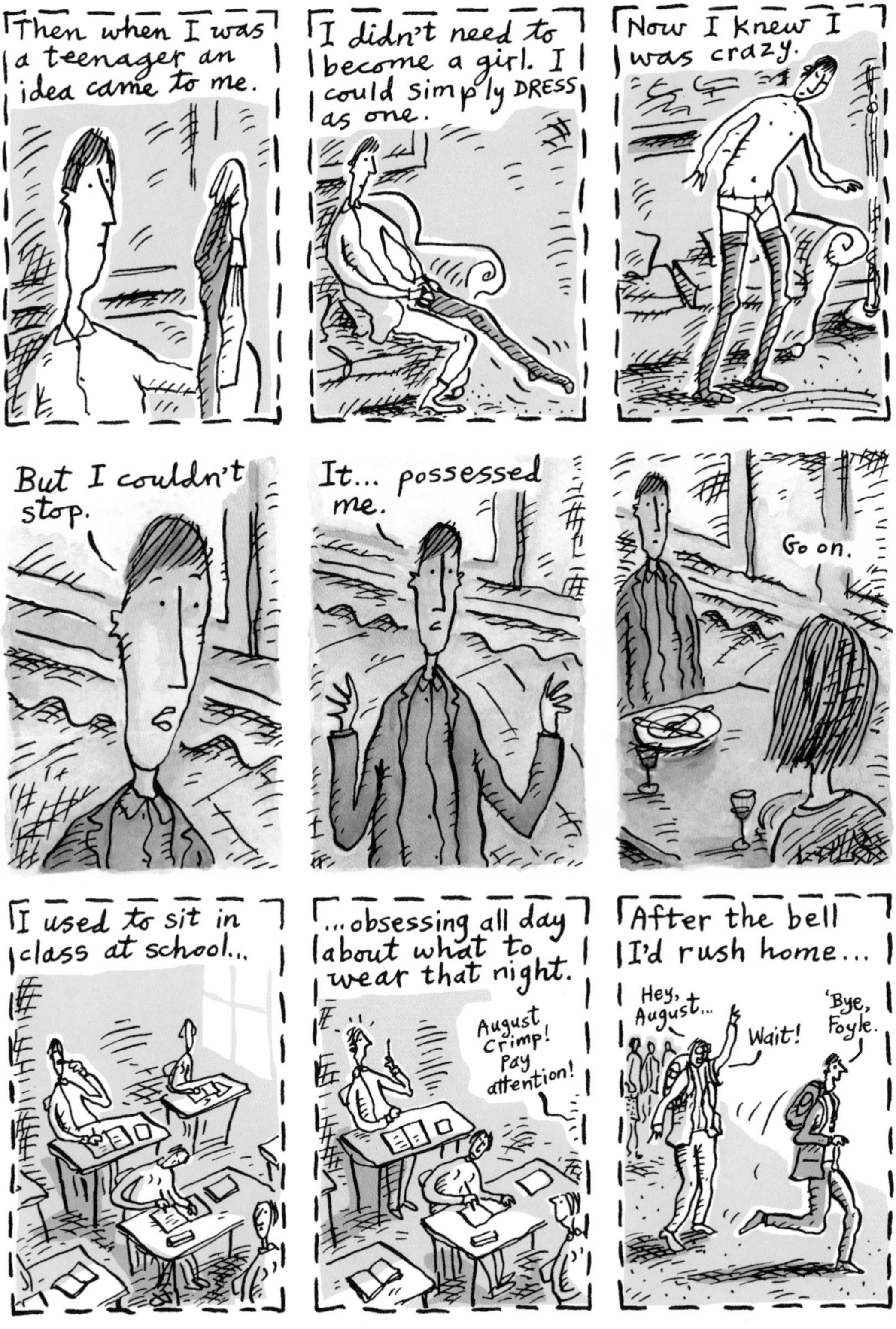

Then when I was a teenager an idea came to me.
I didn't need to become a girl. I could simply DRESS as one.
Now I knew I was crazy.
But I couldn't stop.
It... possessed me.
Go on.
I used to sit in class at school...
...obsessing all day about what to wear that night.
August Crimp! Pay attention!
After the bell I'd rush home...
Hey, August...
Wait!
'Bye, Foyle.

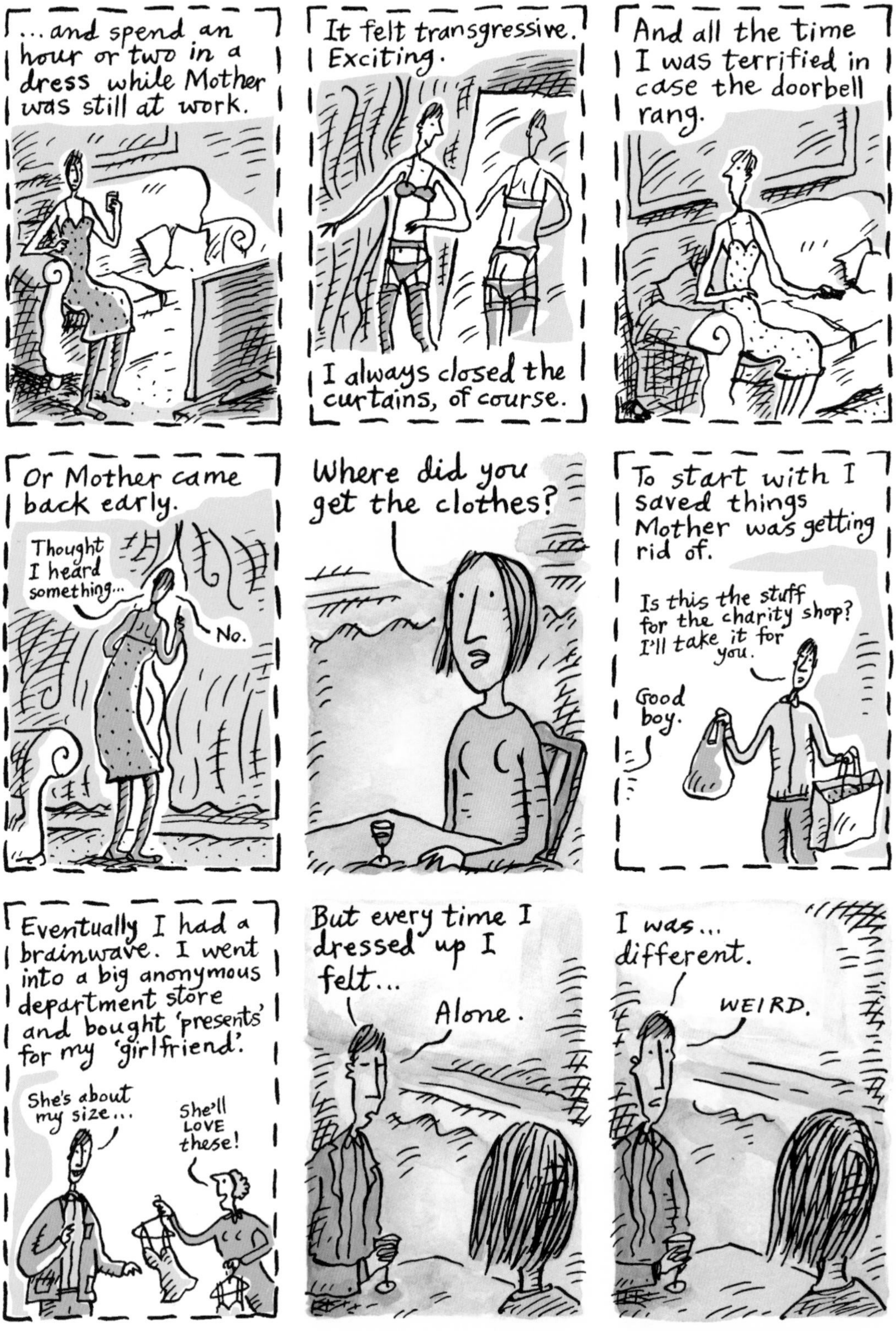
...and spend an hour or two in a dress while Mother was still at work.
It felt transgressive. Exciting.
I always closed the curtains, of course.
And all the time I was terrified in case the doorbell rang.
Or Mother came back early.
Thought I heard something...
No.
Where did you get the clothes?
To start with I saved things Mother was getting rid of.
Is this the stuff for the charity shop? I'll take it for you.
Good boy.
Eventually I had a brainwave. I went into a big anonymous department store and bought 'presents' for my 'girlfriend'.
She's about my size...
She'll LOVE these!
But every time I dressed up I felt...
Alone.
I was... different.
WEIRD.

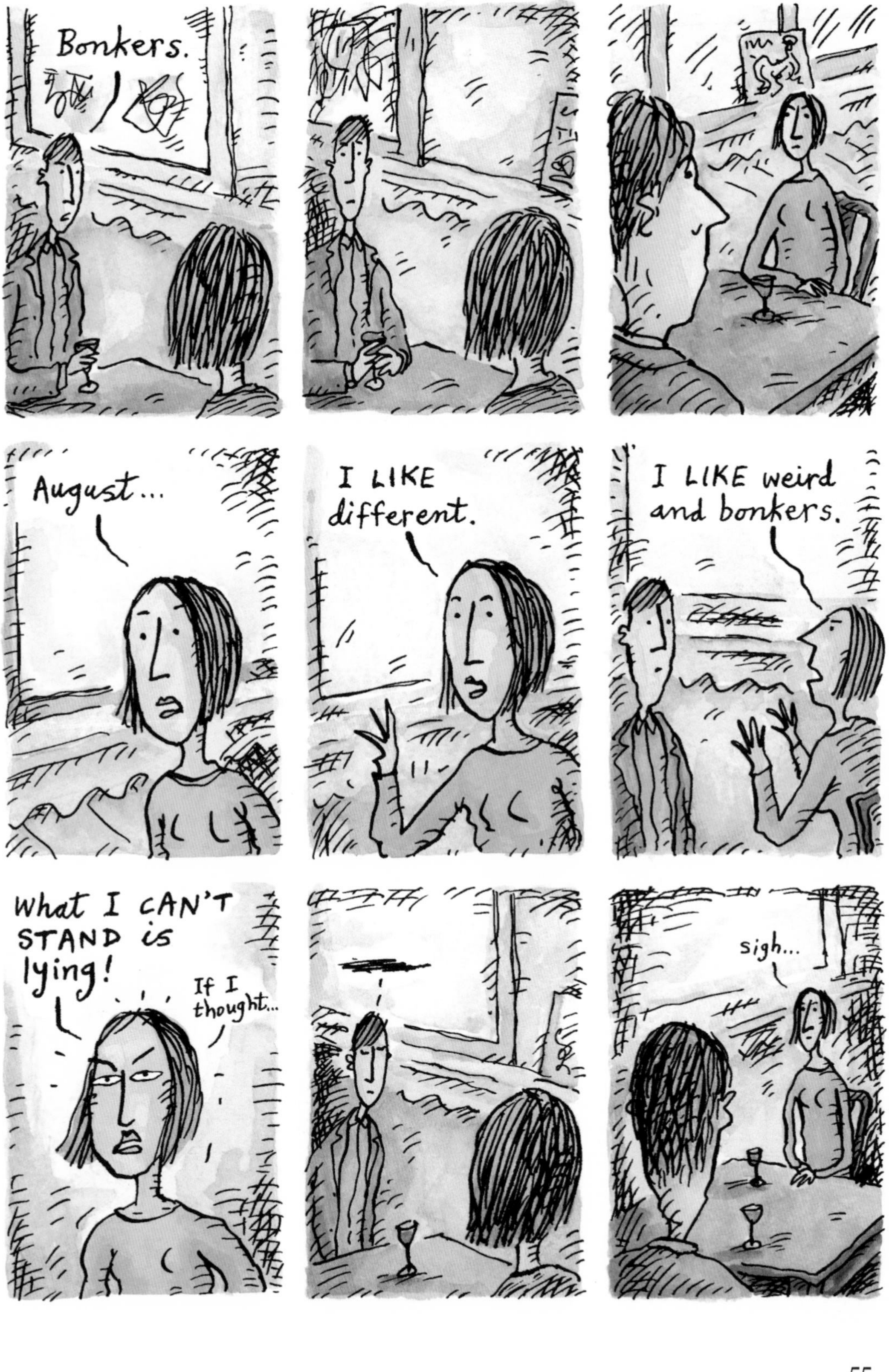

Bonkers.
August...
I LIKE different.
I LIKE weird and bonkers.
What I CAN'T STAND is lying!
If I thought...
sigh...

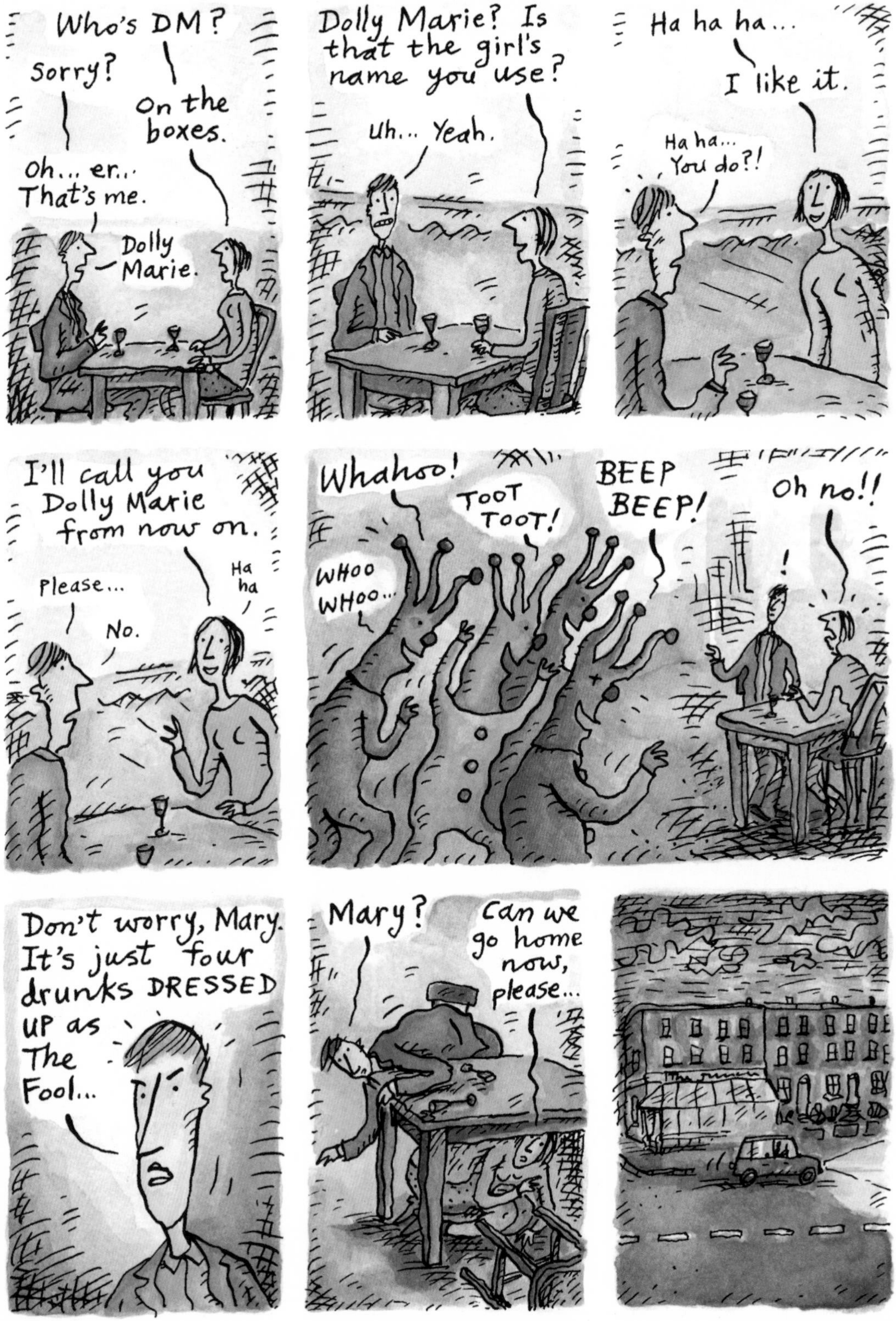
Who's DM?
Sorry?
On the boxes.
Oh... er.. That's me.
Dolly Marie.
Dolly Marie? Is that the girl's name you use?
Uh... Yeah.
Ha ha ha...
I like it.
Ha ha... You do?!
I'll call you Dolly Marie from now on.
Ha ha
Please...
No.
Whahoo!
TOOT TOOT!
BEEP BEEP!
Oh no!!
WHOO WHOO...
!
Don't worry, Mary. It's just four drunks DRESSED UP as The Fool...
Mary?
Can we go home now, please...

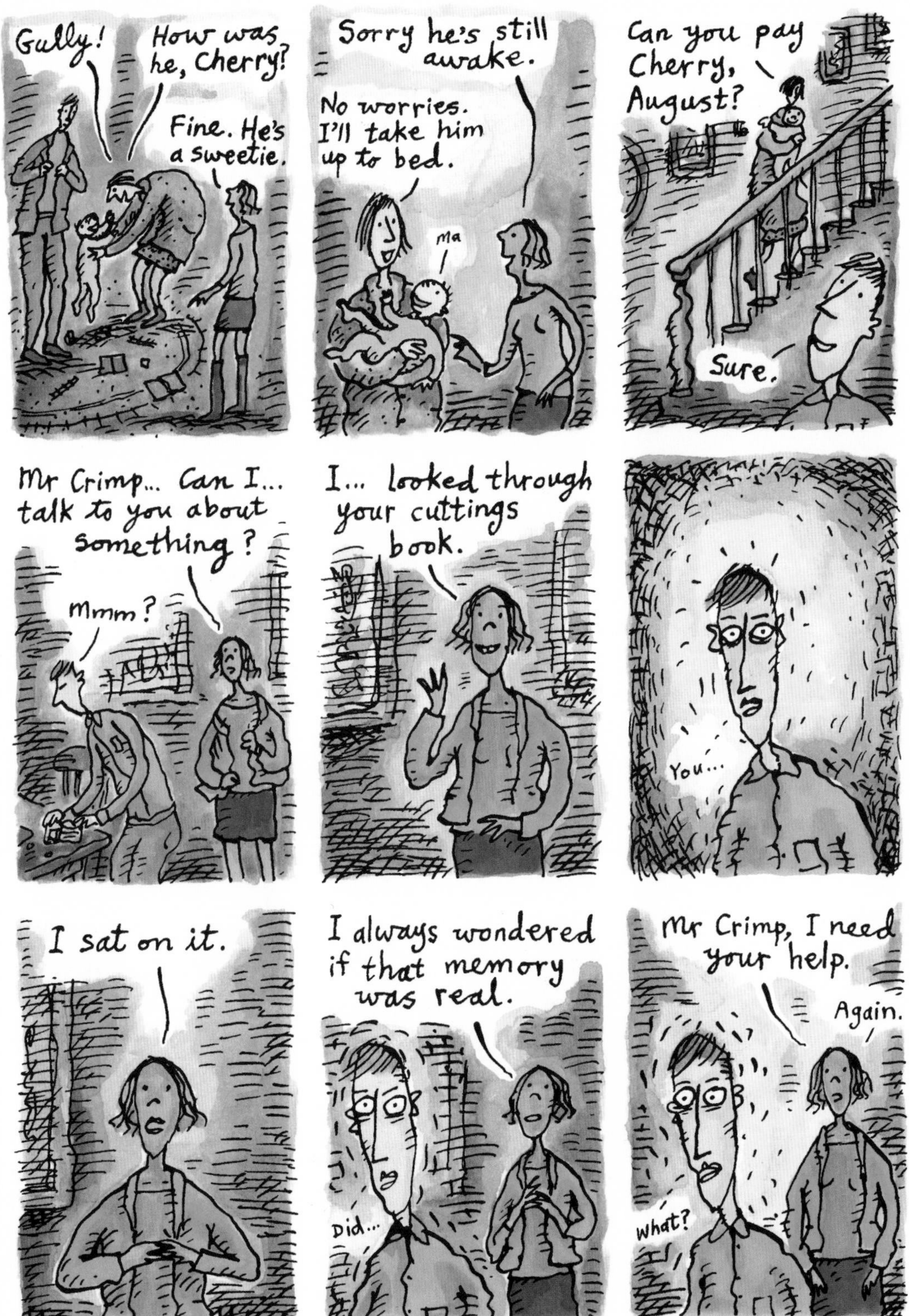
Gully!
How was he, Cherry?
Fine. He's a sweetie.
Sorry he's still awake.
No worries. I'll take him up to bed.
Ma
Can you pay Cherry, August?
Sure.
Mr Crimp... Can I... talk to you about something?
Mmm?
I... looked through your cuttings book.
You...
I sat on it.
I always wondered if that memory was real.
Did...
Mr Crimp, I need your help.
Again.
What?

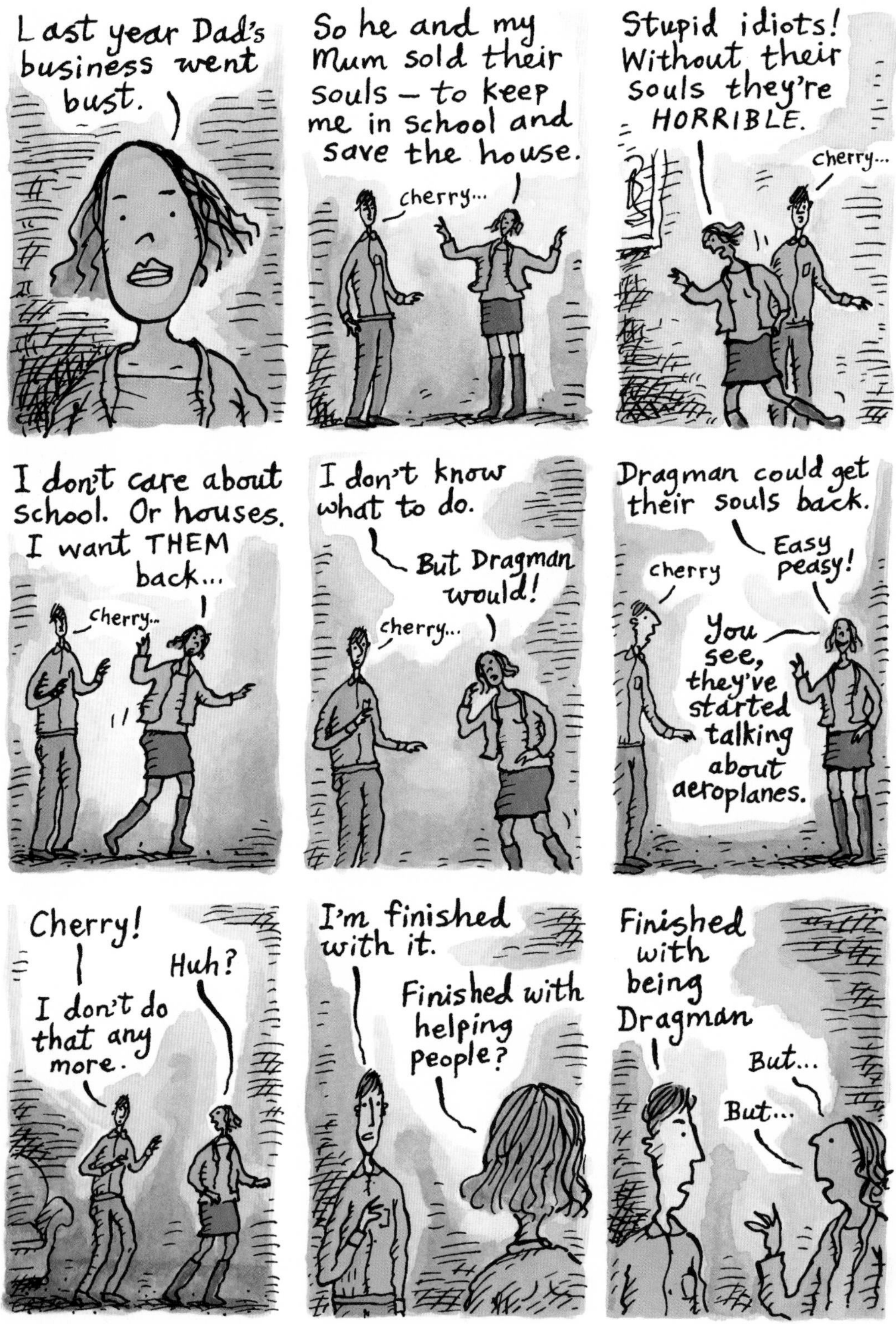
Last year Dad's business went bust.
So he and my Mum sold their souls – to keep me in school and save the house.
cherry...
Stupid idiots! Without their souls they're HORRIBLE.
cherry...
I don't care about school. Or houses. I want THEM back...
cherry..
I don't know what to do.
But Dragman would!
cherry...
Dragman could get their souls back.
Easy peasy!
cherry
You see, they've started talking about aeroplanes.
Cherry!
I don't do that any more.
Huh?
I'm finished with it.
Finished with helping people?
Finished with being Dragman
But...
But...

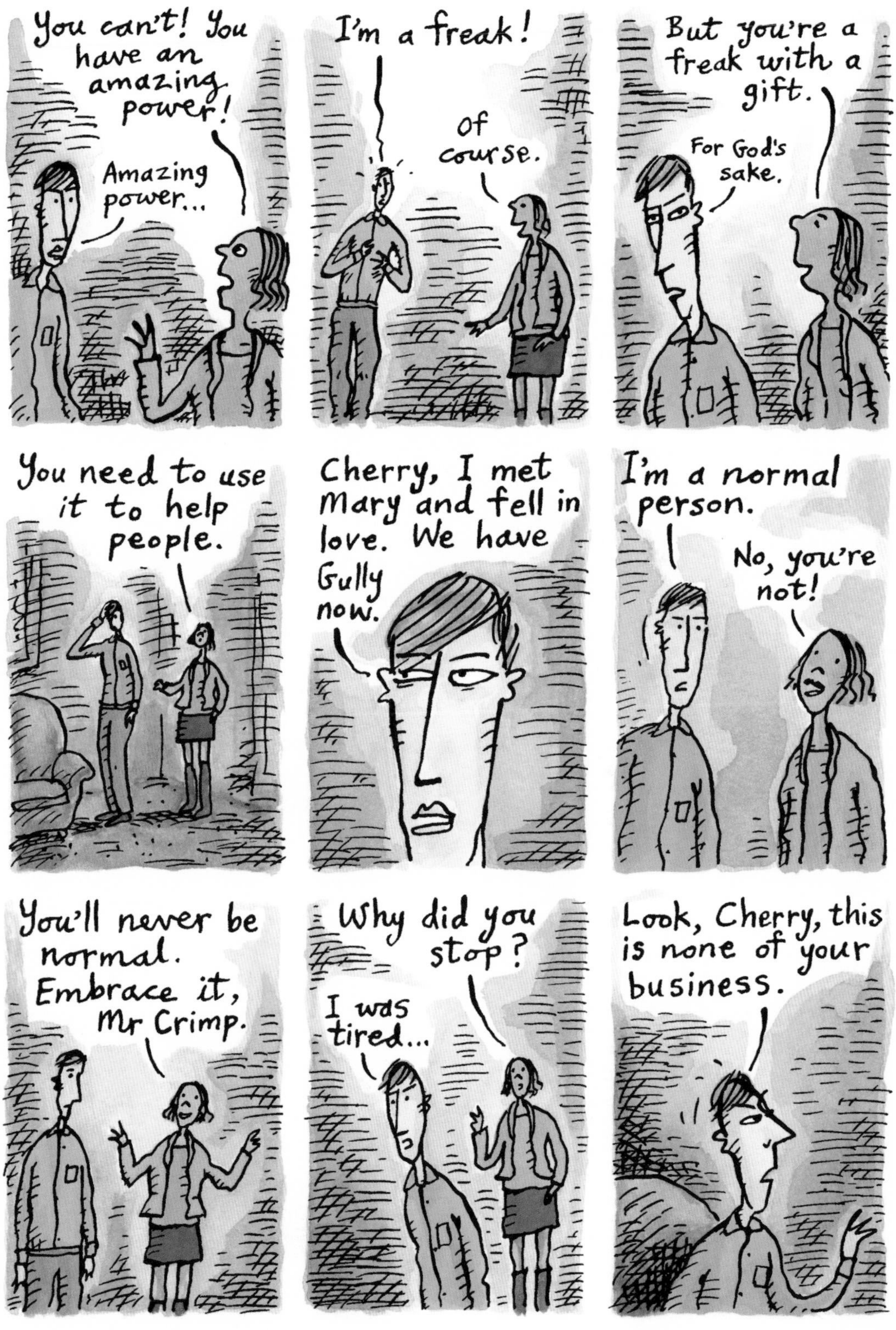

You can't! You have an amazing power!
Amazing power...
I'm a freak!
Of course.
But you're a freak with a gift.
For God's sake.
You need to use it to help people.
Cherry, I met Mary and fell in love. We have Gully now.
I'm a normal person.
No, you're not!
You'll never be normal. Embrace it, Mr Crimp.
Why did you stop?
I was tired...
Look, Cherry, this is none of your business.

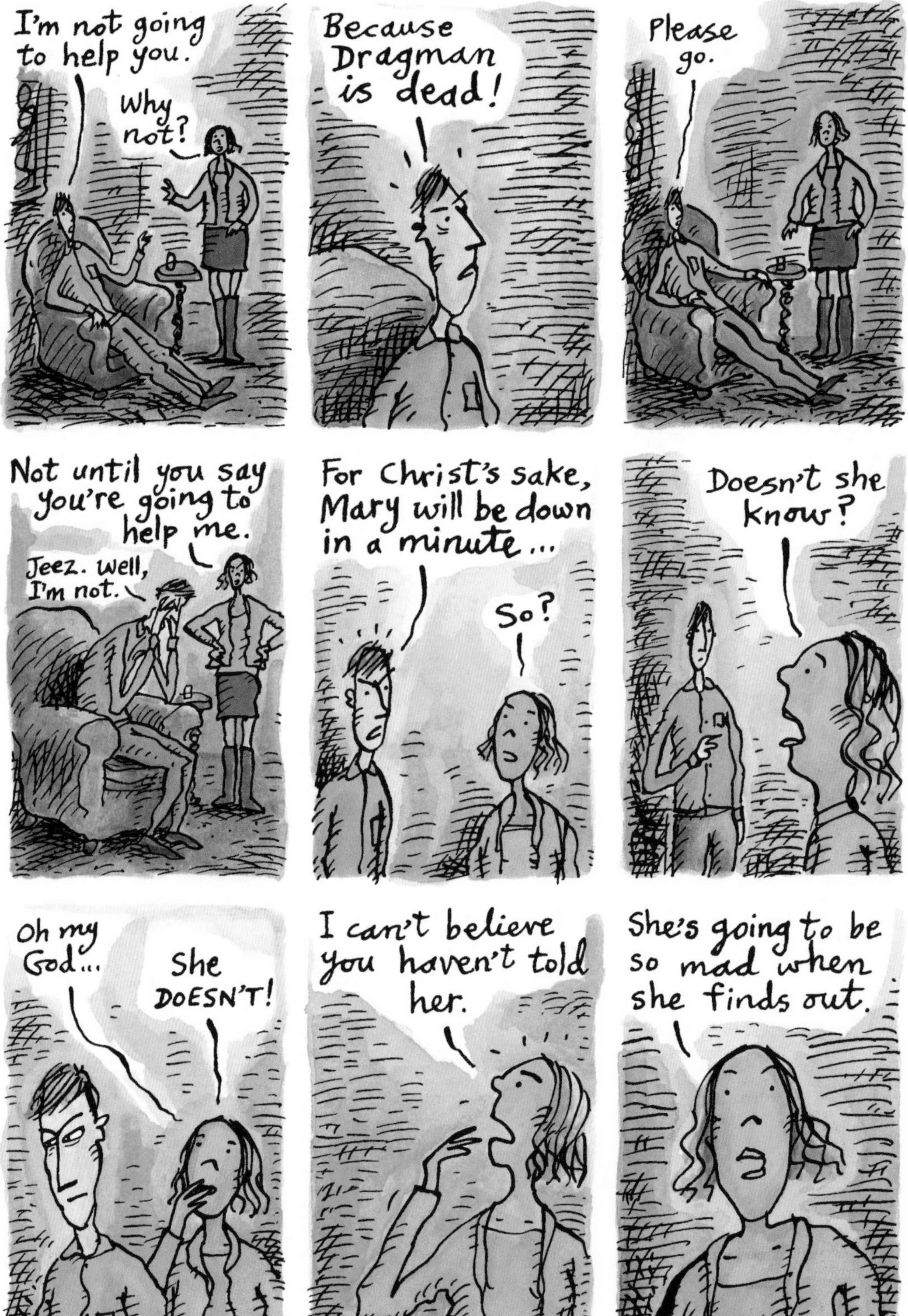
I'm not going to help you.
Why not?
Because Dragman is dead!
Please go.
Not until you say you're going to help me.
Jeez. Well, I'm not.
For Christ's sake, Mary will be down in a minute...
So?
Doesn't she know?
Oh my God...
She DOESN'T!
I can't believe you haven't told her.
She's going to be so mad when she finds out.

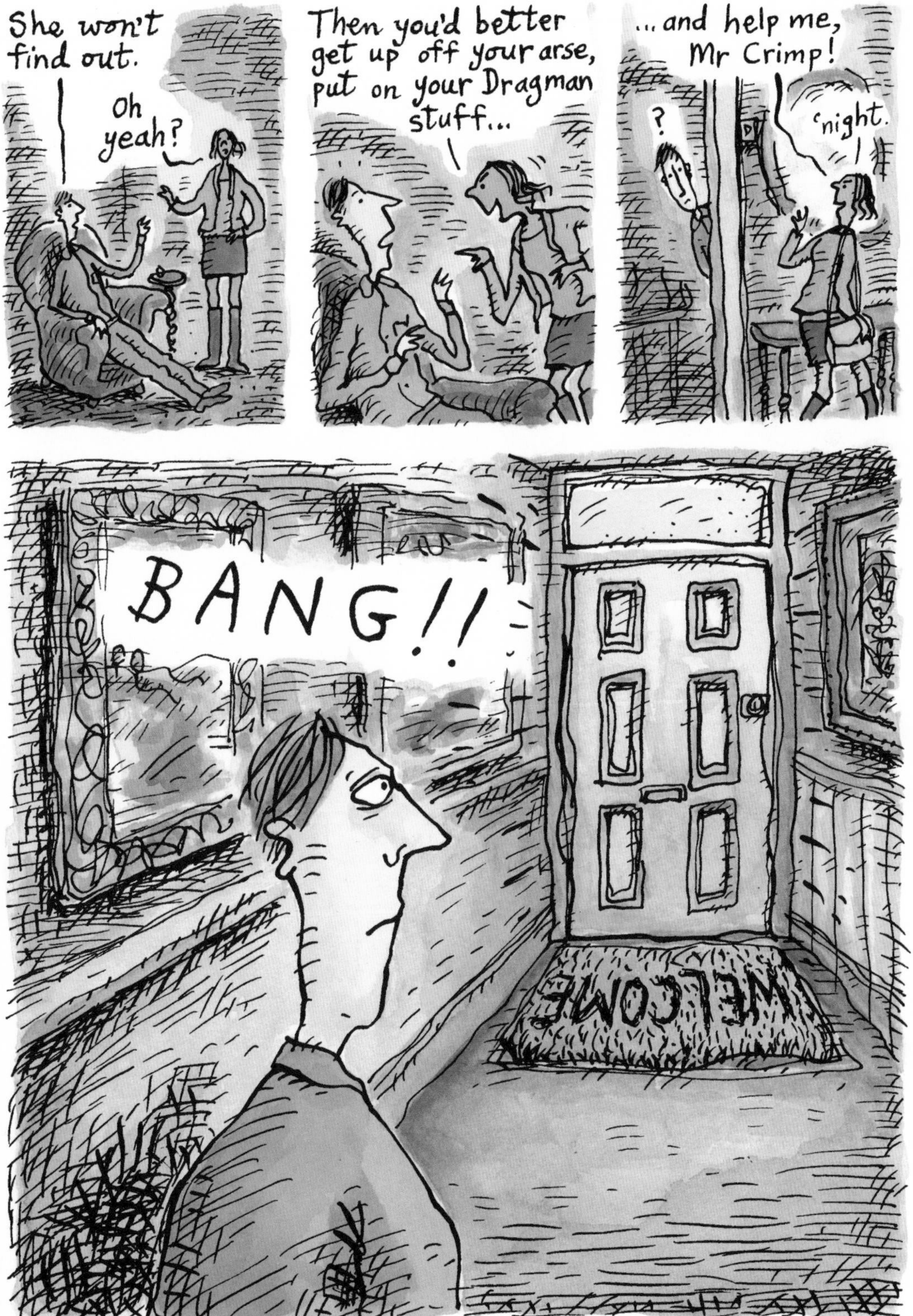
She won't find out.
Oh yeah?
Then you'd better get up off your arse, put on your Dragman stuff...
?
...and help me, Mr Crimp!
'night.
BANG!!
WELCOME

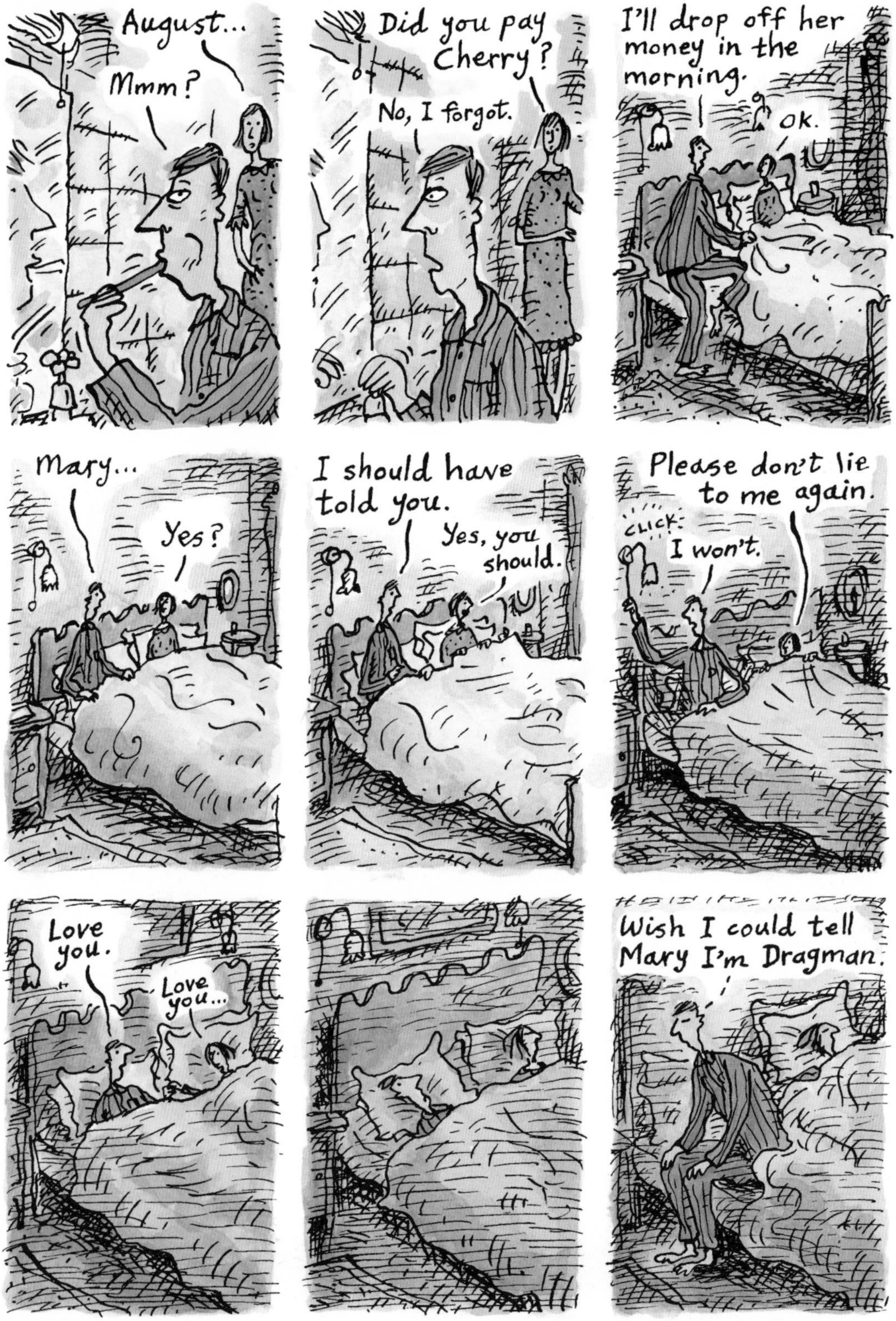
August...
Mmm?
Did you pay Cherry?
No, I forgot.
I'll drop off her money in the morning.
OK.
Mary...
Yes?
I should have told you.
Yes, you should.
Please don't lie to me again.
CLICK
I won't.
Love you.
Love you...
Wish I could tell Mary I'm Dragman.

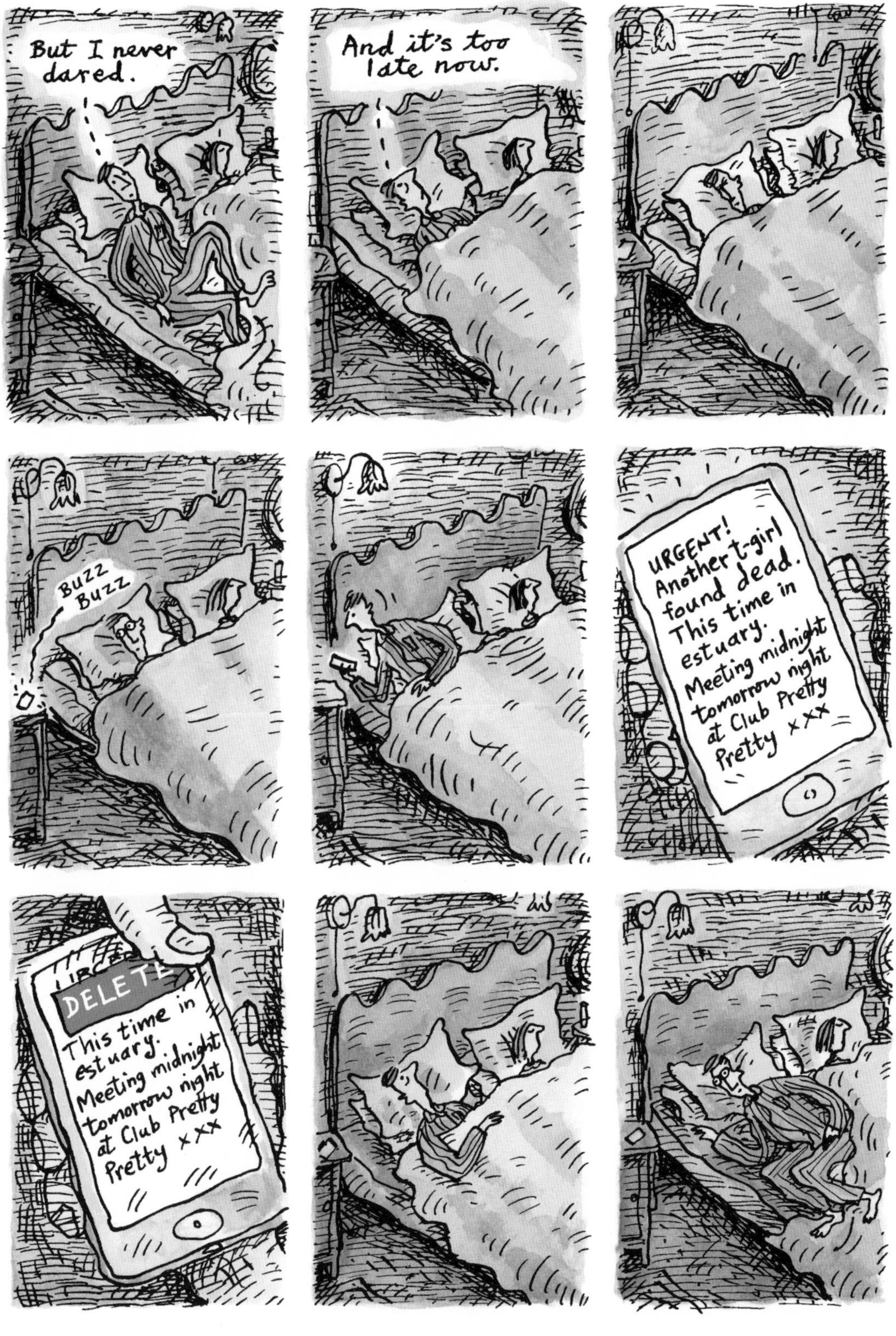
But I never dared.
And it's too late now.
BUZZ BUZZ
URGENT! Another t-girl found dead. This time in estuary. Meeting midnight tomorrow night at Club Pretty Pretty xxx
DELETE
This time in estuary. Meeting midnight tomorrow night at Club Pretty Pretty xxx

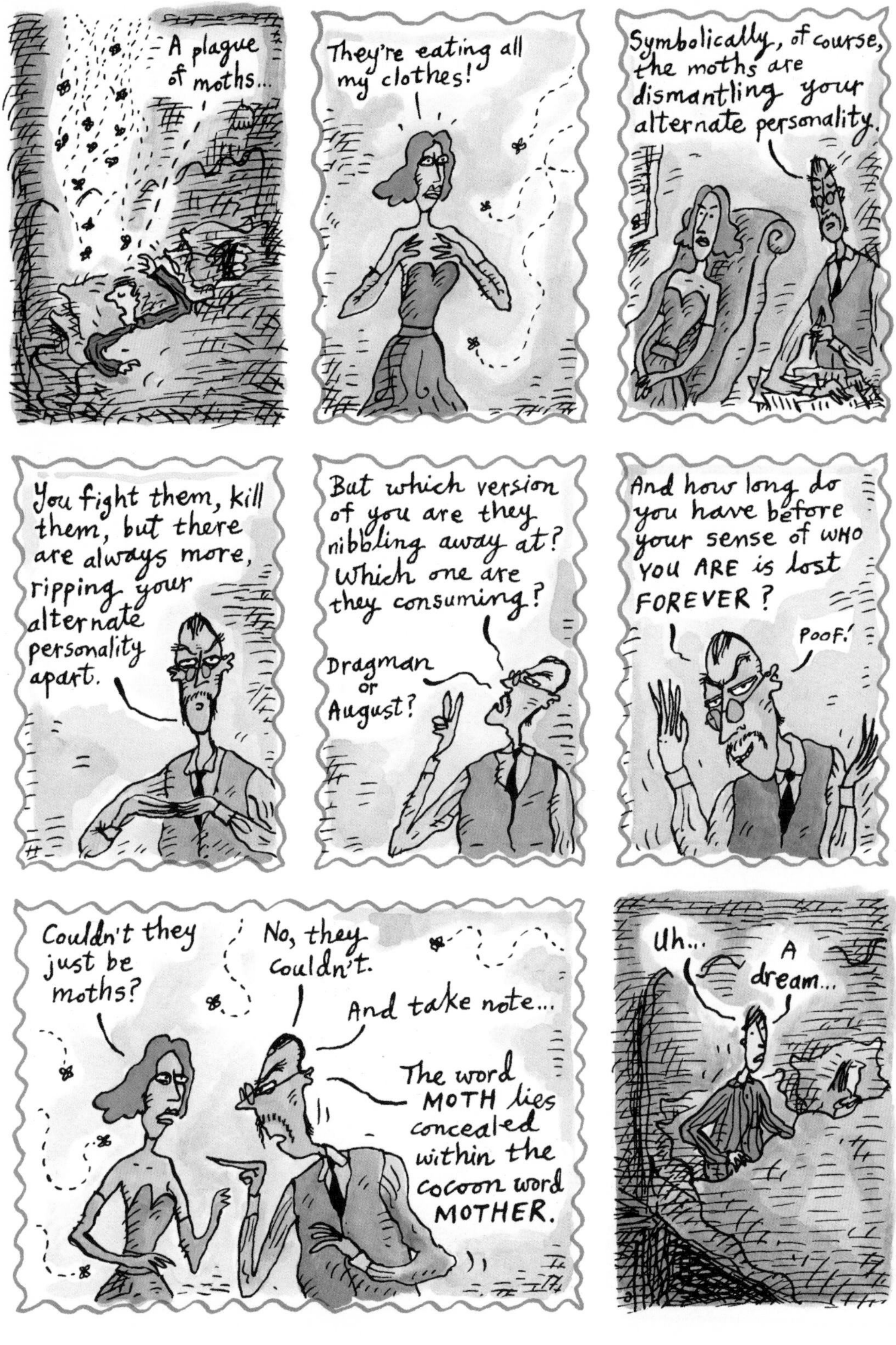
A plague of moths...
They're eating all my clothes!
Symbolically, of course, the moths are dismantling your alternate personality.
You fight them, kill them, but there are always more, ripping your alternate personality apart.
But which version of you are they nibbling away at? Which one are they consuming?
Dragman or August?
And how long do you have before your sense of WHO YOU ARE is lost FOREVER?
POOF!
Couldn't they just be moths?
No, they couldn't.
And take note...
The word MOTH lies concealed within the cocoon word MOTHER.
Uh...
A dream...

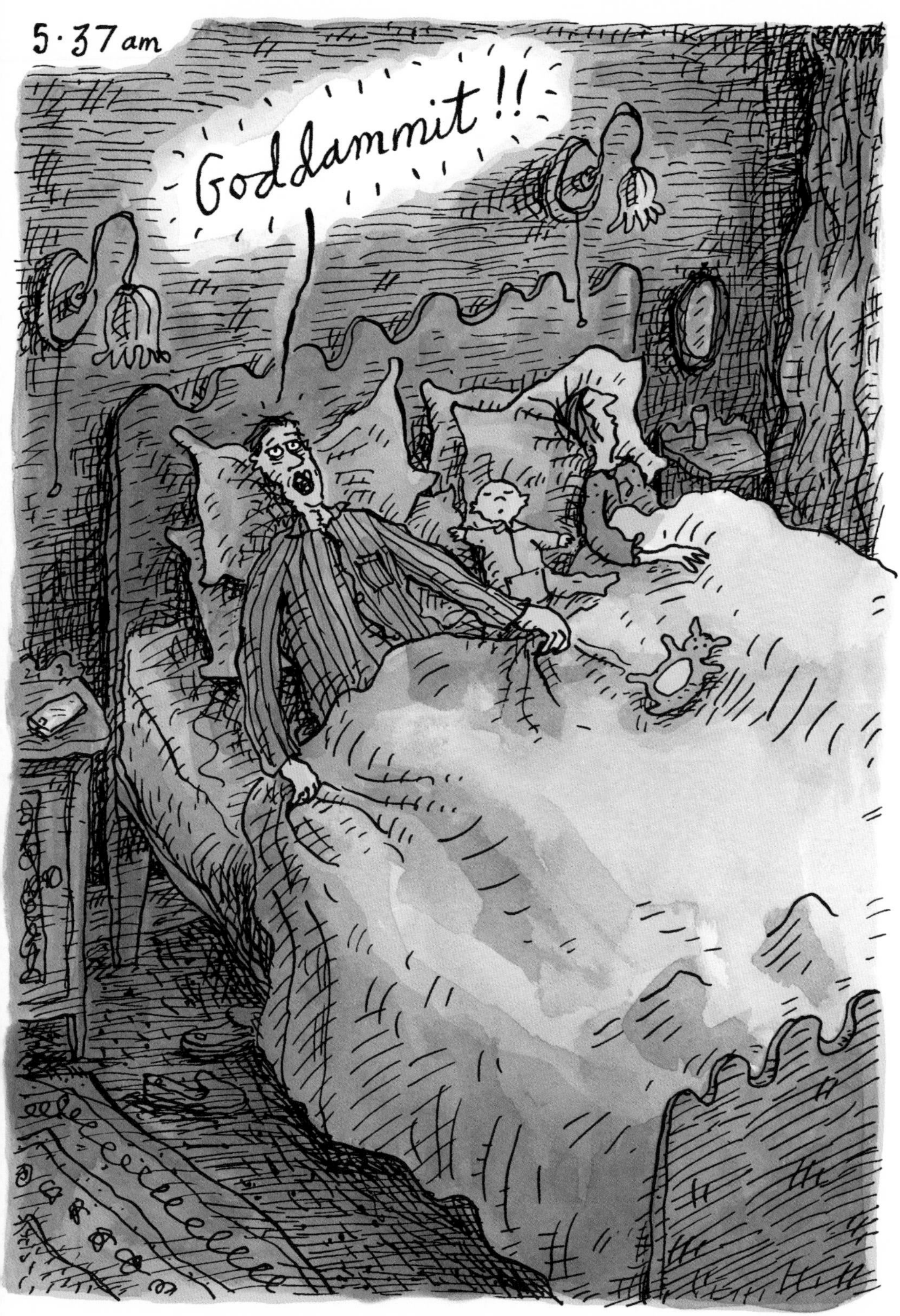
5·37 am
Goddammit!!

Saturday

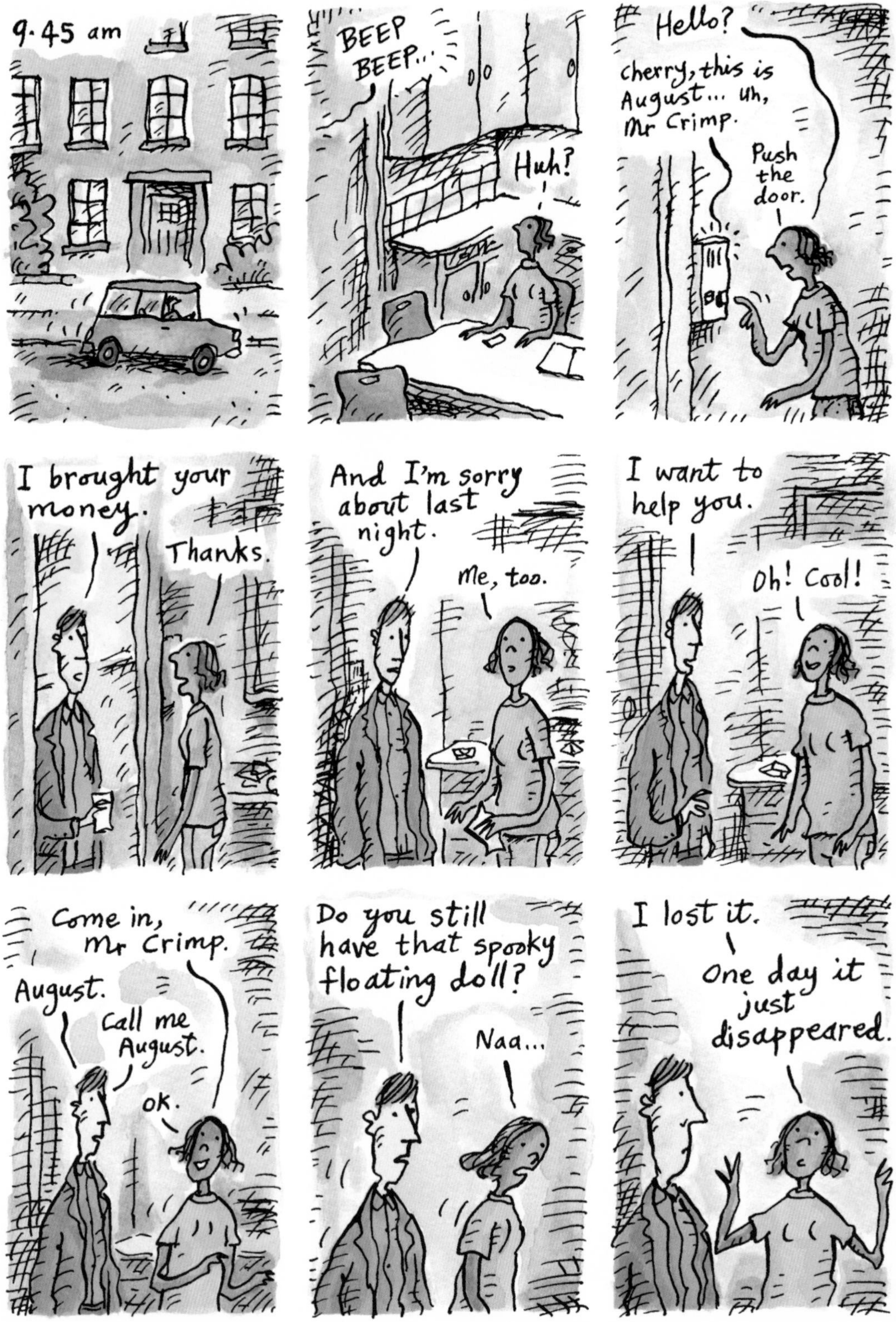
9.45 am
BEEP BEEP...
Huh?
Hello?
Cherry, this is August... uh, Mr Crimp.
Push the door.
I brought your money.
Thanks.
And I'm sorry about last night.
Me, too.
I want to help you.
Oh! Cool!
Come in, Mr Crimp.
August.
Call me August.
OK.
Do you still have that spooky floating doll?
Naa...
I lost it.
One day it just disappeared.

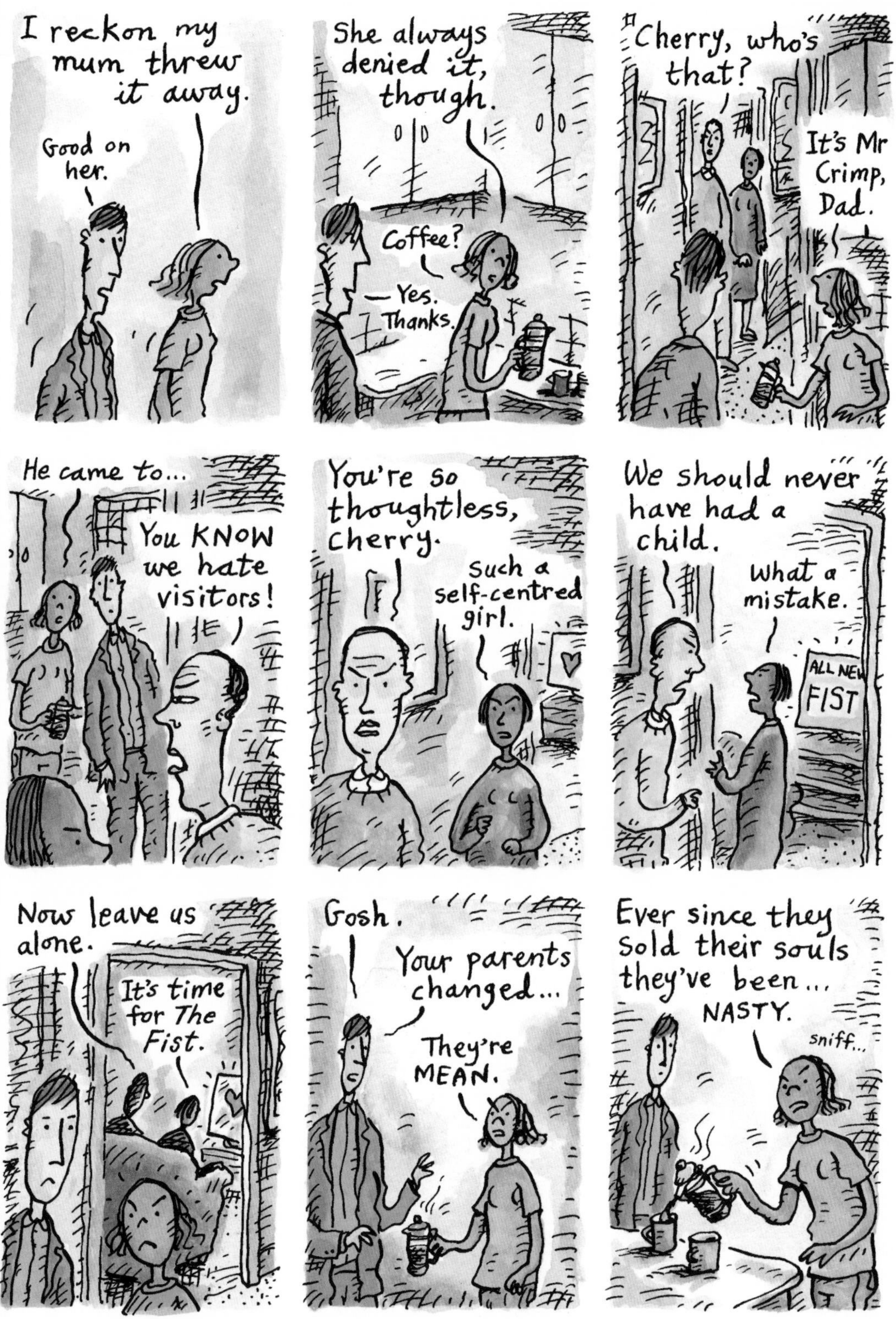
I reckon my mum threw it away.
Good on her.
She always denied it, though.
Coffee?
Yes. Thanks.
Cherry, who's that?
It's Mr Crimp, Dad.
He came to...
You KNOW we hate visitors!
You're so thoughtless, cherry.
Such a self-centred girl.
We should never have had a child.
What a mistake.
ALL NEW FIST
Now leave us alone.
It's time for The Fist.
Gosh.
Your parents changed...
They're MEAN.
Ever since they sold their souls they've been...
NASTY.
sniff...

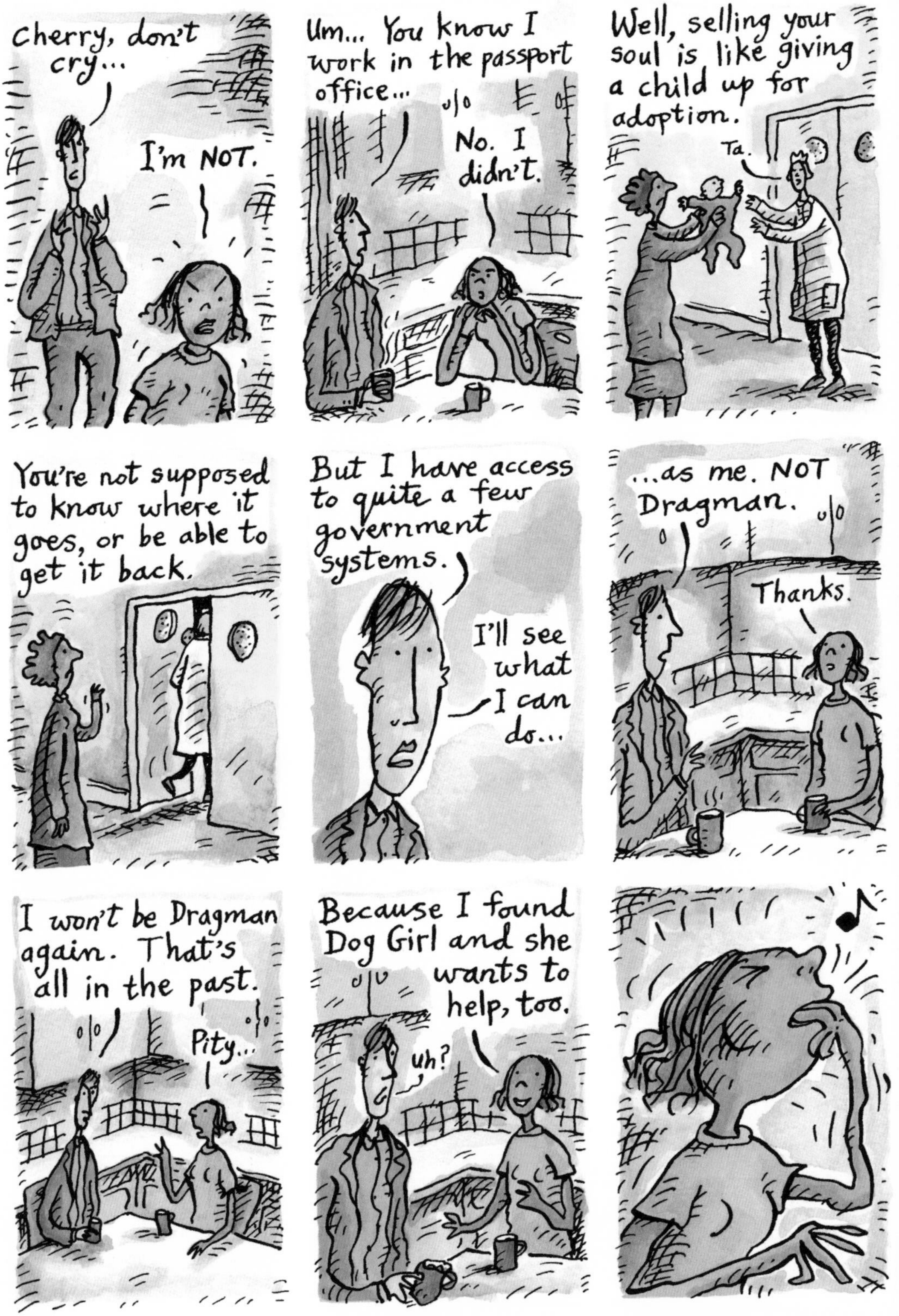
Cherry, don't cry...
I'm NOT.
Um... You know I work in the passport office...
No. I didn't.
Well, selling your soul is like giving a child up for adoption.
Ta.
You're not supposed to know where it goes, or be able to get it back.
But I have access to quite a few government systems.
I'll see what I can do...
...as me. NOT Dragman.
Thanks.
I won't be Dragman again. That's all in the past.
Pity...
Because I found Dog Girl and she wants to help, too.
uh?

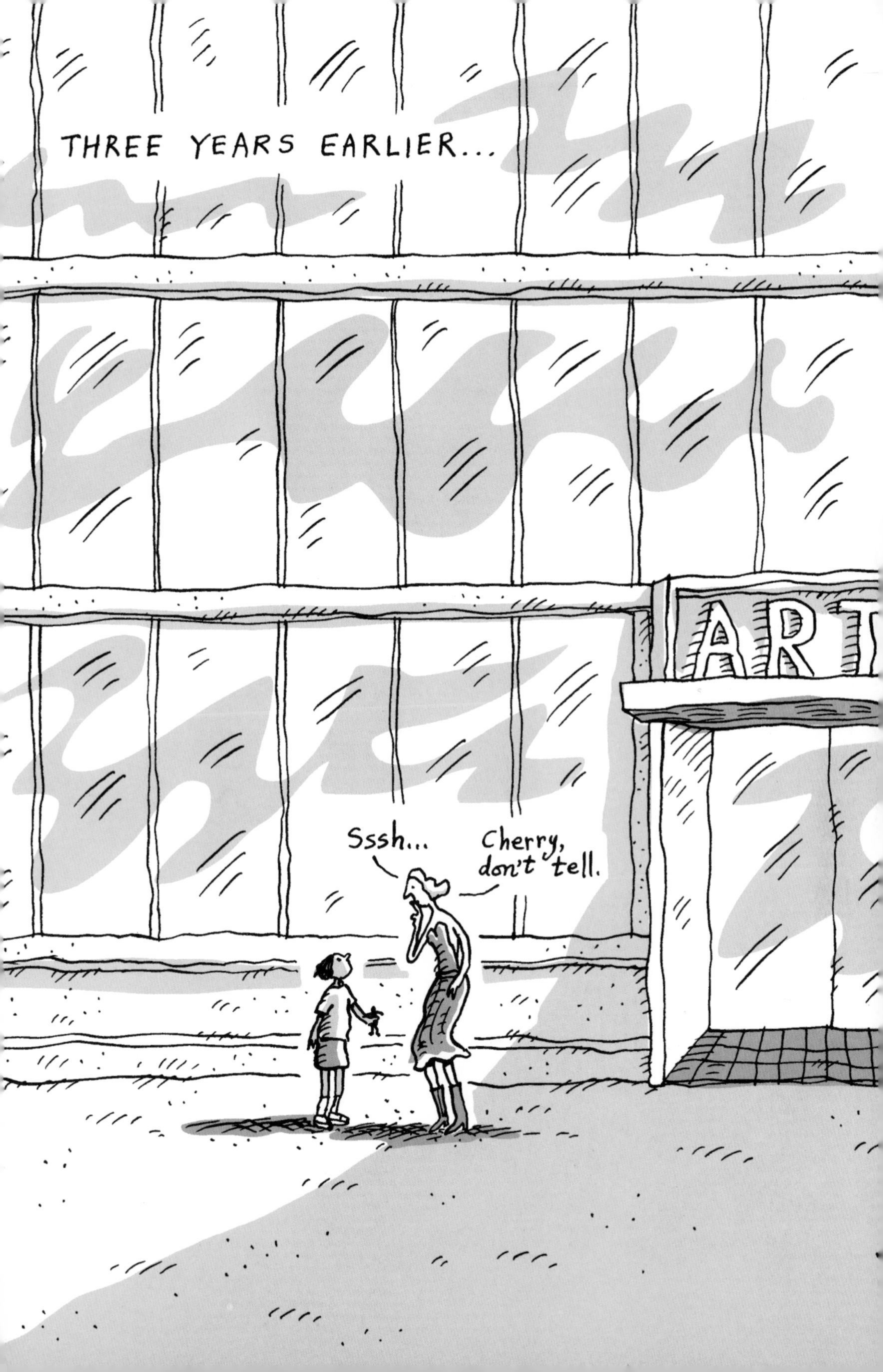
THREE YEARS EARLIER...
ART
Sssh...
Cherry, don't tell.

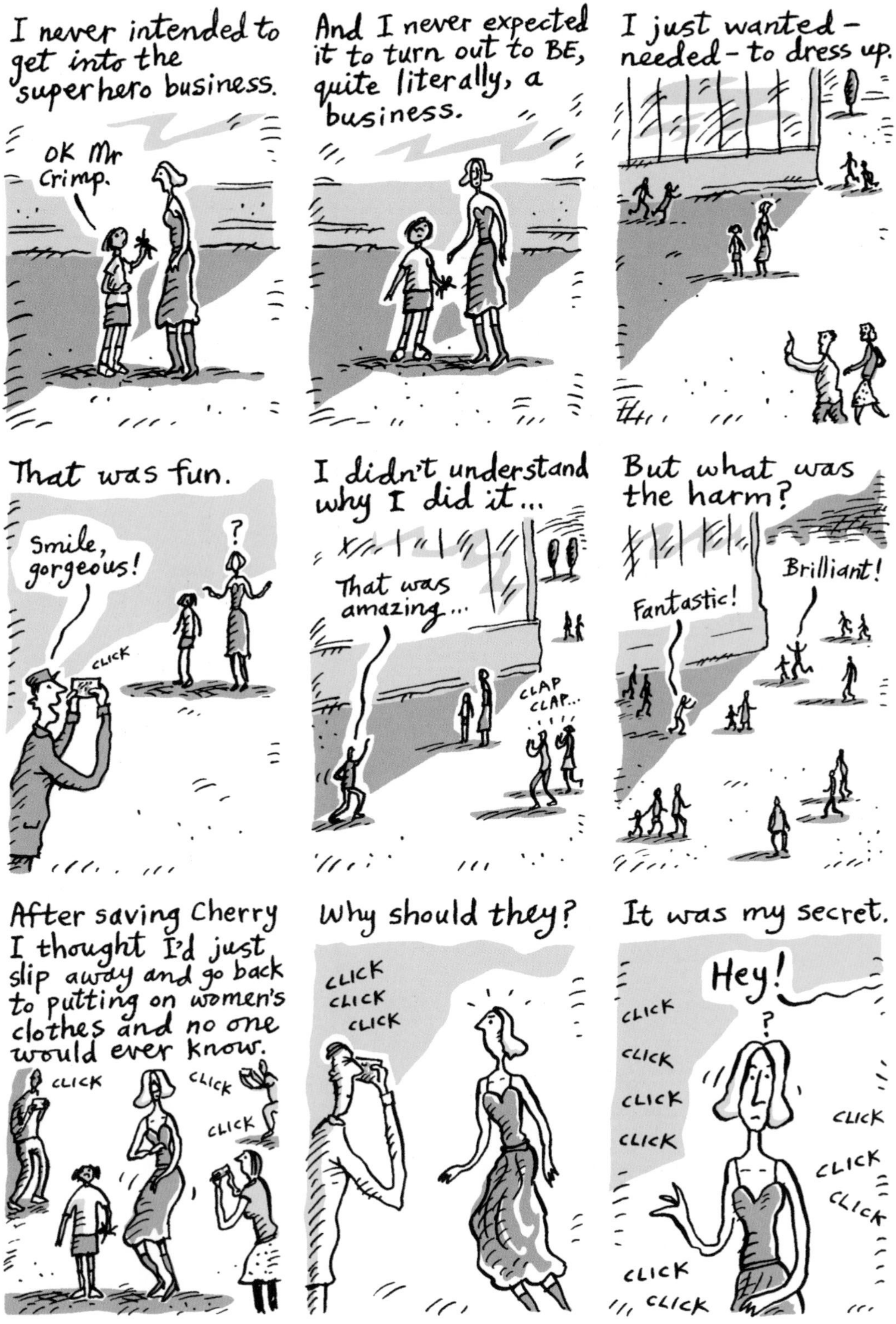
I never intended to get into the superhero business.
OK Mr Crimp.
And I never expected it to turn out to BE, quite literally, a business.
I just wanted – needed – to dress up.
That was fun.
Smile, gorgeous!
CLICK
?
I didn't understand why I did it...
That was amazing...
CLAP CLAP...
But what was the harm?
Fantastic!
Brilliant!
After saving Cherry I thought I'd just slip away and go back to putting on women's clothes and no one would ever know.
CLICK
CLICK
CLICK
Why should they?
CLICK
CLICK
CLICK
It was my secret.
Hey!
?
CLICK
CLICK
CLICK
CLICK
CLICK
CLICK
CLICK
CLICK
CLICK

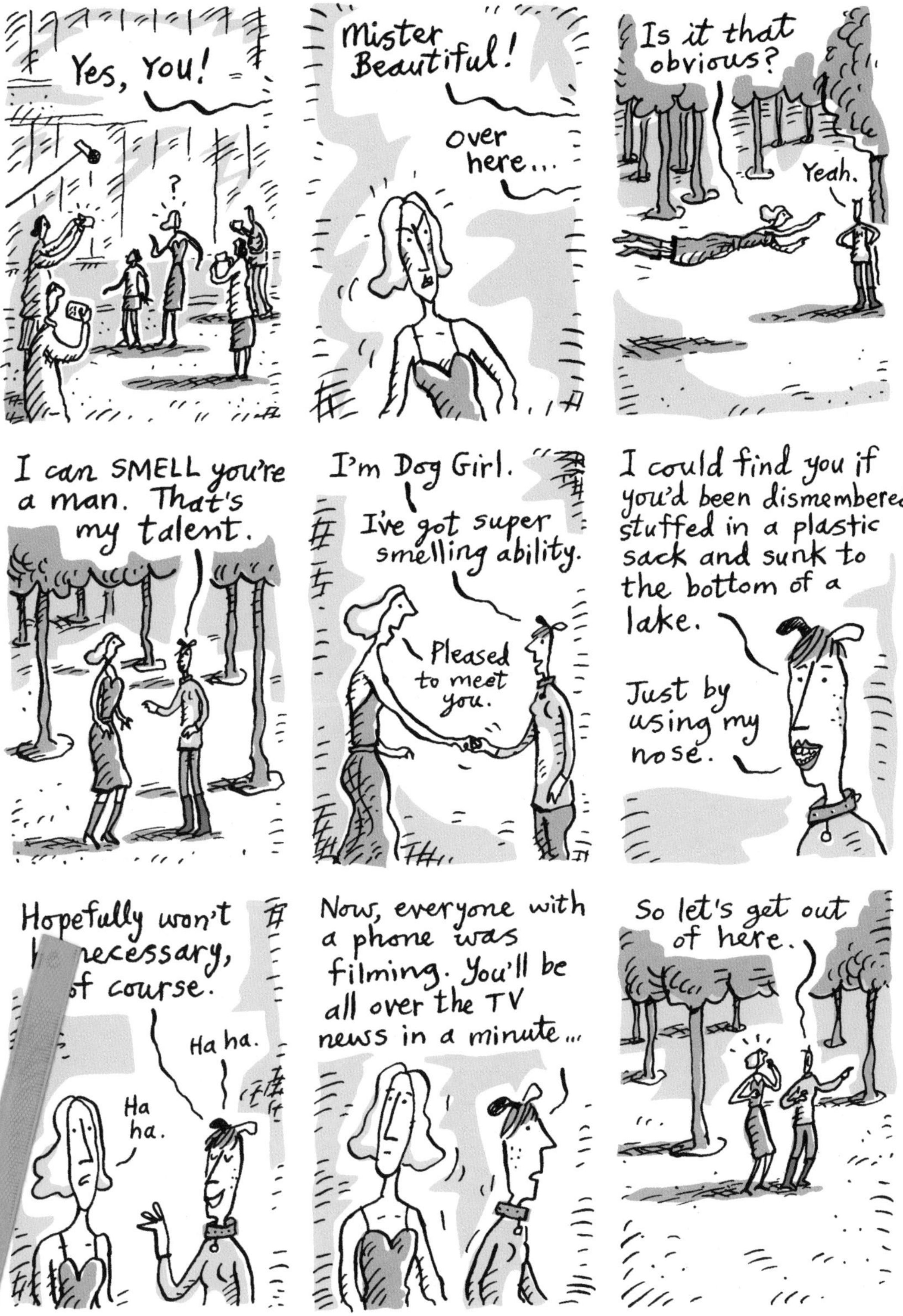
Yes, YOU!
Mister Beautiful!
over here...
Is it that obvious?
Yeah.
I can SMELL you're a man. That's my talent.
I'm Dog Girl.
I've got super smelling ability.
Pleased to meet you.
I could find you if you'd been dismembered, stuffed in a plastic sack and sunk to the bottom of a lake.
Just by using my nose.
Hopefully won't
ecessary,
f course.
Ha ha.
Ha ha.
Now, everyone with a phone was filming. You'll be all over the TV news in a minute...
So let's get out of here.

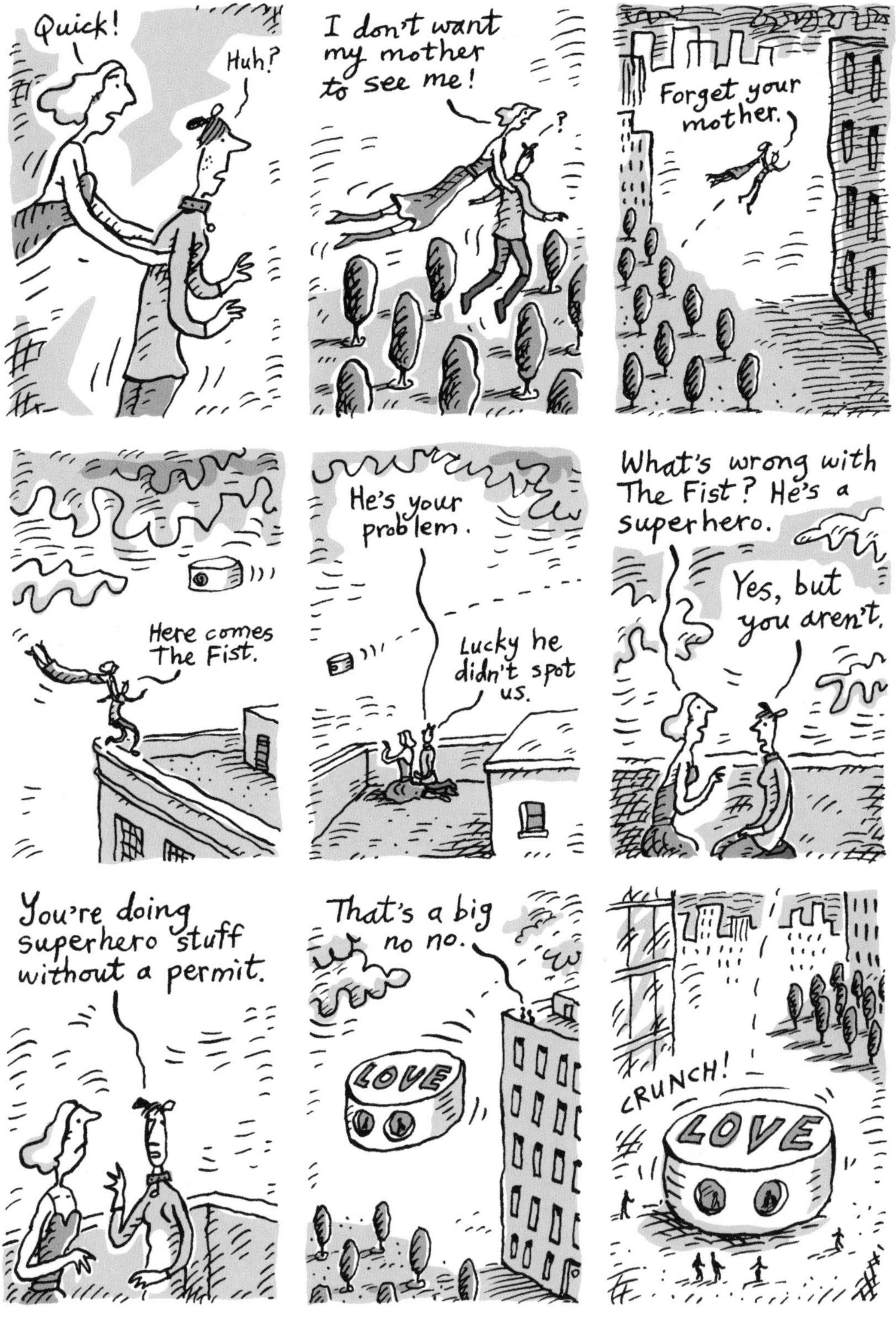
Quick!
Huh?
I don't want my mother to see me!
?
Forget your mother.
Here comes The Fist.
He's your problem.
Lucky he didn't spot us.
What's wrong with The Fist? He's a superhero.
Yes, but you aren't.
You're doing superhero stuff without a permit.
That's a big no no.
LOVE
CRUNCH!
LOVE

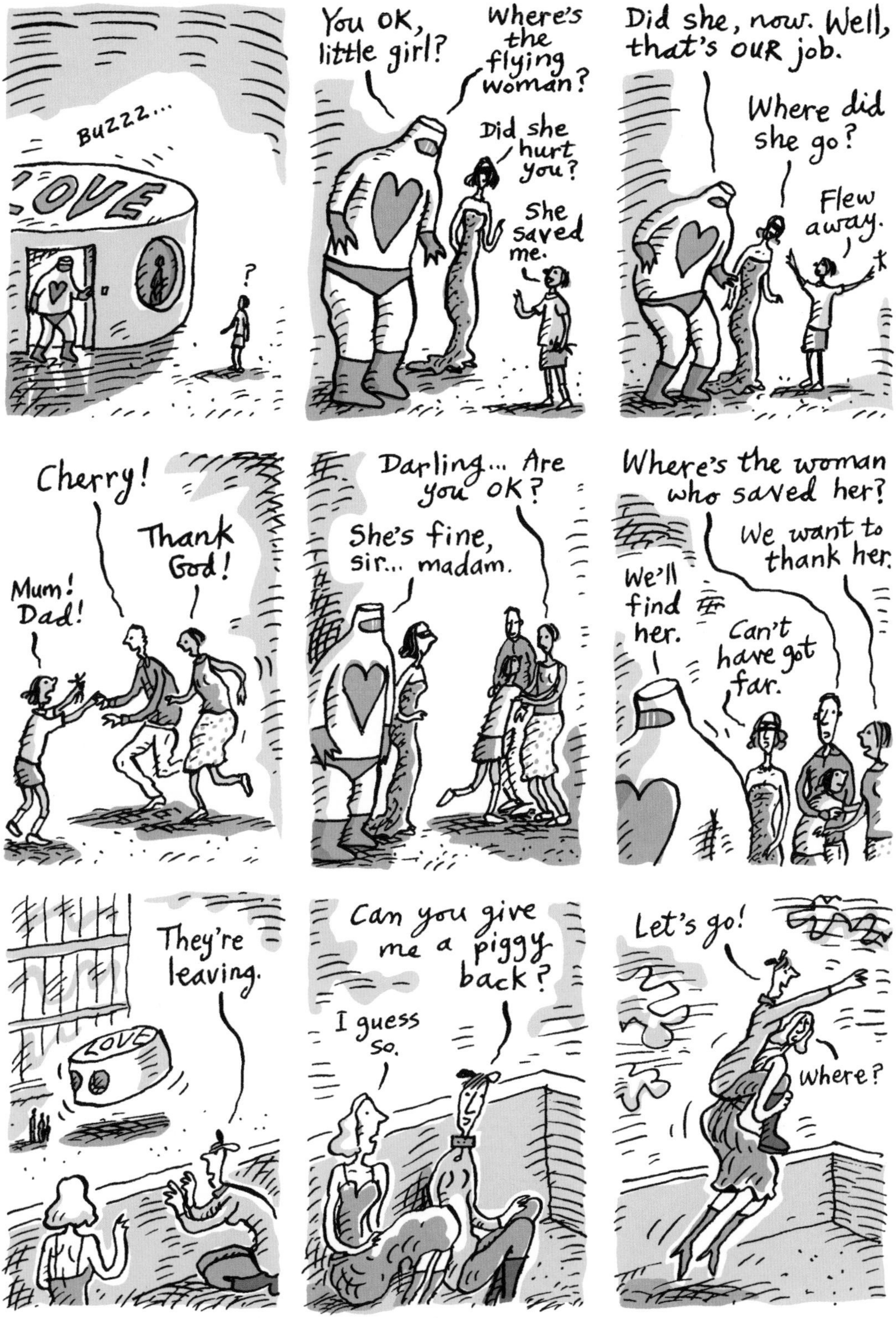

BUZZZ...
LOVE
?
You OK, little girl?
Where's the flying woman?
Did she hurt you?
She saved me.
Did she, now. Well, that's OUR job.
Where did she go?
Flew away.
Cherry!
Thank God!
Mum! Dad!
Darling... Are you OK?
She's fine, sir... madam.
Where's the woman who saved her?
We want to thank her.
We'll find her.
Can't have got far.
They're leaving.
LOVE
Can you give me a piggy back?
I guess so.
Let's go!
Where?

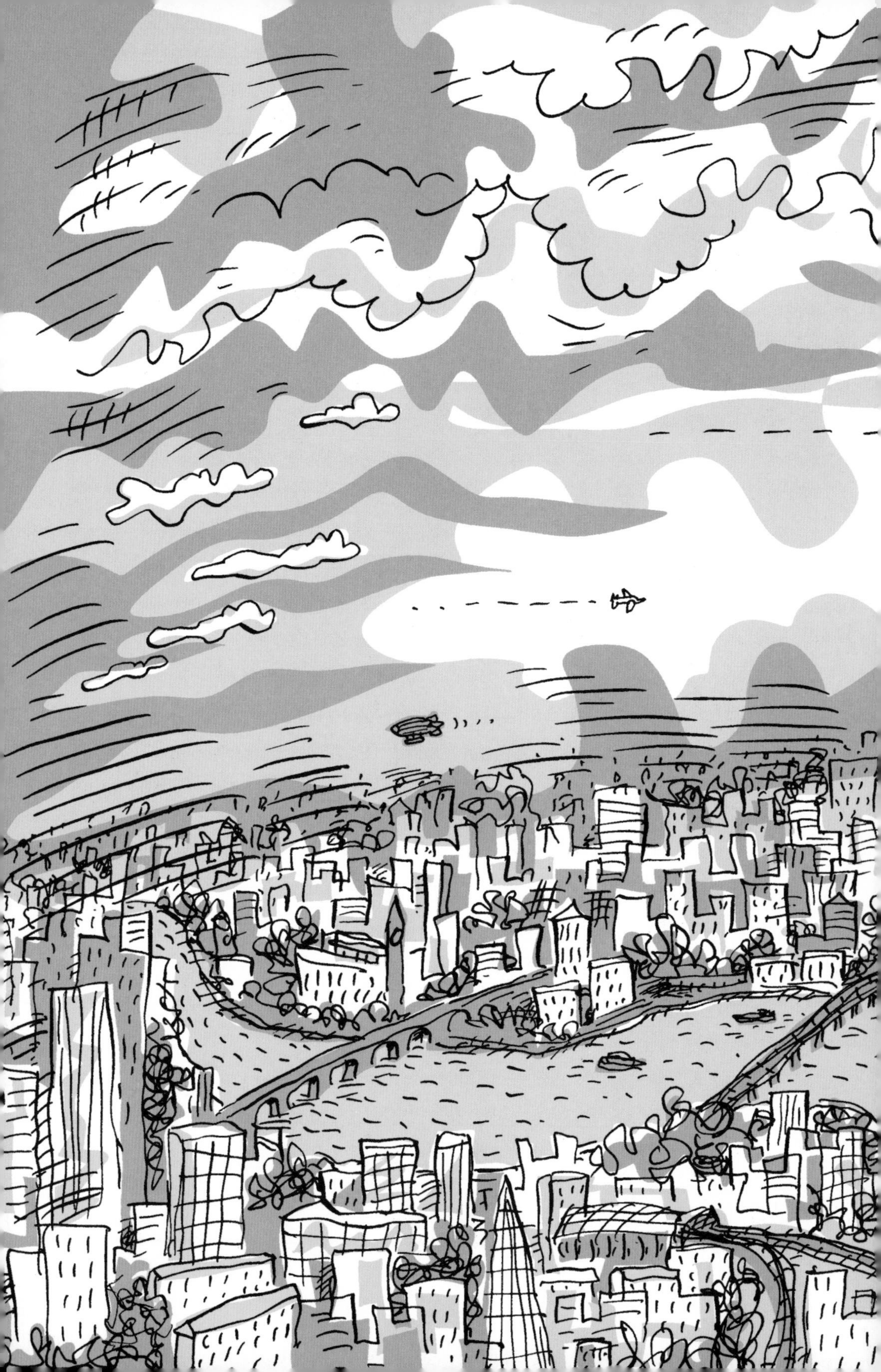

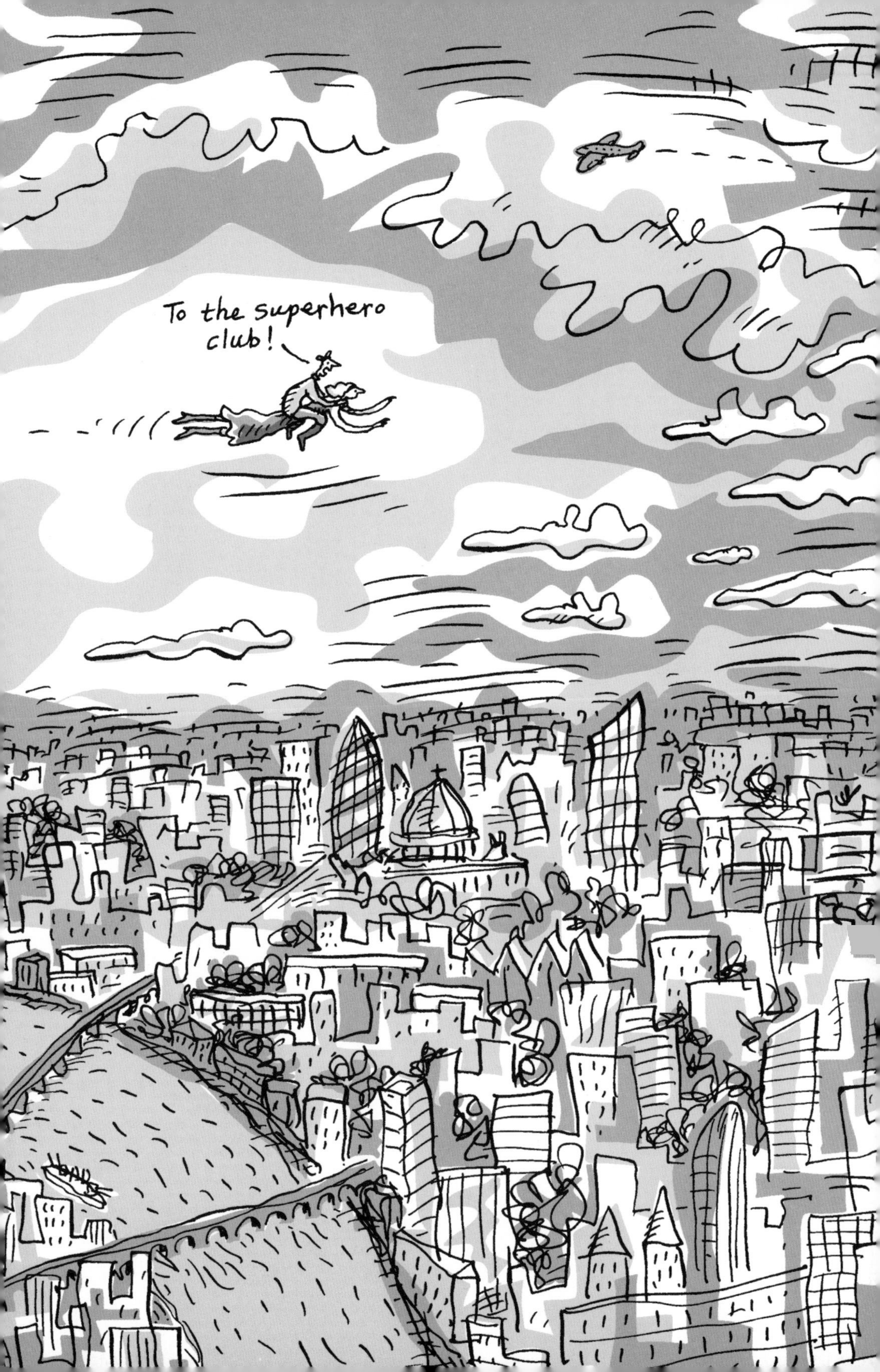
To the superhero club!

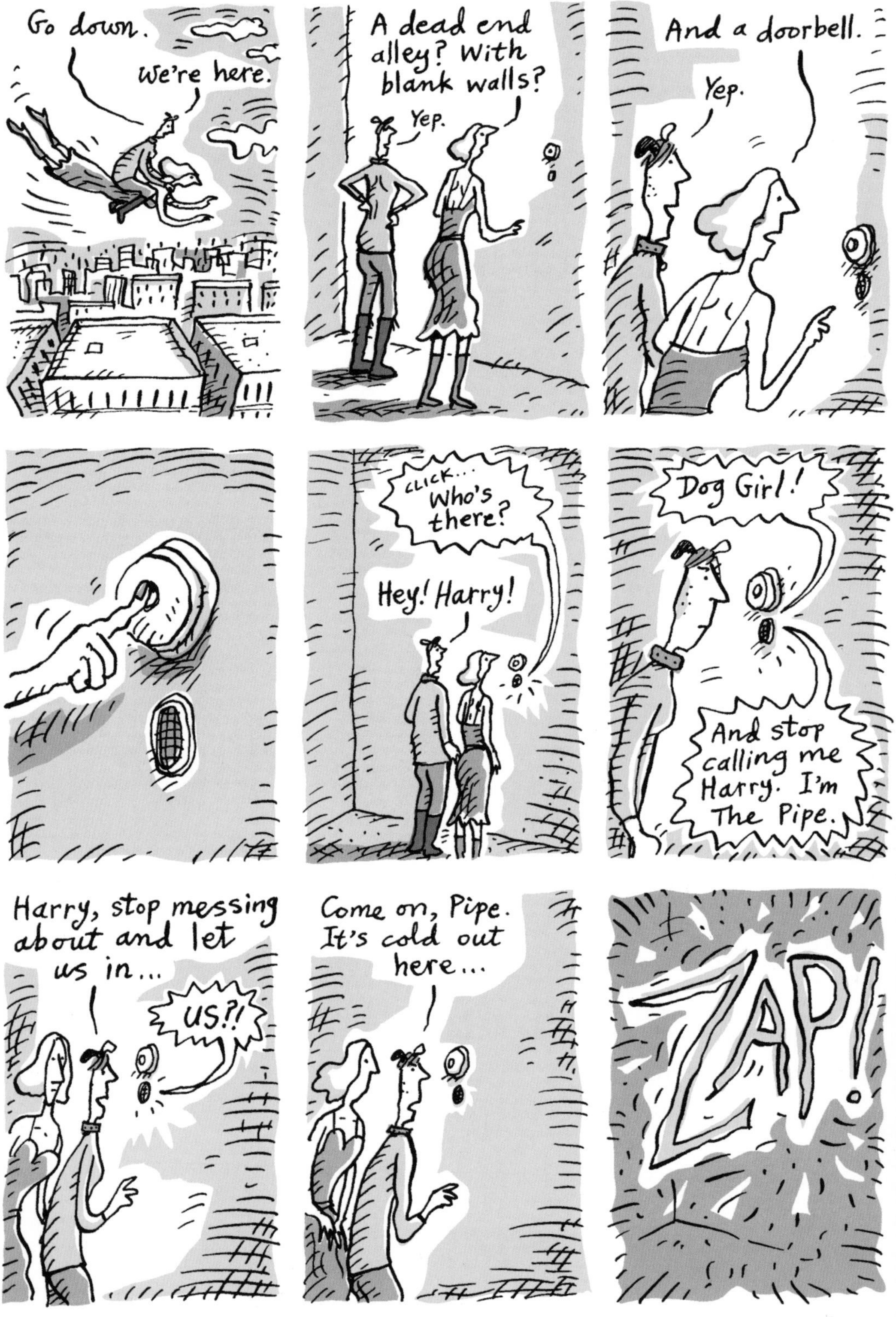
Go down.
We're here.
A dead end alley? With blank walls?
Yep.
And a doorbell.
Yep.
CLICK... Who's there?
Hey! Harry!
Dog Girl!
And stop calling me Harry. I'm The Pipe.
Harry, stop messing about and let us in...
US?!
Come on, Pipe. It's cold out here...
ZAP!

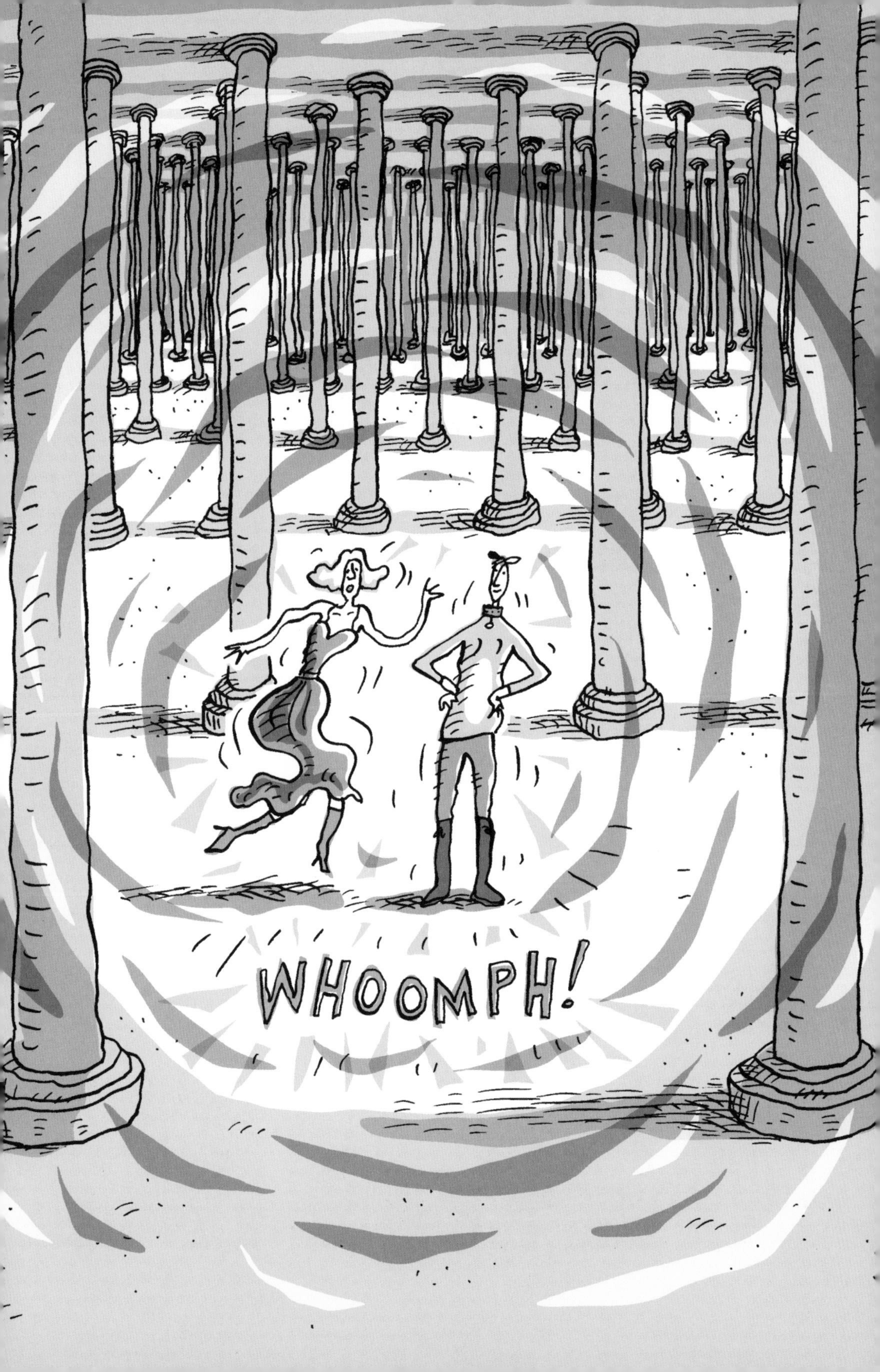
WHOOMPH!

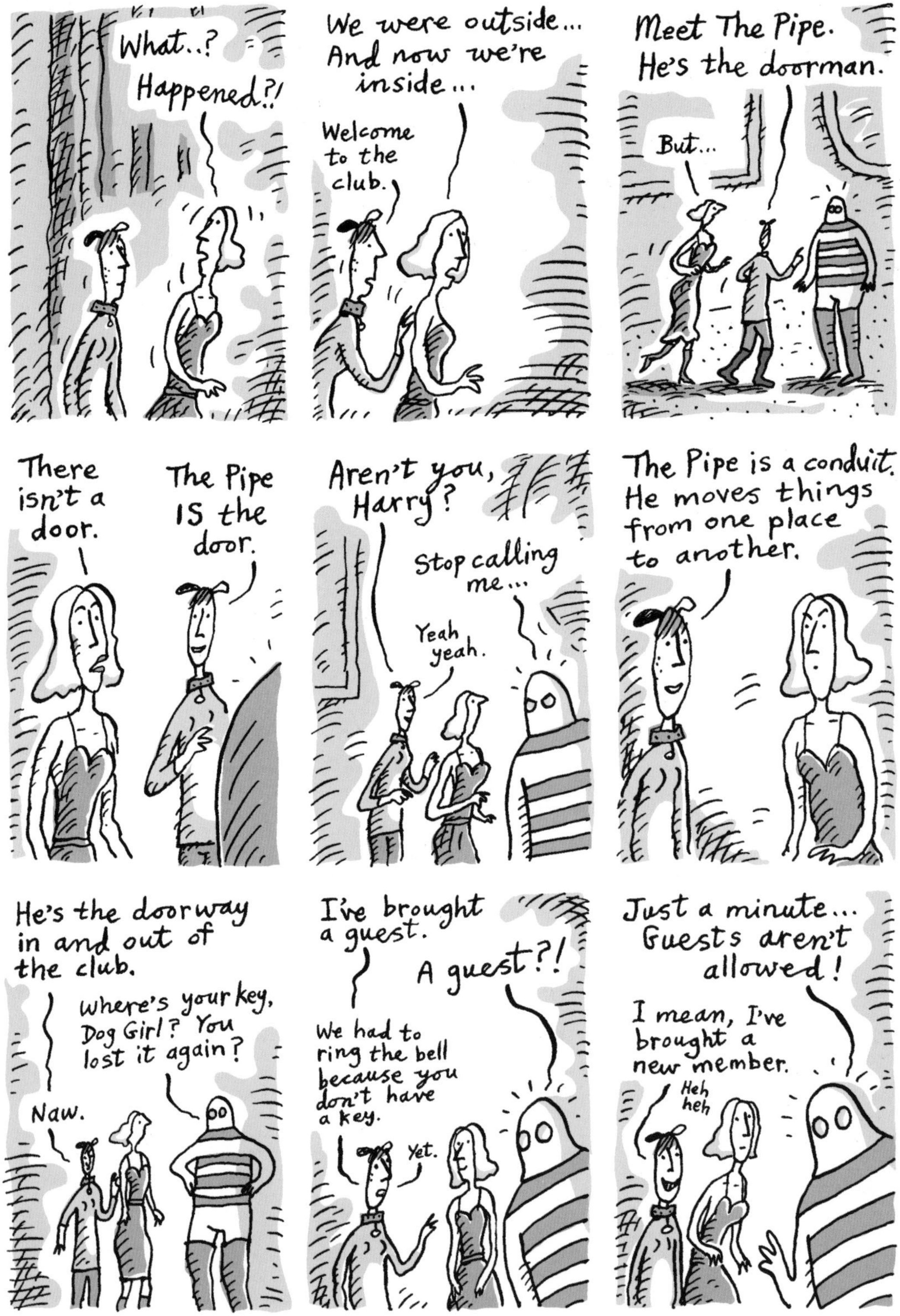
What..?
Happened?!
We were outside... And now we're inside...
Welcome to the club.
Meet The Pipe. He's the doorman.
But...
There isn't a door.
The Pipe IS the door.
Aren't you, Harry?
Stop calling me...
Yeah yeah.
The Pipe is a conduit. He moves things from one place to another.
He's the doorway in and out of the club.
Where's your key, Dog Girl? You lost it again?
Naw.
I've brought a guest.
A guest?!
We had to ring the bell because you don't have a key.
Yet.
Just a minute... Guests aren't allowed!
I mean, I've brought a new member.
Heh heh

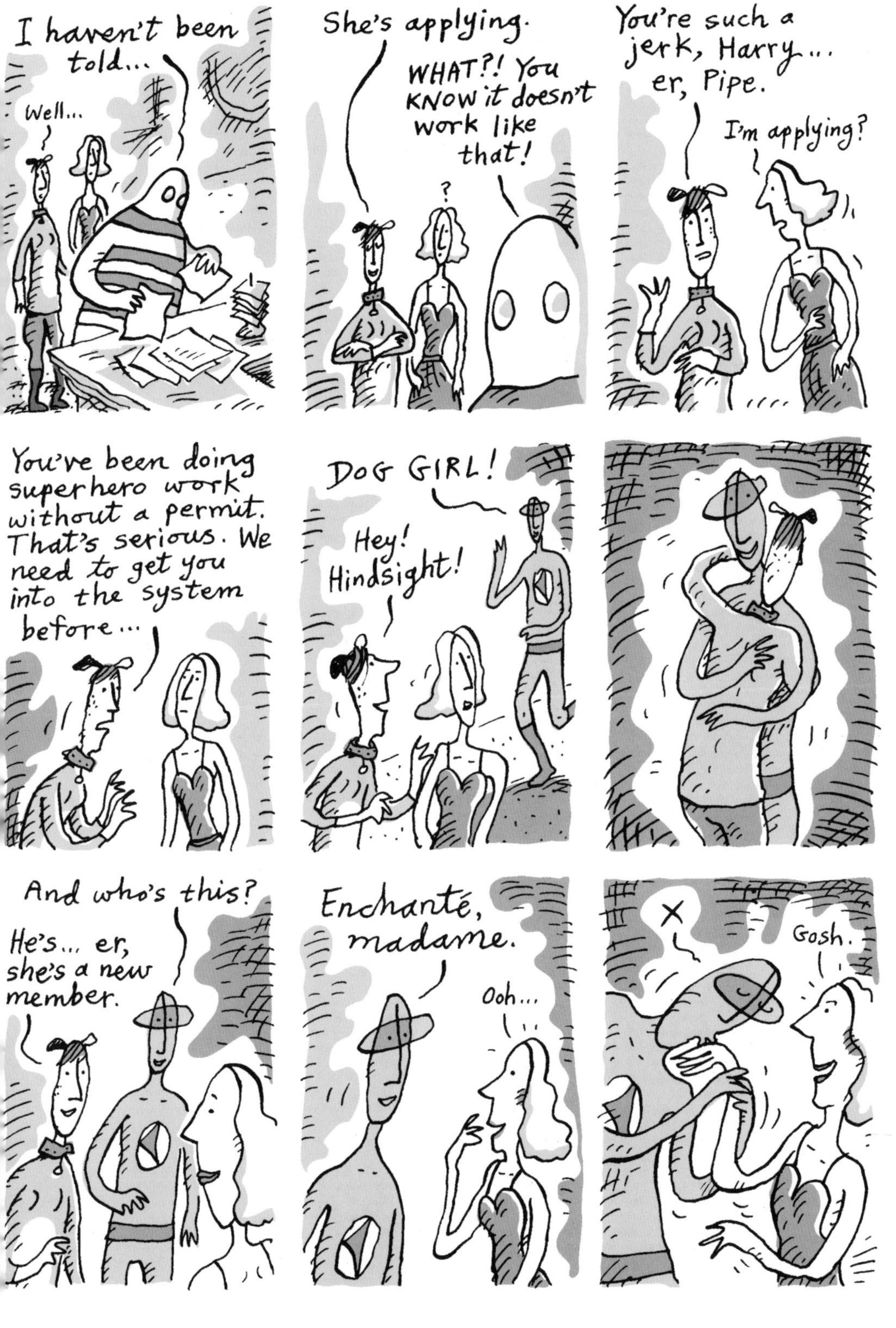
I haven't been told...
Well...
She's applying.
WHAT?! You KNOW it doesn't work like that!
?
You're such a jerk, Harry... er, Pipe.
I'm applying?
You've been doing superhero work without a permit. That's serious. We need to get you into the system before...
DOG GIRL!
Hey! Hindsight!
And who's this?
He's... er, she's a new member.
Enchanté, madame.
Ooh...
X
Gosh.

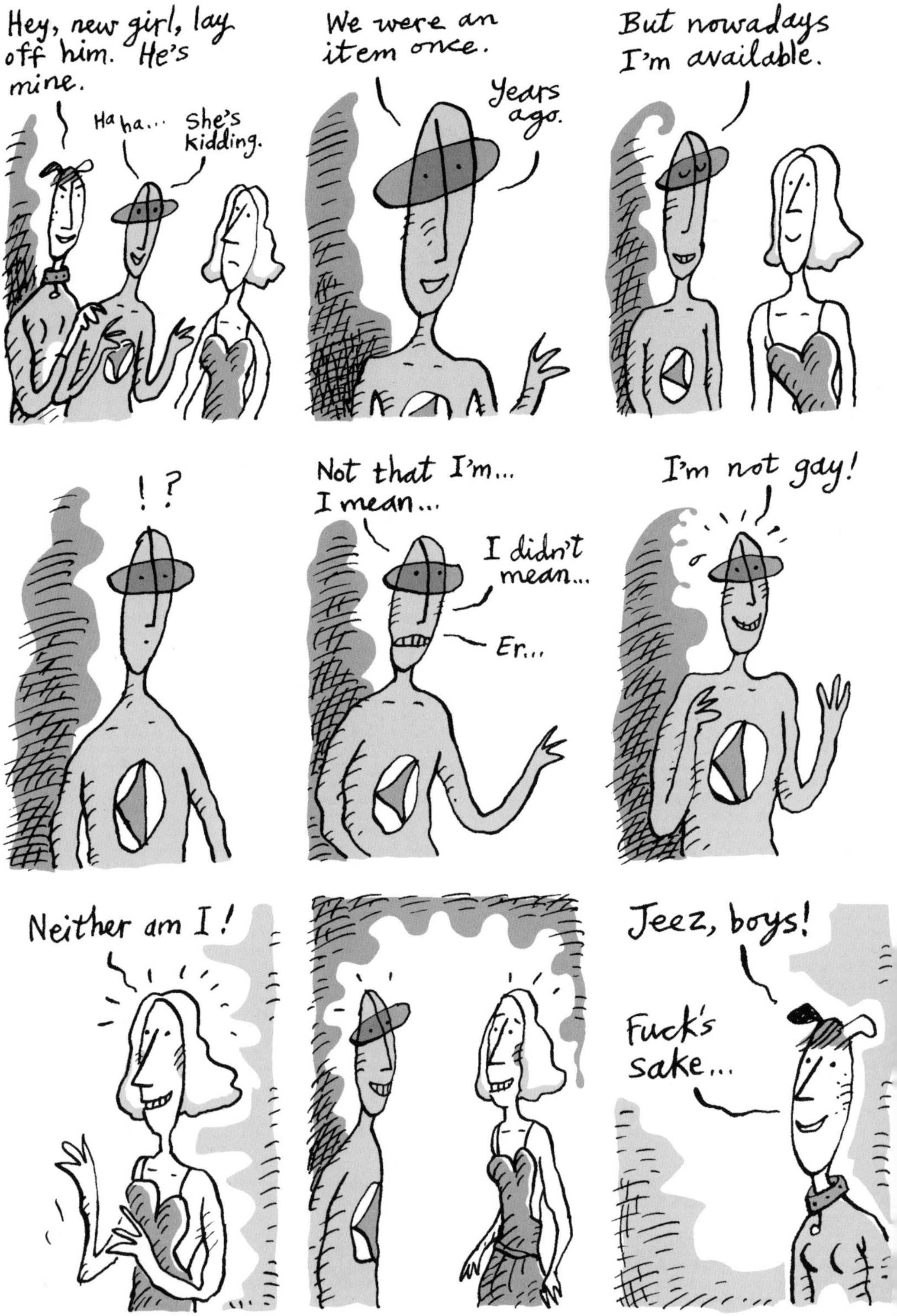
Hey, new girl, lay off him. He's mine.
Ha ha...
She's kidding.
We were an item once.
Years ago.
But nowadays I'm available.
! ?
Not that I'm... I mean...
I didn't mean...
Er...
I'm not gay!
Neither am I!
Jeez, boys!
Fuck's sake...

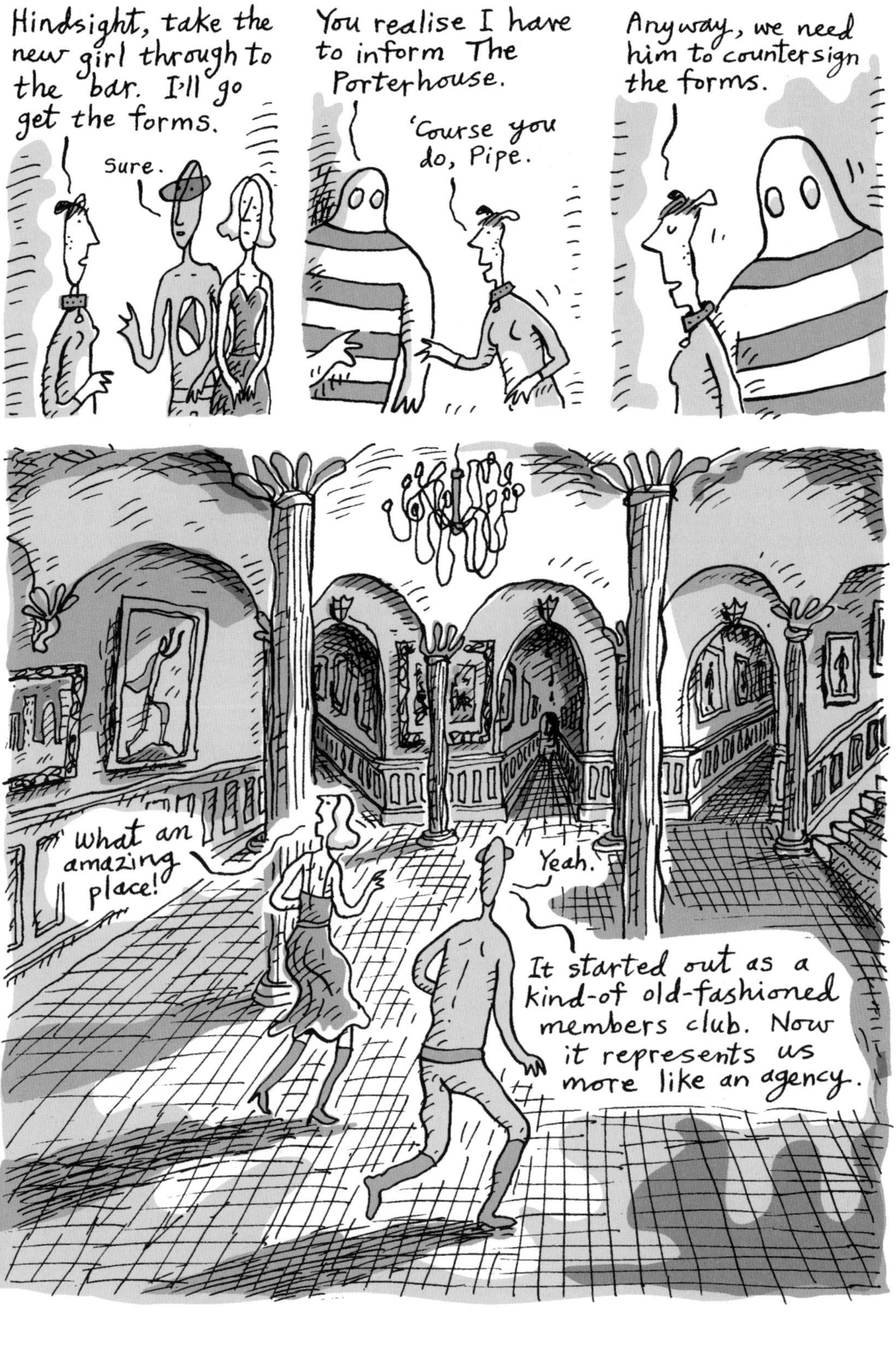
Hindsight, take the new girl through to the bar. I'll go get the forms.
Sure.
You realise I have to inform The Porterhouse.
'Course you do, Pipe.
Anyway, we need him to countersign the forms.
What an amazing place!
Yeah.
It started out as a kind-of old-fashioned members club. Now it represents us more like an agency.

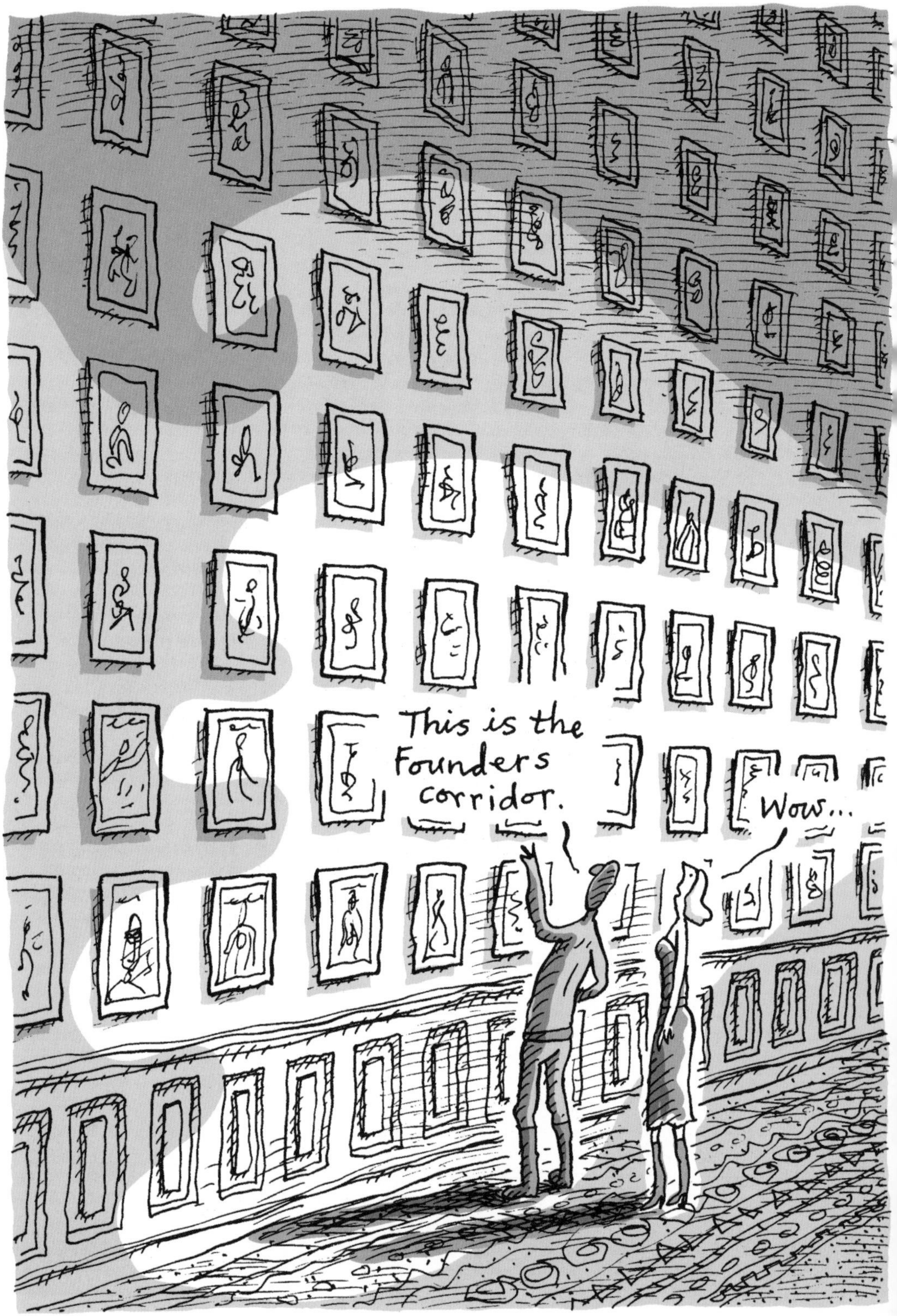
This is the Founders corridor.
Wow...

Framed copies of all their comic books.

Yeah, the club licensed all its heroes back then.

Never licensed me, sadly. I'd have liked my own comic.

Did you collect superhero comics when you were a kid?

A few. But my mother hated them.

Used to throw them out.

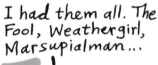

I had them all. The Fool, Weathergirl, Marsupialman...

Remember his catch phrase?

Yeah...

What's in my manpouch today, scumbags?

Oh look... A Browning submachine gun.

Bad luck, suckers.

Ha ha ha ha ha...

Budda budda budda budda budda...

Marsupialman was a bit over the top...

A bit?! He was a total psycho!

Eventually someone shot him while he recited his catch phrase. Almost killed him.

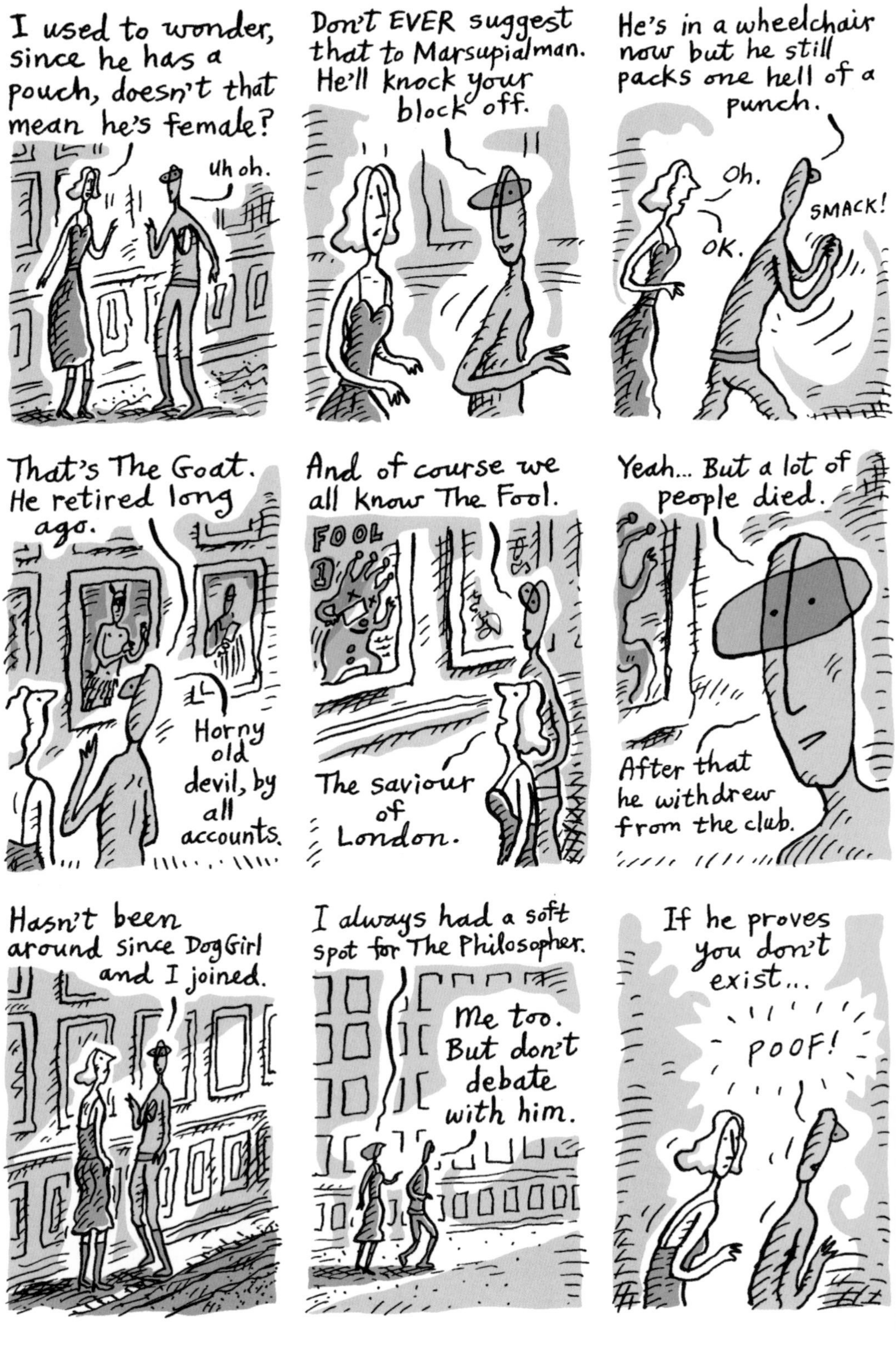
I used to wonder, since he has a pouch, doesn't that mean he's female?
Uh oh.
Don't EVER suggest that to Marsupialman. He'll knock your block off.
He's in a wheelchair now but he still packs one hell of a punch.
Oh.
OK.
SMACK!
That's The Goat. He retired long ago.
Horny old devil, by all accounts.
And of course we all know The Fool.
FOOL
The saviour of London.
Yeah... But a lot of people died.
After that he withdrew from the club.
Hasn't been around since DogGirl and I joined.
I always had a soft spot for The Philosopher.
Me too. But don't debate with him.
If he proves you don't exist...
POOF!

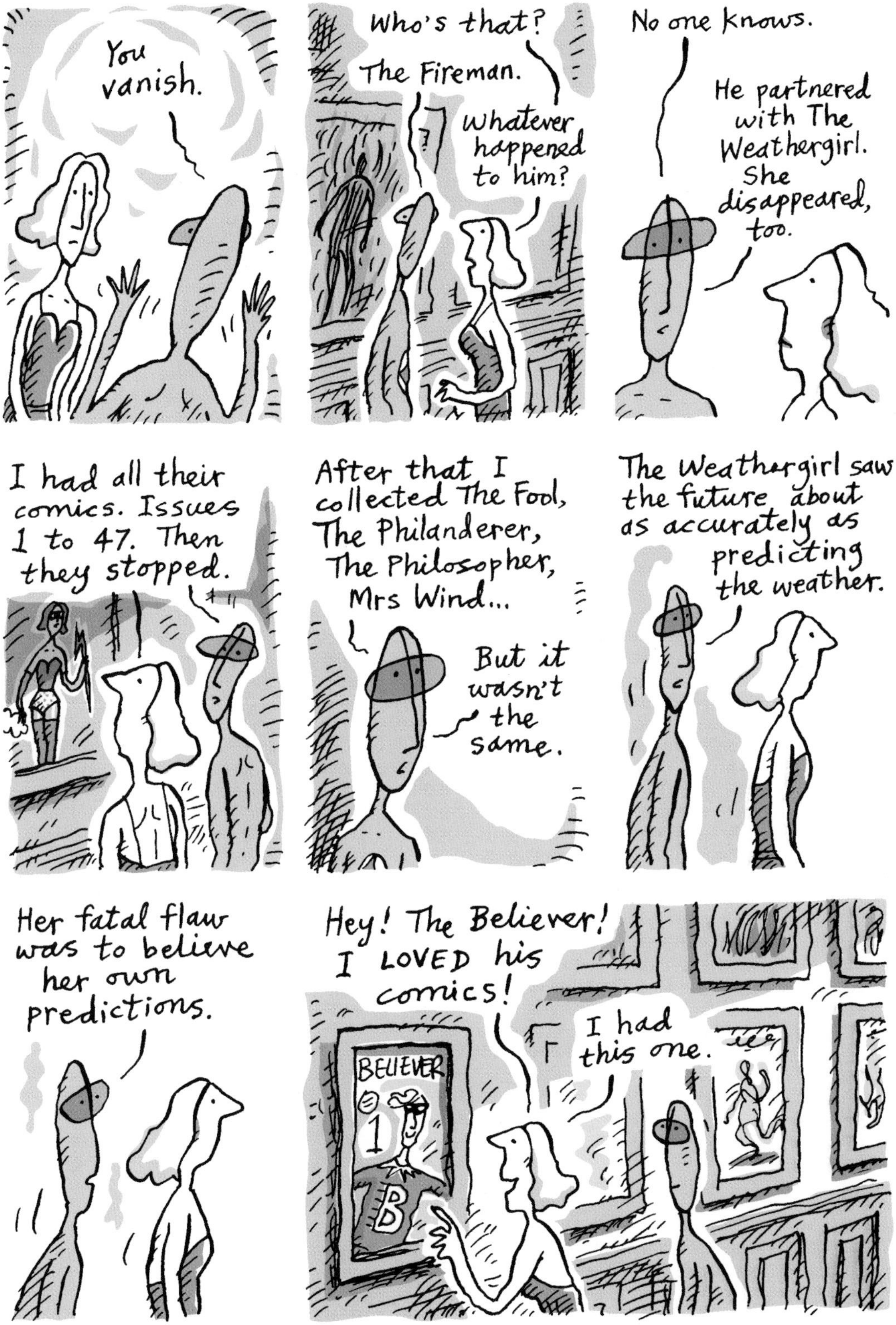
You vanish.
Who's that?
The Fireman.
Whatever happened to him?
No one knows.
He partnered with The Weathergirl. She disappeared, too.
I had all their comics. Issues 1 to 47. Then they stopped.
After that I collected The Fool, The Philanderer, The Philosopher, Mrs Wind...
But it wasn't the same.
The Weathergirl saw the future about as accurately as predicting the weather.
Her fatal flaw was to believe her own predictions.
Hey! The Believer! I LOVED his comics!
I had this one.
BELIEVER
1
B

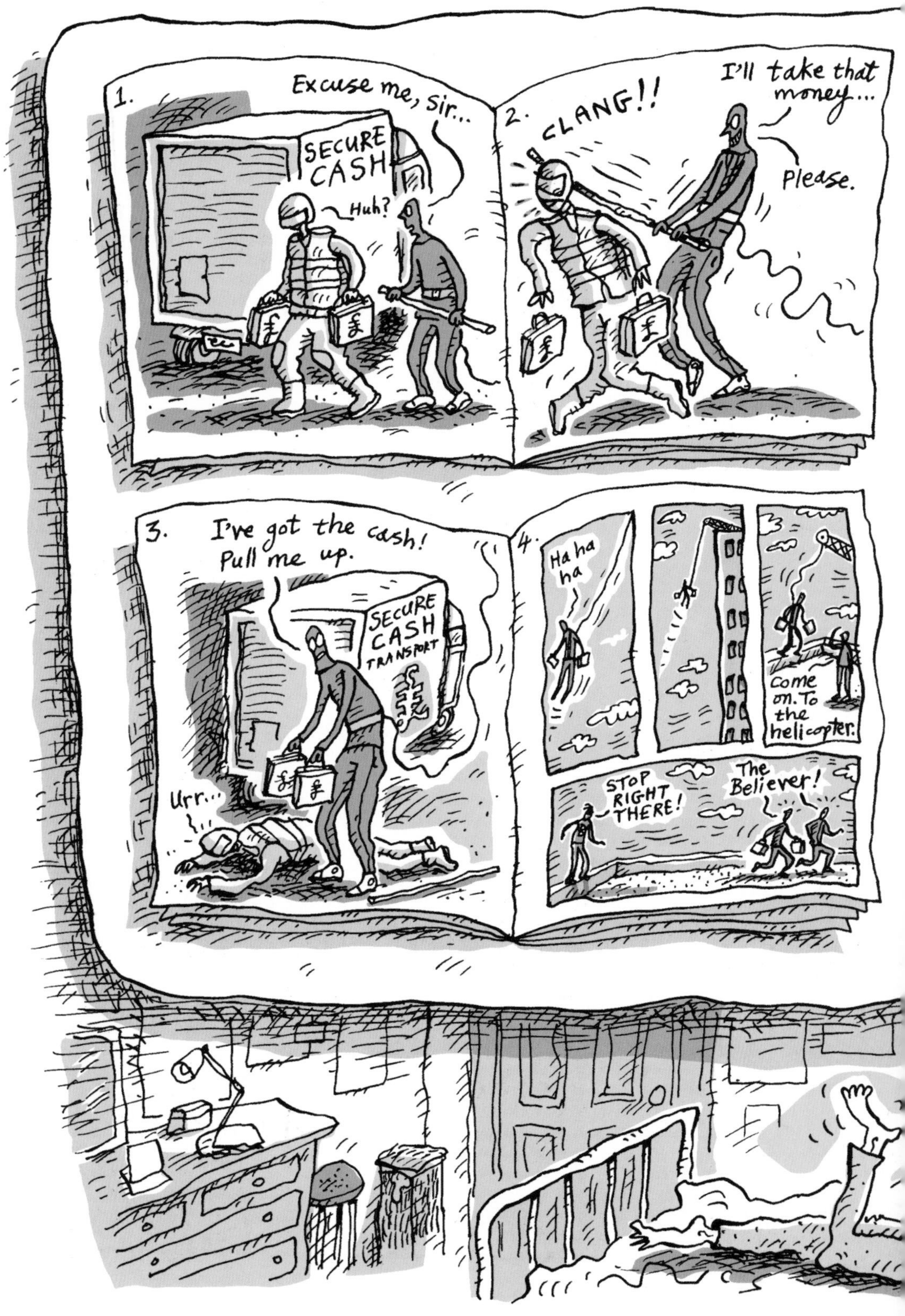
1.
Excuse me, sir...
SECURE CASH
Huh?
2.
CLANG!!
I'll take that money...
Please.
3.
I've got the cash! Pull me up.
SECURE CASH TRANSPORT
Urr...
4.
Ha ha ha
Come on. To the helicopter.
STOP RIGHT THERE!
The Believer!

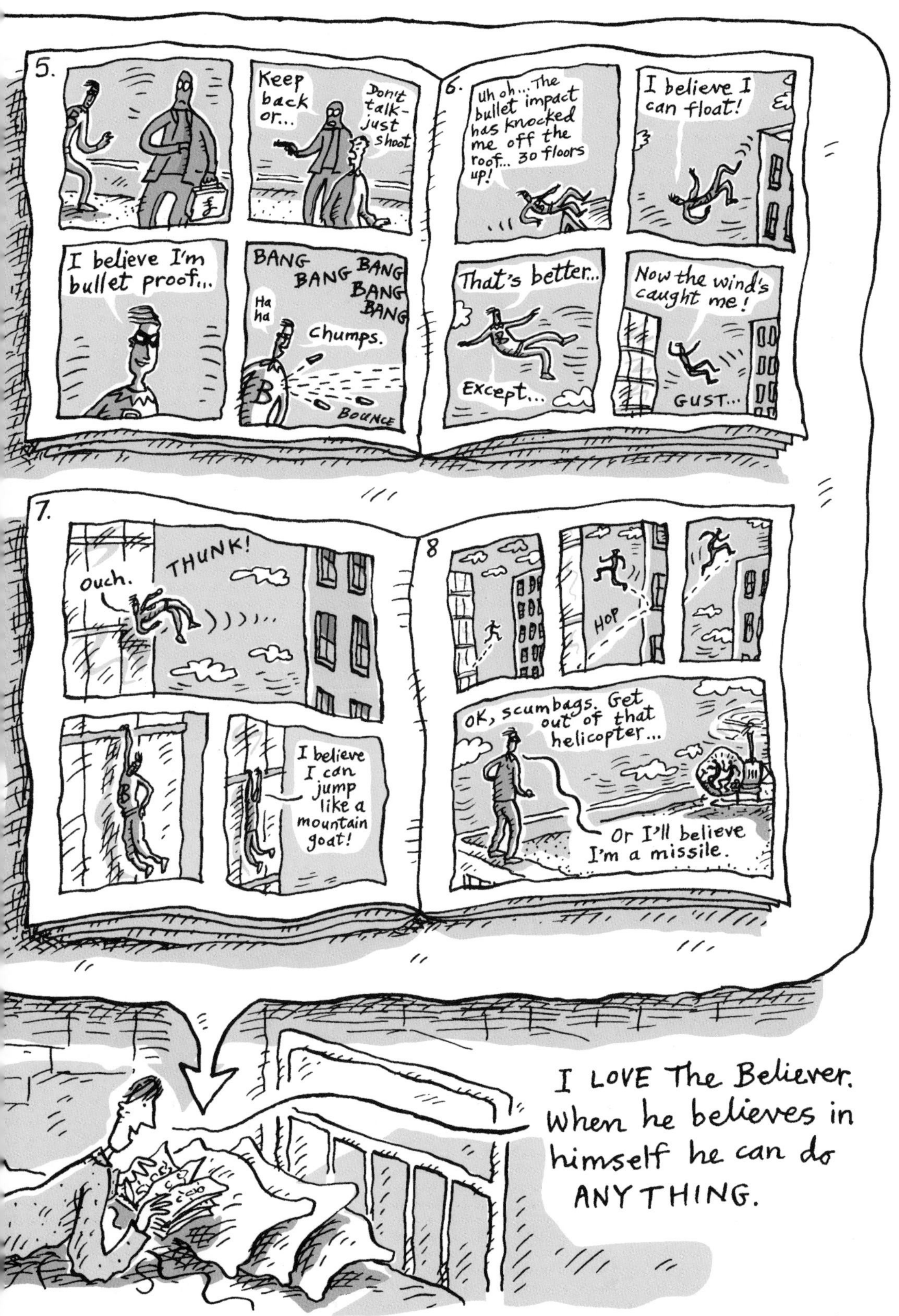
5.
Keep back or...
Don't talk- just shoot
I believe I'm bullet proof...
BANG BANG BANG BANG BANG
Ha ha
Chumps.
BOUNCE
6.
Uh oh... The bullet impact has knocked me off the roof... 30 floors up!
I believe I can float!
That's better...
Except...
Now the wind's caught me!
GUST...
7.
THUNK!
Ouch.
I believe I can jump like a mountain goat!
8
HOP
OK, scumbags. Get out of that helicopter...
Or I'll believe I'm a missile.
I LOVE The Believer. When he believes in himself he can do ANYTHING.

You'll meet him.

He's usually in the bar.

And here we are.

Where is everyone?

Oh...

They'll be out doing superhero stuff.

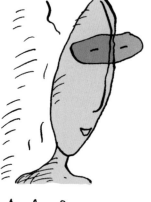

Flypaper is opening a supermarket. The Fool is filming a car ad.

Mrs Wind is doing a fashion shoot and The Philosopher is reviewing a new boutique hotel.

Nice job.

And, of course, The Fist will be making his TV show.

What'll you have?

Urr...

Um... I'm flying... so just a coffee.

Coffee? Christ. I'll have another vodka, Hindsight.

Sure, Believer.

Believer?!

That's me. The one. The only. The true Believer.

I have the power to believe in things.

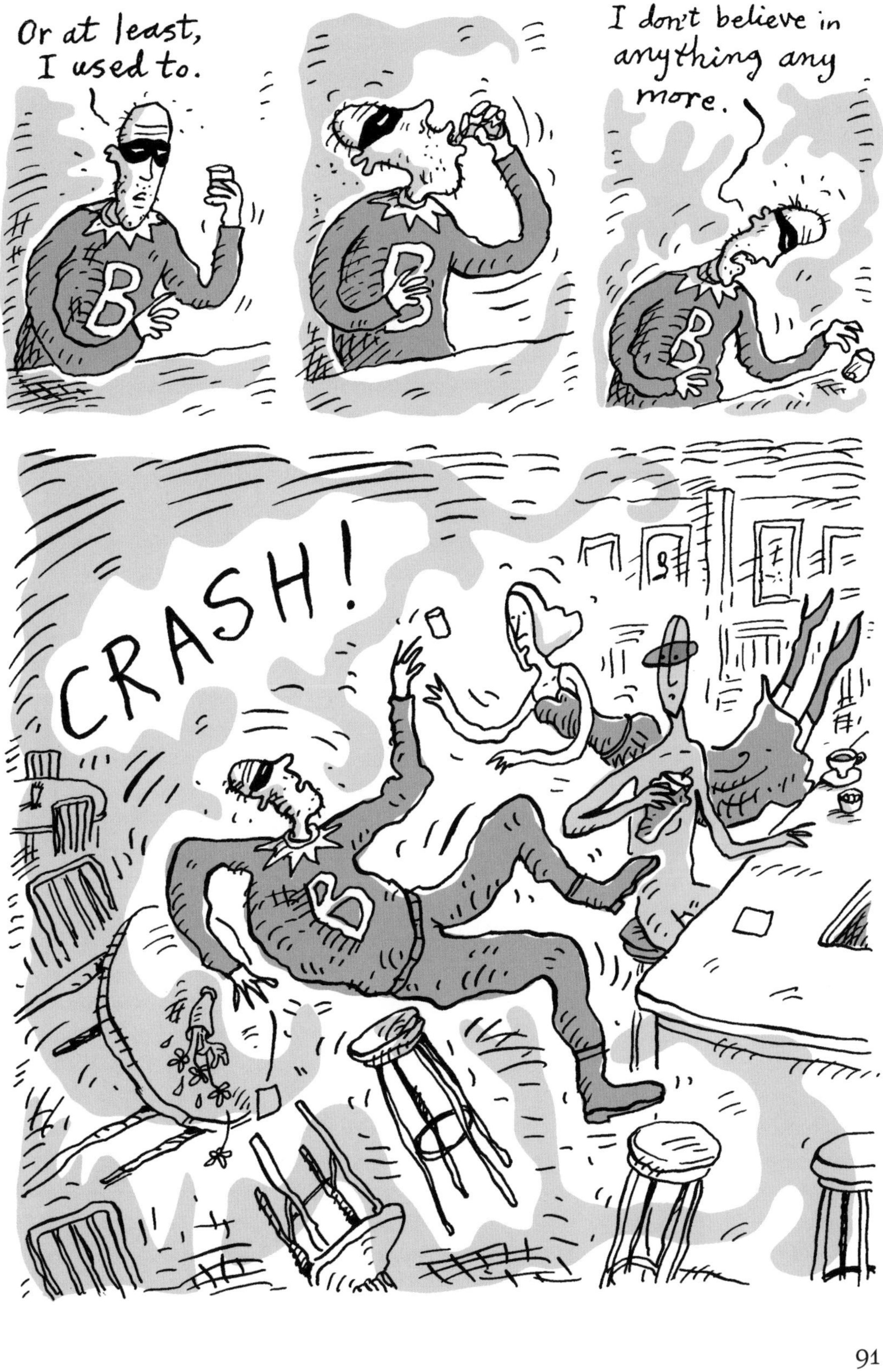
Or at least, I used to.
I don't believe in anything any more.
CRASH!

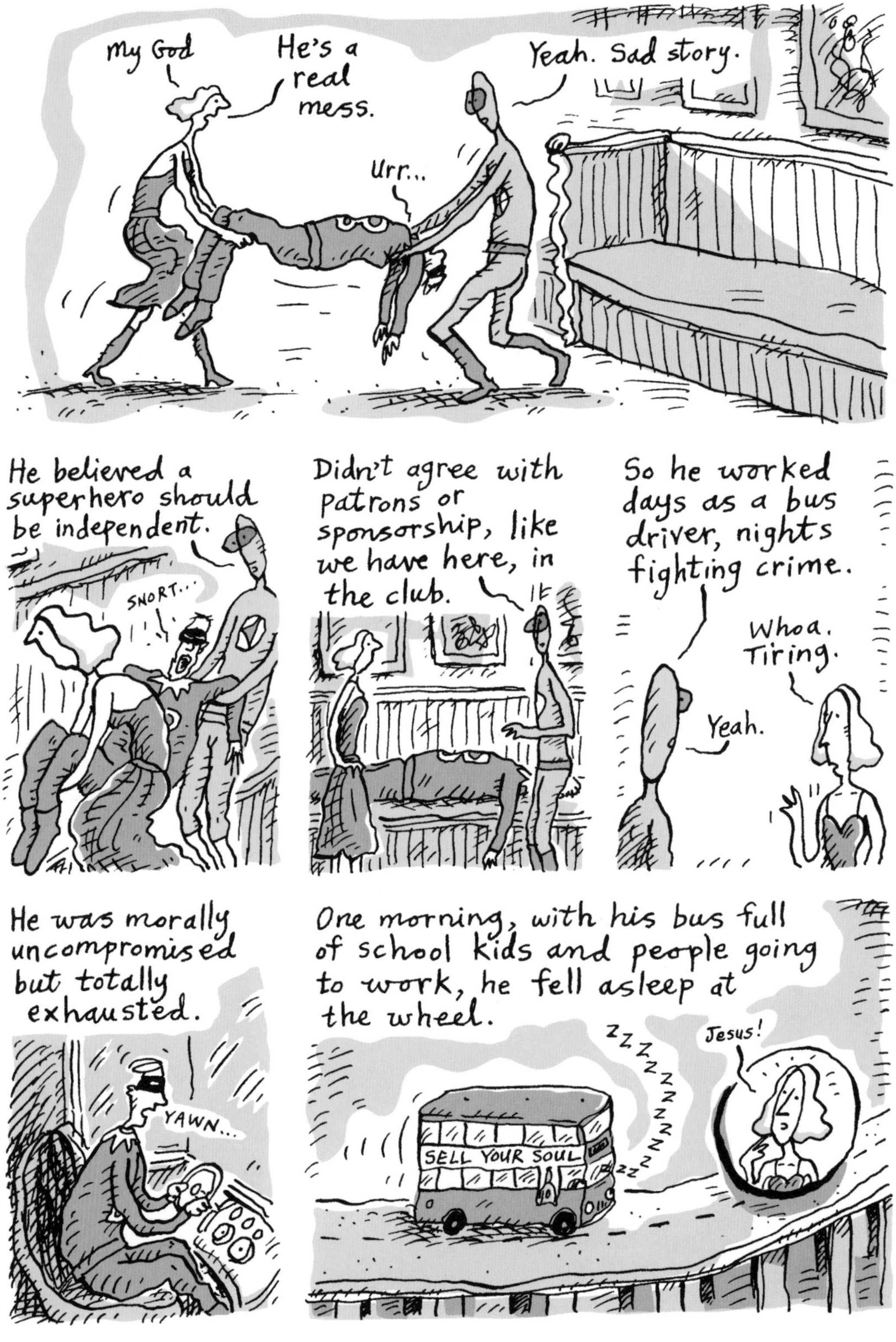
My God
He's a real mess.
Yeah. Sad story.
Urr...
He believed a superhero should be independent.
SNORT...
Didn't agree with patrons or sponsorship, like we have here, in the club.
So he worked days as a bus driver, nights fighting crime.
Whoa. Tiring.
Yeah.
He was morally uncompromised but totally exhausted.
YAWN...
One morning, with his bus full of school kids and people going to work, he fell asleep at the wheel.
ZZZZZZZZZZZZ
Jesus!
SELL YOUR SOUL

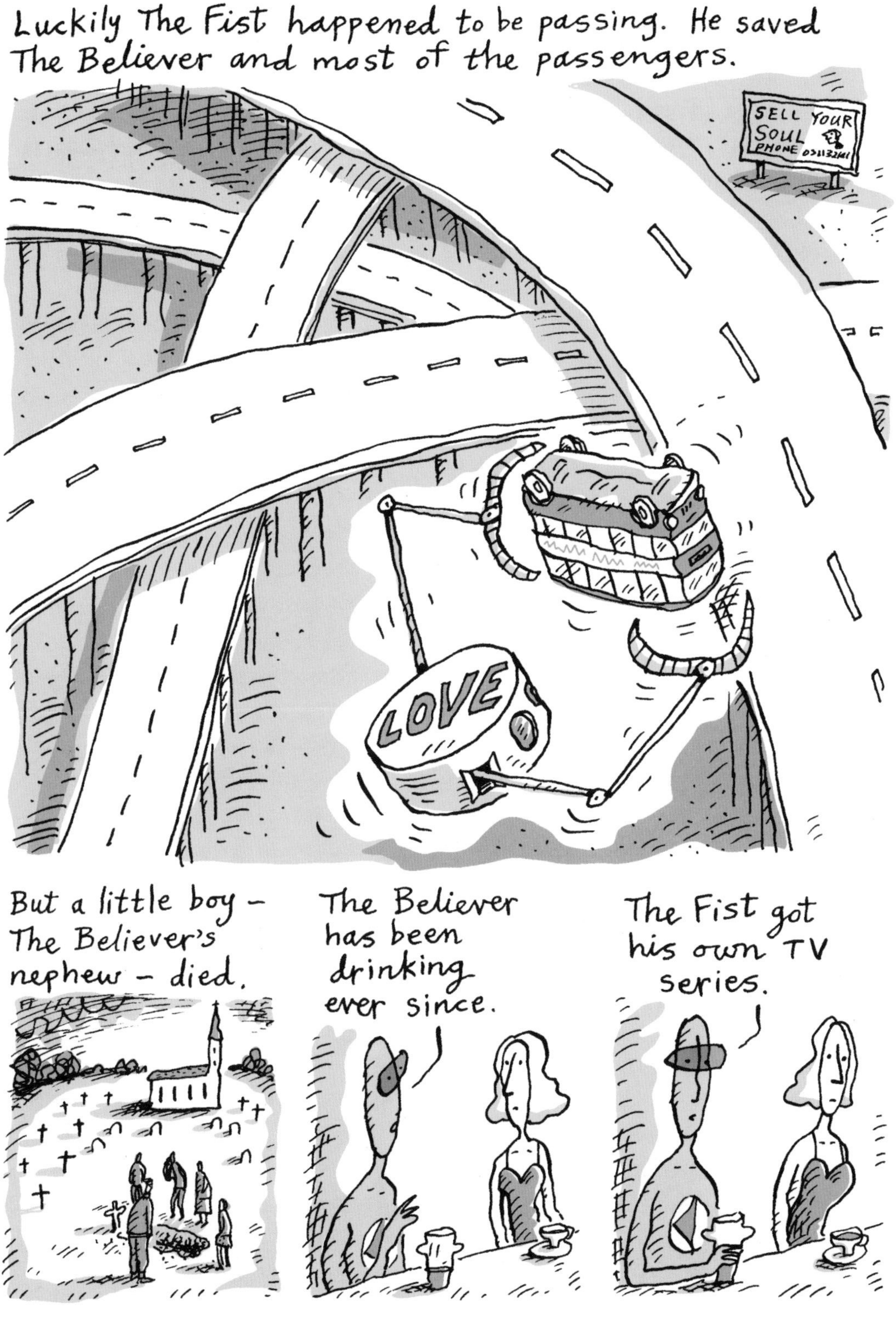
Luckily The Fist happened to be passing. He saved The Believer and most of the passengers.
SELL YOUR SOUL
LOVE
But a little boy – The Believer's nephew – died.
The Believer has been drinking ever since.
The Fist got his own TV series.

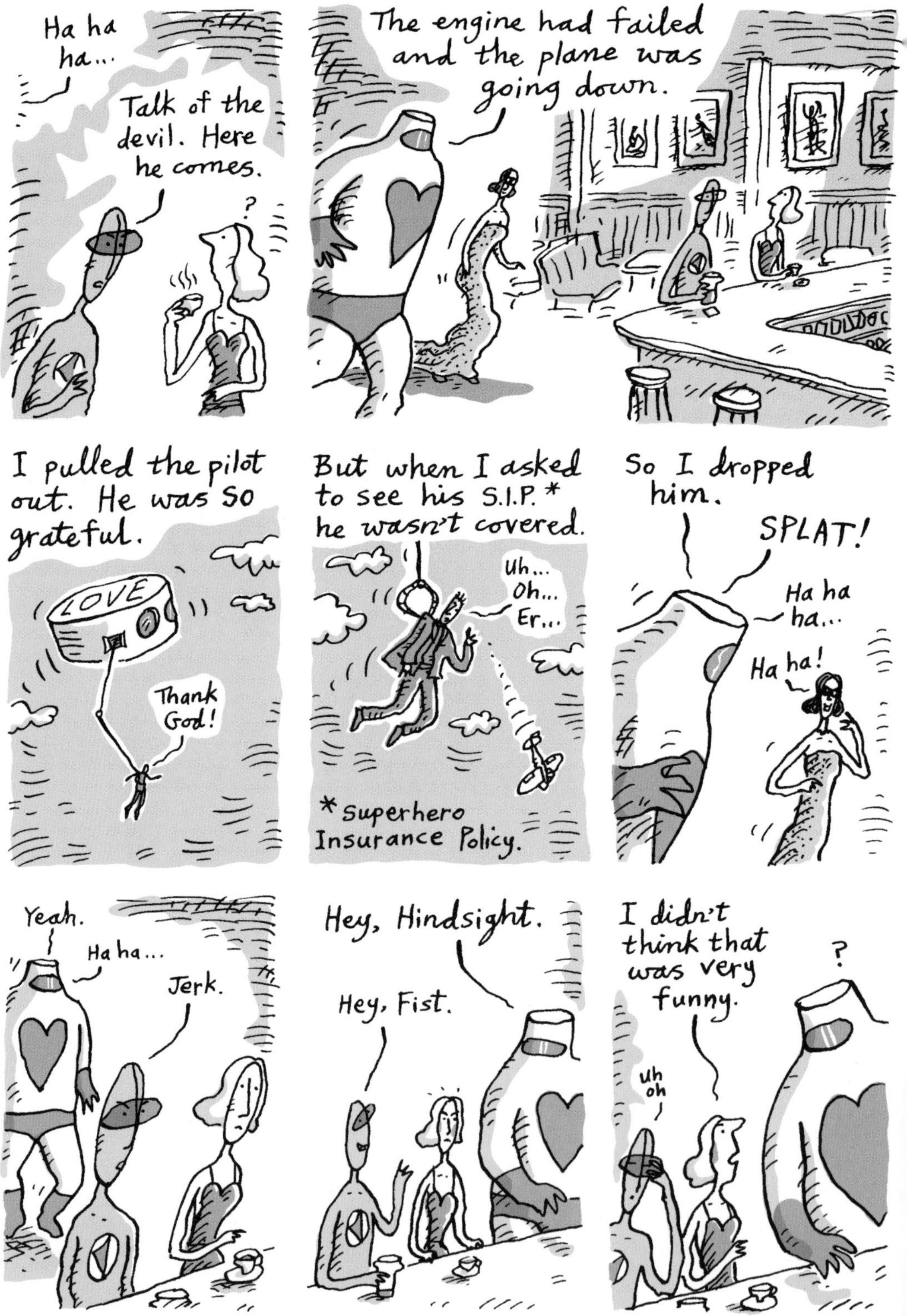

Ha ha ha...
Talk of the devil. Here he comes.
?
The engine had failed and the plane was going down.
I pulled the pilot out. He was so grateful.
LOVE
Thank God!
But when I asked to see his S.I.P.* he wasn't covered.
Uh... Oh... Er...
*Superhero Insurance Policy.
So I dropped him.
SPLAT!
Ha ha ha...
Ha ha!
Yeah.
Ha ha...
Jerk.
Hey, Hindsight.
Hey, Fist.
I didn't think that was very funny.
uh oh
?

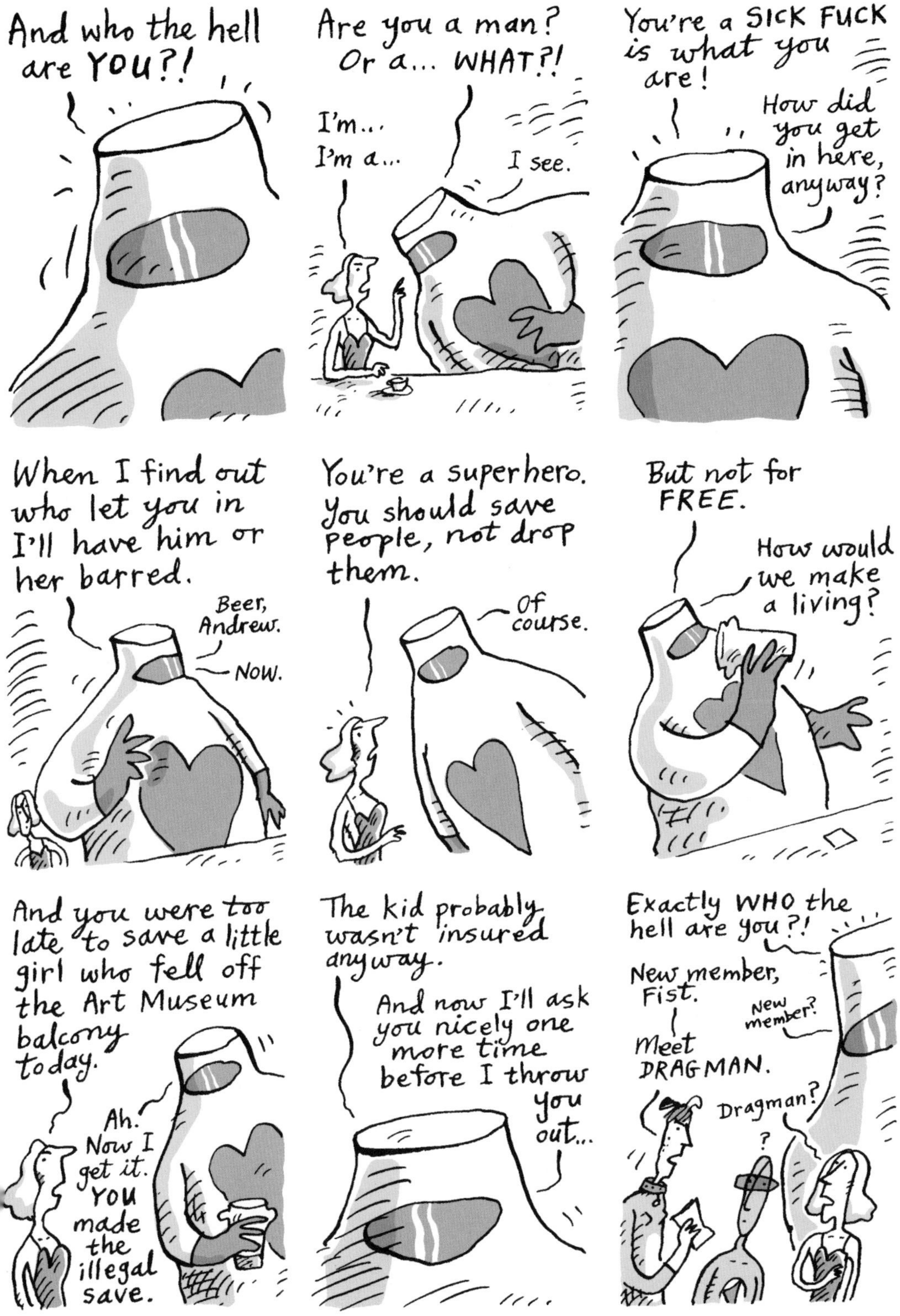
And who the hell are YOU?!
Are you a man? Or a... WHAT?!
I'm... I'm a...
I see.
You're a SICK FUCK is what you are!
How did you get in here, anyway?
When I find out who let you in I'll have him or her barred.
Beer, Andrew.
NOW.
You're a superhero. You should save people, not drop them.
Of course.
But not for FREE.
How would we make a living?
And you were too late to save a little girl who fell off the Art Museum balcony today.
Ah. Now I get it. YOU made the illegal save.
The kid probably wasn't insured anyway.
And now I'll ask you nicely one more time before I throw you out...
Exactly WHO the hell are you?!
New member, Fist.
New member?
Meet DRAGMAN.
Dragman?
?

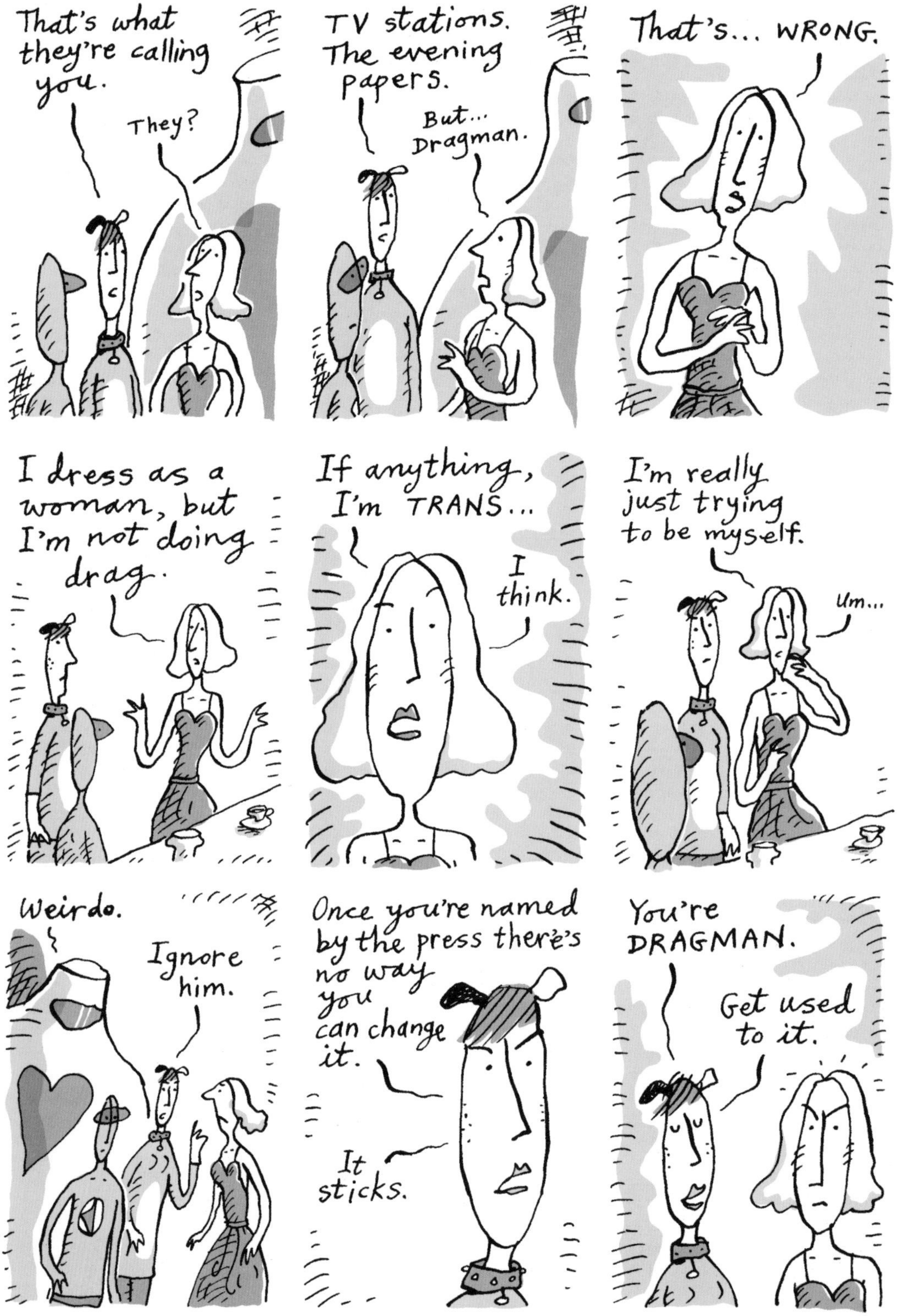
That's what they're calling you.
They?
TV stations. The evening papers.
But... Dragman.
That's... WRONG.
I dress as a woman, but I'm not doing drag.
If anything, I'm TRANS...
I think.
I'm really just trying to be myself.
Um...
Weirdo.
Ignore him.
Once you're named by the press there's no way you can change it.
It sticks.
You're DRAGMAN.
Get used to it.

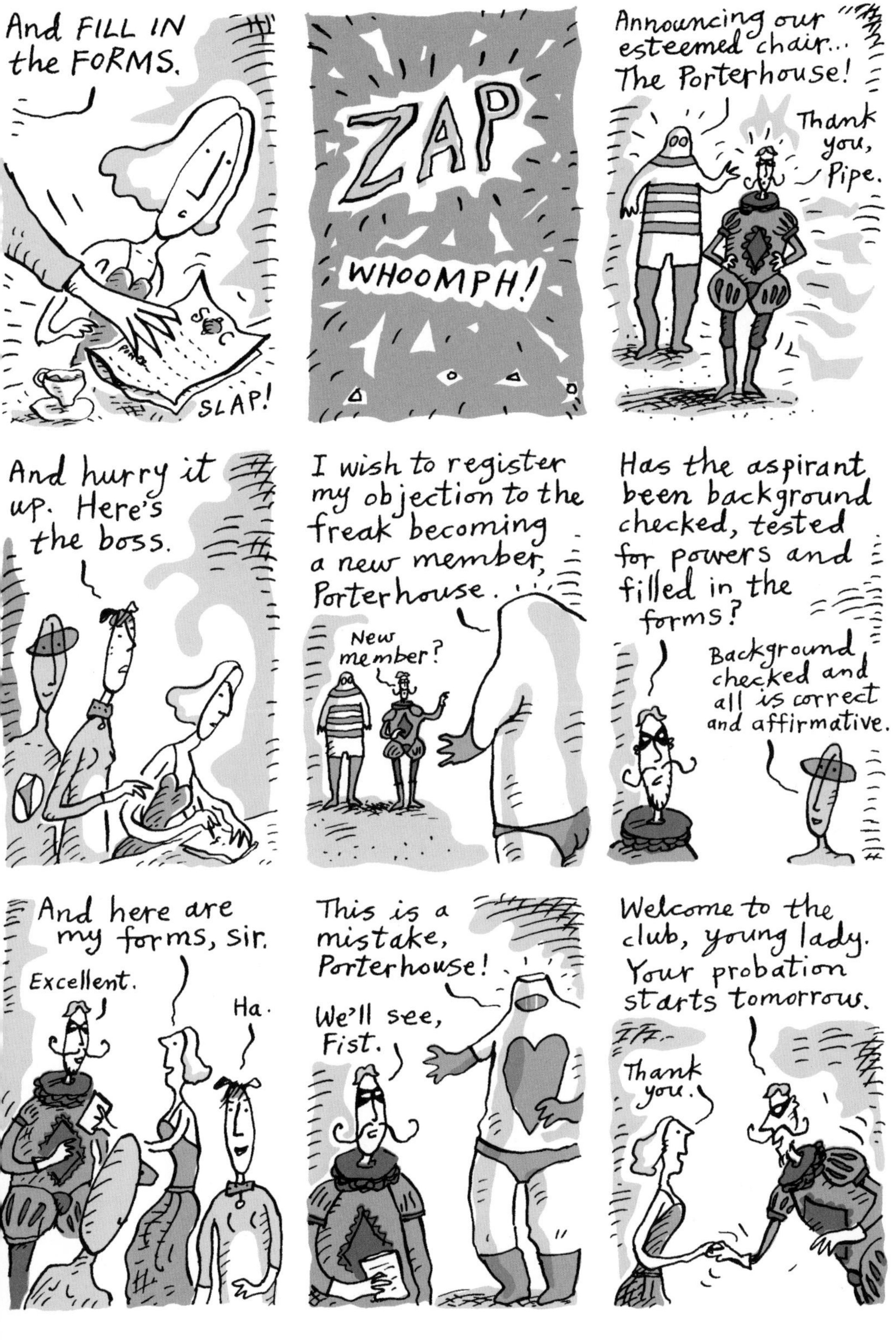
And FILL IN the FORMS.
SLAP!
ZAP
WHOOMPH!
Announcing our esteemed chair... The Porterhouse!
Thank you, Pipe.
And hurry it up. Here's the boss.
I wish to register my objection to the freak becoming a new member, Porterhouse.
New member?
Has the aspirant been background checked, tested for powers and filled in the forms?
Background checked and all is correct and affirmative.
And here are my forms, sir.
Excellent.
Ha.
This is a mistake, Porterhouse!
We'll see, Fist.
Welcome to the club, young lady. Your probation starts tomorrow.
Thank you.

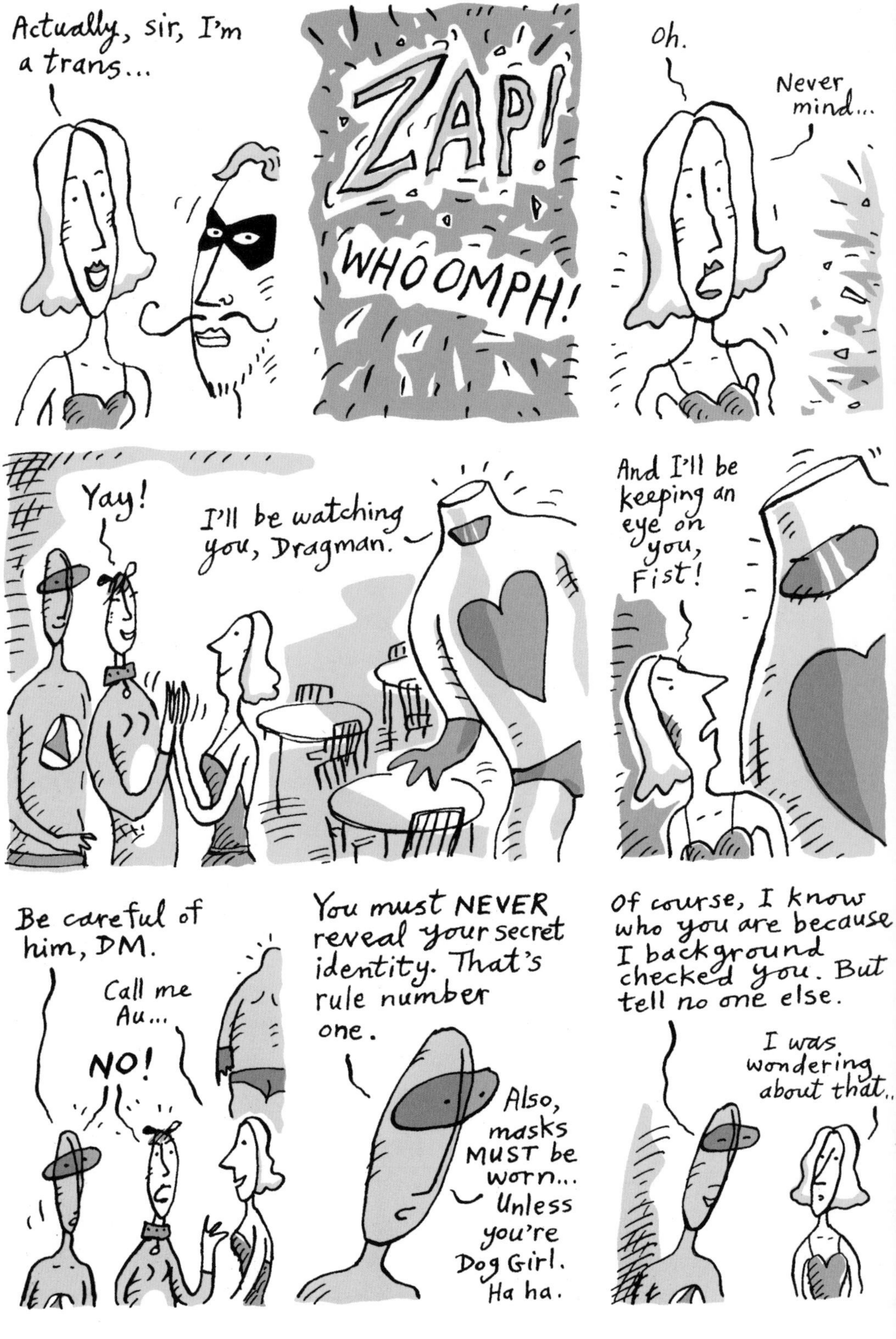

Actually, sir, I'm a trans...
ZAP!
WHOOMPH!
Oh.
Never mind...
Yay!
I'll be watching you, Dragman.
And I'll be keeping an eye on you, Fist!
Be careful of him, DM.
Call me Au...
NO!
You must NEVER reveal your secret identity. That's rule number one.
Also, masks MUST be worn... Unless you're Dog Girl. Ha ha.
Of course, I know who you are because I background checked you. But tell no one else.
I was wondering about that...

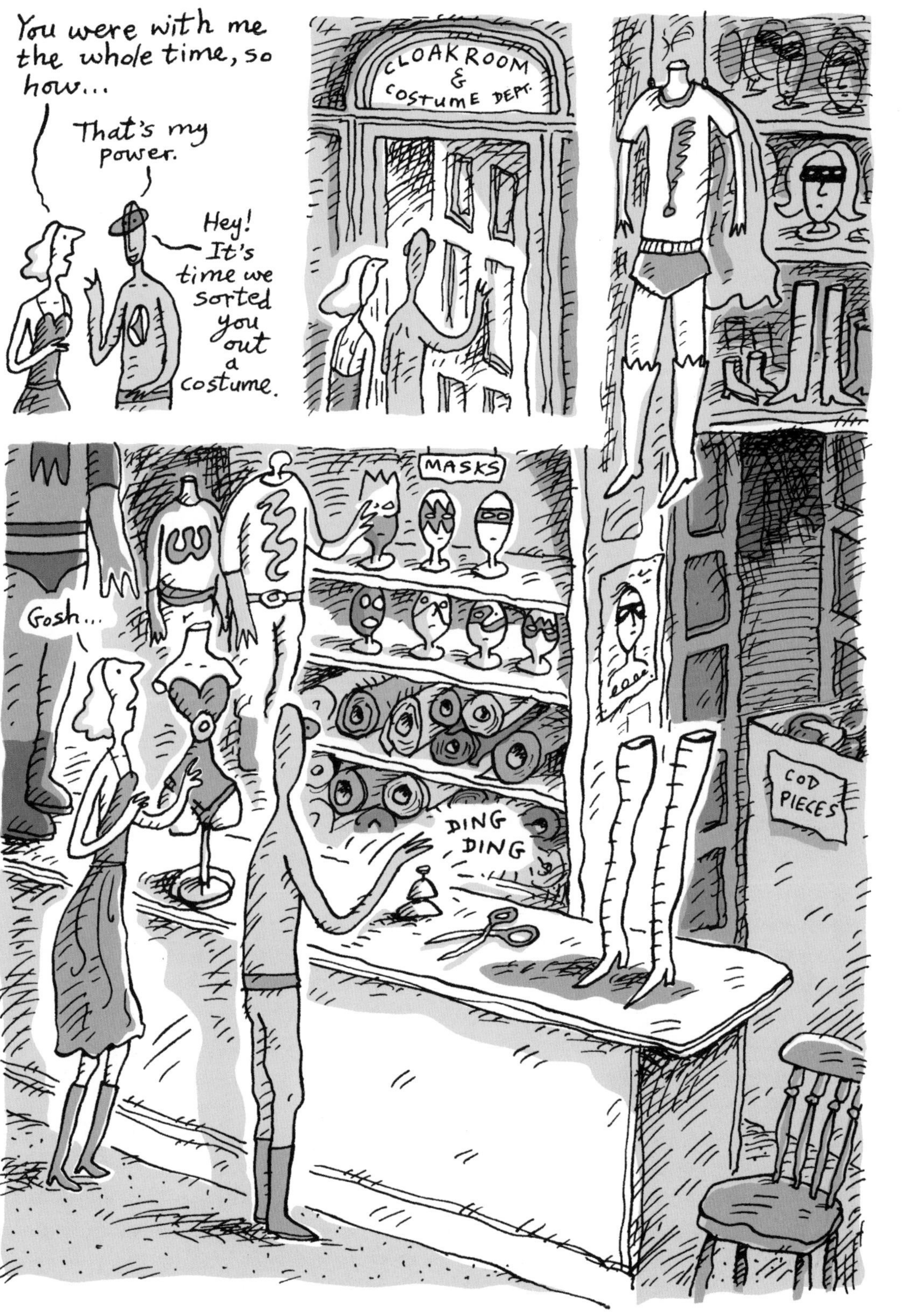
You were with me the whole time, so how...
That's my power.
Hey! It's time we sorted you out a costume.
CLOAKROOM & COSTUME DEPT.
MASKS
Gosh...
DING DING
COD PIECES

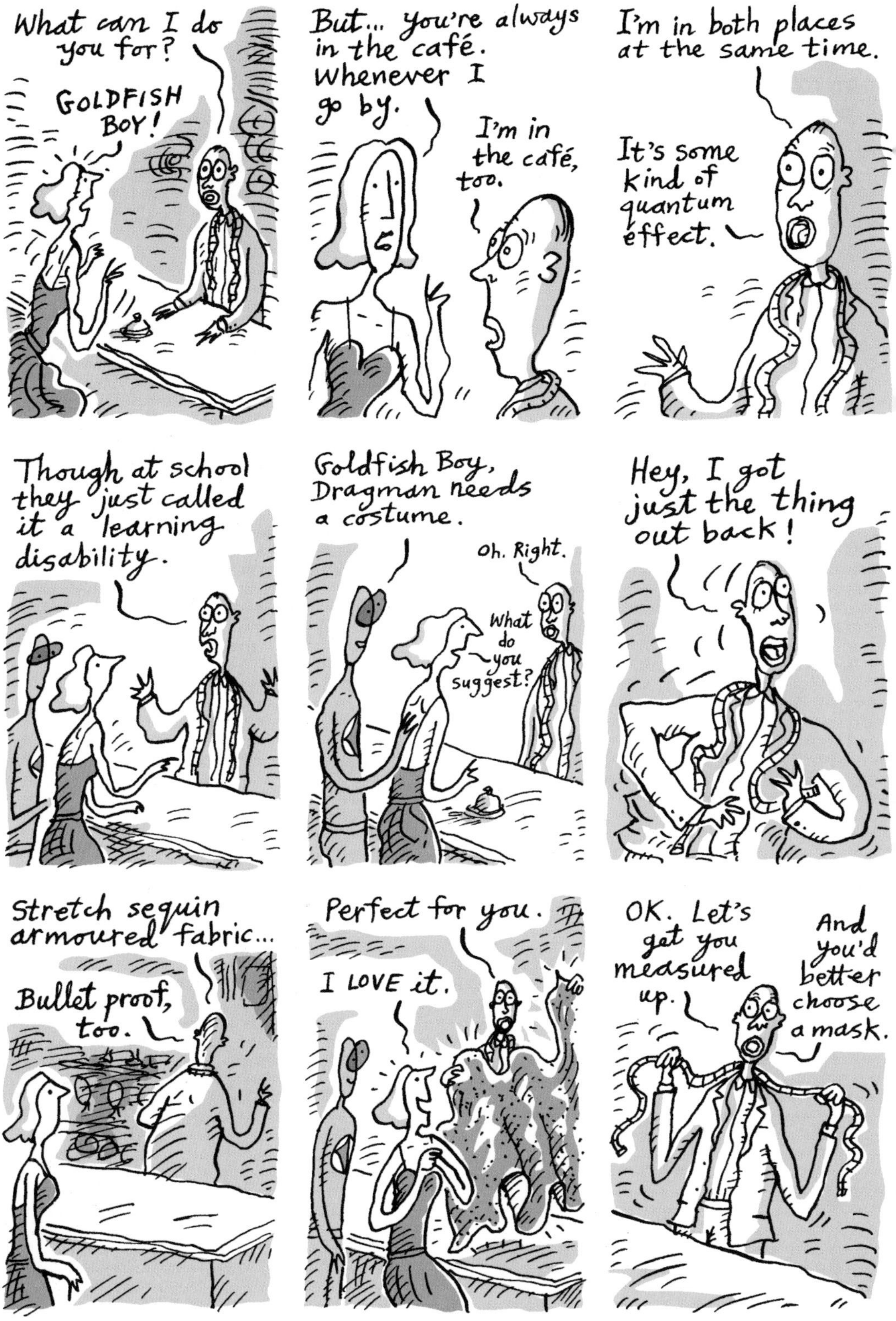
What can I do you for?
GOLDFISH BOY!
But... you're always in the café. Whenever I go by.
I'm in the café, too.
I'm in both places at the same time.
It's some kind of quantum effect.
Though at school they just called it a learning disability.
Goldfish Boy, Dragman needs a costume.
Oh. Right.
What do you suggest?
Hey, I got just the thing out back!
Stretch sequin armoured fabric...
Bullet proof, too.
Perfect for you.
I LOVE it.
OK. Let's get you measured up.
And you'd better choose a mask.

BACK IN THE BAR

What about you, Hindsight? What's your power?

Ha. Well...

I have the power to SEE the past.

The past?

Yeah. I know.

Seeing the future would be useful.

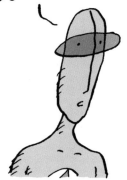

I'd be able to avert disasters before they happened. Stop crimes before they were even planned.

Seeing the past is pretty pointless.

No, no...

You don't have to be nice, Dragman.

I can't punch through walls like The Fist.

Or fly, like you.

But that's fine.

I do all the background checks.

And I run the club's lost property department.

I can look back into the past and see where someone left their coat...

101

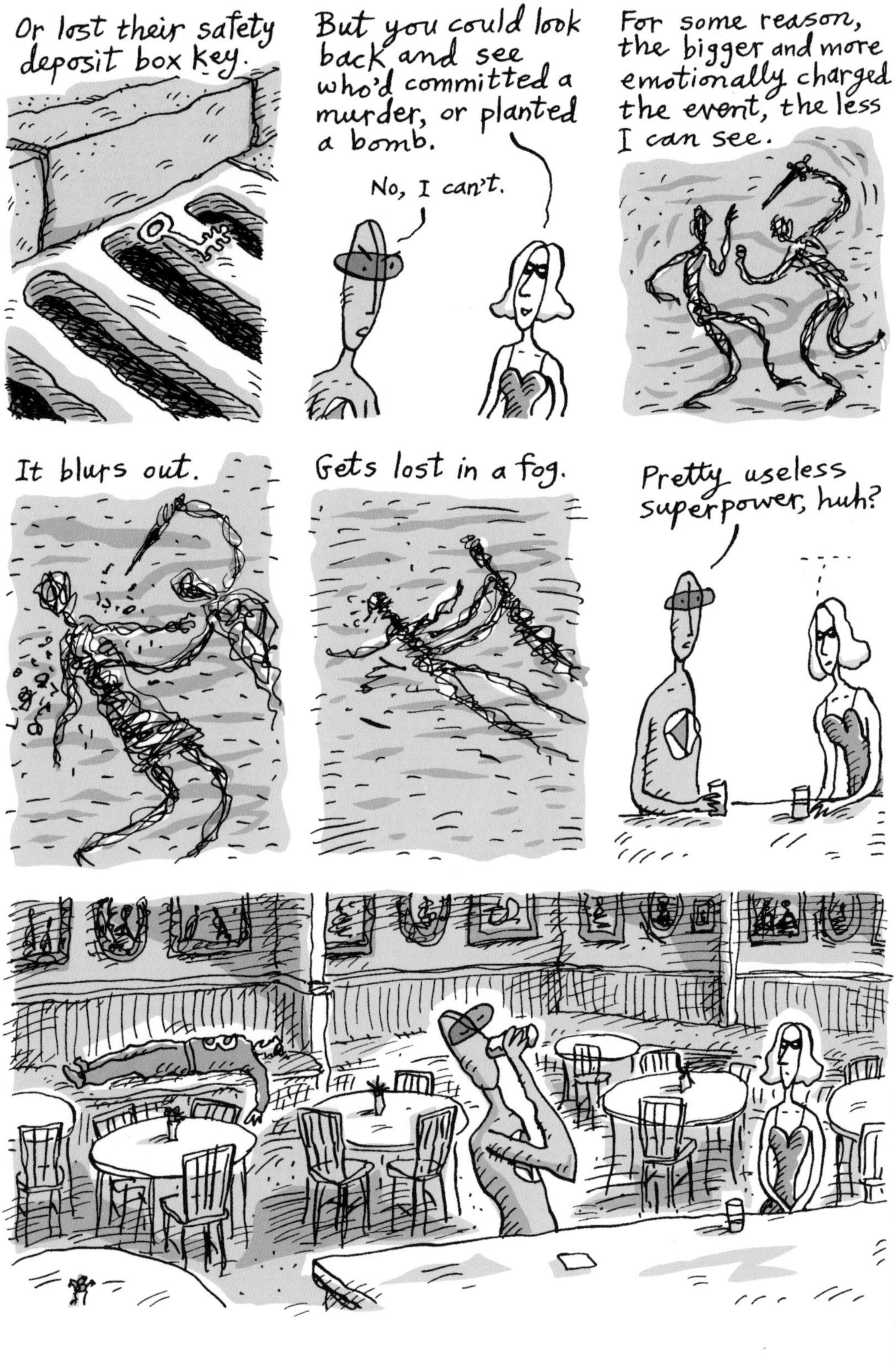

Or lost their safety deposit box key.
But you could look back and see who'd committed a murder, or planted a bomb.
No, I can't.
For some reason, the bigger and more emotionally charged the event, the less I can see.
It blurs out.
Gets lost in a fog.
Pretty useless superpower, huh?

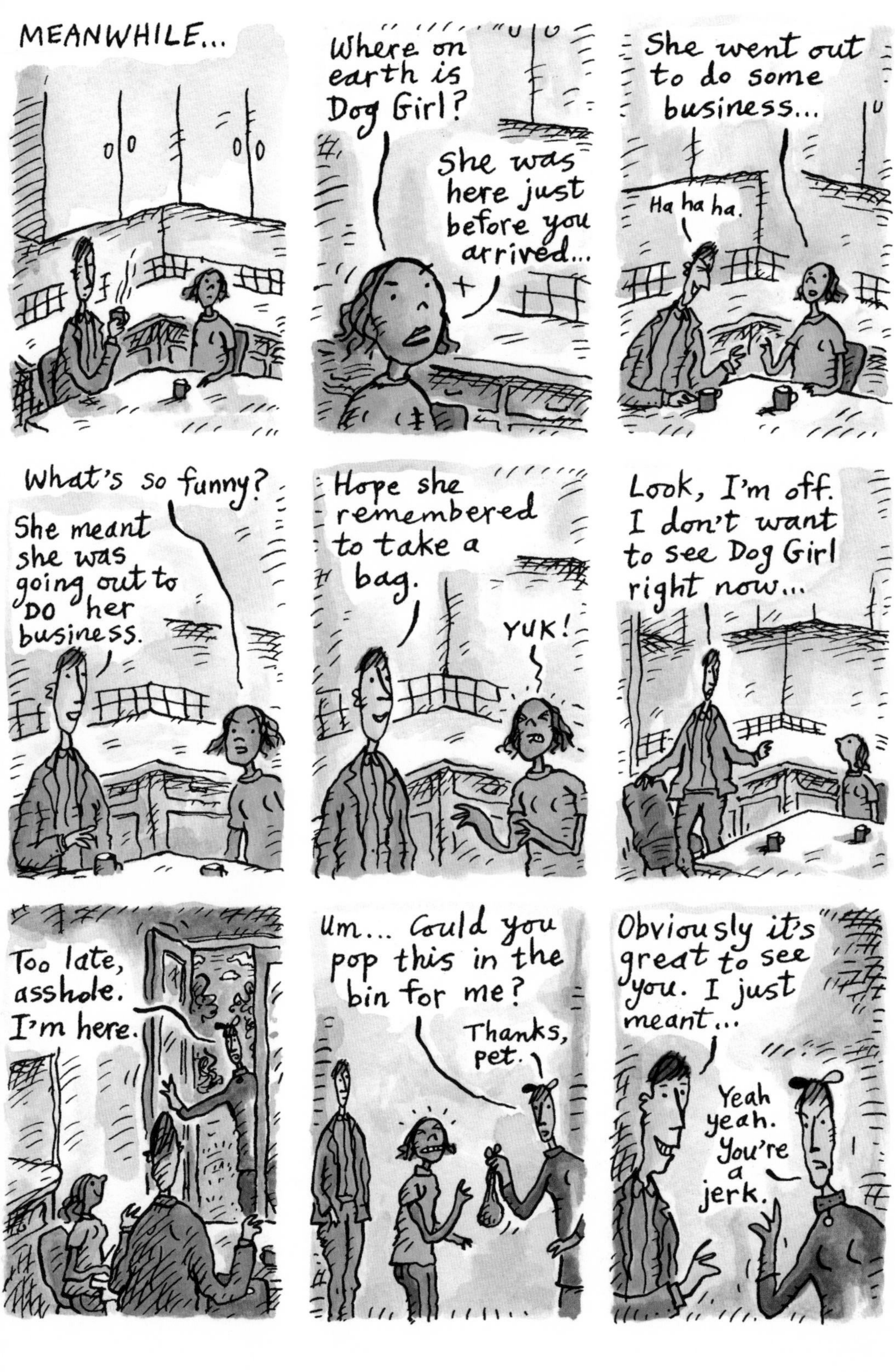
MEANWHILE...
Where on earth is Dog Girl?
She was here just before you arrived...
She went out to do some business...
Ha ha ha.
What's so funny?
She meant she was going out to DO her business.
Hope she remembered to take a bag.
YUK!
Look, I'm off. I don't want to see Dog Girl right now...
Too late, asshole. I'm here.
Um... Could you pop this in the bin for me?
Thanks, pet.
Obviously it's great to see you. I just meant...
Yeah yeah. You're a jerk.

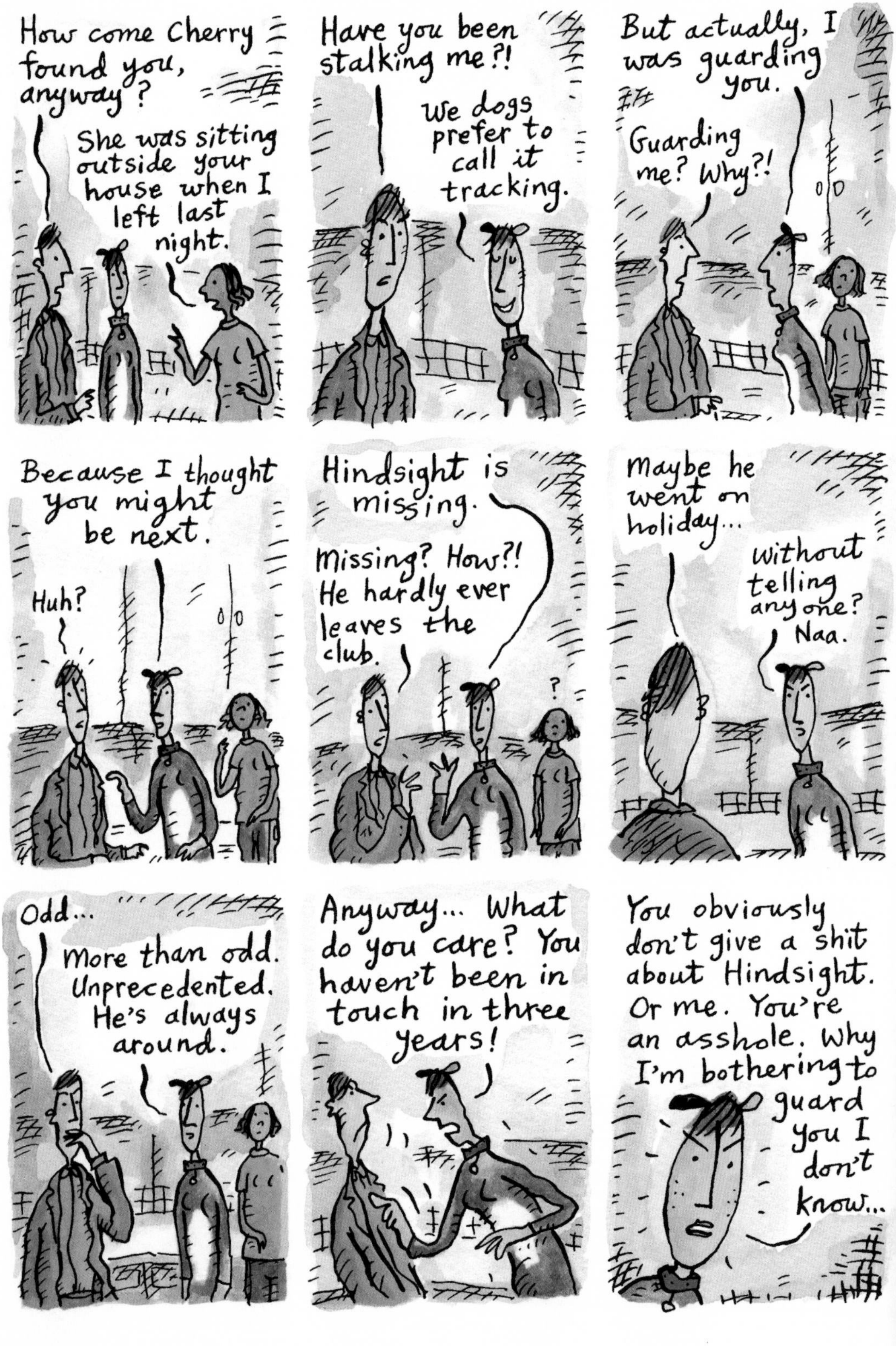
How come Cherry found you, anyway?
She was sitting outside your house when I left last night.
Have you been stalking me?!
We dogs prefer to call it tracking.
But actually, I was guarding you.
Guarding me? Why?!
Because I thought you might be next.
Huh?
Hindsight is missing.
Missing? How?! He hardly ever leaves the club.
?
Maybe he went on holiday...
Without telling anyone? Naa.
Odd...
More than odd. Unprecedented. He's always around.
Anyway... What do you care? You haven't been in touch in three years!
You obviously don't give a shit about Hindsight. Or me. You're an asshole. Why I'm bothering to guard you I don't know...

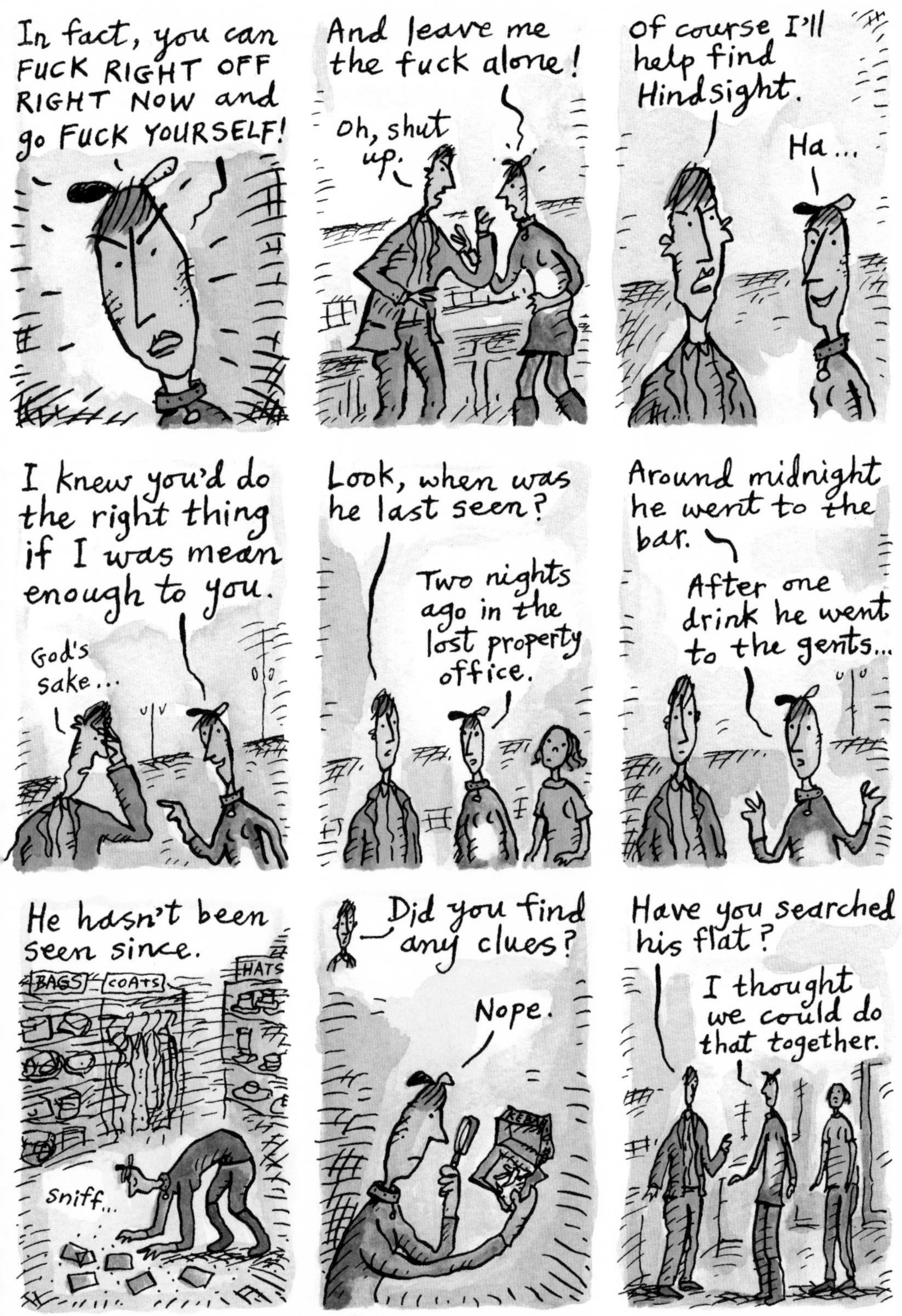
In fact, you can FUCK RIGHT OFF RIGHT NOW and go FUCK YOURSELF!
And leave me the fuck alone!
Oh, shut up.
Of course I'll help find Hindsight.
Ha...
I knew you'd do the right thing if I was mean enough to you.
God's sake...
Look, when was he last seen?
Two nights ago in the lost property office.
Around midnight he went to the bar.
After one drink he went to the gents...
He hasn't been seen since.
BAGS
COATS
HATS
sniff...
Did you find any clues?
Nope.
KEBAB
Have you searched his flat?
I thought we could do that together.

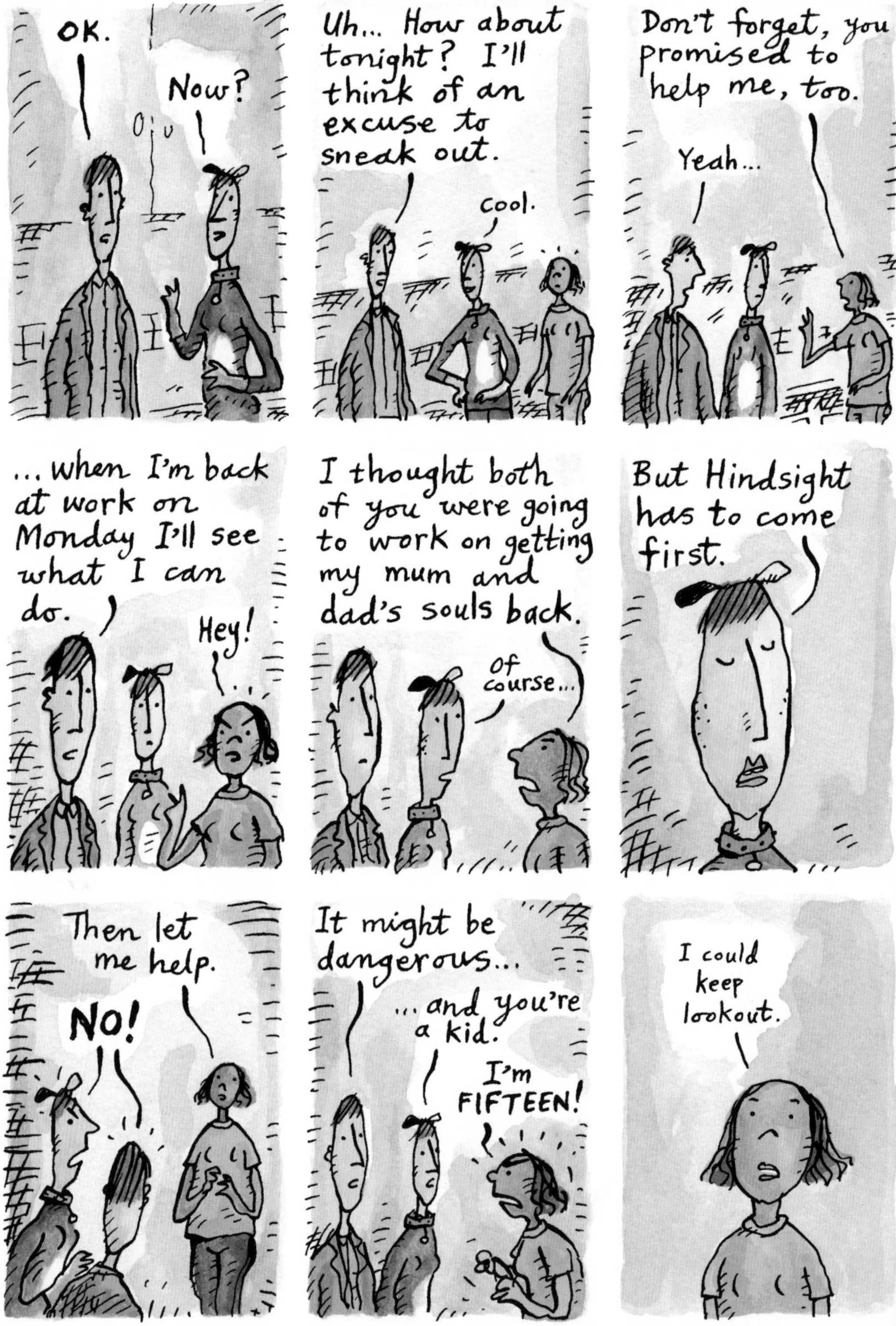
OK.
Now?
Uh... How about tonight? I'll think of an excuse to sneak out.
Cool.
Don't forget, you promised to help me, too.
Yeah...
...when I'm back at work on Monday I'll see what I can do.
Hey!
I thought both of you were going to work on getting my mum and dad's souls back.
Of course...
But Hindsight has to come first.
Then let me help.
NO!
It might be dangerous...
...and you're a kid.
I'm FIFTEEN!
I could keep lookout.

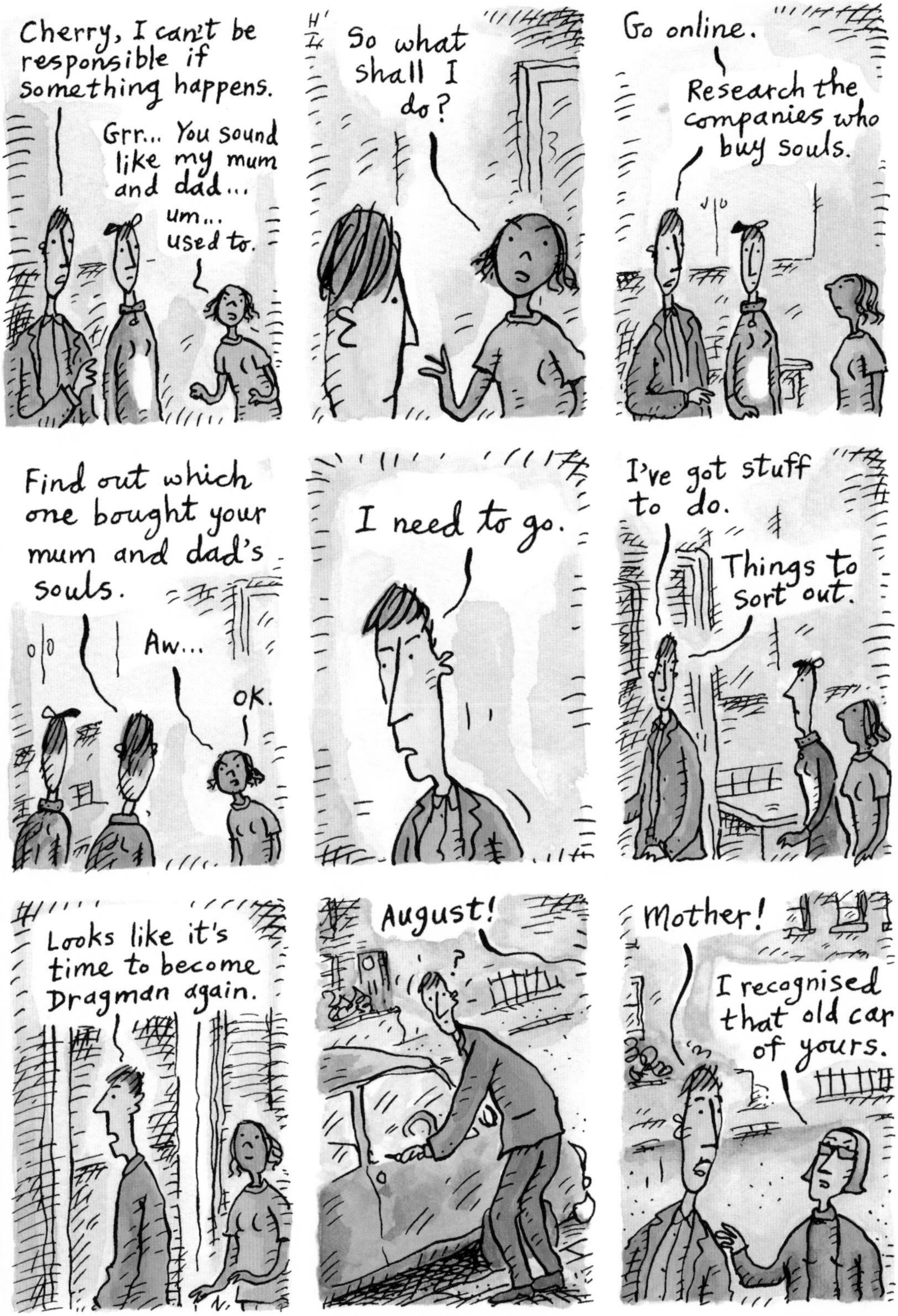
Cherry, I can't be responsible if something happens.
Grr... You sound like my mum and dad...
um... used to.
So what shall I do?
Go online.
Research the companies who buy souls.
Find out which one bought your mum and dad's souls.
Aw...
OK.
I need to go.
I've got stuff to do.
Things to sort out.
Looks like it's time to become Dragman again.
August!
?
Mother!
I recognised that old car of yours.

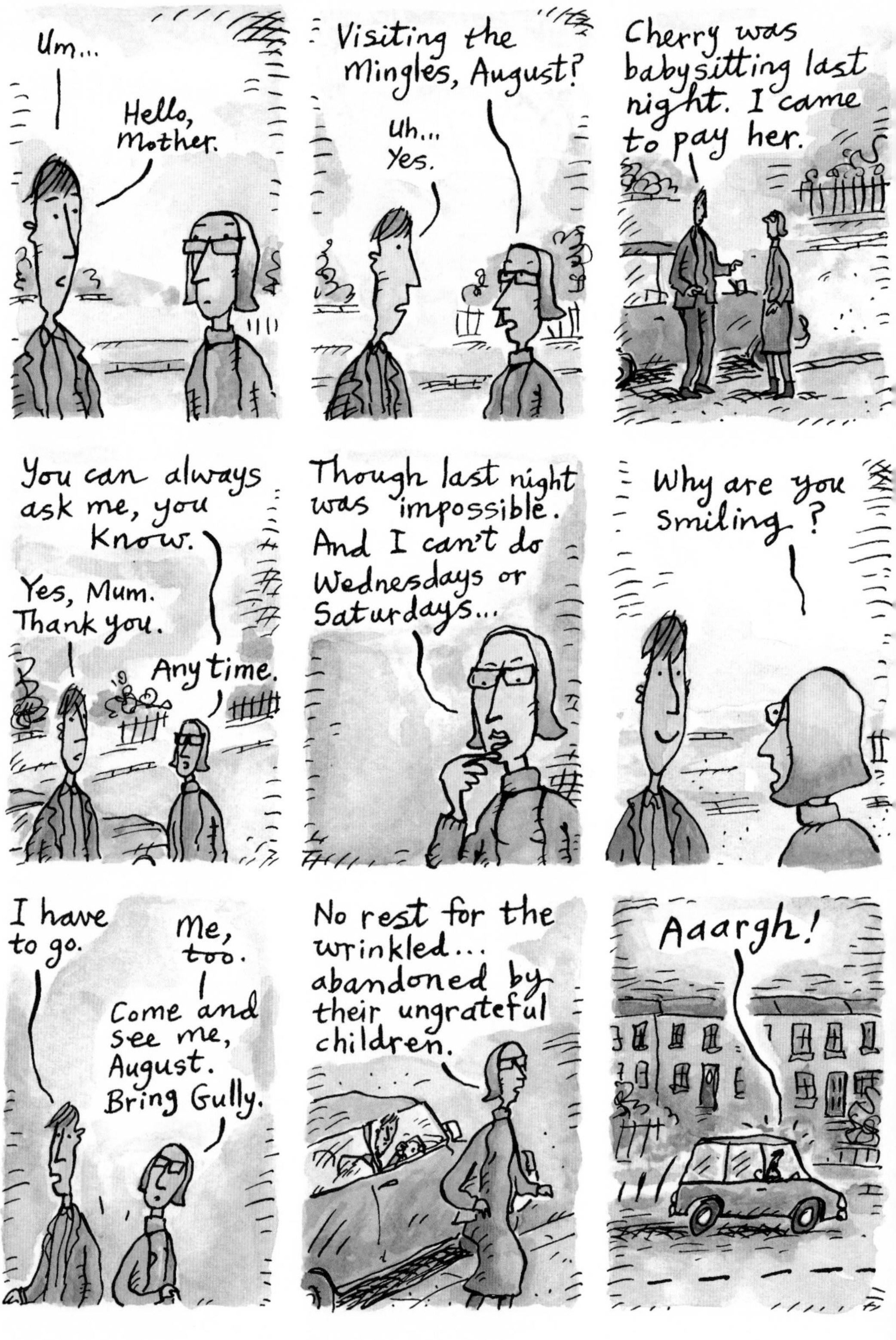
Um...
Hello, Mother.
Visiting the Mingles, August?
Uh... Yes.
Cherry was babysitting last night. I came to pay her.
You can always ask me, you know.
Yes, Mum. Thank you.
Any time.
Though last night was impossible. And I can't do Wednesdays or Saturdays...
Why are you smiling?
I have to go.
Me, too.
Come and see me, August. Bring Gully.
No rest for the wrinkled... abandoned by their ungrateful children.
Aaargh!

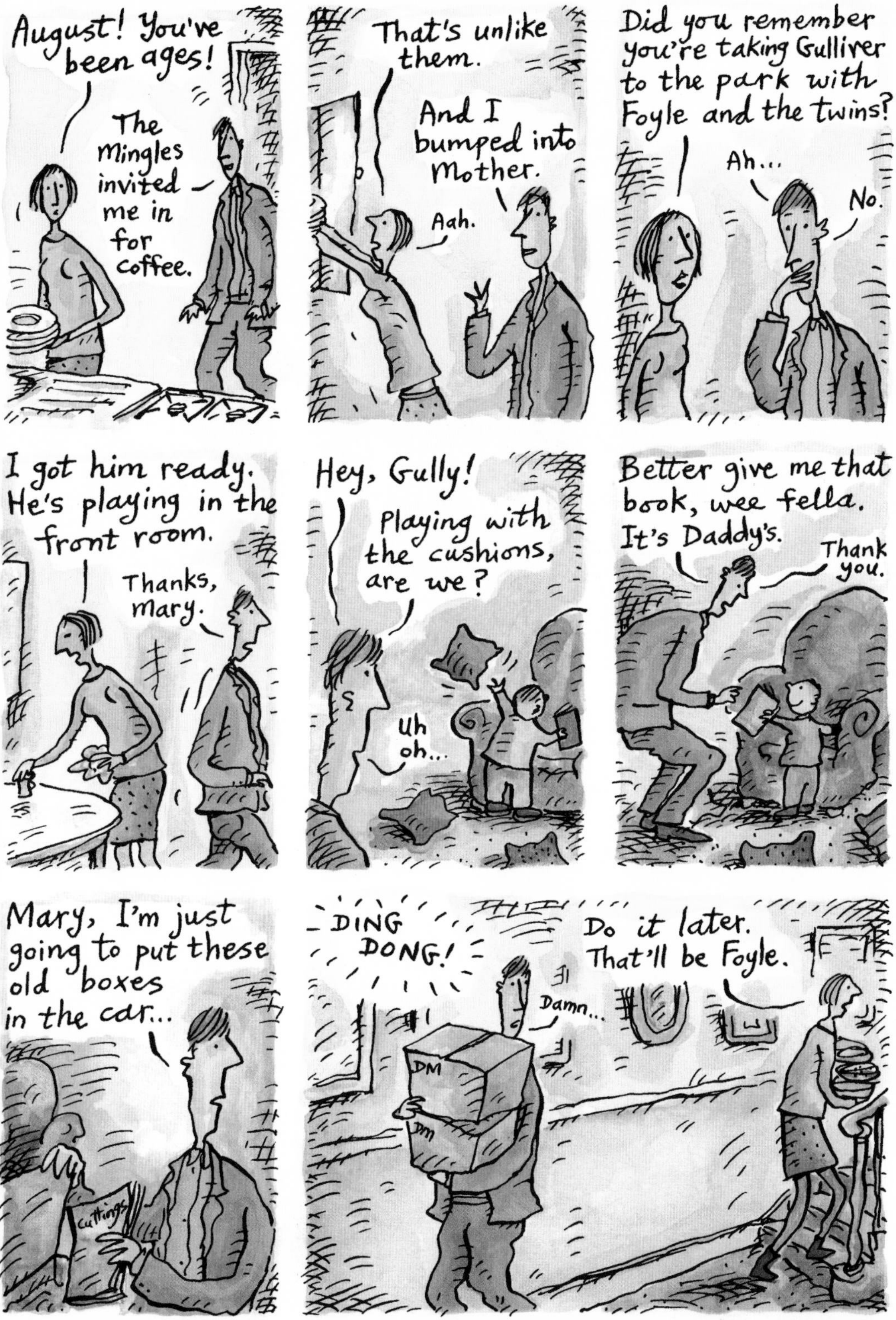
August! You've been ages!
The Mingles invited me in for coffee.
That's unlike them.
And I bumped into Mother.
Aah.
Did you remember you're taking Gulliver to the park with Foyle and the twins?
Ah...
No.
I got him ready. He's playing in the front room.
Thanks, Mary.
Hey, Gully!
Playing with the cushions, are we?
Uh oh...
Better give me that book, wee fella. It's Daddy's.
Thank you.
Mary, I'm just going to put these old boxes in the car...
cuttings
DING DONG!
Damn...
DM
DM
Do it later. That'll be Foyle.

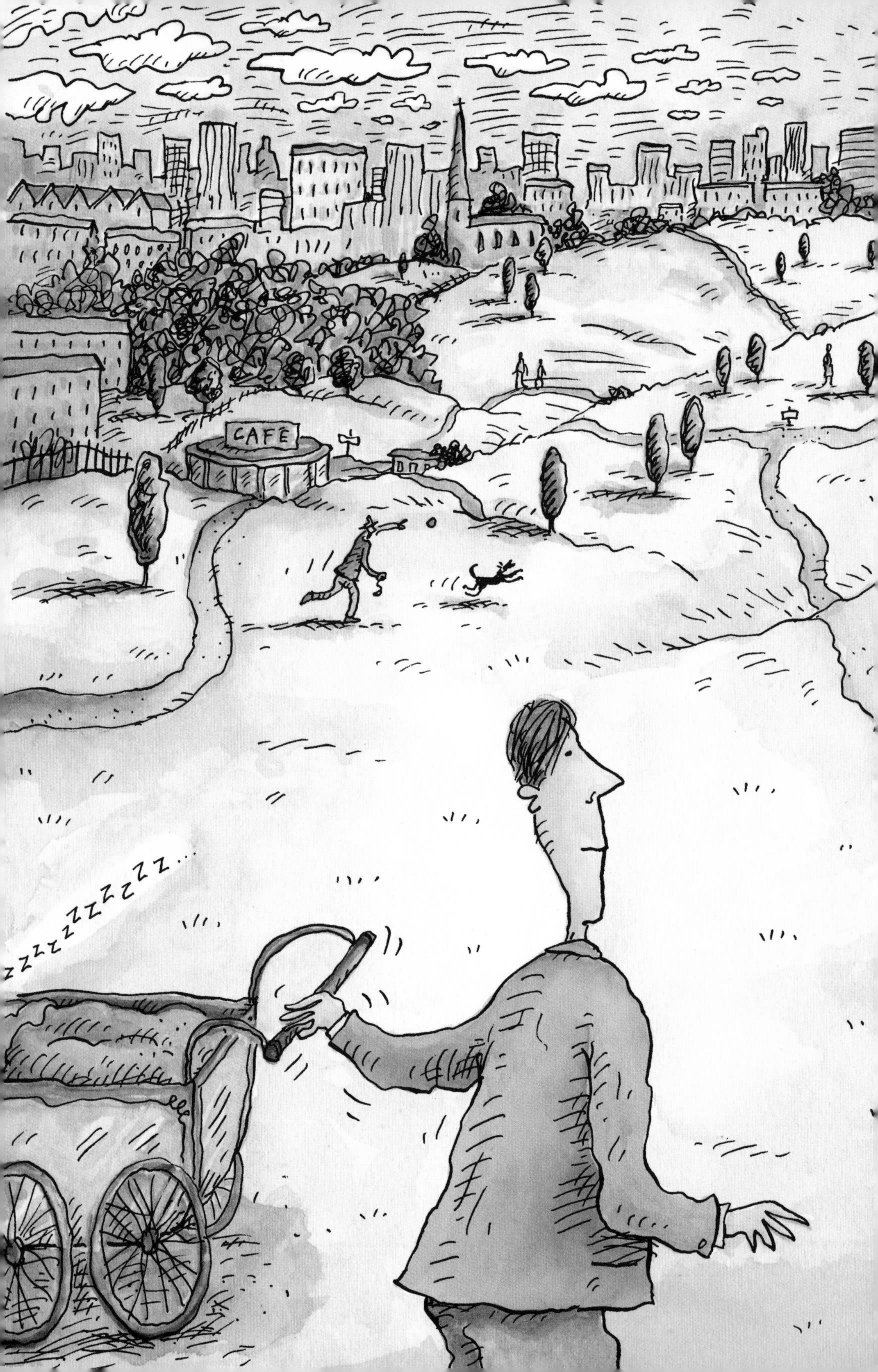
CAFÉ
zzzzzzzzzzzz...

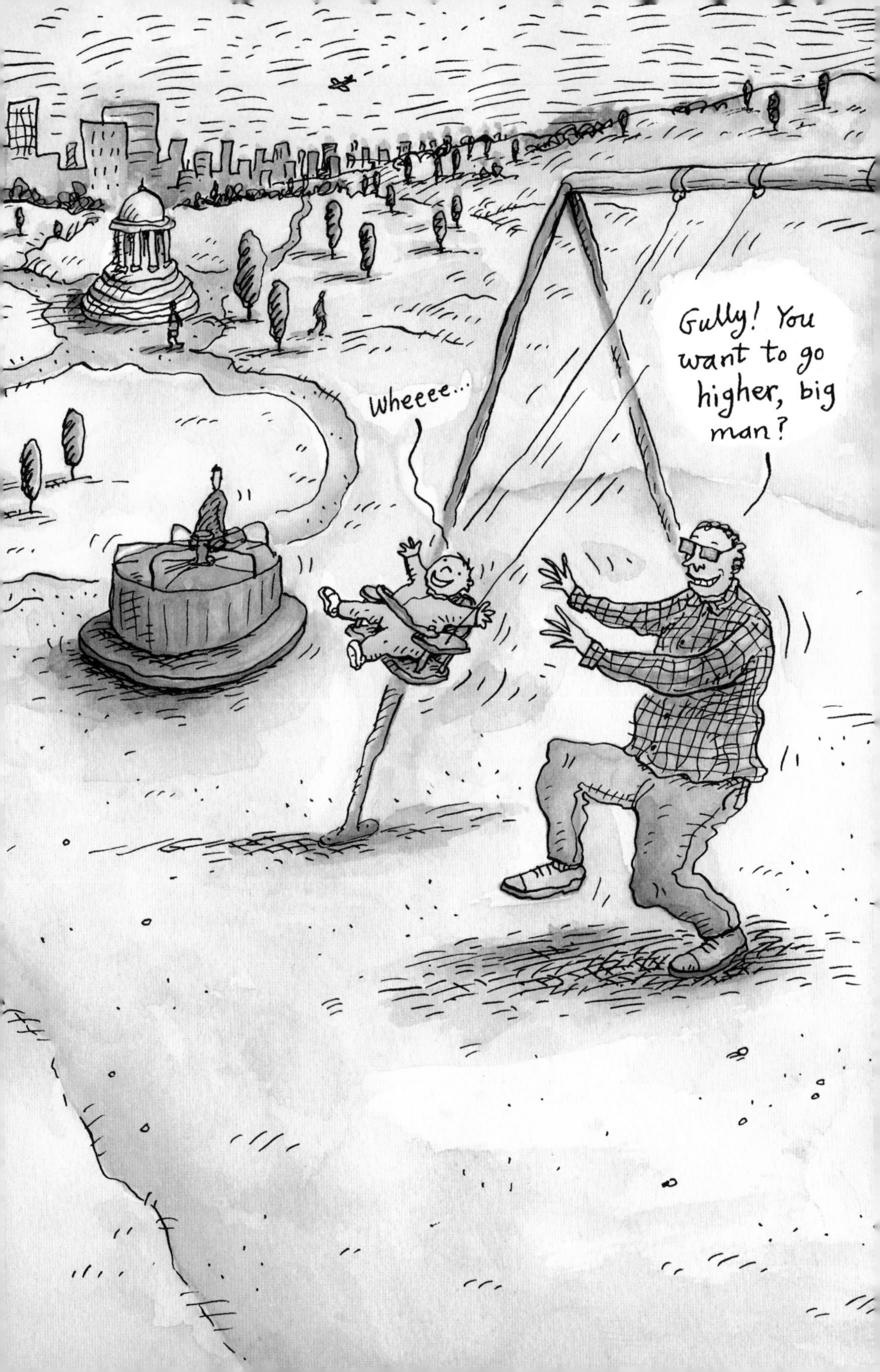
Wheeee...
Gully! You want to go higher, big man?

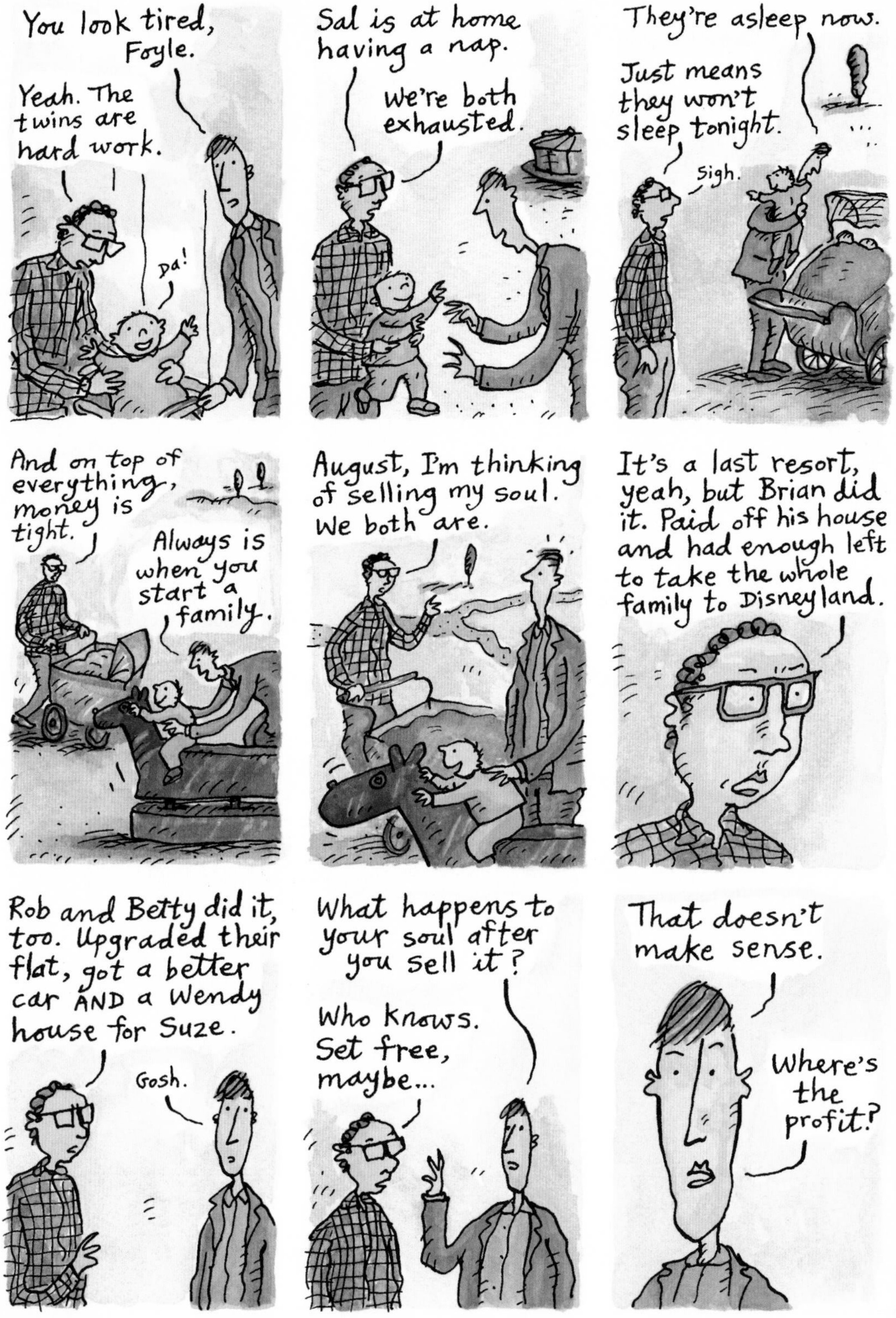
You look tired, Foyle.
Yeah. The twins are hard work.
Da!
Sal is at home having a nap.
We're both exhausted.
They're asleep now.
Just means they won't sleep tonight.
Sigh.
And on top of everything, money is tight.
Always is when you start a family.
August, I'm thinking of selling my soul. We both are.
It's a last resort, yeah, but Brian did it. Paid off his house and had enough left to take the whole family to Disneyland.
Rob and Betty did it, too. Upgraded their flat, got a better car AND a Wendy house for Suze.
Gosh.
What happens to your soul after you sell it?
Who knows. Set free, maybe...
That doesn't make sense.
Where's the profit?

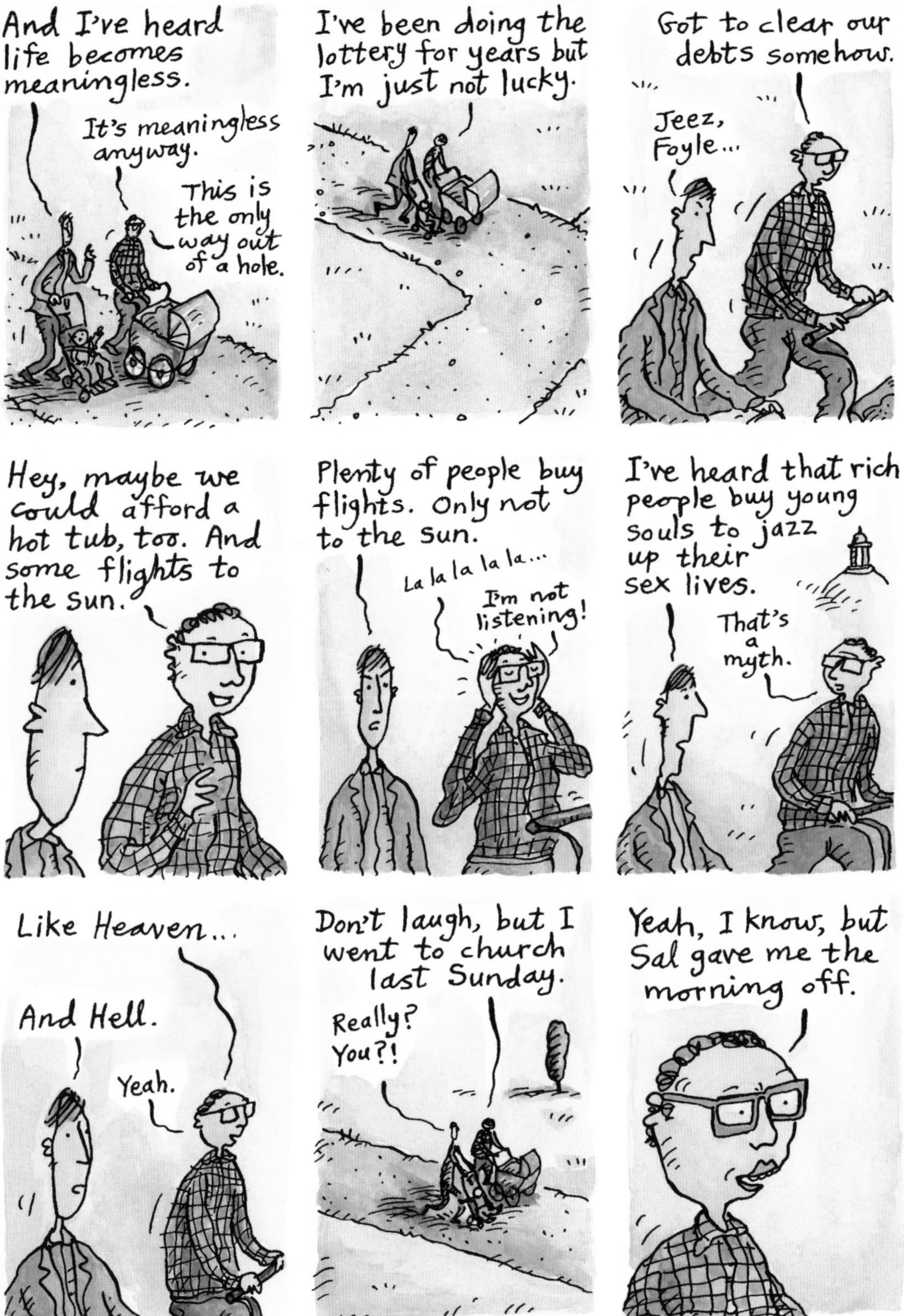
And I've heard life becomes meaningless.
It's meaningless anyway.
This is the only way out of a hole.
I've been doing the lottery for years but I'm just not lucky.
Got to clear our debts somehow.
Jeez, Foyle...
Hey, maybe we could afford a hot tub, too. And some flights to the sun.
Plenty of people buy flights. Only not to the sun.
La la la la la...
I'm not listening!
I've heard that rich people buy young souls to jazz up their sex lives.
That's a myth.
Like Heaven...
And Hell.
Yeah.
Don't laugh, but I went to church last Sunday.
Really? You?!
Yeah, I know, but Sal gave me the morning off.

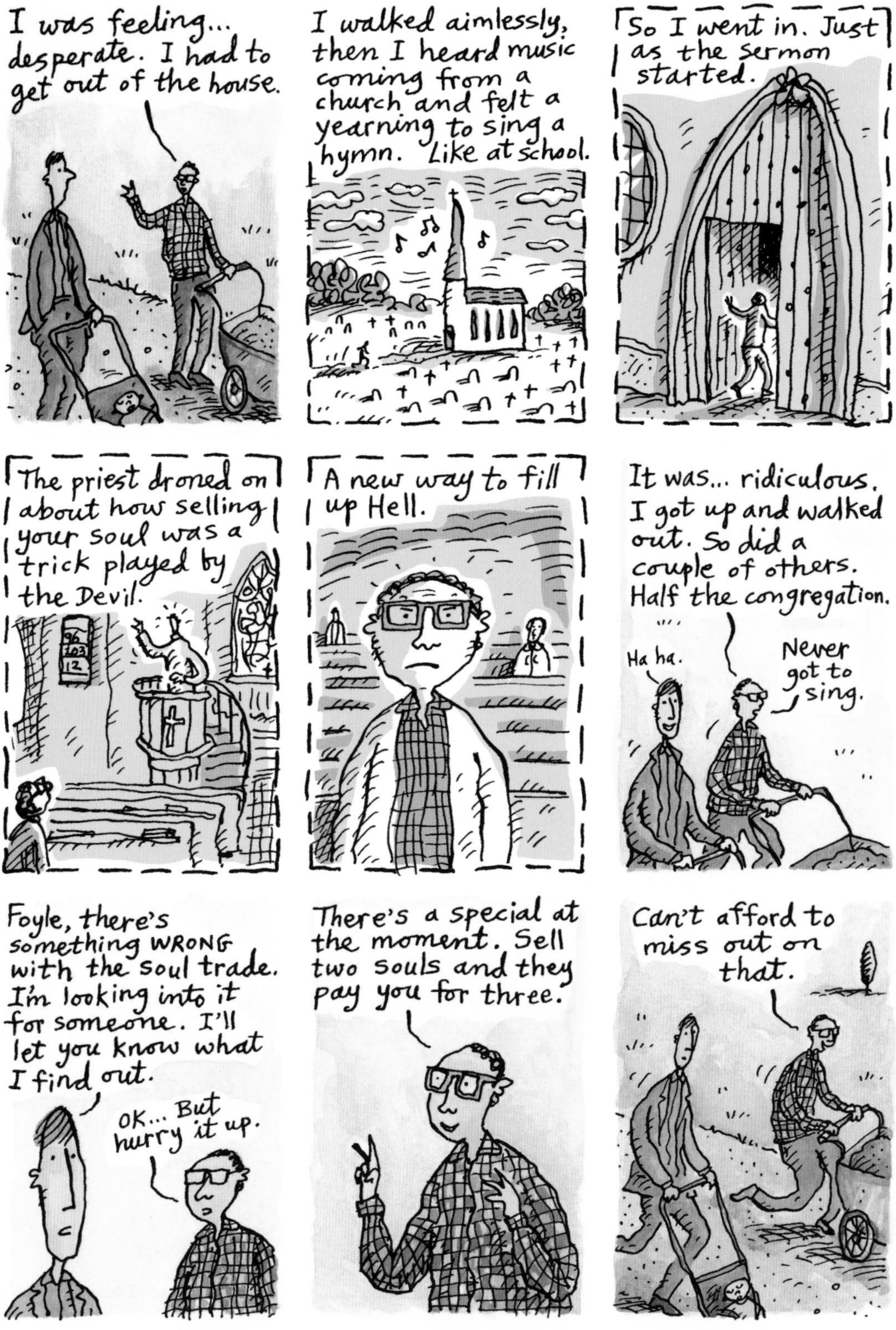

I was feeling... desperate. I had to get out of the house.
I walked aimlessly, then I heard music coming from a church and felt a yearning to sing a hymn. Like at school.
So I went in. Just as the sermon started.
The priest droned on about how selling your soul was a trick played by the Devil.
96
103
12
A new way to fill up Hell.
It was... ridiculous. I got up and walked out. So did a couple of others. Half the congregation.
Ha ha.
Never got to sing.
Foyle, there's something WRONG with the soul trade. I'm looking into it for someone. I'll let you know what I find out.
OK... But hurry it up.
There's a special at the moment. Sell two souls and they pay you for three.
Can't afford to miss out on that.

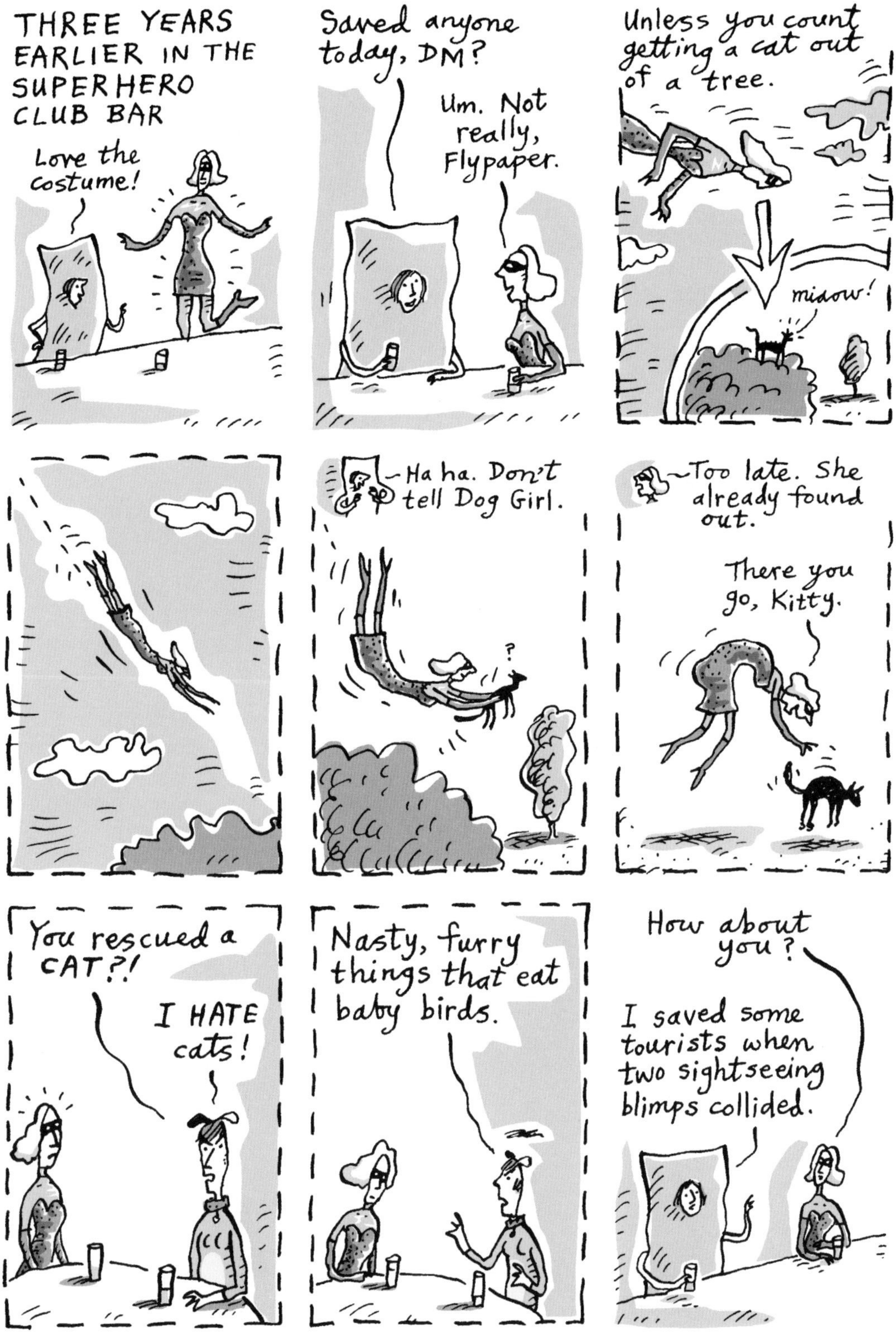

THREE YEARS EARLIER IN THE SUPERHERO CLUB BAR
Love the costume!
Saved anyone today, DM?
Um. Not really, Flypaper.
Unless you count getting a cat out of a tree.
miaow!
Ha ha. Don't tell Dog Girl.
?
Too late. She already found out.
There you go, Kitty.
You rescued a CAT?!
I HATE cats!
Nasty, furry things that eat baby birds.
How about you?
I saved some tourists when two sightseeing blimps collided.

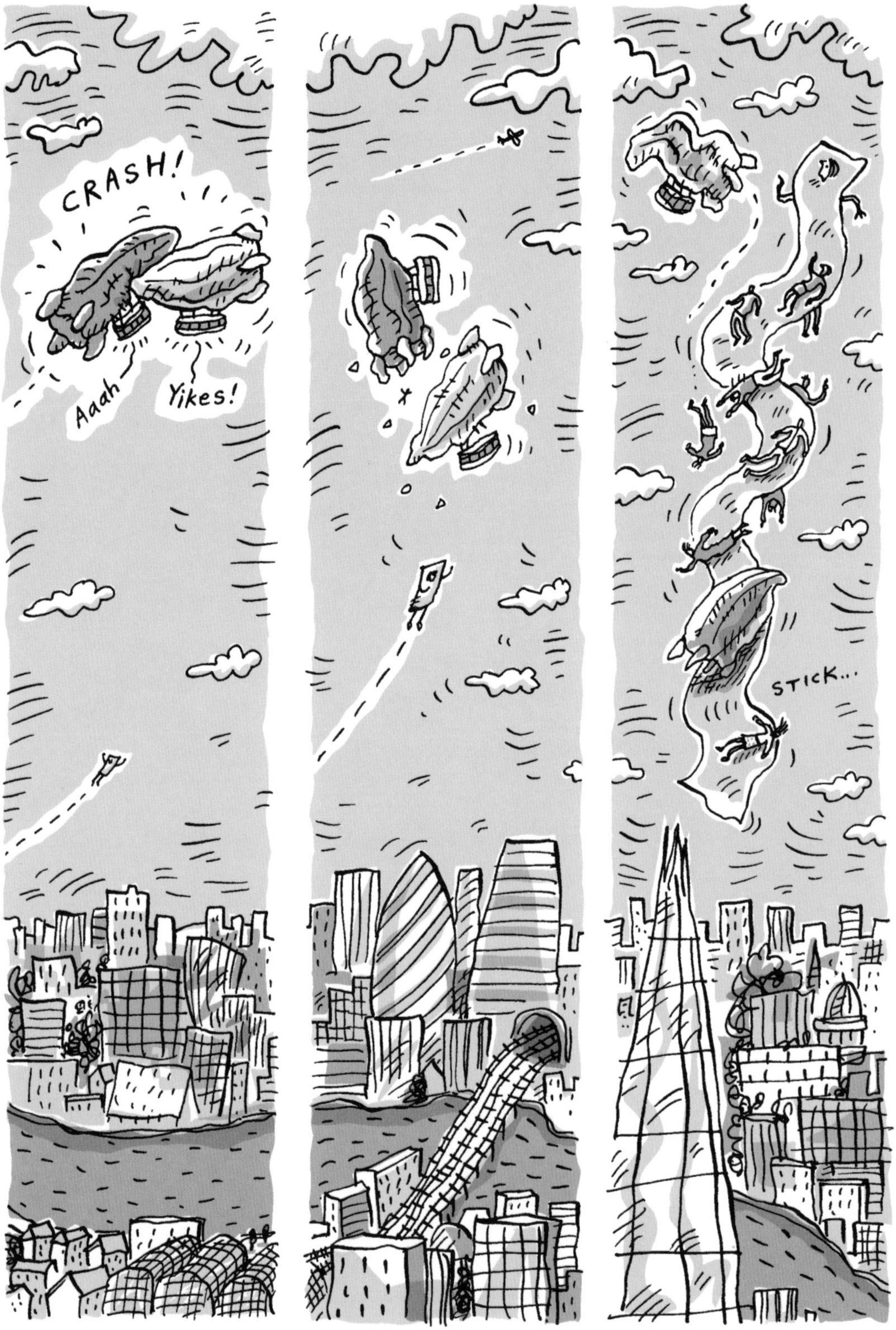
CRASH!
Aaah
Yikes!
STICK...

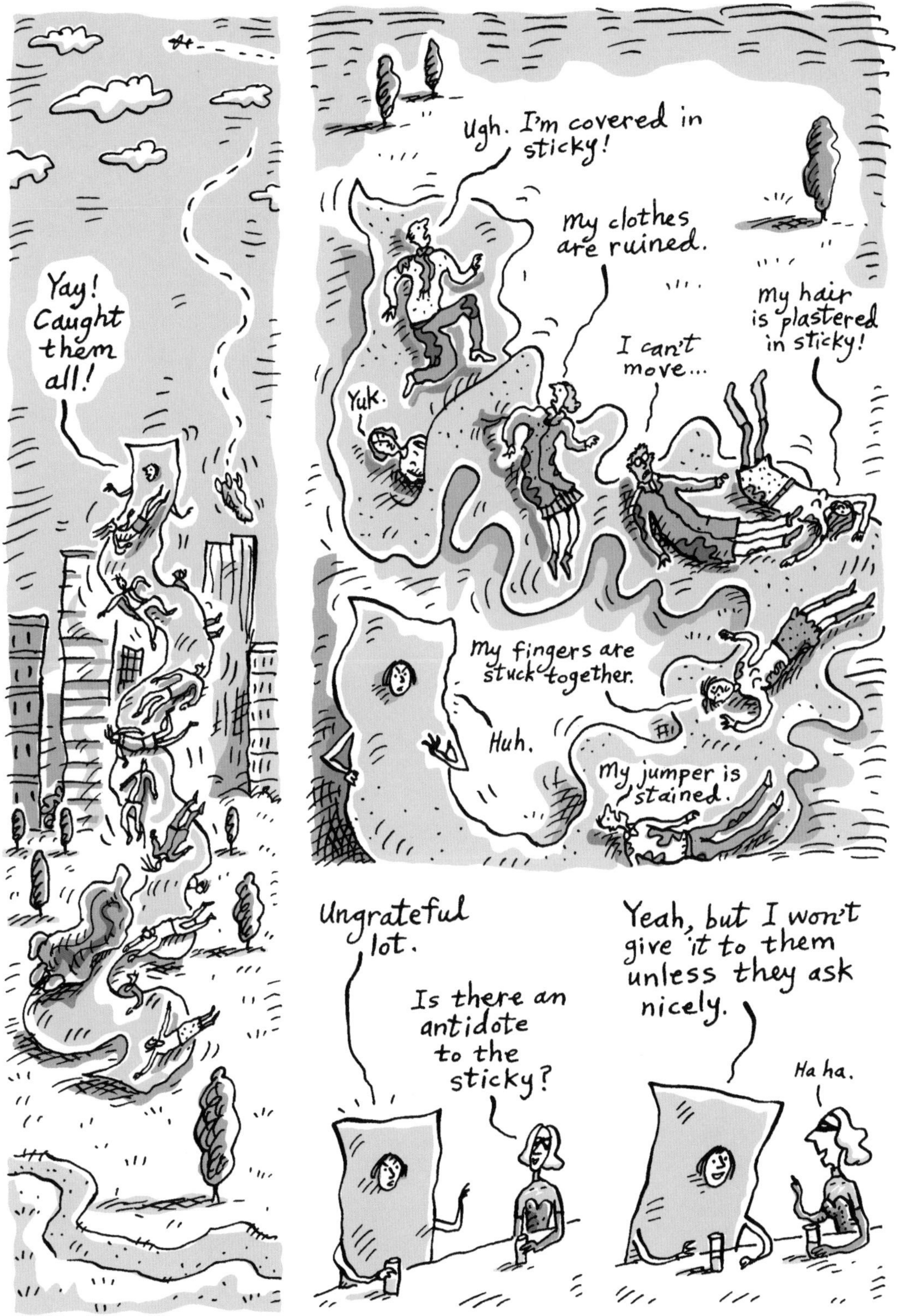
Yay! Caught them all!
Ugh. I'm covered in sticky!
My clothes are ruined.
Yuk.
I can't move...
My hair is plastered in sticky!
My fingers are stuck together.
Huh.
My jumper is stained.
Ungrateful lot.
Is there an antidote to the sticky?
Yeah, but I won't give it to them unless they ask nicely.
Ha ha.

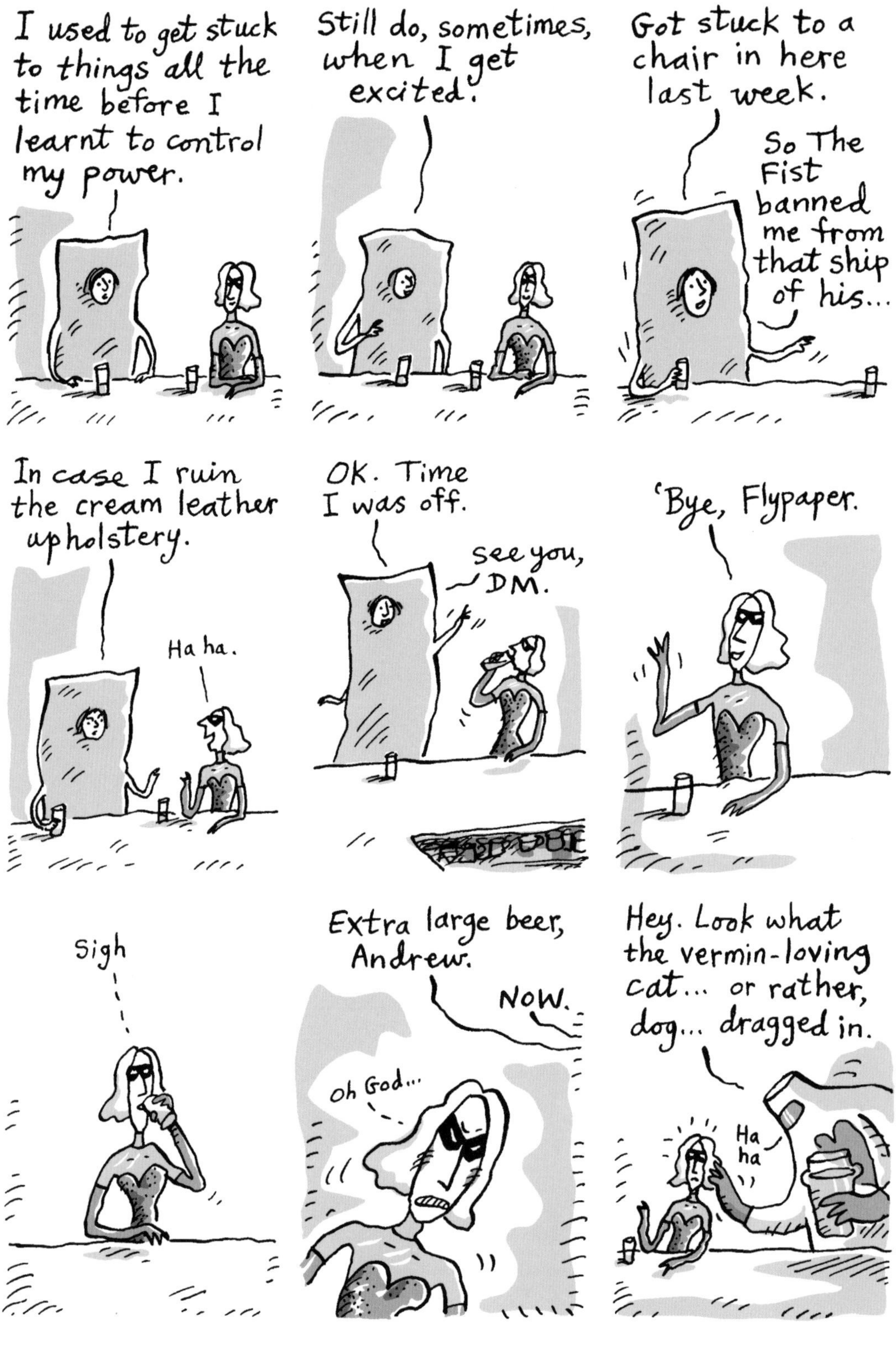
I used to get stuck to things all the time before I learnt to control my power.
Still do, sometimes, when I get excited.
Got stuck to a chair in here last week.
So The Fist banned me from that ship of his...
In case I ruin the cream leather upholstery.
Ha ha.
OK. Time I was off.
See you, DM.
'Bye, Flypaper.
Sigh
Extra large beer, Andrew.
NOW.
Oh God...
Hey. Look what the vermin-loving cat... or rather, dog... dragged in.
Ha ha

Something foul and maggot-infested.

SNIFF SNIFF

Stinky, too!

That's Eu de Dragman. A perfume line I'm developing.

Forget it.

There'll be no perfume line.

Or cosmetic franchise.

?

There'll be no fashion brand. No comic books.

What do you mean?

BELCH!

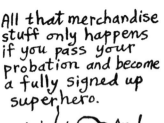

All that merchandise stuff only happens if you pass your probation and become a fully signed up superhero.

And guess who's on your tribunal?

Yup. ME!

And there's NO WAY I'm letting a SICK WEIRDO like YOU join this club.

You... You...

You what, sicko?

Shall I squeeze your head off?

Gak...

Urr... what's going on, boys?

Nothing, Believer.

DROP...

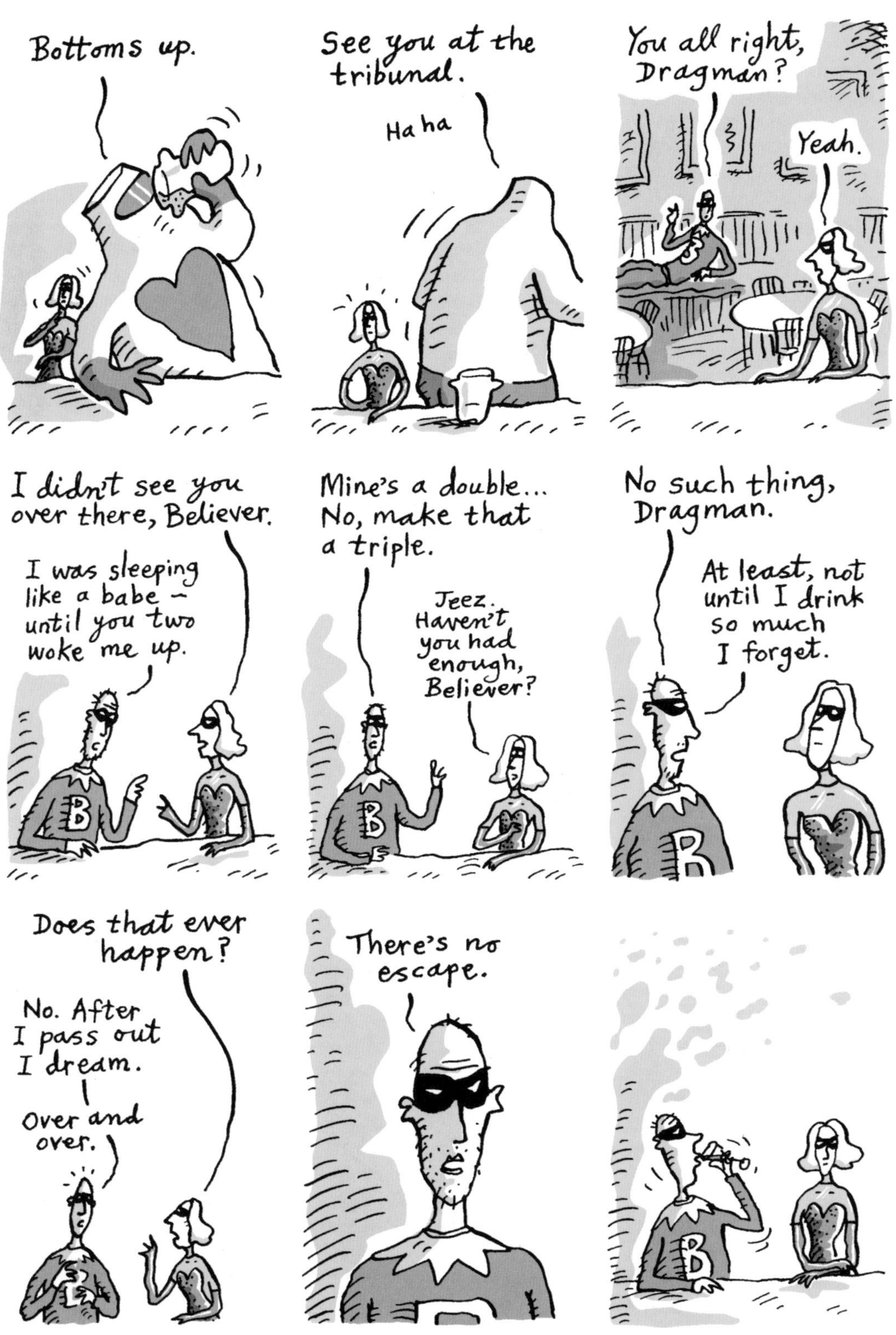
Bottoms up.
See you at the tribunal.
Ha ha
You all right, Dragman?
Yeah.
I didn't see you over there, Believer.
I was sleeping like a babe – until you two woke me up.
Mine's a double... No, make that a triple.
Jeez. Haven't you had enough, Believer?
No such thing, Dragman.
At least, not until I drink so much I forget.
Does that ever happen?
No. After I pass out I dream.
Over and over.
There's no escape.

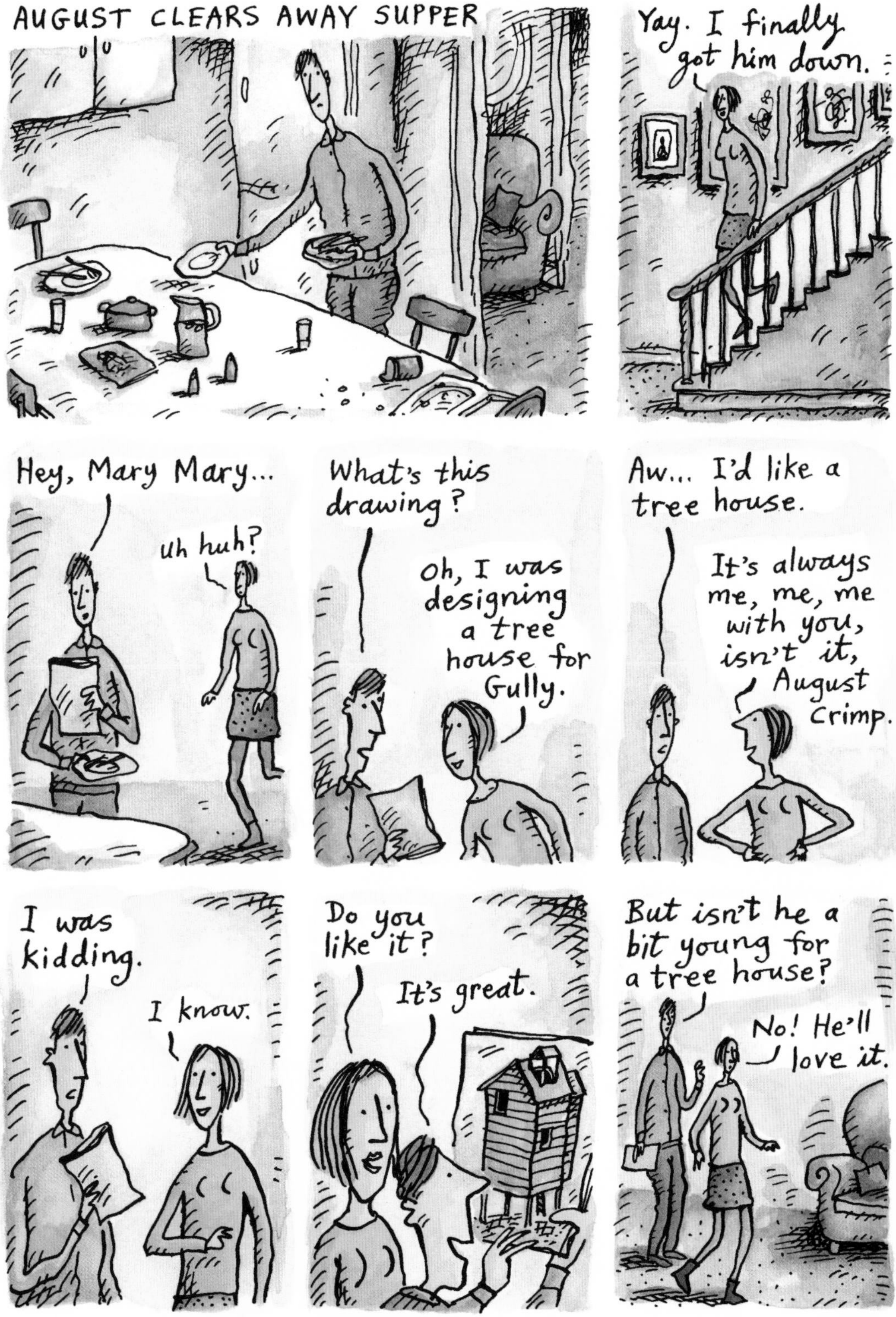
AUGUST CLEARS AWAY SUPPER
Yay. I finally got him down.
Hey, Mary Mary...
uh huh?
What's this drawing?
Oh, I was designing a tree house for Gully.
Aw... I'd like a tree house.
It's always me, me, me with you, isn't it, August Crimp.
I was kidding.
I know.
Do you like it?
It's great.
But isn't he a bit young for a tree house?
No! He'll love it.

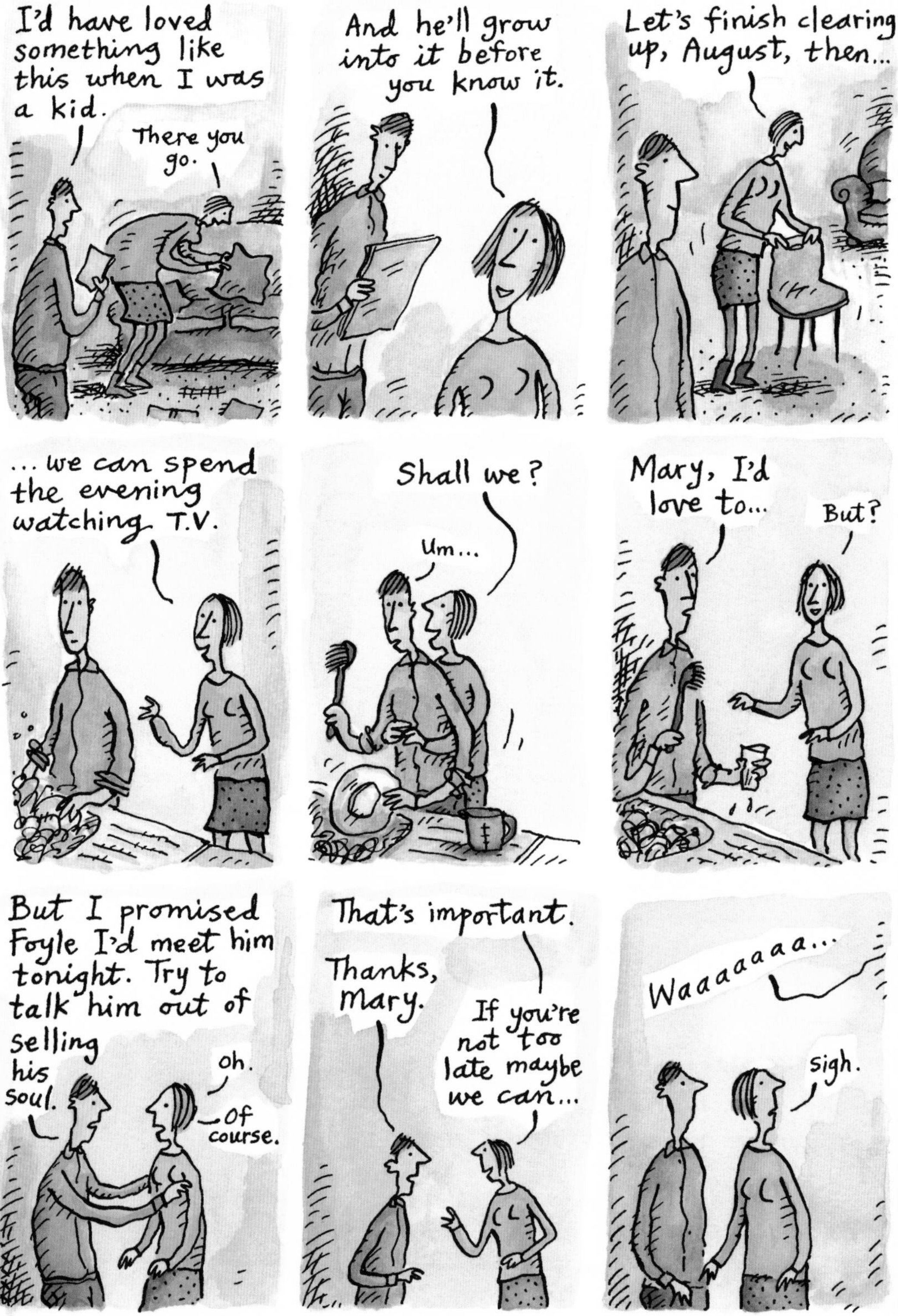
I'd have loved something like this when I was a kid.
There you go.
And he'll grow into it before you know it.
Let's finish clearing up, August, then...
... we can spend the evening watching T.V.
Shall we?
Um...
Mary, I'd love to...
But?
But I promised Foyle I'd meet him tonight. Try to talk him out of selling his soul.
Oh.
Of course.
That's important.
Thanks, Mary.
If you're not too late maybe we can...
Waaaaaaa...
Sigh.

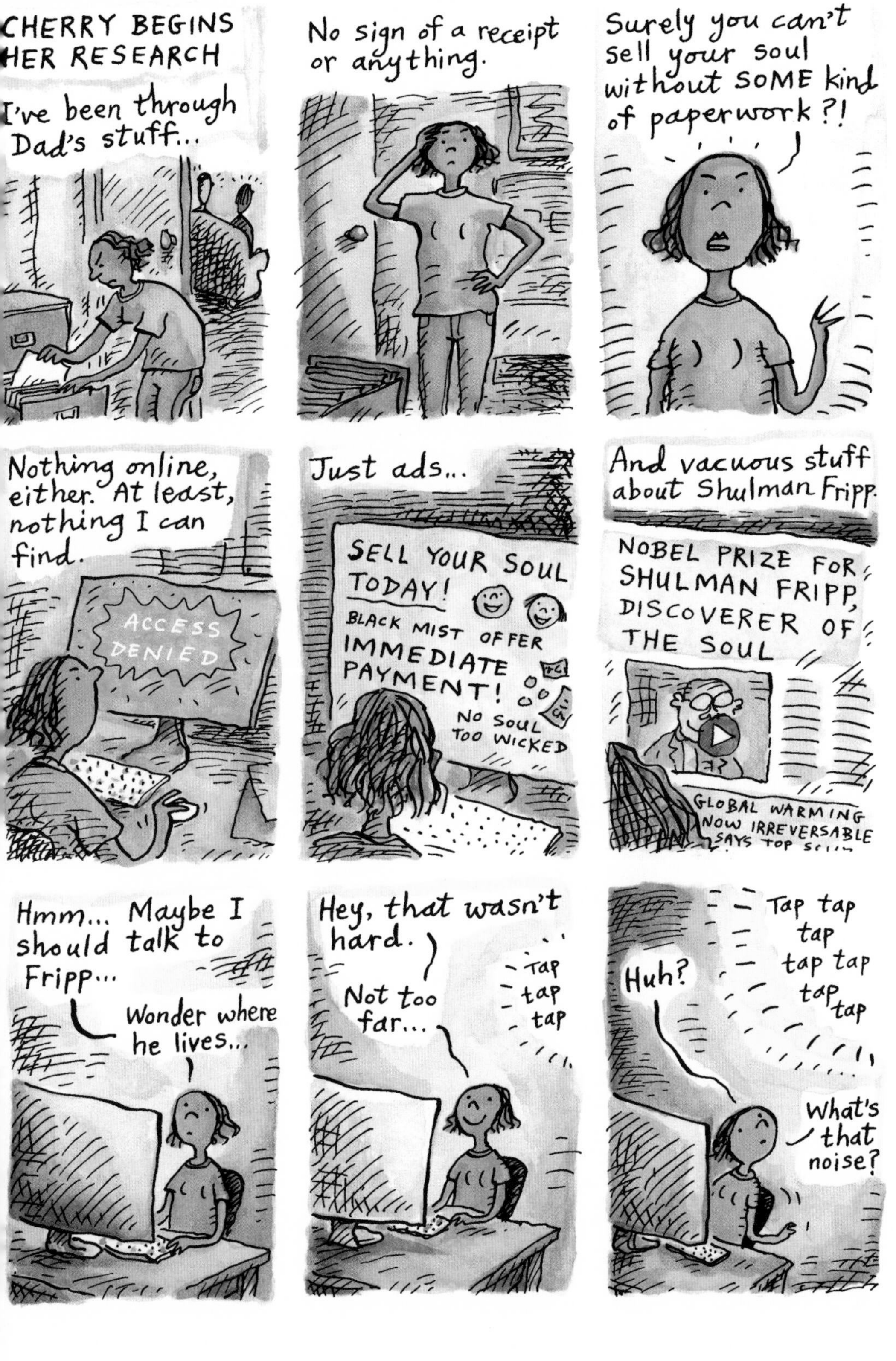
CHERRY BEGINS HER RESEARCH
I've been through Dad's stuff...
No sign of a receipt or anything.
Surely you can't sell your soul without SOME kind of paperwork?!
Nothing online, either. At least, nothing I can find.
ACCESS DENIED
Just ads...
SELL YOUR SOUL TODAY!
BLACK MIST OFFER IMMEDIATE PAYMENT!
NO SOUL TOO WICKED
And vacuous stuff about Shulman Fripp.
NOBEL PRIZE FOR SHULMAN FRIPP, DISCOVERER OF THE SOUL
GLOBAL WARMING NOW IRREVERSABLE
Hmm... Maybe I should talk to Fripp...
Wonder where he lives...
Hey, that wasn't hard.
Not too far...
tap tap tap
Tap tap tap tap tap tap tap
Huh?
What's that noise?

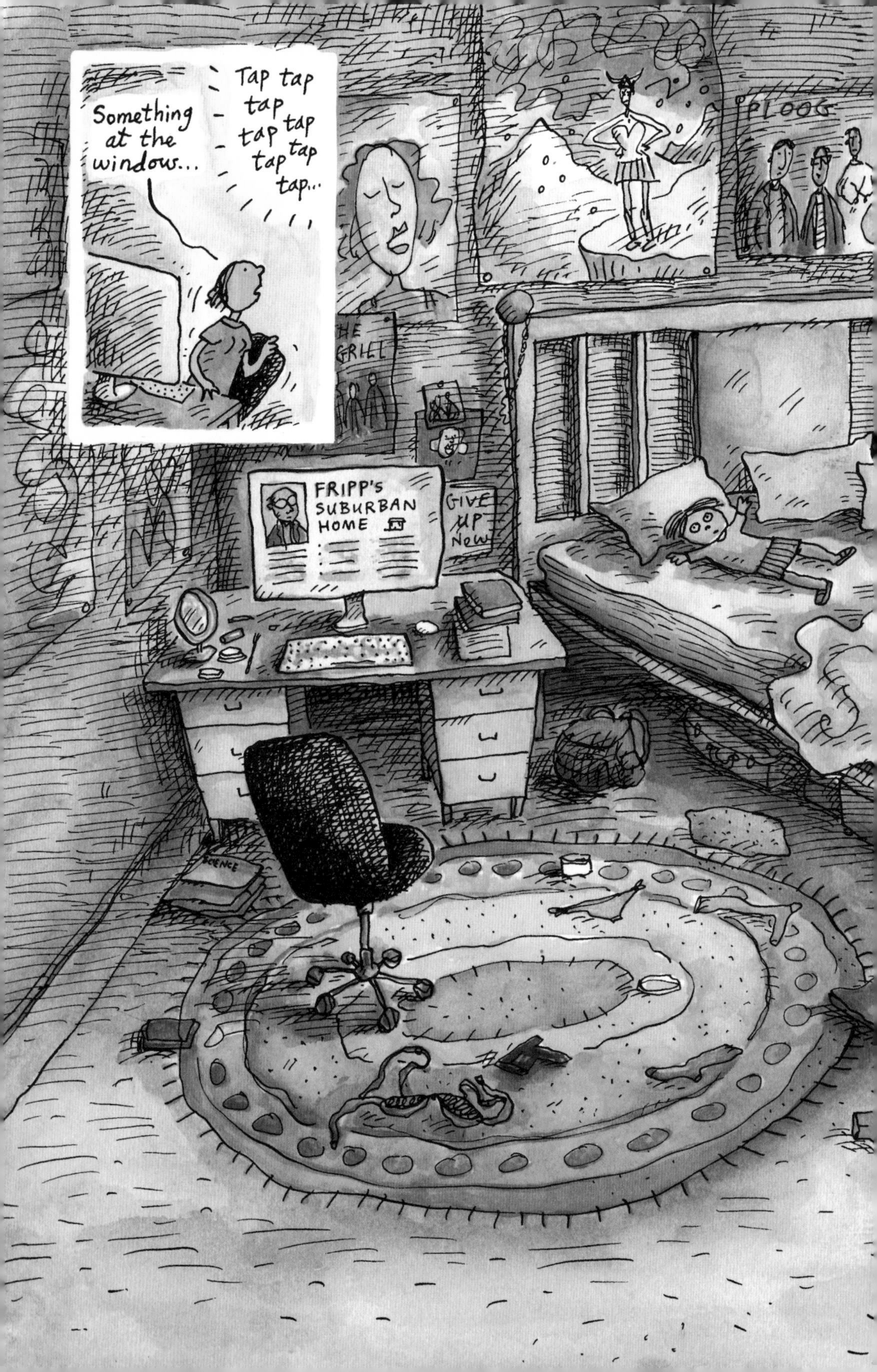

Something at the window...
Tap tap tap tap tap tap tap tap tap...
PLOOG
THE GRILL
FRIPP'S SUBURBAN HOME
GIVE UP NOW
SCIENCE

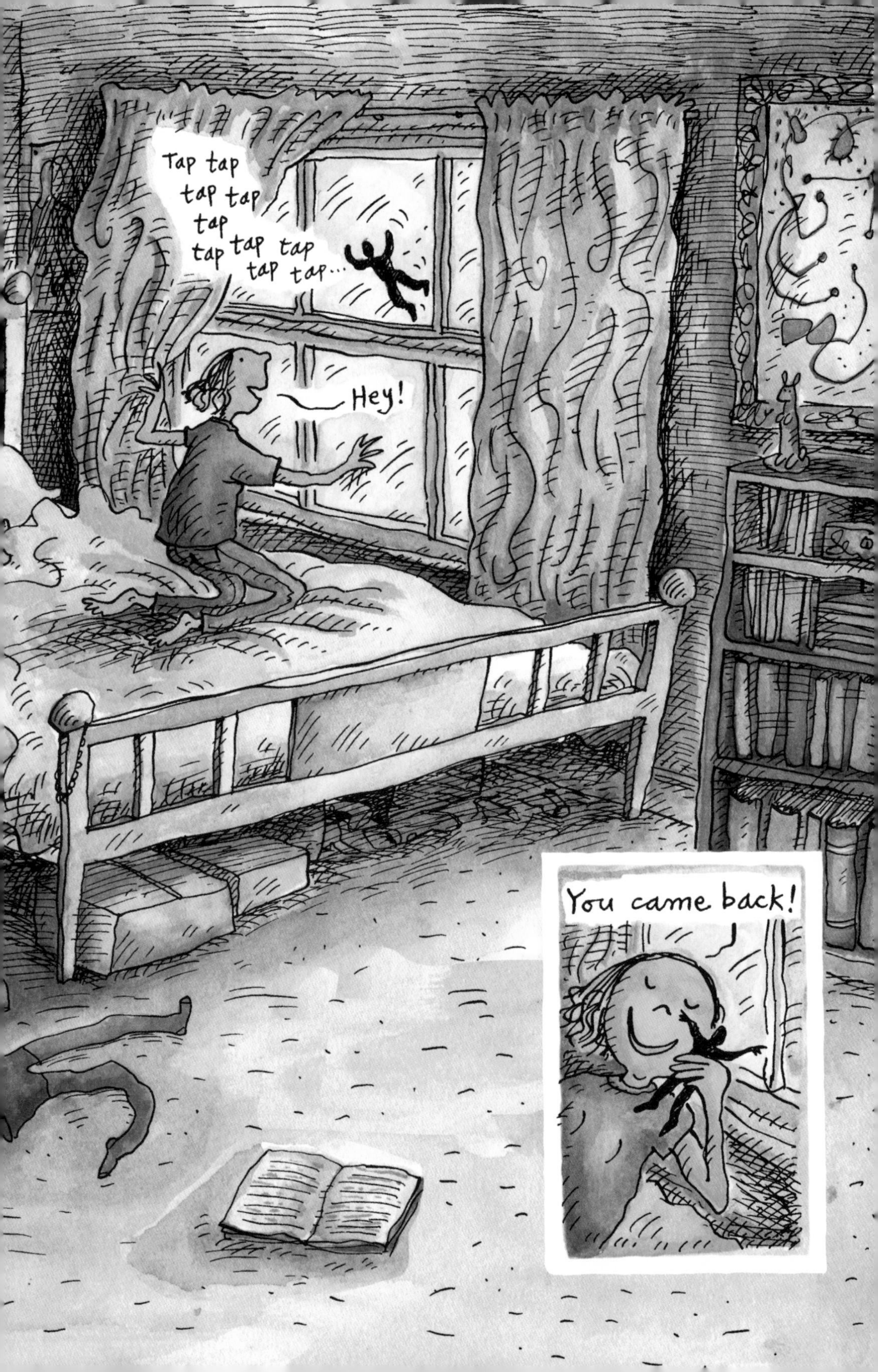
Tap tap
tap tap
tap
tap tap tap
tap tap...
Hey!
You came back!

10·23 pm

HIGH ABOVE THE CITY clouds dissolve into drizzle as descending airliners, so low you can see the screws holding them together, roar like thunder as they slide down the sky towards the airport. It's almost dark and sirens wail. Time to hit the town…

The man full of ghosts parks in a quiet street just off Kingsland Road and watches as a fat transvestite, shoulders like a builder's and boobs like basketballs, limps past, teetering through the moist dusk in scarlet stilettos towards an anonymous doorway under a railway arch. She rings the bell, the door opens and she topples inside.

Sitting in his car the man anticipates a night of fun in the crimson, dimly lit mock bedrooms of Club Pretty Pretty and feels the familiar trickle of pleasure drip down his spine. The man is popular with the girls despite being average-looking because he's been blessed with the ability to stay firm and functional for hours and the girls, despite loving to chit-chat with their friends in the bar, are really at the club for one reason only.

'Dirty bitches,' the man says to himself, smiling. 'Pretty like a girl, dirty like a boy…'

As he thinks this he marvels that beneath the wigs, false eyelashes, powder and paint these part-time girls are men like himself. It's trompe l'oeil. Sleight of hand. A collusion in which the girls, when dressed, get to bask in the lust of the men and see themselves reflected as beautiful and desirable mythological creatures. Which they are.

Tonight the man hopes to find a girl who'll suggest things he hasn't tried yet. Things he hasn't even imagined. And when he finds her he'll enjoy her and kill her and take her soul to add to his collection. The man has quite an archive of souls now and feels no guilt about how he acquires them and no intention of stopping his hobby any time soon because, deep down, he knows he is supplying his victims with their darkest desire.

He takes a small, oblong device from his pocket and inserts the plastic and metal disc containing the ghost he has selected for tonight. Then he leans forward, holds the device behind him near his spine and presses the button. Immediately the wriggle of warmth and electricity spreads as the soul speeds through his cells, and he closes his eyes.

There's nothing quite so sublime as the frisson
he gets when the soul of a dirty girl slides into his
system, twists through his mind and amplifies his
emotions.

A few moments later the man with a ghost inside
him, wearing cheap, generic, supermarket clothes
and shoes deliberately a size too big, gets out of his car
and walks to the anonymous door leaving dark, liquid
footprints in the film of mist that has settled on the
pavement. He rings the unmarked doorbell and the
door buzzes.

He pushes it open and steps inside.

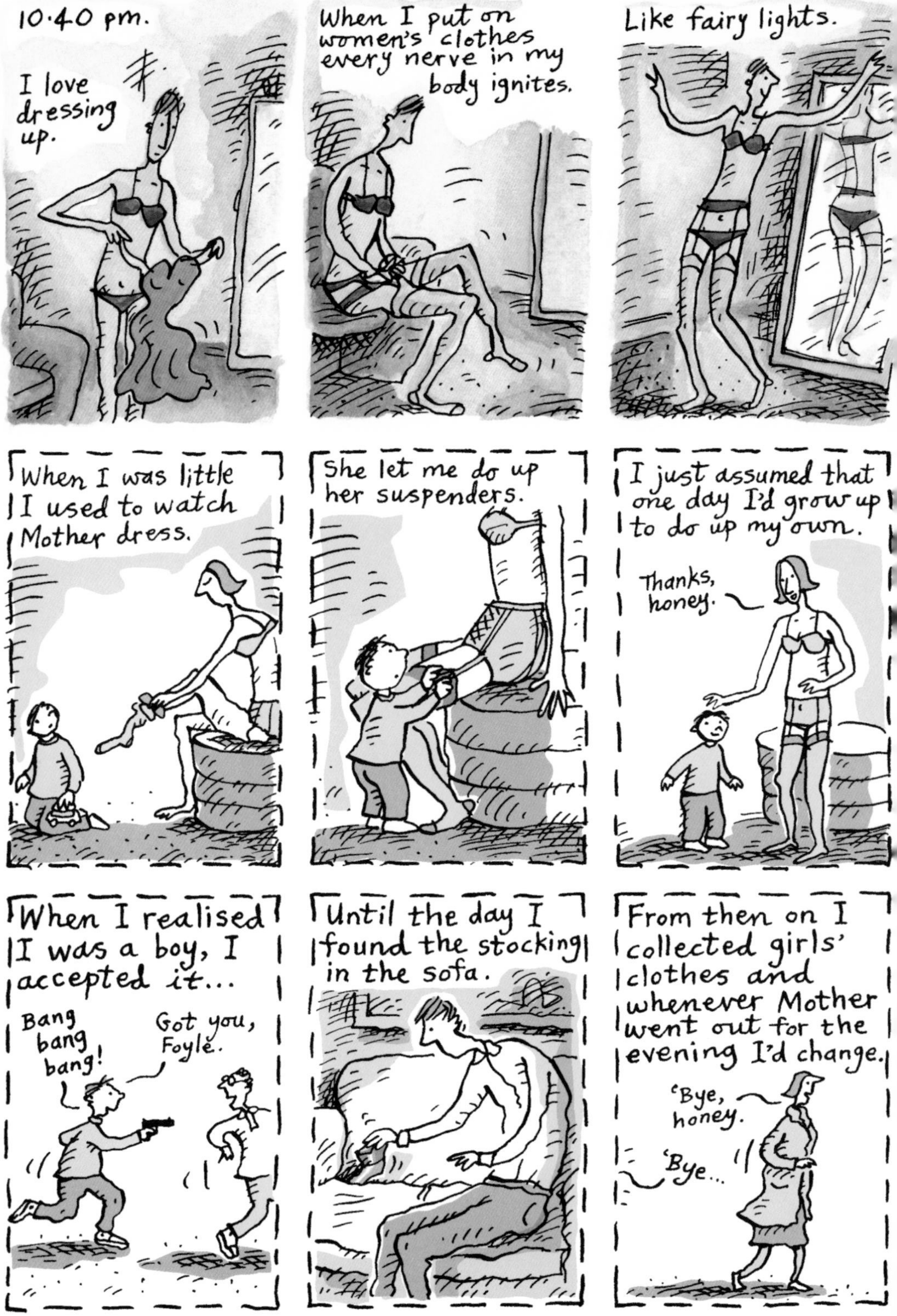
10.40 pm.
I love dressing up.
When I put on women's clothes every nerve in my body ignites.
Like fairy lights.
When I was little I used to watch Mother dress.
She let me do up her suspenders.
I just assumed that one day I'd grow up to do up my own.
Thanks, honey.
When I realised I was a boy, I accepted it...
Bang bang bang!
Got you, Foyle.
Until the day I found the stocking in the sofa.
From then on I collected girls' clothes and whenever Mother went out for the evening I'd change.
'Bye, honey.
'Bye...

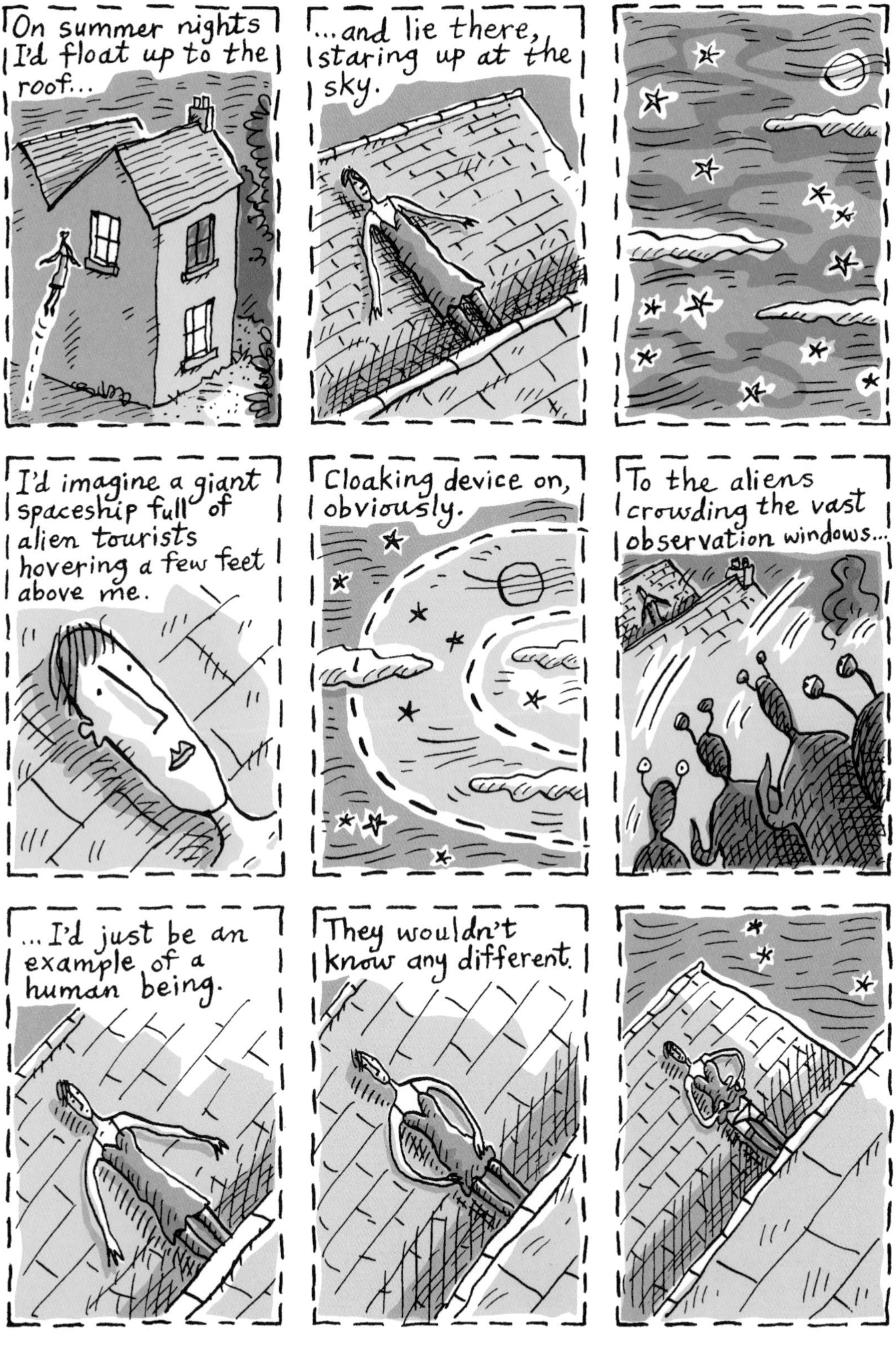
On summer nights I'd float up to the roof...
...and lie there, staring up at the sky.
I'd imagine a giant spaceship full of alien tourists hovering a few feet above me.
Cloaking device on, obviously.
To the aliens crowding the vast observation windows...
...I'd just be an example of a human being.
They wouldn't know any different.

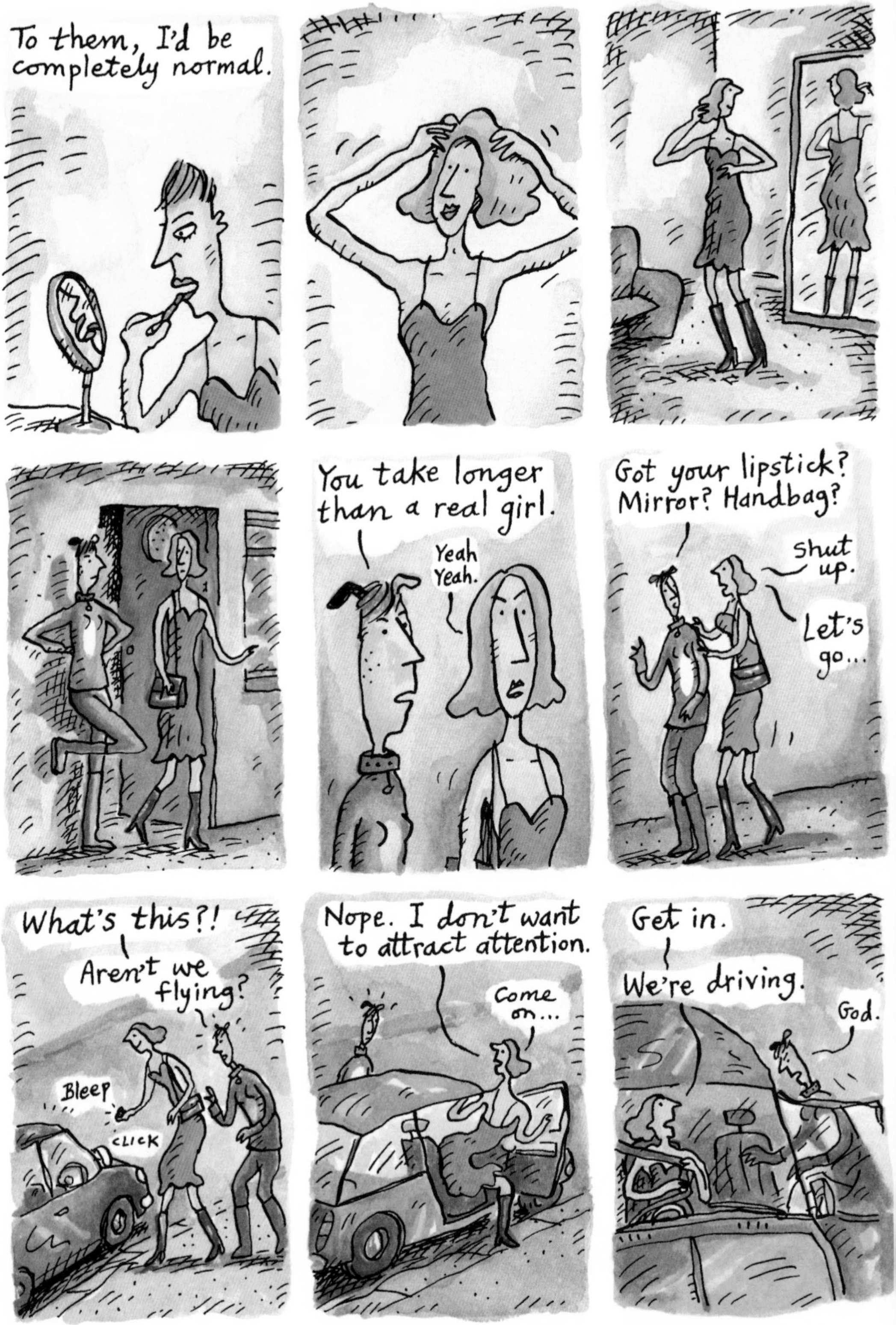
To them, I'd be completely normal.
You take longer than a real girl.
Yeah Yeah.
Got your lipstick? Mirror? Handbag?
Shut up.
Let's go...
What's this?!
Aren't we flying?
Bleep
CLICK
Nope. I don't want to attract attention.
Come on...
Get in.
We're driving.
God.

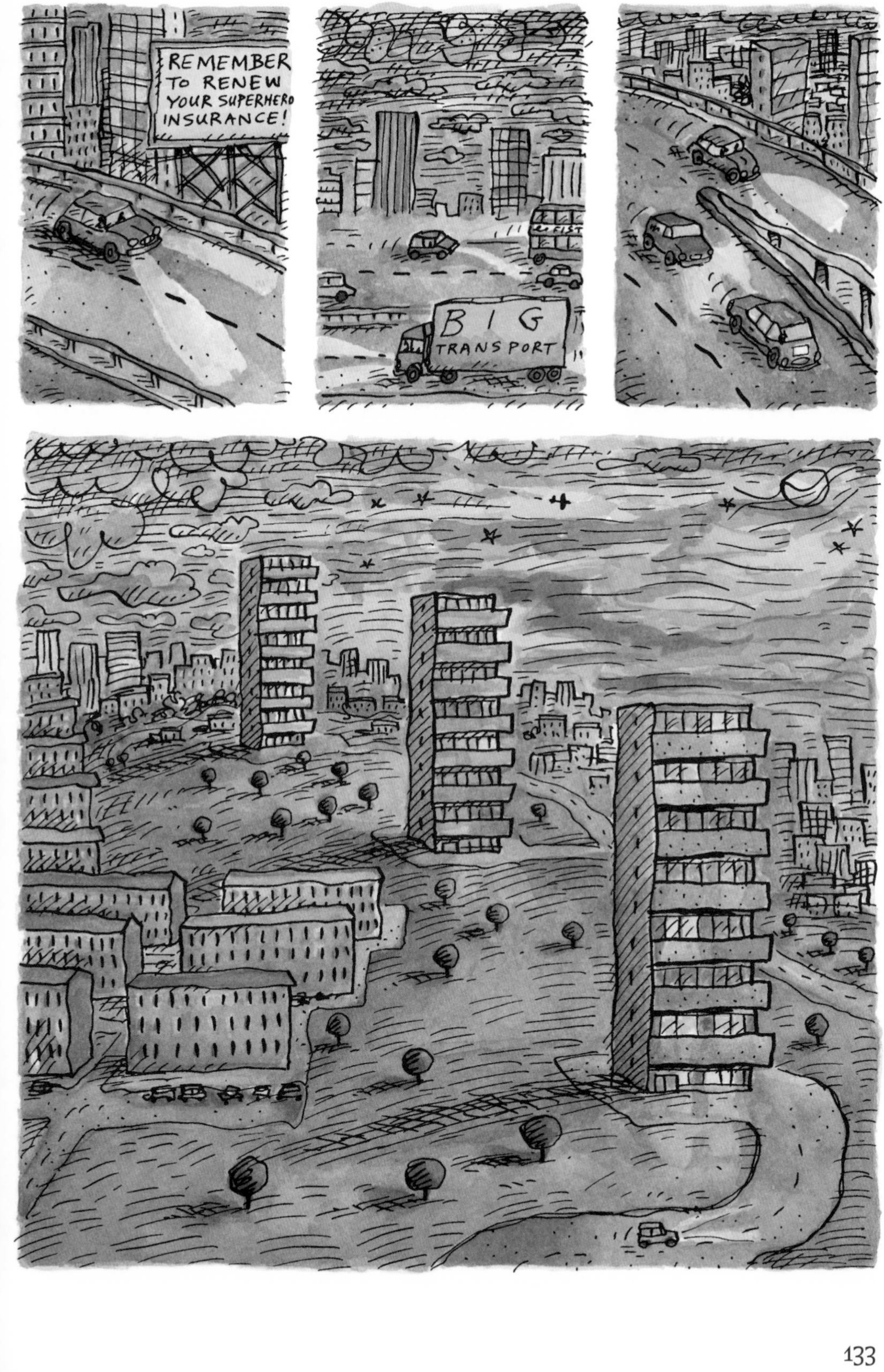
REMEMBER TO RENEW YOUR SUPERHERO INSURANCE!
BIG TRANSPORT

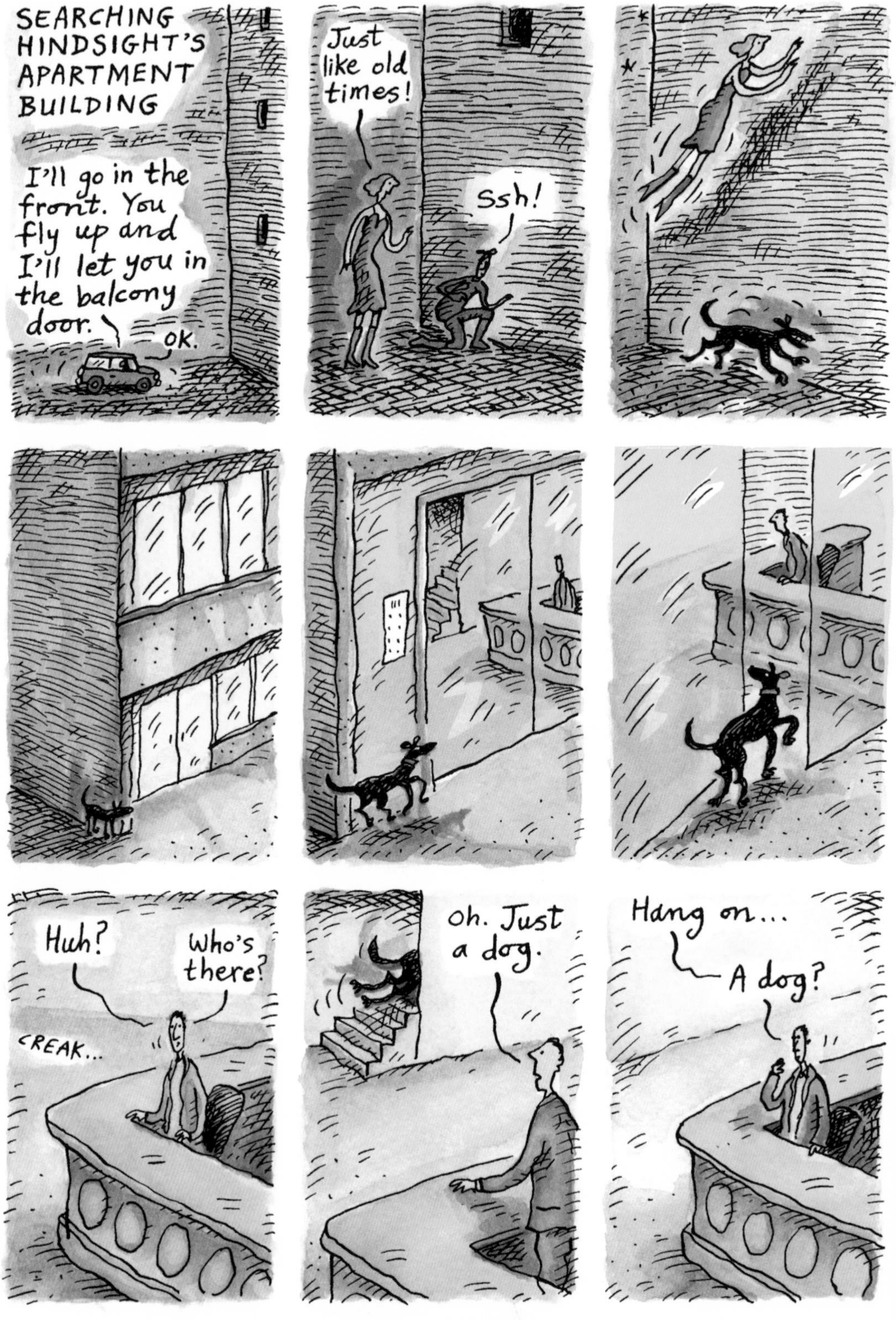
SEARCHING HINDSIGHT'S APARTMENT BUILDING
I'll go in the front. You fly up and I'll let you in the balcony door.
OK.
Just like old times!
Ssh!
Huh?
Who's there?
CREAK...
Oh. Just a dog.
Hang on...
A dog?

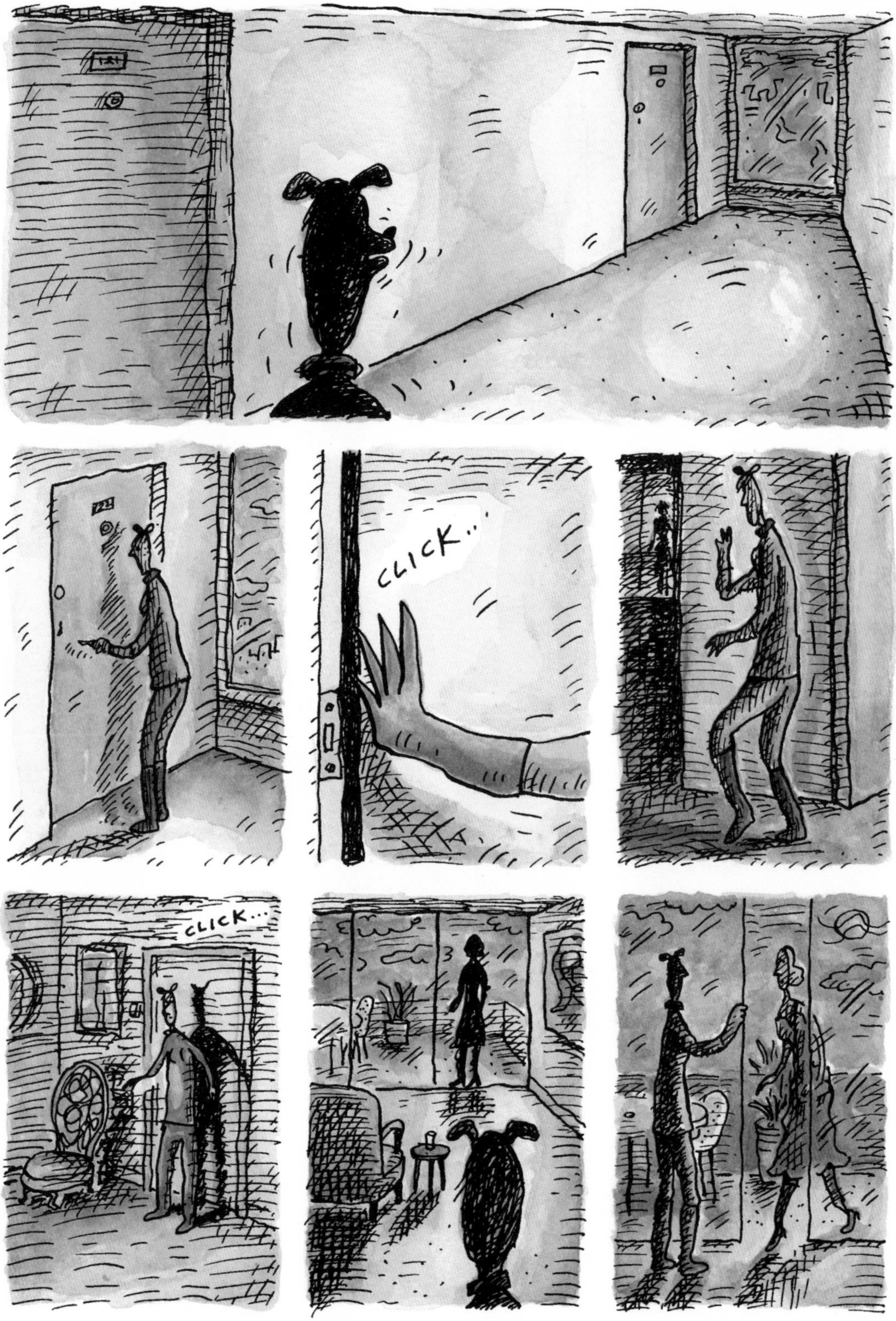
CLICK...
CLICK...

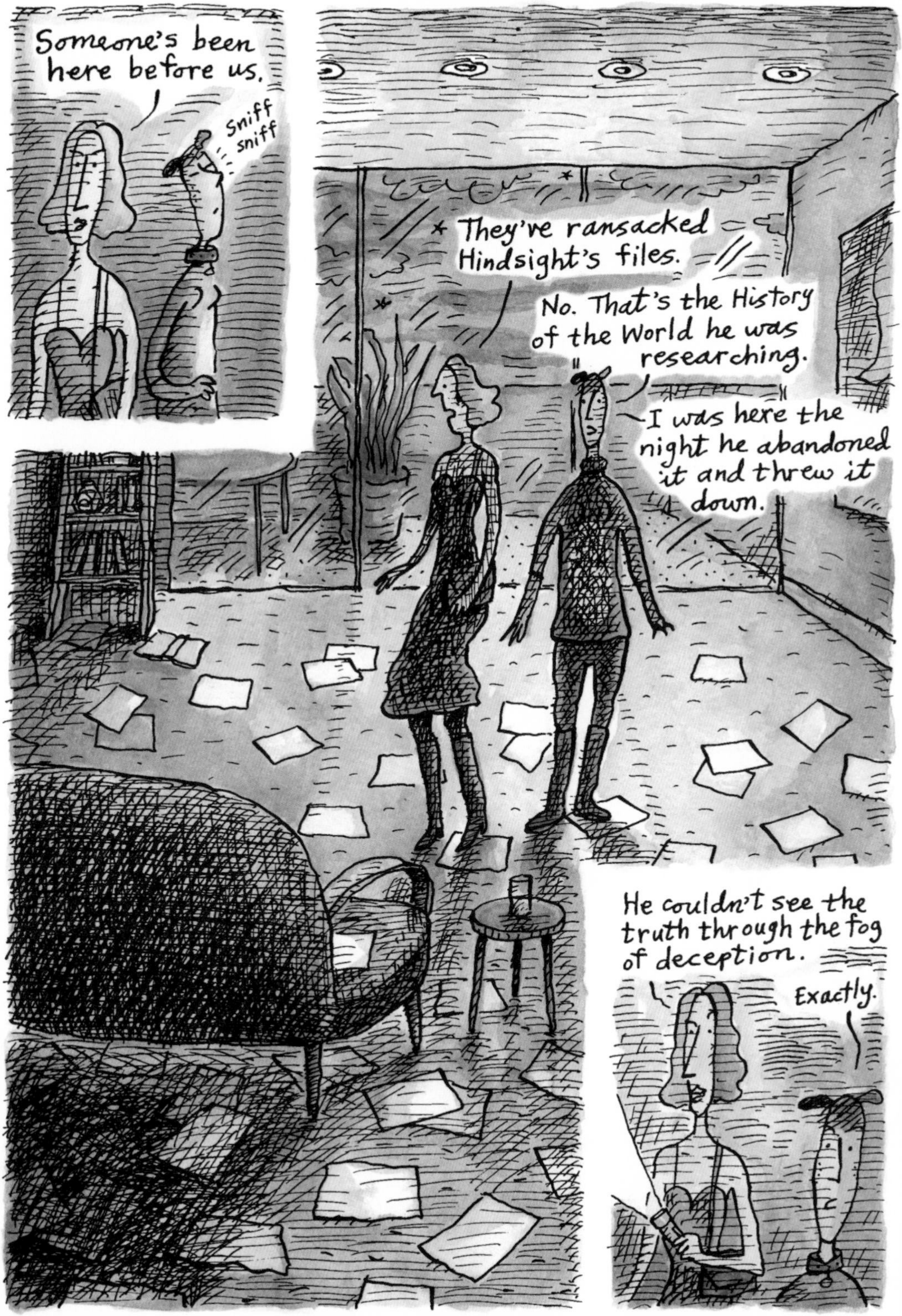

Someone's been here before us.
Sniff sniff
They've ransacked Hindsight's files.
No. That's the History of the World he was researching.
I was here the night he abandoned it and threw it down.
He couldn't see the truth through the fog of deception.
Exactly.

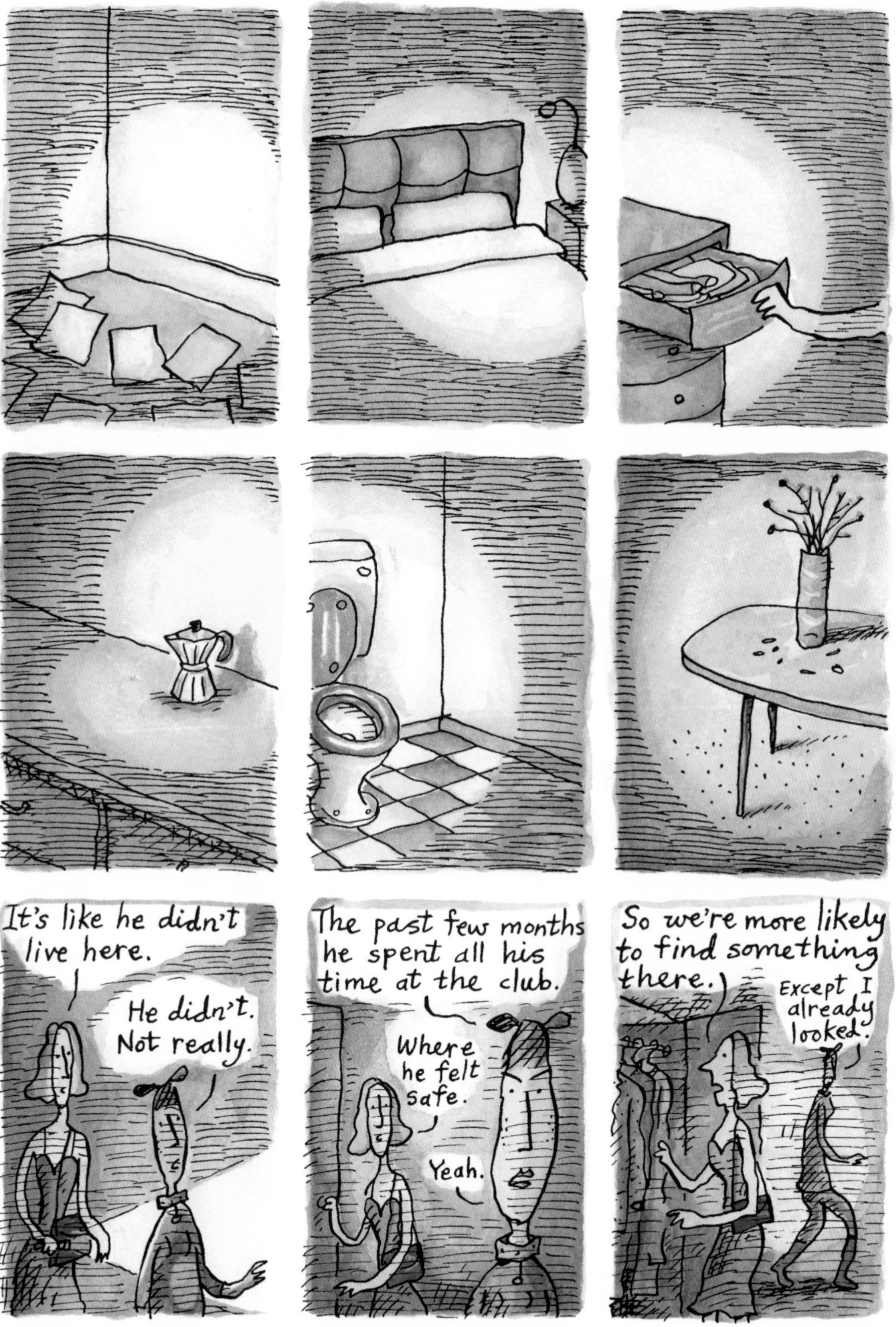
It's like he didn't live here.
He didn't. Not really.
The past few months he spent all his time at the club.
Where he felt safe.
Yeah.
So we're more likely to find something there.
Except I already looked.

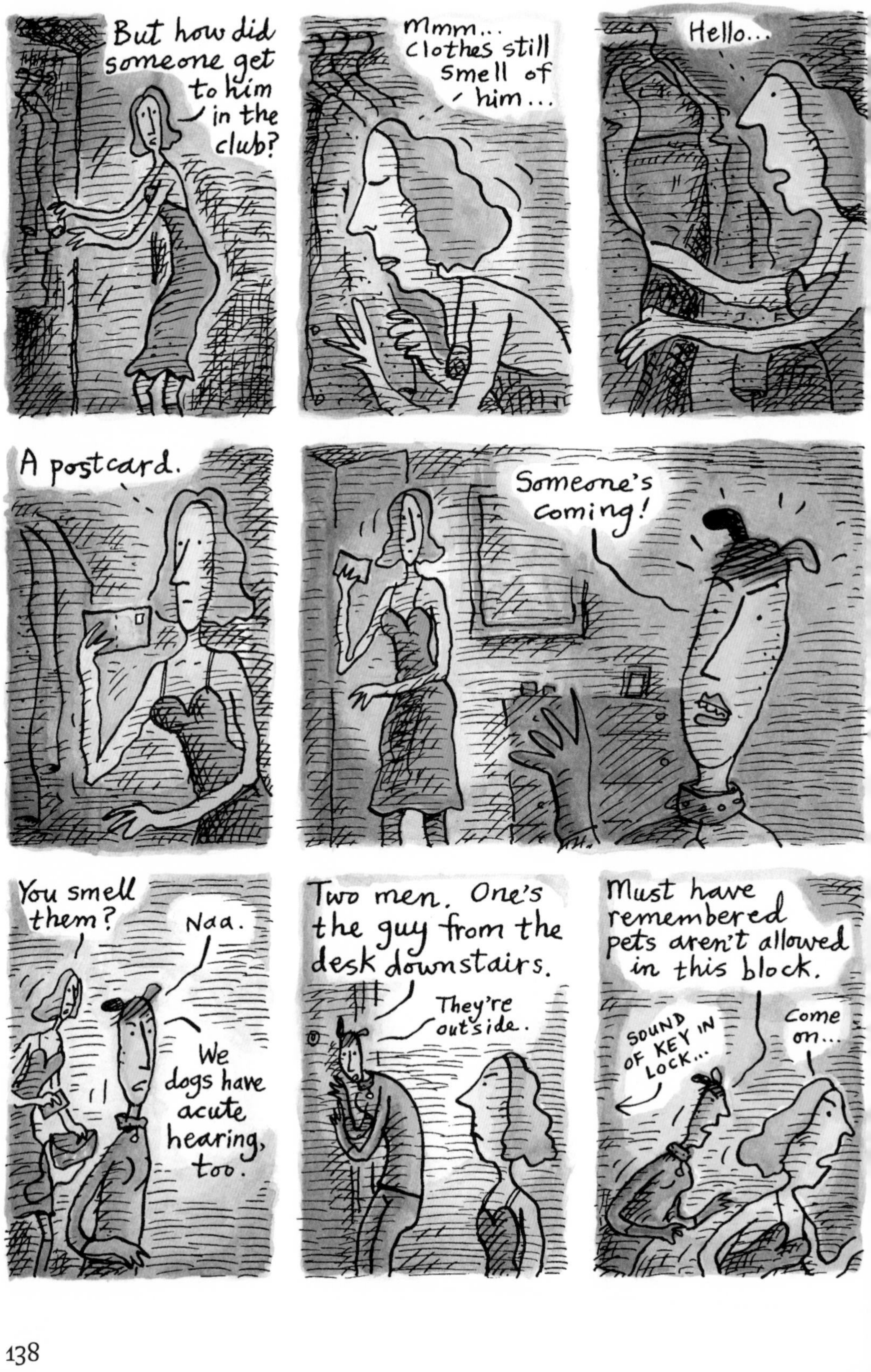

But how did someone get to him in the club?
Mmm... Clothes still smell of him...
Hello...
A postcard.
Someone's coming!
You smell them?
Naa.
We dogs have acute hearing, too.
Two men. One's the guy from the desk downstairs.
They're outside.
Must have remembered pets aren't allowed in this block.
SOUND OF KEY IN LOCK...
Come on...

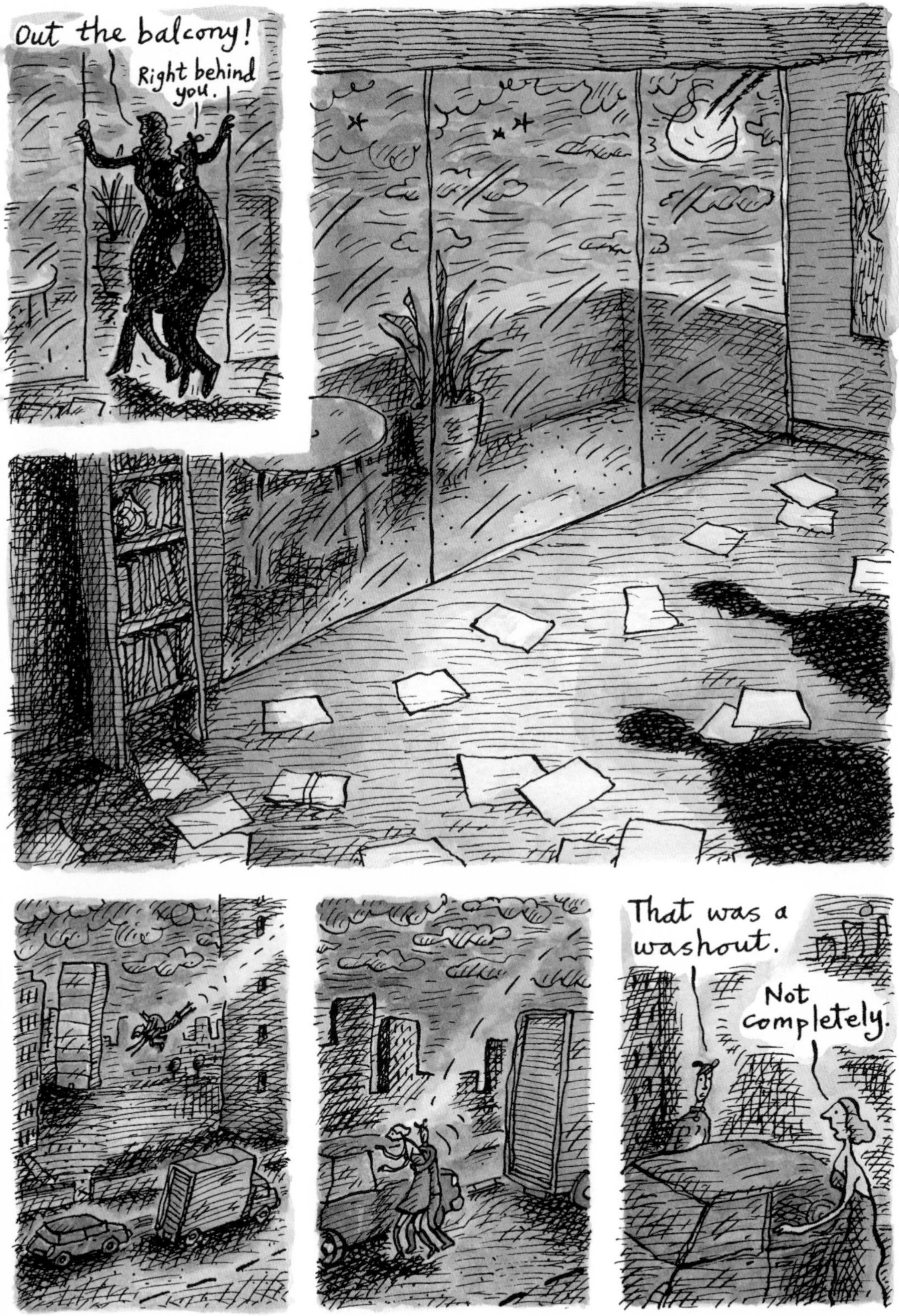
Out the balcony!
Right behind you.
That was a washout.
Not completely.

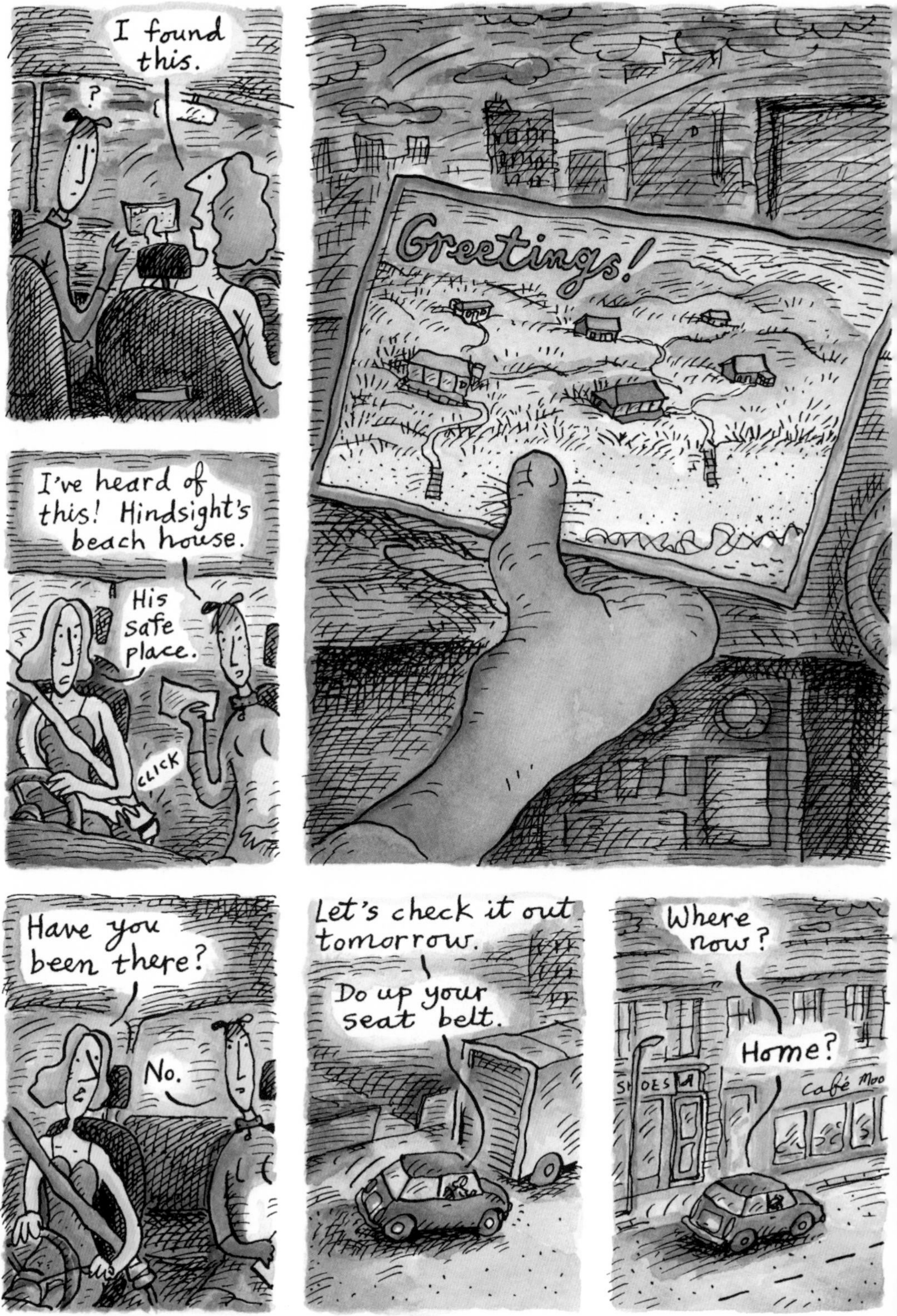
I found this.
?
Greetings!
I've heard of this! Hindsight's beach house.
His safe place.
CLICK
Have you been there?
No.
Let's check it out tomorrow.
Do up your seat belt.
Where now?
Home?
SHOES
Café Moo

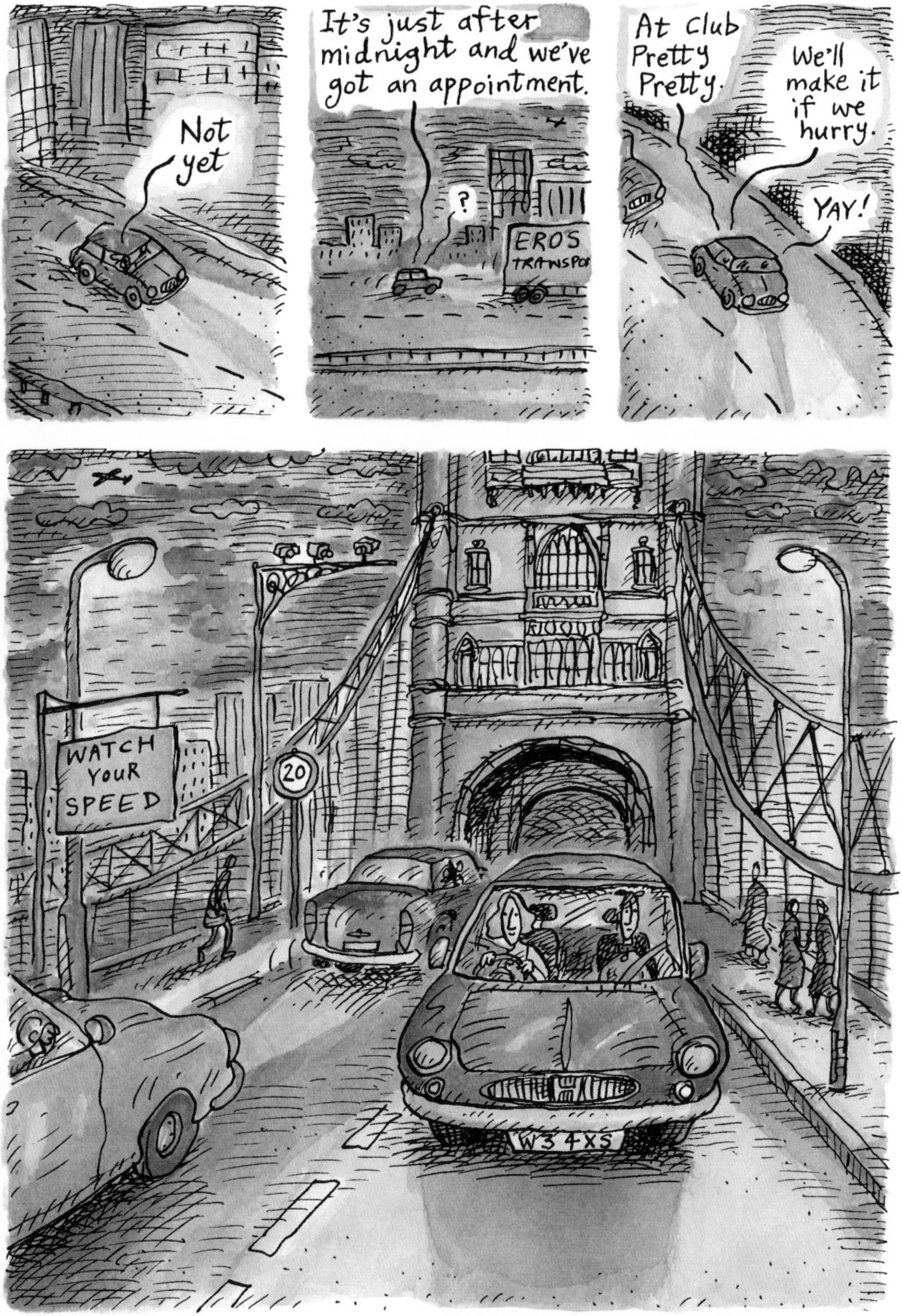
Not yet
It's just after midnight and we've got an appointment.
?
EROS TRANSPOR
At Club Pretty Pretty.
We'll make it if we hurry.
YAY!
WATCH YOUR SPEED
20
W34XS

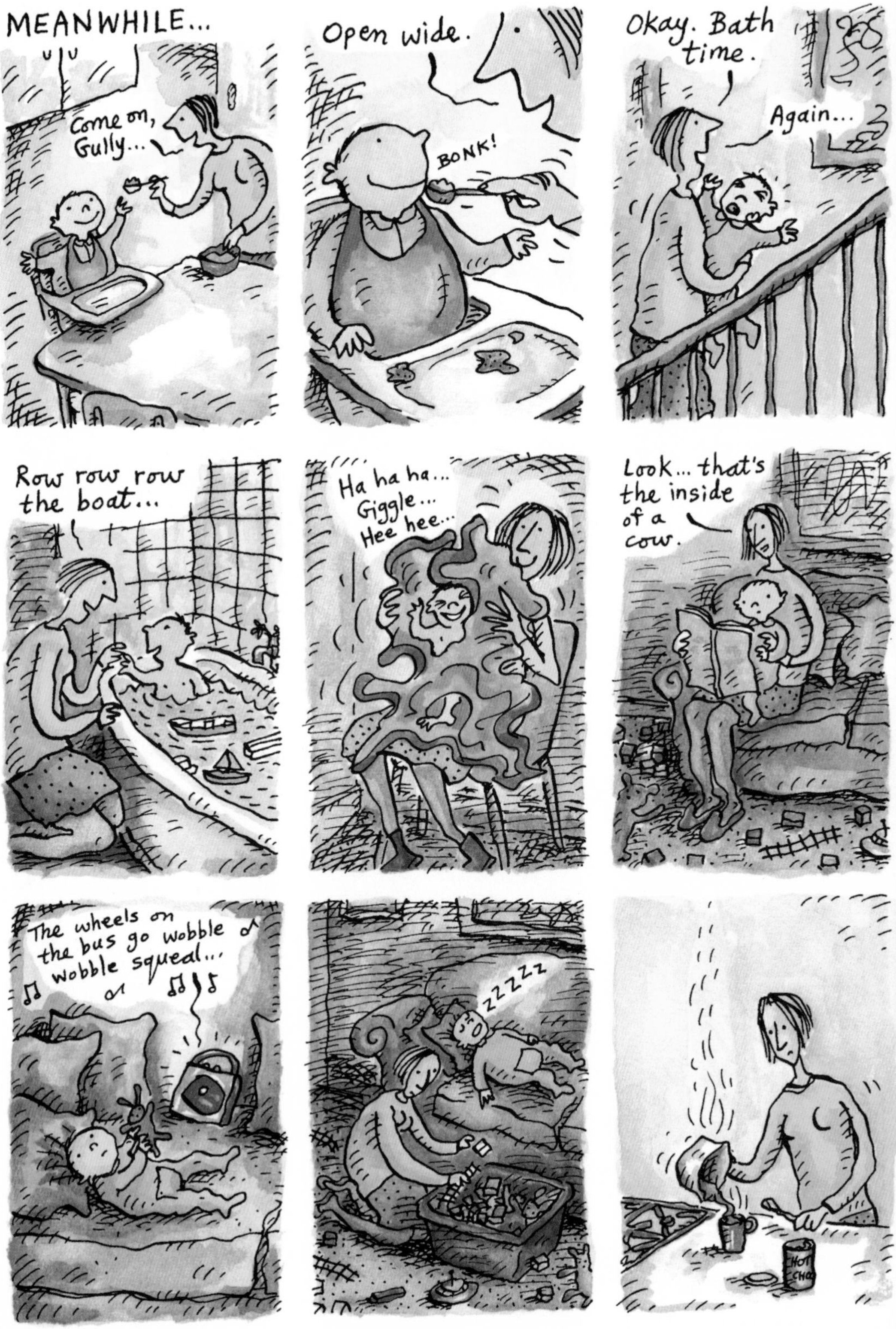
MEANWHILE...
Come on, Gully...
Open wide.
BONK!
Okay. Bath time.
Again...
Row row row the boat...
Ha ha ha... Giggle... Hee hee...
Look... that's the inside of a cow.
The wheels on the bus go wobble wobble squeal...
ZZZZZ
HOT CHOC

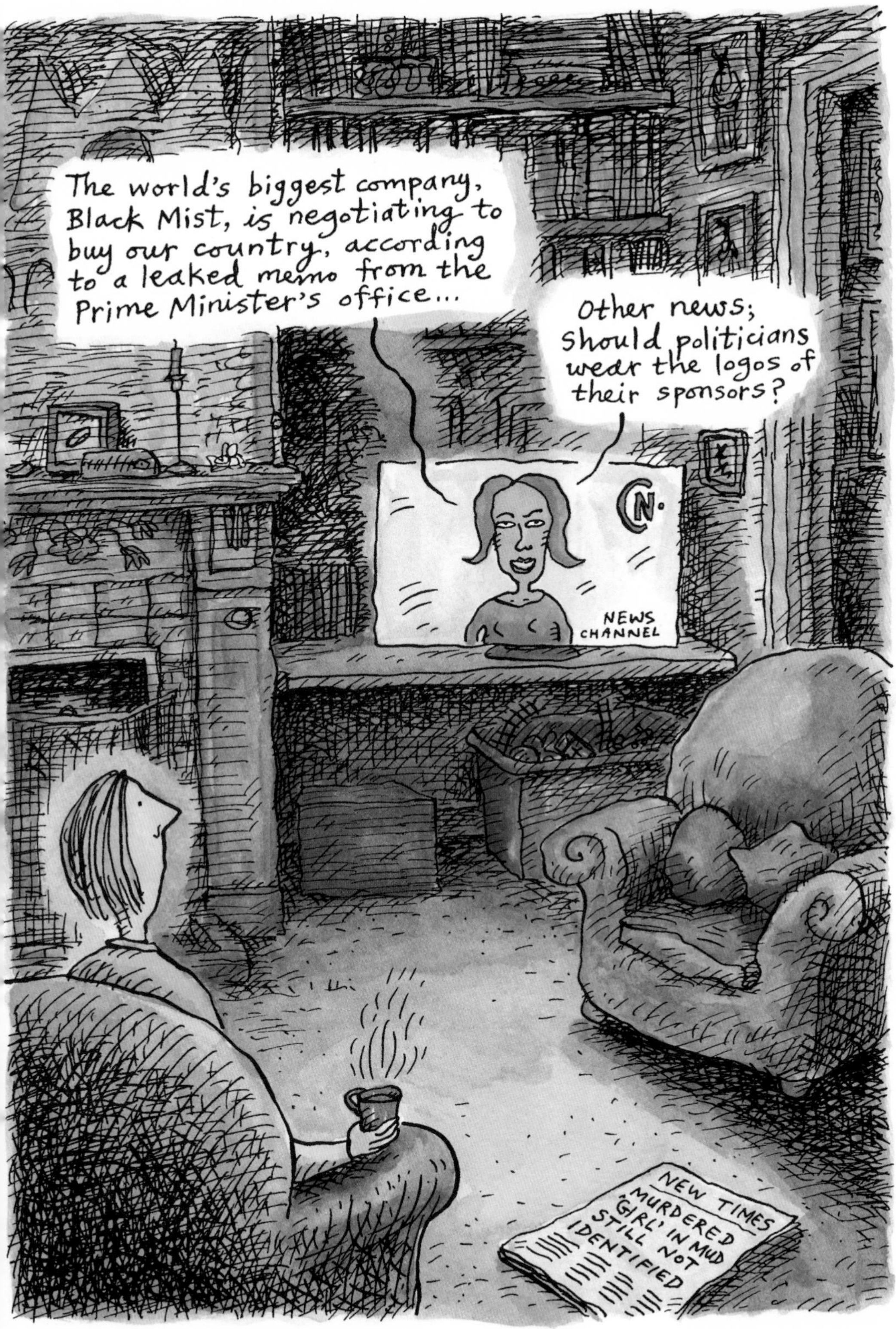
The world's biggest company, Black Mist, is negotiating to buy our country, according to a leaked memo from the Prime Minister's office...
Other news; Should politicians wear the logos of their sponsors?
CN
NEWS CHANNEL
NEW TIMES
MURDERED 'GIRL' IN MUD STILL NOT IDENTIFIED

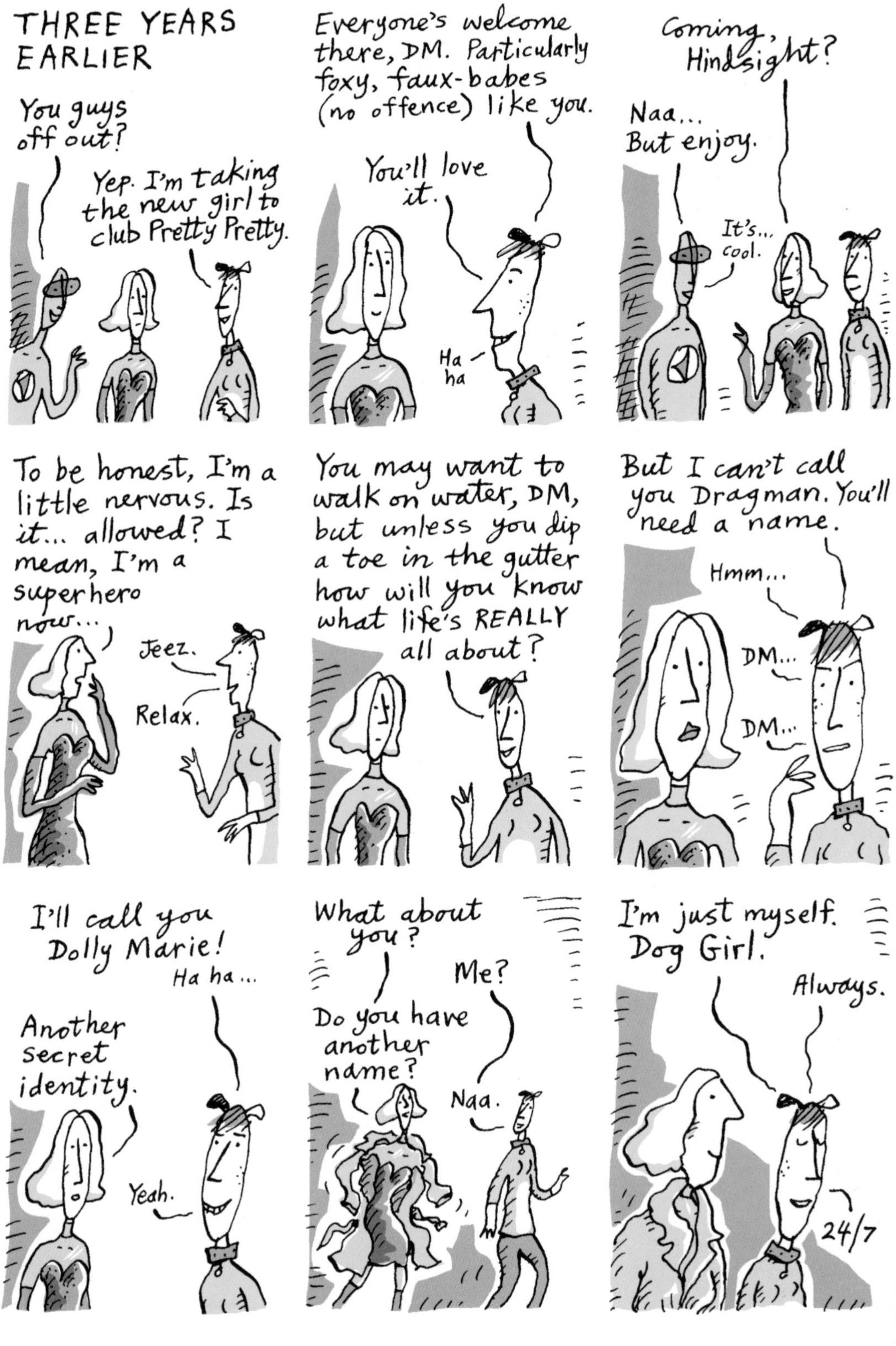
THREE YEARS EARLIER
You guys off out?
Yep. I'm taking the new girl to club Pretty Pretty.
Everyone's welcome there, DM. Particularly foxy, faux-babes (no offence) like you.
You'll love it.
Ha ha
Coming, Hindsight?
Naa... But enjoy.
It's... cool.
To be honest, I'm a little nervous. Is it... allowed? I mean, I'm a superhero now...
Jeez.
Relax.
You may want to walk on water, DM, but unless you dip a toe in the gutter how will you know what life's REALLY all about?
But I can't call you Dragman. You'll need a name.
Hmm...
DM...
DM...
I'll call you Dolly Marie!
Ha ha...
Another secret identity.
Yeah.
What about you?
Me?
Do you have another name?
Naa.
I'm just myself. Dog Girl.
Always.
24/7

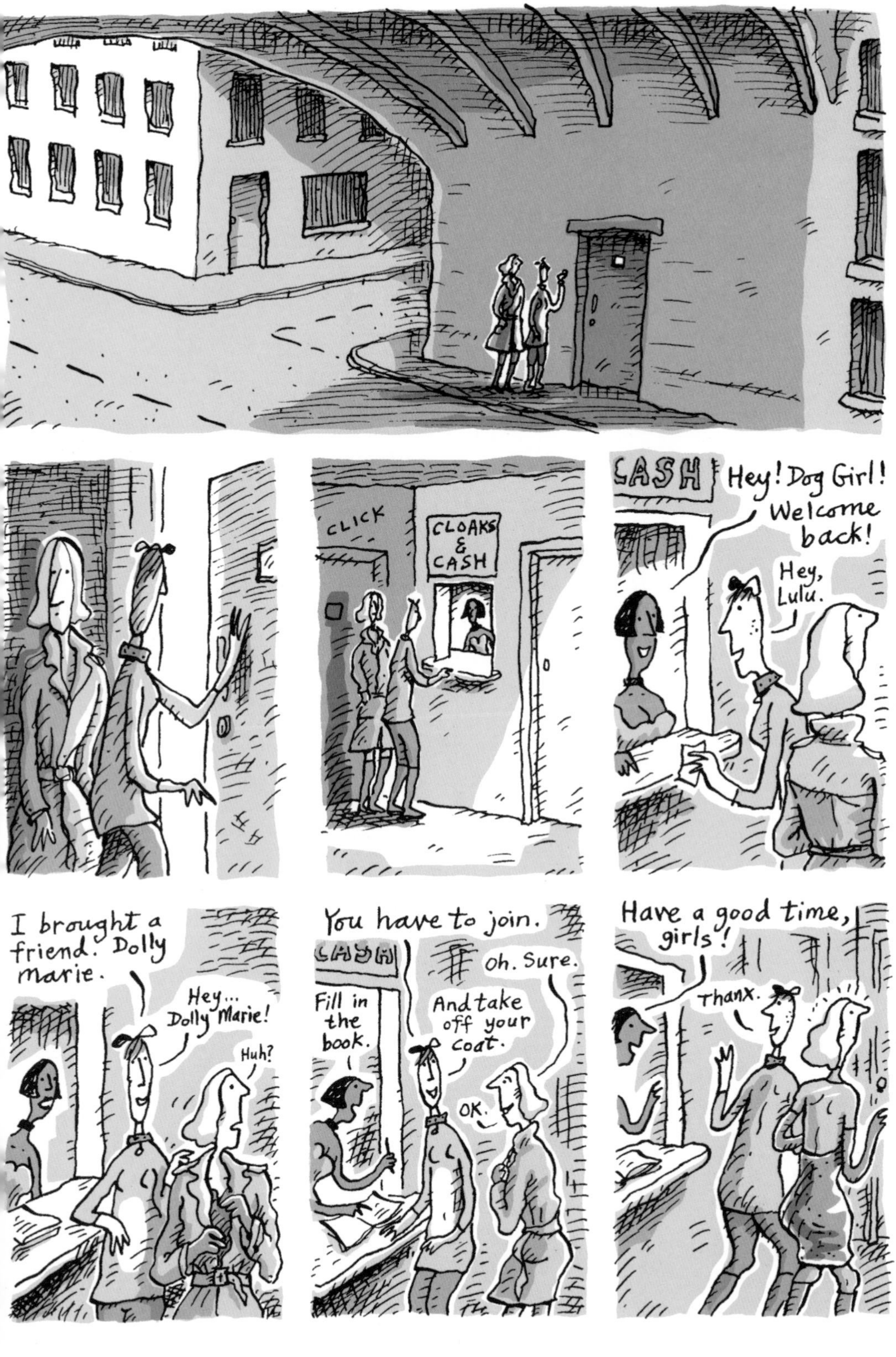
CLICK
CLOAKS & CASH
CASH
Hey! Dog Girl! Welcome back!
Hey, Lulu.
I brought a friend. Dolly marie.
Hey... Dolly Marie!
Huh?
You have to join.
CASH
Fill in the book.
Oh. Sure.
And take off your coat.
OK.
Have a good time, girls!
Thanx.

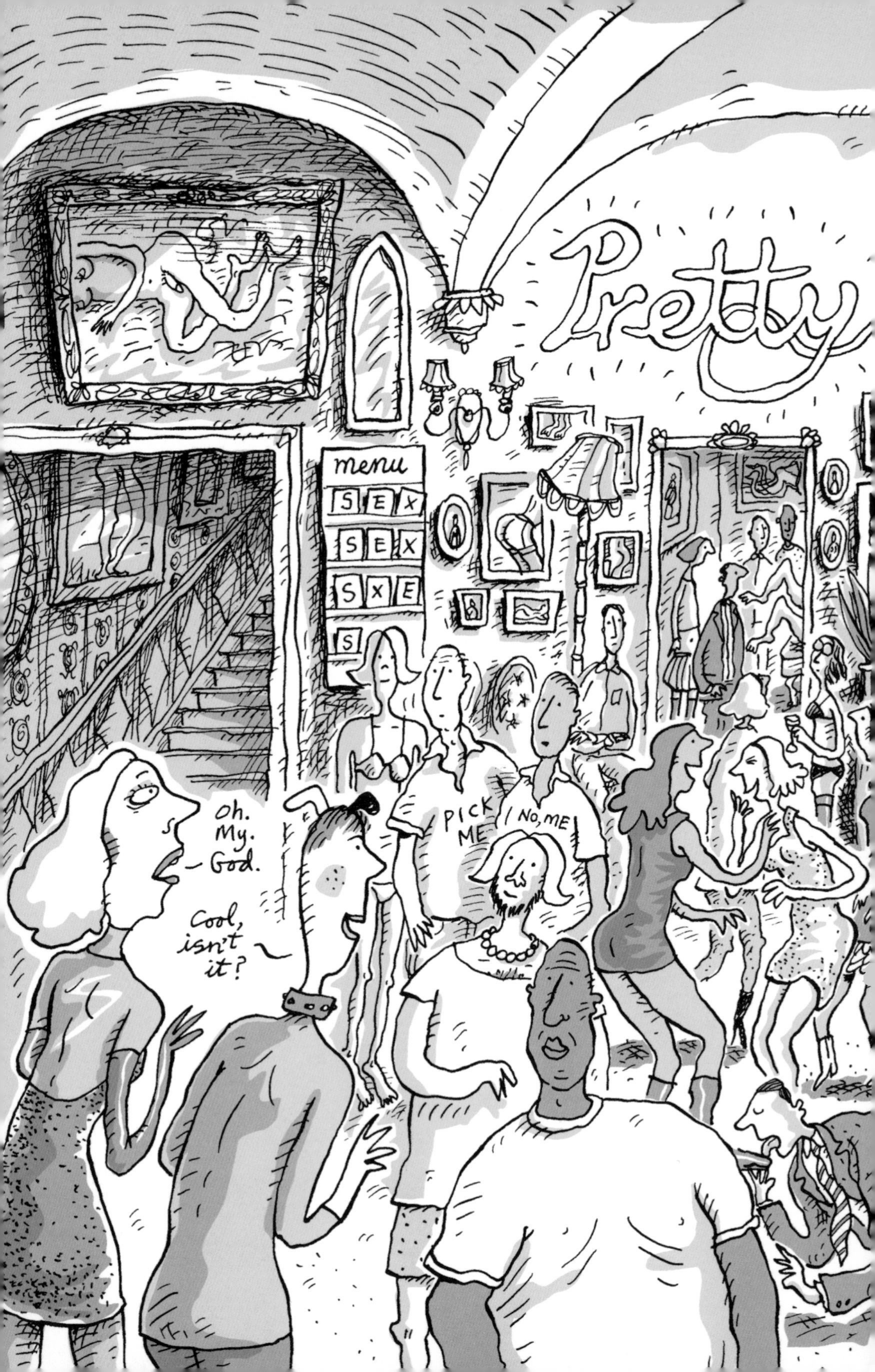
Pretty
menu
SEX
SEX
SXE
S
PICK ME
NO, ME
Oh. My. God.
Cool, isn't it?

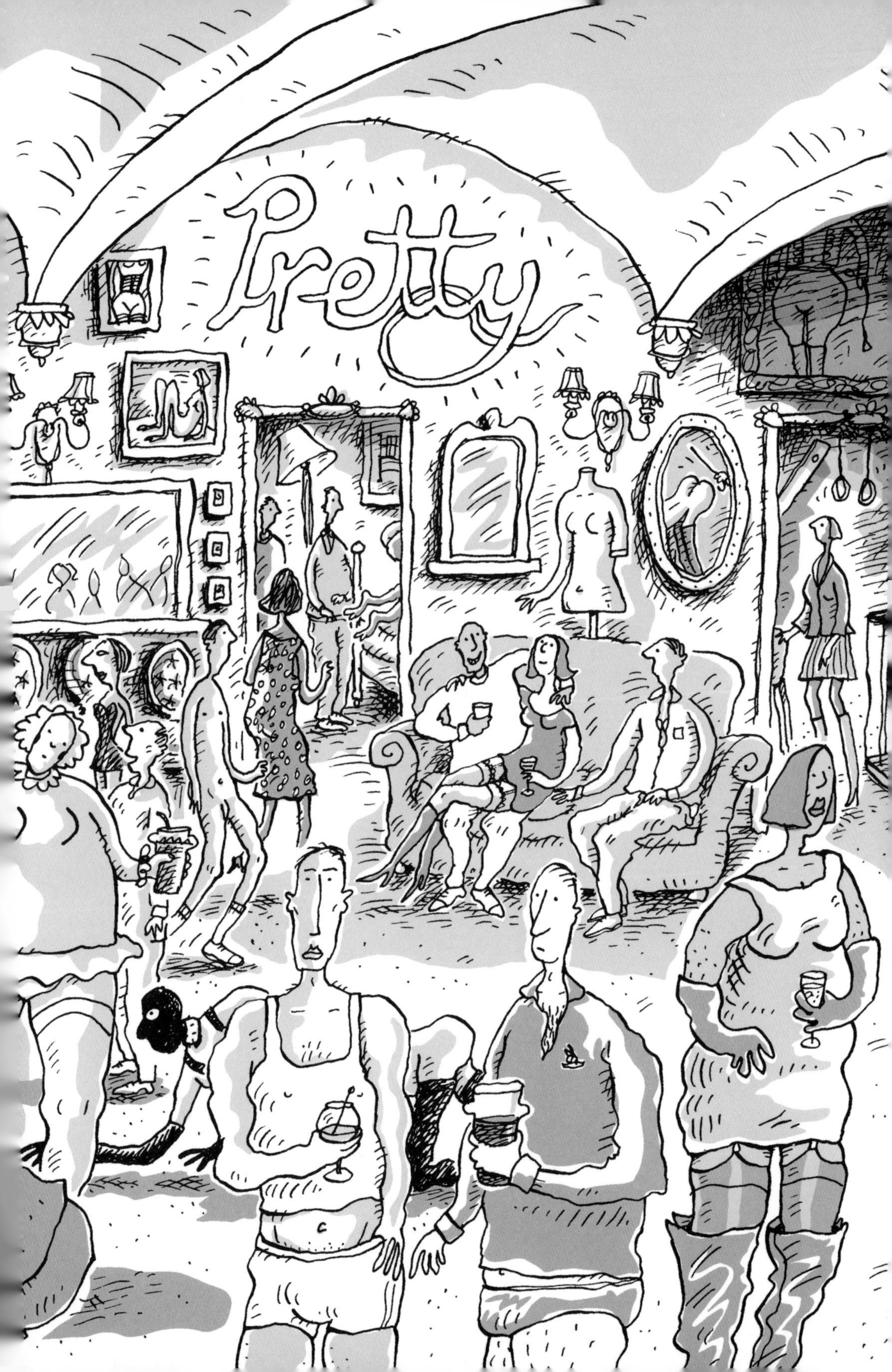
Pretty

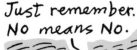
Just remember.
No means No.

And you'll be fine

Uh...

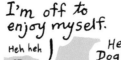
I'm off to enjoy myself.

Heh heh

Hey, Dog Girl!

Wait...

Hullo, boys...

Hello, sexy...

New here?

Hello sweetheart...

Hello hello hello.

Hiya, Babe...

Want to be rescued?

Oh yes!

Please...

A FEW MINUTES LATER...

So I was doing this DIY job wearing a practical skirt, old jumper and my biggest boobs...

I climbed up into the loft to turn off the water and got stuck in the hatch.

148

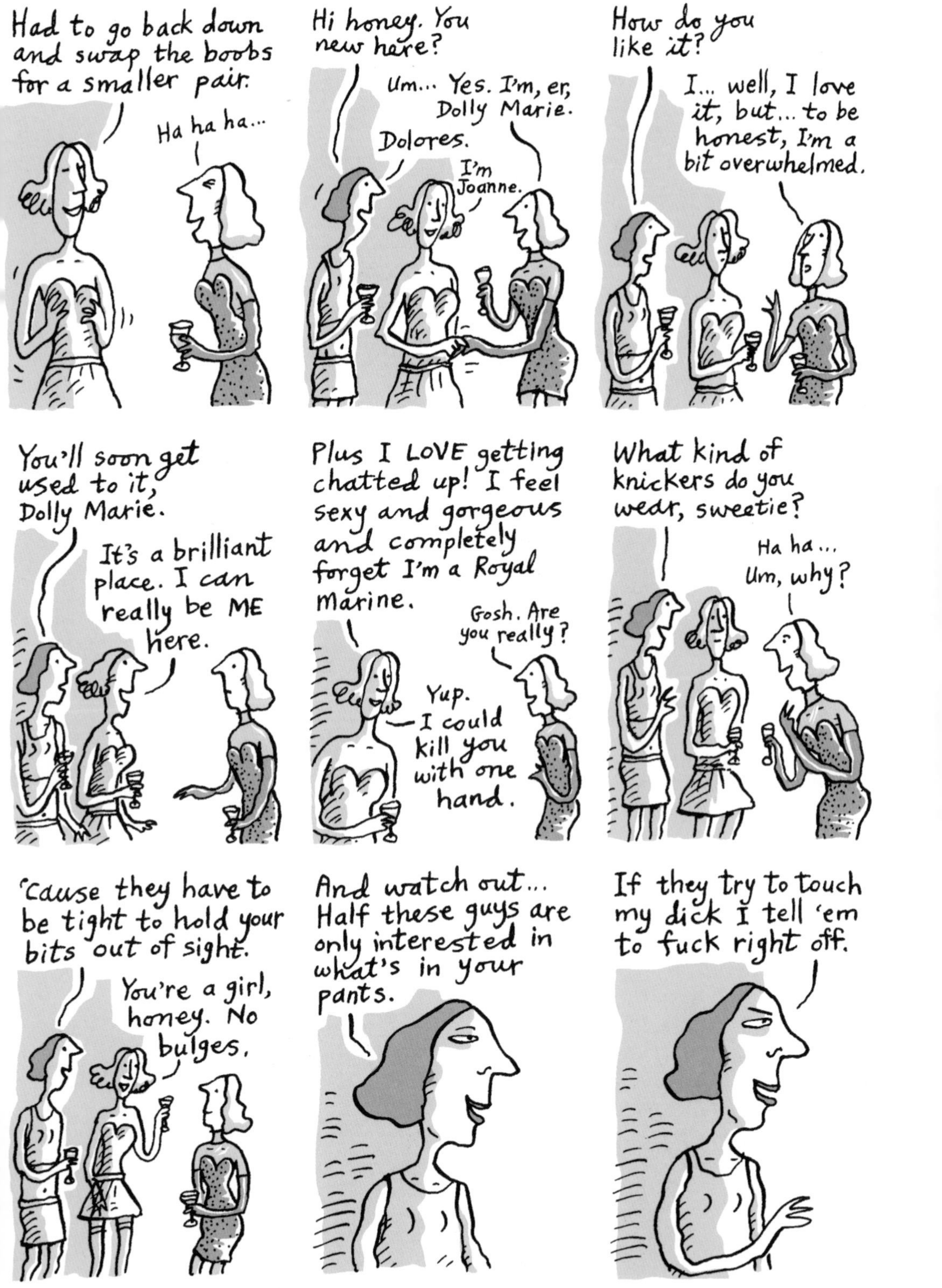
Had to go back down and swap the boobs for a smaller pair.
Ha ha ha...
Hi honey. You new here?
Um... Yes. I'm, er, Dolly Marie.
Dolores.
I'm Joanne.
How do you like it?
I... well, I love it, but... to be honest, I'm a bit overwhelmed.
You'll soon get used to it, Dolly Marie.
It's a brilliant place. I can really be ME here.
Plus I LOVE getting chatted up! I feel sexy and gorgeous and completely forget I'm a Royal Marine.
Gosh. Are you really?
Yup. I could kill you with one hand.
What kind of knickers do you wear, sweetie?
Ha ha... Um, why?
'Cause they have to be tight to hold your bits out of sight.
You're a girl, honey. No bulges.
And watch out... Half these guys are only interested in what's in your pants.
If they try to touch my dick I tell 'em to fuck right off.

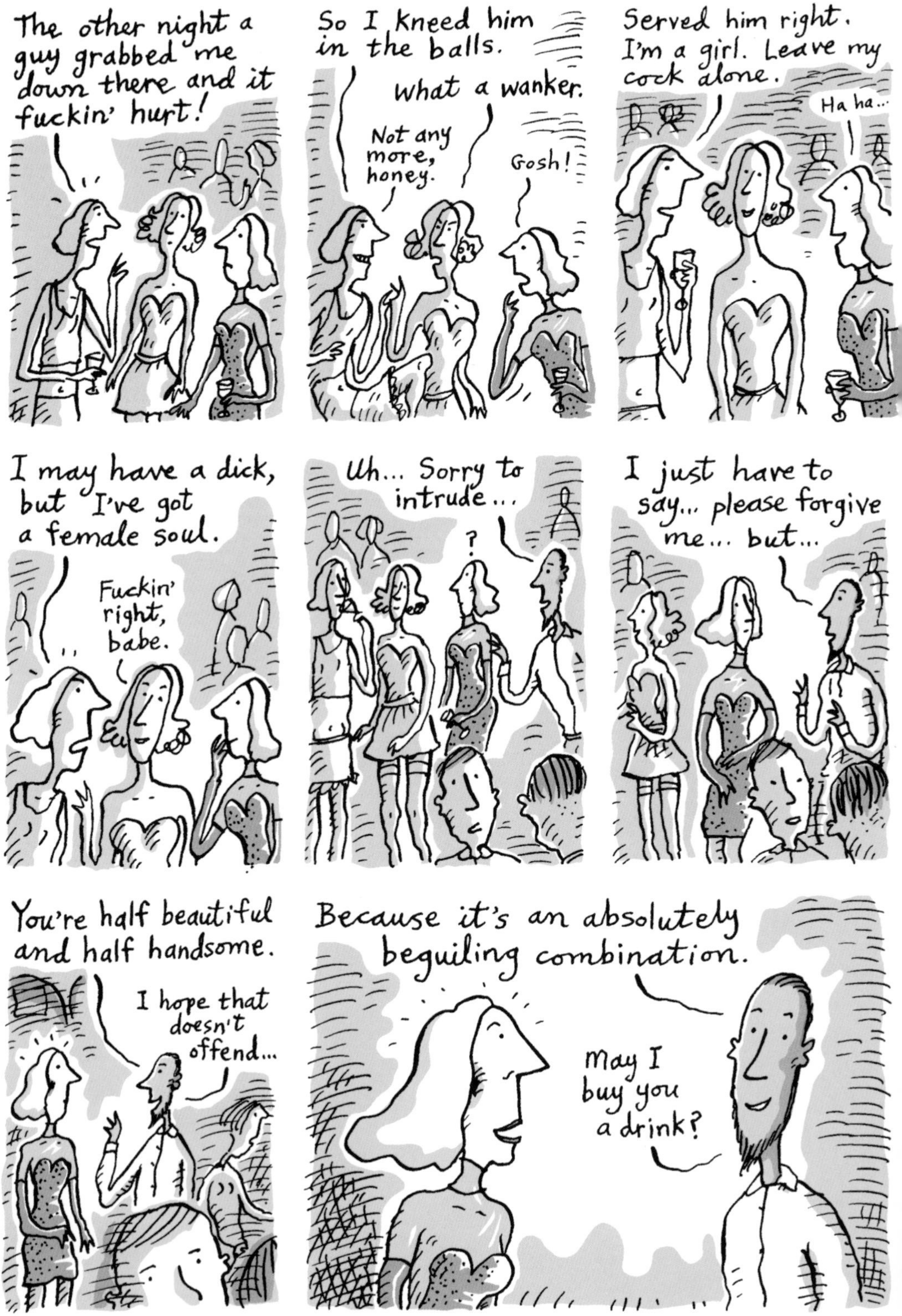

The other night a guy grabbed me down there and it fuckin' hurt!
So I kneed him in the balls.
What a wanker.
Not any more, honey.
Gosh!
Served him right. I'm a girl. Leave my cock alone.
Ha ha...
I may have a dick, but I've got a female soul.
Fuckin' right, babe.
Uh... Sorry to intrude...
?
I just have to say... please forgive me... but...
You're half beautiful and half handsome.
I hope that doesn't offend...
Because it's an absolutely beguiling combination.
May I buy you a drink?

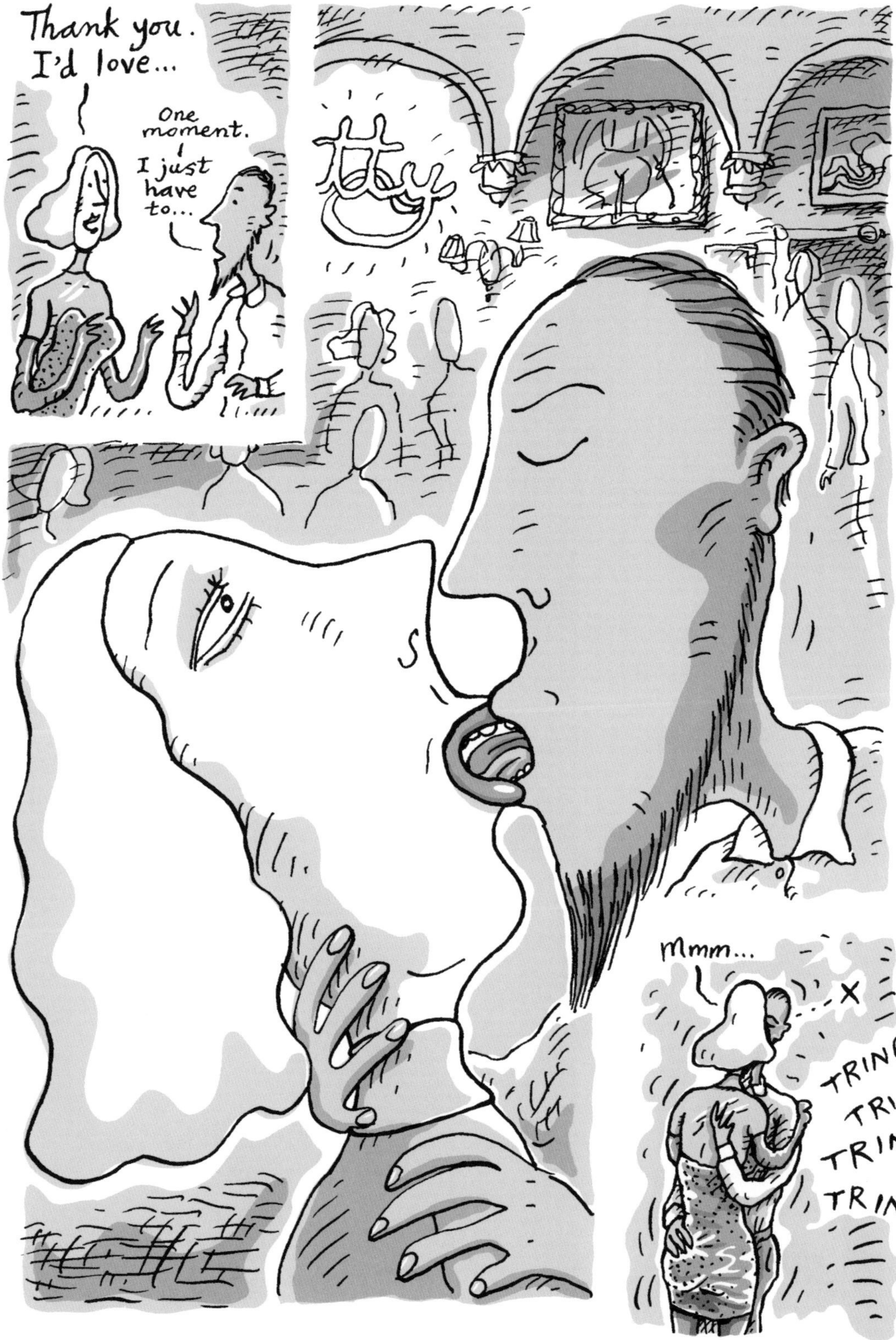
Thank you. I'd love...
One moment. I just have to...
Mmm...
TRING! TRING! TRING! TRING!

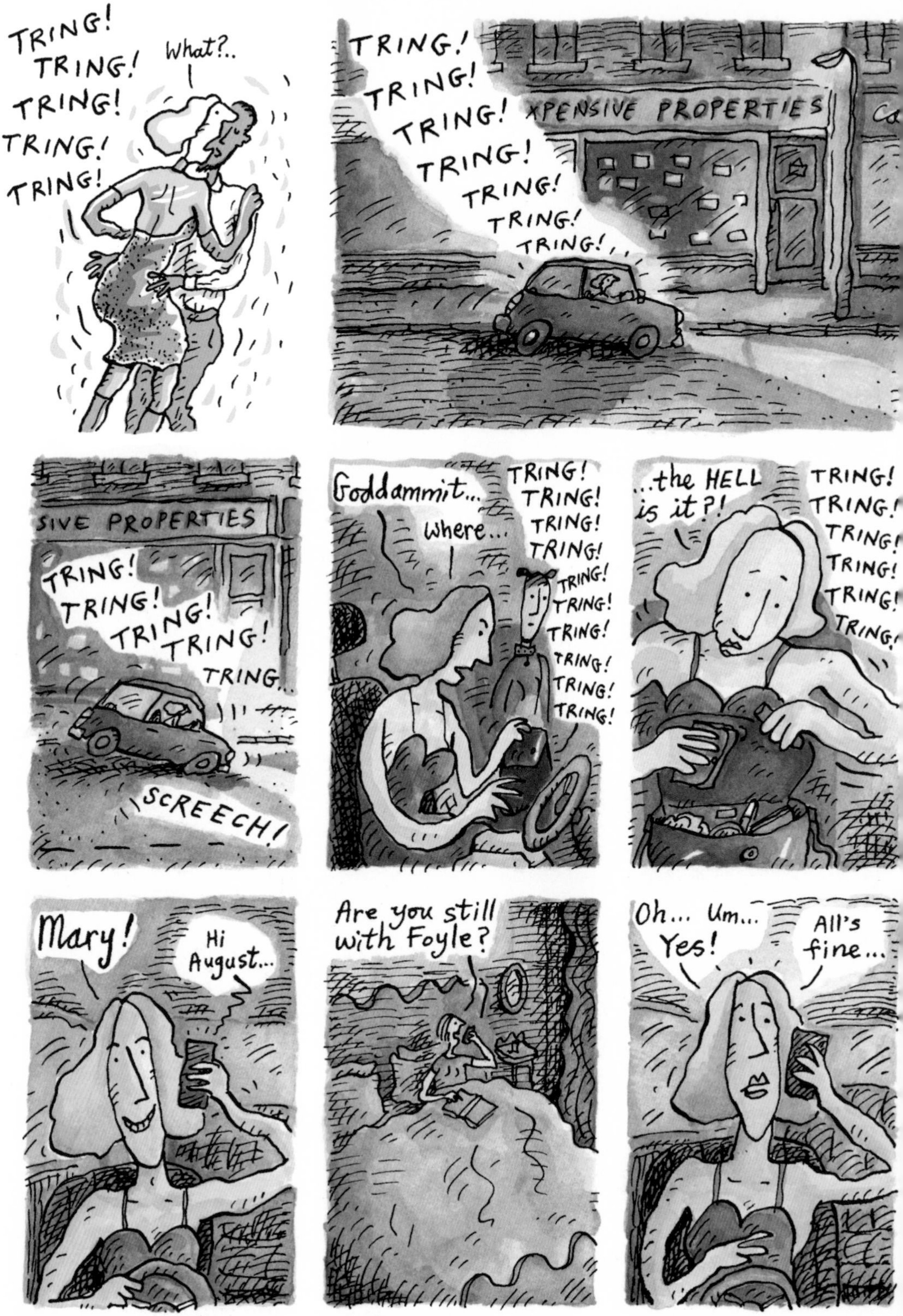
TRING! TRING! TRING! TRING! TRING!
What?..
TRING! TRING! TRING! TRING! TRING! TRING! TRING!
XPENSIVE PROPERTIES
SIVE PROPERTIES
TRING! TRING! TRING! TRING! TRING...
SCREECH!
Goddammit...
Where...
TRING! TRING! TRING! TRING! TRING! TRING! TRING! TRING! TRING! TRING!
...the HELL is it?!
TRING! TRING! TRING! TRING! TRING! TRING!
Mary!
Hi August...
Are you still with Foyle?
Oh... Um... Yes!
All's fine...

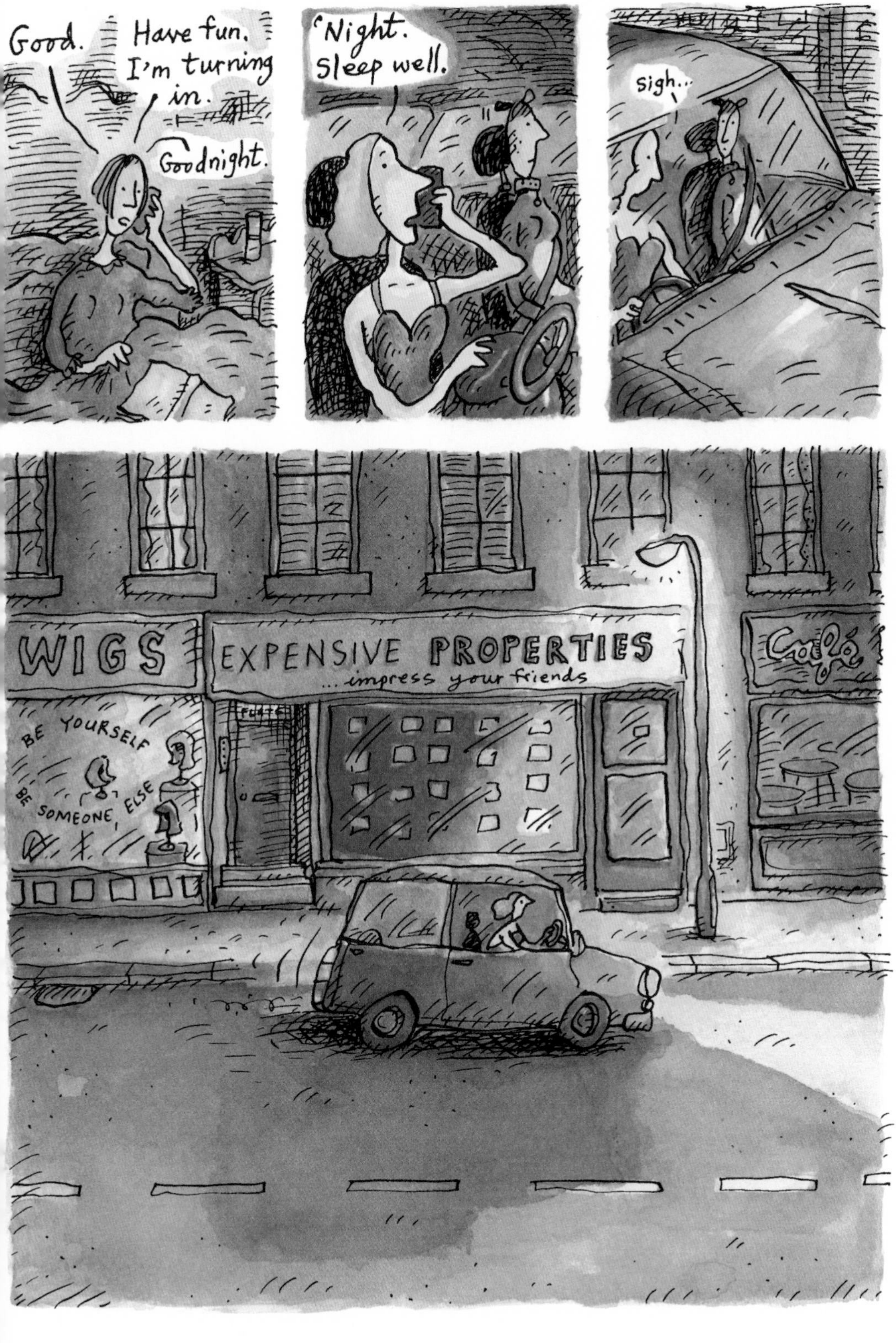

Good.
Have fun. I'm turning in.
Goodnight.
'Night. Sleep well.
Sigh...
WIGS
EXPENSIVE PROPERTIES
...impress your friends
Café
BE YOURSELF
BE SOMEONE, ELSE

11·59 pm

THE MAN FULL OF GHOSTS is in the Pretty Pretty harem room, one of his favourite places, and he's just getting into it and enjoying himself when the music stops and Filly, one of the owners of the club, comes on the sound system and makes an announcement.

'Girls, boys and everyone somewhere in between, I'm sorry to interrupt your fun,' she says, 'but it's midnight, so please can you gather in the lounge because the special meeting is about to begin...'

'What the fuck..?' thinks the man, but the girls around him drift out of the room, including the blonde girl he heard someone call Cindy who he's decided might be good value for later, so he zips up and follows.

The overhead lights are on in the main lounge which rather spoils the atmosphere so the man hangs back in a doorway and Cindy, seeing him there in the shadows, comes up behind him and starts kissing his neck, which isn't what she should be doing right now when Filly is up on a chair thanking them all for coming, but never mind, Cindy's a nice distraction.

Filly says something about the recent trans murders and suddenly the man is listening hard, despite Cindy, as he realises this meeting is about him, though of course he's the only one who knows that and hopefully it'll stay that way.

'We all want to play safe and stay safe,' Filly is saying, 'so let's pool information and catch the bastard preying on our community.'

The man pauses Cindy who is now nibbling his ear, which is a shame, but he wants to follow what's being said, which turns out to be not much because, despite five trans-girls being murdered – and he smiles because actually it's eleven – the police have identified the bodies from their fingerprints and whatnot and arrived at their male names which are, of course, the names on all their documentation, so it's like those part-time girls have vanished as if they never existed in the first place and now won't ever exist. Meaning there's nothing to connect them to this world of Pretty Pretty – and therefore to him.

At which point the door to the outside world opens and two girls arrive late. A tall, foxy one and a smaller, cute one dressed as a dog.

They both look like they'd be pretty good fun if only the tall one would stop eyeballing the crowd and lose that serious expression and the little one would stop sniffing like she has a drug problem. Cindy, seeing where the man is looking, whispers.

'That's Dog Girl. She's often here. I don't know her friend…'

The man puts his hand over Cindy's mouth and she starts sucking and biting his thumb. Yeah, he thinks, Cindy is definitely a keeper.

Someone is saying that when a trans-girl hasn't been seen for a few weeks or a few months – or even a year – it doesn't mean she died. It's often that her wife discovered her secret life, or she got ill and dropped out of the scene, or she moved away, or her tastes moved on, or maybe, full of self-disgust, she simply decided, as most do from time to time, to give the whole thing up, throw away her clothes and wigs and stop dressing. Someone else points out that when a part-time T-girl takes off her clothes she disappears like Cinderella at midnight, which doesn't mean she's been murdered.

All in all, no one at Pretty Pretty can work out if they knew any of the victims or not, because all the trans-girls and most of the guys in the room, including himself, use scene names, meaning their secret lives and their real lives, or whichever way round you want to think of it, don't connect up.

Two and two doesn't add up to... well, anything.

The man leans deeper into the shadows and watches until the meeting breaks up, the lights are dimmed, the music comes back on and the crowd return to their hedonistic pleasures. At which point the new arrivals disappear into the office with Filly and the man suggests to Cindy that she take him back to her place, to which she greedily agrees, so they collect their coats and slip away out into the real world where the real murders take place.

And no one notices them go.

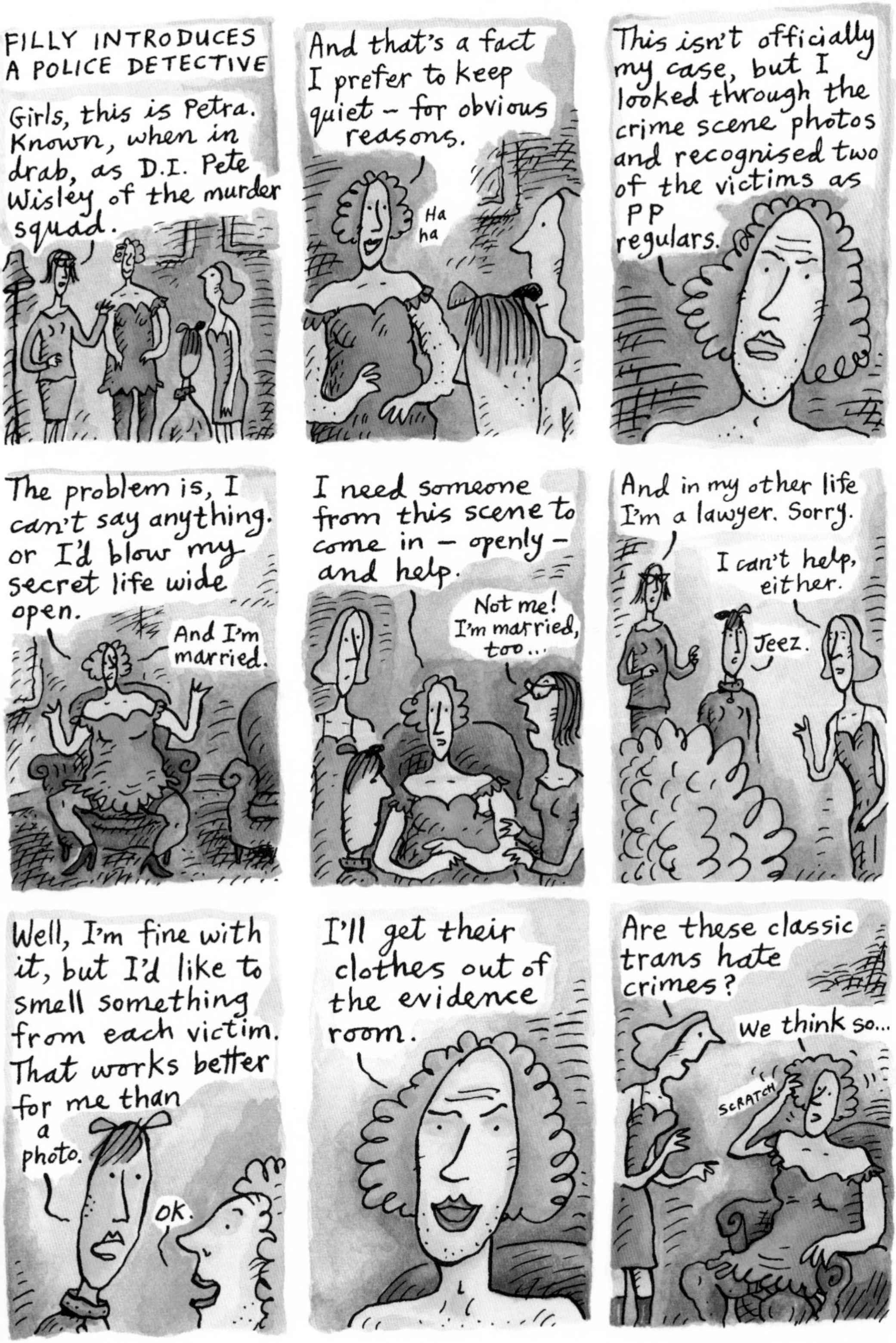
FILLY INTRODUCES A POLICE DETECTIVE
Girls, this is Petra. Known, when in drab, as D.I. Pete Wisley of the murder squad.
And that's a fact I prefer to keep quiet – for obvious reasons.
Ha ha
This isn't officially my case, but I looked through the crime scene photos and recognised two of the victims as PP regulars.
The problem is, I can't say anything. or I'd blow my secret life wide open.
And I'm married.
I need someone from this scene to come in – openly – and help.
Not me! I'm married, too...
And in my other life I'm a lawyer. Sorry.
I can't help, either.
Jeez.
Well, I'm fine with it, but I'd like to smell something from each victim. That works better for me than a photo.
OK.
I'll get their clothes out of the evidence room.
Are these classic trans hate crimes?
We think so...
SCRATCH

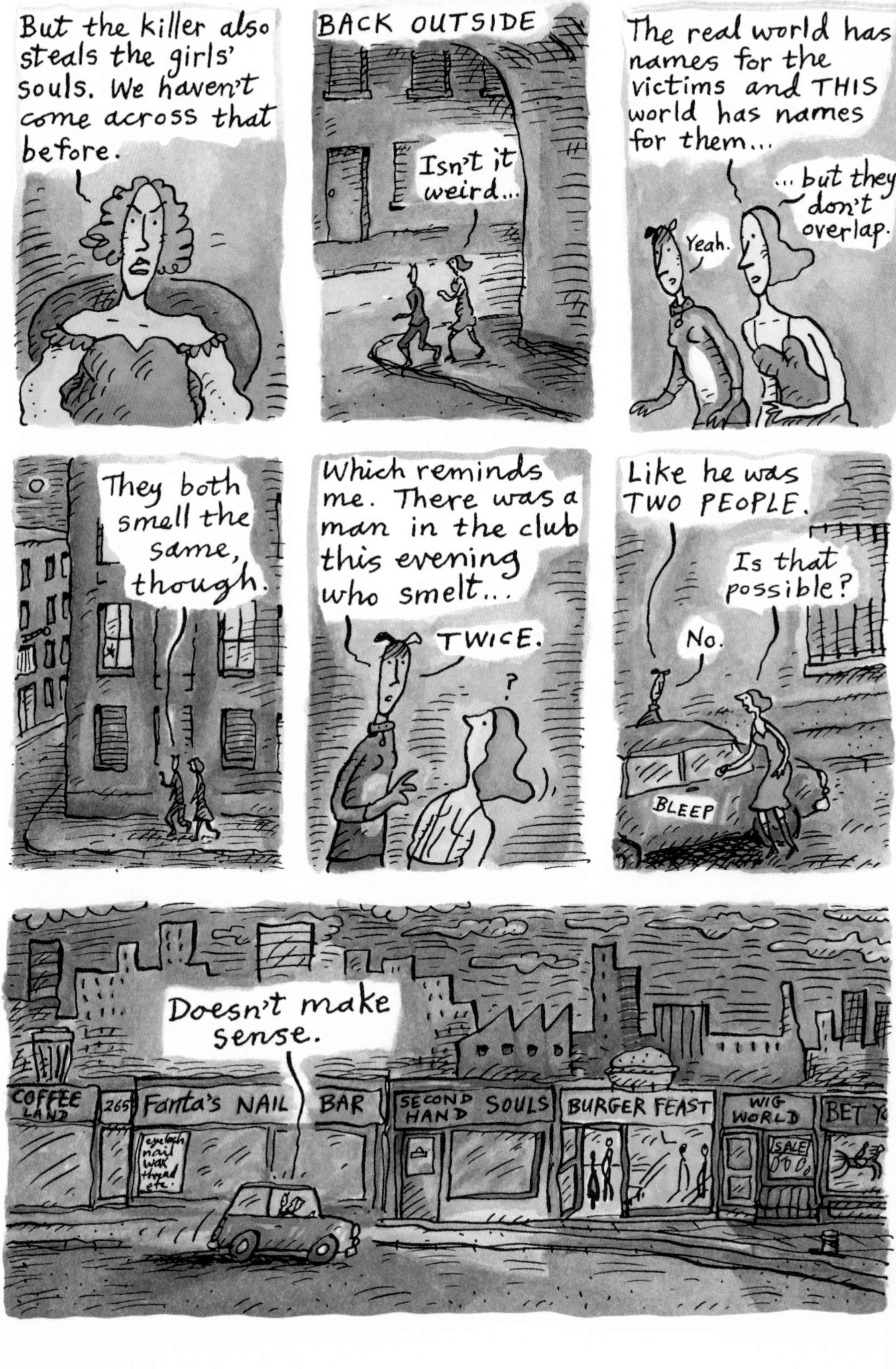
But the killer also steals the girls' souls. We haven't come across that before.
BACK OUTSIDE
Isn't it weird...
The real world has names for the victims and THIS world has names for them...
Yeah.
...but they don't overlap.
They both smell the same, though.
Which reminds me. There was a man in the club this evening who smelt...
TWICE.
?
Like he was TWO PEOPLE.
Is that possible?
No.
BLEEP
Doesn't make sense.
COFFEE LAND
265
Fanta's NAIL BAR
eyelash nail wax thread etc.
SECOND HAND SOULS
BURGER FEAST
WIG WORLD
SALE
BET

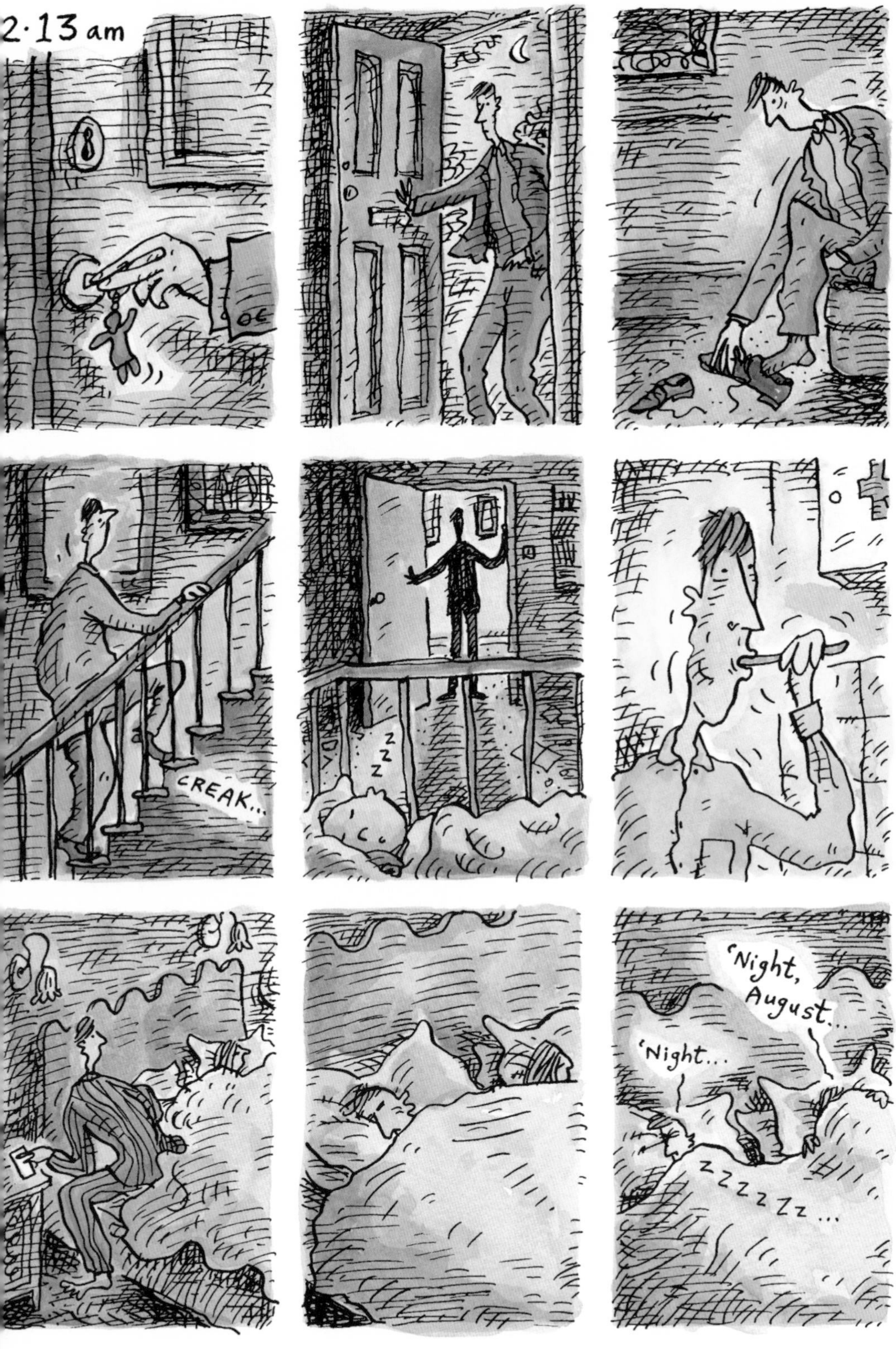
2·13 am
CREAK...
Z
Z
Z
'Night, August...
'Night...
ZZZZZZz...

Sunday

6.07 am

DAWN RISES. As the sky lightens the sounds of vehicles, footsteps, sirens – sparse during the night but never completely absent – become hundreds, then thousands, then hundreds of thousands of sounds that register and overlap and surge and swell until soon, as people wake and argue and run showers and leave home for shopping and work, the cacophony coalesces into the constant backdrop underlying everything in this giant city.

The man in cheap supermarket clothes lets himself out of a ground-floor flat into the stillness of a suburban morning and quietly closes the door. He feels good. A slight ache in the groin and a slight muscular strain in his hands, but then he's spent the night a-fucking and a-killing, so what would you expect? No wonder he has a dull throbbing in his thumb joints. Throttling an adult – particularly a strong, well-built trans-woman – requires muscles he doesn't use all that often. He resolves to buy a small, soft, exercise ball to keep in his pocket.

He'll squeeze it regularly and develop his thumb and finger strength. Just in case. Just in case one of these days he picks up a girl who used to be a soldier, or who takes kick-boxing lessons, or something. Sod's law it'll happen one day and he'd rather not use his gun unless he has to. Though the stirring in his trousers at the thought of shooting a trans-girl in the head just as she ejaculates suggests... well, it's obviously an idea he'll take further at some point.

The sun is weak but bright and, as always, the sight of the sun at all in this grey, bleak, perpetually damp city raises his spirits, meaning there's almost a jauntiness in his step as he walks away from the soiled body of Cindy, arranged like a painting, all lilac and yellow bruises, blushing pinks, purples and splatters of red combined in an almost abstract design against the background of her orange sofa. Beautiful – even though he says so himself. He's walking away but in a sense he isn't leaving her. No, not really. He has her close by, her soul saved on a slim metal and plastic disc in his pocket.

Saved for later.

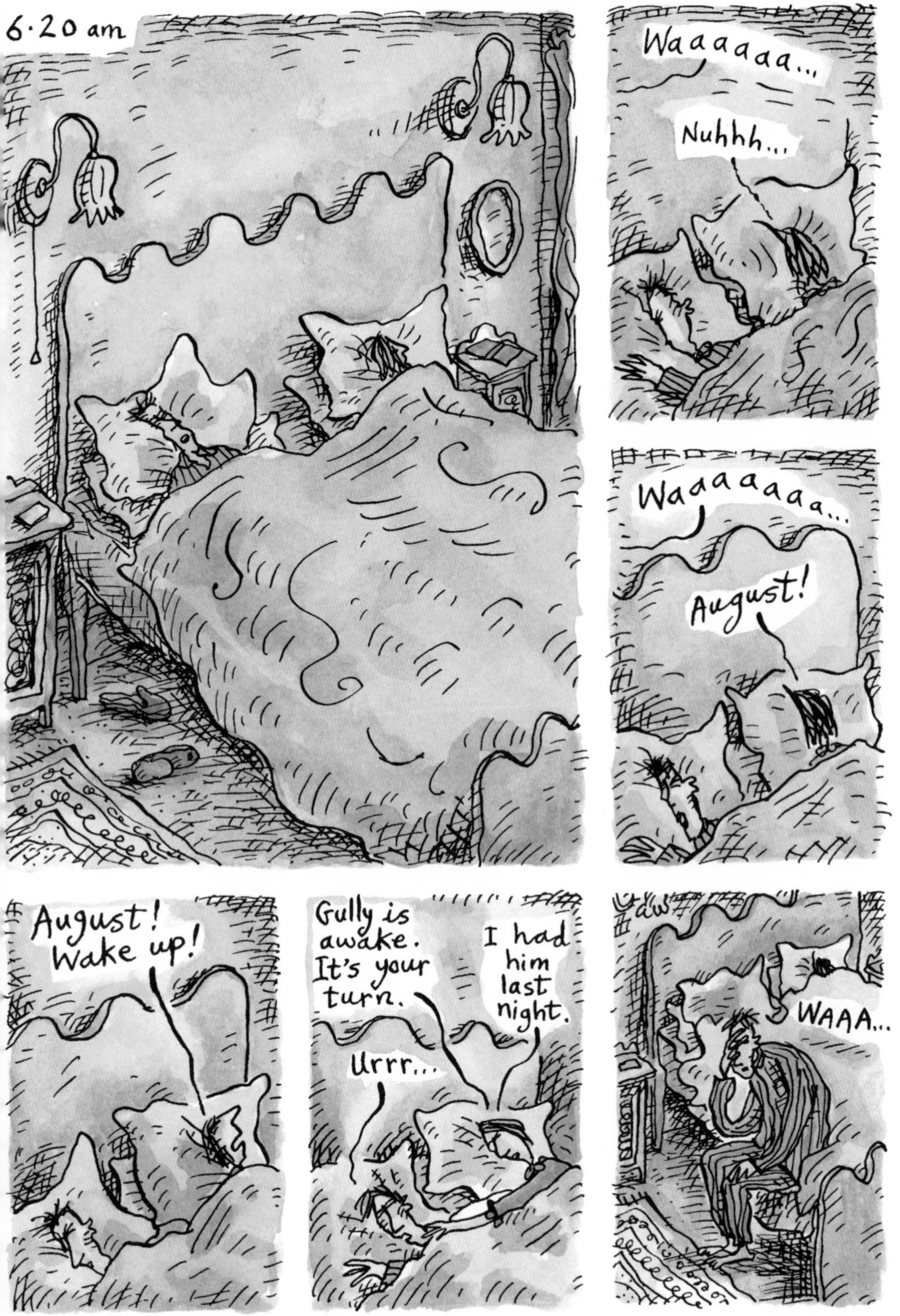
6·20 am
Waaaaaa...
Nuhhh...
Waaaaaaa...
August!
August! Wake up!
Gully is awake. It's your turn.
I had him last night.
Urrr...
WAAA...

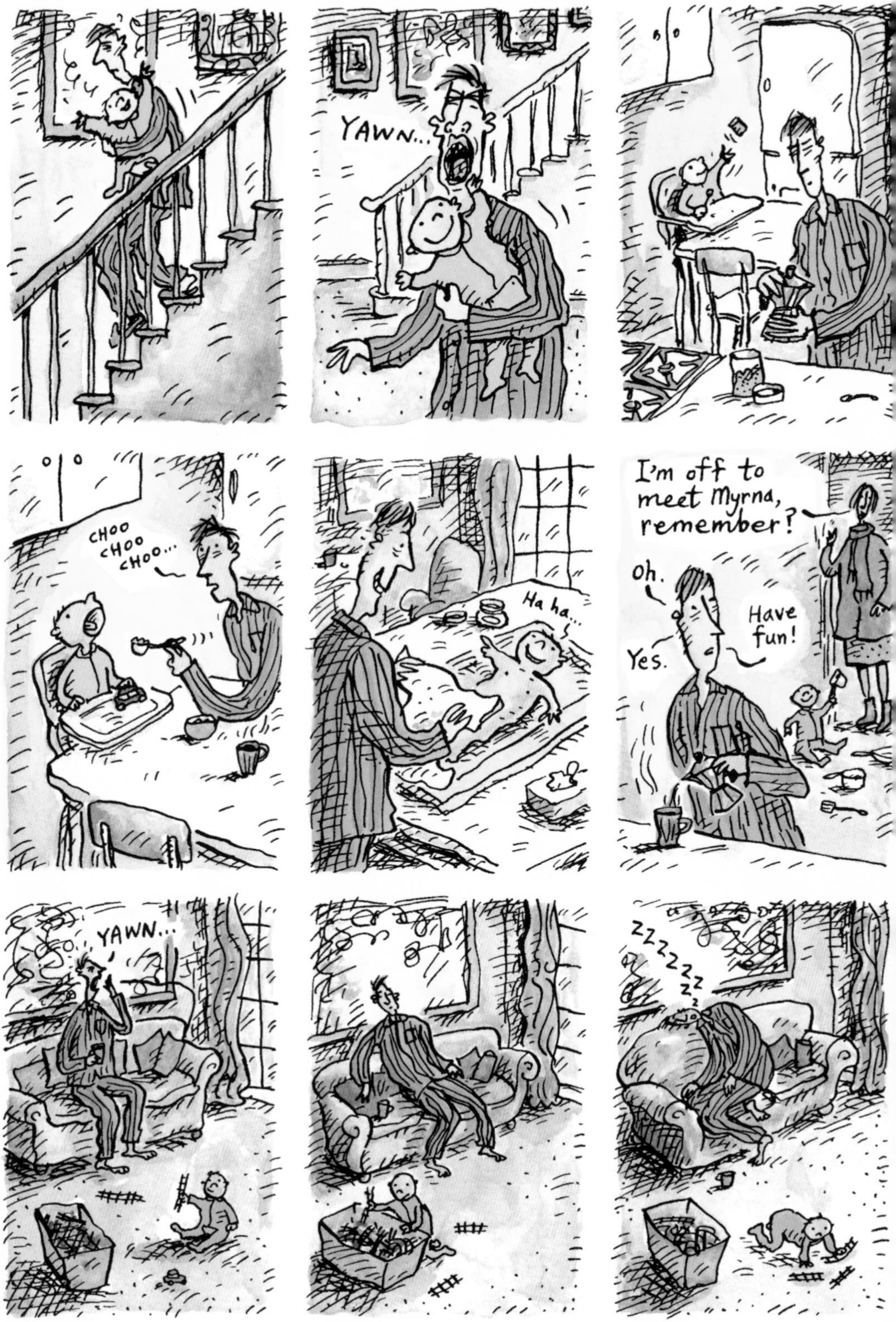
YAWN...
CHOO CHOO CHOO...
Ha ha...
I'm off to meet Myrna, remember?
Oh.
Yes.
Have fun!
YAWN...
ZZZZZZZ

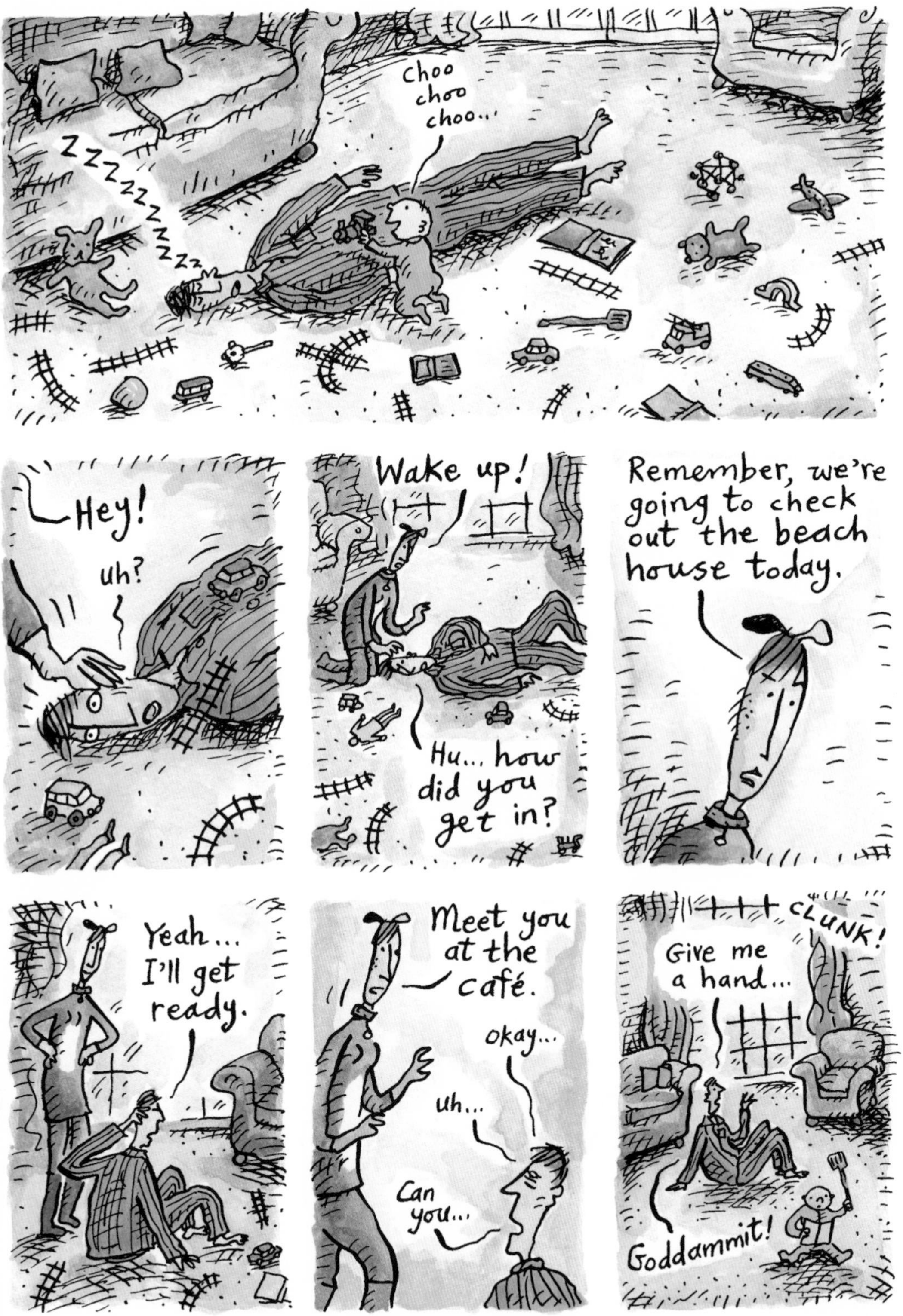
Choo choo choo...
ZZZZZZZZZZzzz
Hey!
uh?
Wake up!
Hu... how did you get in?
Remember, we're going to check out the beach house today.
Yeah... I'll get ready.
Meet you at the café.
Okay...
uh...
Can you...
CLUNK!
Give me a hand...
Goddammit!

The No Hope Café

Where's Cherry?

You brought the baby?!

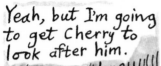

Yeah, but I'm going to get Cherry to look after him.

Here she is.

Hey, Gully! School uniform? Isn't it Sunday today?

Yeah.

I'm in disguise.

You found that doll!

Uh huh. He came back last night.

DOLL... Dog... Soul...

Hey, Joe...

Don't bother the customers.

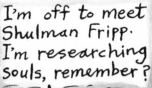

DOG SOUL

Uh, Cherry... I need a favour.

Can you look after Gully while Dog Girl and I...

No way.

Ha ha

I'm off to meet Shulman Fripp. I'm researching souls, remember?

Gotta run... Train to catch.

What now?

Ga!

171

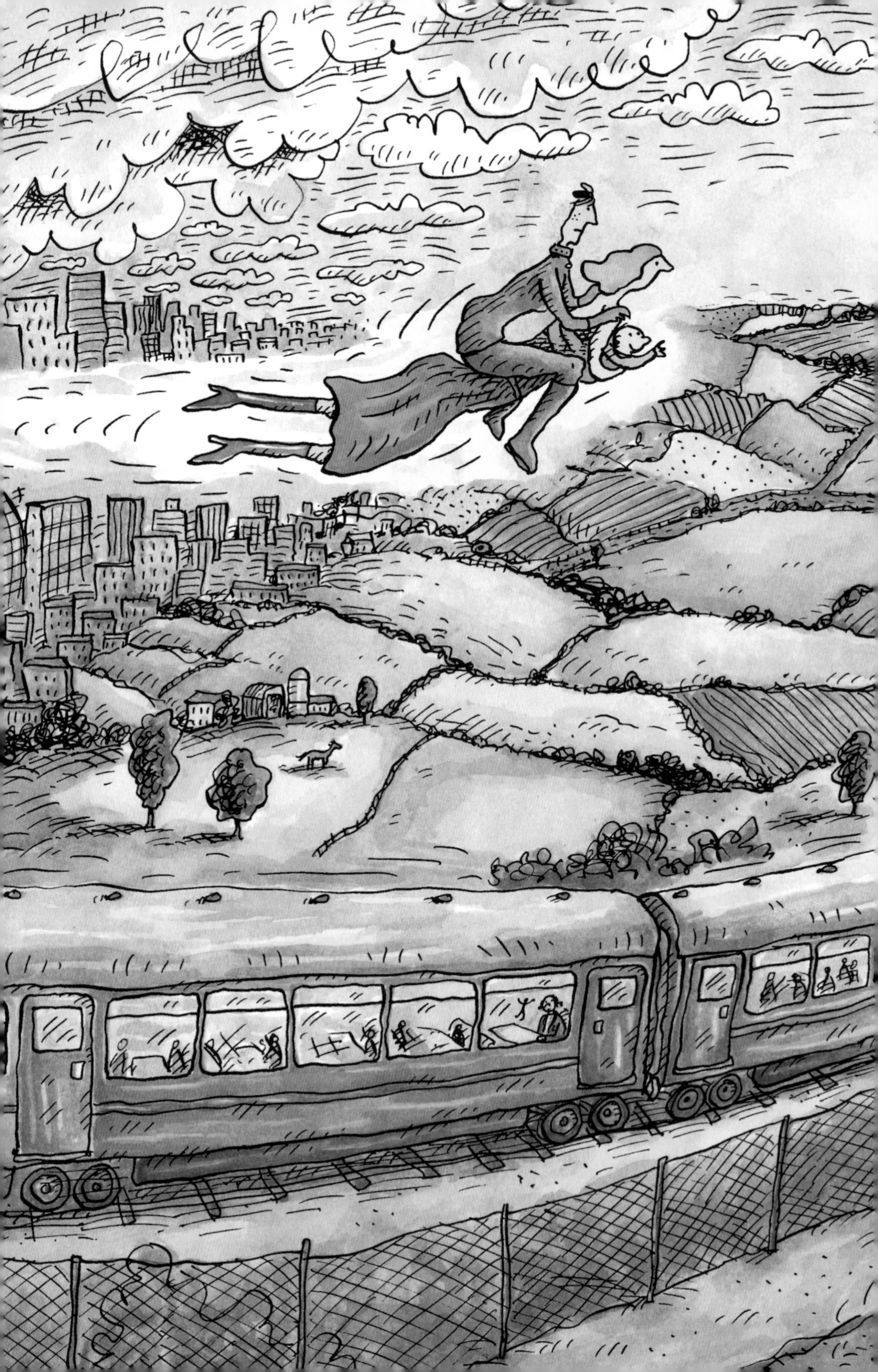

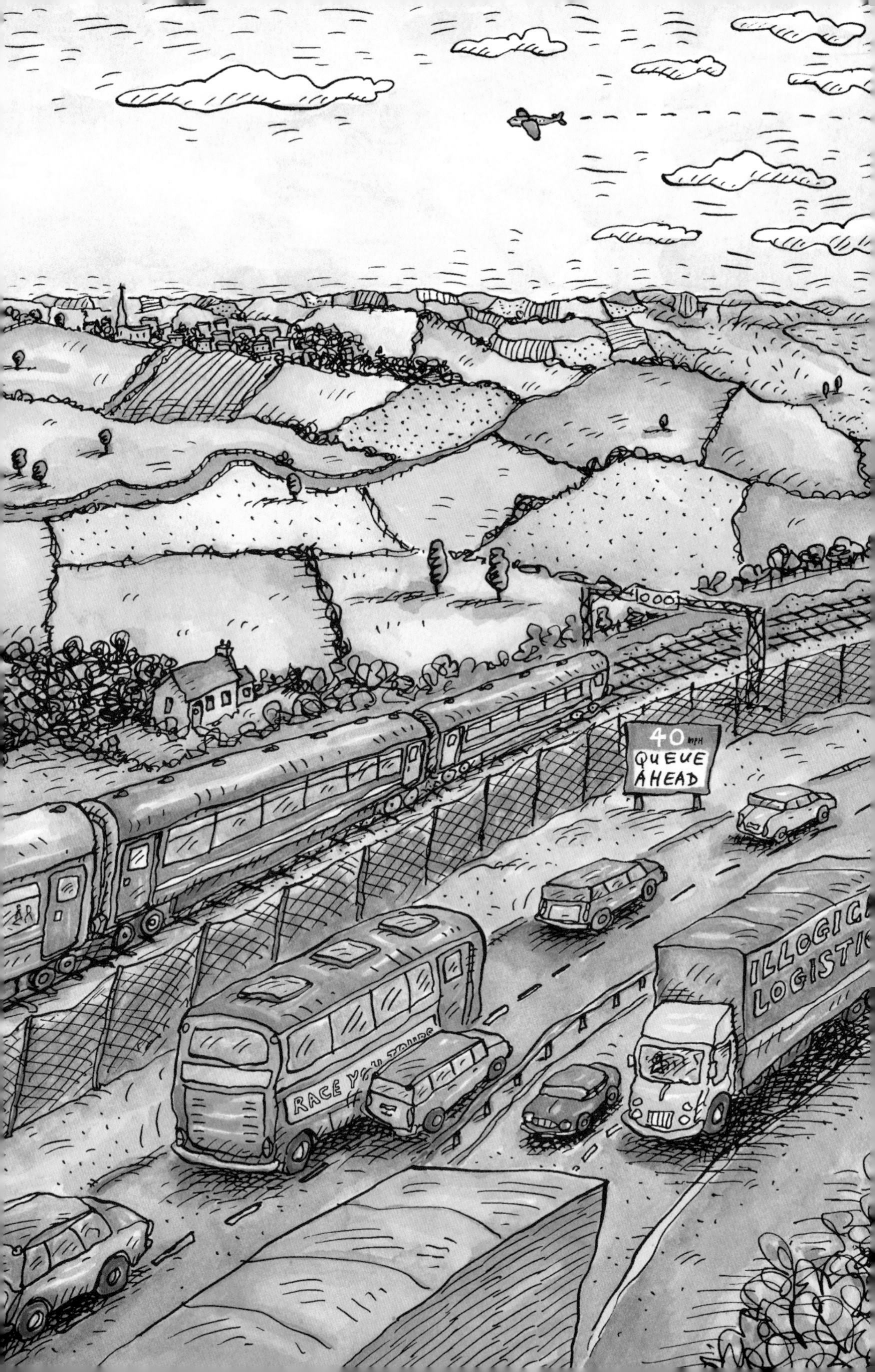
1000
40 mph
QUEUE
AHEAD
ILLOGICA
LOGISTIC
RACE

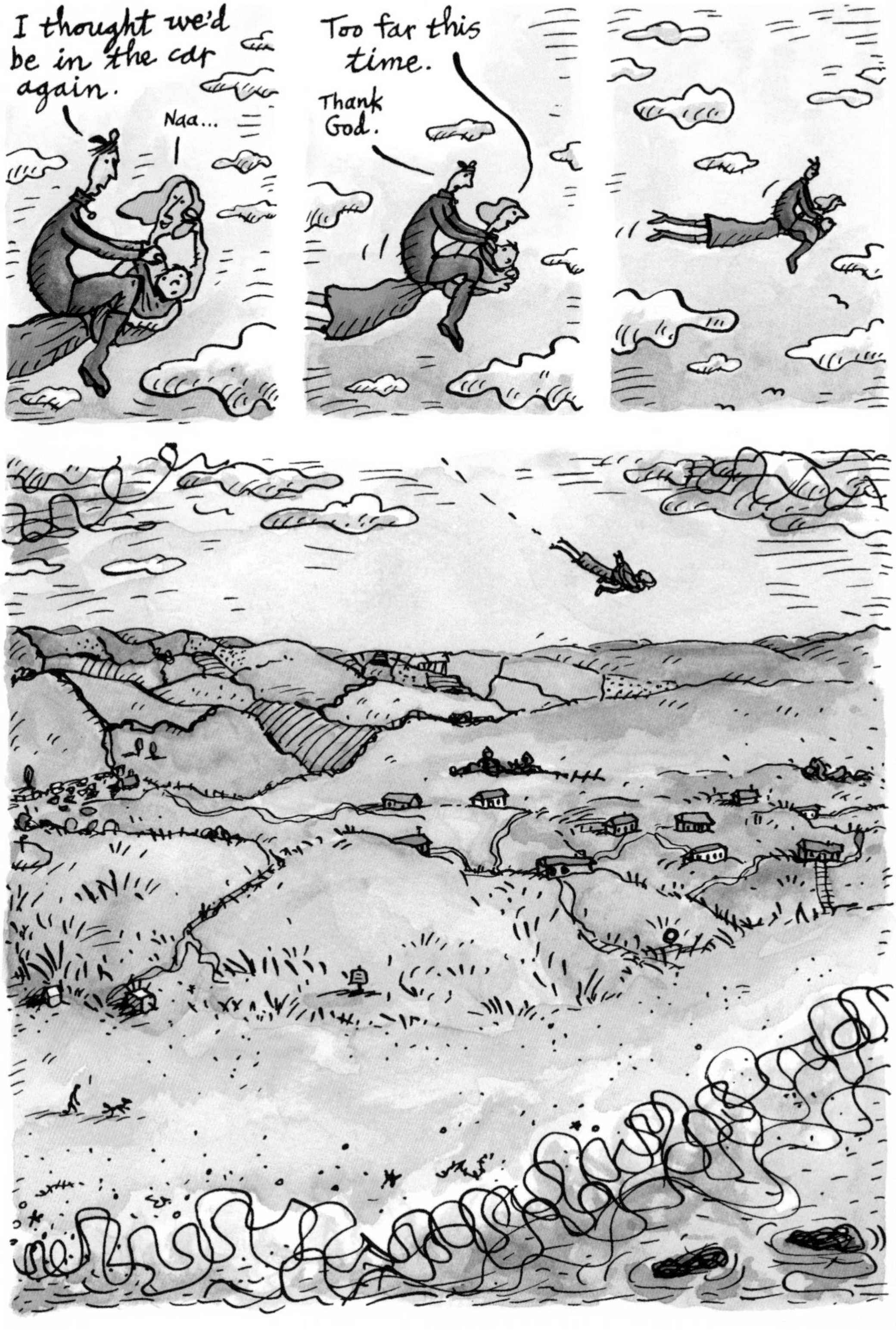
I thought we'd be in the car again.
Naa...
Too far this time.
Thank God.

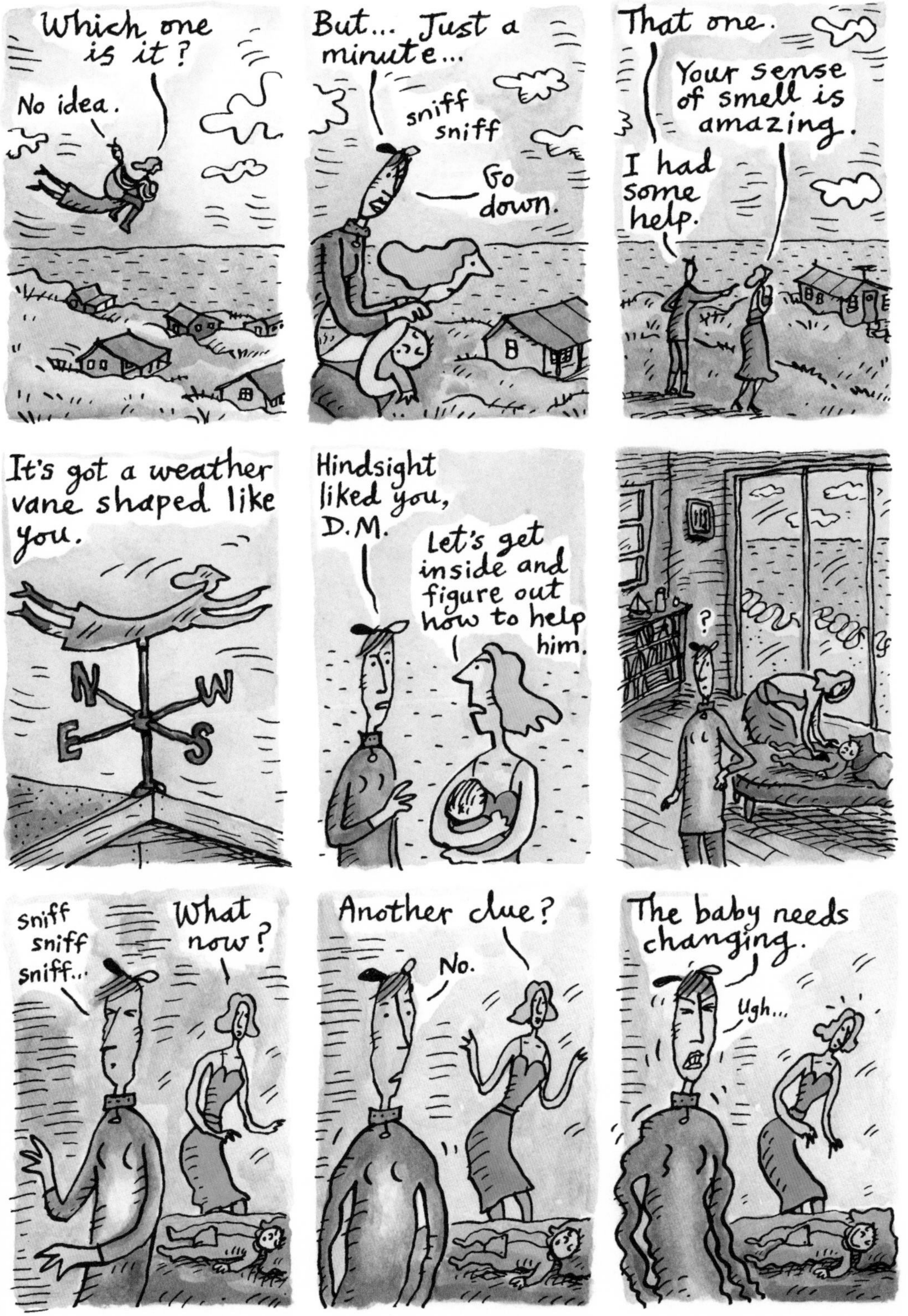
Which one is it?
No idea.
But... Just a minute...
sniff sniff
Go down.
That one.
Your sense of smell is amazing.
I had some help.
It's got a weather vane shaped like you.
N
W
E
S
Hindsight liked you, D.M.
Let's get inside and figure out how to help him.
?
sniff sniff sniff...
What now?
Another clue?
No.
The baby needs changing.
Ugh...

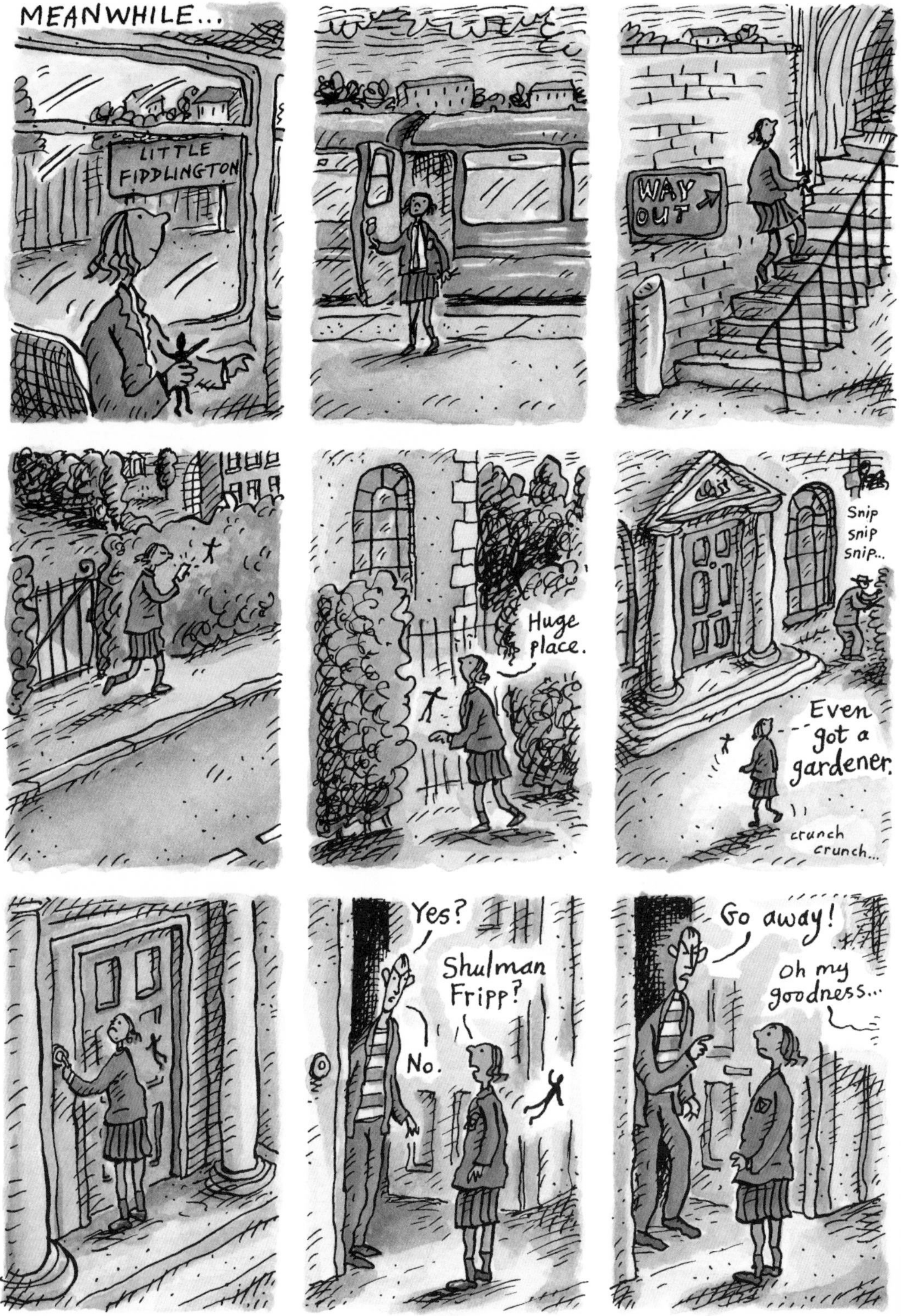
MEANWHILE...
LITTLE FIDDLINGTON
WAY OUT
Huge place.
Snip snip snip...
Even got a gardener.
crunch crunch...
Yes?
Shulman Fripp?
No.
Go away!
Oh my goodness...

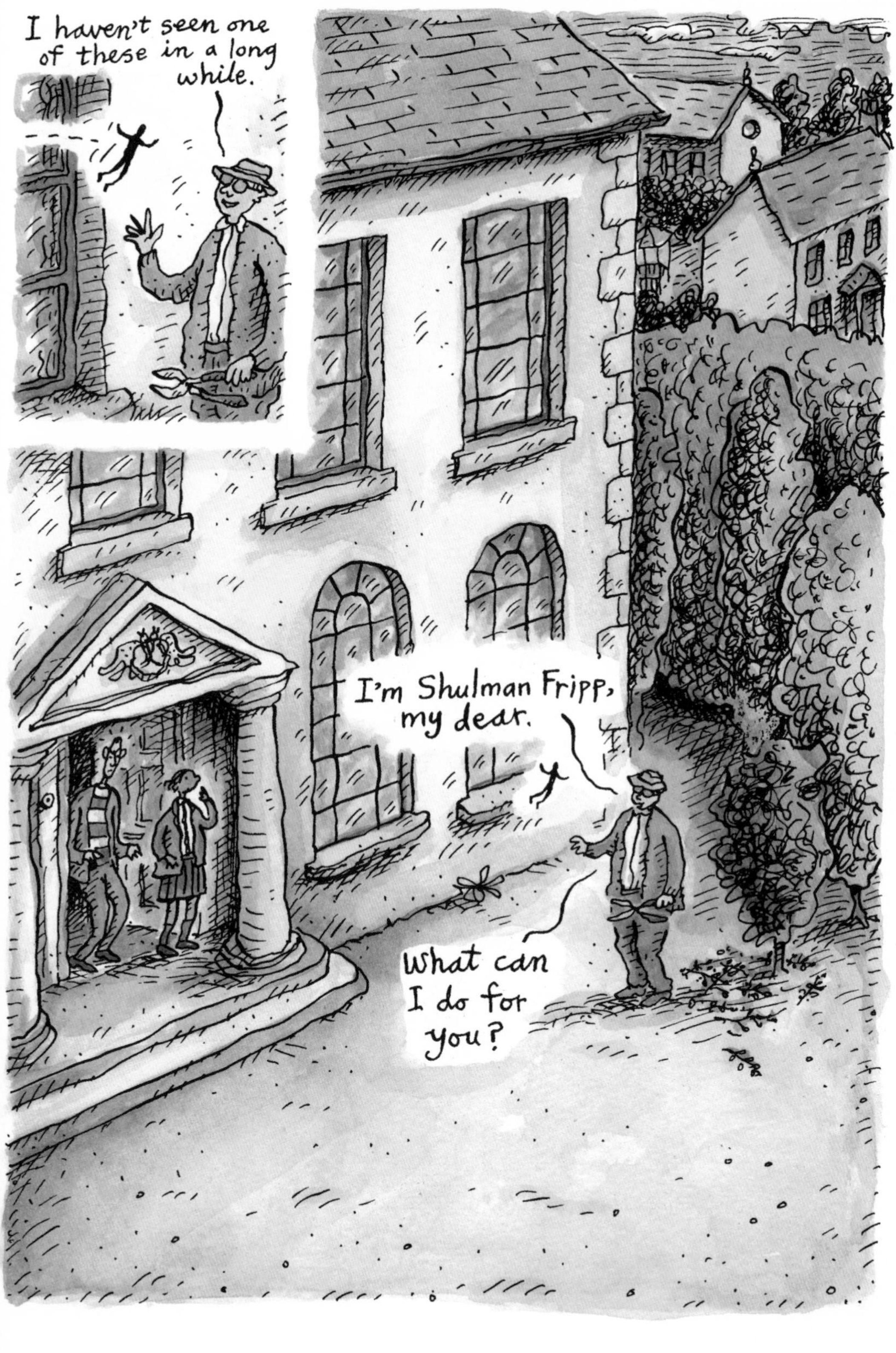
I haven't seen one of these in a long while.
I'm Shulman Fripp, my dear.
What can I do for you?

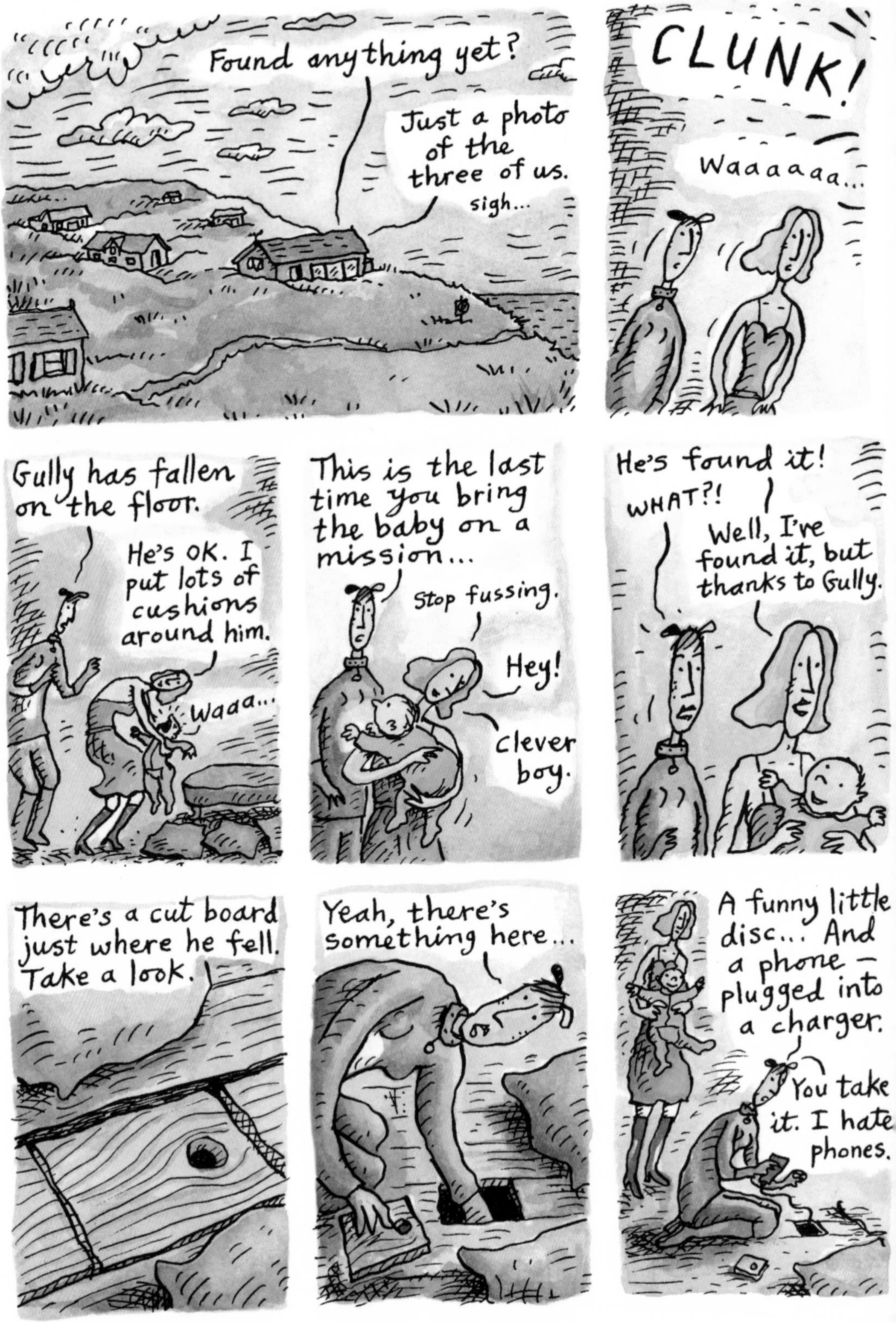
Found anything yet?
Just a photo of the three of us.
sigh...
CLUNK!
Waaaaaa...
Gully has fallen on the floor.
He's OK. I put lots of cushions around him.
Waaa...
This is the last time you bring the baby on a mission...
Stop fussing.
Hey!
Clever boy.
He's found it!
WHAT?!
Well, I've found it, but thanks to Gully.
There's a cut board just where he fell. Take a look.
Yeah, there's something here...
A funny little disc... And a phone — plugged into a charger.
You take it. I hate phones.

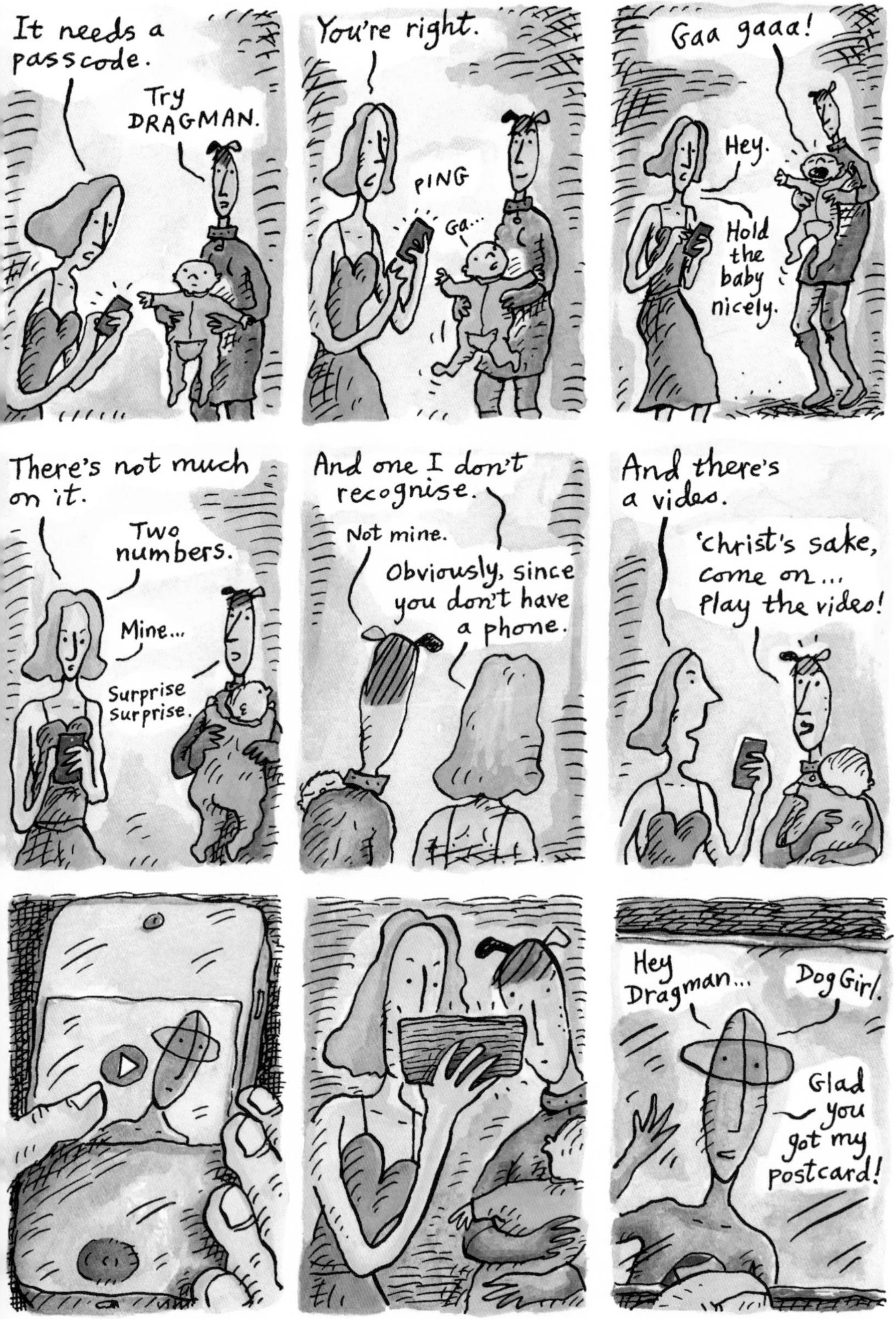
It needs a passcode.
Try DRAGMAN.
You're right.
PING
Ga...
Gaa gaaa!
Hey.
Hold the baby nicely.
There's not much on it.
Two numbers.
Mine...
Surprise surprise.
And one I don't recognise.
Not mine.
Obviously, since you don't have a phone.
And there's a video.
'christ's sake, come on... Play the video!
Hey Dragman...
Dog Girl.
Glad you got my postcard!

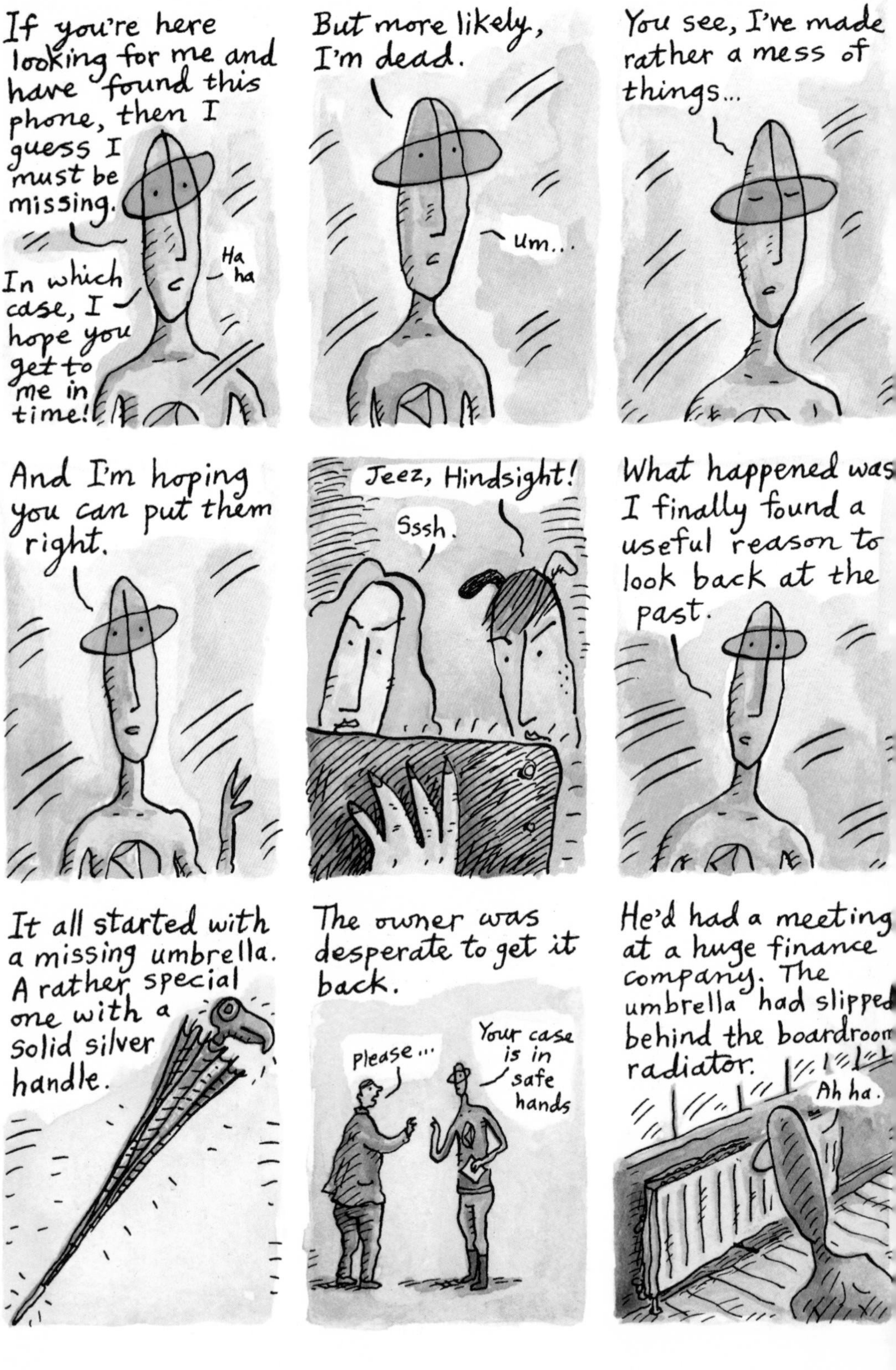

If you're here looking for me and have found this phone, then I guess I must be missing.
In which case, I hope you get to me in time!
Ha ha
But more likely, I'm dead.
um...
You see, I've made rather a mess of things...
And I'm hoping you can put them right.
Jeez, Hindsight!
Sssh.
What happened was I finally found a useful reason to look back at the past.
It all started with a missing umbrella. A rather special one with a solid silver handle.
The owner was desperate to get it back.
Please...
Your case is in safe hands
He'd had a meeting at a huge finance company. The umbrella had slipped behind the boardroom radiator.
Ah ha.

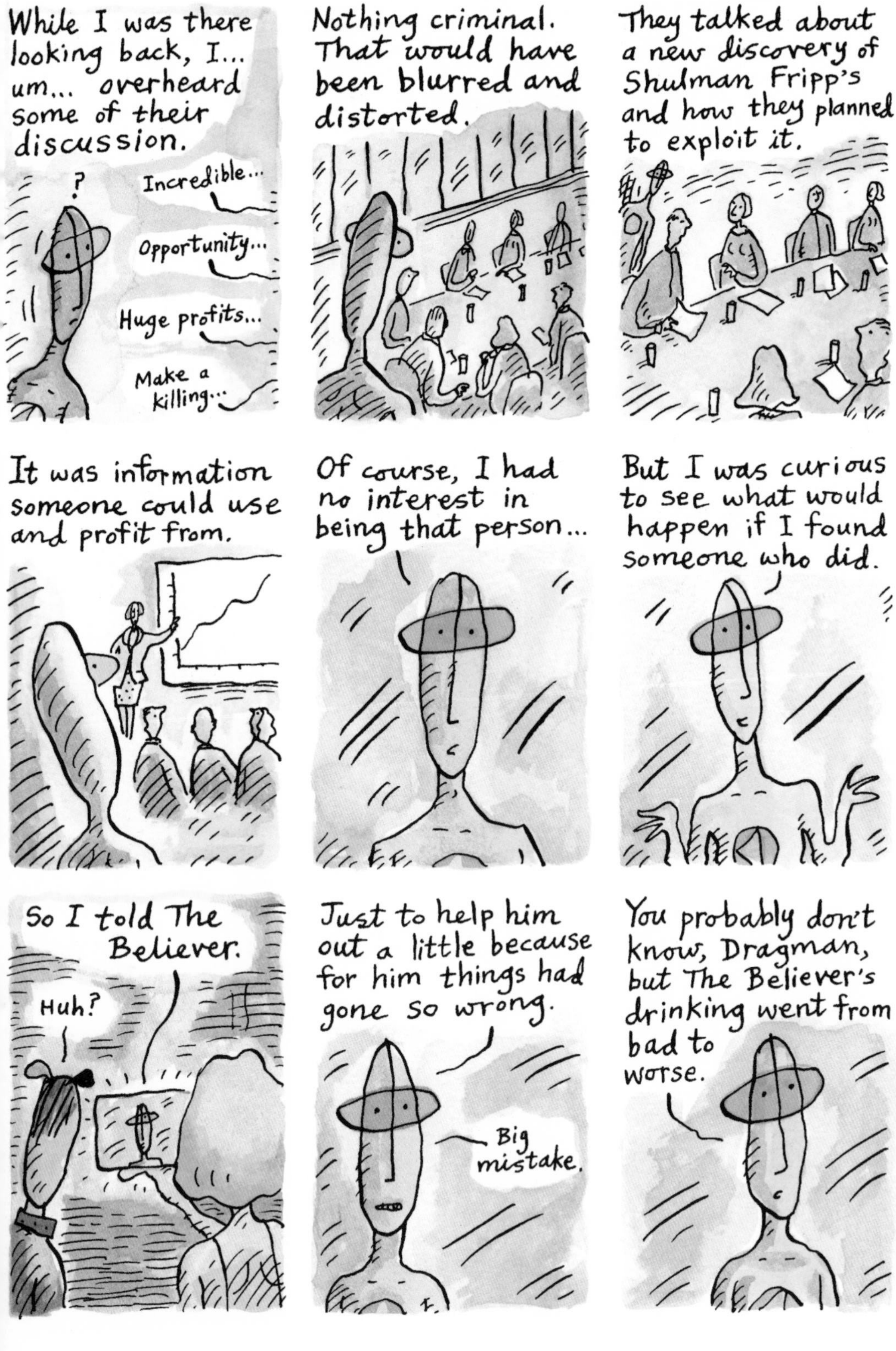
While I was there looking back, I... um... overheard some of their discussion.
?
Incredible...
Opportunity...
Huge profits...
Make a killing...
Nothing criminal. That would have been blurred and distorted.
They talked about a new discovery of Shulman Fripp's and how they planned to exploit it.
It was information someone could use and profit from.
Of course, I had no interest in being that person...
But I was curious to see what would happen if I found someone who did.
So I told The Believer.
Huh?
Just to help him out a little because for him things had gone so wrong.
Big mistake.
You probably don't know, Dragman, but The Believer's drinking went from bad to worse.

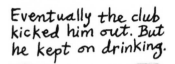
Eventually the club kicked him out. But he kept on drinking.

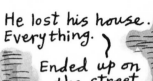
He lost his house. Everything.

Ended up on the street.

Yeah, I saw him from time to time.

Finally he sold his soul. Just for the money to keep buying drink.

But the funny thing was, when he'd got no soul...

He stopped drinking.

Hey, Believer.

Hindsight.

Not drinking?

Naw. Lost interest in it.

So instead of giving him some money for a drink as I usually did...

Hey, Believer!

I gave him information.

Next time I saw him he was wearing a suit.

Hindsight!

Believer? Wow! You look good.

It's a costume. Like yours.

So I gave him more information.

Uh huh.

The time after that he had rented a suite of offices. Soon he owned the building we met in.

What do you think?

Cool...

182

I was pleased for him and I kept giving him useful investment titbits.

Go on.

Then he started asking me specific questions.

There's a social media company I'm curious about...

OK.

In only a couple of years his company, Black Mist, owned communications companies, banks, social media, pharmaceuticals... Too many things to remember.

Nowadays Black Mist own ideas, art, inventions, politicians... You name it.

Including most of the companies who buy and sell souls.

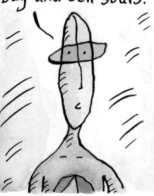

They also fund Shulman Fripp, the scientist...

They even sponsor the superhero club.

All thanks to me.

And too late I started to worry.

And far too late I finally looked back at The Believer's own meetings and boardrooms to see what he was up to...

BLACK MIST

And everything was a blur. Nothing was clear... Except for a notice The Believer had posted on every boardroom door.

POKE YOUR NOSE INTO MY BUSINESS, HINDSIGHT, AND YOU'RE DEAD.

183

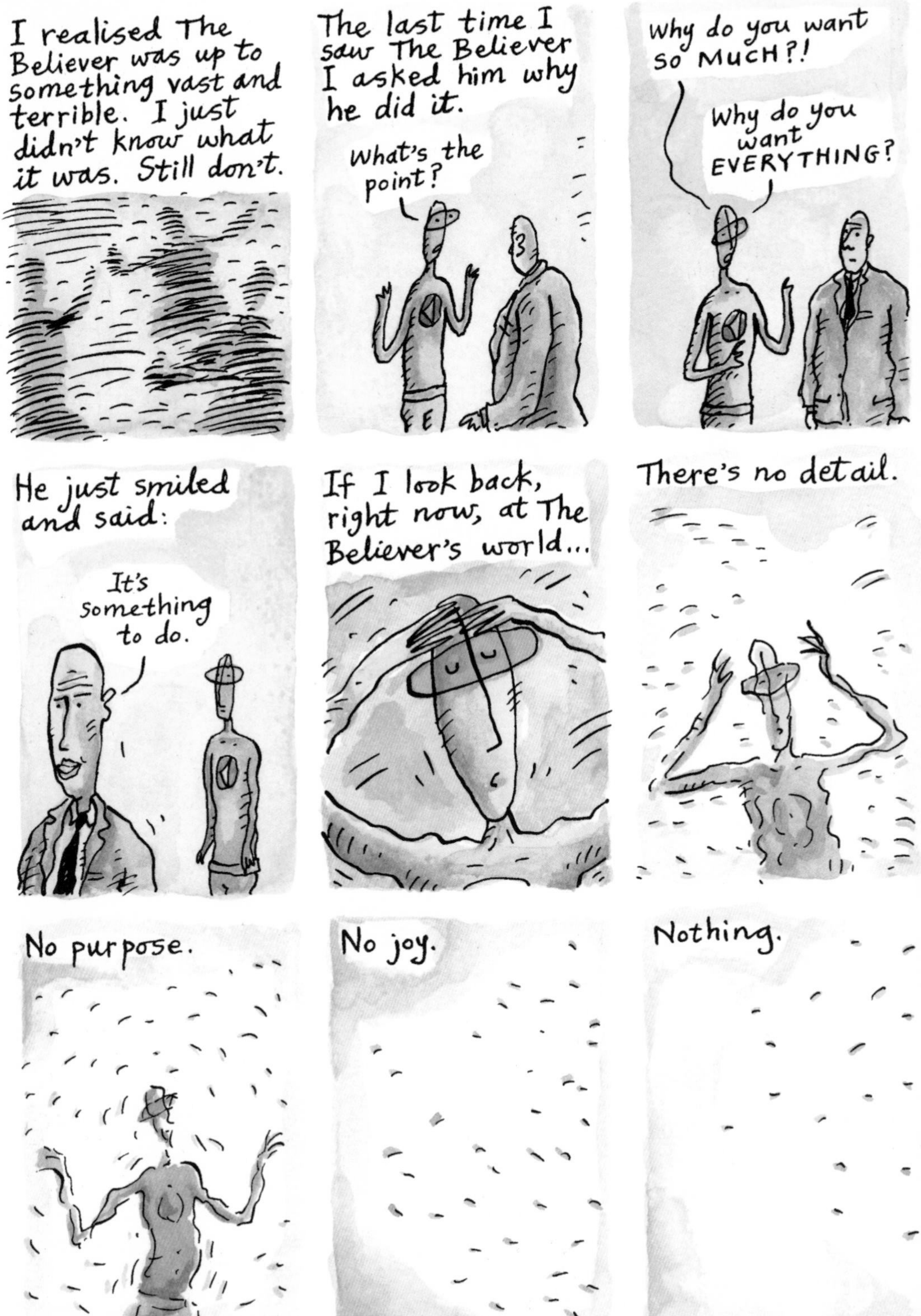
I realised The Believer was up to something vast and terrible. I just didn't know what it was. Still don't.
The last time I saw The Believer I asked him why he did it.
What's the point?
Why do you want so MUCH?!
Why do you want EVERYTHING?
He just smiled and said:
It's something to do.
If I look back, right now, at The Believer's world...
There's no detail.
No purpose.
No joy.
Nothing.

I think I'm finally seeing the future.

And there isn't one.

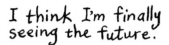

So that's the story.

It's all my fault, so I'm going to confront him. To try and stop him

Wish me luck.

Oh. I forgot. If you're watching this, then I've disappeared and it's too late for luck.

Oh well...

There's one thing in my favour, though...

I looked back a year or so ago and found something The Believer has been searching for.

His soul.

And I've got it.

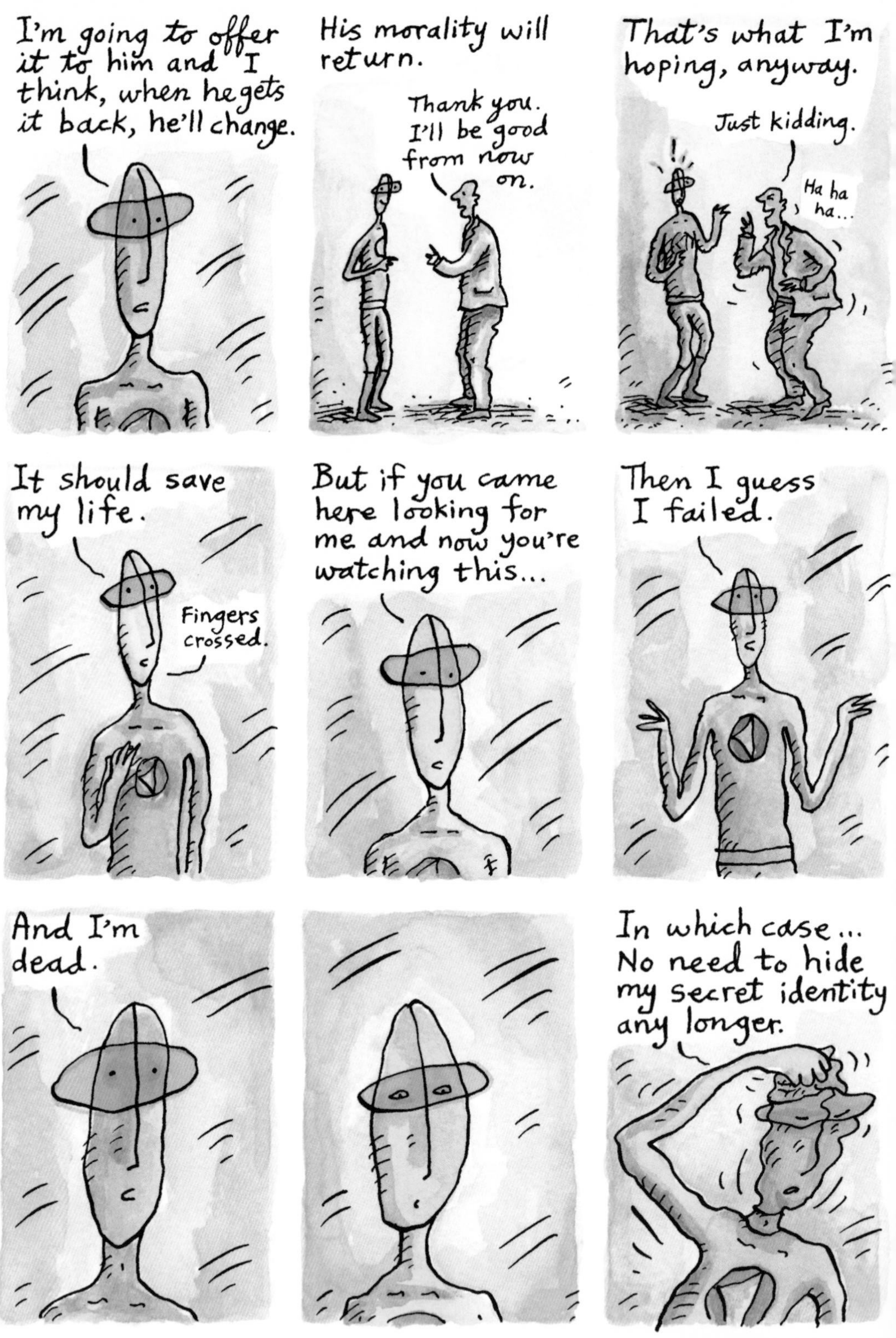
I'm going to offer it to him and I think, when he gets it back, he'll change.
His morality will return.
Thank you. I'll be good from now on.
That's what I'm hoping, anyway.
Just kidding.
Ha ha ha...
It should save my life.
Fingers crossed.
But if you came here looking for me and now you're watching this...
Then I guess I failed.
And I'm dead.
In which case... No need to hide my secret identity any longer.

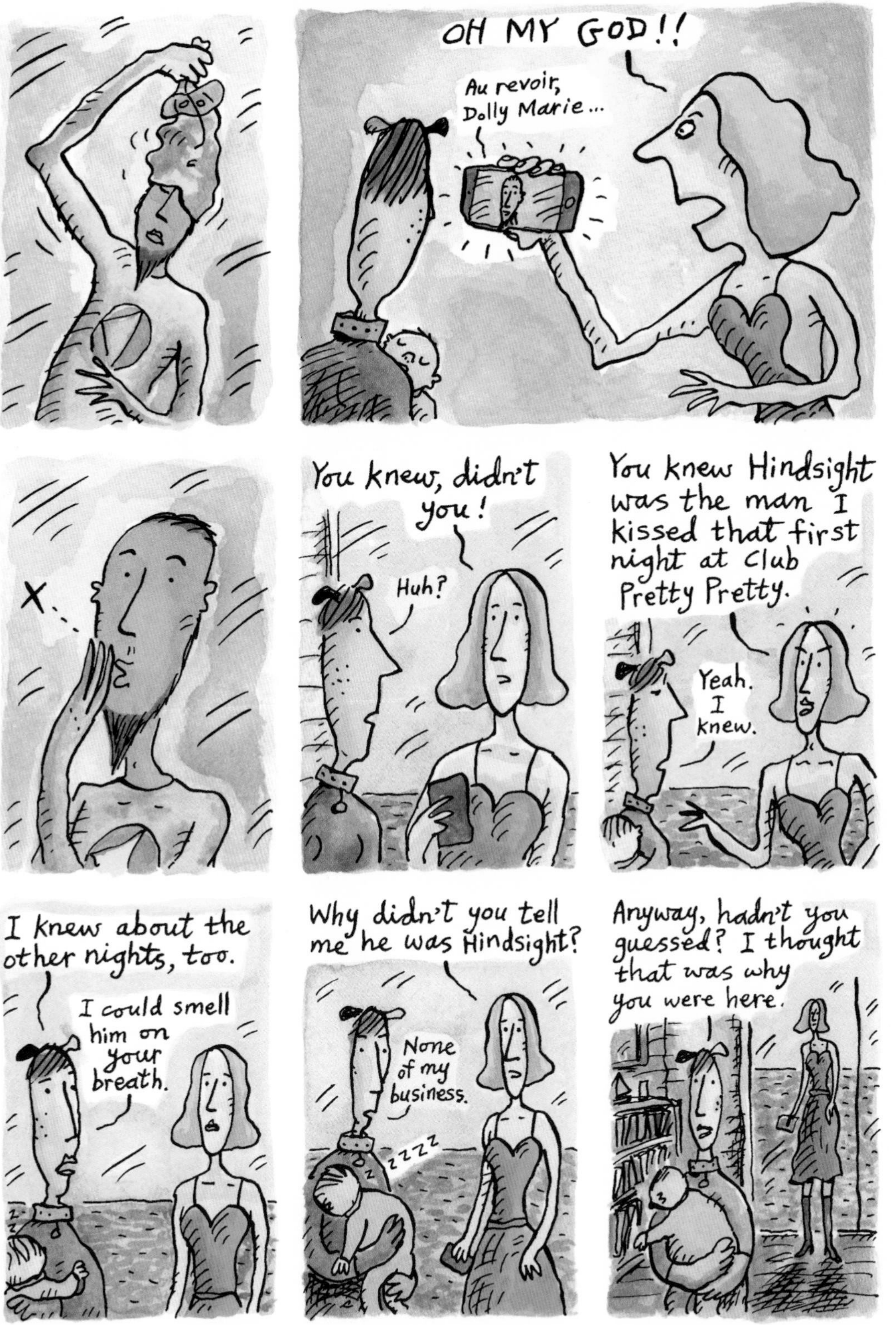
OH MY GOD!!
Au revoir, Dolly Marie...
You knew, didn't you!
Huh?
You knew Hindsight was the man I kissed that first night at Club Pretty Pretty.
Yeah. I knew.
I knew about the other nights, too.
I could smell him on your breath.
Why didn't you tell me he was Hindsight?
None of my business.
ZZZZ
Anyway, hadn't you guessed? I thought that was why you were here.

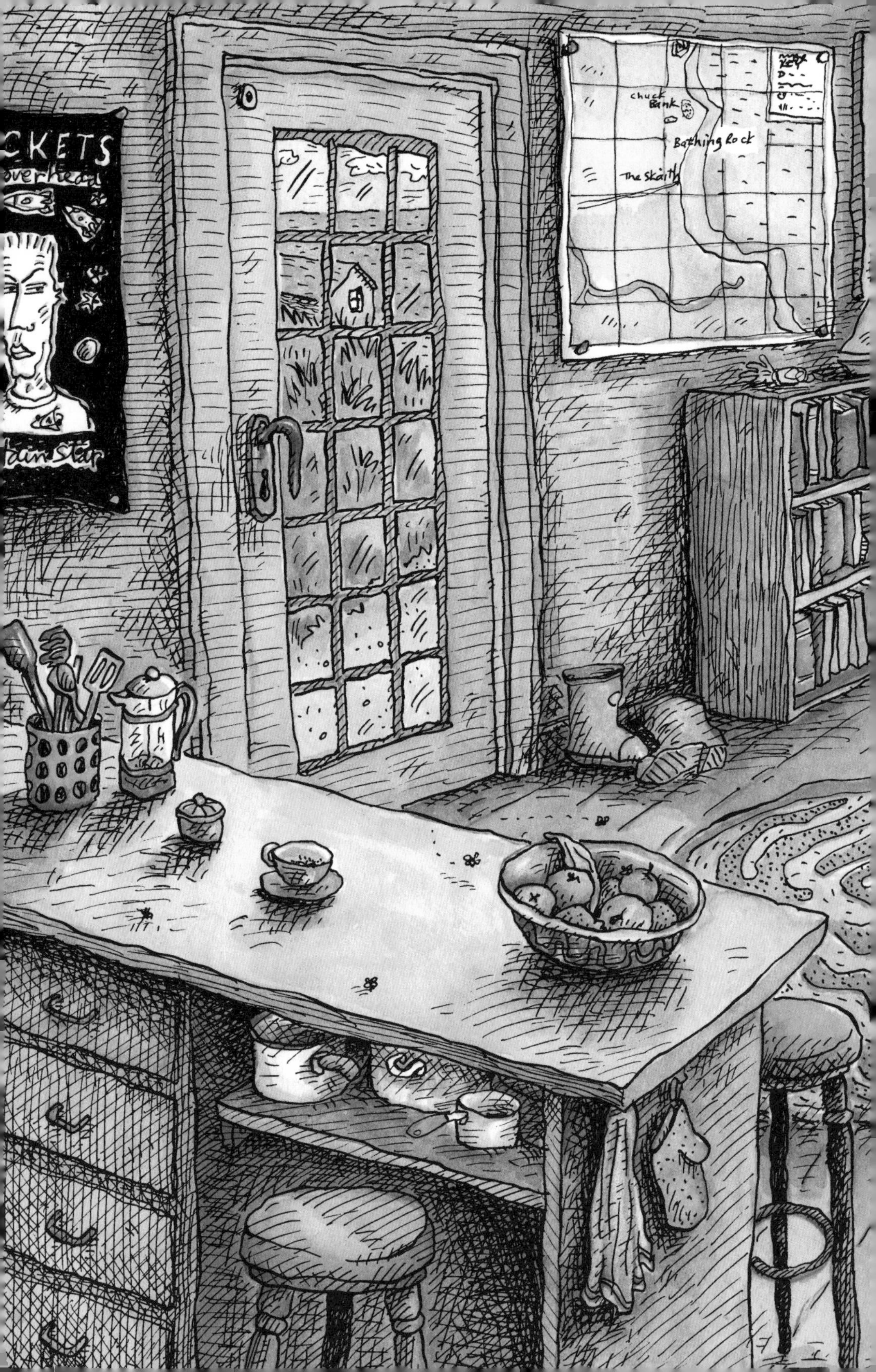
CKETS
overhead
tain Star
chuck Bank
Bathing Rock
The Skaith
KEY

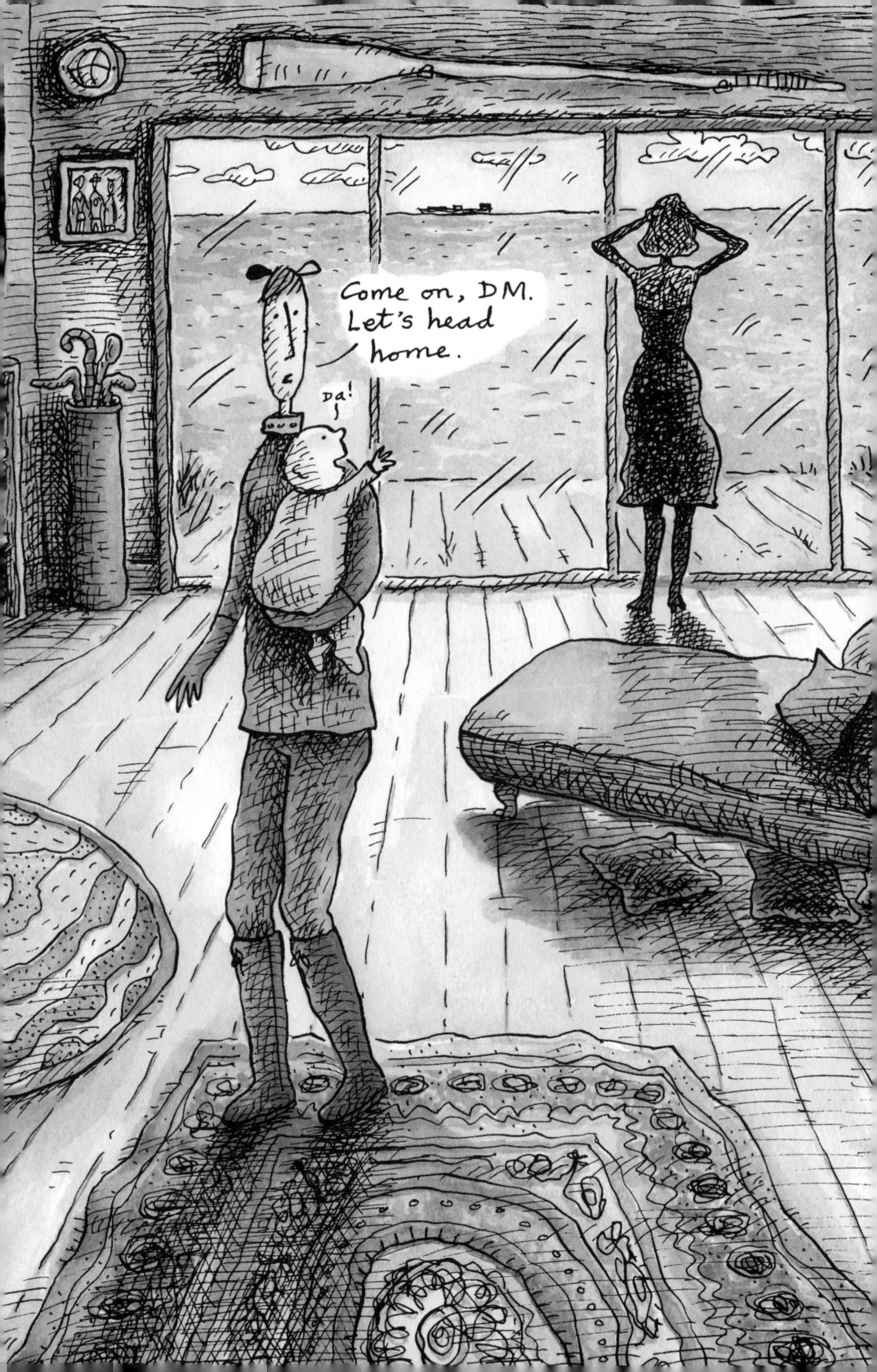
Come on, DM. Let's head home.
Da!

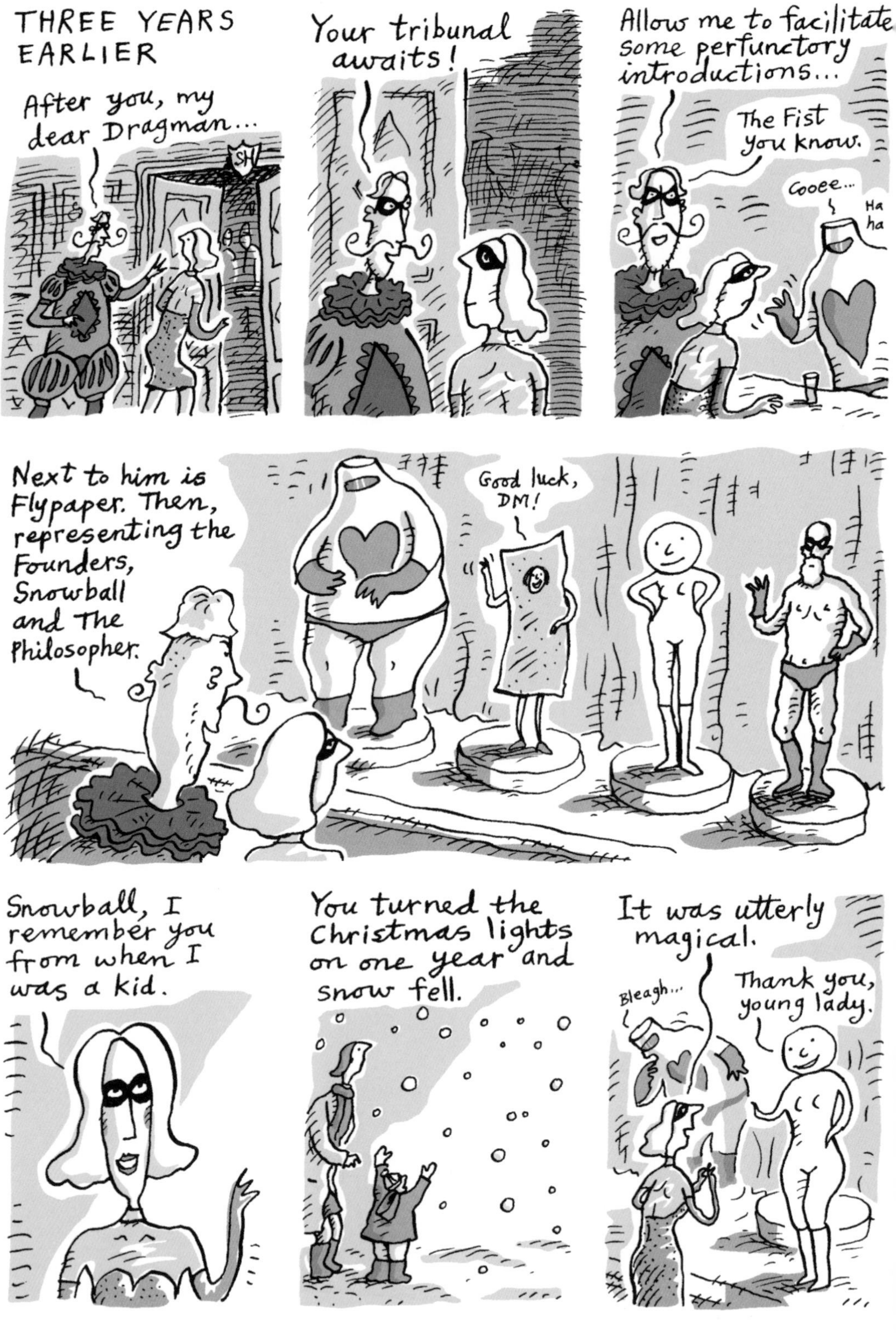
THREE YEARS EARLIER
After you, my dear Dragman...
SH
Your tribunal awaits!
Allow me to facilitate some perfunctory introductions...
The Fist you know.
Cooee...
Ha ha
Next to him is Flypaper. Then, representing the Founders, Snowball and The Philosopher.
Good luck, DM!
Snowball, I remember you from when I was a kid.
You turned the Christmas lights on one year and snow fell.
It was utterly magical.
Bleagh...
Thank you, young lady.

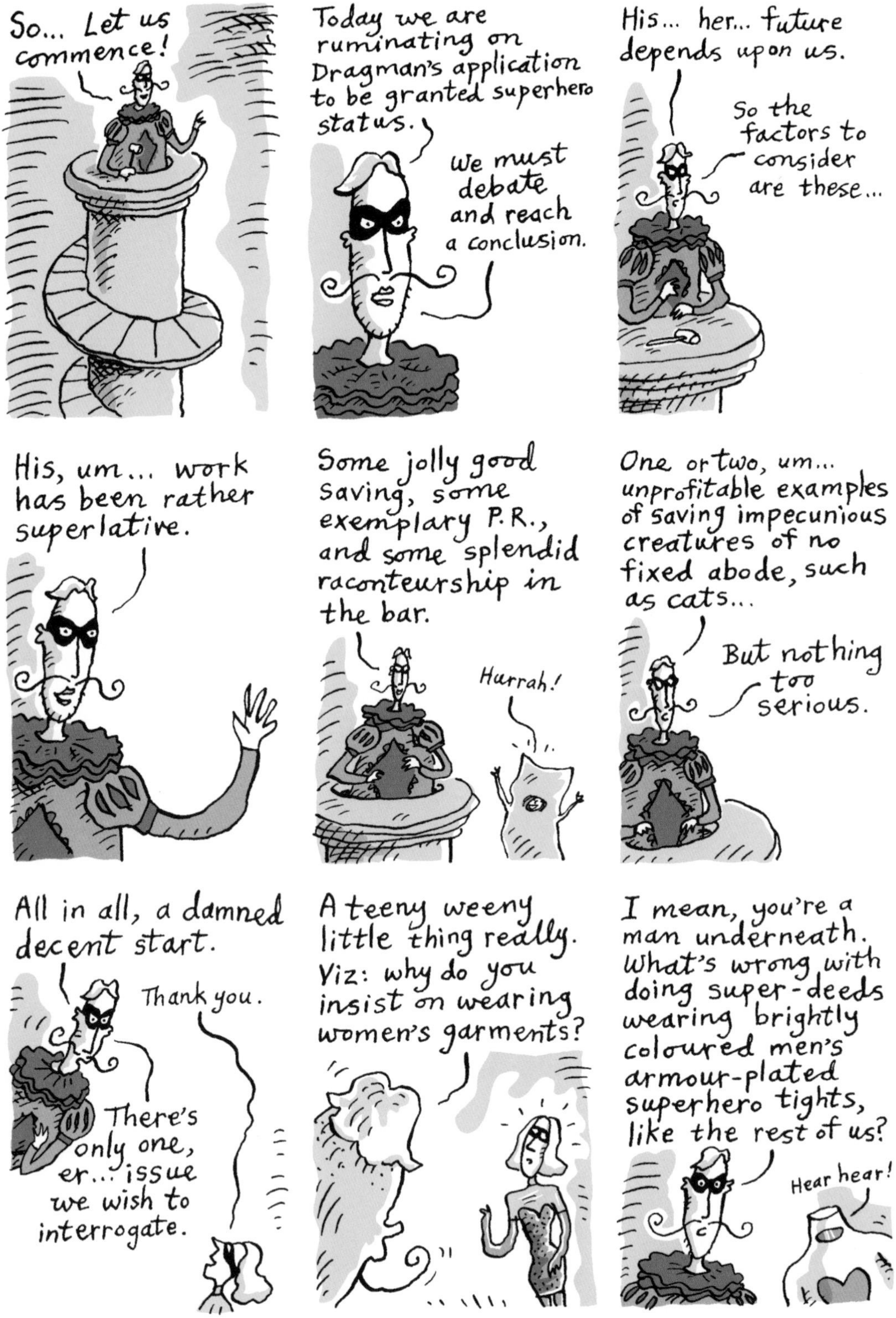
So... Let us commence!
Today we are ruminating on Dragman's application to be granted superhero status.
We must debate and reach a conclusion.
His... her... future depends upon us.
So the factors to consider are these...
His, um... work has been rather superlative.
Some jolly good saving, some exemplary P.R., and some splendid raconteurship in the bar.
Hurrah!
One or two, um... unprofitable examples of saving impecunious creatures of no fixed abode, such as cats...
But nothing too serious.
All in all, a damned decent start.
Thank you.
There's only one, er... issue we wish to interrogate.
A teeny weeny little thing really. Viz: why do you insist on wearing women's garments?
I mean, you're a man underneath. What's wrong with doing super-deeds wearing brightly coloured men's armour-plated superhero tights, like the rest of us?
Hear hear!

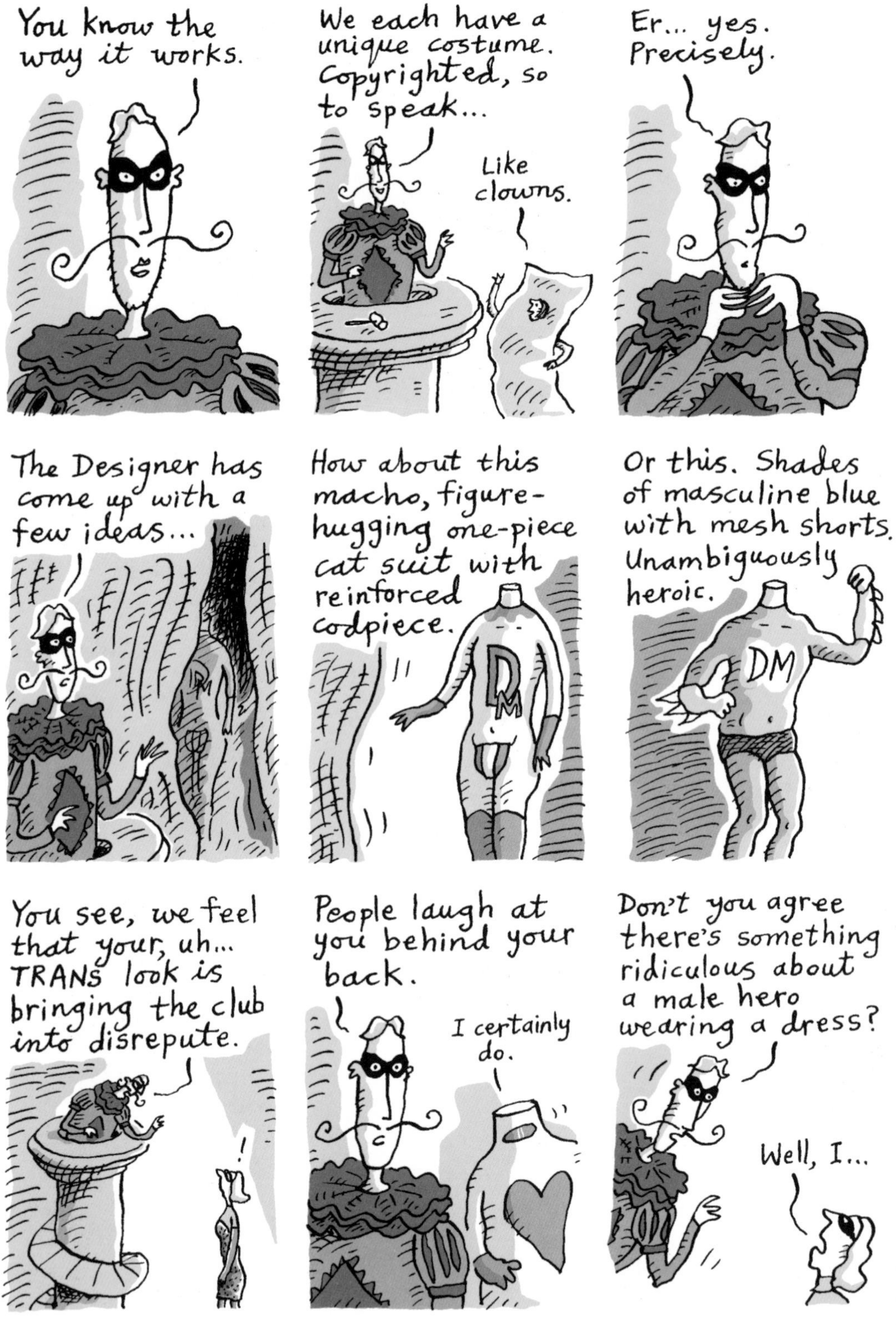
You know the way it works.
We each have a unique costume. Copyrighted, so to speak...
Like clowns.
Er... yes. Precisely.
The Designer has come up with a few ideas...
How about this macho, figure-hugging one-piece cat suit with reinforced codpiece.
Or this. Shades of masculine blue with mesh shorts. Unambiguously heroic.
DM
You see, we feel that your, uh... TRANS look is bringing the club into disrepute.
!
People laugh at you behind your back.
I certainly do.
Don't you agree there's something ridiculous about a male hero wearing a dress?
Well, I...

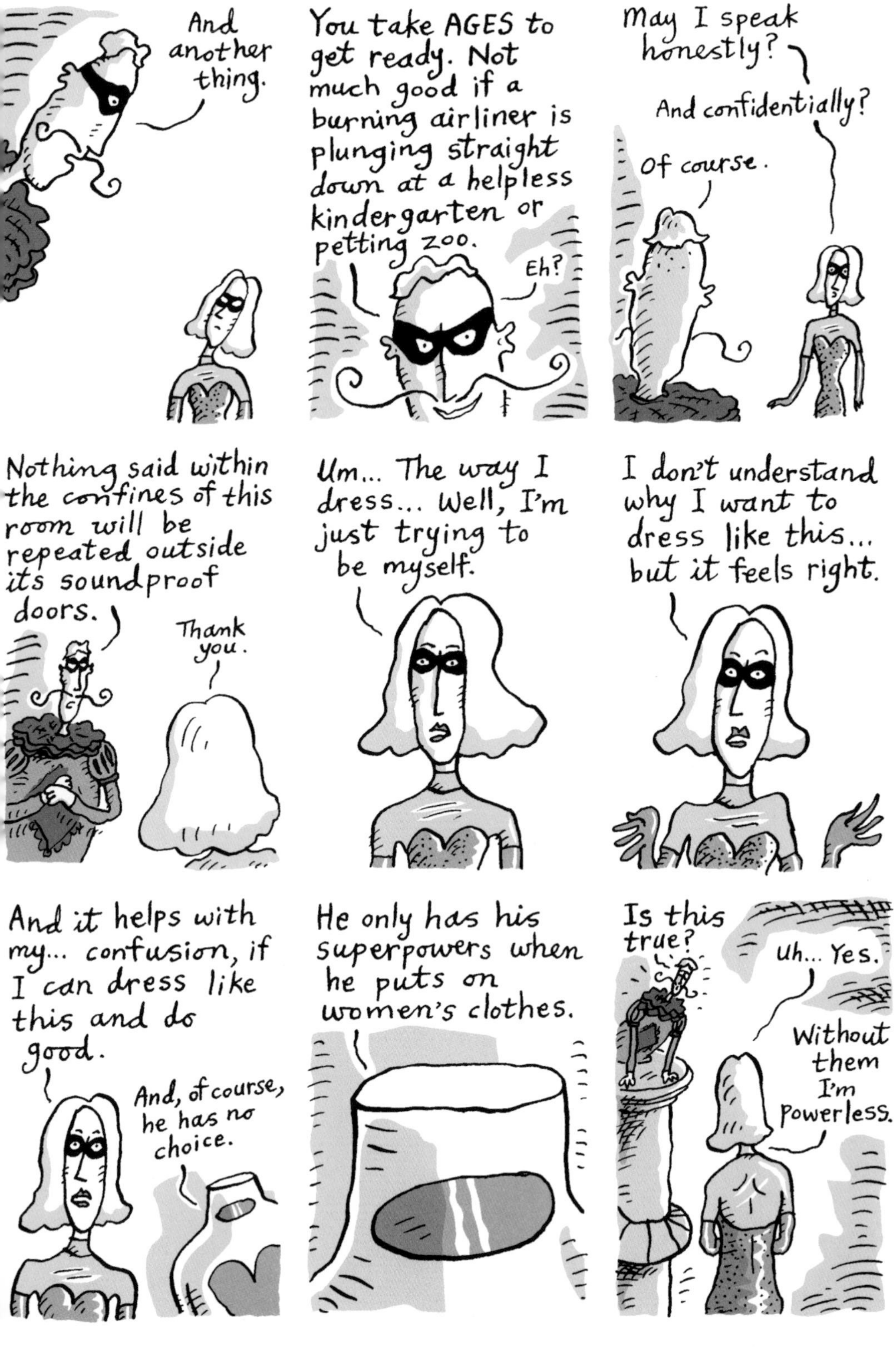

And another thing.
You take AGES to get ready. Not much good if a burning airliner is plunging straight down at a helpless kindergarten or petting zoo.
Eh?
May I speak honestly?
And confidentially?
Of course.
Nothing said within the confines of this room will be repeated outside its soundproof doors.
Thank you.
Um... The way I dress... Well, I'm just trying to be myself.
I don't understand why I want to dress like this... but it feels right.
And it helps with my... confusion, if I can dress like this and do good.
And, of course, he has no choice.
He only has his superpowers when he puts on women's clothes.
Is this true?
Uh... Yes.
Without them I'm powerless.

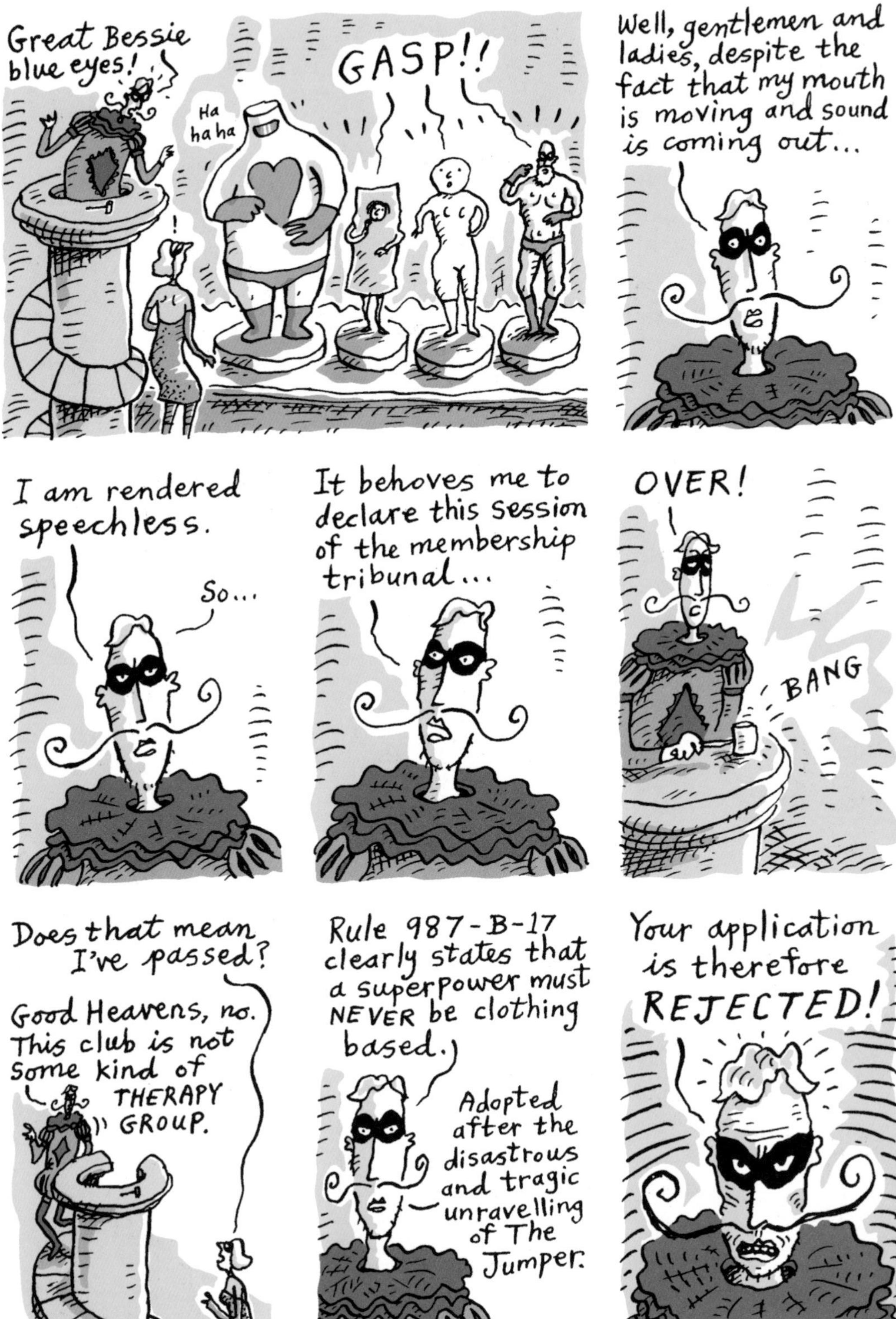
Great Bessie blue eyes!
Ha ha ha
GASP!!
Well, gentlemen and ladies, despite the fact that my mouth is moving and sound is coming out...
I am rendered speechless.
So...
It behoves me to declare this session of the membership tribunal...
OVER!
BANG
Does that mean I've passed?
Good Heavens, no. This club is not some kind of THERAPY GROUP.
Rule 987-B-17 clearly states that a superpower must NEVER be clothing based.
Adopted after the disastrous and tragic unravelling of The Jumper.
Your application is therefore REJECTED!

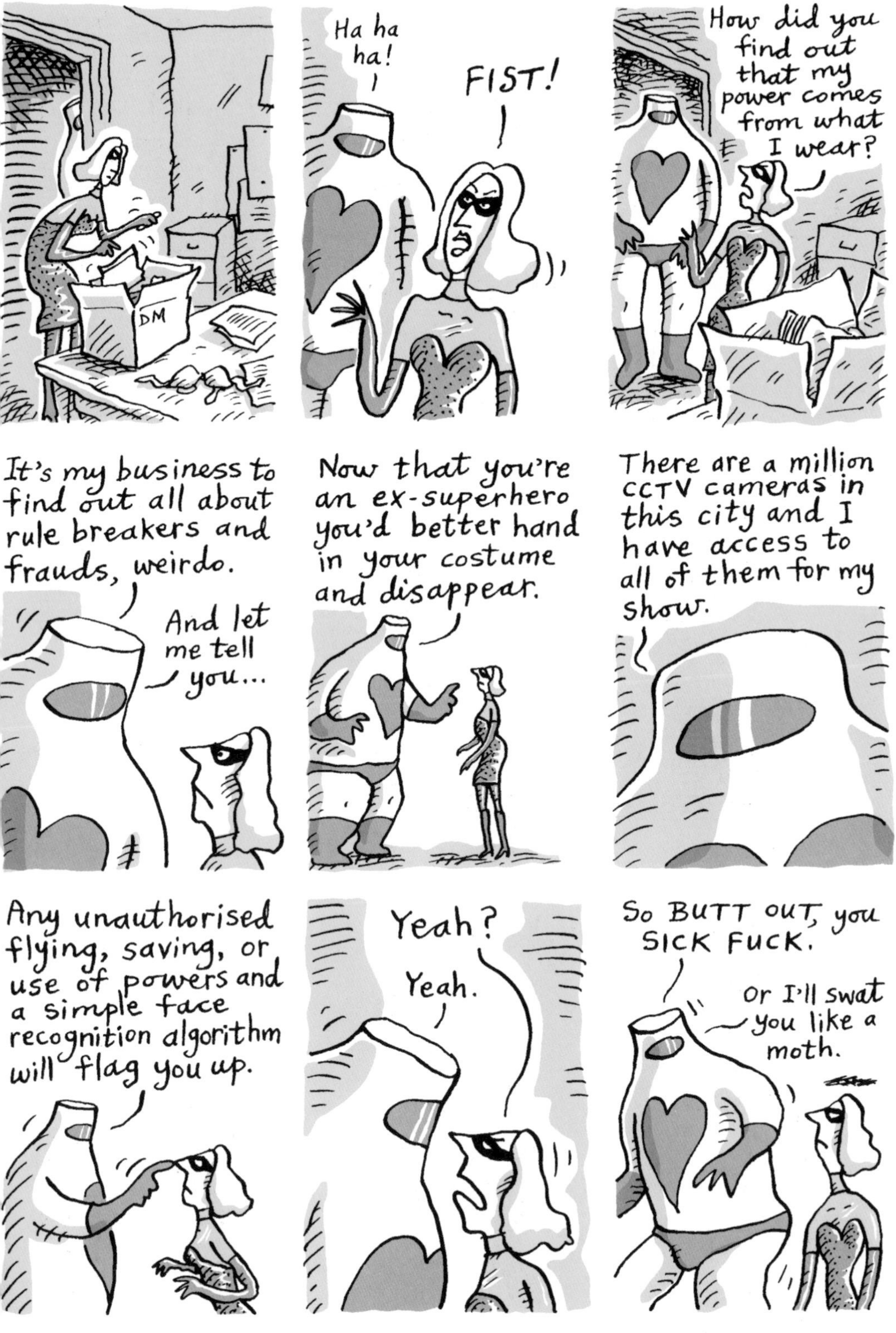
Ha ha ha!
FIST!
How did you find out that my power comes from what I wear?
DM
It's my business to find out all about rule breakers and frauds, weirdo.
And let me tell you...
Now that you're an ex-superhero you'd better hand in your costume and disappear.
There are a million CCTV cameras in this city and I have access to all of them for my show.
Any unauthorised flying, saving, or use of powers and a simple face recognition algorithm will flag you up.
Yeah?
Yeah.
So BUTT OUT, you SICK FUCK.
Or I'll swat you like a moth.

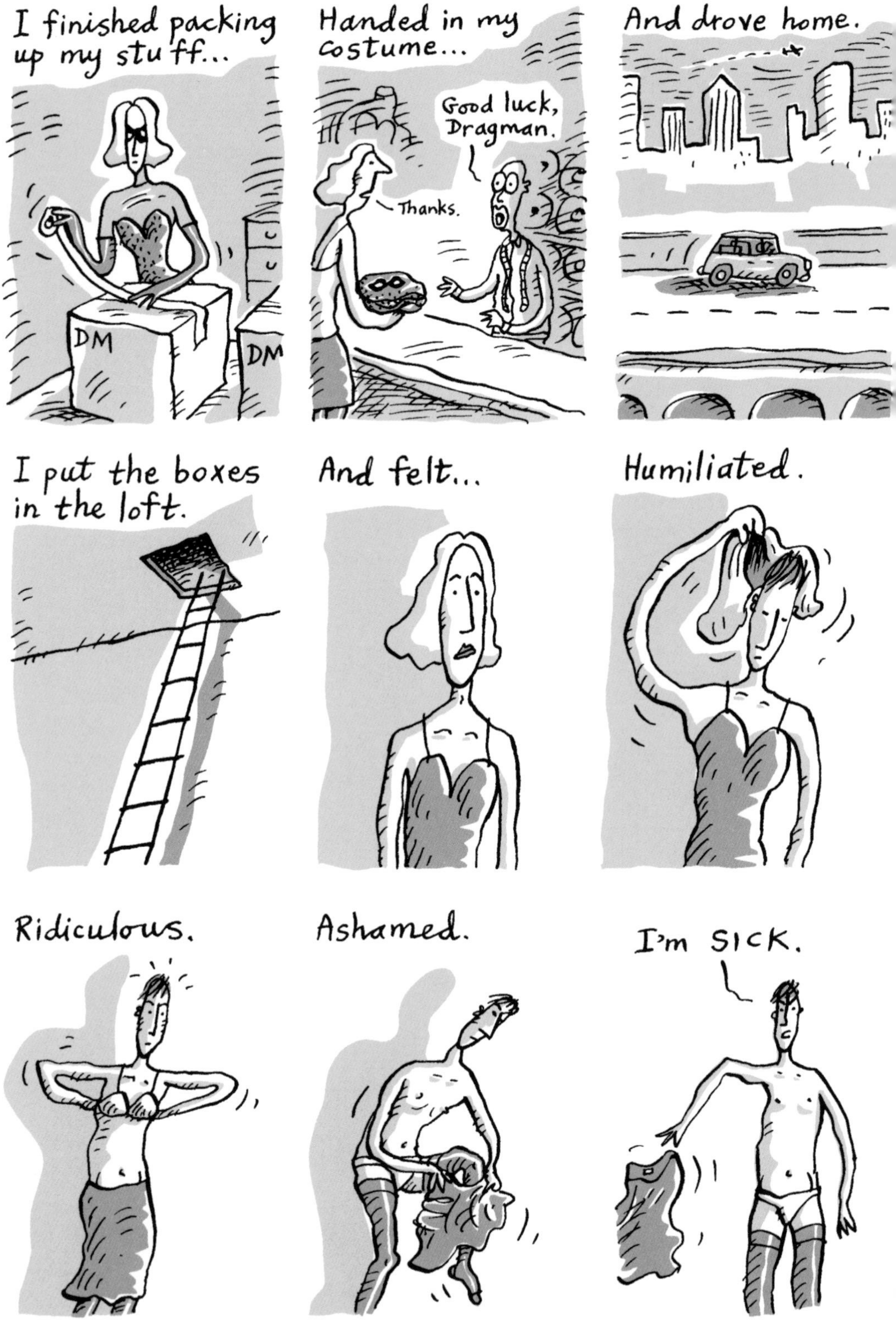
I finished packing up my stuff...
DM
DM
Handed in my costume...
Good luck, Dragman.
Thanks.
And drove home.
I put the boxes in the loft.
And felt...
Humiliated.
Ridiculous.
Ashamed.
I'm SICK.

Disgusting.

A pervert!

CLANG!

Soon after that
I met Mary Mary...

And fell in love.

I tried to forget all
about wearing
women's clothes,
except... I couldn't.

Ha ha ha!

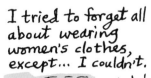

It's there. Always.
It doesn't go away.

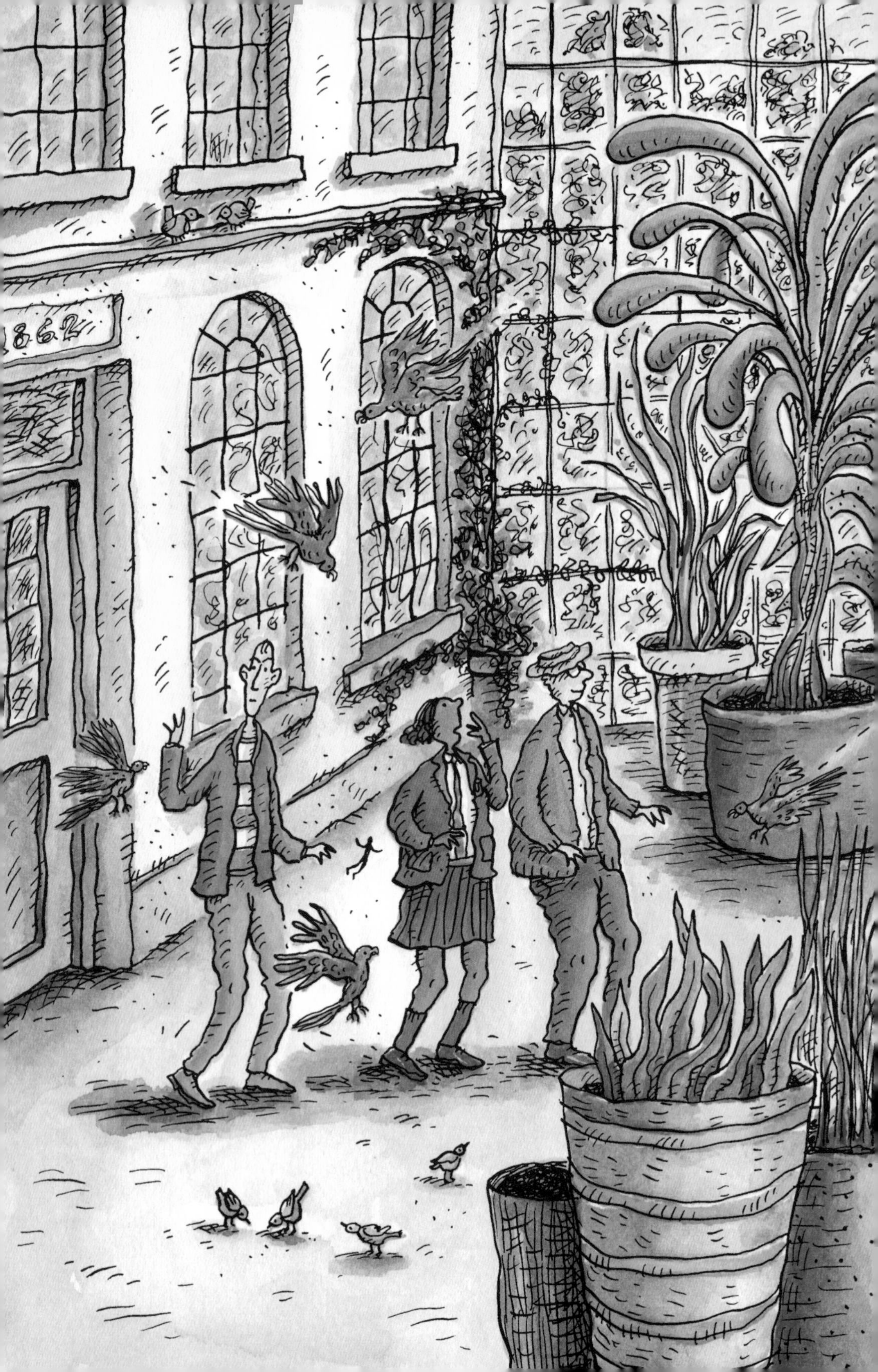

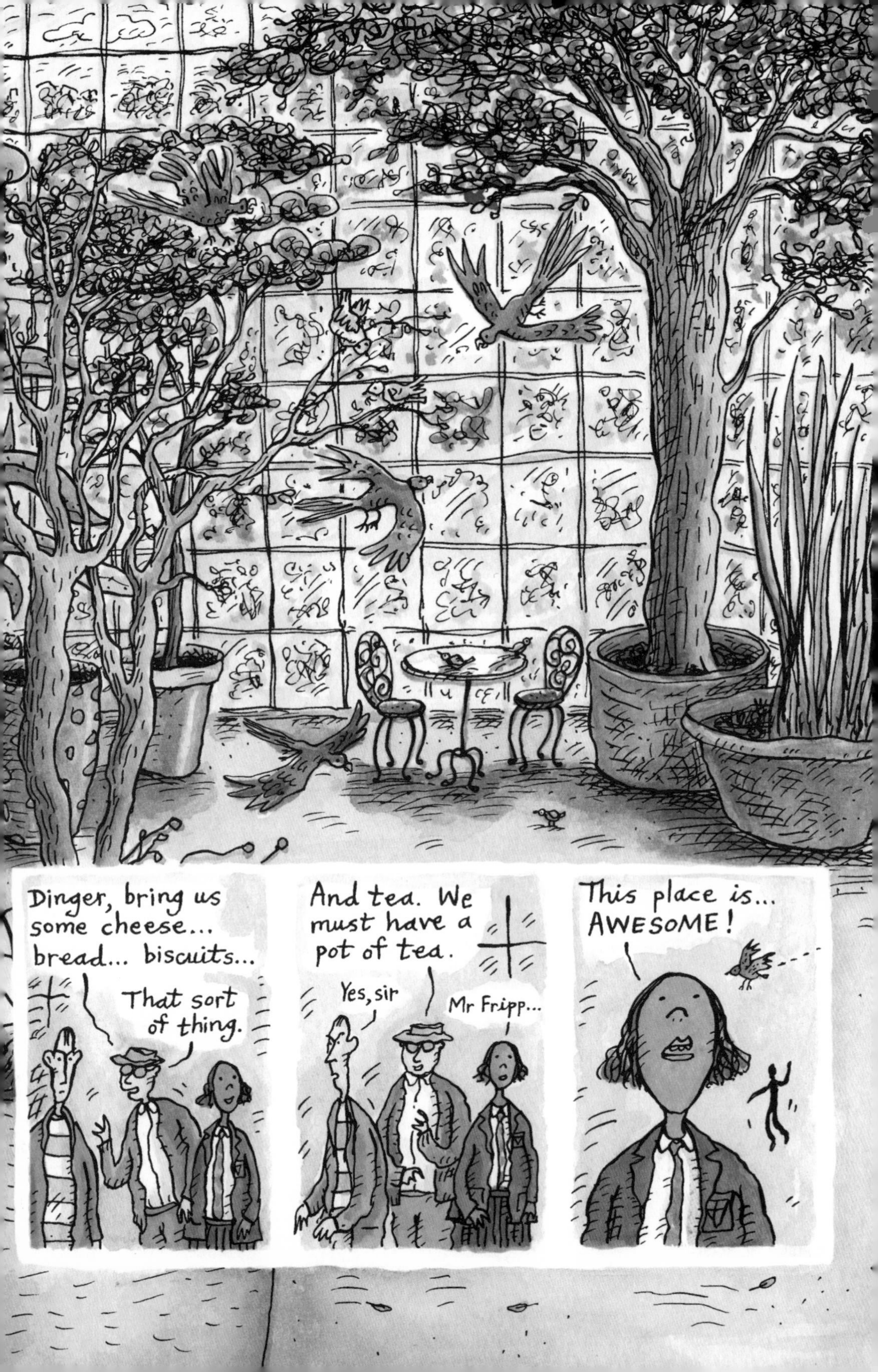
Dinger, bring us some cheese... bread... biscuits...
That sort of thing.
And tea. We must have a pot of tea.
Yes, sir
Mr Fripp...
This place is... AWESOME!

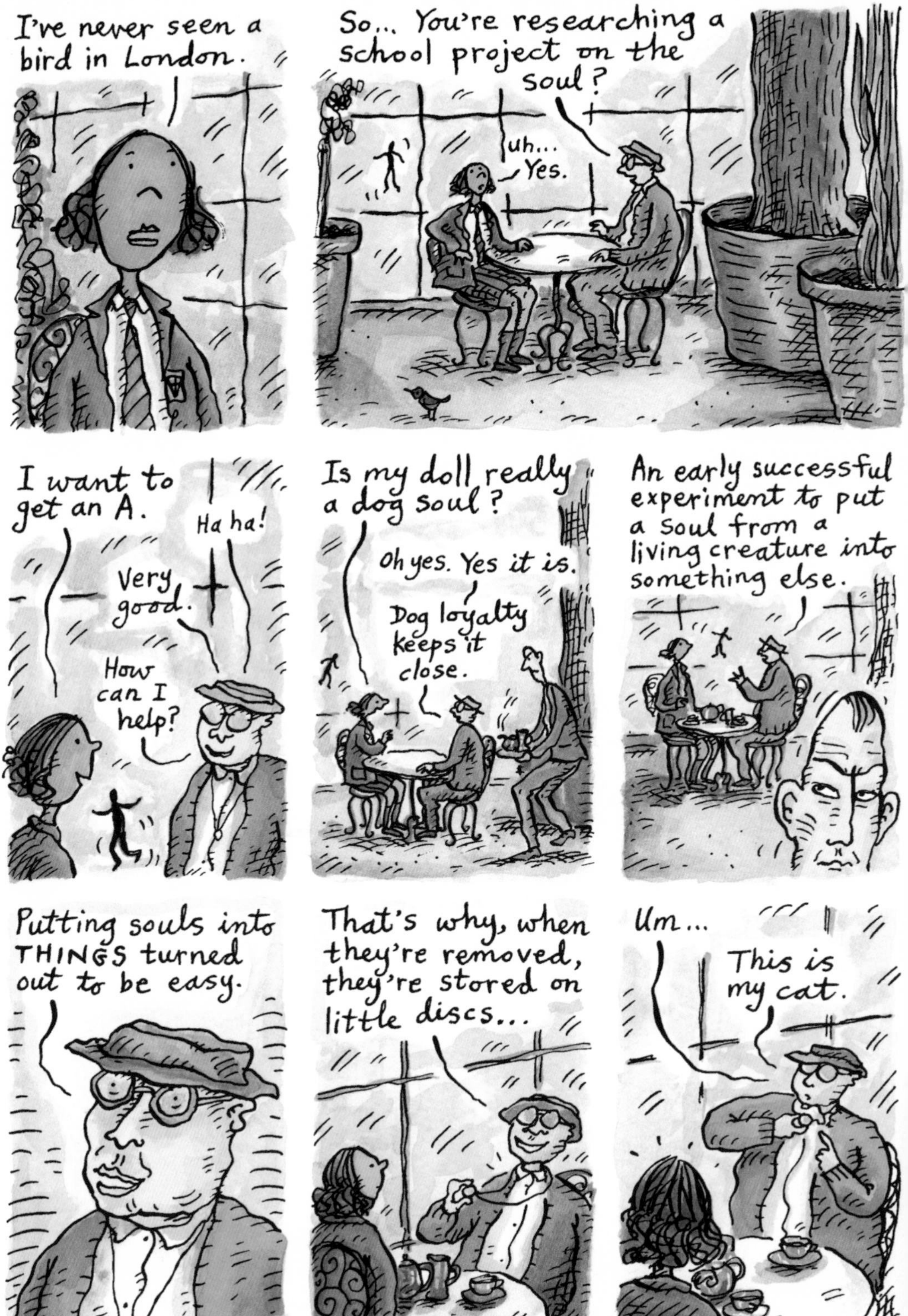
I've never seen a bird in London.
So... You're researching a school project on the soul?
uh... Yes.
I want to get an A.
Ha ha!
Very good.
How can I help?
Is my doll really a dog soul?
Oh yes. Yes it is.
Dog loyalty keeps it close.
An early successful experiment to put a soul from a living creature into something else.
Putting souls into THINGS turned out to be easy.
That's why, when they're removed, they're stored on little discs...
Um...
This is my cat.

I thought maybe human souls were set free.

Oh dear me, no!

Ha ha ha...

Where would be the profit in that?

Money comes into everything, my dear...

Life is a transaction.

So can a human soul be put back into a person?

Oh, yes.

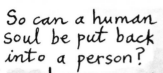

Rich people pay very well for a young, vital, virile soul.

Ha ha.

It's like an aphrodisiac.

Um... Or so they say.

There's also a big demand for creative and intellectual souls.

You have far better dreams.

And, of course, the existence of the soul implies that Heaven and Hell exist, too.

I'm talking scientifically. Quantum mechanics, parallel worlds, and so on and so forth.

Ha ha...

Fascinating stuff...

But I digress.

Clear the table, Dinger.

Yes sir.

That's all confidential information.

SIR.

Owned, patented, and trade marked by Black mist.

Oh, don't fuss, Dinger.

She's a schoolgirl! Where's the harm?

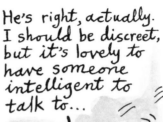

He's right, actually. I should be discreet, but it's lovely to have someone intelligent to talk to...

So ask away, my dear. What do you want to know?

Ha ha

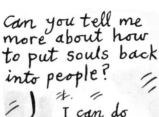

Can you tell me more about how to put souls back into people?

I can do better than that...

I'll show you.

Follow me, Ms Mingle...

I'm going to give you a tour of my laboratory.

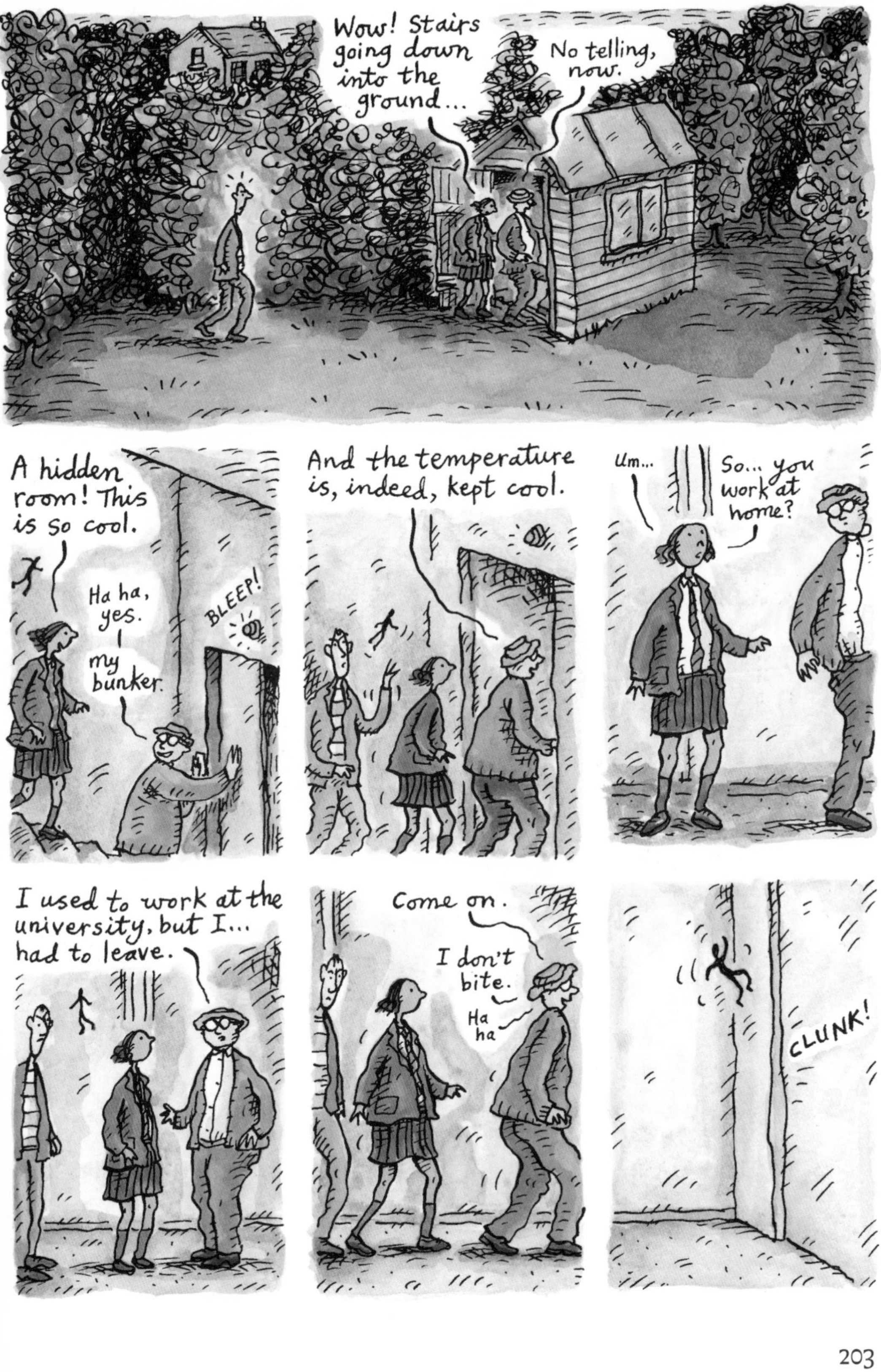
Wow! Stairs going down into the ground...
No telling, now.
A hidden room! This is so cool.
Ha ha, yes.
my bunker.
BLEEP!
And the temperature is, indeed, kept cool.
Um...
So... you work at home?
I used to work at the university, but I... had to leave.
Come on.
I don't bite.
Ha ha
CLUNK!

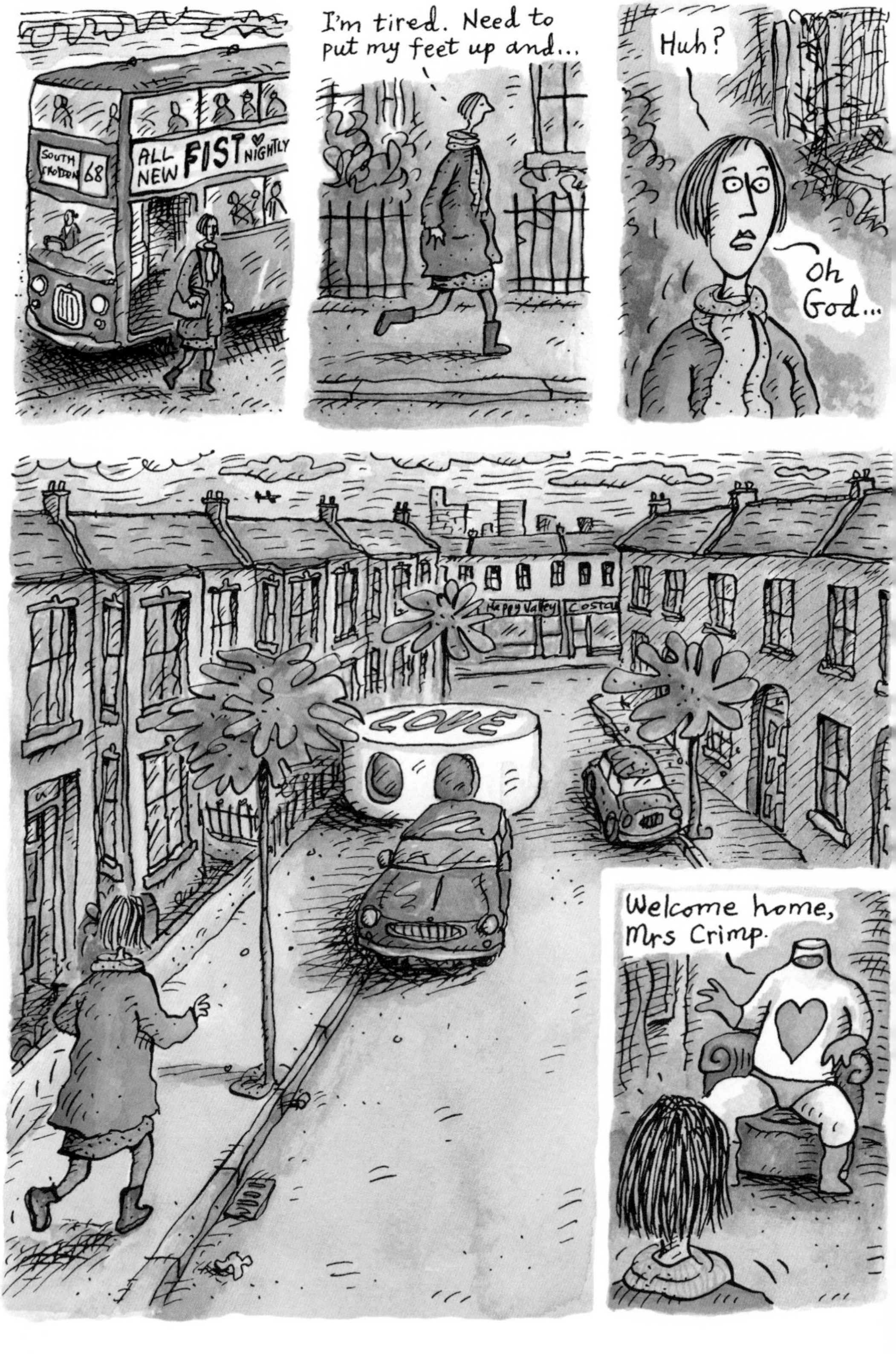
SOUTH CRODDON 68
ALL NEW FIST NIGHTLY
I'm tired. Need to put my feet up and...
Huh?
Oh God...
Happy Valley
Costcu
LOVE
Welcome home, Mrs Crimp.

What's happened? Where's Gulliver? And August?!

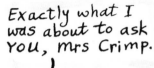

Exactly what I was about to ask YOU, mrs Crimp.

I've no idea.

The Actress and I are here to deliver a speeding ticket.

So we'll wait.

Where... are the cameras?

No cameras, mrs Crimp.

We're certainly not going to film THIS for the show.

Eh, Actress?

Ha ha ha ha...

Now, why don't you take off your coat, mrs Crimp, and make a pot of tea.

Then we'll all sit down and wait for, um... August. And wee Gulliver.

SNAP!

OK?

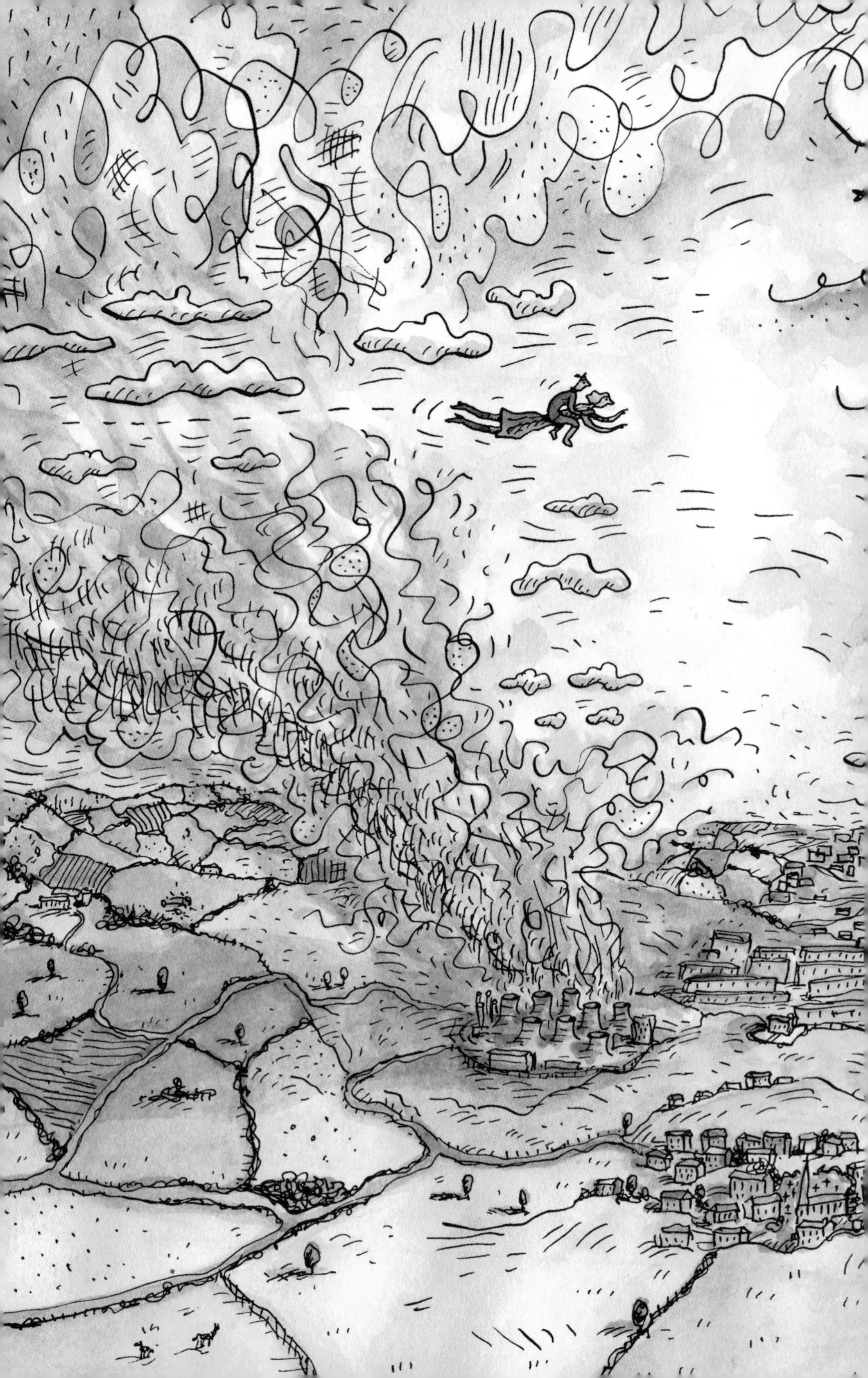

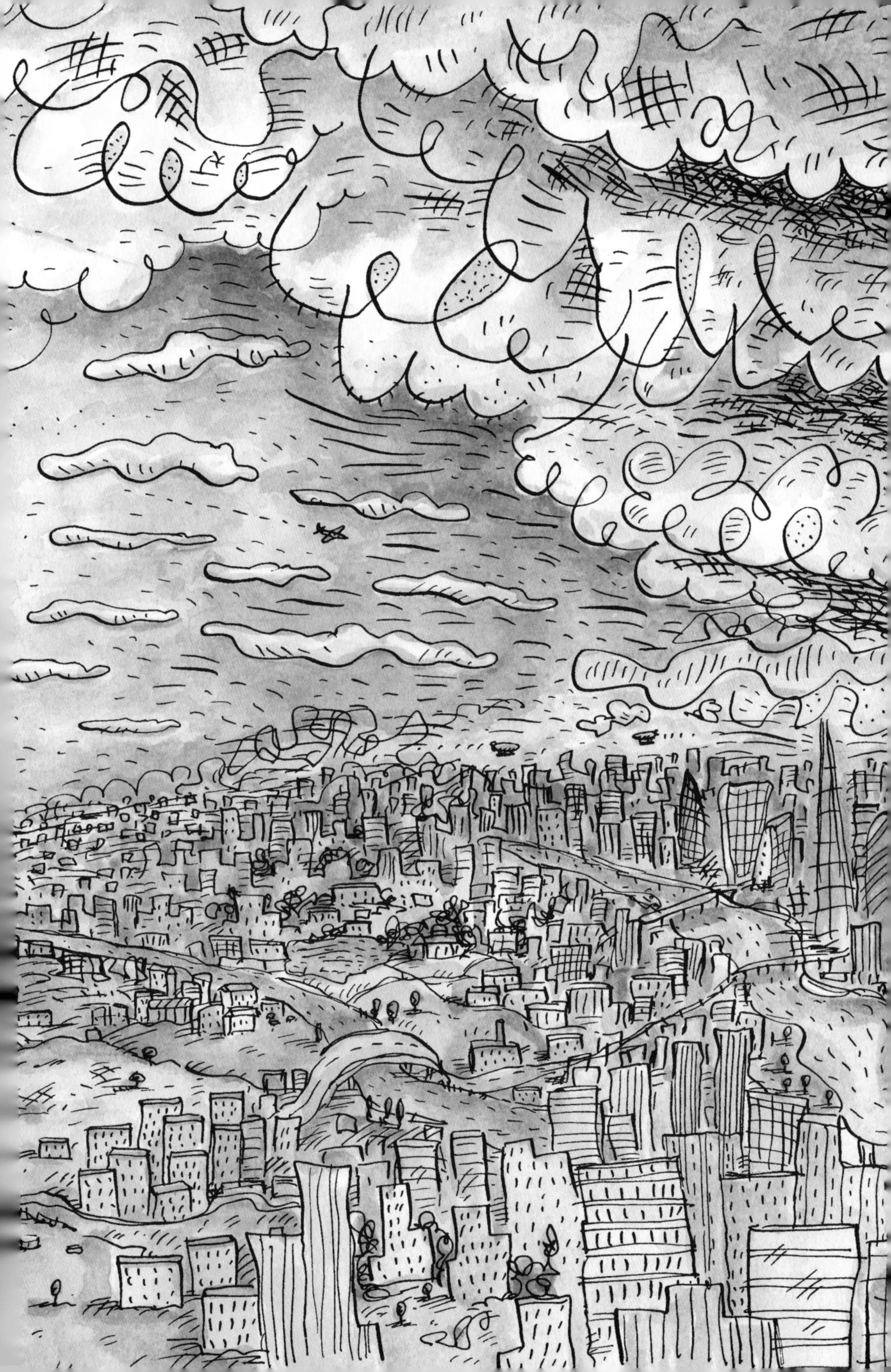

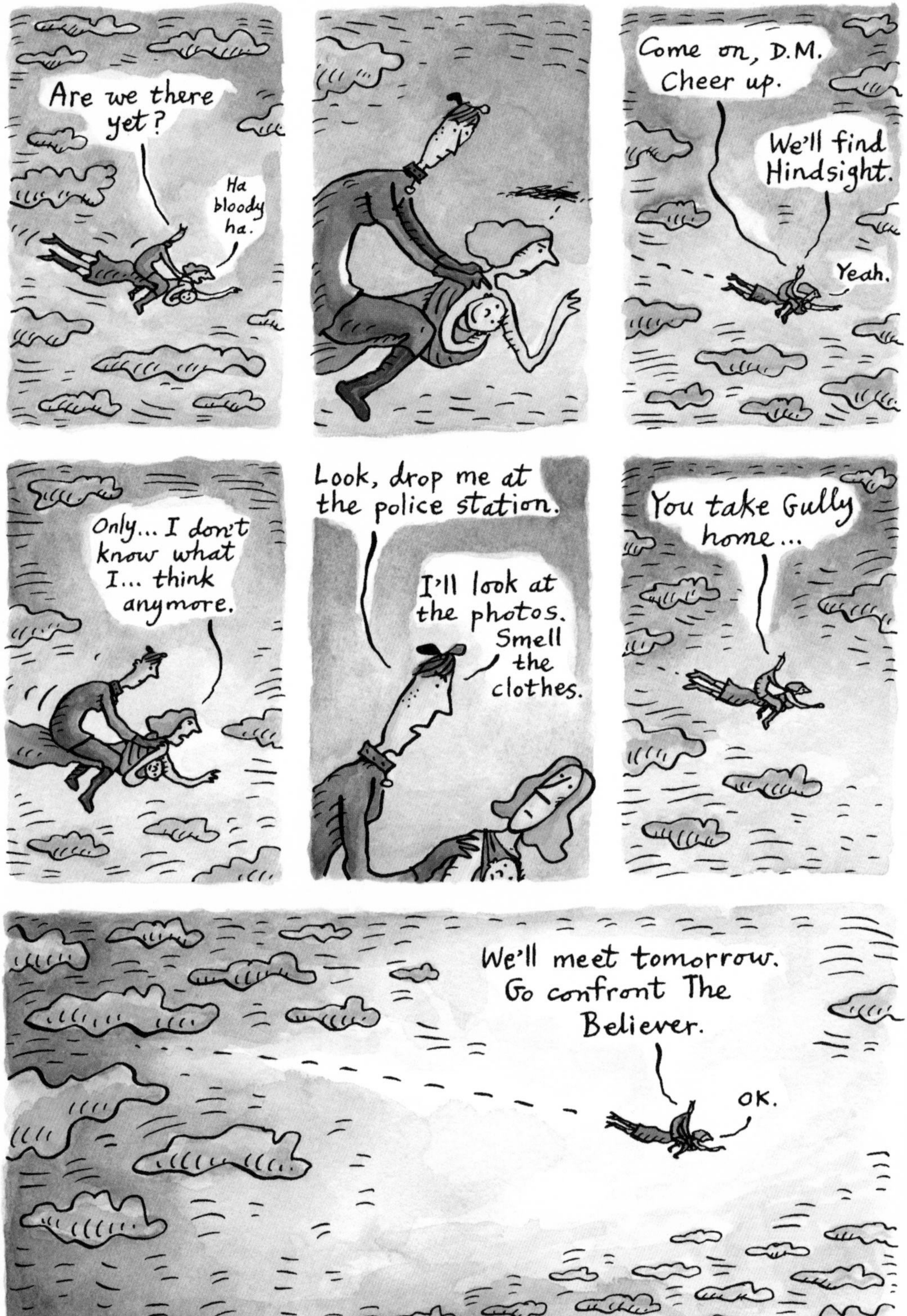
Are we there yet?
Ha bloody ha.
Come on, D.M. Cheer up.
We'll find Hindsight.
Yeah.
Only... I don't know what I... think anymore.
Look, drop me at the police station.
I'll look at the photos.
Smell the clothes.
You take Gully home...
We'll meet tomorrow. Go confront The Believer.
OK.

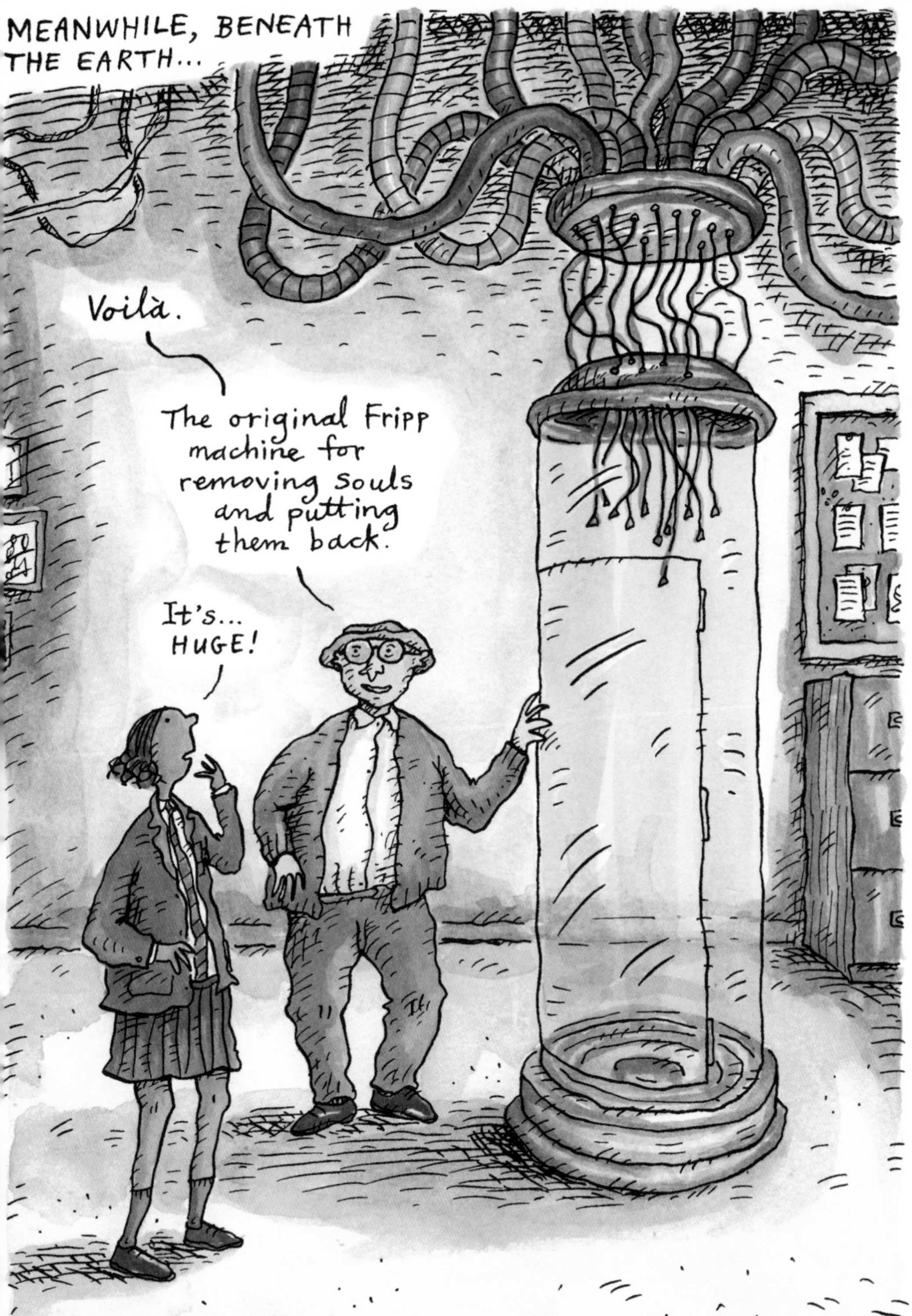
MEANWHILE, BENEATH THE EARTH...
Voilà.
The original Fripp machine for removing souls and putting them back.
It's... HUGE!

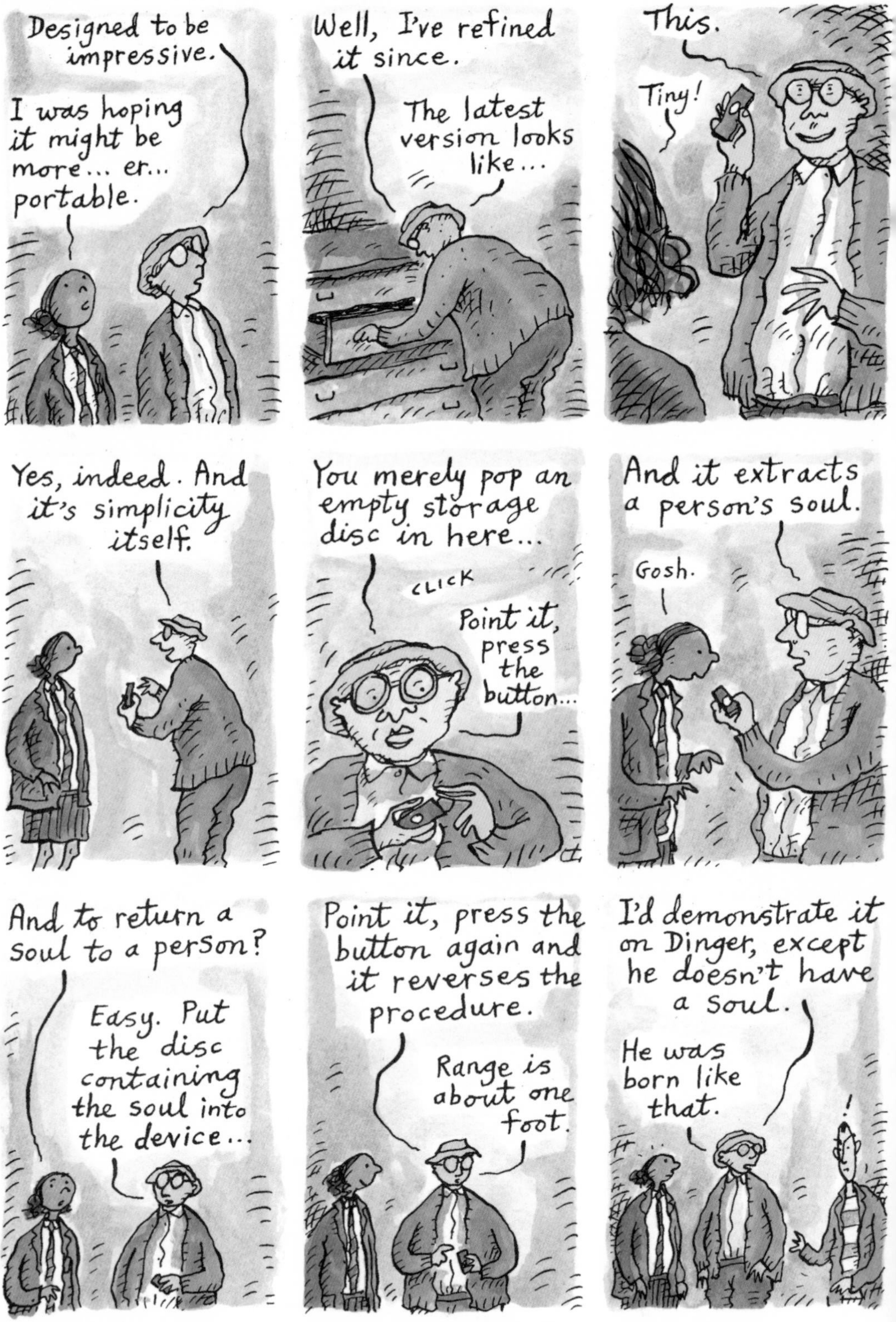
Designed to be impressive.
I was hoping it might be more... er... portable.
Well, I've refined it since.
The latest version looks like...
This.
Tiny!
Yes, indeed. And it's simplicity itself.
You merely pop an empty storage disc in here...
CLICK
Point it, press the button...
And it extracts a person's soul.
Gosh.
And to return a soul to a person?
Easy. Put the disc containing the soul into the device...
Point it, press the button again and it reverses the procedure.
Range is about one foot.
I'd demonstrate it on Dinger, except he doesn't have a soul.
He was born like that.
!

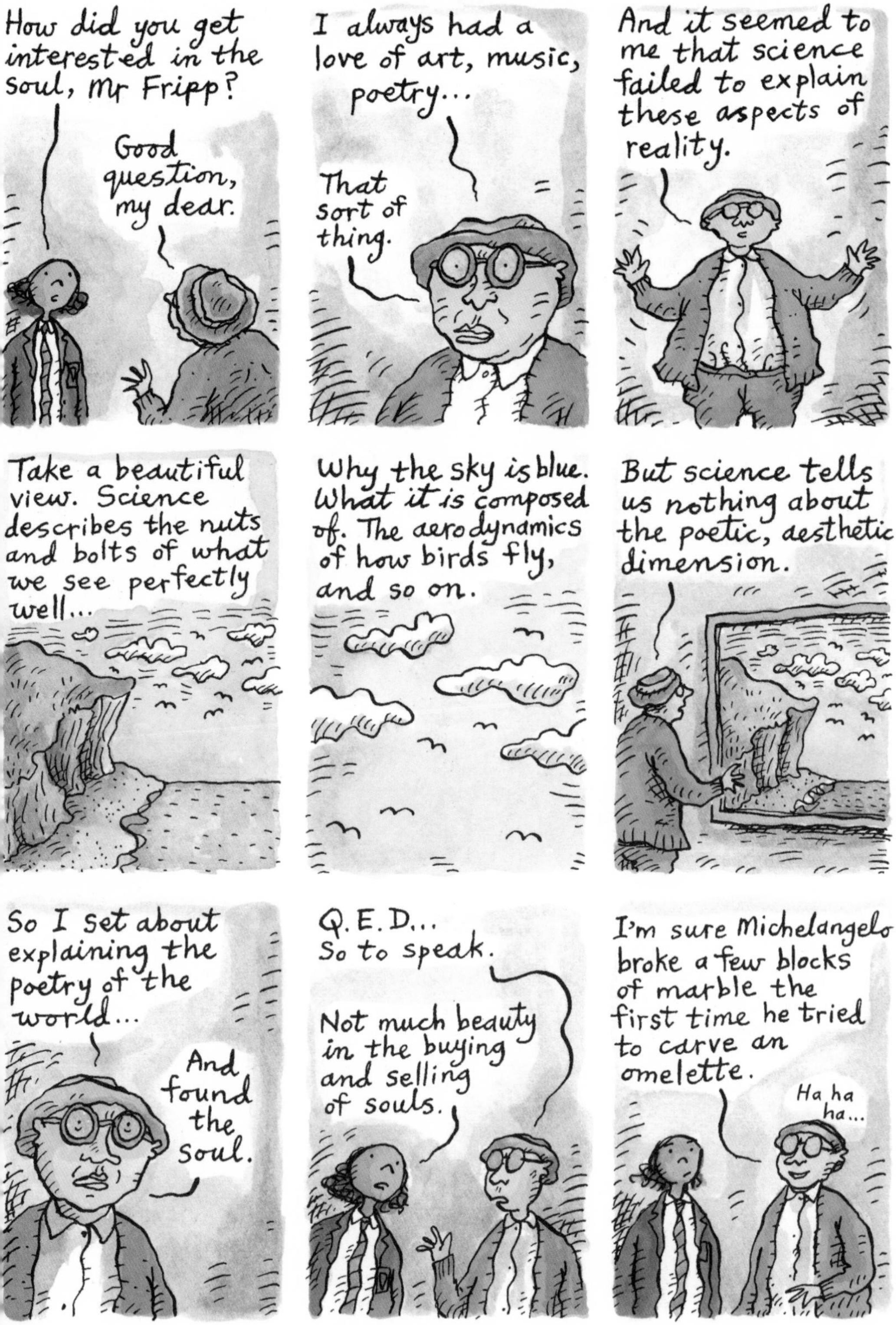
How did you get interested in the soul, Mr Fripp?
Good question, my dear.
I always had a love of art, music, poetry...
That sort of thing.
And it seemed to me that science failed to explain these aspects of reality.
Take a beautiful view. Science describes the nuts and bolts of what we see perfectly well...
Why the sky is blue. What it is composed of. The aerodynamics of how birds fly, and so on.
But science tells us nothing about the poetic, aesthetic dimension.
So I set about explaining the poetry of the world...
And found the soul.
Q.E.D... So to speak.
Not much beauty in the buying and selling of souls.
I'm sure Michelangelo broke a few blocks of marble the first time he tried to carve an omelette.
Ha ha ha...

Hey, Mr Fripp...

NOBEL PRIZE award to S. FRIPP

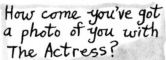

How come you've got a photo of you with The Actress?

What? Oh, no. That's a photo of my team back at the university.

That woman is The Actress.

who?

NOBEL PRIZE awarded to...

She's a superhero. Rubbish. That's Jenny. One of my students.

Lovely girl.

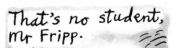

That's no student, Mr Fripp.

I see The Actress every day on The Fist's TV show.

That's The Actress alright.

For sure.

Then... Then...

She must have been protecting me, or something.

Spying, more like.

That's... crazy.

Why? You're funded by Black Mist. Well, so is The Fist's show.

And The Actress can play any role... Sidekick. Scientist. Student. Seductress...

Seductress?!

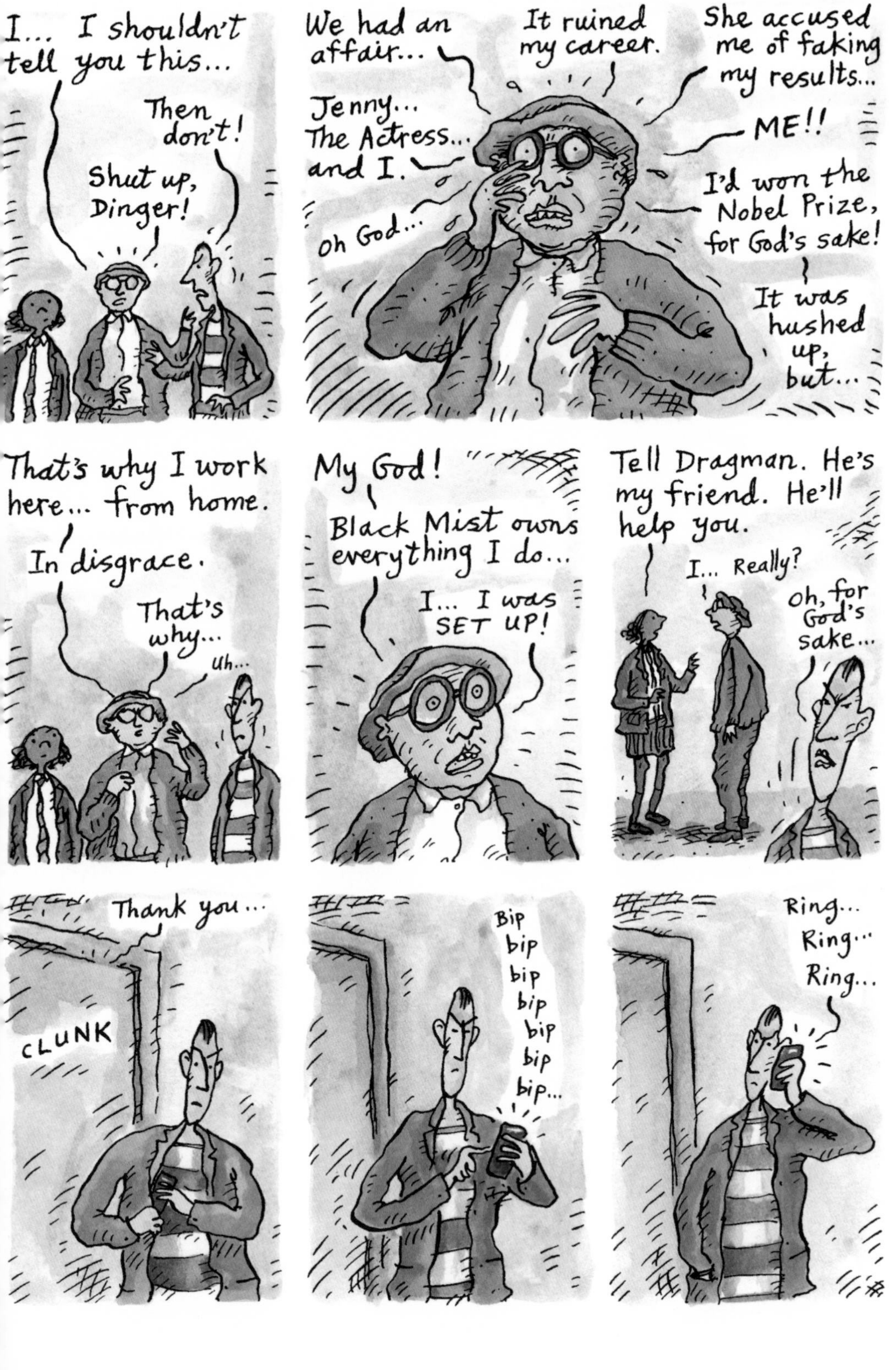
I... I shouldn't tell you this...
Then don't!
Shut up, Dinger!
We had an affair...
Jenny... The Actress... and I.
Oh God...
It ruined my career.
She accused me of faking my results...
ME!!
I'd won the Nobel Prize, for God's sake!
It was hushed up, but...
That's why I work here... from home.
In disgrace.
That's why...
Uh...
My God!
Black Mist owns everything I do...
I... I was SET UP!
Tell Dragman. He's my friend. He'll help you.
I... Really?
Oh, for God's sake...
Thank you...
CLUNK
Bip bip bip bip bip bip bip...
Ring... Ring... Ring...

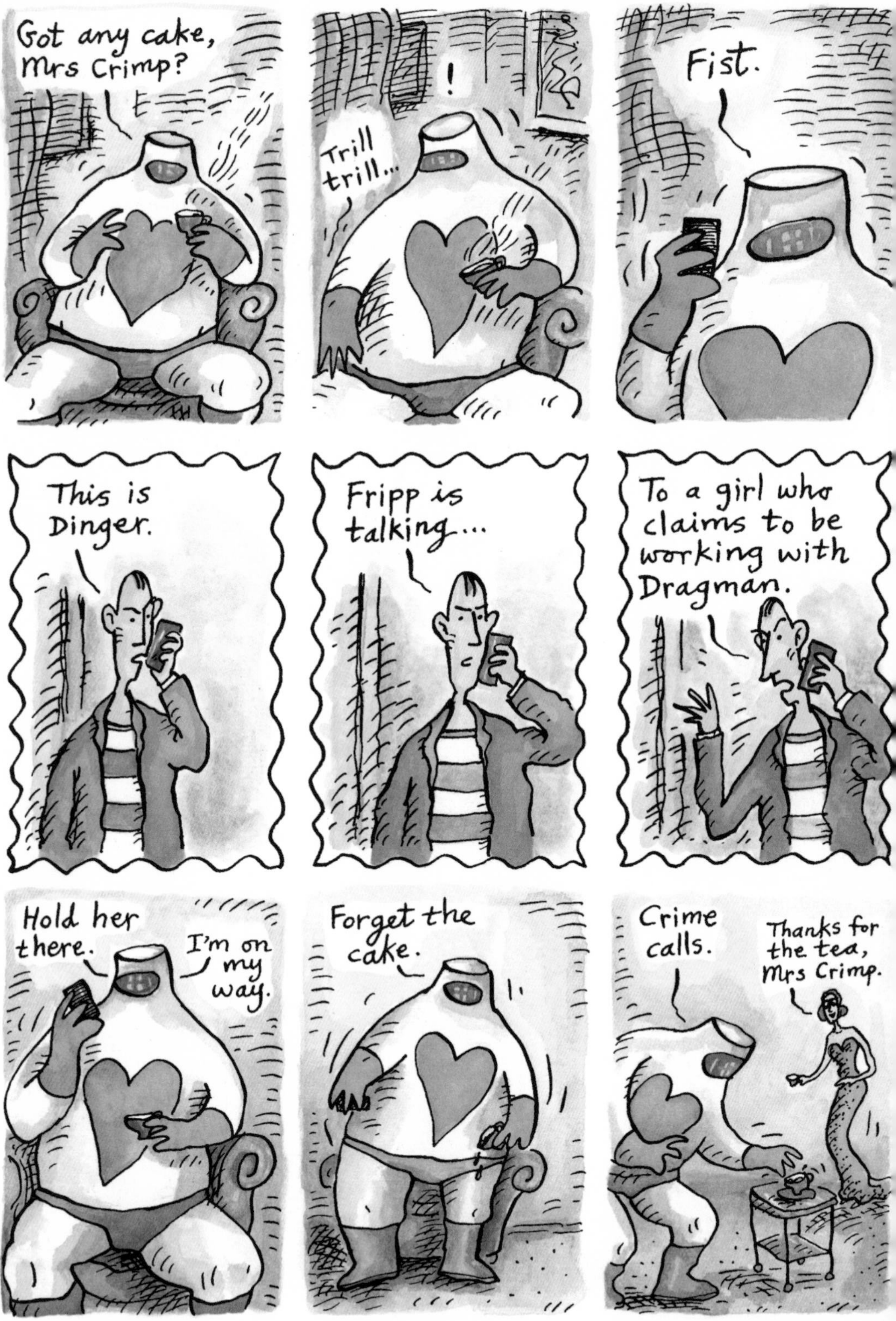
Got any cake, Mrs Crimp?
!
Trill trill...
Fist.
This is Dinger.
Fripp is talking...
To a girl who claims to be working with Dragman.
Hold her there.
I'm on my way.
Forget the cake.
Crime calls.
Thanks for the tea, Mrs Crimp.

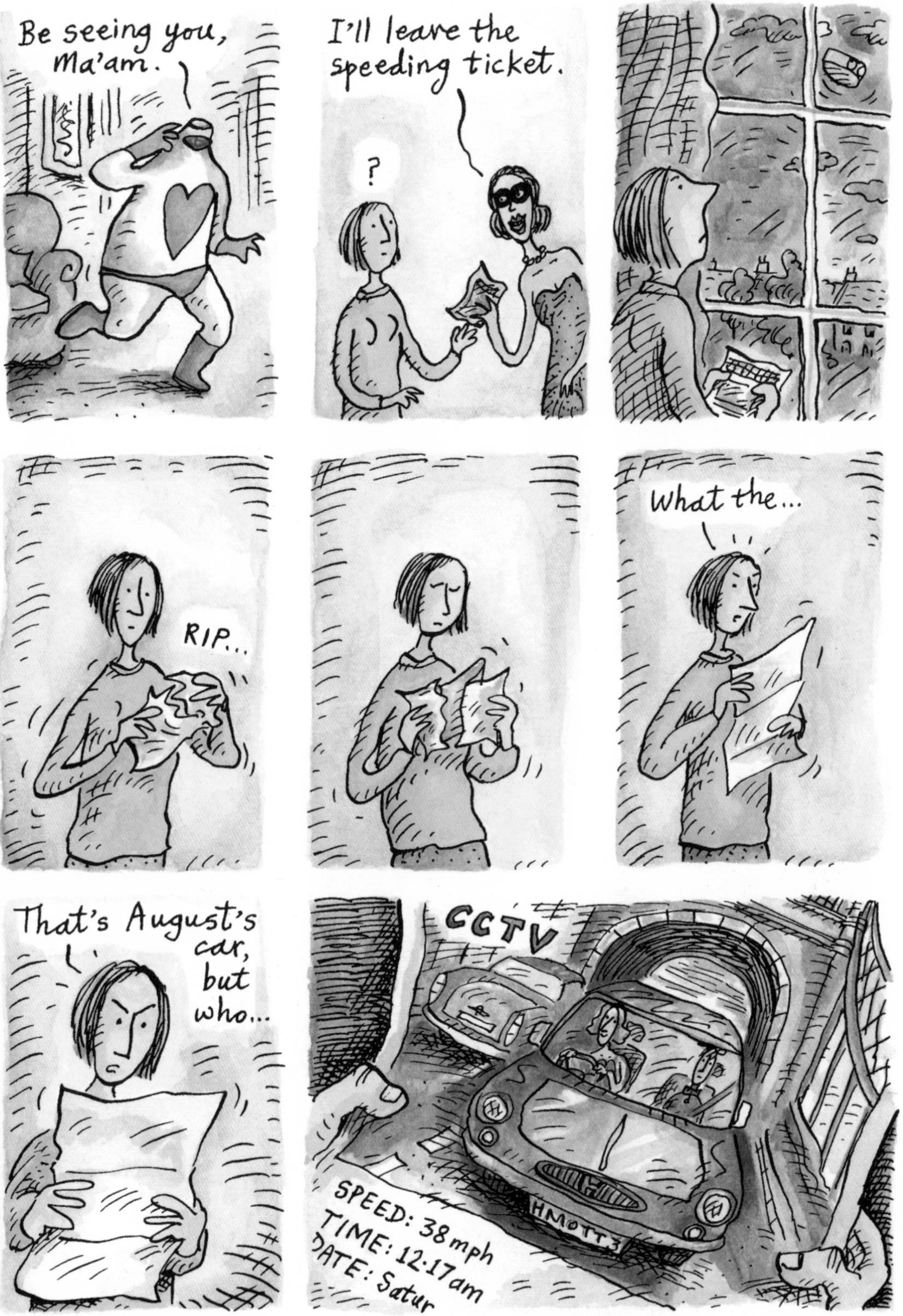
Be seeing you, Ma'am.
I'll leave the speeding ticket.
?
RIP...
What the...
That's August's car, but who...
CCTV
SPEED: 38 mph
TIME: 12:17 am
DATE: Satur
HMOTT3

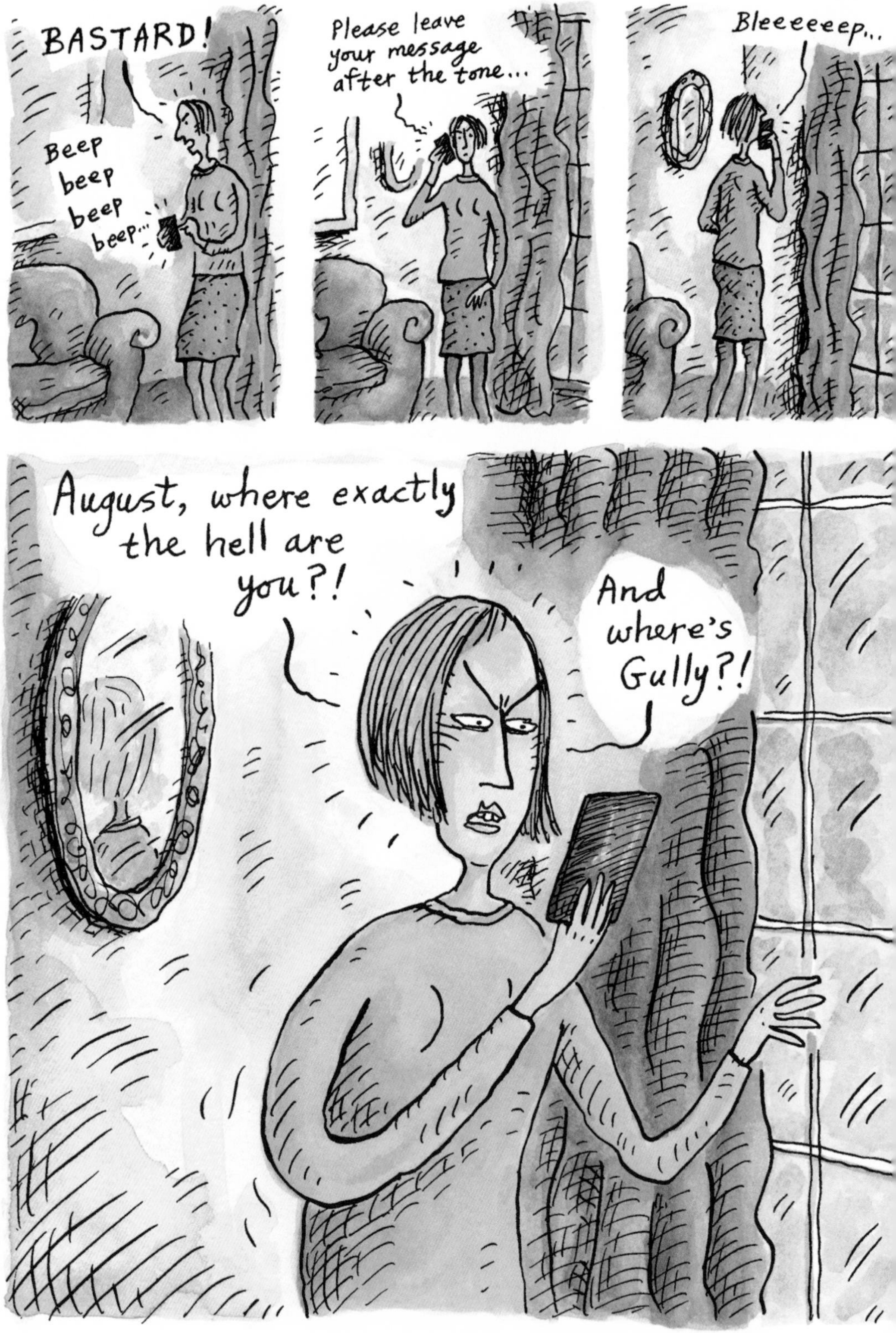
BASTARD!
Beep beep beep beep...
Please leave your message after the tone...
Bleeeeeeep...
August, where exactly the hell are you?!
And where's Gully?!

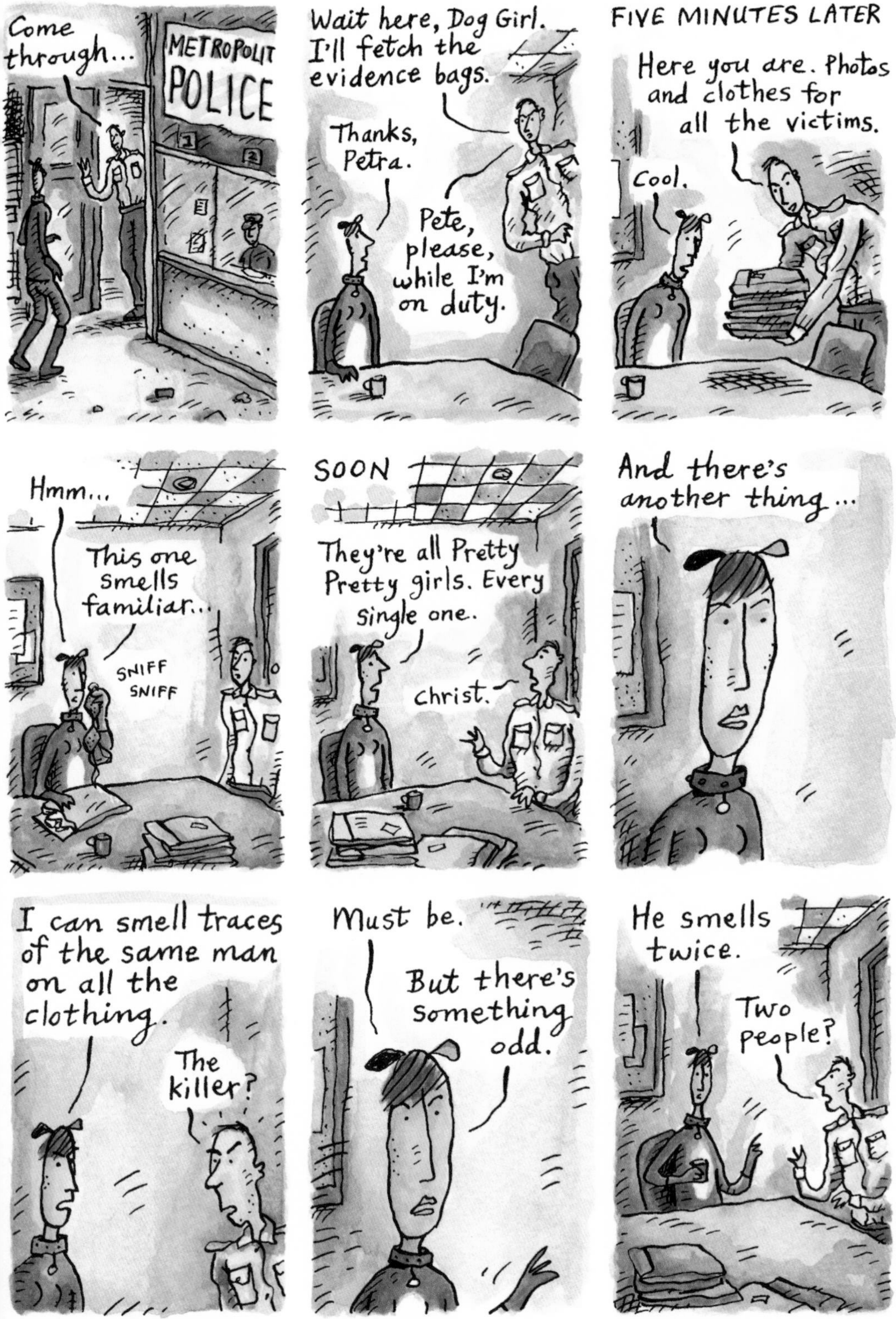
Come through...
METROPOLIT
POLICE
Wait here, Dog Girl. I'll fetch the evidence bags.
Thanks, Petra.
Pete, please, while I'm on duty.
FIVE MINUTES LATER
Here you are. Photos and clothes for all the victims.
Cool.
Hmm...
This one smells familiar...
SNIFF
SNIFF
SOON
They're all Pretty Pretty girls. Every single one.
Christ.
And there's another thing...
I can smell traces of the same man on all the clothing.
The killer?
Must be.
But there's something odd.
He smells twice.
Two people?

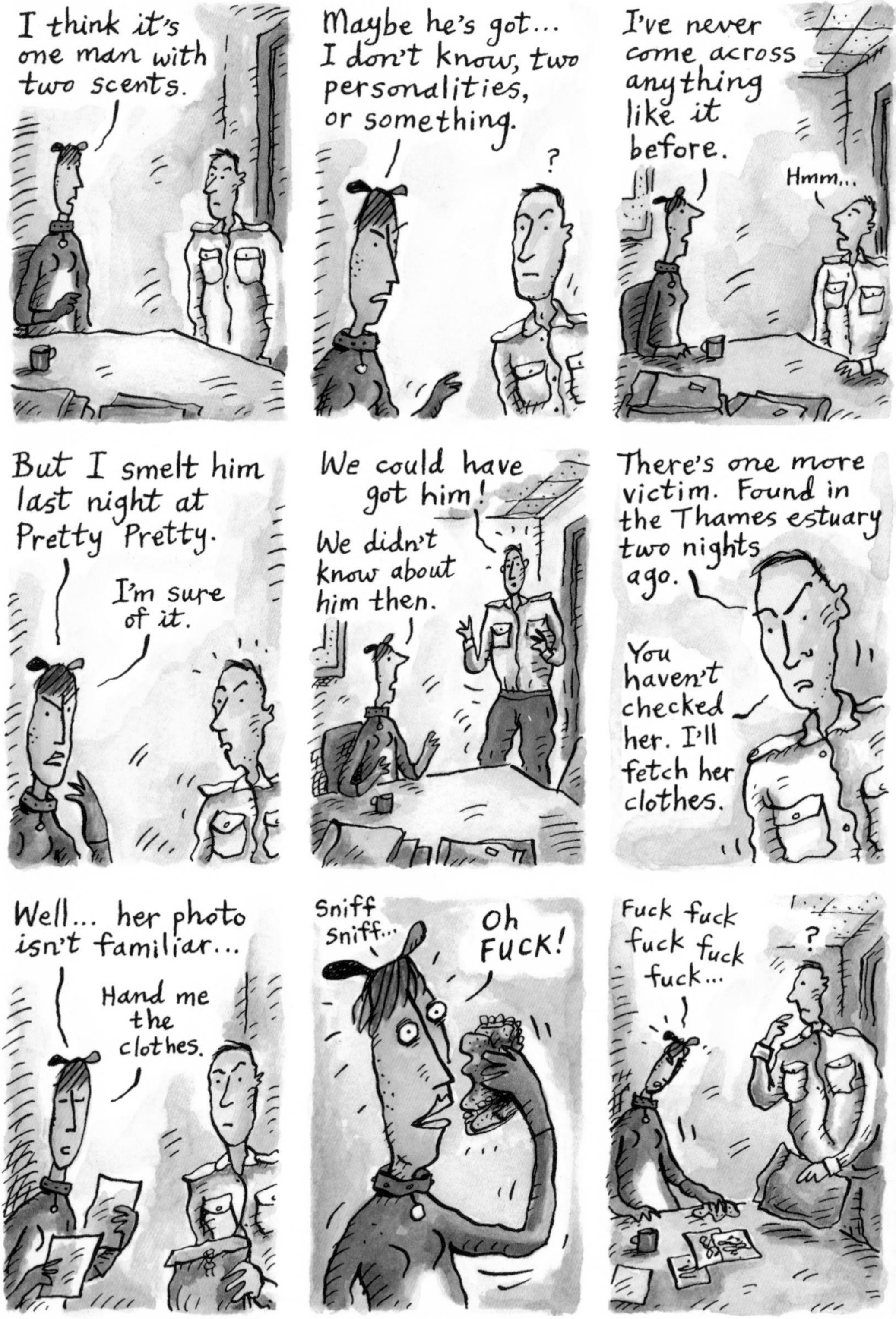
I think it's one man with two scents.
Maybe he's got... I don't know, two personalities, or something.
?
I've never come across anything like it before.
Hmm...
But I smelt him last night at Pretty Pretty.
I'm sure of it.
We could have got him!
We didn't know about him then.
There's one more victim. Found in the Thames estuary two nights ago.
You haven't checked her. I'll fetch her clothes.
Well... her photo isn't familiar...
Hand me the clothes.
Sniff sniff...
Oh FUCK!
Fuck fuck fuck fuck fuck...
?

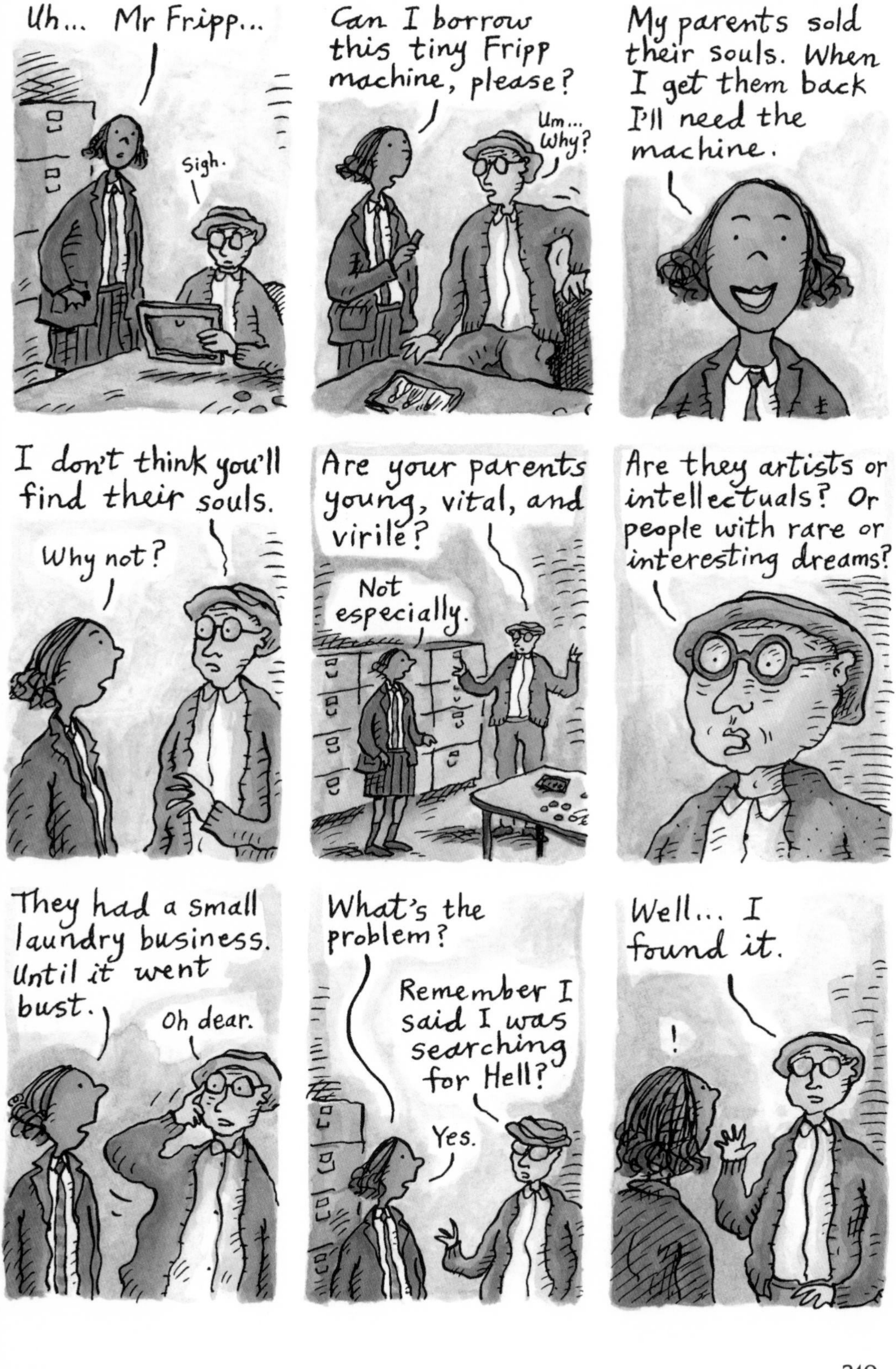
Uh... Mr Fripp...
Sigh.
Can I borrow this tiny Fripp machine, please?
Um... Why?
My parents sold their souls. When I get them back I'll need the machine.
I don't think you'll find their souls.
Why not?
Are your parents young, vital, and virile?
Not especially.
Are they artists or intellectuals? Or people with rare or interesting dreams?
They had a small laundry business. Until it went bust.
Oh dear.
What's the problem?
Remember I said I was searching for Hell?
Yes.
Well... I found it.
!

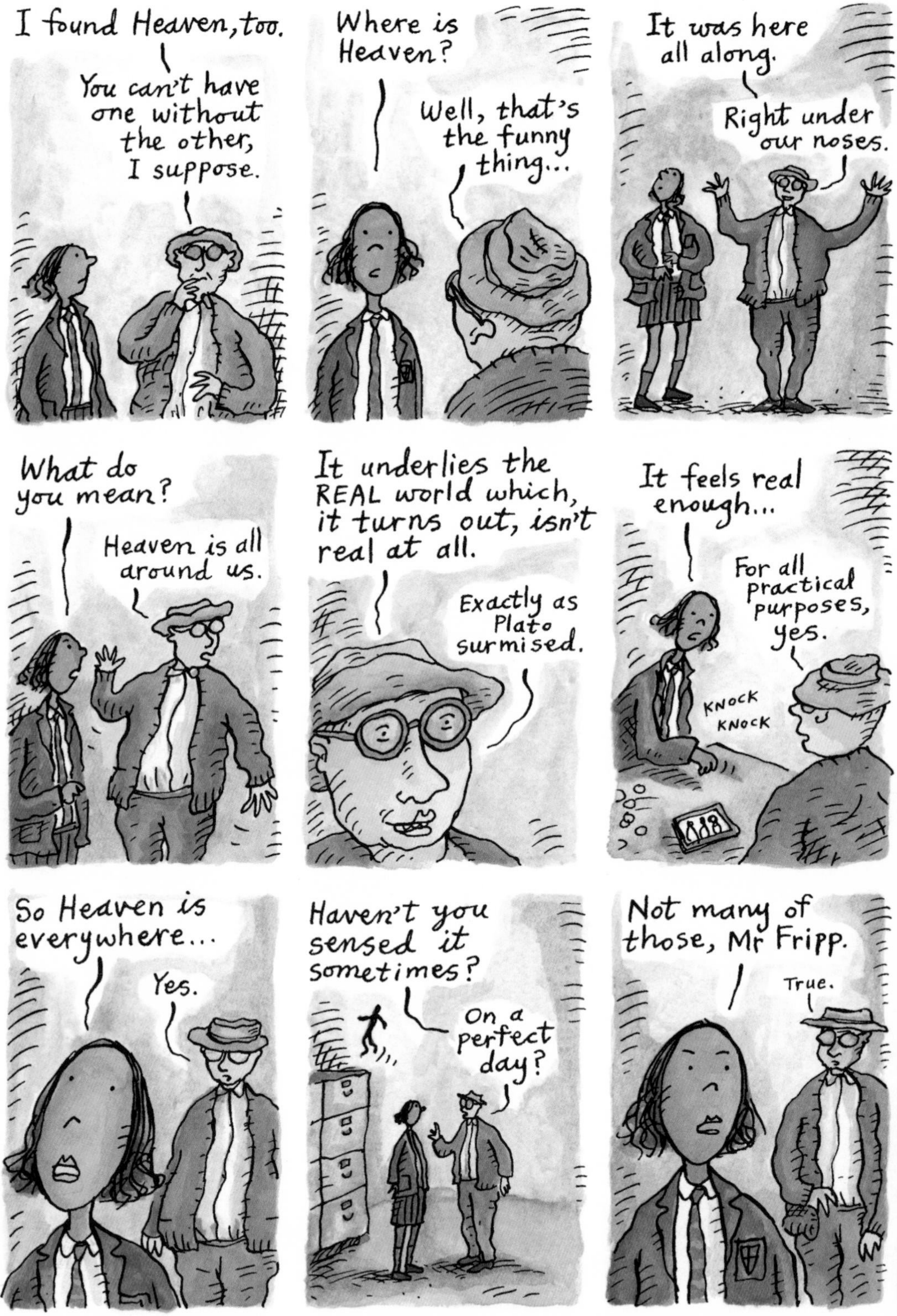

I found Heaven, too.
You can't have one without the other, I suppose.
Where is Heaven?
Well, that's the funny thing...
It was here all along.
Right under our noses.
What do you mean?
Heaven is all around us.
It underlies the REAL world which, it turns out, isn't real at all.
Exactly as Plato surmised.
It feels real enough...
For all practical purposes, yes.
KNOCK
KNOCK
So Heaven is everywhere...
Yes.
Haven't you sensed it sometimes?
On a perfect day?
Not many of those, Mr Fripp.
True.

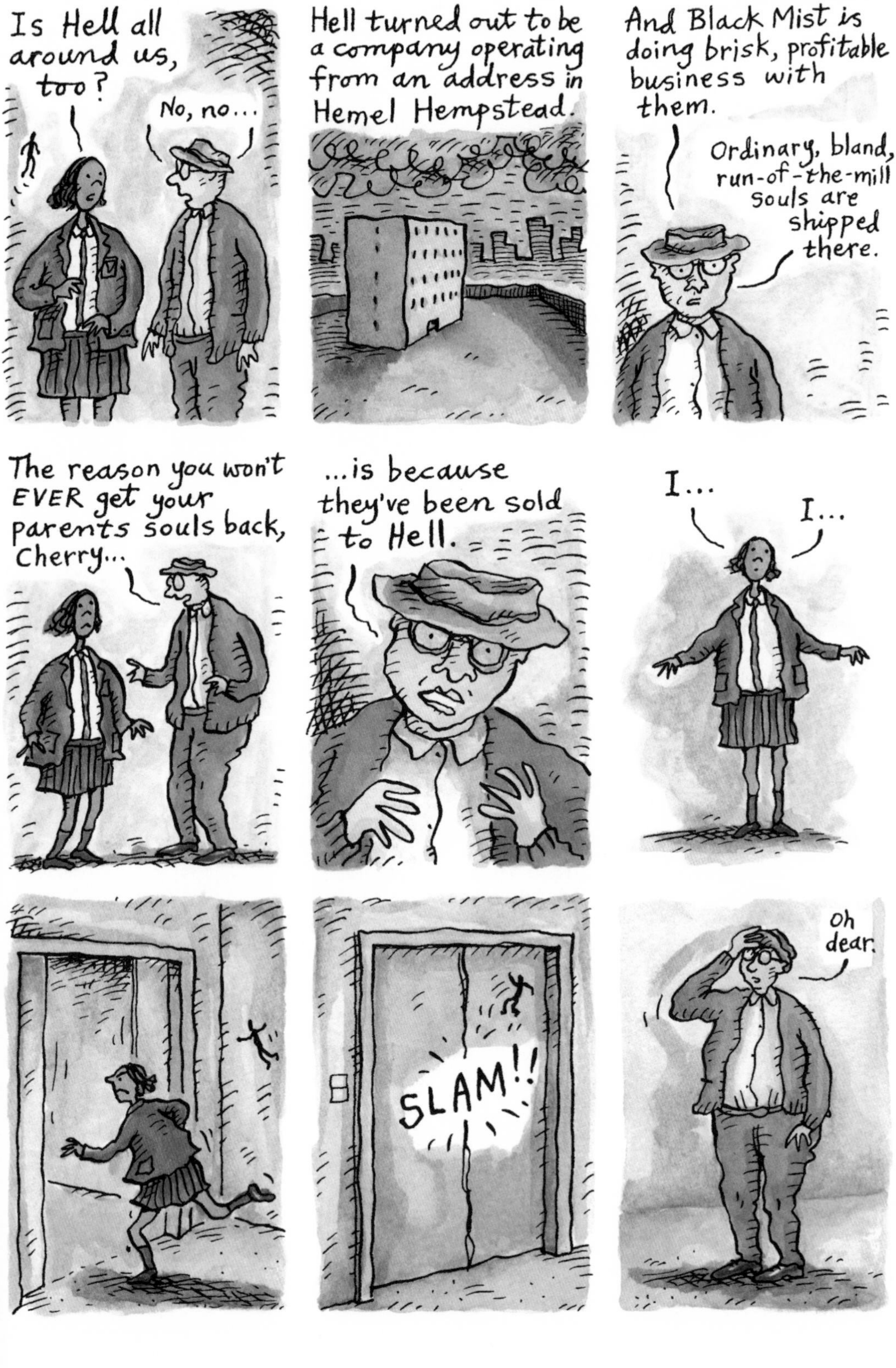
Is Hell all around us, too?
No, no...
Hell turned out to be a company operating from an address in Hemel Hempstead.
And Black Mist is doing brisk, profitable business with them.
Ordinary, bland, run-of-the-mill souls are shipped there.
The reason you won't EVER get your parents souls back, Cherry...
...is because they've been sold to Hell.
I...
I...
SLAM!!
Oh dear.

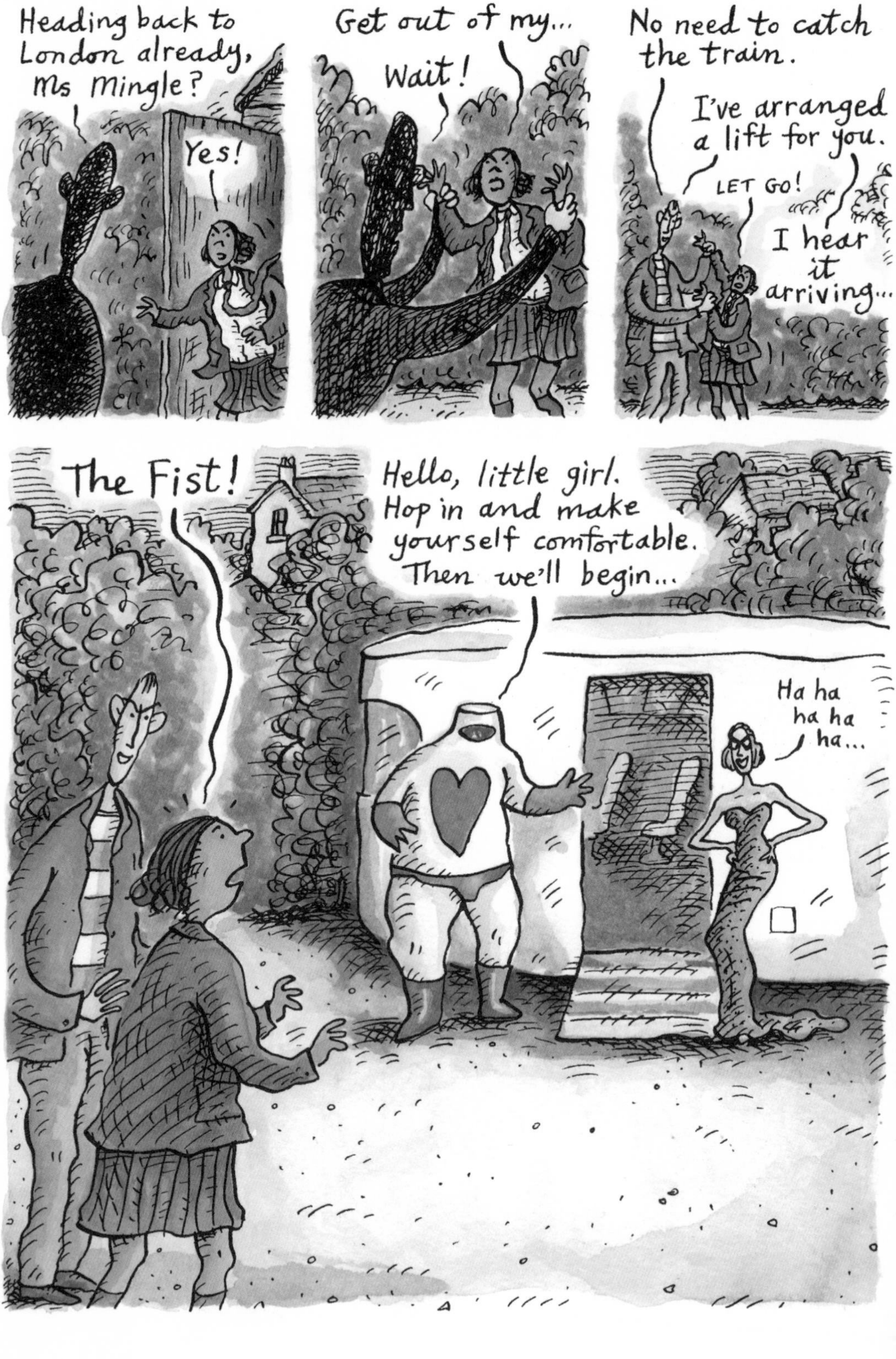
Heading back to London already, Ms Mingle?
Yes!
Get out of my...
Wait!
No need to catch the train.
I've arranged a lift for you.
LET GO!
I hear it arriving...
The Fist!
Hello, little girl. Hop in and make yourself comfortable. Then we'll begin...
Ha ha ha ha ha...

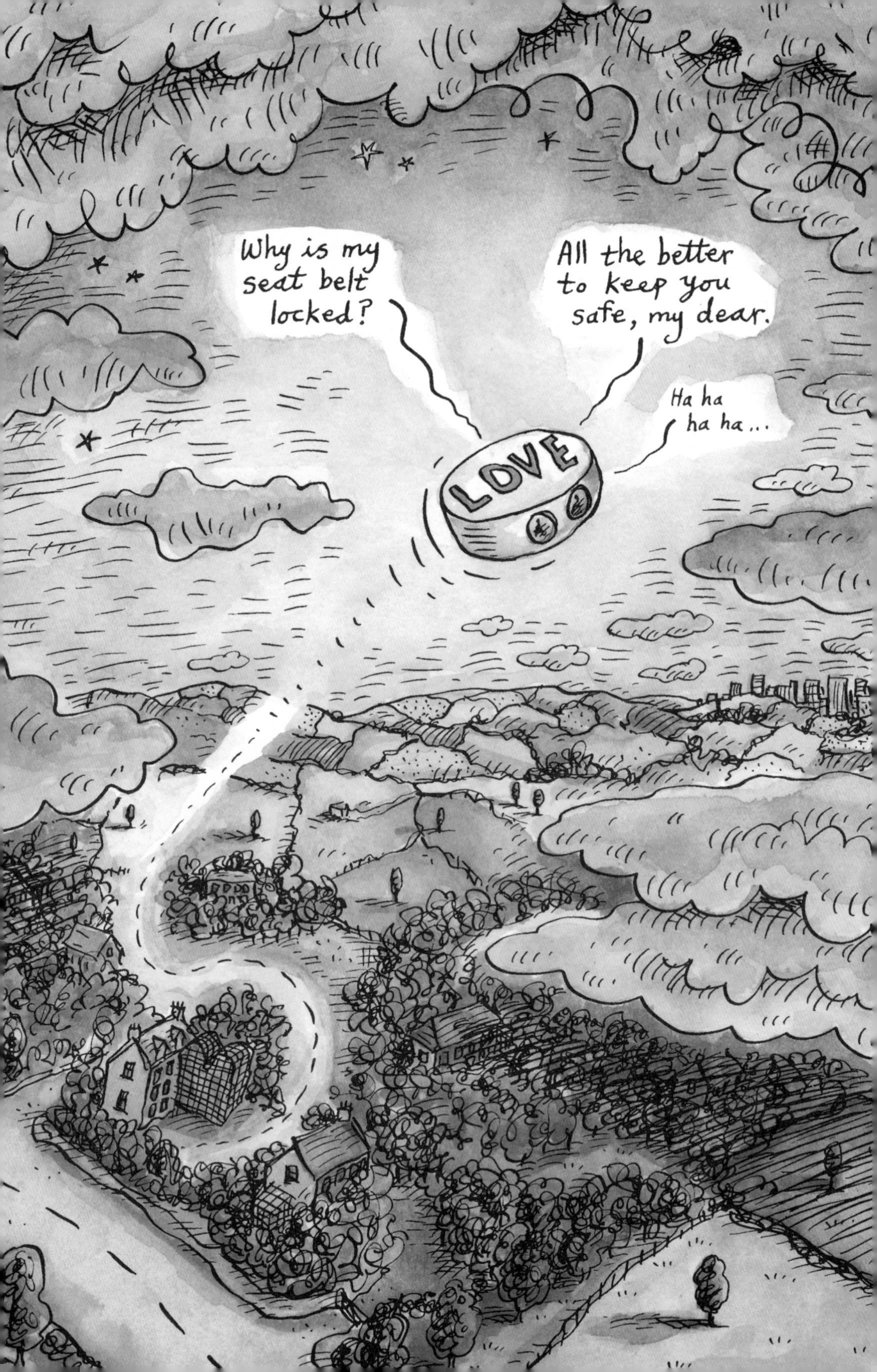
Why is my seat belt locked?
All the better to keep you safe, my dear.
Ha ha ha ha...
LOVE

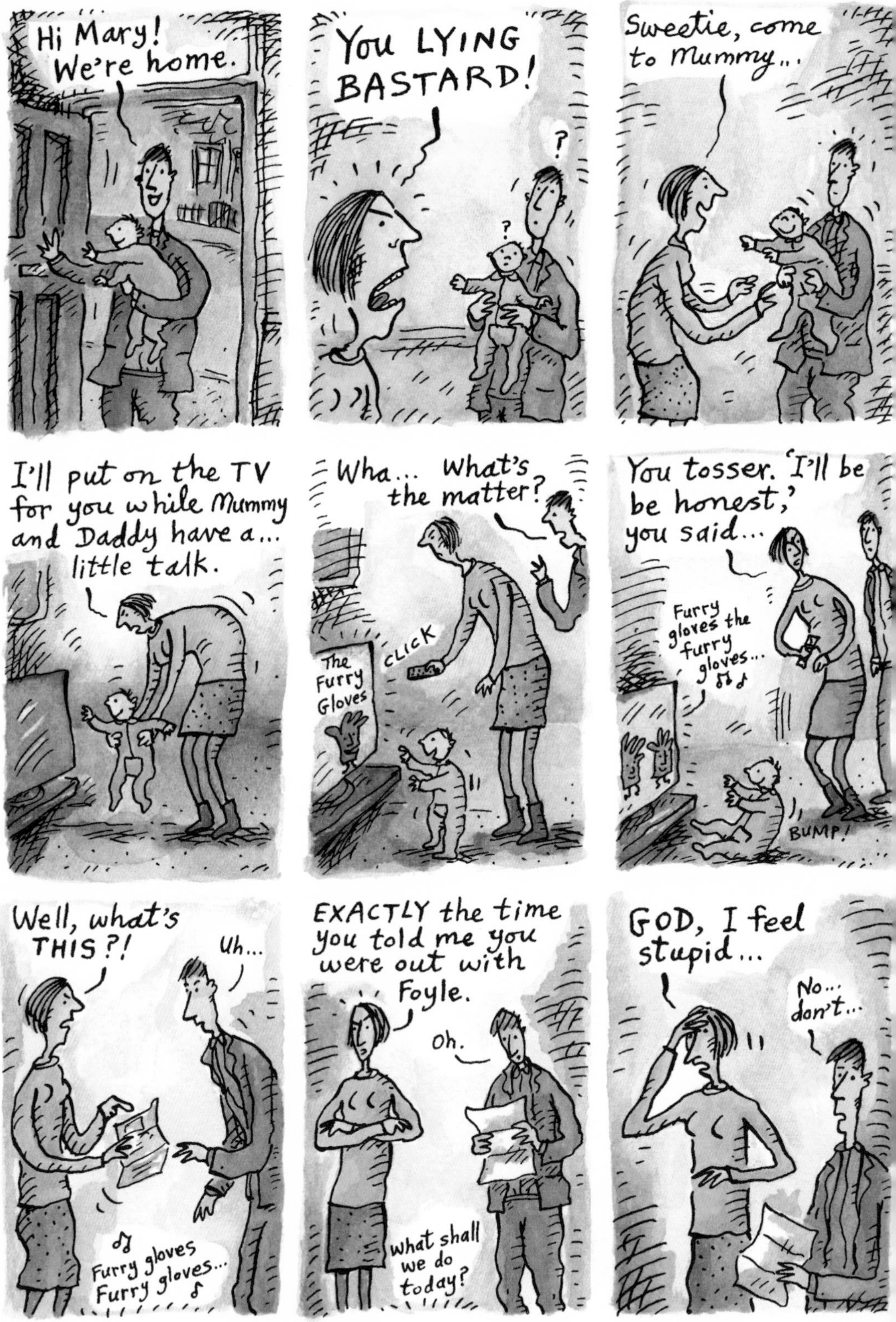

Hi Mary! We're home.
You LYING BASTARD!
?
?
Sweetie, come to Mummy...
I'll put on the TV for you while Mummy and Daddy have a... little talk.
Wha... What's the matter?
The Furry Gloves
CLICK
You tosser. 'I'll be be honest,' you said...
Furry gloves the furry gloves...
BUMP!
Well, what's THIS?!
Uh...
Furry gloves Furry gloves...
EXACTLY the time you told me you were out with Foyle.
Oh.
What shall we do today?
GOD, I feel stupid...
No... don't...

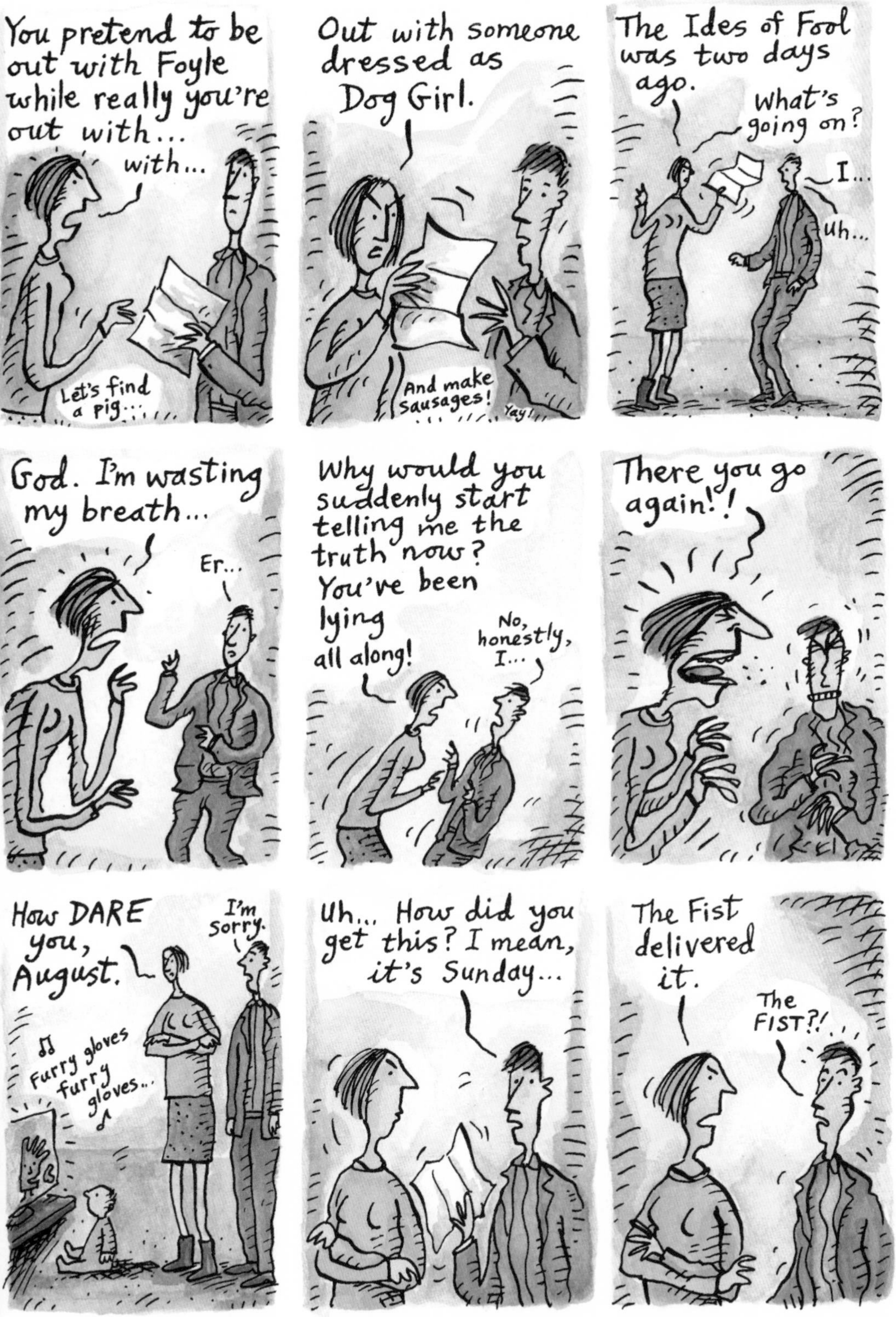
You pretend to be out with Foyle while really you're out with...
with...
Let's find a pig...
Out with someone dressed as Dog Girl.
And make sausages!
Yay!
The Ides of Fool was two days ago.
What's going on?
I...
Uh...
God. I'm wasting my breath...
Er...
Why would you suddenly start telling me the truth now? You've been lying all along!
No, honestly, I...
There you go again!!
How DARE you, August.
I'm sorry.
Furry gloves furry gloves...
Uh... How did you get this? I mean, it's Sunday...
The Fist delivered it.
The FIST?!

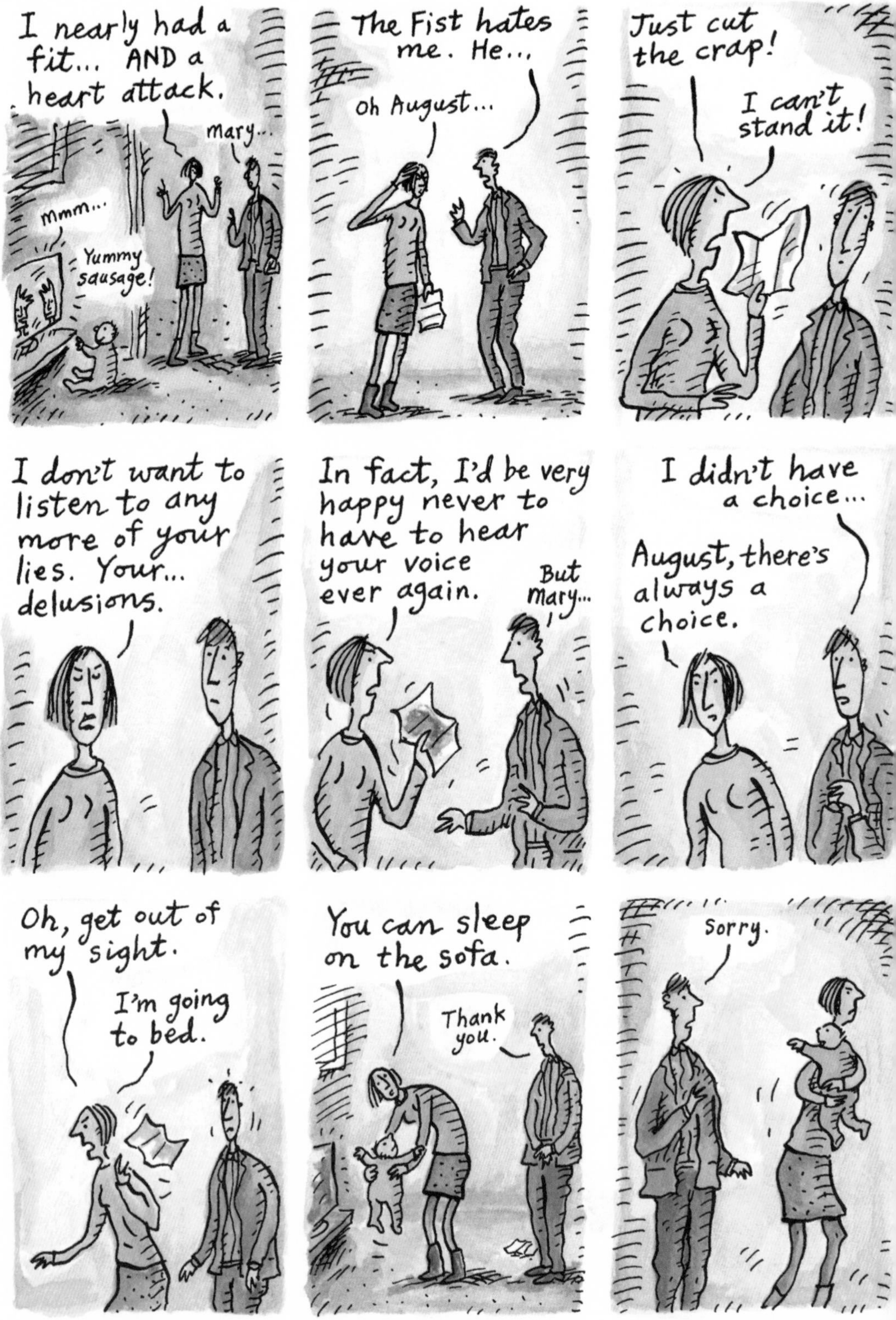
I nearly had a fit... AND a heart attack.
mary...
mmm...
Yummy sausage!
The Fist hates me. He...
Oh August...
Just cut the crap!
I can't stand it!
I don't want to listen to any more of your lies. Your... delusions.
In fact, I'd be very happy never to have to hear your voice ever again.
But mary...
I didn't have a choice...
August, there's always a choice.
Oh, get out of my sight.
I'm going to bed.
You can sleep on the sofa.
Thank you.
Sorry.

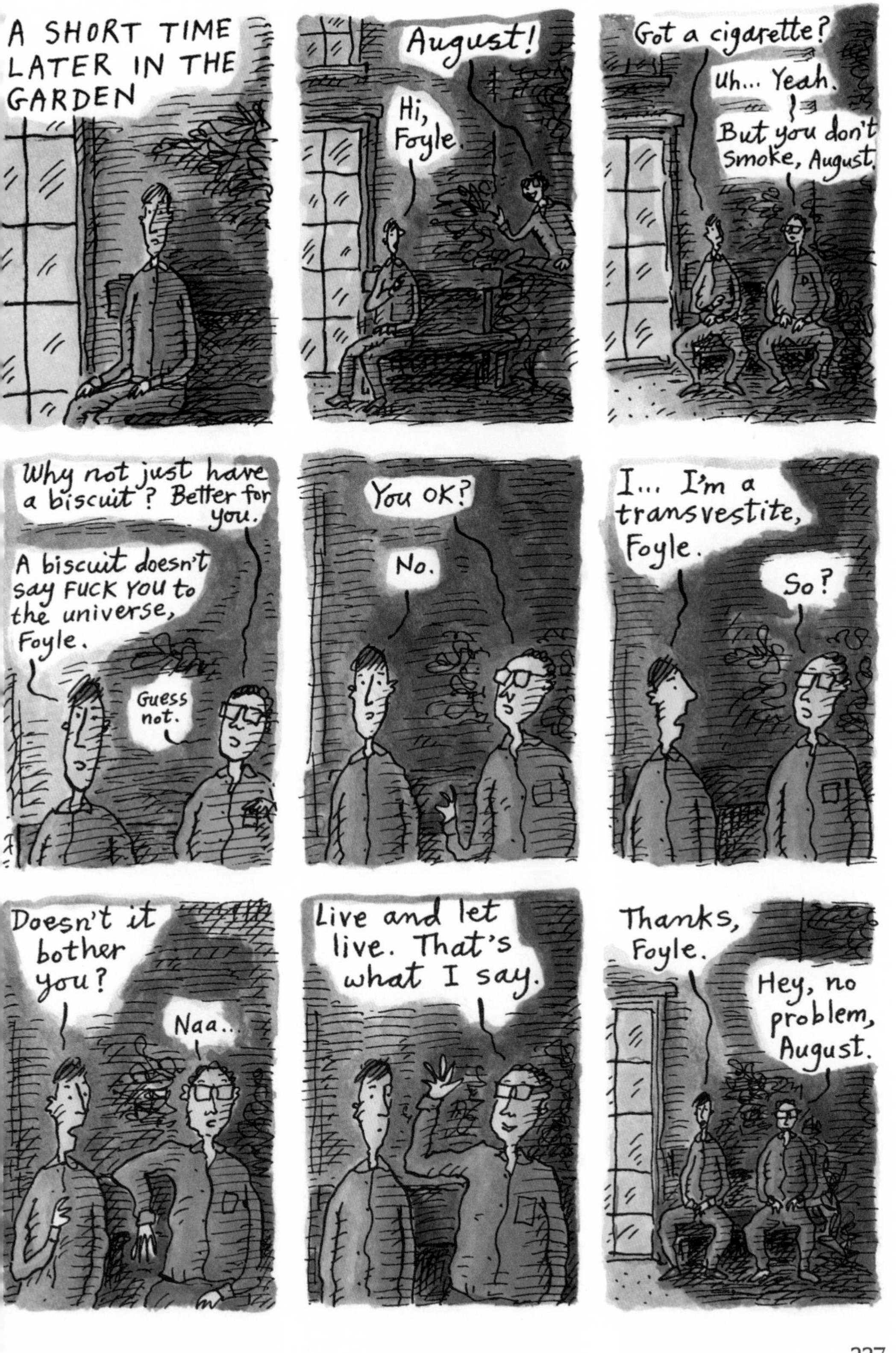
A SHORT TIME LATER IN THE GARDEN
August!
Hi, Foyle.
Got a cigarette?
Uh... Yeah.
But you don't smoke, August.
Why not just have a biscuit? Better for you.
A biscuit doesn't say FUCK YOU to the universe, Foyle.
Guess not.
You OK?
No.
I... I'm a transvestite, Foyle.
So?
Doesn't it bother you?
Naa...
Live and let live. That's what I say.
Thanks, Foyle.
Hey, no problem, August.

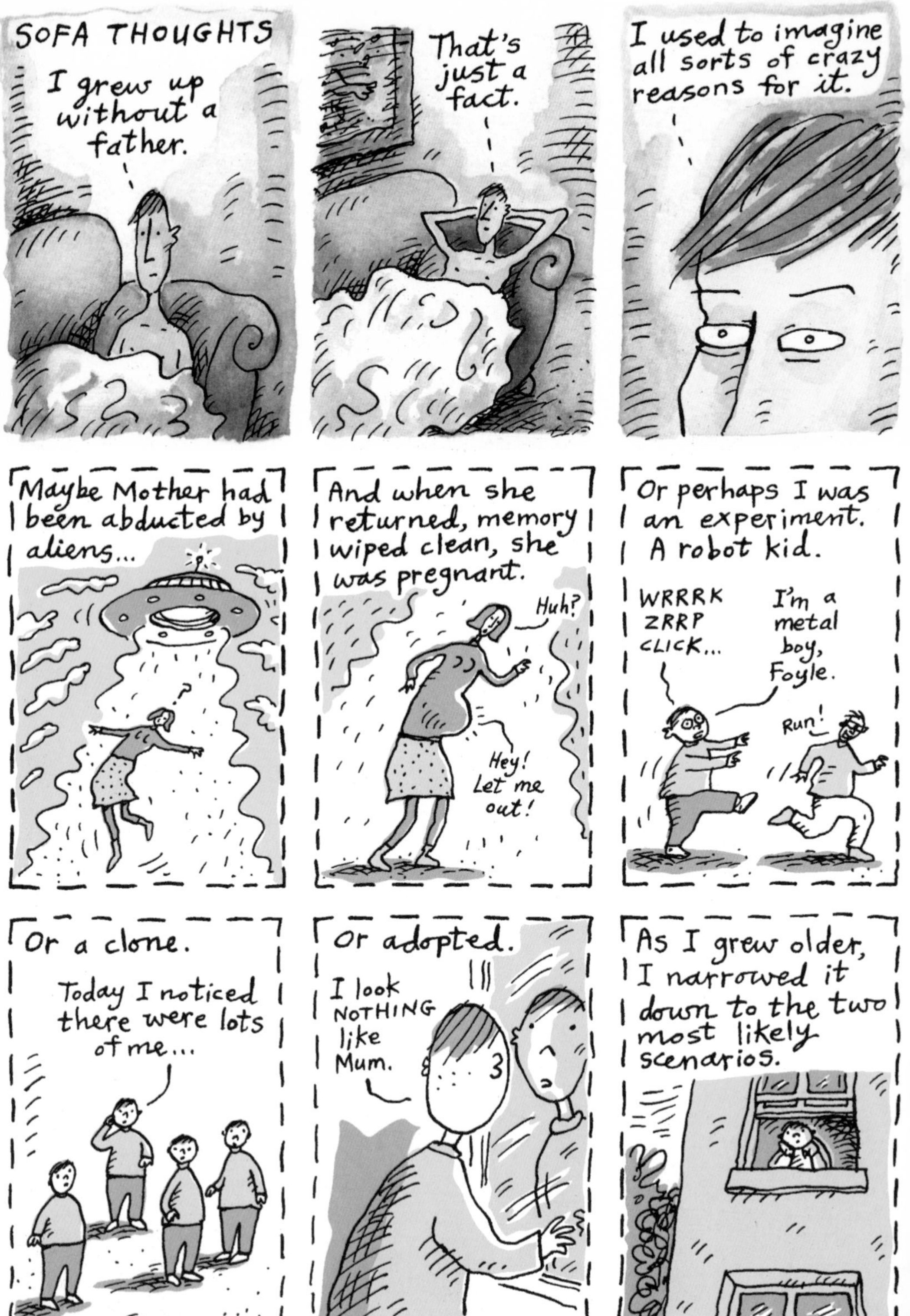
SOFA THOUGHTS
I grew up without a father.
That's just a fact.
I used to imagine all sorts of crazy reasons for it.
Maybe Mother had been abducted by aliens...
?
And when she returned, memory wiped clean, she was pregnant.
Huh?
Hey! Let me out!
Or perhaps I was an experiment. A robot kid.
WRRRK ZRRP CLICK...
I'm a metal boy, Foyle.
Run!
Or a clone.
Today I noticed there were lots of me...
Or adopted.
I look NOTHING like Mum.
As I grew older, I narrowed it down to the two most likely scenarios.

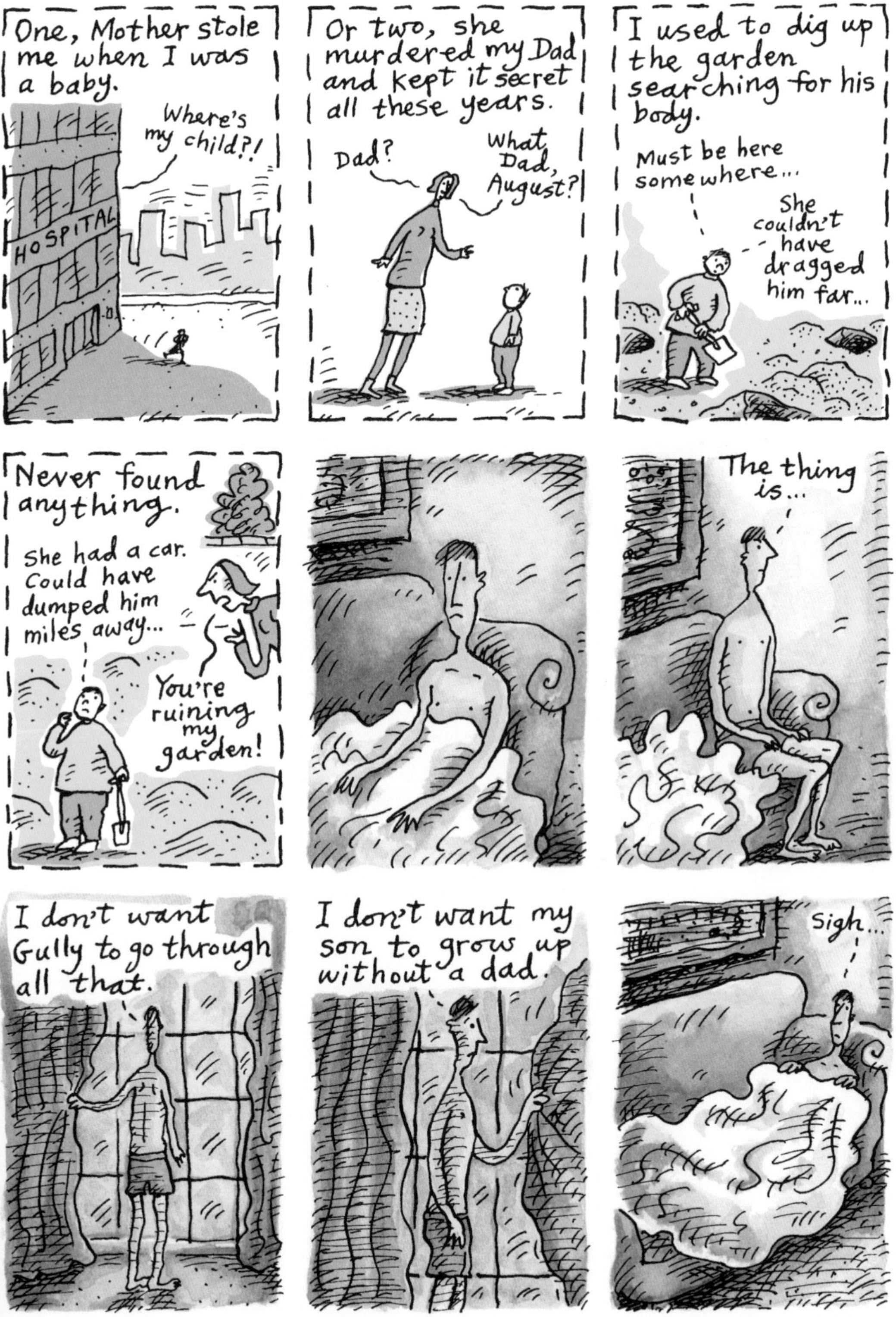
One, Mother stole me when I was a baby.
Where's my child?!
HOSPITAL
Or two, she murdered my Dad and kept it secret all these years.
Dad?
What Dad, August?
I used to dig up the garden searching for his body.
Must be here somewhere...
She couldn't have dragged him far...
Never found anything.
She had a car. Could have dumped him miles away...
You're ruining my garden!
The thing is...
I don't want Gully to go through all that.
I don't want my son to grow up without a dad.
Sigh...

Monday

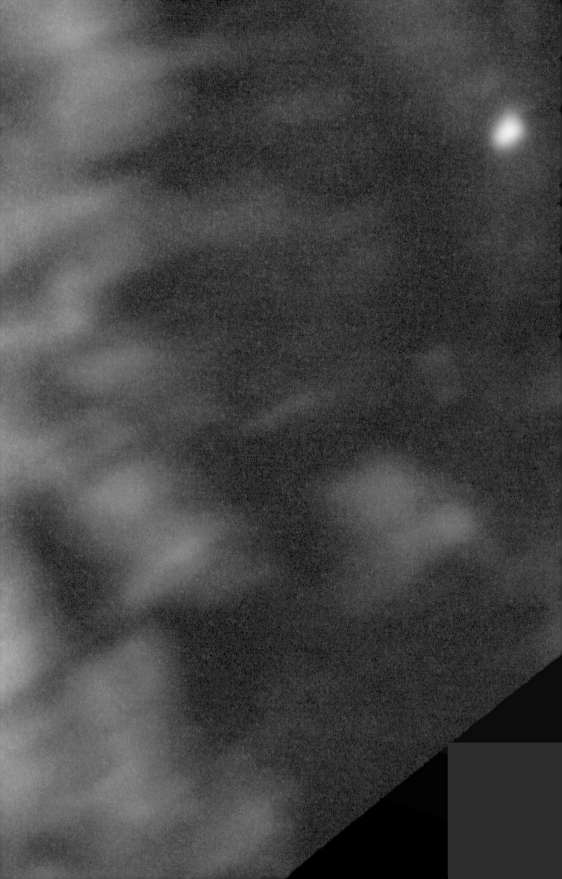

5·53 am

The dream starts...

It's a dream I remember from being a child, but it doesn't feel like a dream. In fact, it never felt like a dream. At least, not my dream.

I'm looking down on a little district of the city called Pity Me, probably in the past, or maybe in the future – whenever it was that the world was going to Hell so fast the Devil himself could hardly keep up. In those days, whenever they were, the people were awoken every night by shouts and cries as the Devil went past pushing his handcart piled high with the damned. But despite this, and the fact that nothing grew properly there, so that when healthy things arrived they soon waned and withered and died... Despite all this, Pity Me was criss-crossed by narrow streets lined with small, grey, detached houses where people like you and me lived. They had little gardens front and back planted up with dead things and washing lines. There was a small, ash-grey, soot-covered park; a few shops, lit up during the day by tarnished yellow electric light, and a few factories backing onto the canal, into which they tipped their dirty water and anything else they'd used up and didn't want any more. The days in Pity Me were never fully light and the nights never fully dark, so a life spent in Pity Me was a life lived in permanent dusk.

On one of the streets, in a grey house just like all the others, lived a baby boy with his cute, sensible Mummy and his wild, crazy Daddy. The Daddy was sterile and set fire to buildings for a living. The Mummy, knowing that the Daddy knew he was sterile, lived in constant fear. But the Daddy seemed to love the baby boy, or at least to like him, since he paid him no attention at all. So the baby boy loved his Mummy and his Daddy and life carried along in a truce of shopping, burning buildings and walks to the park.

One particular night – night according to the clock, since, as I said before, the light is much the same all the twenty-four hours long due to the fires and the smoke and whatnot – the Daddy arrives home from work covered in soot as usual, except that tonight he is burning inside. The Mummy can see the hot coals glowing out from deep inside his tired, grey, ash-coloured eyes. Without a word, the Daddy picks up the baby boy, puts him in his pram and pushes him out of the door. When the Mummy starts putting on her coat to follow, the Daddy says; 'Get supper ready.'

Then he goes, slamming the door behind him.
The Mummy hears the key turn in the lock and through the window sees the Daddy disappear down the street in the opposite direction to the park.

The Mummy looks in the Daddy's bag and sees that he has brought home only enough food for two, so she feels for her front door key but it isn't in her pocket, then she looks for the spare front-door key but it isn't on the hook. Feeling panic, as if the fire inside the Daddy has started a second little fire in her breast, the Mummy opens the sitting-room window and climbs out into the garden, snapping the dead grass as she lands and leaving dead footprints across the lawn. She hurries up the street in the direction the Daddy went but she can't see him, and the little fire inside her starts to crackle as it catches and begins to blaze.

The next street is empty, and so is the next, and now there are cross streets and side streets and where, in Pity Me, could the Daddy have disappeared to, oh so quickly? Then the Mummy sees the damp marks of pram wheels leaving a puddle of ash and petrol heading towards Coal Street, and she hurries on. Up ahead a building burns – are those the Daddy's friends? Is this where he's gone? The flames flickering inside the Mummy's chest start to roar, as if doused in paraffin, but no, these men work for a rival company which is bigger and busier than the Daddy's, causing him to huff and puff and hit the wall, leaving the prints of his fists in soot to be cleaned off later.

The Mummy hurries round the corner and there, up ahead, stands the Daddy next to the pram. Just staring into the canal where the short street ends at a wharf. Just standing. Just staring.

'Where's the baby?' screams the Mummy. 'What the fuck have you done with my baby?!'

The Daddy turns, pauses for a moment as if he might have something to say, then he smiles a little smile – which is unusual for him, because he doesn't smile very much – and pushes the pram into the canal.

The Mummy howls, like tearing metal, and runs straight into the canal, fighting her way through the thick, waist-deep water to the pram... but it's empty.

At that point, as always, I wake up sweating in my childhood bed, and am so shaken with fear that I have to turn on the little bedside light shaped like a sailing ship and pull the blankets up to my neck. And then, as always, I hear a sound and, sitting up, see my mother by the ship's dim glow, lying on the rug on the floor beside my bed, arms wrapped around her knees, rocking and moaning and crying in her sleep as, for her, the dream continues.

This time, though, things change and, as I watch, Mother stops sobbing and opens her eyes. Then she gets to her feet and stands, staring at me, and I realise that I'm not in my childhood bedroom at all.

I'm lying on the sofa in my adult house surrounded by the ruins of my family and, as I'm thinking this, Mother speaks.

'I'm sorry, August. I was wrong.'

She picks up the cuttings book from the floor, where I know it wasn't lying, and turns the pages.

'I've been trying to protect you but that was a mistake. You have to do things for yourself.'

She puts the book on the chair and turns to me.

'I love you, August. Just exactly as you are.'

And she is gone.

I look around and realise I'm still asleep, and this is still a dream. But whose dream is it?

I also realise, because the pillow is wet, that I am crying.

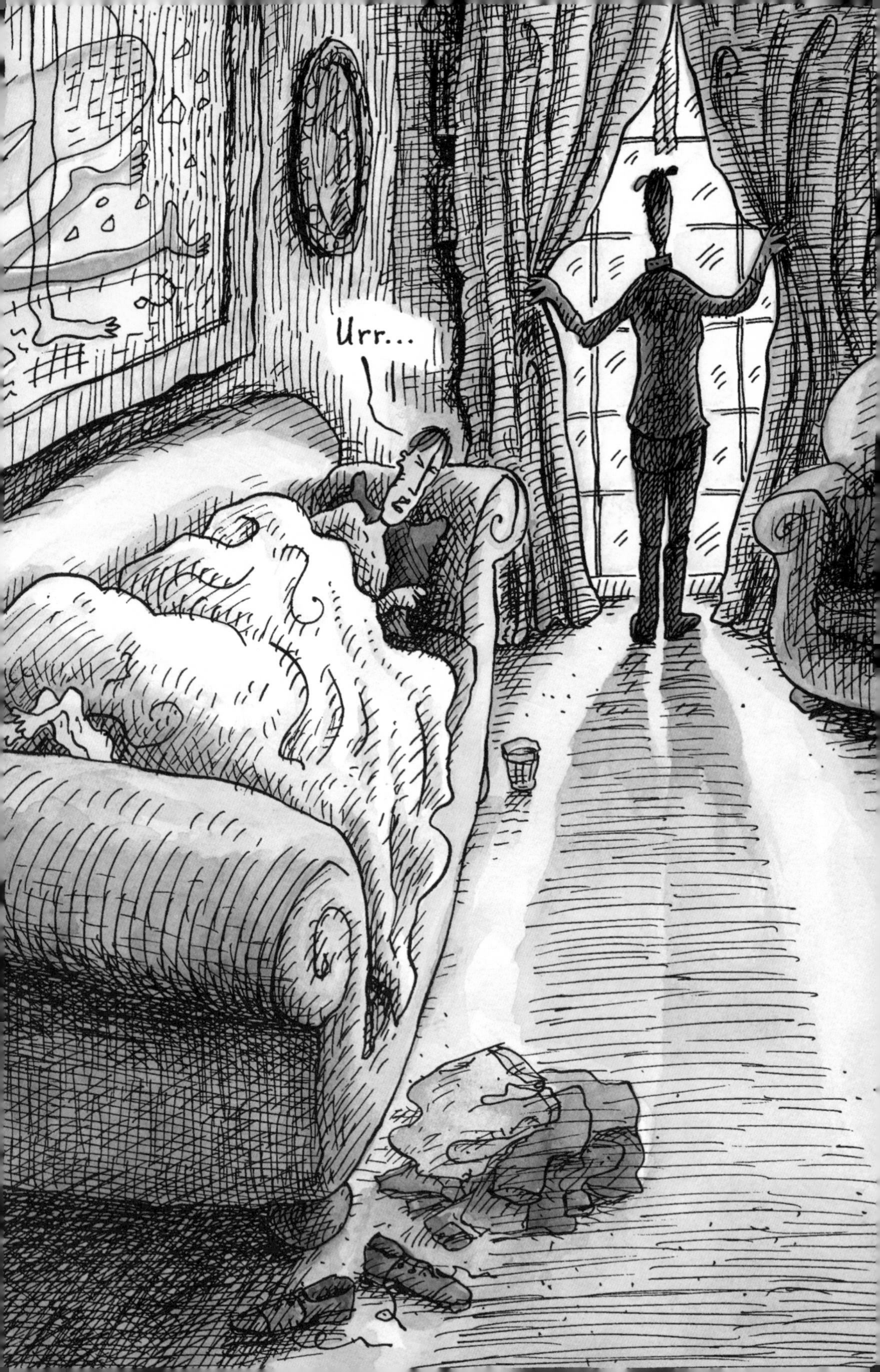
Urr...

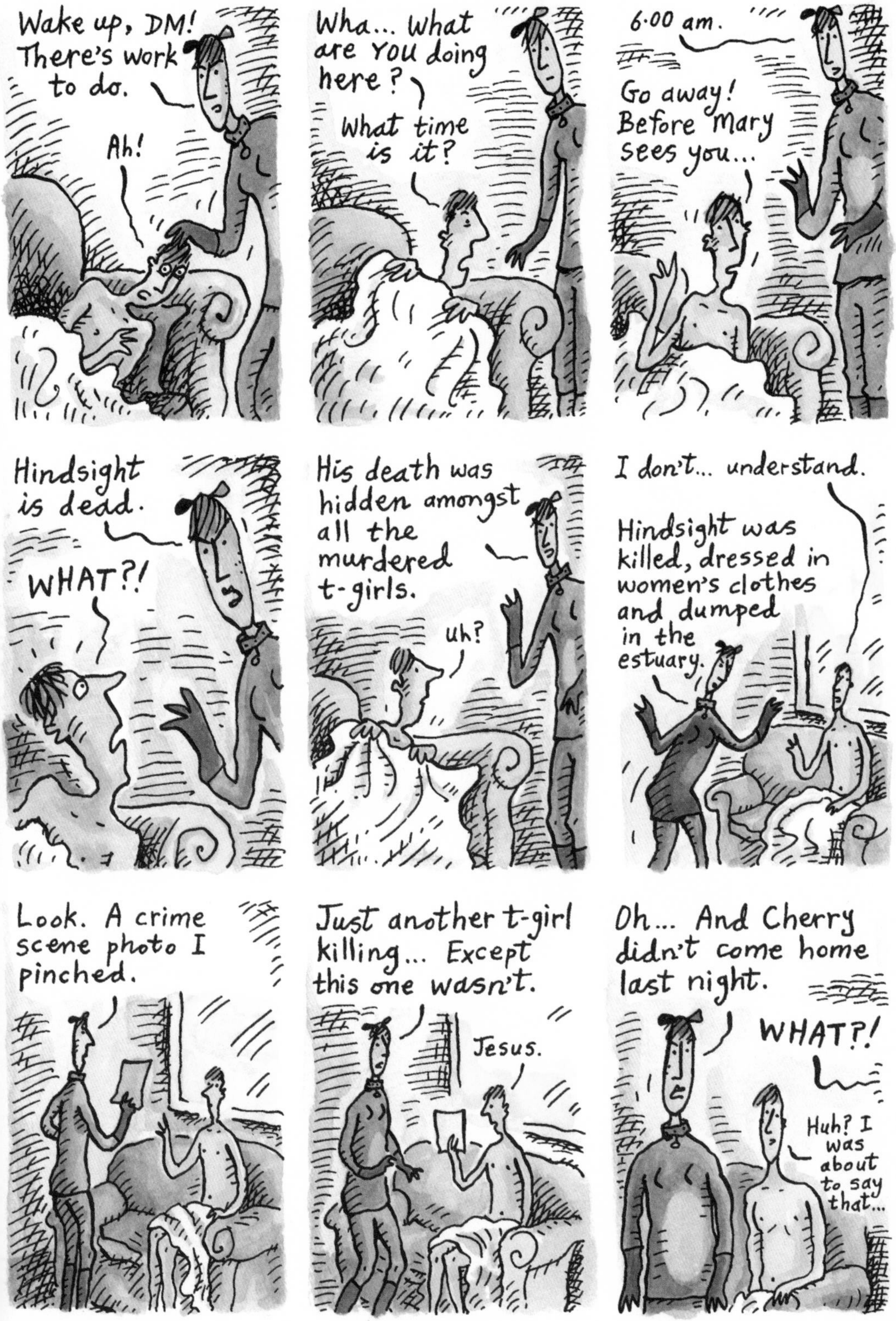
Wake up, DM! There's work to do.
Ah!
Wha... What are YOU doing here?
What time is it?
6.00 am.
Go away! Before Mary sees you...
Hindsight is dead.
WHAT?!
His death was hidden amongst all the murdered t-girls.
Uh?
I don't... understand.
Hindsight was killed, dressed in women's clothes and dumped in the estuary.
Look. A crime scene photo I pinched.
Just another t-girl killing... Except this one wasn't.
Jesus.
Oh... And Cherry didn't come home last night.
WHAT?!
Huh? I was about to say that...

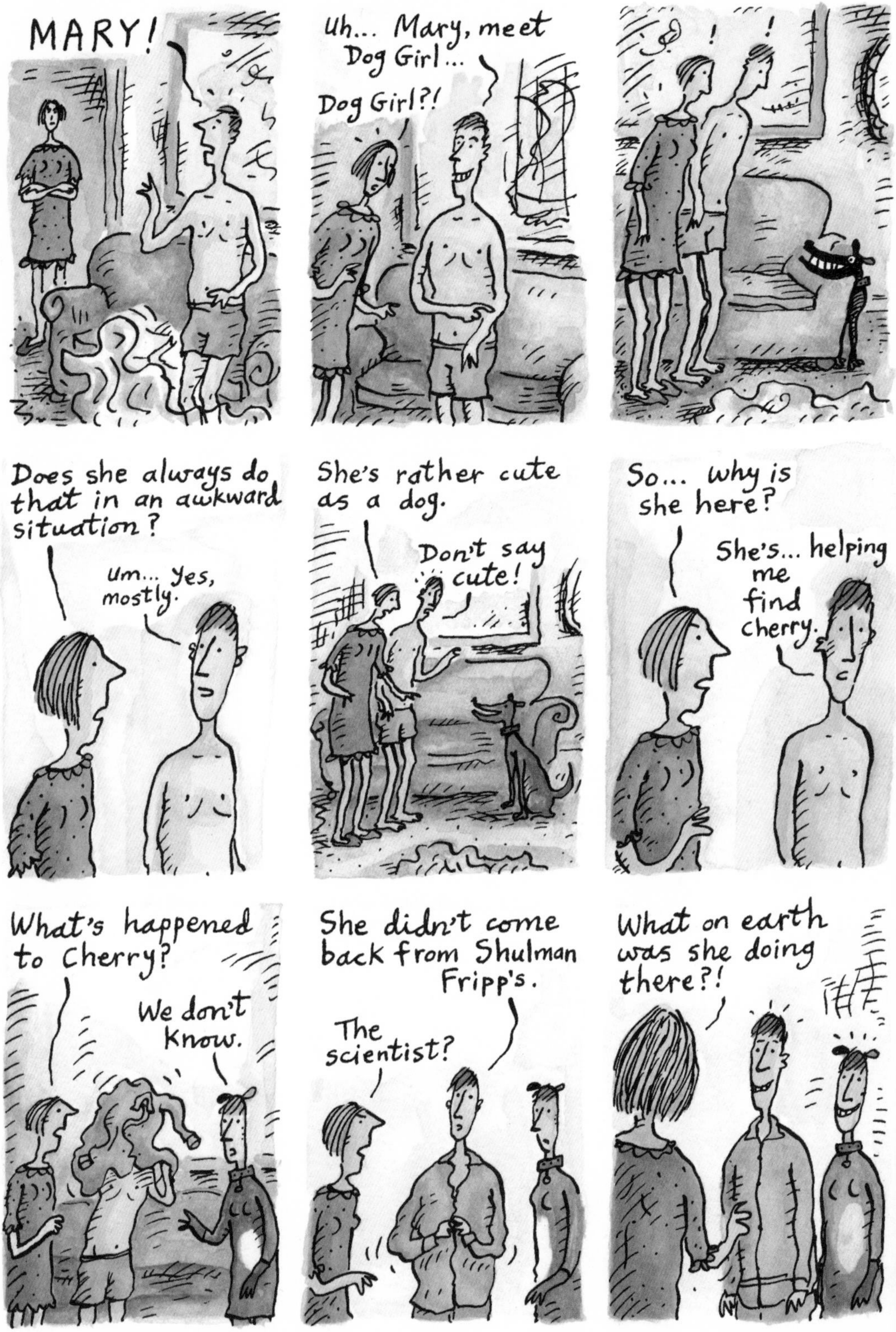
MARY!
Uh... Mary, meet Dog Girl...
Dog Girl?!
Does she always do that in an awkward situation?
Um... Yes, mostly.
She's rather cute as a dog.
Don't say cute!
So... why is she here?
She's... helping me find Cherry.
What's happened to Cherry?
We don't know.
She didn't come back from Shulman Fripp's.
The scientist?
What on earth was she doing there?!

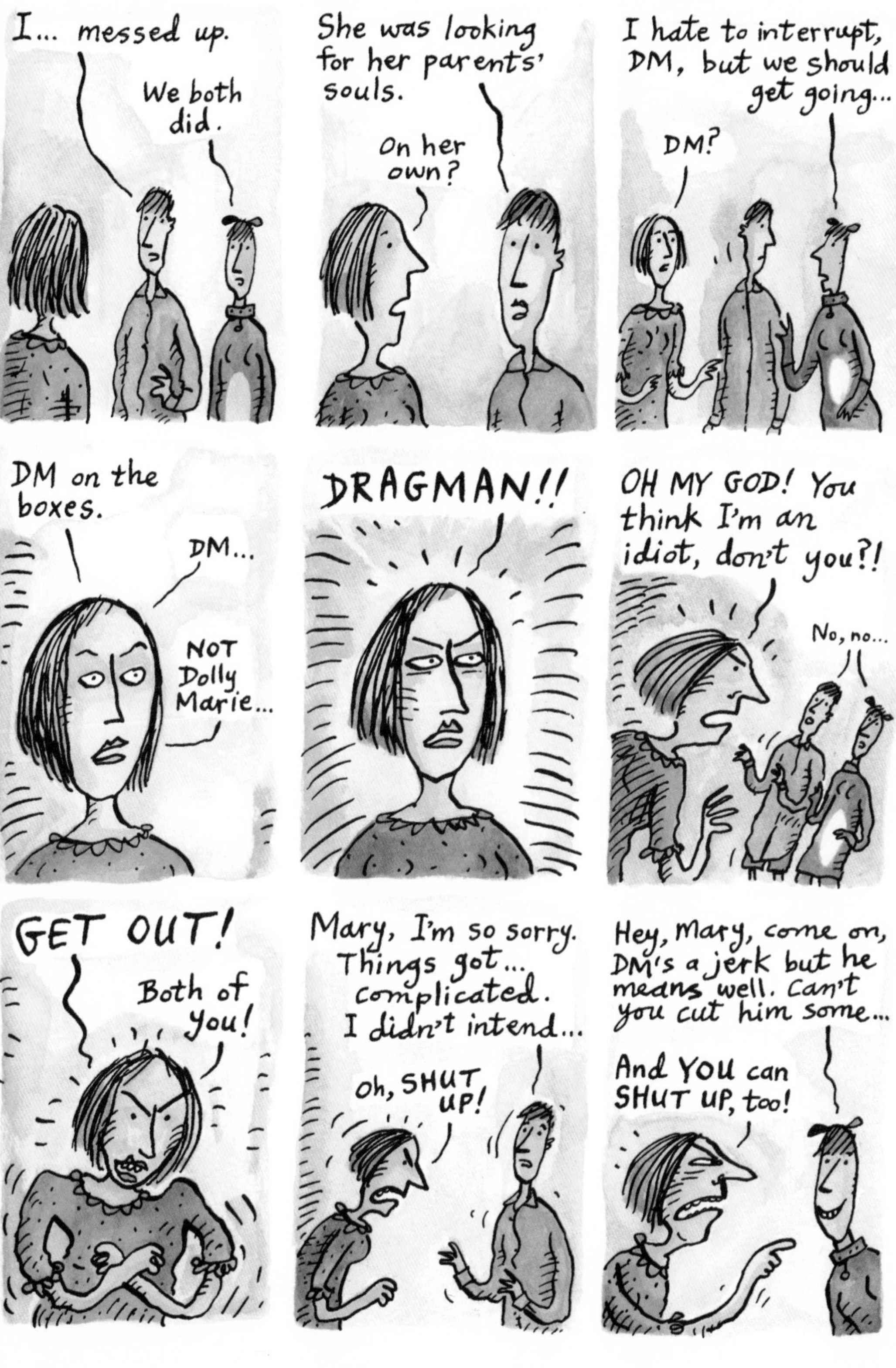
I... messed up.
We both did.
She was looking for her parents' souls.
On her own?
I hate to interrupt, DM, but we should get going...
DM?
DM on the boxes.
DM...
NOT Dolly Marie...
DRAGMAN!!
OH MY GOD! You think I'm an idiot, don't you?!
No, no...
GET OUT!
Both of you!
Mary, I'm so sorry. Things got... complicated. I didn't intend...
Oh, SHUT UP!
Hey, Mary, come on, DM's a jerk but he means well. Can't you cut him some...
And YOU can SHUT UP, too!

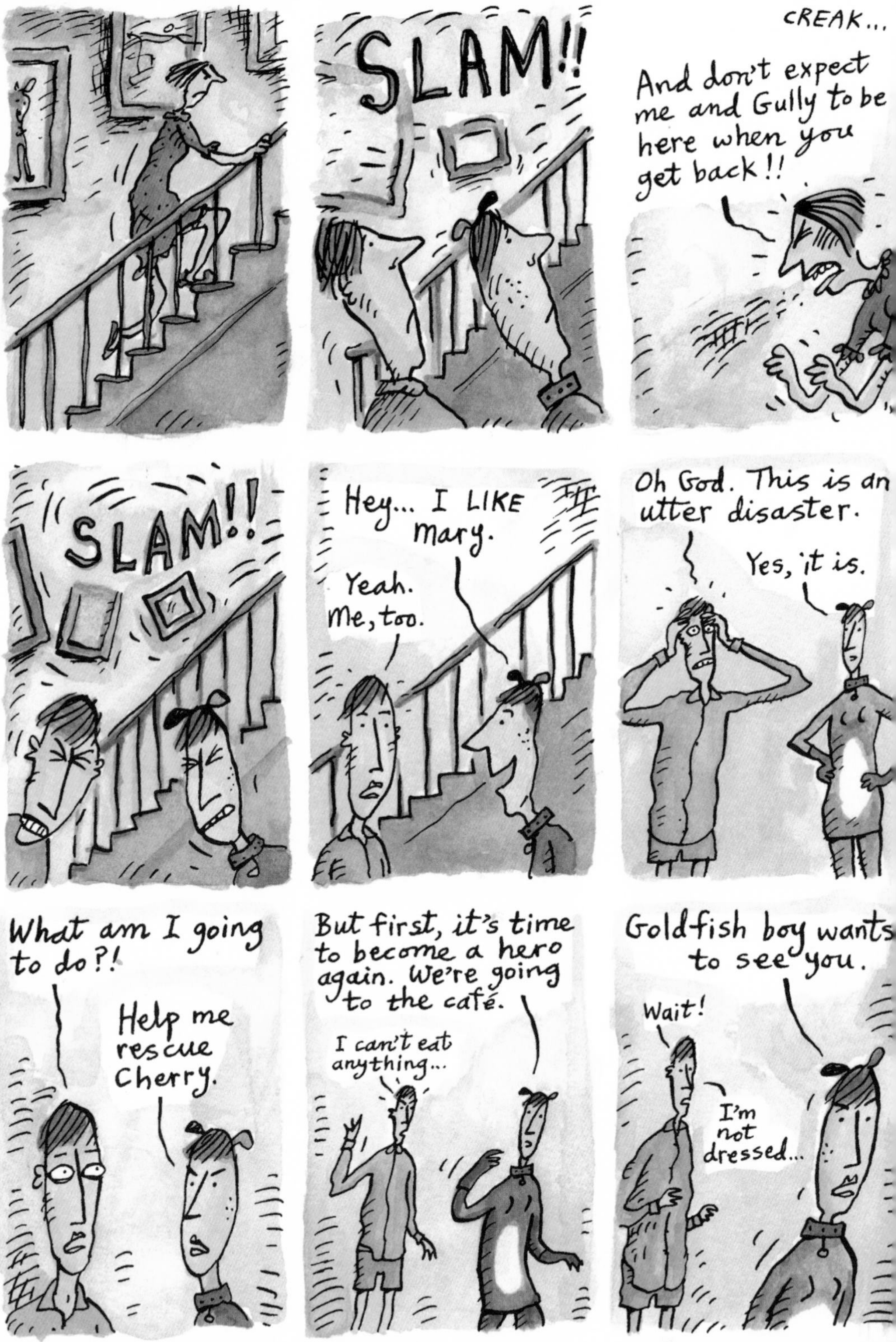
SLAM!!
CREAK...
And don't expect me and Gully to be here when you get back!!
SLAM!!
Hey... I LIKE mary.
Yeah. me, too.
Oh God. This is an utter disaster.
Yes, it is.
What am I going to do?!
Help me rescue Cherry.
But first, it's time to become a hero again. We're going to the café.
I can't eat anything...
Goldfish boy wants to see you.
Wait!
I'm not dressed...

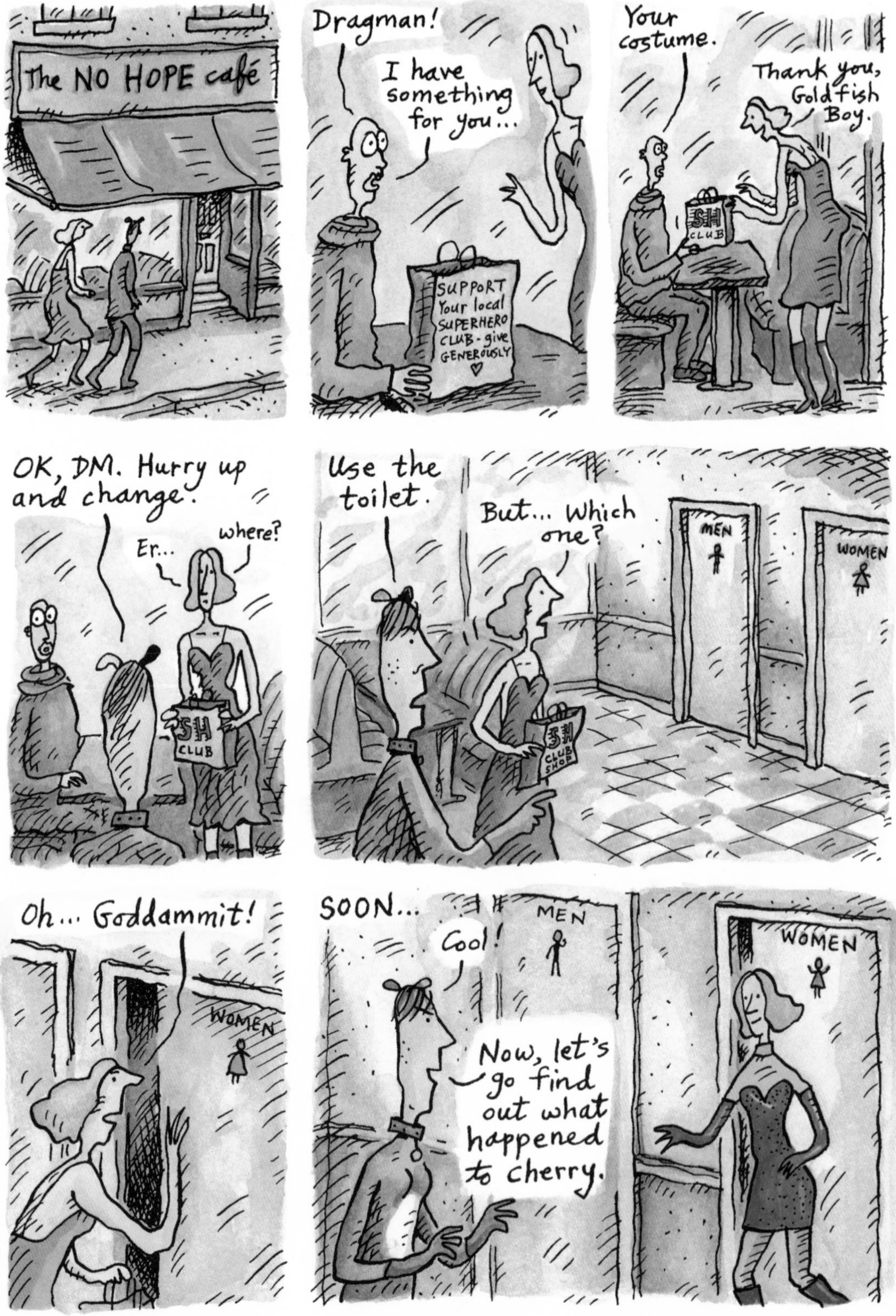
The NO HOPE café
Dragman!
I have something for you...
SUPPORT Your local SUPERHERO CLUB - give GENEROUSLY
Your costume.
Thank you, Goldfish Boy.
SH CLUB
OK, DM. Hurry up and change.
Er...
where?
SH CLUB
Use the toilet.
But... Which one?
MEN
WOMEN
SH CLUB SHOP
Oh... Goddammit!
WOMEN
SOON...
Cool!
MEN
WOMEN
Now, let's go find out what happened to cherry.

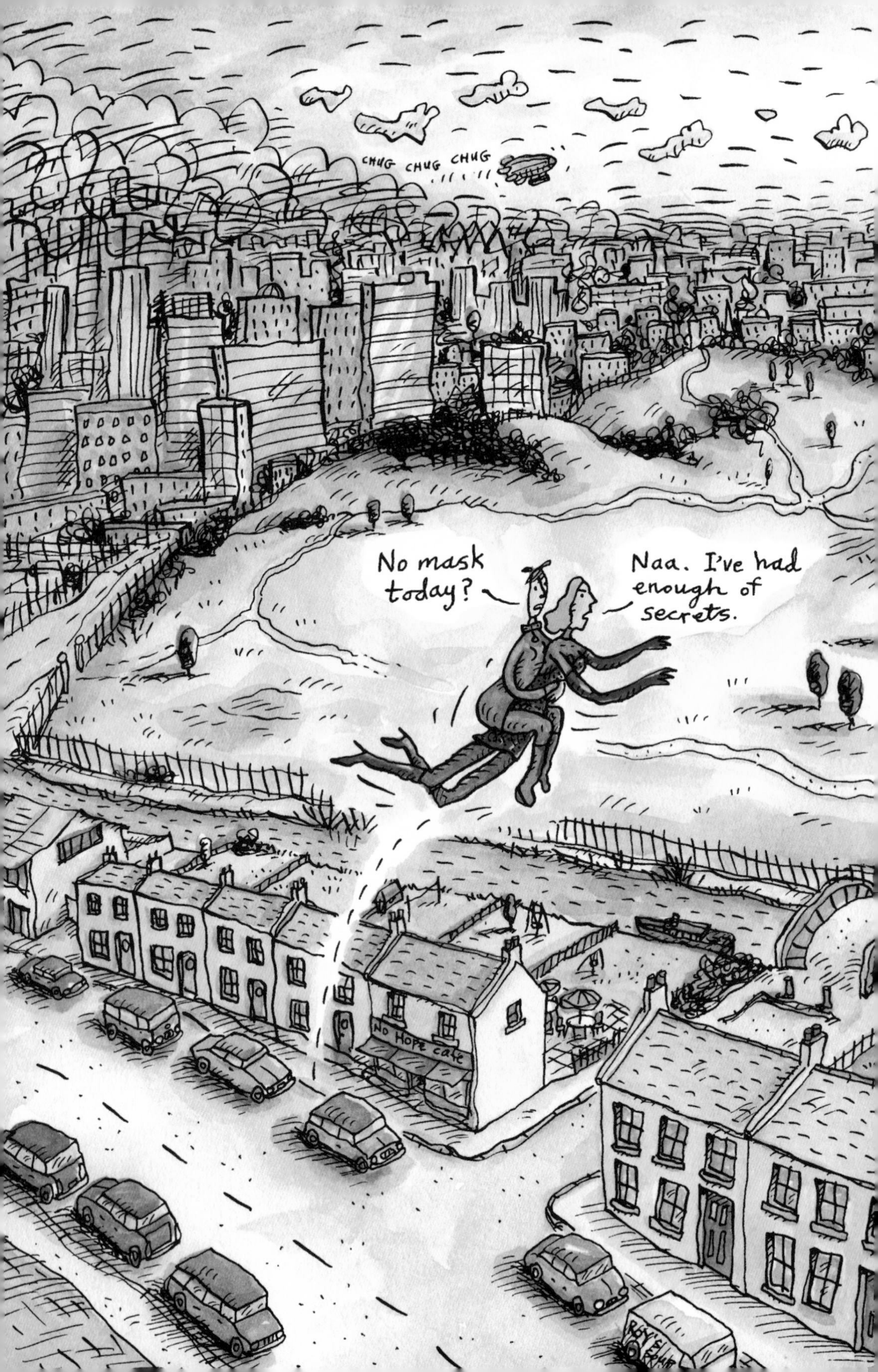
CHUG CHUG CHUG
No mask today?
Naa. I've had enough of secrets.
NO HOPE café

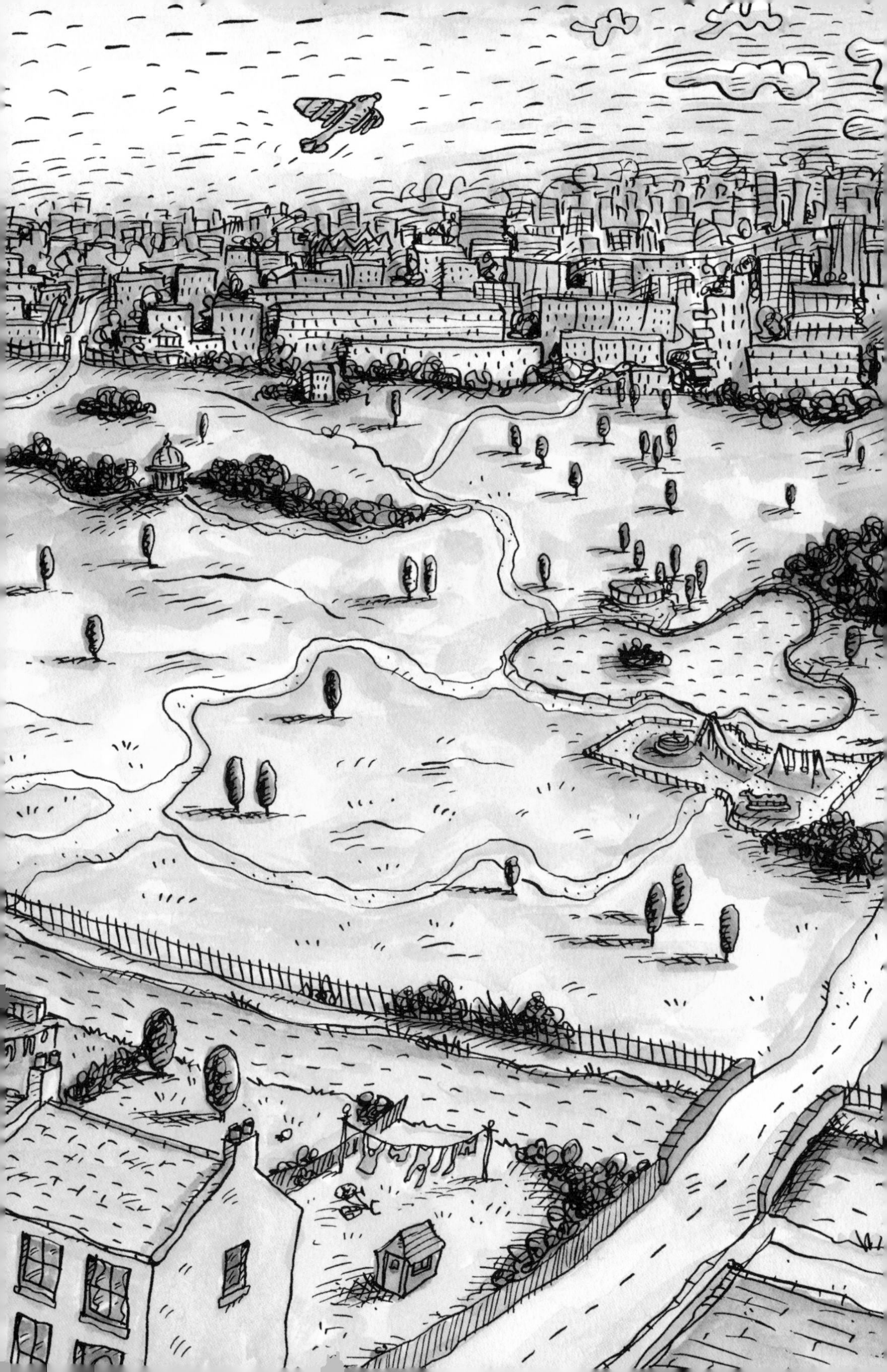

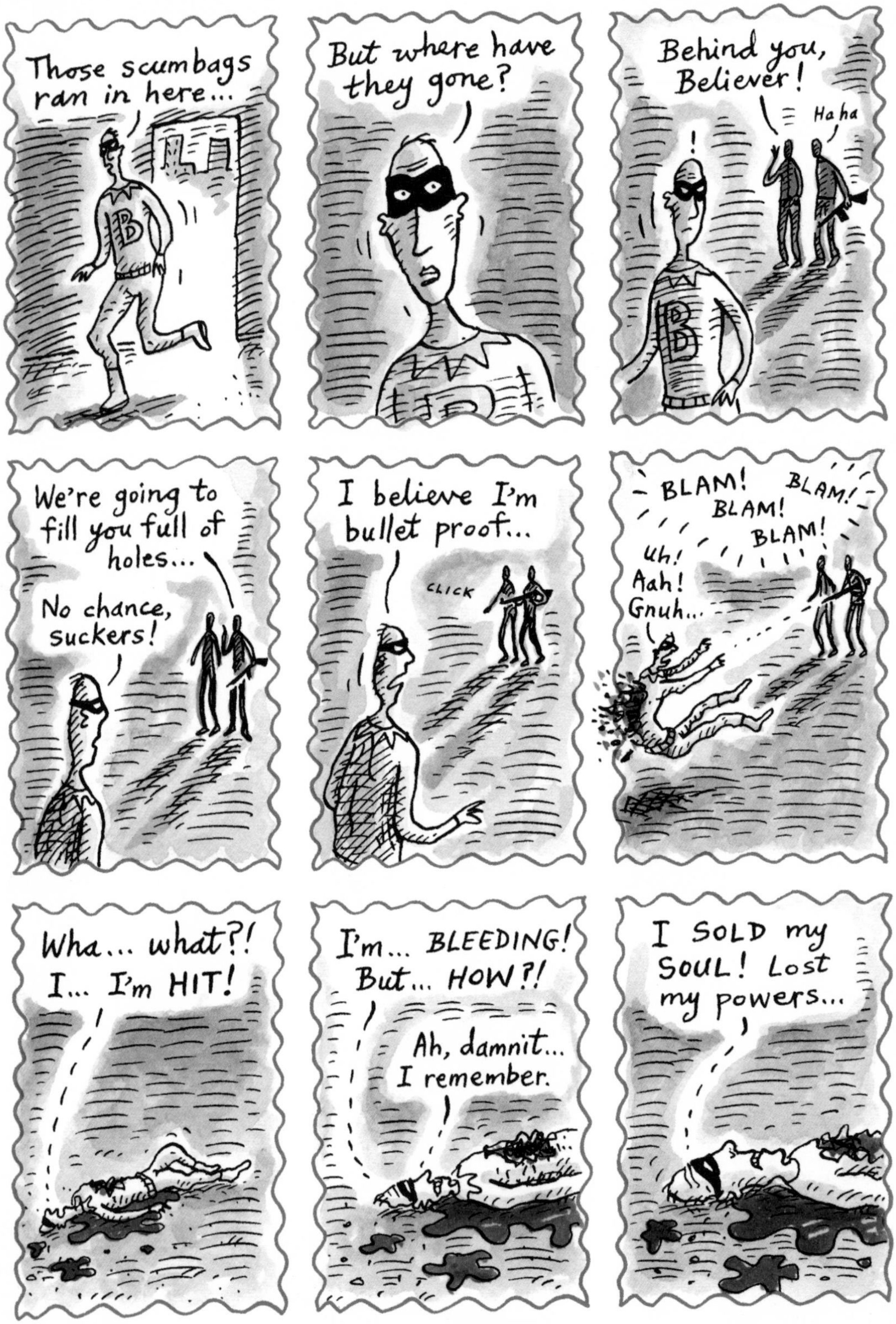
Those scumbags ran in here...
But where have they gone?
Behind you, Believer!
Haha
We're going to fill you full of holes...
No chance, suckers!
I believe I'm bullet proof...
CLICK
BLAM! BLAM! BLAM! BLAM!
Uh! Aah! Gnuh...
Wha... what?! I... I'm HIT!
I'm... BLEEDING! But... HOW?!
Ah, damnit... I remember.
I SOLD my SOUL! Lost my powers...

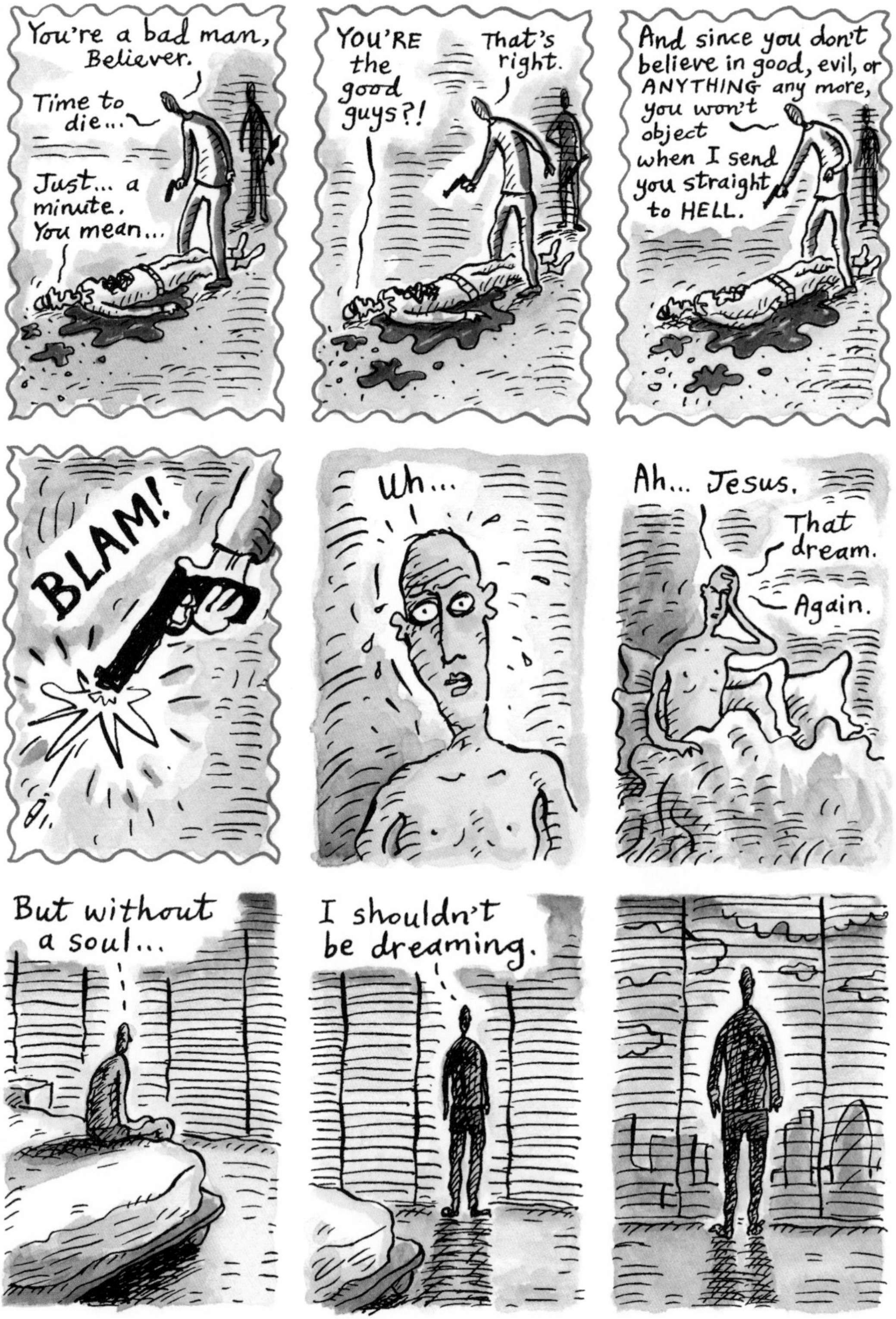
You're a bad man, Believer.
Time to die...
Just... a minute. You mean...
YOU'RE the good guys?!
That's right.
And since you don't believe in good, evil, or ANYTHING any more, you won't object when I send you straight to HELL.
BLAM!
Uh...
Ah... Jesus.
That dream.
Again.
But without a soul...
I shouldn't be dreaming.

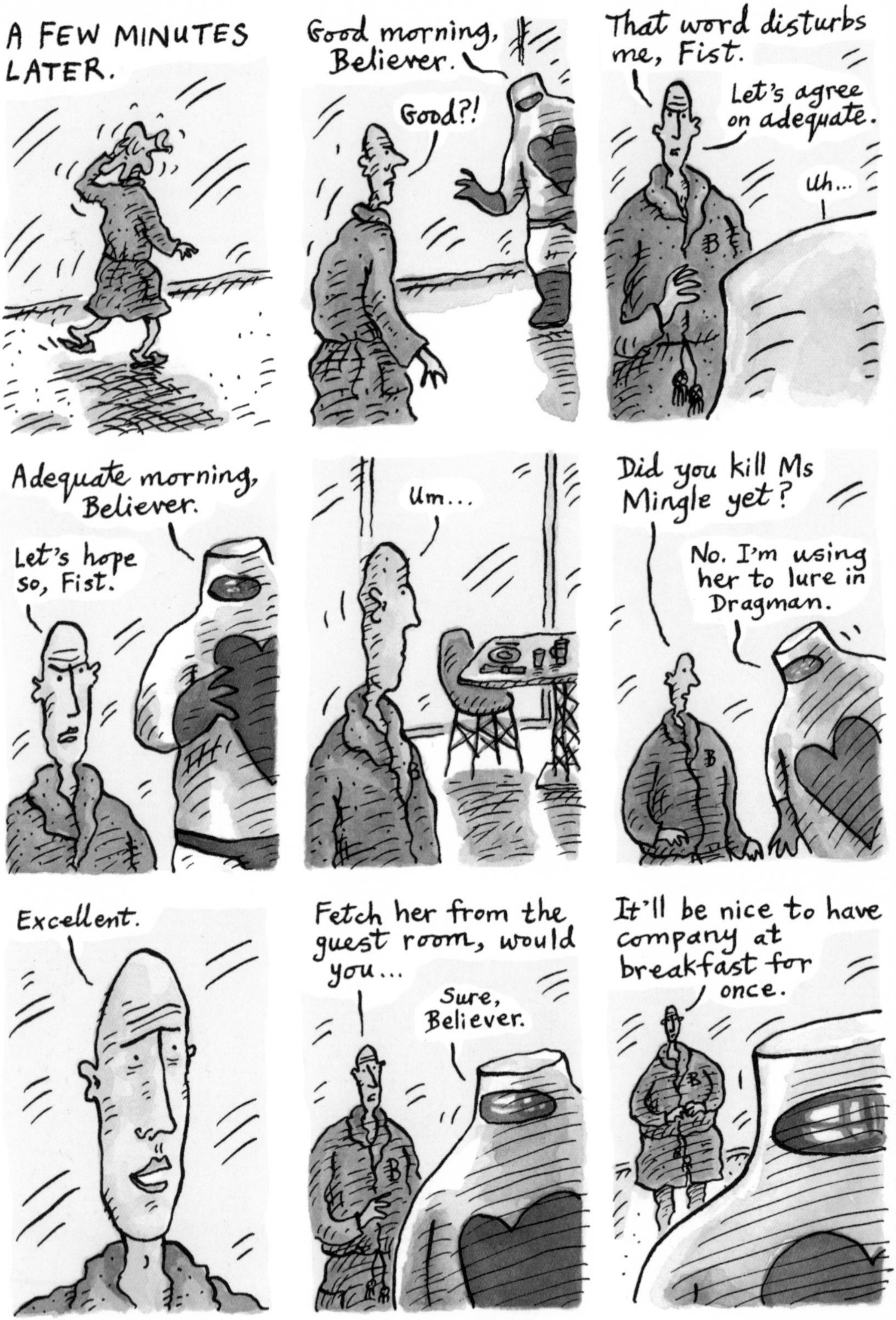
A FEW MINUTES LATER.
Good morning, Believer.
Good?!
That word disturbs me, Fist.
Let's agree on adequate.
Uh...
Adequate morning, Believer.
Let's hope so, Fist.
Um...
Did you kill Ms Mingle yet?
No. I'm using her to lure in Dragman.
Excellent.
Fetch her from the guest room, would you...
Sure, Believer.
It'll be nice to have company at breakfast for once.

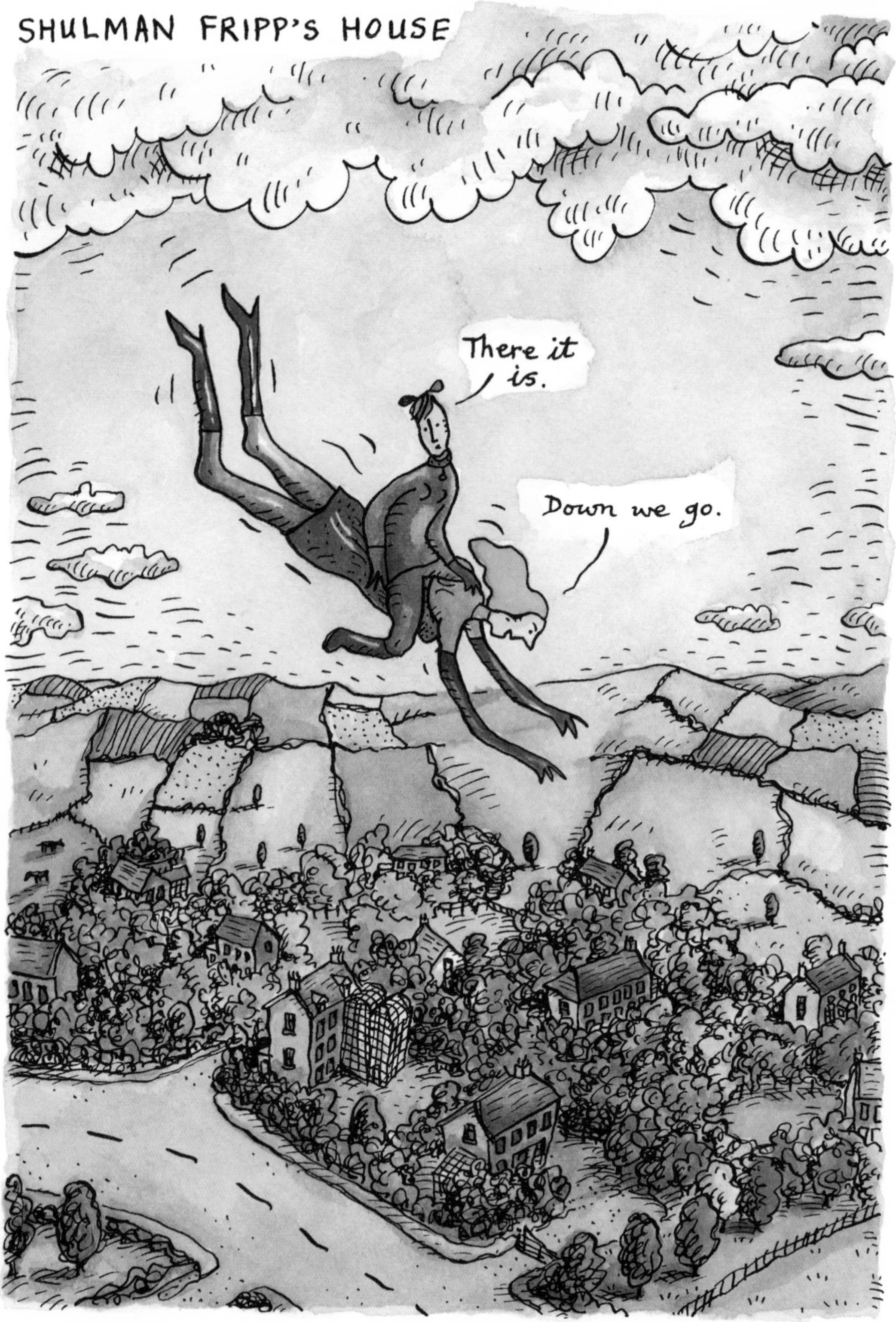
SHULMAN FRIPP'S HOUSE
There it is.
Down we go.

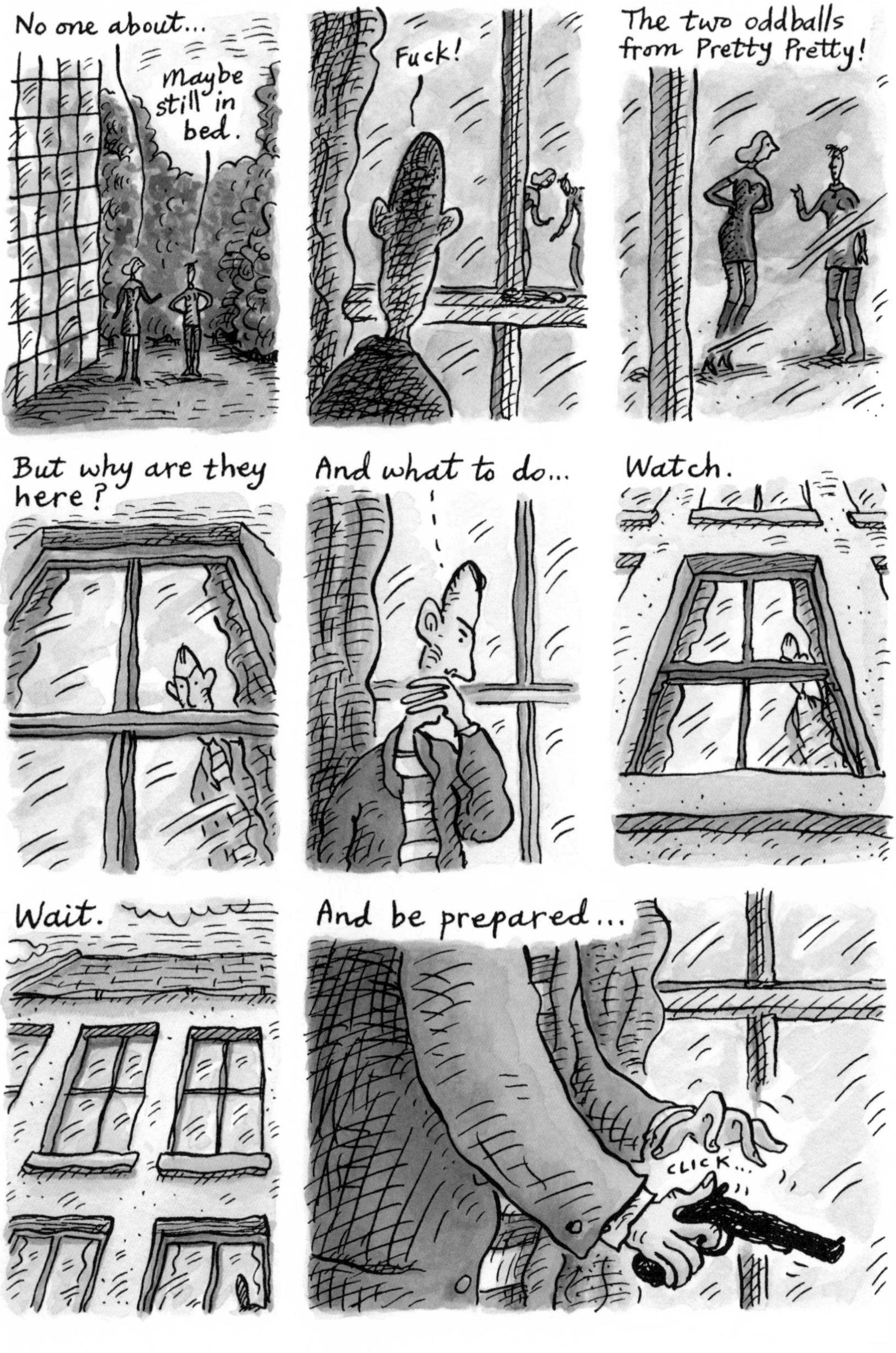
No one about...
Maybe still in bed.
Fuck!
The two oddballs from Pretty Pretty!
But why are they here?
And what to do...
Watch.
Wait.
And be prepared...
CLICK...

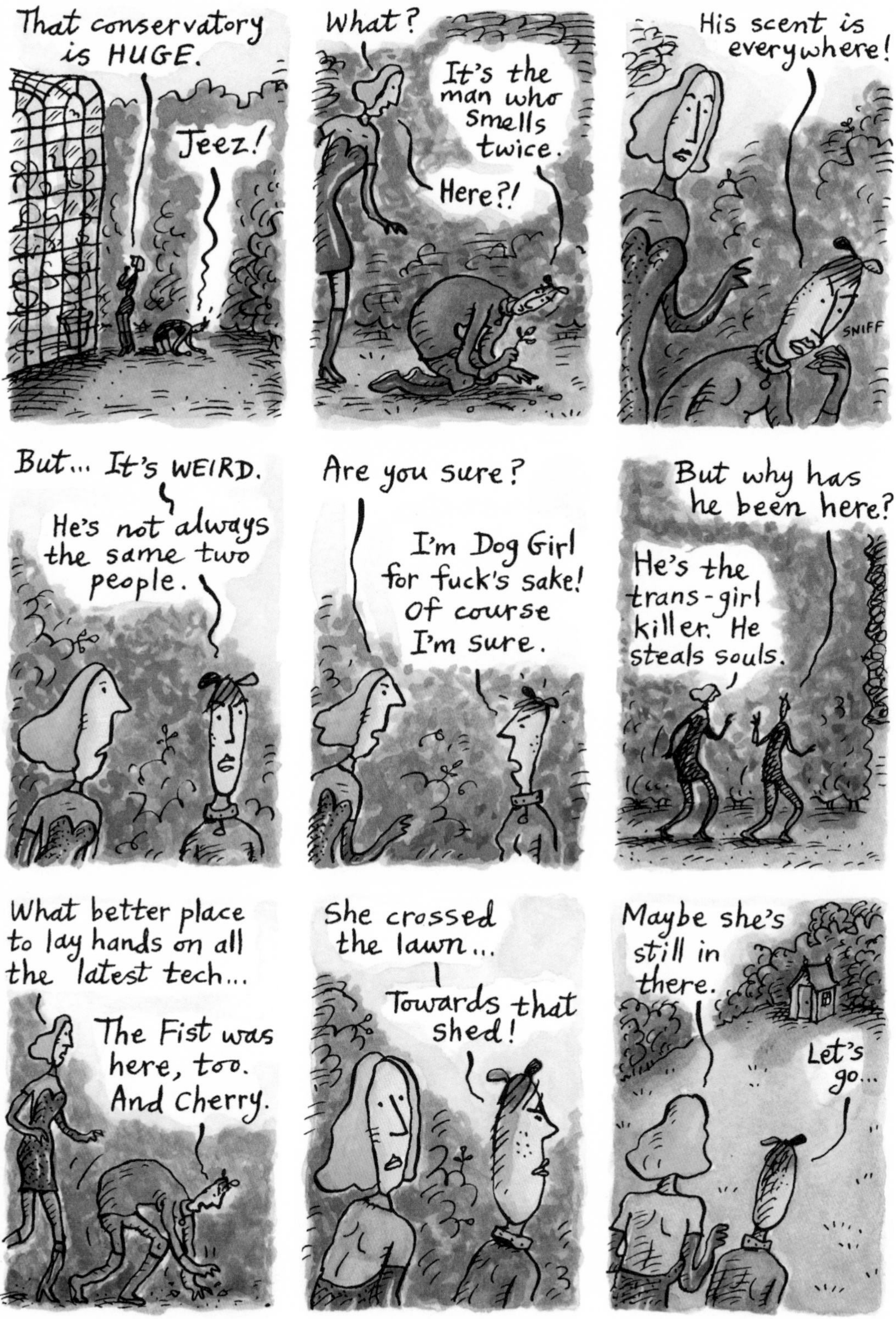
That conservatory is HUGE.
Jeez!
What?
It's the man who smells twice.
Here?!
His scent is everywhere!
SNIFF
But... It's WEIRD.
He's not always the same two people.
Are you sure?
I'm Dog Girl for fuck's sake! Of course I'm sure.
But why has he been here?
He's the trans-girl killer. He steals souls.
What better place to lay hands on all the latest tech...
The Fist was here, too. And Cherry.
She crossed the lawn...
Towards that shed!
Maybe she's still in there.
Let's go...

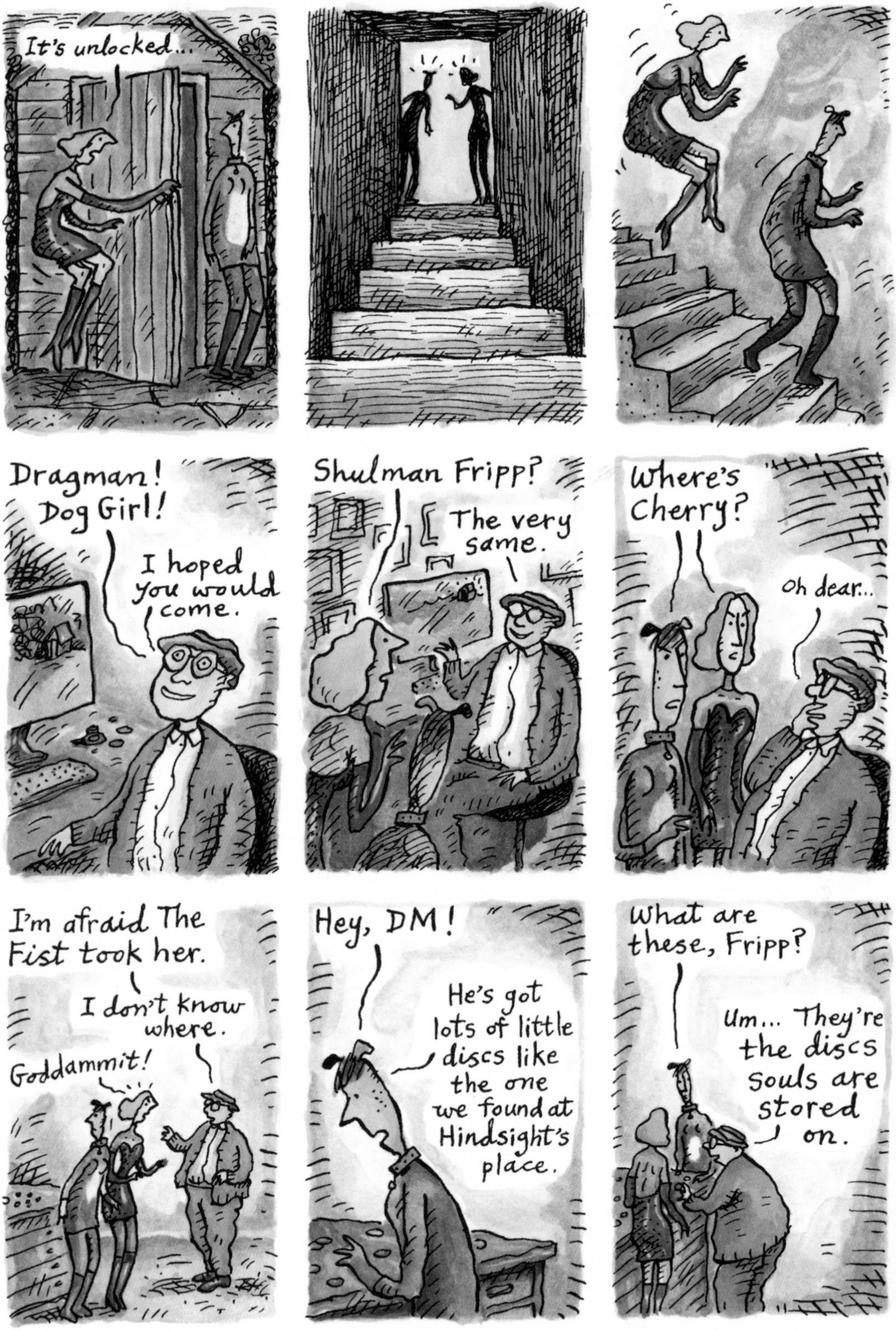
It's unlocked...
Dragman! Dog Girl!
I hoped you would come.
Shulman Fripp?
The very same.
Where's Cherry?
Oh dear...
I'm afraid The Fist took her.
I don't know where.
Goddammit!
Hey, DM!
He's got lots of little discs like the one we found at Hindsight's place.
What are these, Fripp?
Um... They're the discs Souls are stored on.

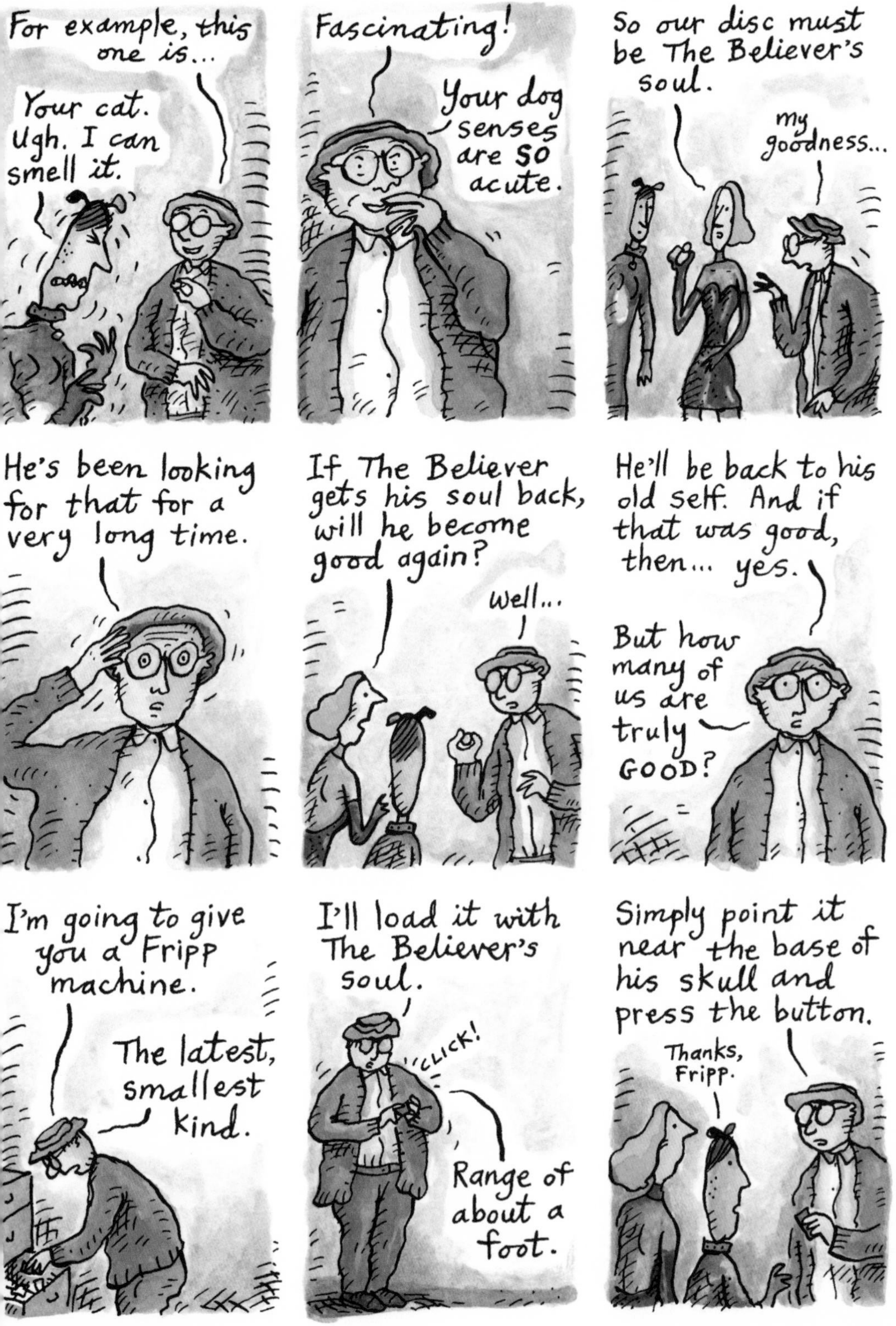
For example, this one is...
Your cat. Ugh. I can smell it.
Fascinating!
Your dog senses are SO acute.
So our disc must be The Believer's soul.
my goodness...
He's been looking for that for a very long time.
If The Believer gets his soul back, will he become good again?
Well...
He'll be back to his old self. And if that was good, then... yes.
But how many of us are truly GOOD?
I'm going to give you a Fripp machine.
The latest, smallest kind.
I'll load it with The Believer's soul.
CLICK!
Range of about a foot.
Simply point it near the base of his skull and press the button.
Thanks, Fripp.

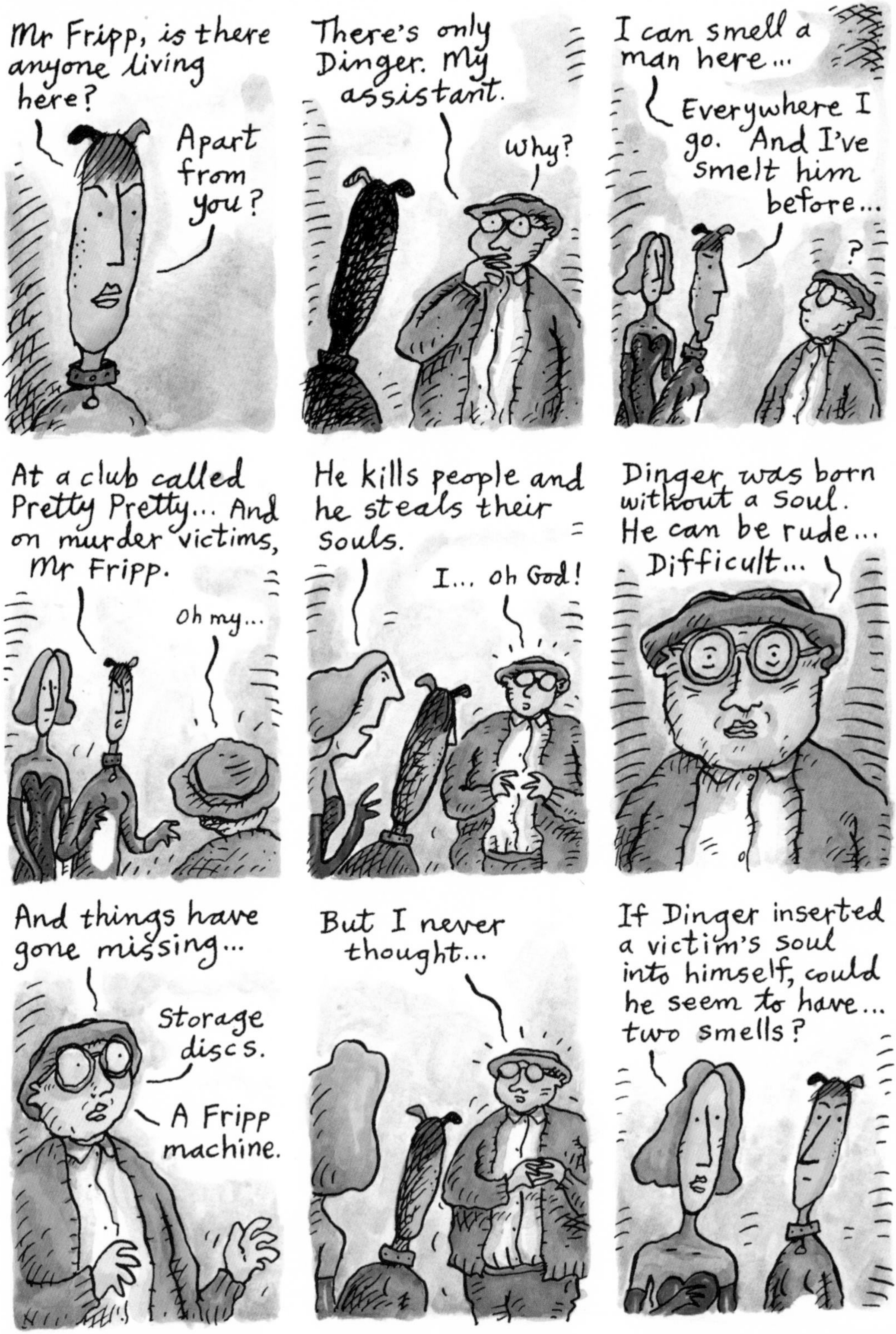
Mr Fripp, is there anyone living here?
Apart from you?
There's only Dinger. My assistant.
Why?
I can smell a man here...
Everywhere I go. And I've smelt him before...
?
At a club called Pretty Pretty... And on murder victims, Mr Fripp.
Oh my...
He kills people and he steals their souls.
I... oh God!
Dinger was born without a soul. He can be rude... Difficult...
And things have gone missing...
Storage discs.
A Fripp machine.
But I never thought...
If Dinger inserted a victim's soul into himself, could he seem to have... two smells?

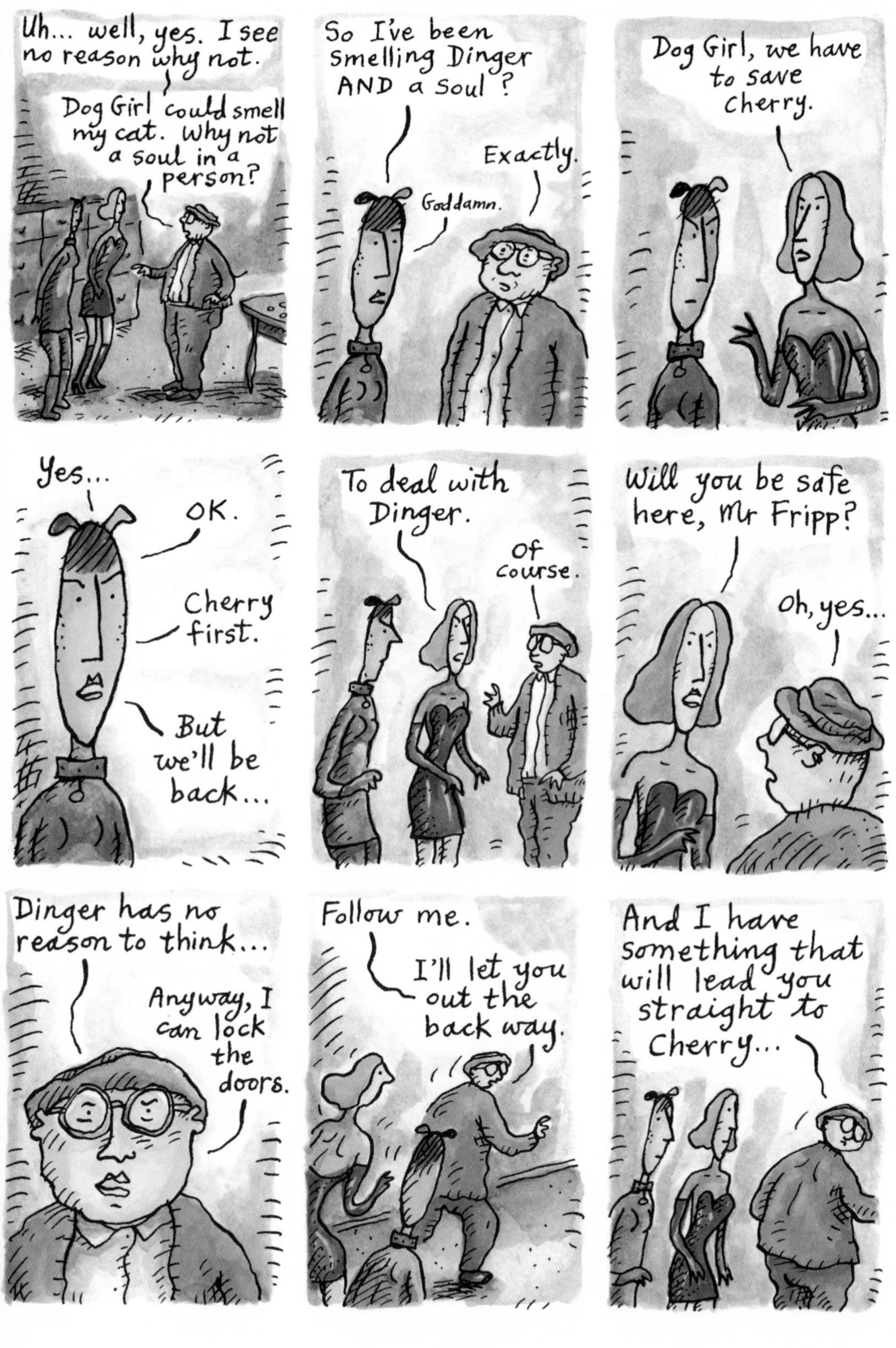
Uh... well, yes. I see no reason why not.
Dog Girl could smell my cat. Why not a soul in a person?
So I've been smelling Dinger AND a soul?
Goddamn.
Exactly.
Dog Girl, we have to save Cherry.
Yes...
OK.
Cherry first.
But we'll be back...
To deal with Dinger.
Of course.
Will you be safe here, Mr Fripp?
Oh, yes...
Dinger has no reason to think...
Anyway, I can lock the doors.
Follow me.
I'll let you out the back way.
And I have something that will lead you straight to Cherry...

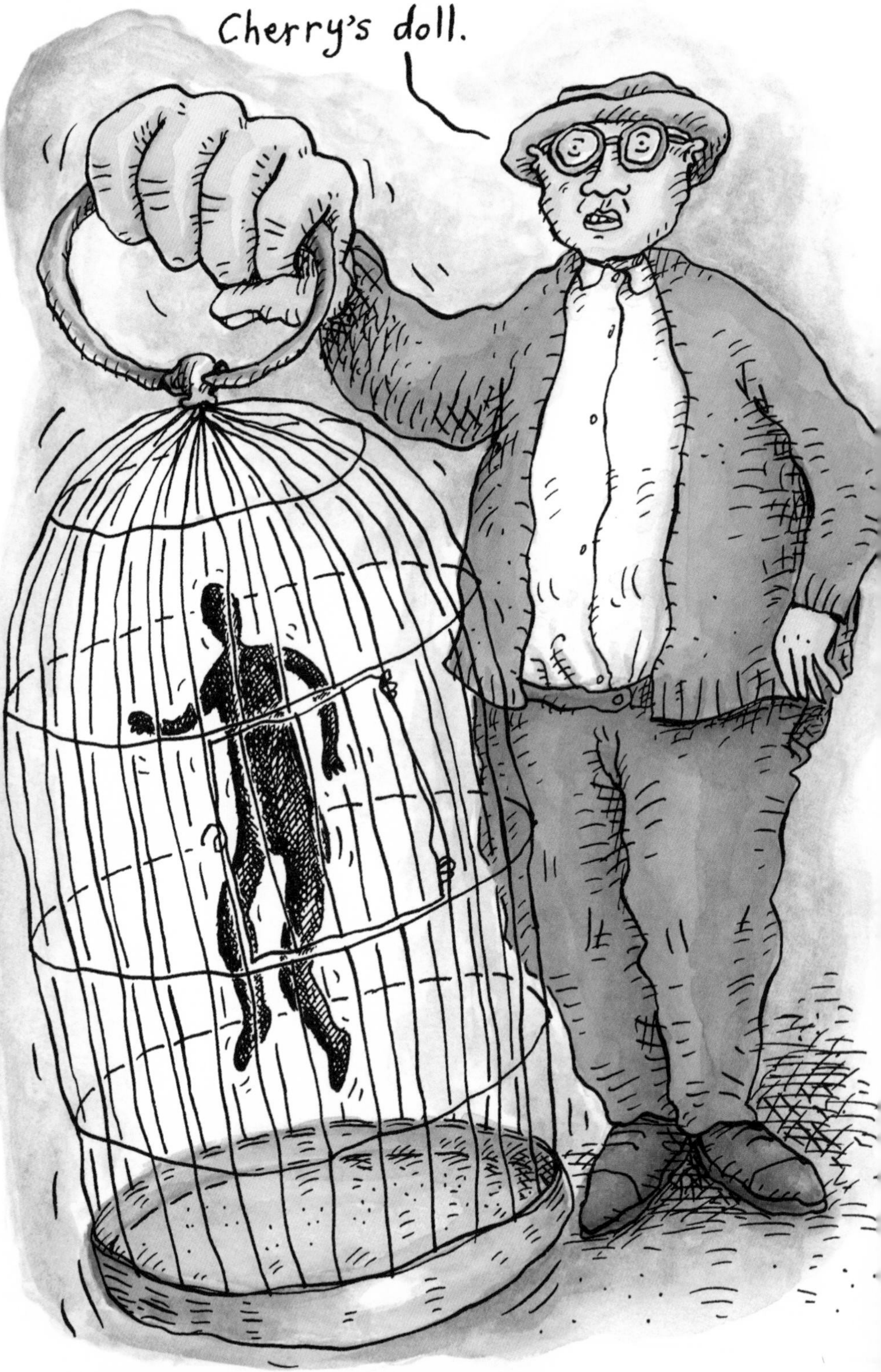
Cherry's doll.

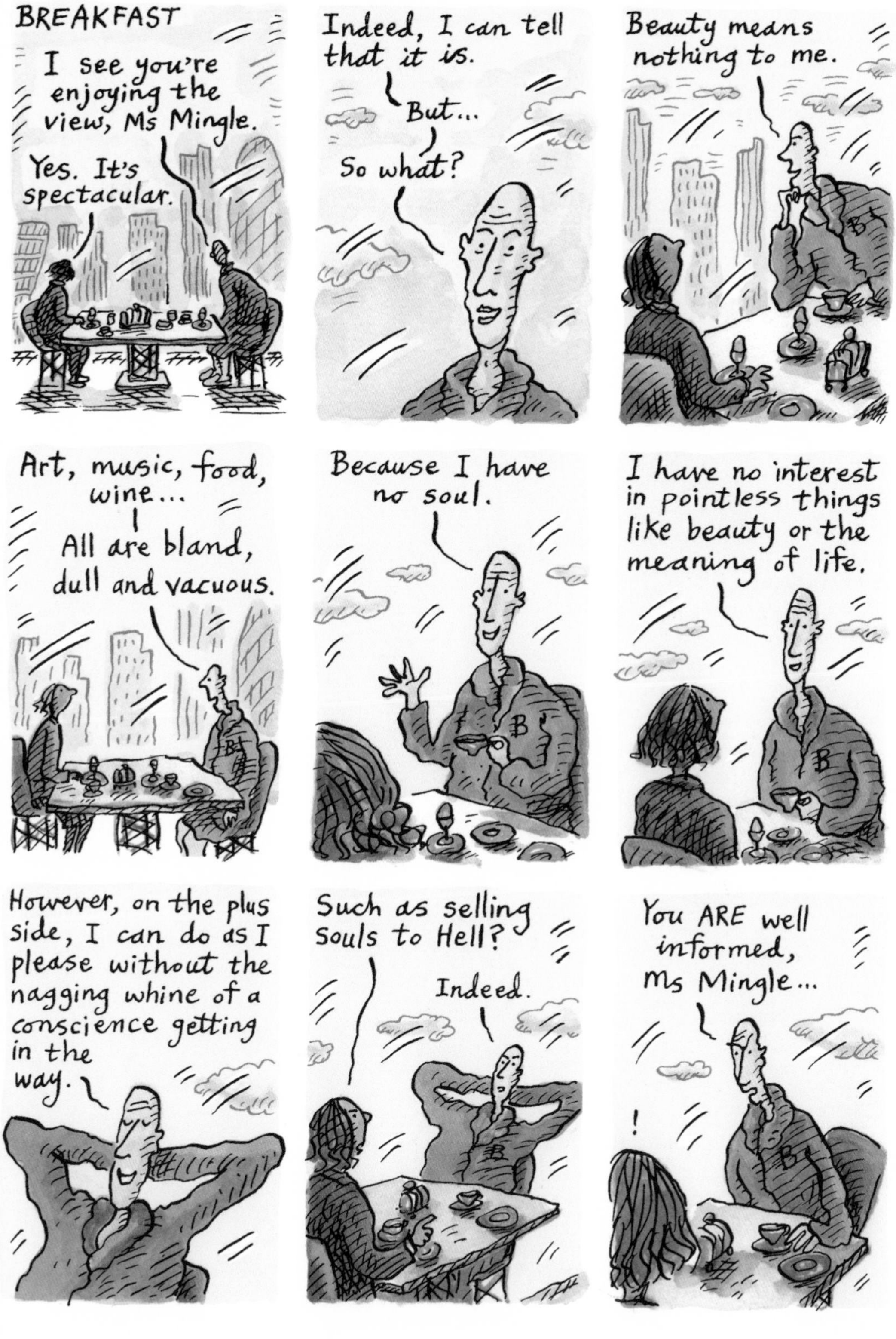
BREAKFAST
I see you're enjoying the view, Ms Mingle.
Yes. It's spectacular.
Indeed, I can tell that it is.
But...
So what?
Beauty means nothing to me.
Art, music, food, wine...
All are bland, dull and vacuous.
Because I have no soul.
I have no interest in pointless things like beauty or the meaning of life.
However, on the plus side, I can do as I please without the nagging whine of a conscience getting in the way.
Such as selling souls to Hell?
Indeed.
You ARE well informed, Ms Mingle...
!

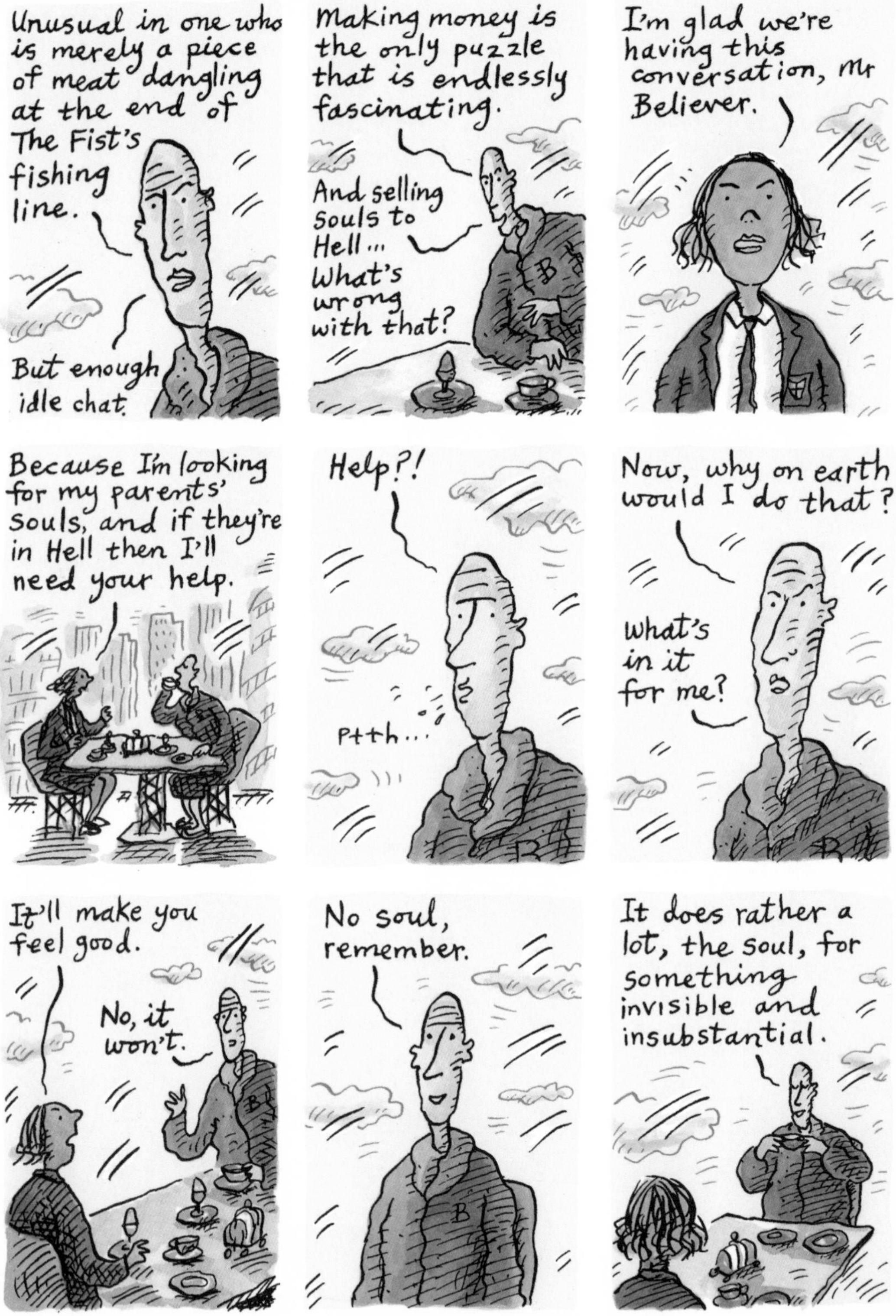

Unusual in one who is merely a piece of meat dangling at the end of The Fist's fishing line.
But enough idle chat.
Making money is the only puzzle that is endlessly fascinating.
And selling souls to Hell... What's wrong with that?
I'm glad we're having this conversation, Mr Believer.
Because I'm looking for my parents' souls, and if they're in Hell then I'll need your help.
Help?!
Ptth...
Now, why on earth would I do that?
What's in it for me?
It'll make you feel good.
No, it won't.
No soul, remember.
It does rather a lot, the soul, for something invisible and insubstantial.

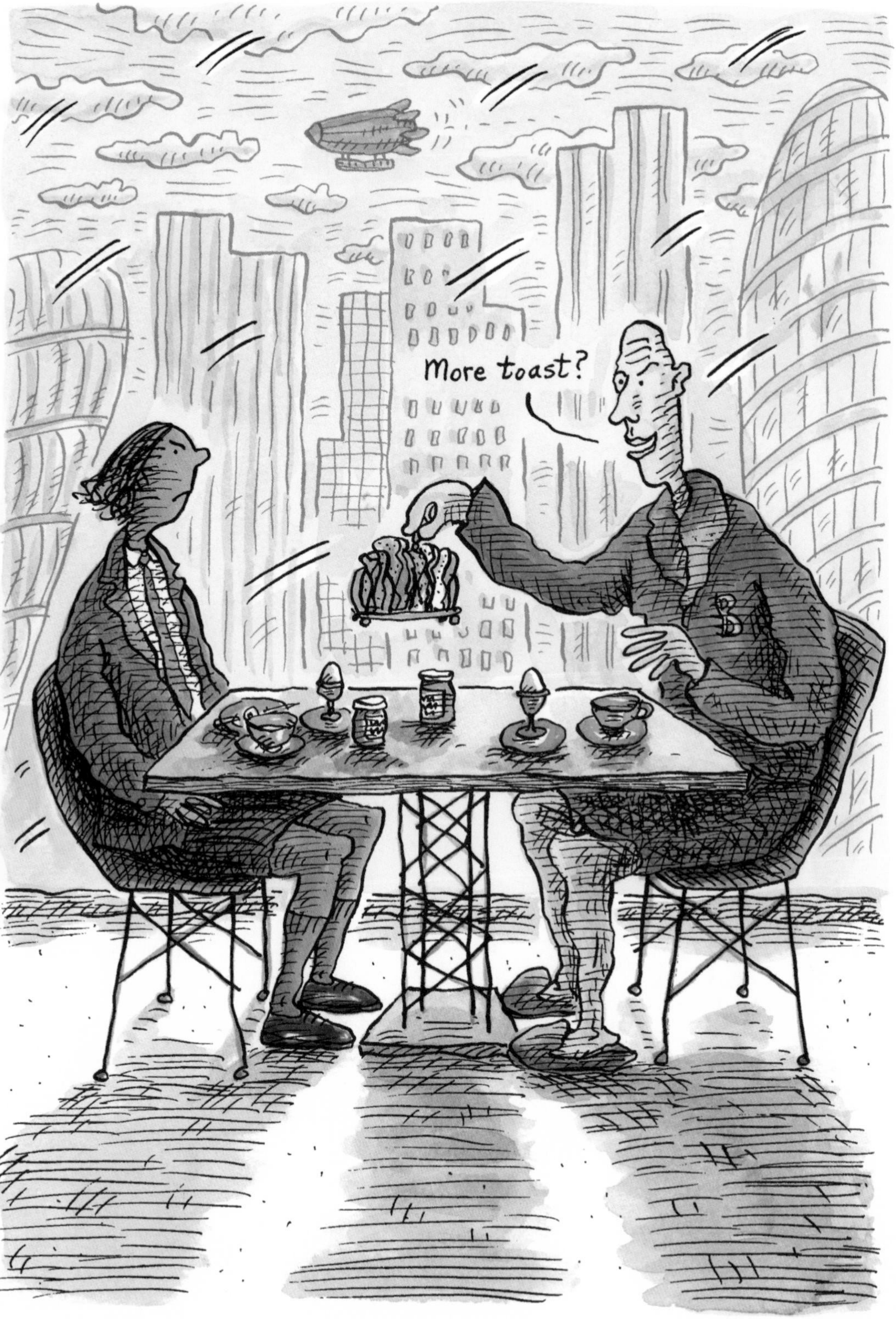
More toast?

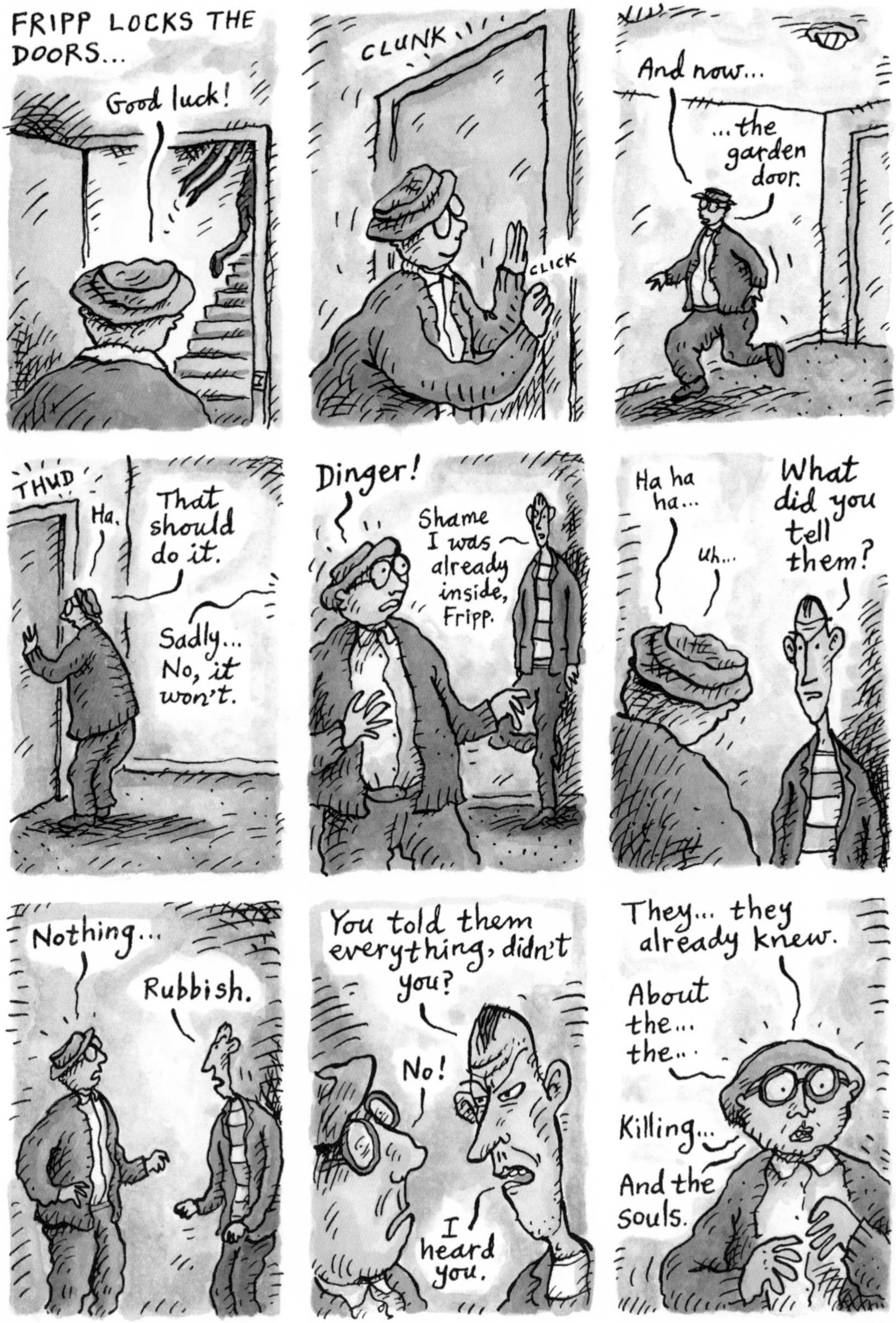

FRIPP LOCKS THE DOORS...
Good luck!
CLUNK
CLICK
And now...
...the garden door.
THUD
Ha.
That should do it.
Sadly... No, it won't.
Dinger!
Shame I was already inside, Fripp.
Ha ha ha...
Uh...
What did you tell them?
Nothing...
Rubbish.
You told them everything, didn't you?
No!
I heard you.
They... they already knew.
About the... the... the...
Killing...
And the souls.

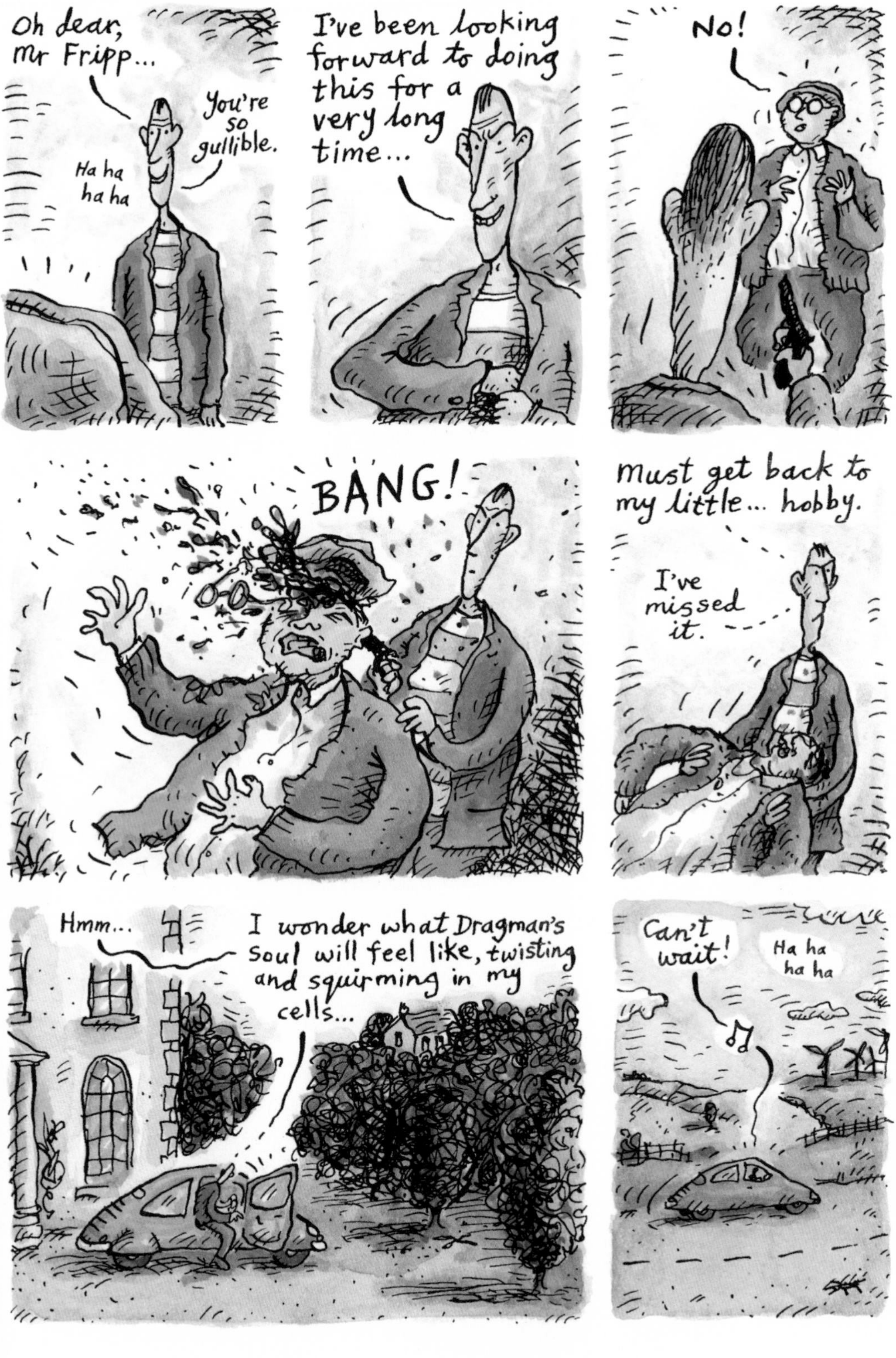
Oh dear, Mr Fripp...
You're so gullible.
Ha ha ha ha
I've been looking forward to doing this for a very long time...
No!
BANG!
Must get back to my little... hobby.
I've missed it.
Hmm...
I wonder what Dragman's soul will feel like, twisting and squirming in my cells...
Can't wait!
Ha ha ha ha

FOLLOWING THE DOLL
Funny man...
Very helpful, though.
Not sure I trust him.
Funny eyes...
Ssh. The doll's heading back to London.

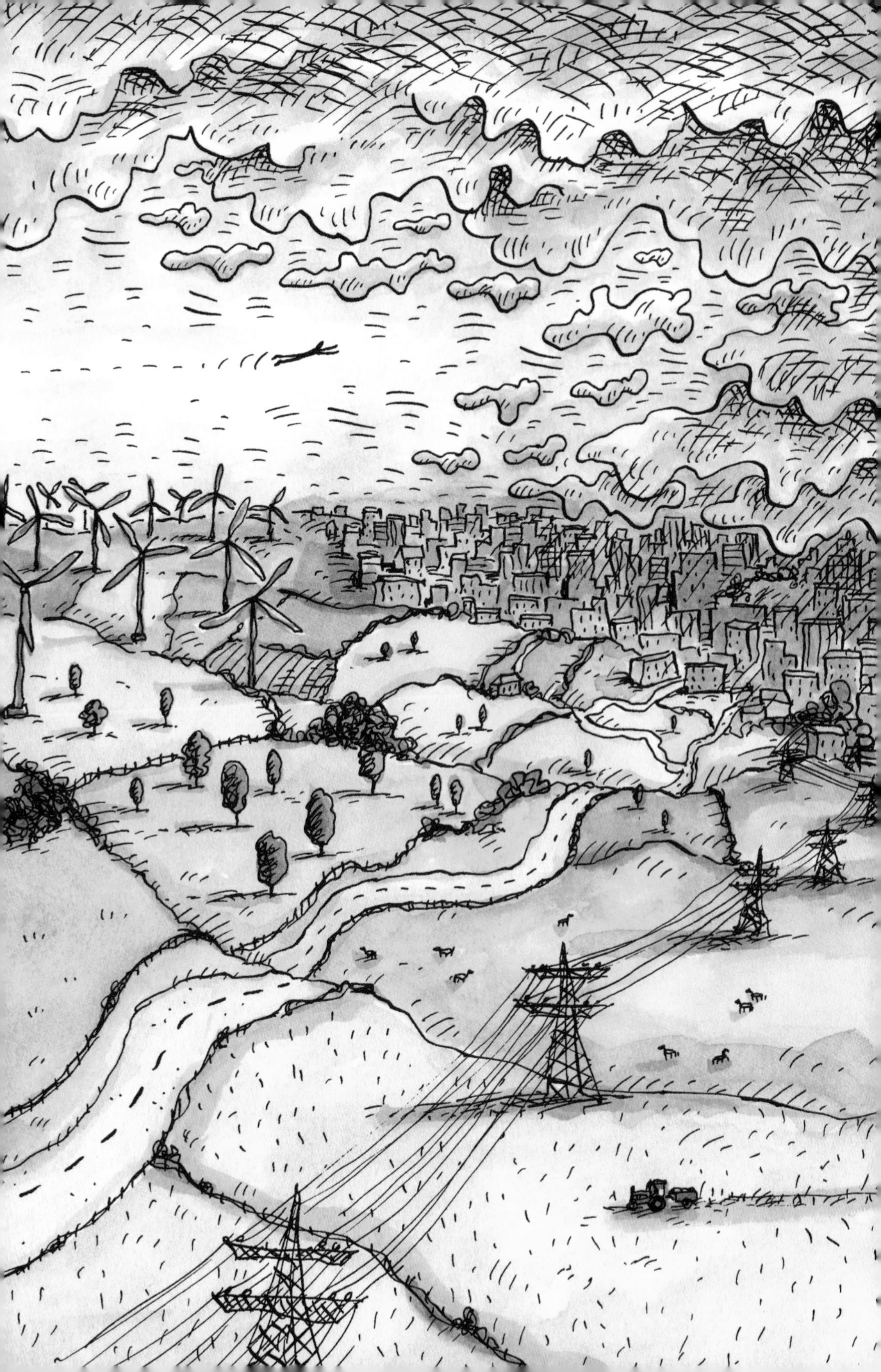

8·15 am

DINGER, THE MAN FULL OF GHOSTS, drives towards the yellow-green smear on the horizon that is London. He drives fast, foot heavy on the accelerator, passing trucks, vans, coaches, cars and, when the traffic slows, pulling onto the hard shoulder and speeding past on the inside. He feels omnipotent. A tiny Fripp machine is in his pocket and the leather, foam-lined case in which he keeps his collection of souls sits on the passenger seat beside him. He plugs in his phone, touches a name on the speed-dial list and, as the ringing tone fills the car, imagines a phone trilling in a pocket up ahead in London.

'Fist.'

'This is Dinger. Dragman is on his way.'

'Good.'

The phone disconnects and Dinger taps a rhythm on the steering wheel. Flecks of blood and bone spatter his jacket and speckle his hair, but a shower and a change of clothes will soon deal with that and make it as if it never happened. He wonders if Shulman Fripp's soul is in Heaven, and has a momentary pang of regret that it doesn't reside on one of the discs in the leather case. He shouldn't have killed him so efficiently.

'Too impulsive,' he thinks. 'Let my feelings take over...'

But then, isn't the ability to show his feelings and get impulsively carried away exactly what the Pretty Pretty girls find deliciously charming and fall head over heels for, over and over and over again?

An image of somersaulting corpses appears in his mind and he smiles. And speeds. And as the corpses perform jerky cartwheels in never-ending loops, London grows steadily from a smear on the horizon into a smudge until finally it becomes a city of concrete and clay into which he vanishes, still moving forward as fast as he can.

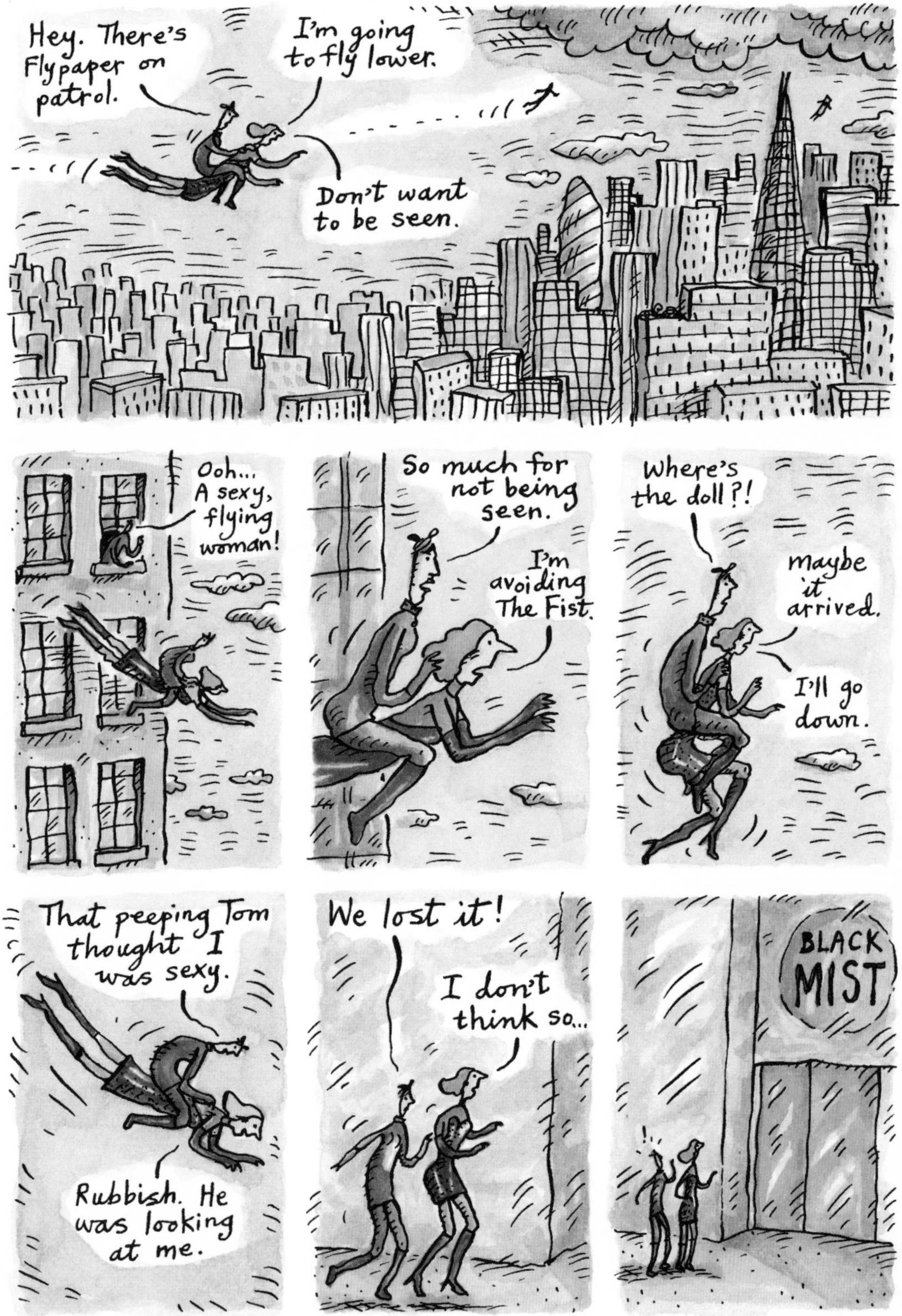

Hey. There's Flypaper on patrol.
I'm going to fly lower.
Don't want to be seen.
Ooh... A sexy, flying woman!
So much for not being seen.
I'm avoiding The Fist.
Where's the doll?!
maybe it arrived.
I'll go down.
That peeping Tom thought I was sexy.
Rubbish. He was looking at me.
We lost it!
I don't think so...
BLACK MIST

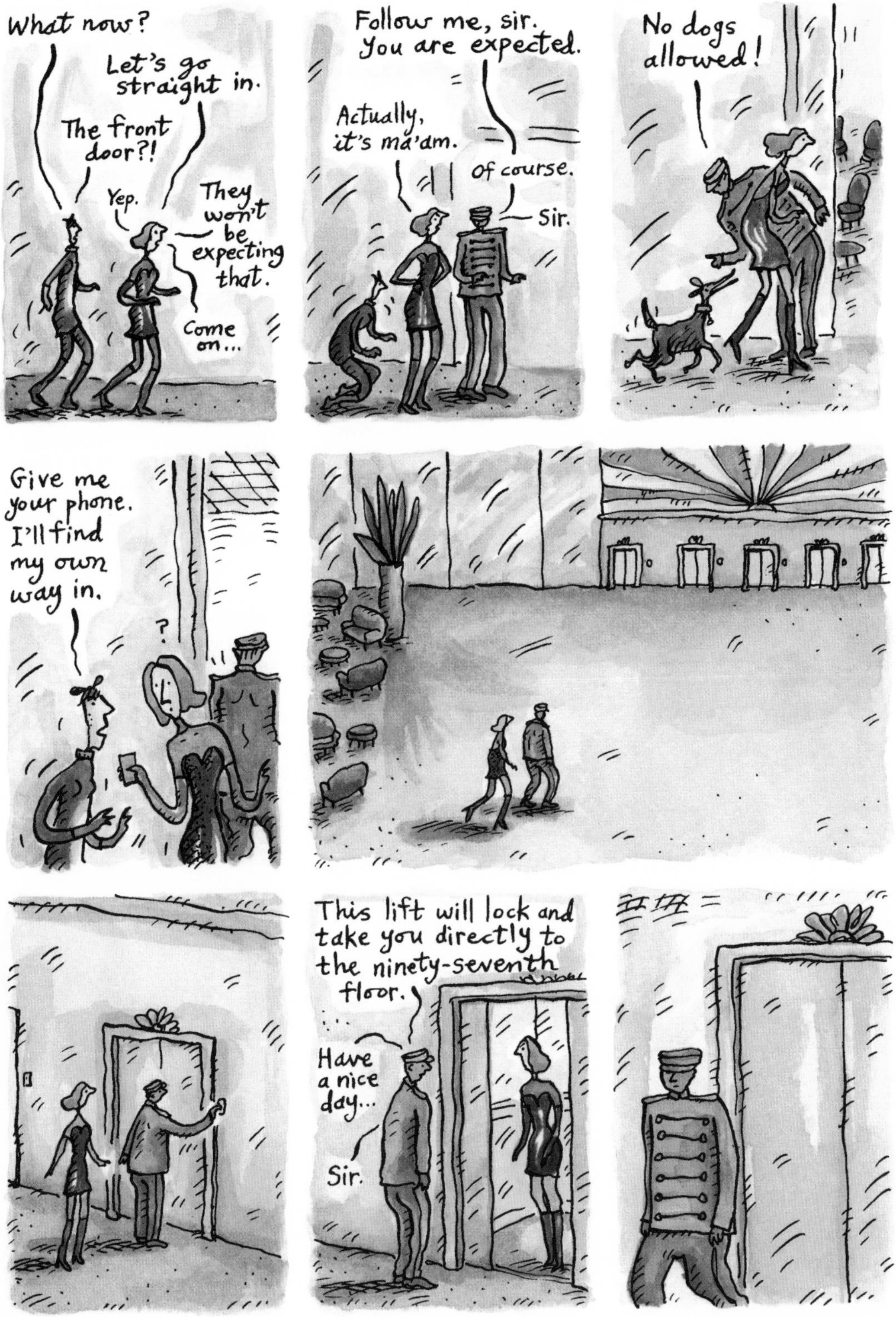
What now?
Let's go straight in.
The front door?!
Yep.
They won't be expecting that.
Come on...
Follow me, sir. You are expected.
Actually, it's ma'am.
Of course.
Sir.
No dogs allowed!
Give me your phone. I'll find my own way in.
?
This lift will lock and take you directly to the ninety-seventh floor.
Have a nice day...
Sir.

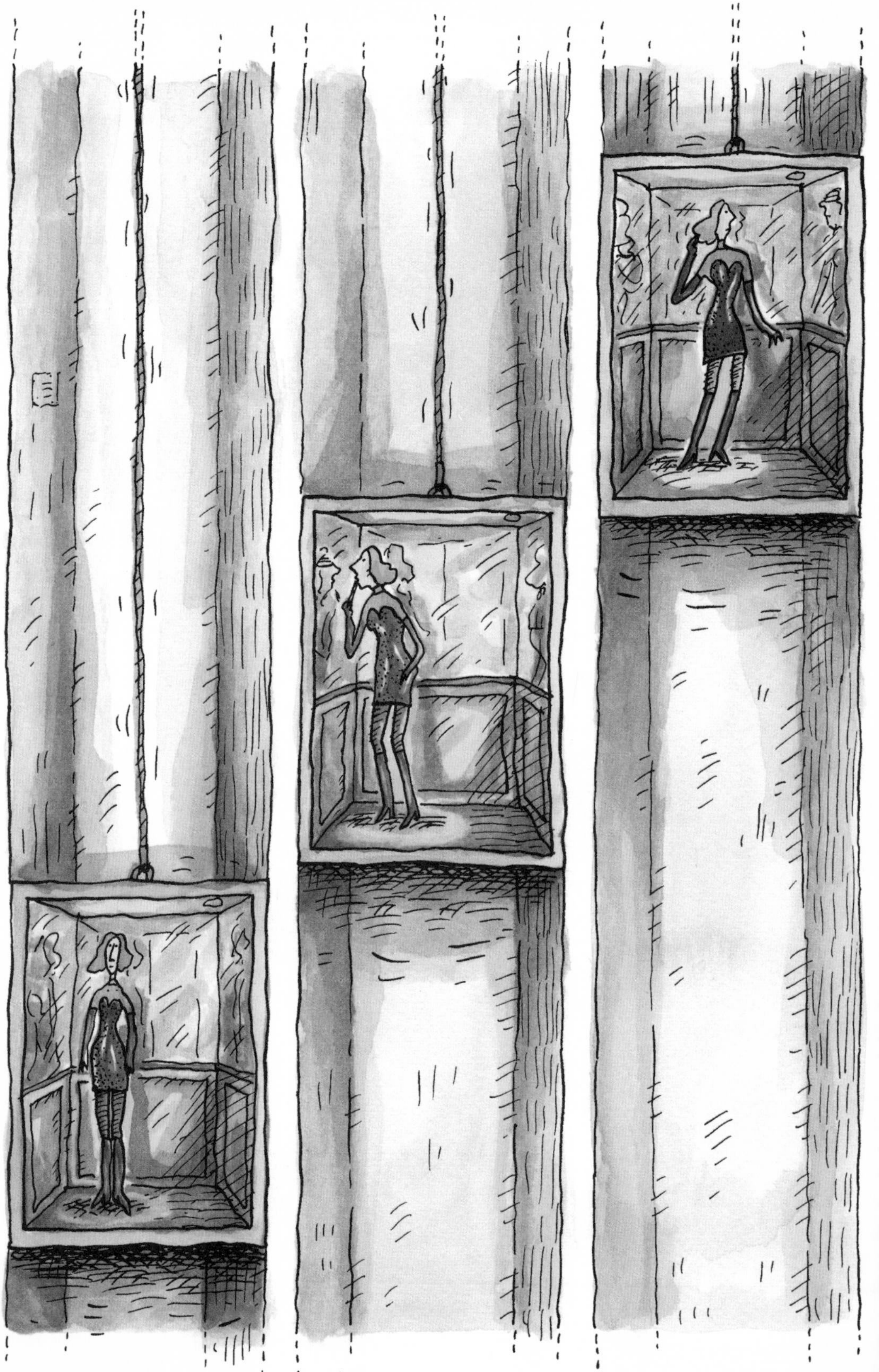

CLUNK...
Dragman. Welcome...
Now, before you exit the lift I want you to remove every article of clothing.
Or I'm sure you can imagine what I'll do to Ms Mingle.
I'll happily do it for you, Believer.
So thoughtful, Fist.
Of course you may.
Wig too.
Don't be shy.

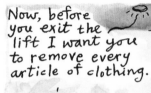

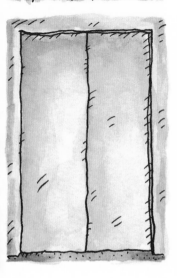

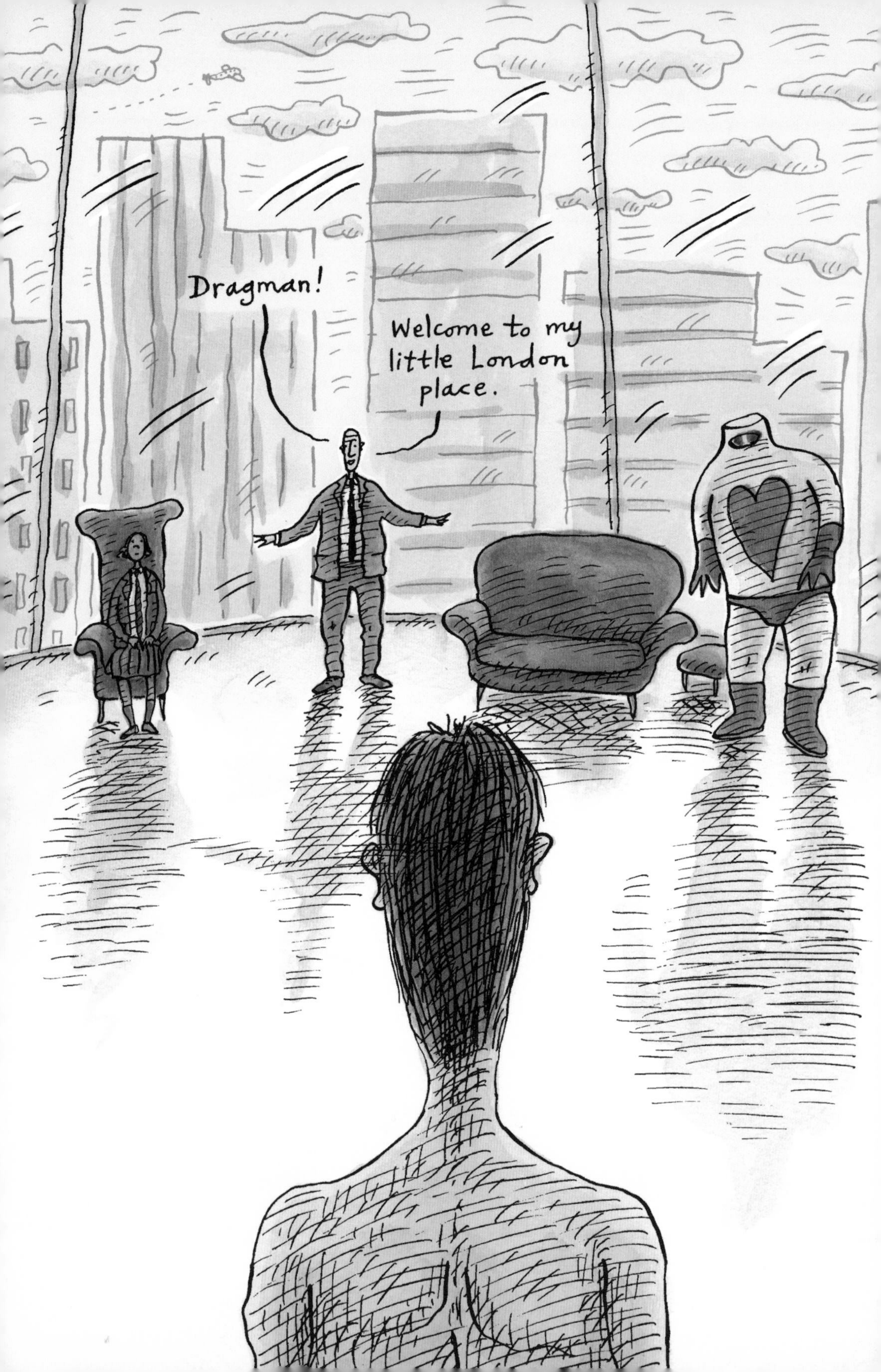
Dragman!
Welcome to my little London place.

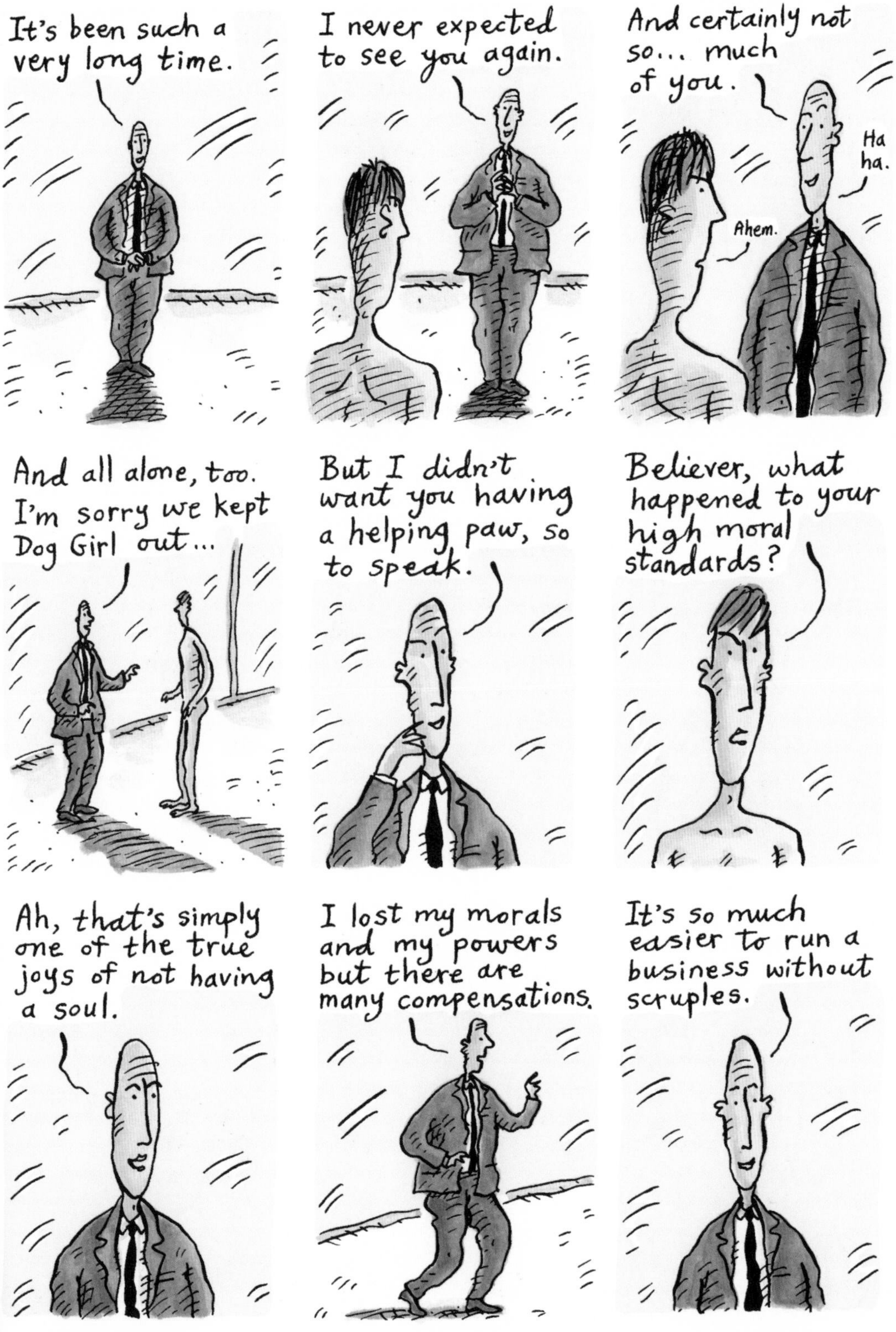
It's been such a very long time.
I never expected to see you again.
And certainly not so... much of you.
Ahem.
Ha ha.
And all alone, too. I'm sorry we kept Dog Girl out...
But I didn't want you having a helping paw, so to speak.
Believer, what happened to your high moral standards?
Ah, that's simply one of the true joys of not having a soul.
I lost my morals and my powers but there are many compensations.
It's so much easier to run a business without scruples.

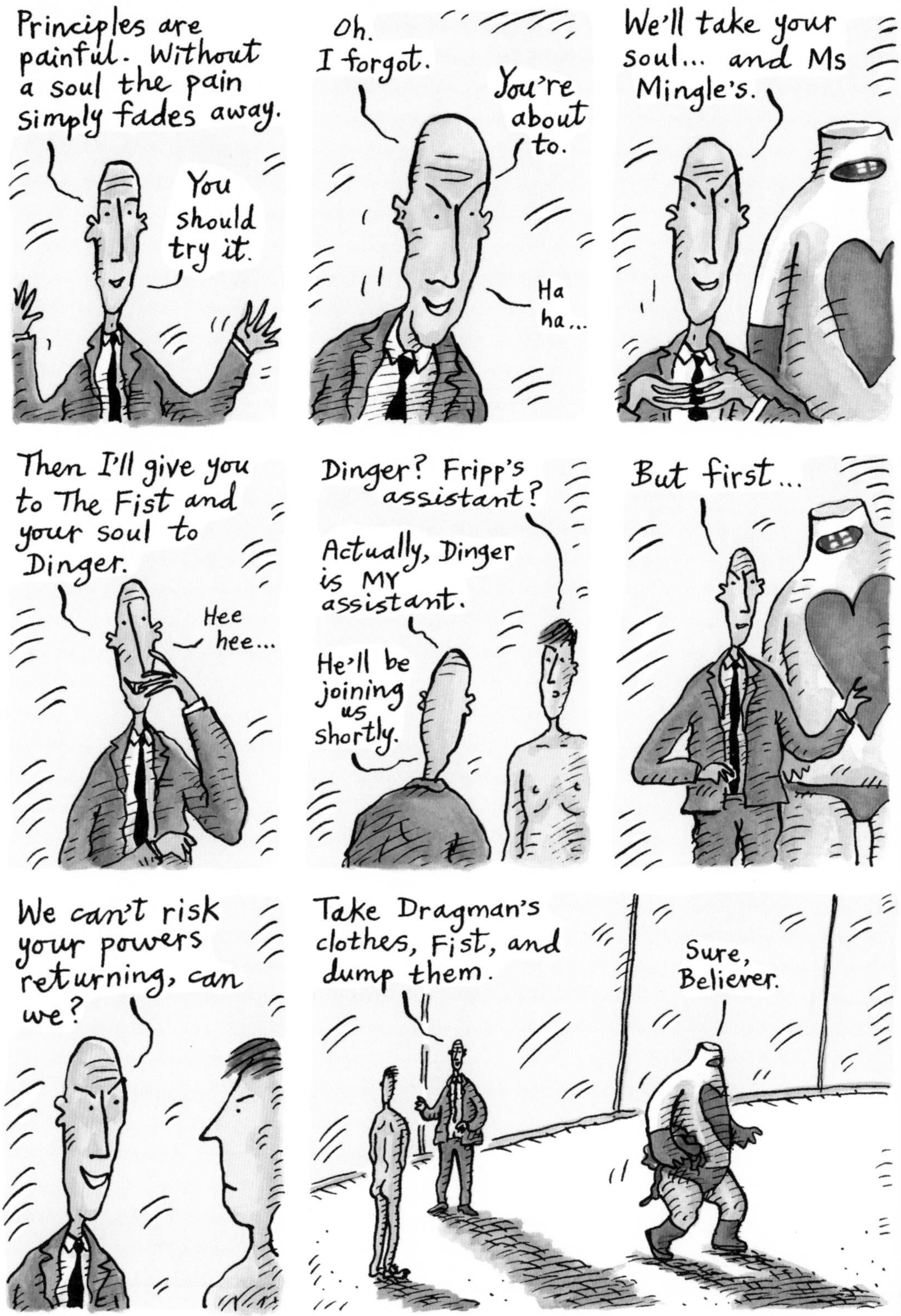
Principles are painful. Without a soul the pain simply fades away.
You should try it.
Oh. I forgot.
You're about to.
Ha ha...
We'll take your soul... and Ms Mingle's.
Then I'll give you to The Fist and your soul to Dinger.
Hee hee...
Dinger? Fripp's assistant?
Actually, Dinger is MY assistant.
He'll be joining us shortly.
But first...
We can't risk your powers returning, can we?
Take Dragman's clothes, Fist, and dump them.
Sure, Believer.

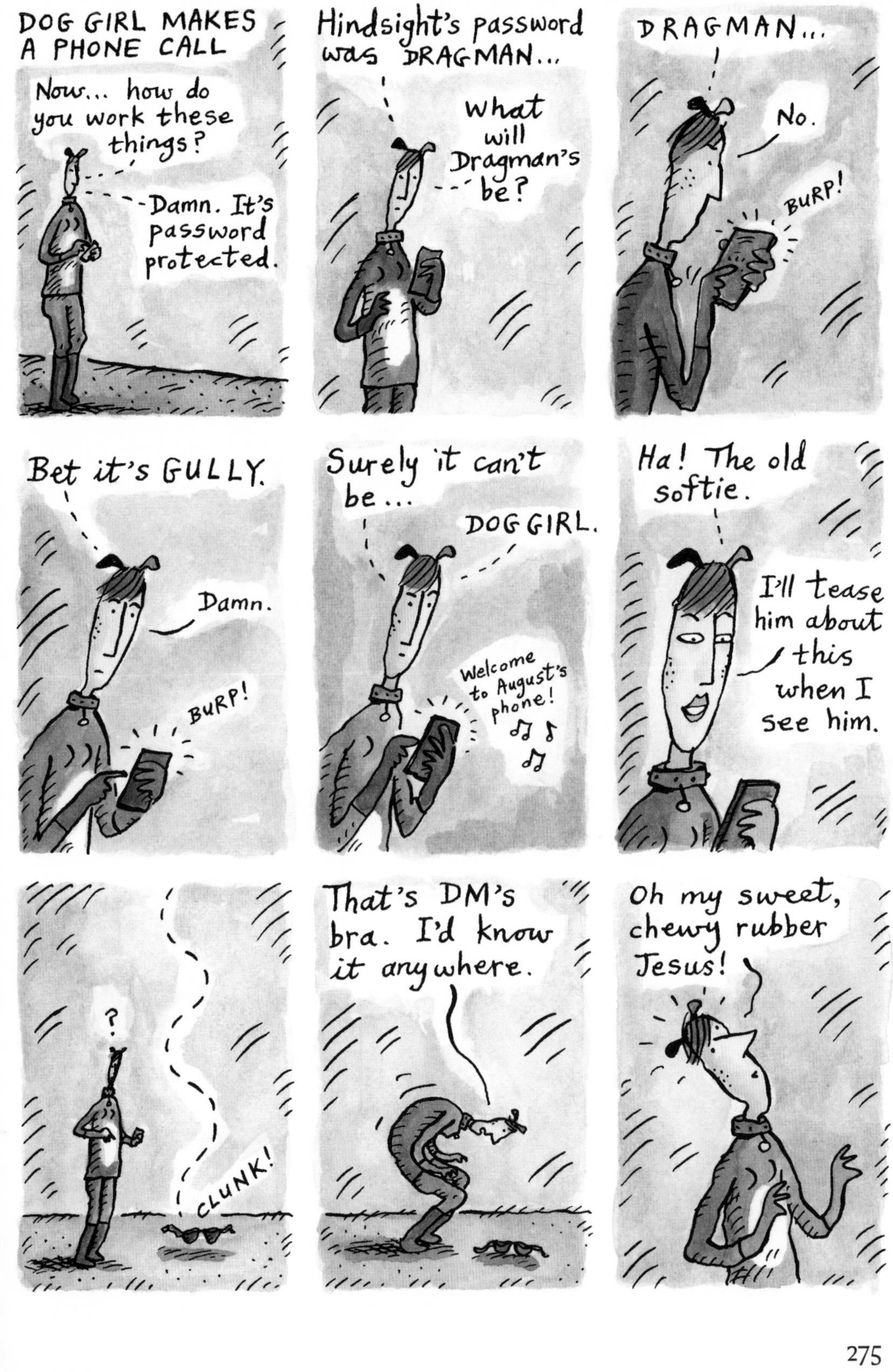
DOG GIRL MAKES A PHONE CALL
Now... how do you work these things?
Damn. It's password protected.
Hindsight's password was DRAGMAN...
What will Dragman's be?
DRAGMAN...
No.
BURP!
Bet it's GULLY.
Damn.
BURP!
Surely it can't be...
DOG GIRL.
Welcome to August's phone!
Ha! The old softie.
I'll tease him about this when I see him.
?
CLUNK!
That's DM's bra. I'd know it anywhere.
Oh my sweet, chewy rubber Jesus!

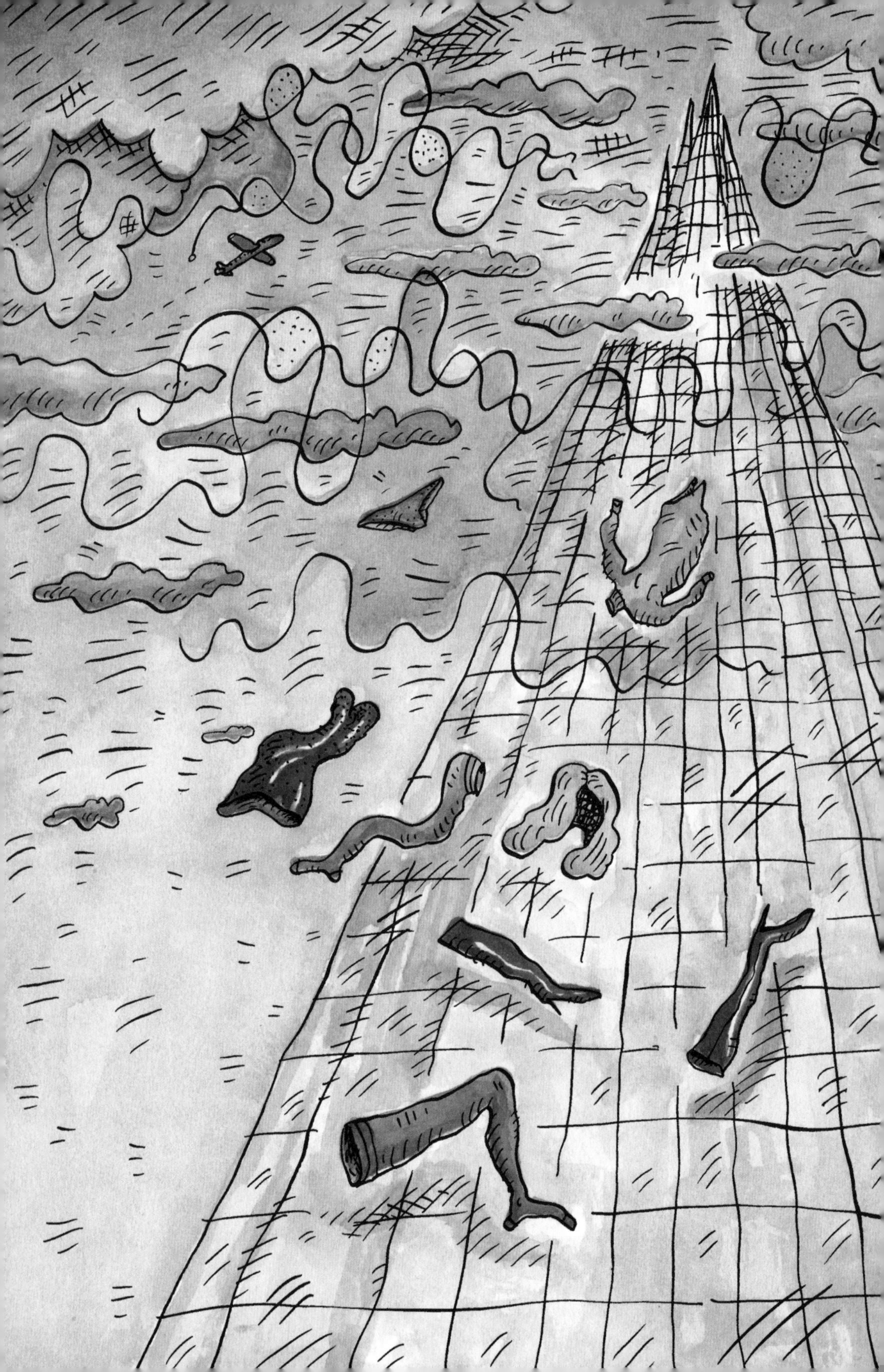

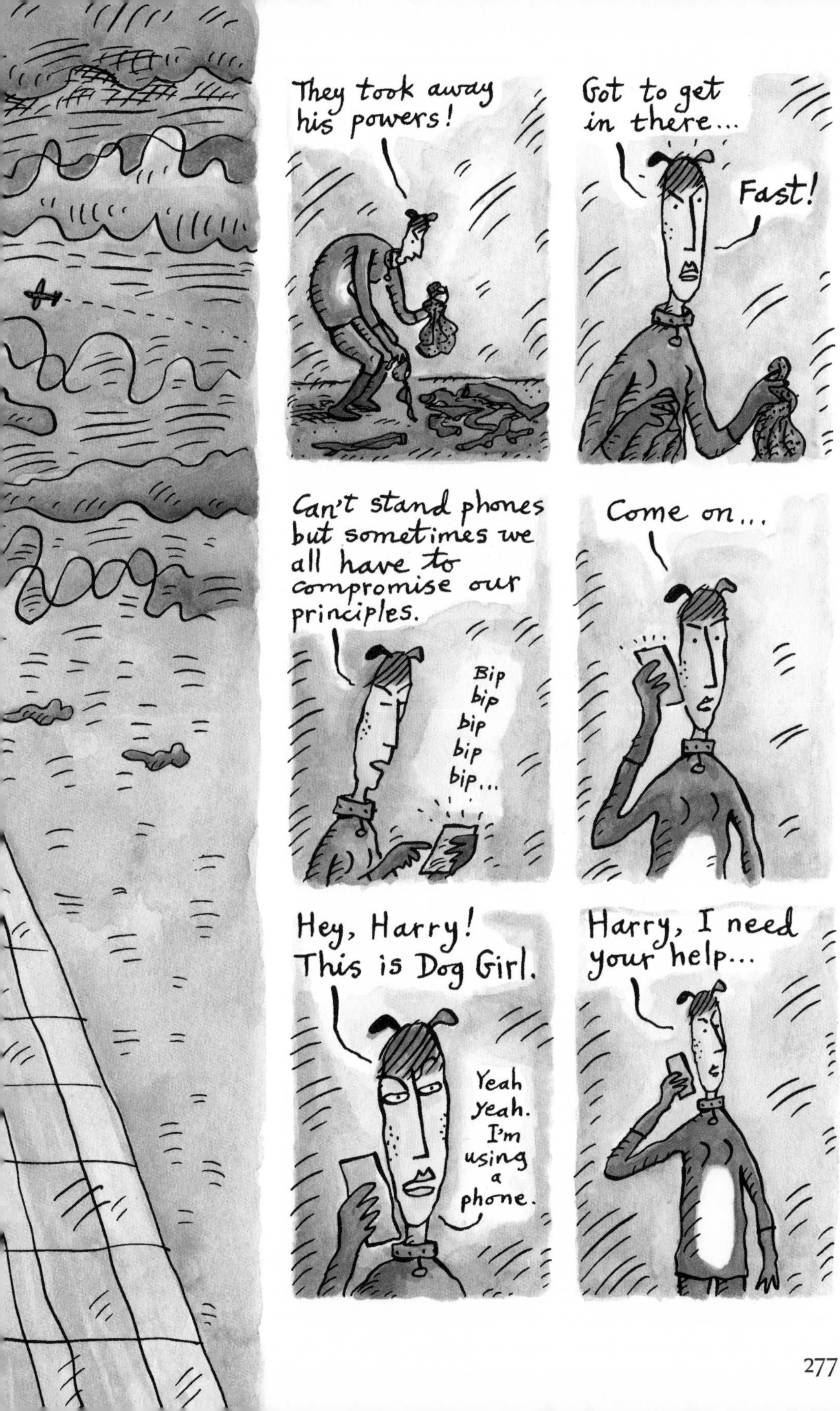
They took away his powers!
Got to get in there...
Fast!
Can't stand phones but sometimes we all have to compromise our principles.
Bip bip bip bip bip...
Come on...
Hey, Harry! This is Dog Girl.
Yeah Yeah. I'm using a phone.
Harry, I need your help...

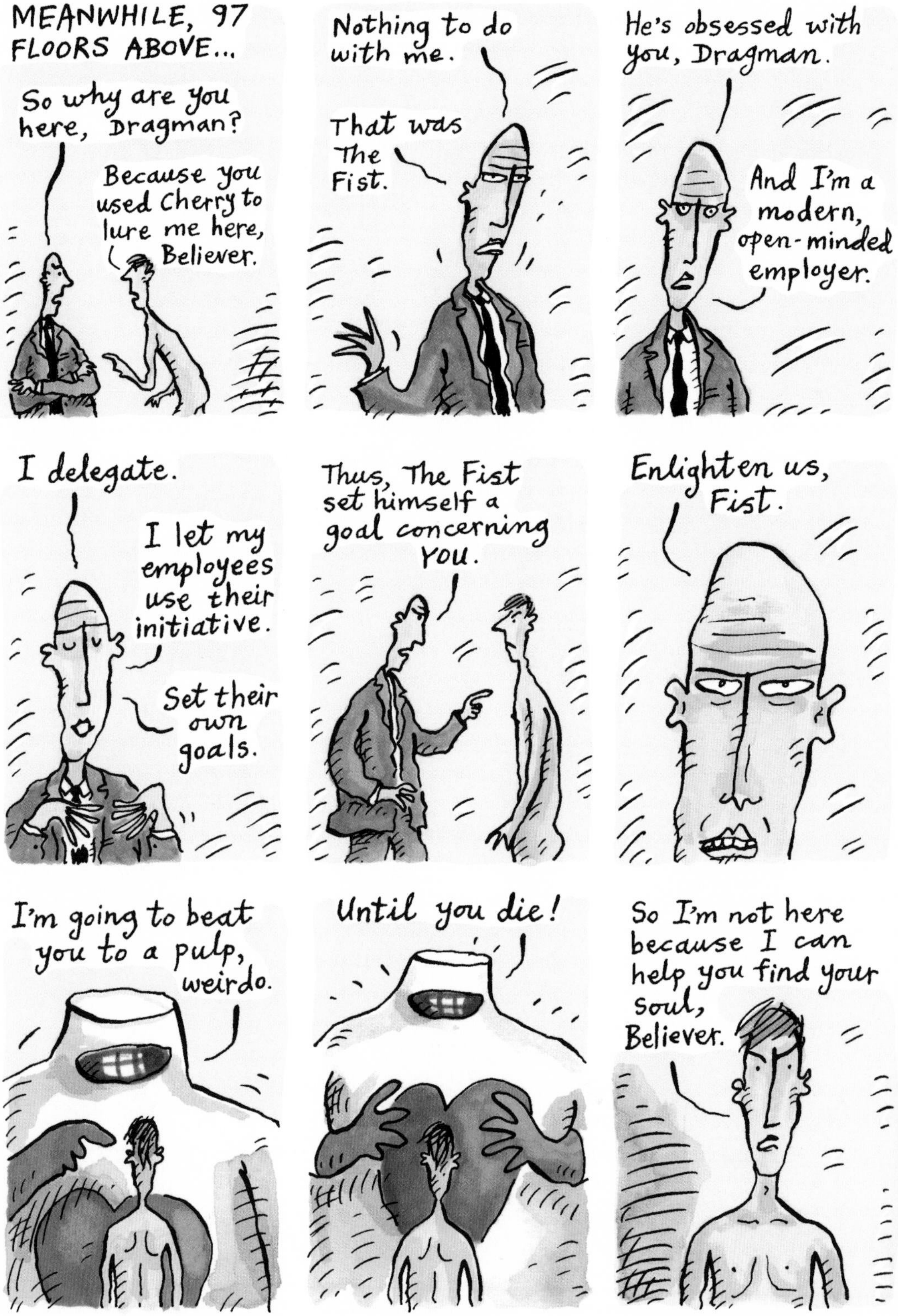
MEANWHILE, 97 FLOORS ABOVE...
So why are you here, Dragman?
Because you used Cherry to lure me here, Believer.
Nothing to do with me.
That was The Fist.
He's obsessed with you, Dragman.
And I'm a modern, open-minded employer.
I delegate.
I let my employees use their initiative.
Set their own goals.
Thus, The Fist set himself a goal concerning YOU.
Enlighten us, Fist.
I'm going to beat you to a pulp, weirdo.
Until you die!
So I'm not here because I can help you find your soul, Believer.

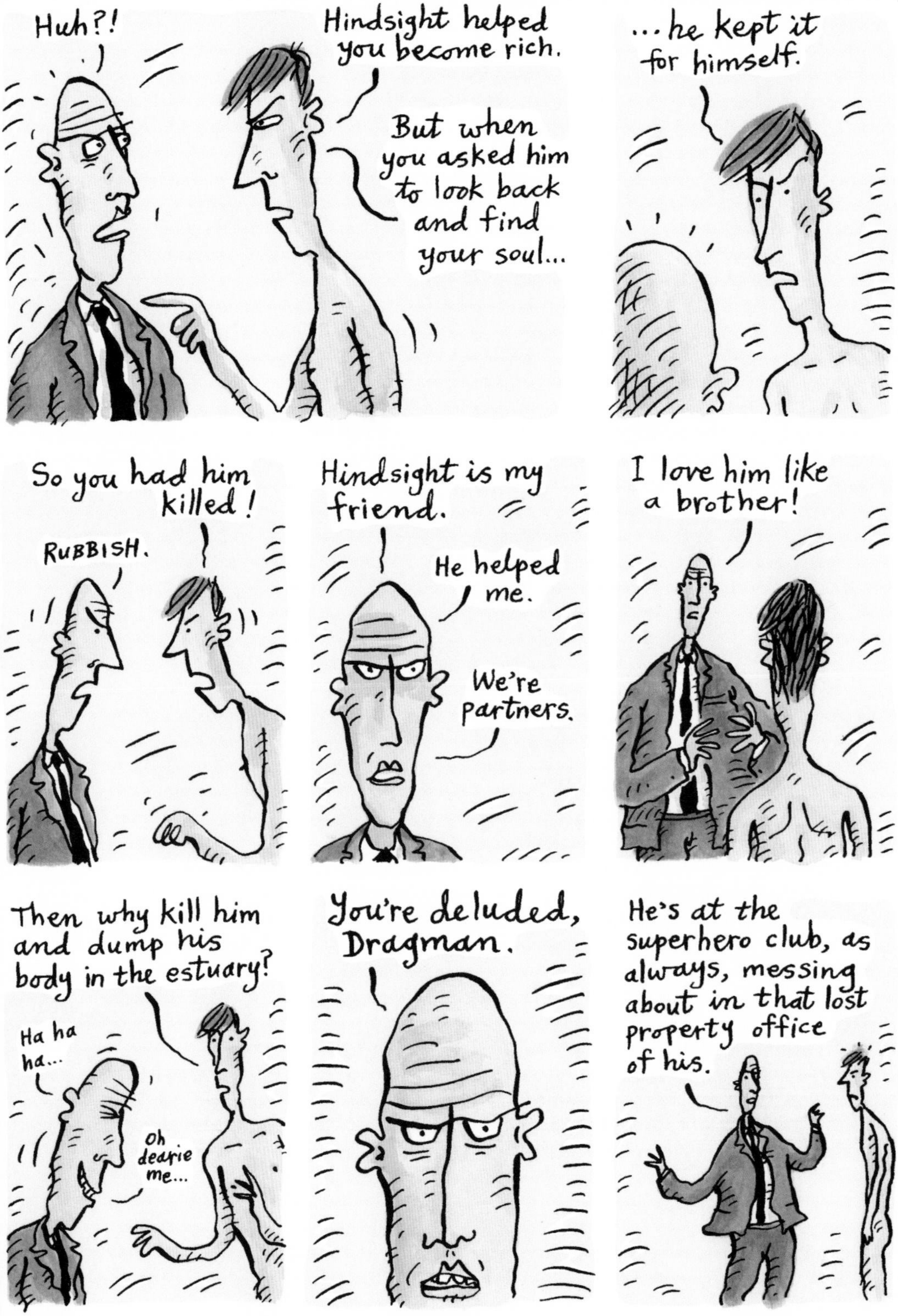
Huh?!
Hindsight helped you become rich.
But when you asked him to look back and find your soul...
...he kept it for himself.
So you had him killed!
RUBBISH.
Hindsight is my friend.
He helped me.
We're partners.
I love him like a brother!
Then why kill him and dump his body in the estuary?
Ha ha ha...
Oh dearie me...
You're deluded, Dragman.
He's at the superhero club, as always, messing about in that lost property office of his.

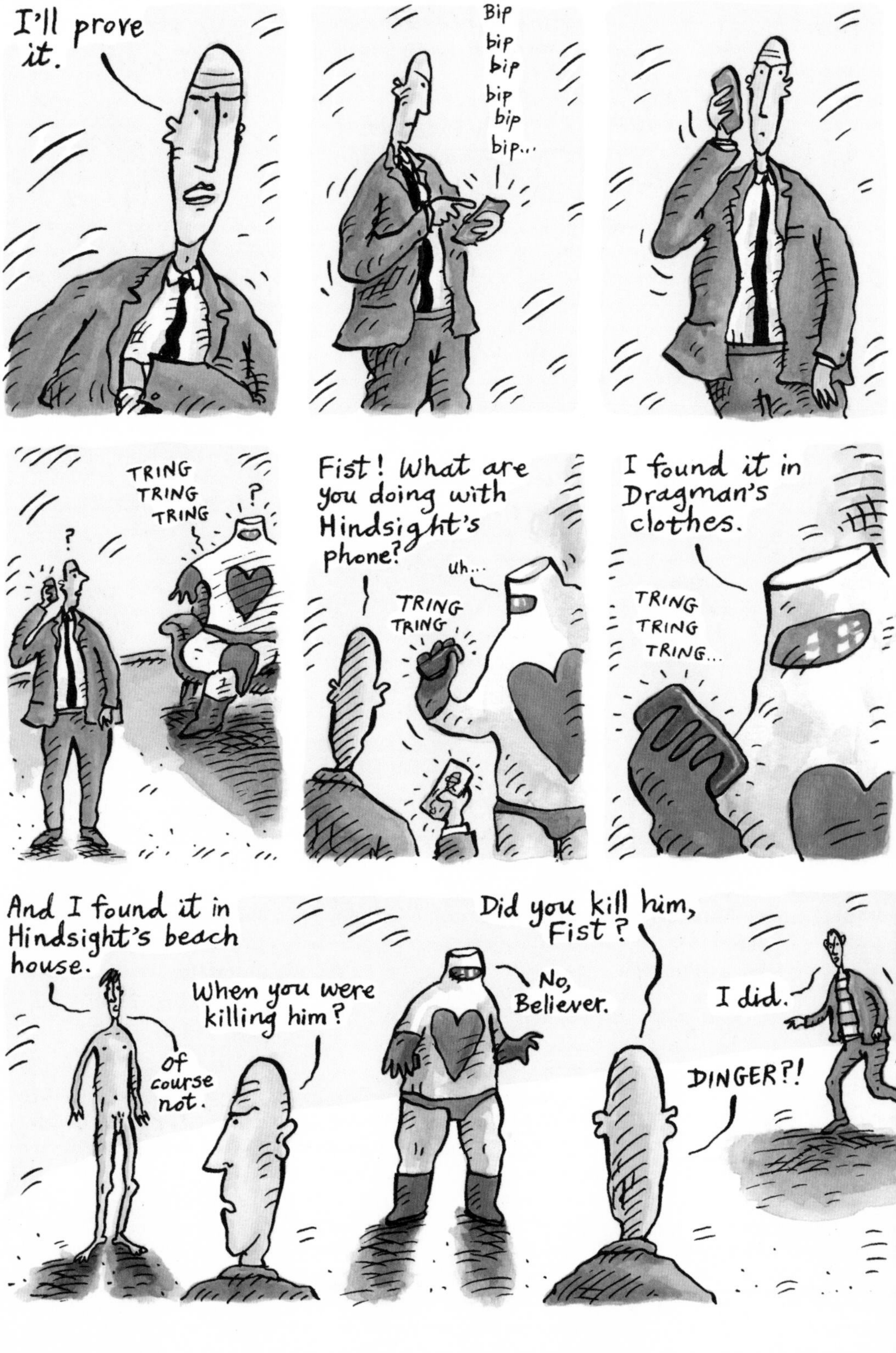

I'll prove it.
Bip
bip
bip
bip
bip
bip...
TRING
TRING
TRING
?
?
Fist! What are you doing with Hindsight's phone?
uh...
TRING
TRING
I found it in Dragman's clothes.
TRING
TRING
TRING...
And I found it in Hindsight's beach house.
Of course not.
When you were killing him?
Did you kill him, Fist?
No, Believer.
I did.
DINGER?!

Why?!

He came to see you, Believer, and I happened to be here.

He was agitated. We'd met before, but this time he called me by the wrong name.

Hi, Harvey.

My secret name.

Your Pretty Pretty name!

uh... Yes.

How did you..?

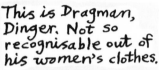

This is Dragman, Dinger. Not so recognisable out of his women's clothes.

And less powerful.

Ha ha ha...

Well, I couldn't have Hindsight knowing my secret name. One day he'd start making connections. I couldn't have that.

Is The Believer around, Harvey?

So I strangled him. And dressed his body as a girl. Hid him in plain sight, so to speak.

Akk... kk...

One corpse among many.

Well that's that.

C'est la vie.

Thank you, Dinger.

But... Hindsight was your FRIEND!

Another benefit of not having a soul, Dragman.

A murder simply feels like breaking a favourite vase.

281

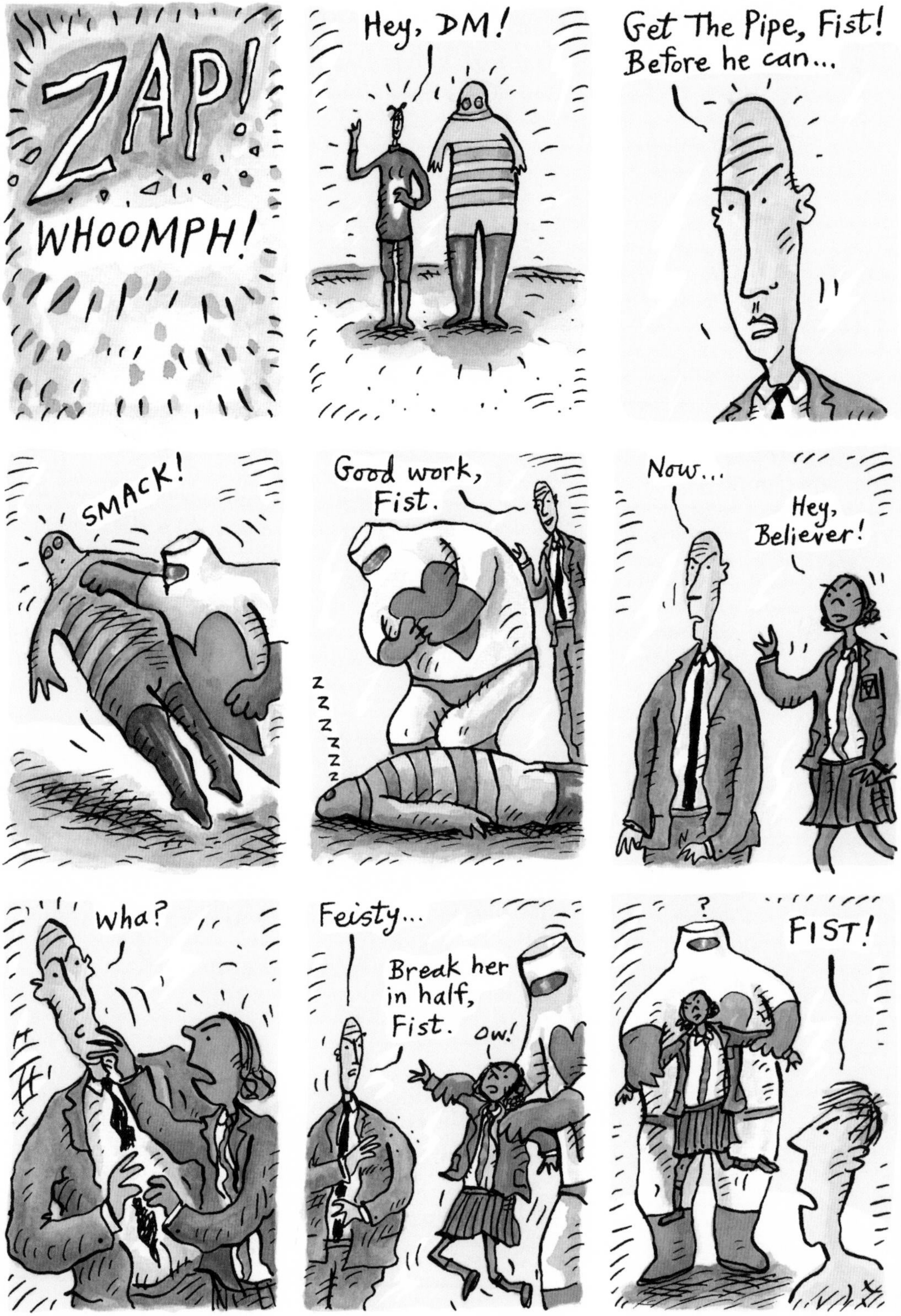
ZAP!
WHOOMPH!
Hey, DM!
Get The Pipe, Fist! Before he can...
SMACK!
Good work, Fist.
z z z z z z
Now...
Hey, Believer!
Wha?
Feisty...
Break her in half, Fist.
OW!
?
FIST!

Leave Cherry alone!

If you want to pick on someone, pick on me.

What a good idea.

TOSS

You could take off your strong suit. Make it a fairer fight.

No. I couldn't do that.

Because I intend to beat the living shit out of you, weirdo.

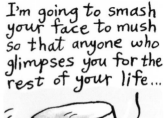

I'm going to smash your face to mush so that anyone who glimpses you for the rest of your life...

Will turn away and throw up at the sight.

I'm going to...

Raaaaa...

283

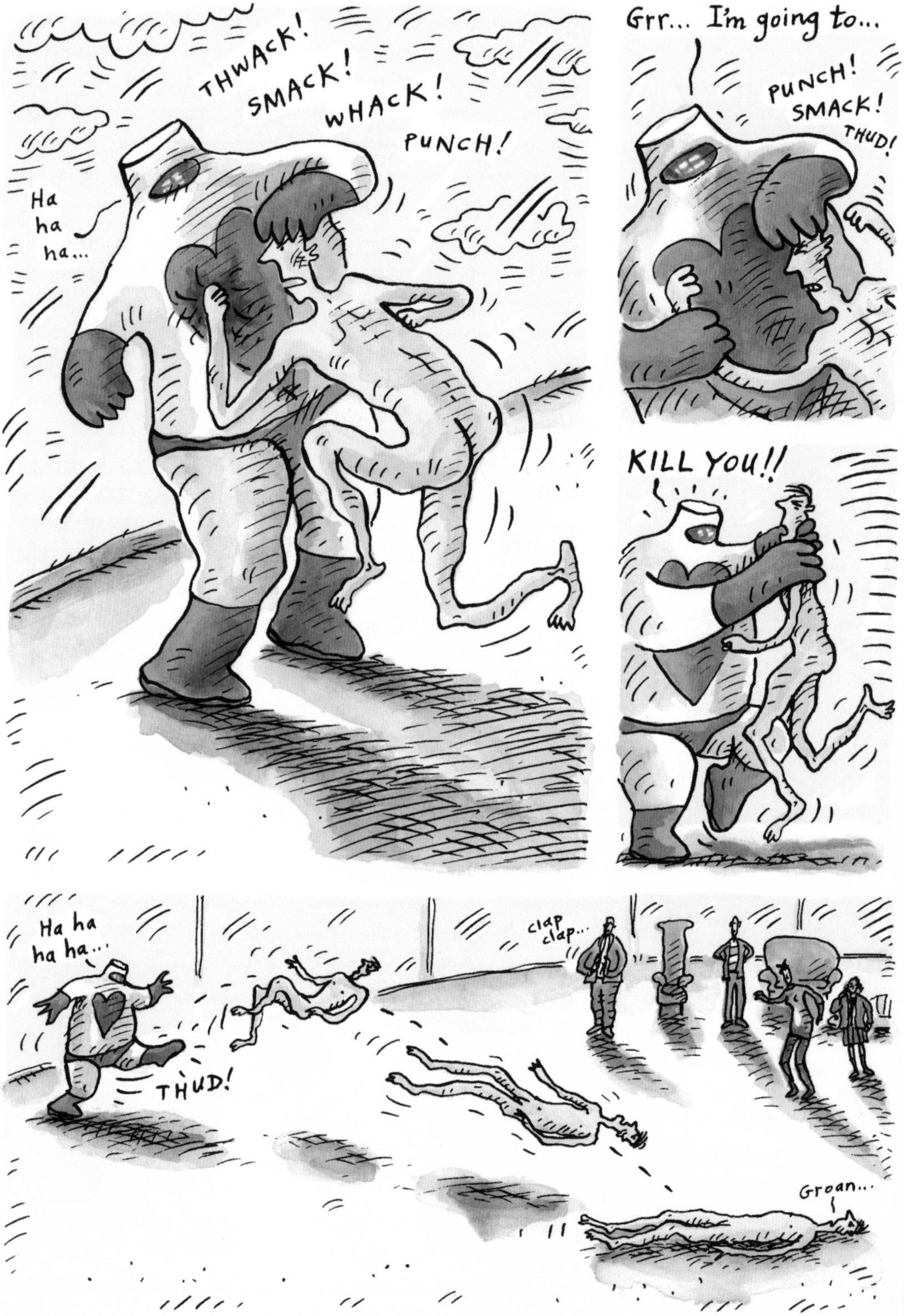
THWACK!
SMACK!
WHACK!
PUNCH!
Ha ha ha...
Grr... I'm going to...
PUNCH!
SMACK!
THUD!
KILL YOU!!
Ha ha ha ha...
THUD!
clap clap...
Groan...

Interlude

I wake up to see Mother sitting in her usual chair, staring at me. It's disconcerting.

'Um...' I say, and her mouth starts moving but I can't hear anything. And she just keeps on staring.

The piano is playing but I can't see anyone sitting at it. And the keyboard lid is shut.

'August!'
I realise that my eyes have closed again. I keep drifting off. I open them.
'August! Pay attention!'
With a huge effort I stare back at Mother. She's leaning forward as if she has something very important to say. I concentrate.
'Yes, Mother?'
'While you and The Fist were creating a distraction, Dog Girl managed to slip the tiny Fripp machine to Cherry. Cherry knows how to use it and she knows she has to use it on The Believer.'

The piano is still playing. I try to look at it but Mother snaps her fingers so I look at them instead.

'Mary Mary and Gulliver are fine. I'm in the process of feeding Gully toast fingers dipped in a boiled egg, which he seems to love.'

She's right. Gully does indeed love toast fingers dipped in egg. I can hear Gully's voice in the background and I want to cry.

'August! It's time to wake up. You have to attack The Fist again. You have to give Cherry a chance to get at The Believer.'

Mother smiles.

'Remember, you're Dragman, August. And you'll be fine.'

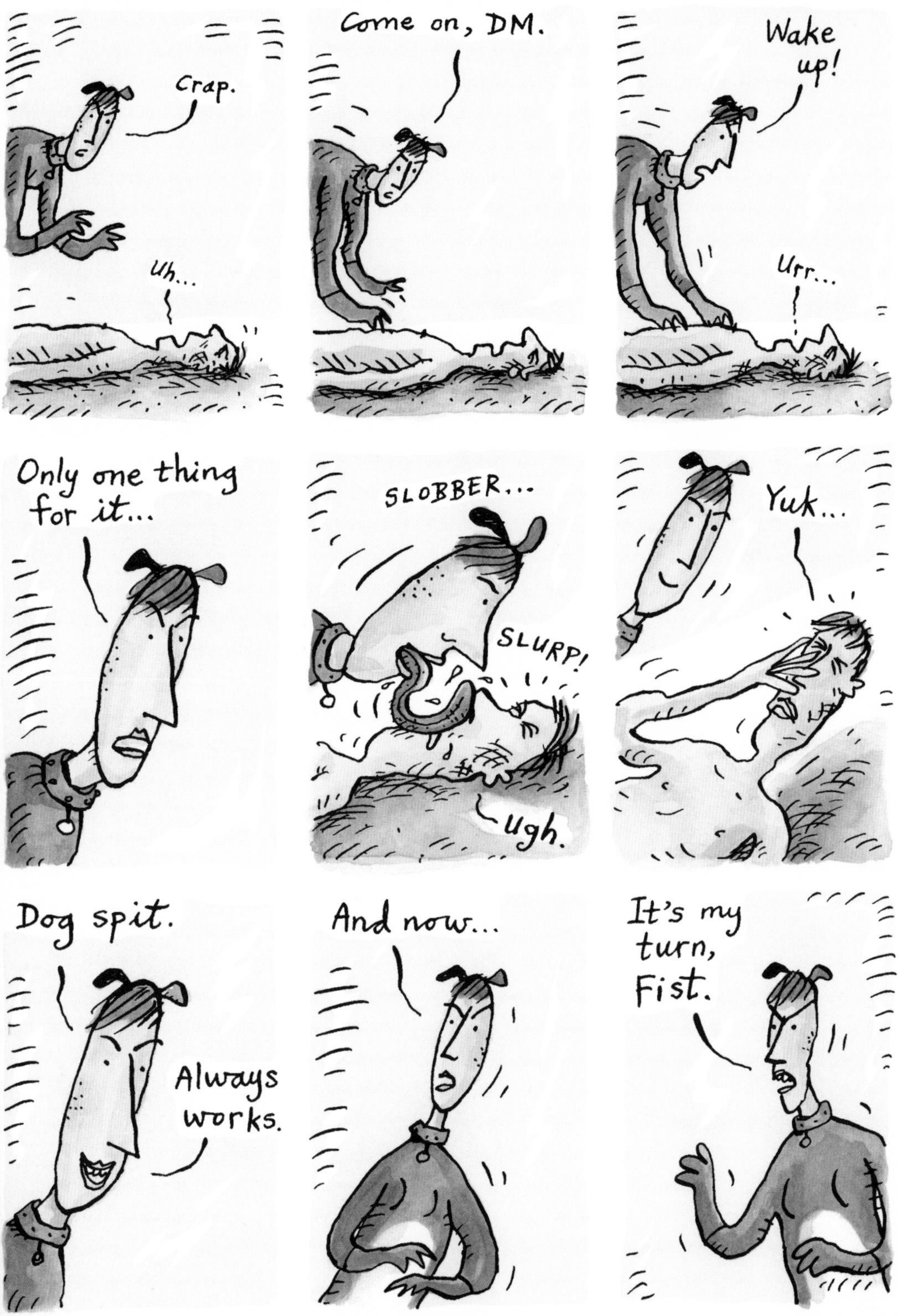
Crap.
Uh...
Come on, DM.
Wake up!
Urr...
Only one thing for it...
SLOBBER...
SLURP!
Ugh.
Yuk...
Dog spit.
Always works.
And now...
It's my turn, Fist.

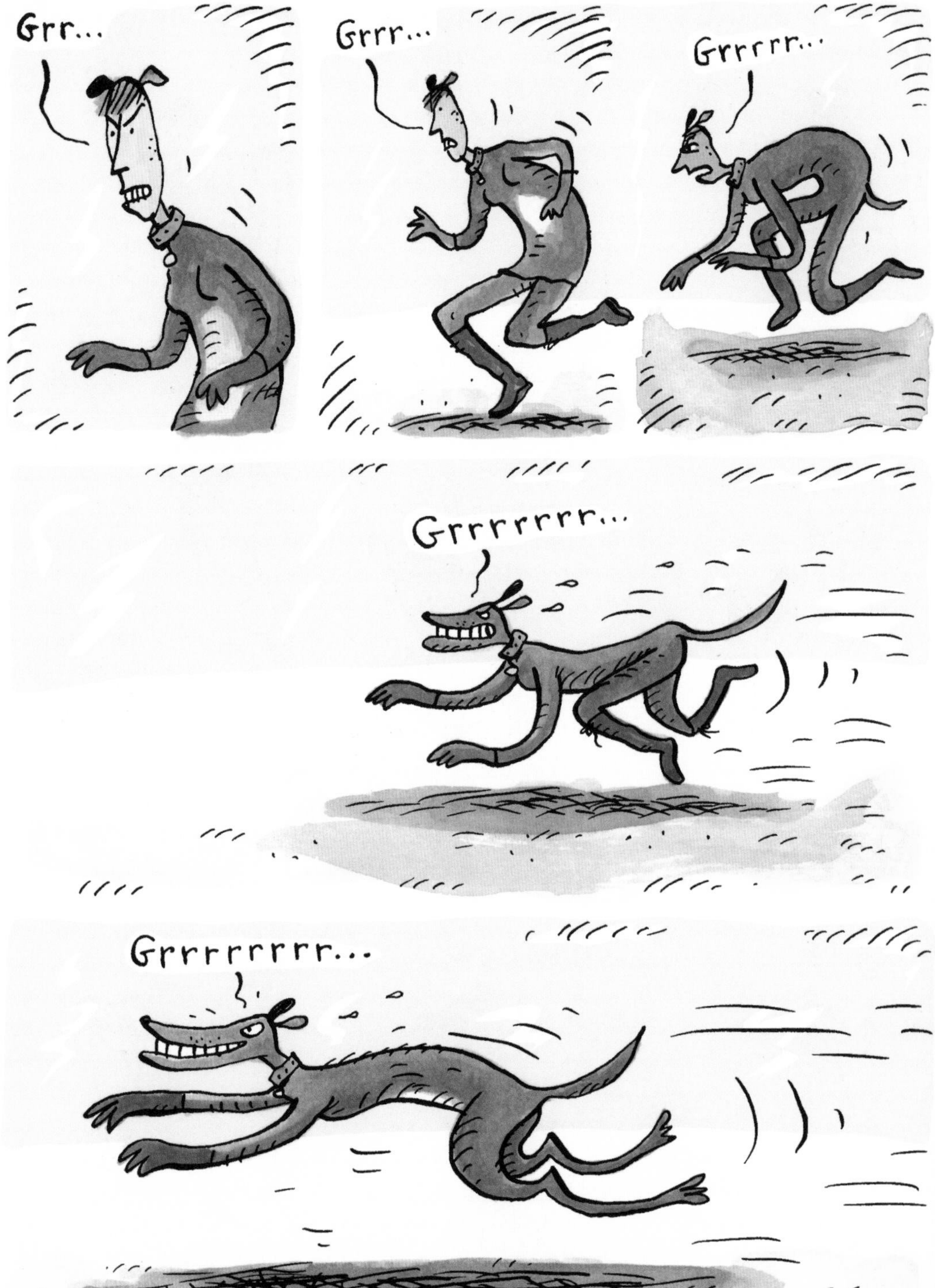
Grr...
Grrr...
Grrrrr...
Grrrrrrr...
Grrrrrrrr...

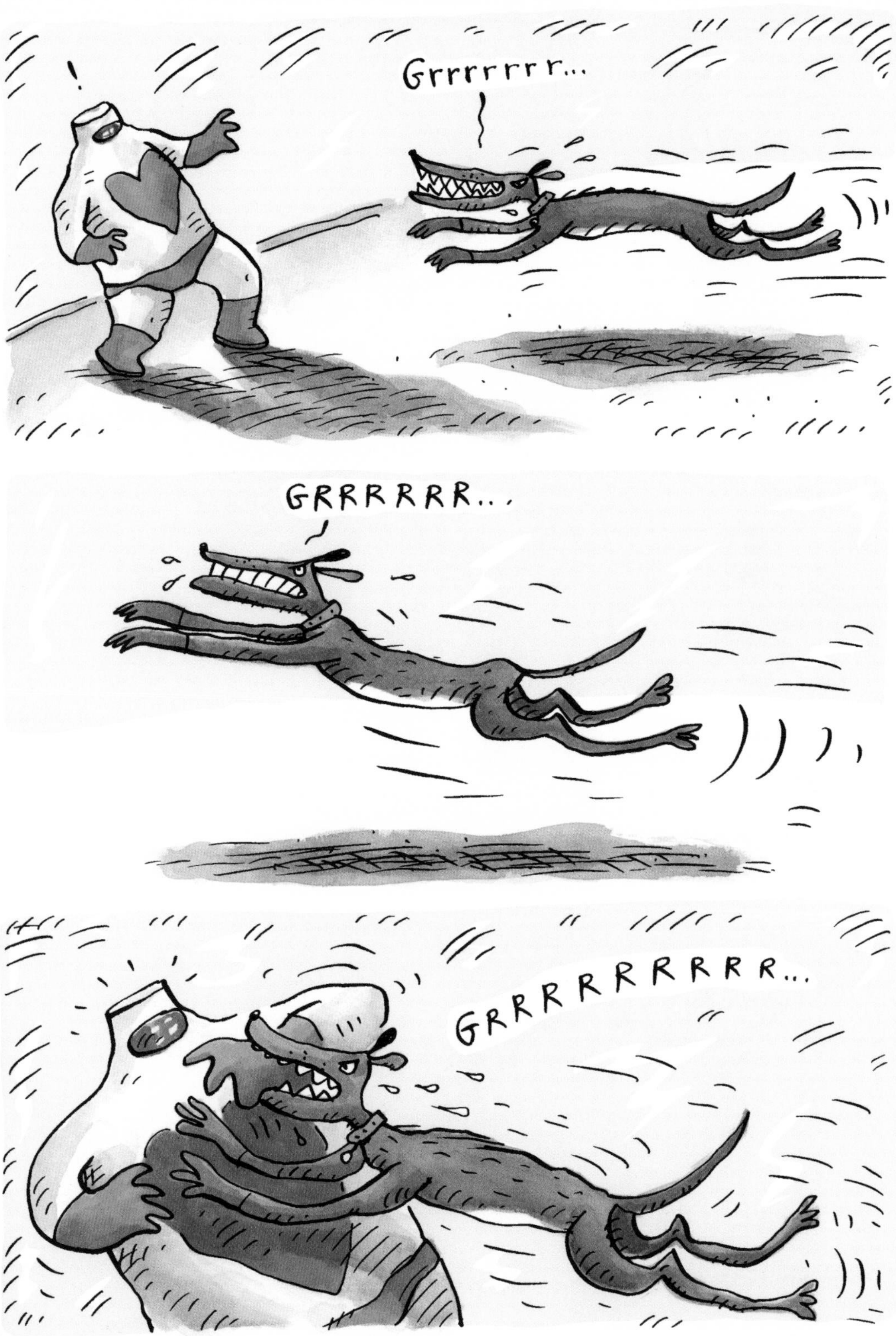
!
Grrrrrrr...
GRRRRRR...
GRRRRRRRRRR...

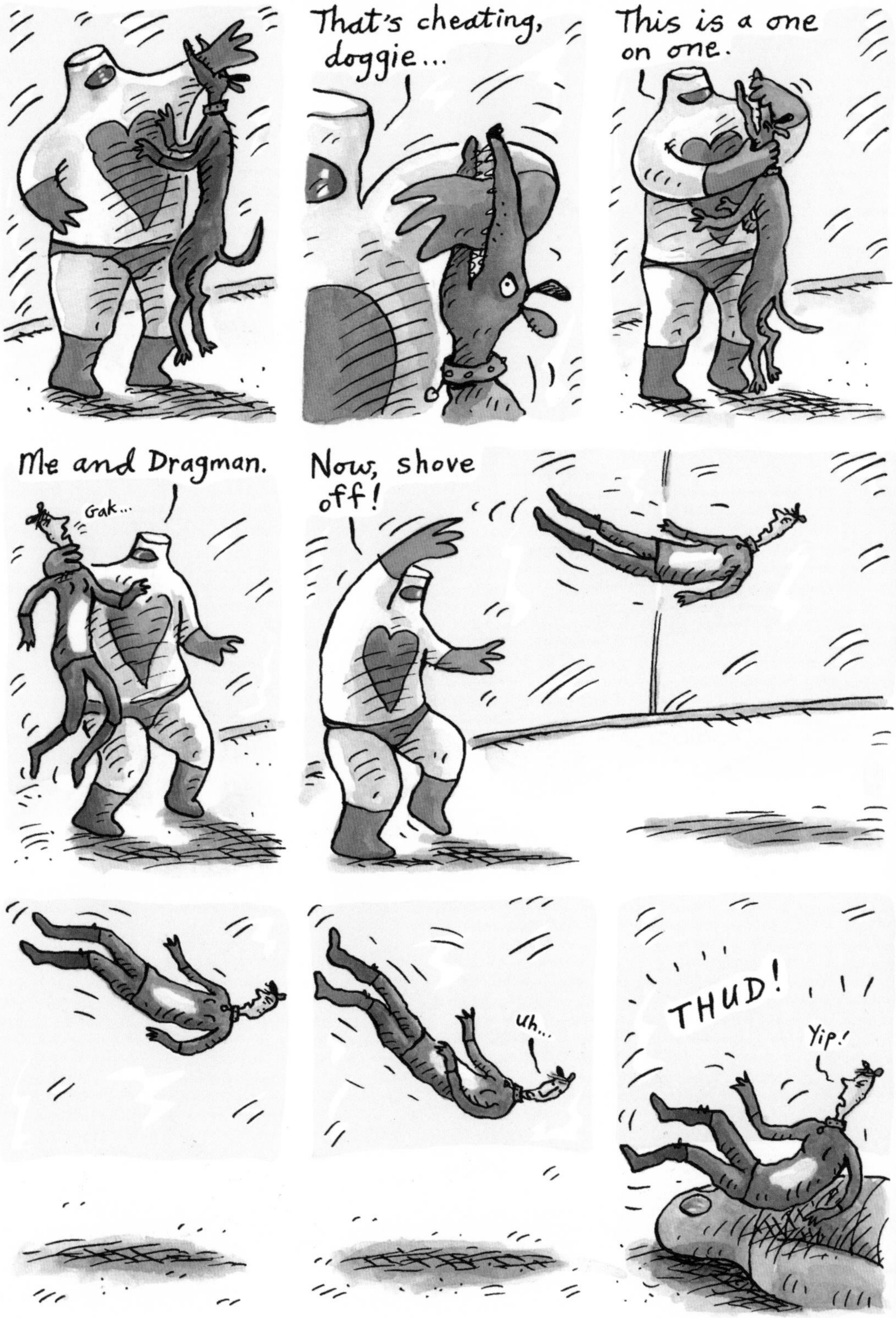
That's cheating, doggie...
This is a one on one.
Me and Dragman.
Gak...
Now, shove off!
Uh...
THUD!
Yip!

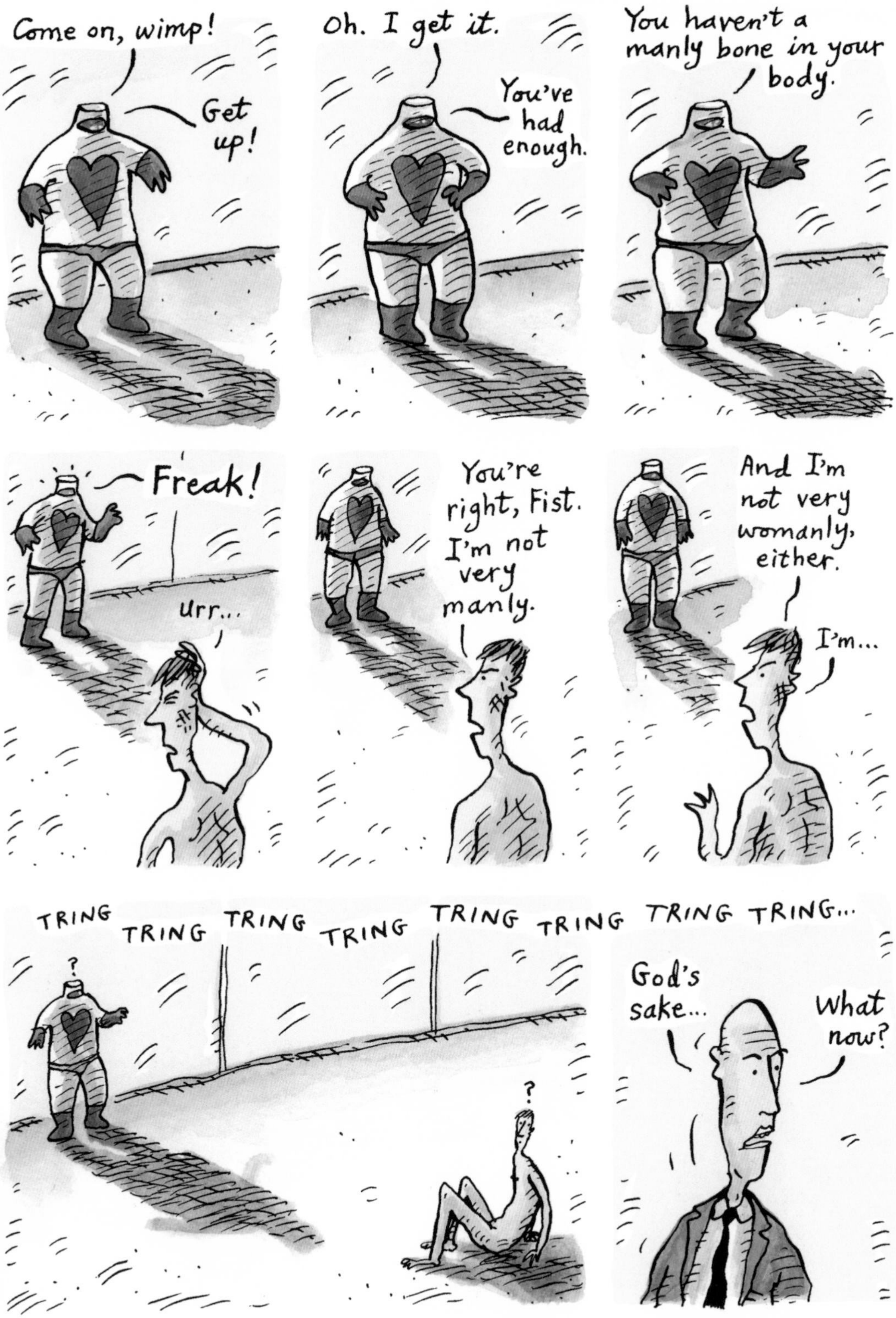
Come on, wimp!
Get up!
Oh. I get it.
You've had enough.
You haven't a manly bone in your body.
Freak!
Urr...
You're right, Fist. I'm not very manly.
And I'm not very womanly, either.
I'm...
TRING TRING TRING TRING TRING TRING TRING TRING...
?
?
God's sake...
What now?

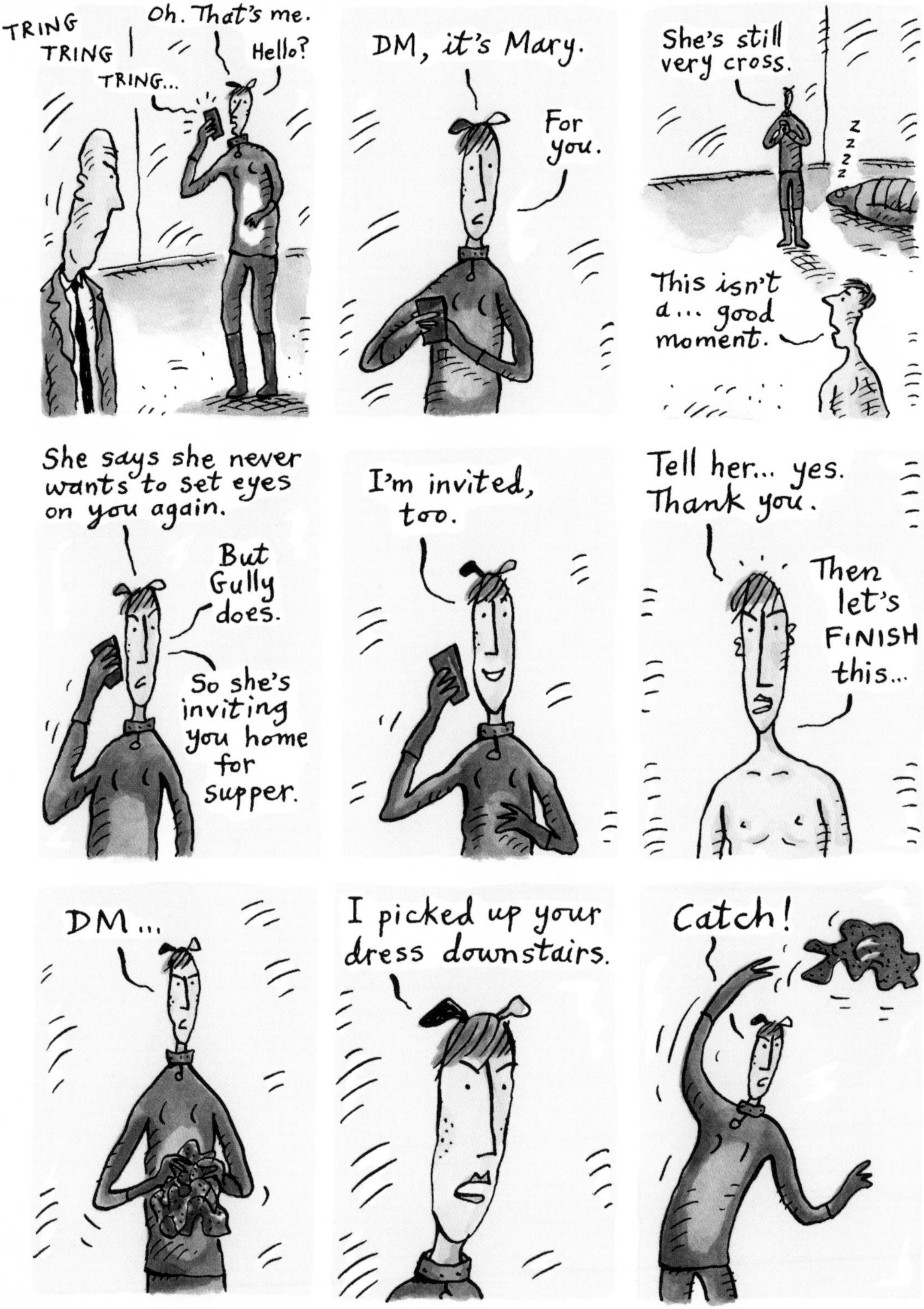
TRING
TRING
TRING...
Oh. That's me.
Hello?
DM, it's Mary.
For you.
She's still very cross.
This isn't a... good moment.
She says she never wants to set eyes on you again.
But Gully does.
So she's inviting you home for supper.
I'm invited, too.
Tell her... yes. Thank you.
Then let's FINISH this...
DM...
I picked up your dress downstairs.
Catch!

Thanks, Dog Girl.

But I don't need it.

I was... never very good at being a man.

And I don't think I'll ever feel truly right as a woman.

I'm something else, Fist.

I'm ME!

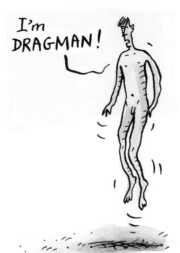
I'm DRAGMAN!

That's who I am...

293

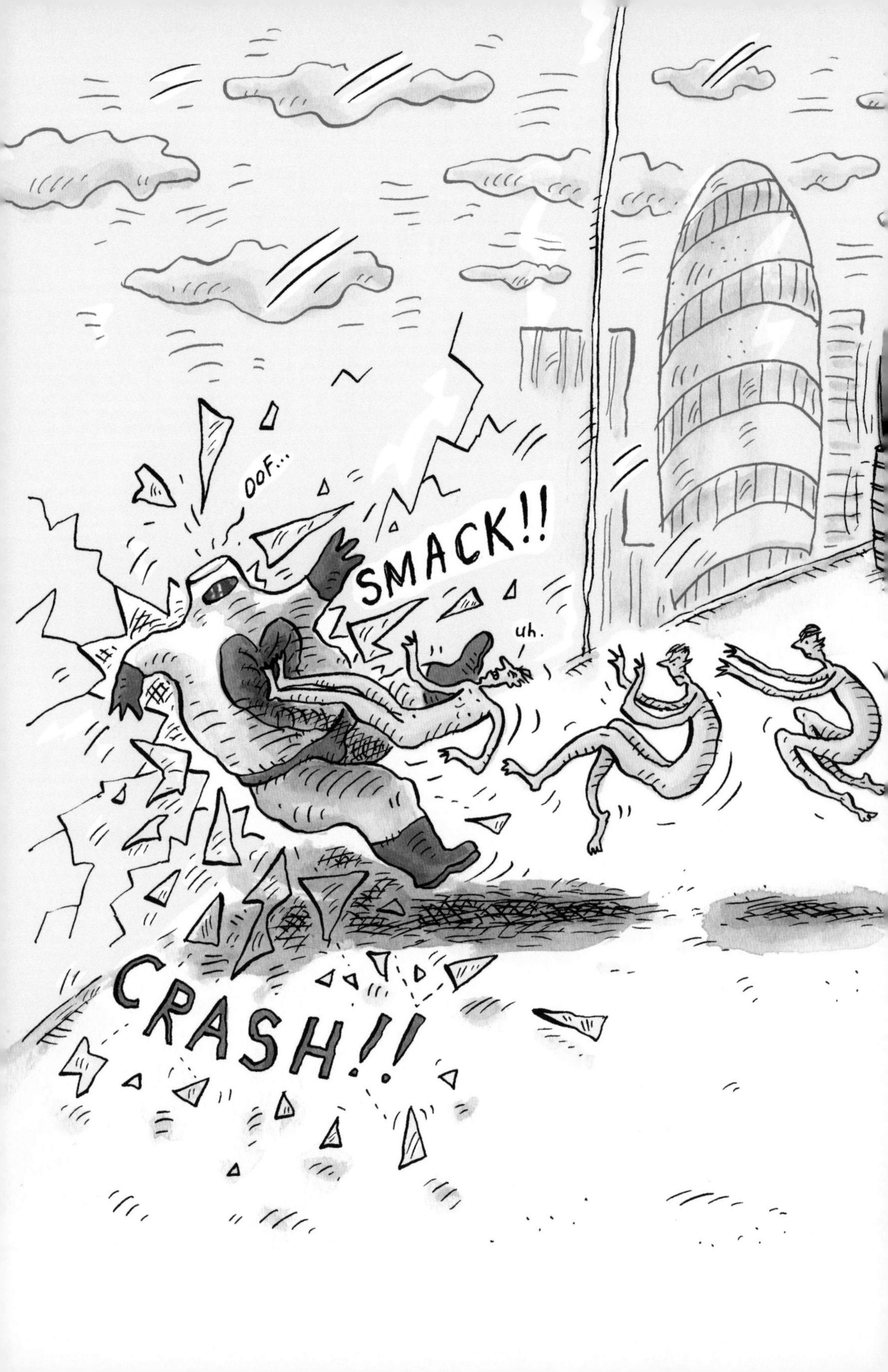
OOF...
SMACK!!
uh.
CRASH!!

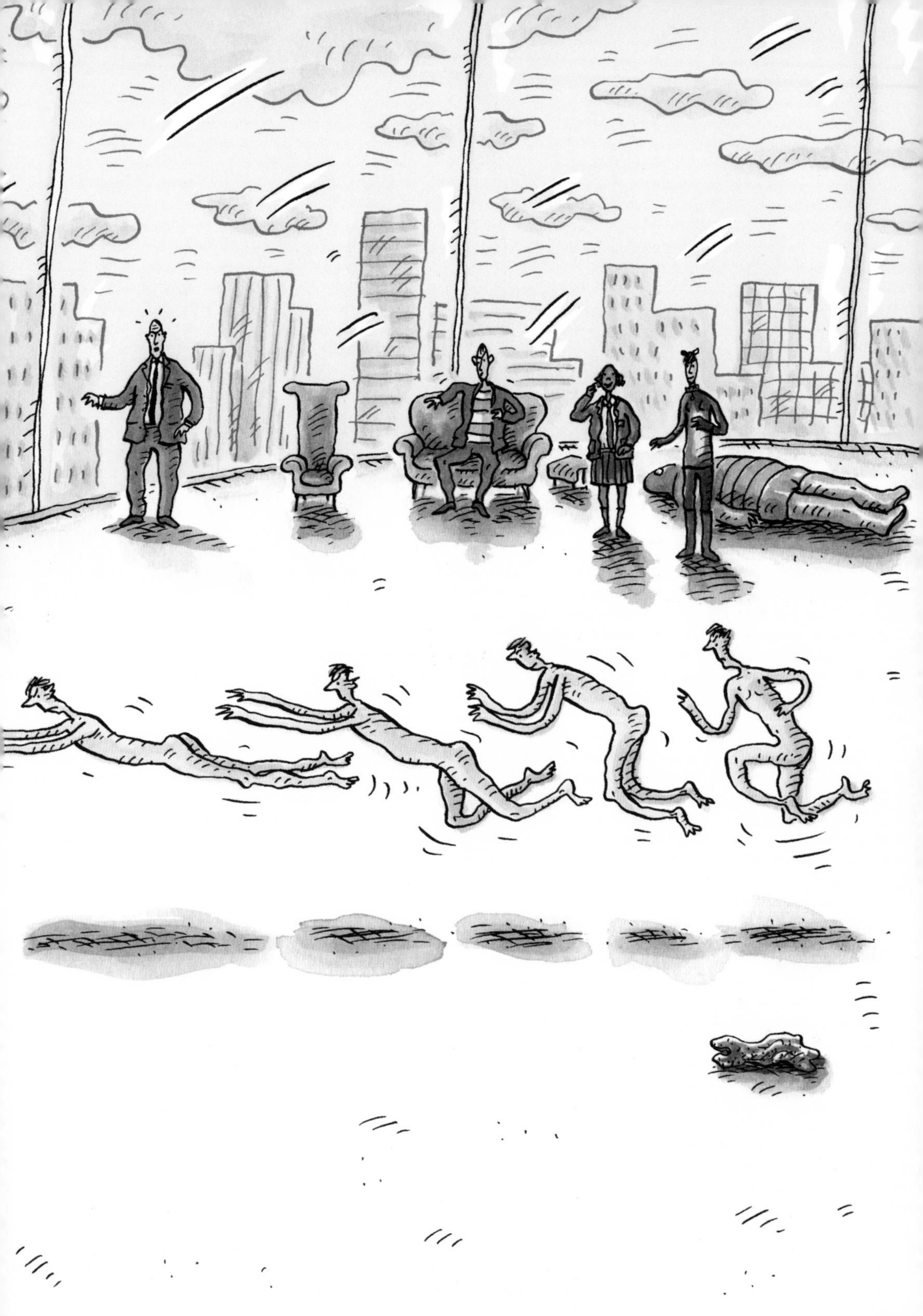

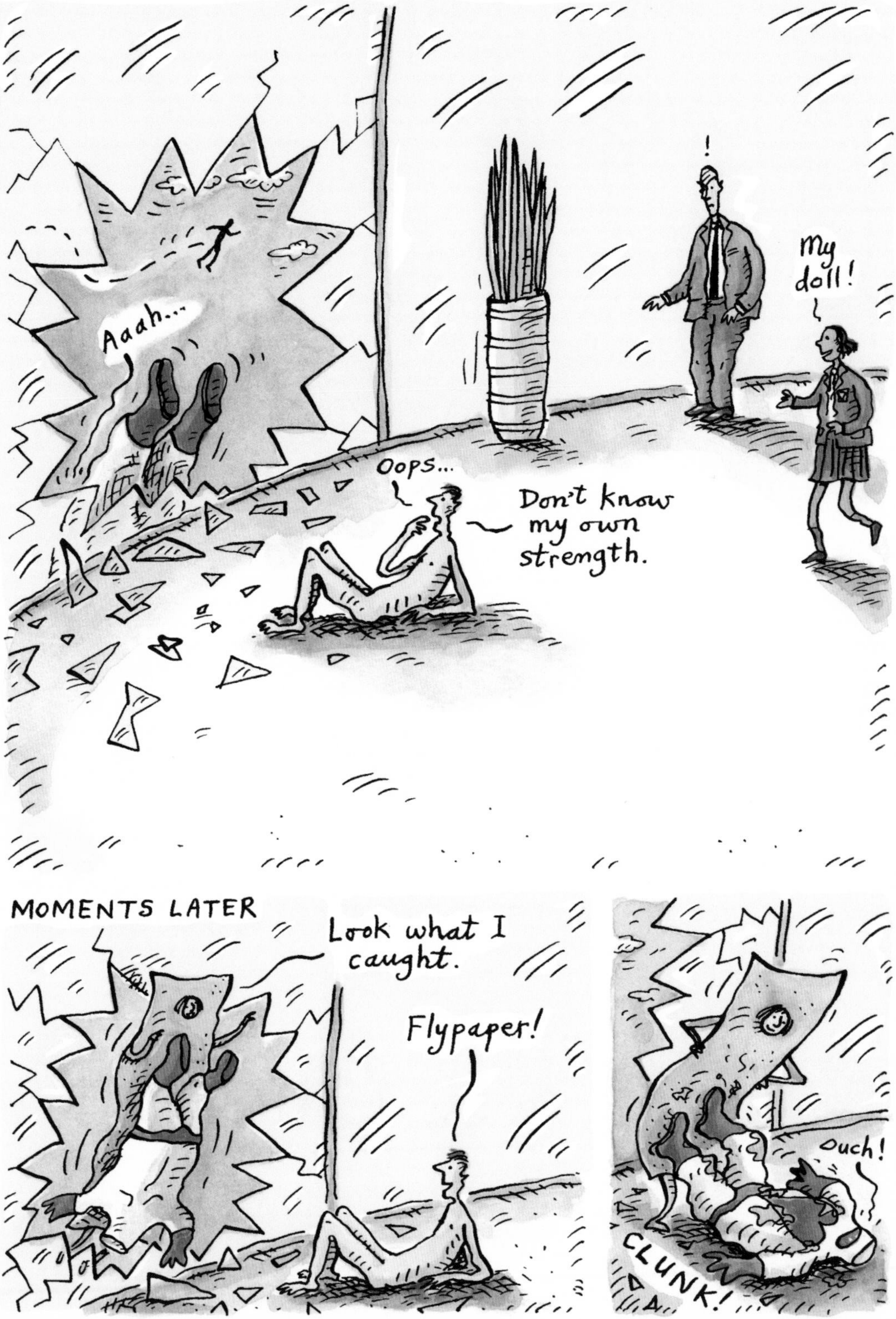
Aaah...
!
My doll!
Oops...
Don't know my own strength.
MOMENTS LATER
Look what I caught.
Flypaper!
Ouch!
CLUNK!

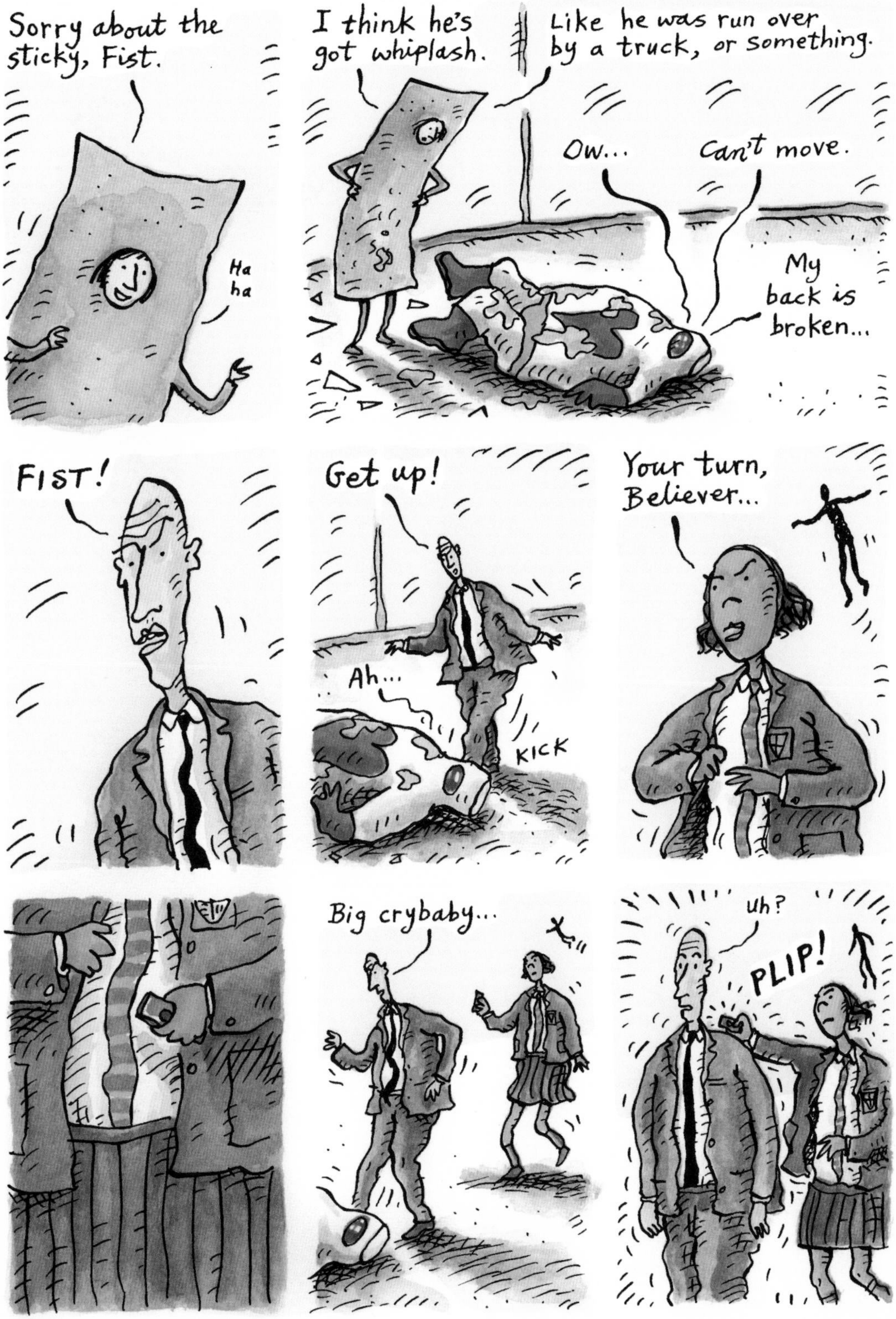
Sorry about the sticky, Fist.
Ha ha
I think he's got whiplash.
Like he was run over by a truck, or something.
Ow...
Can't move.
My back is broken...
FIST!
Get up!
Ah...
KICK
Your turn, Believer...
Big crybaby...
Uh?
PLIP!

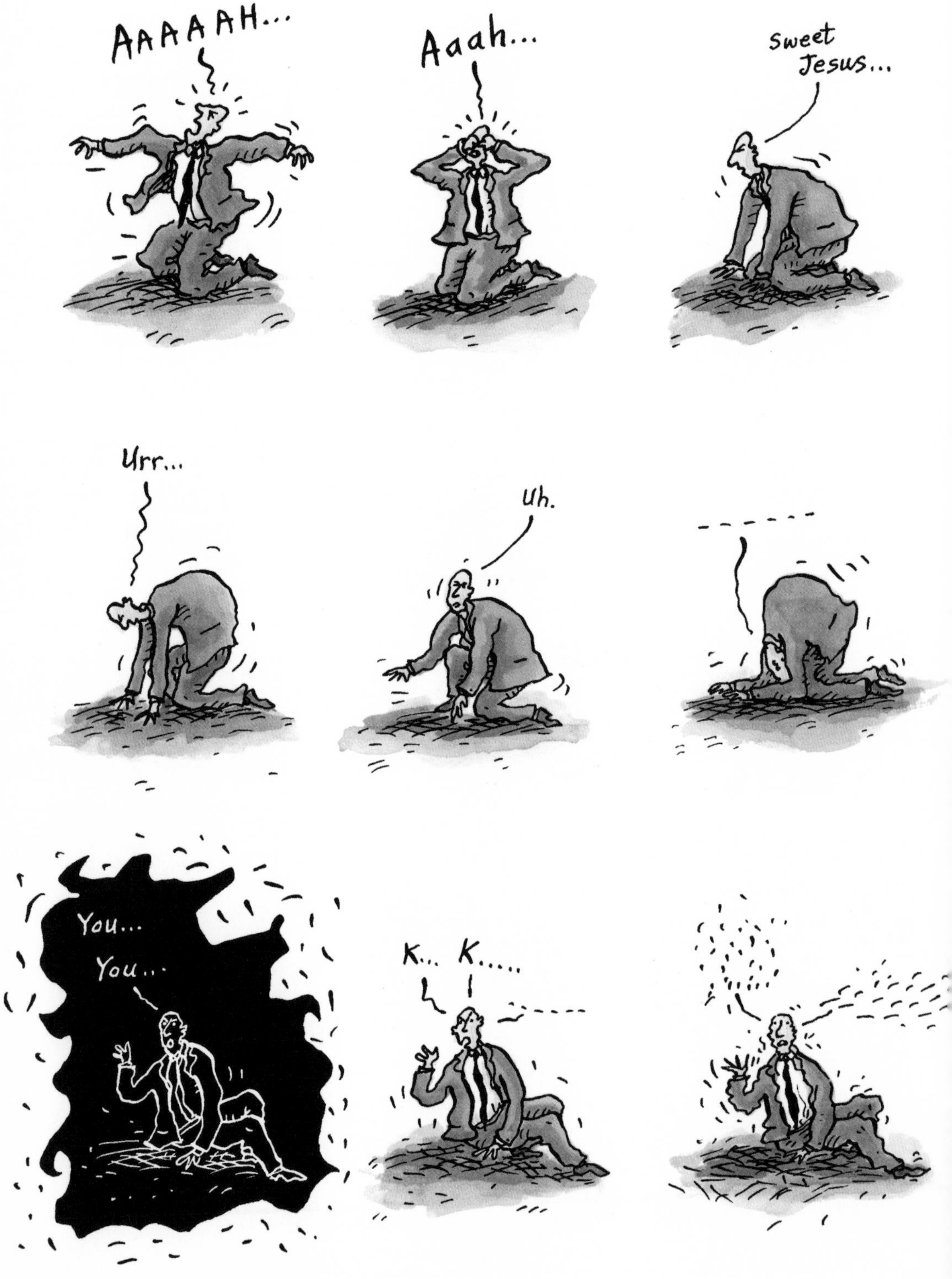
AAAAAH...
Aaah...
Sweet Jesus...
Urr...
Uh.
You... You...
K... K.....

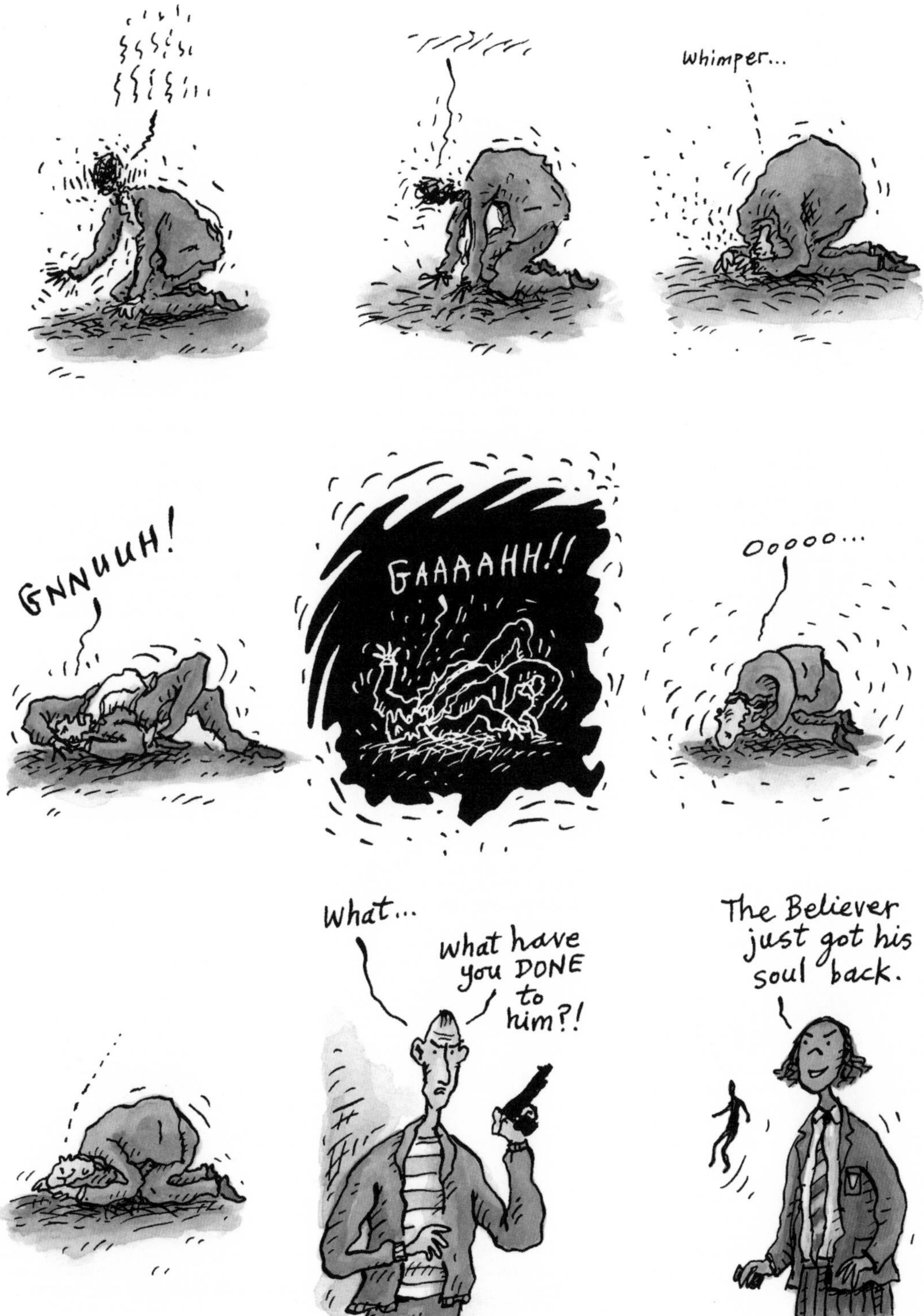
whimper...
GNNUUH!
GAAAAHH!!
Ooooo...
What...
What have you DONE to him?!
The Believer just got his soul back.

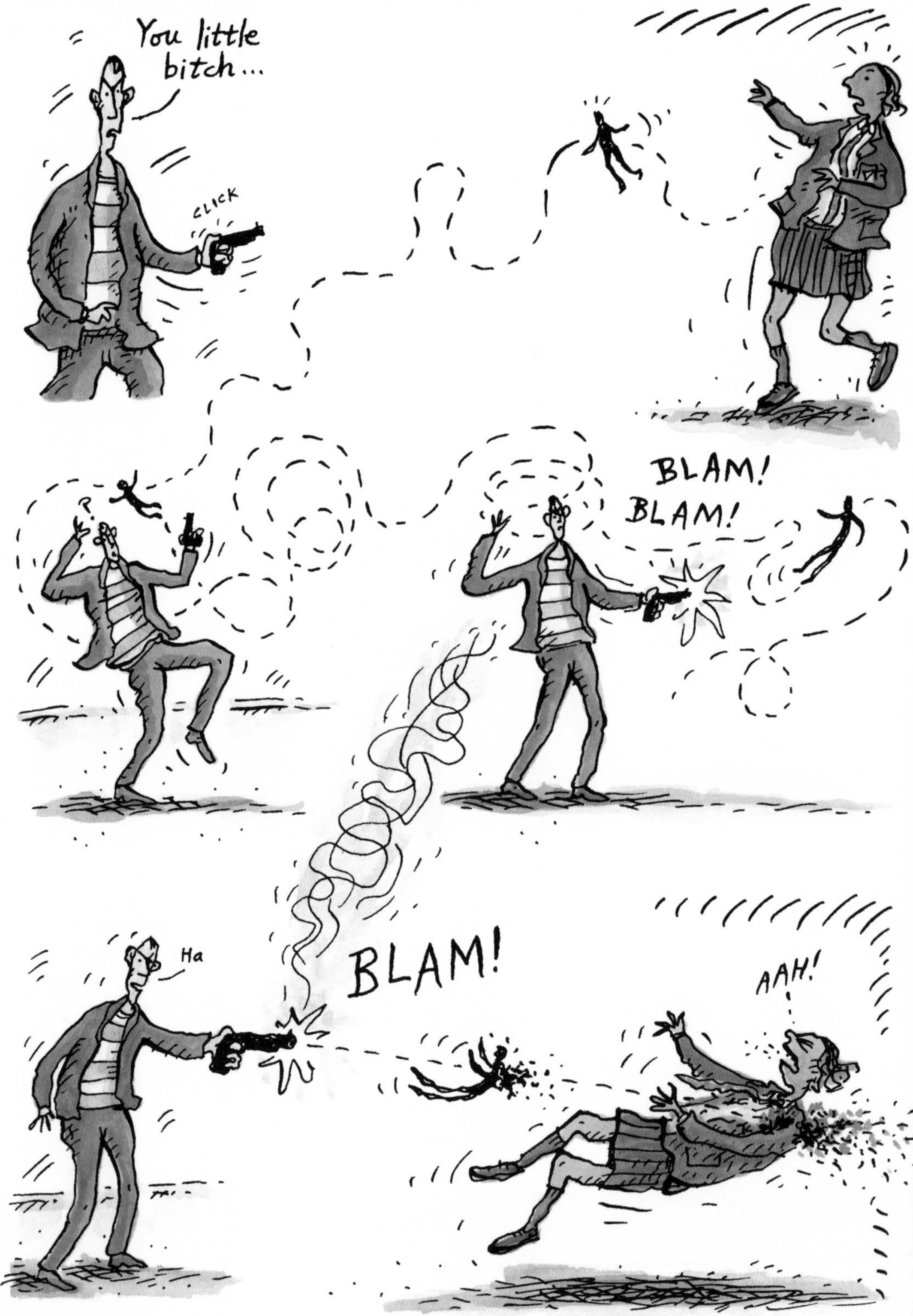
You little bitch...
CLICK
BLAM!
BLAM!
Ha
BLAM!
AAH!

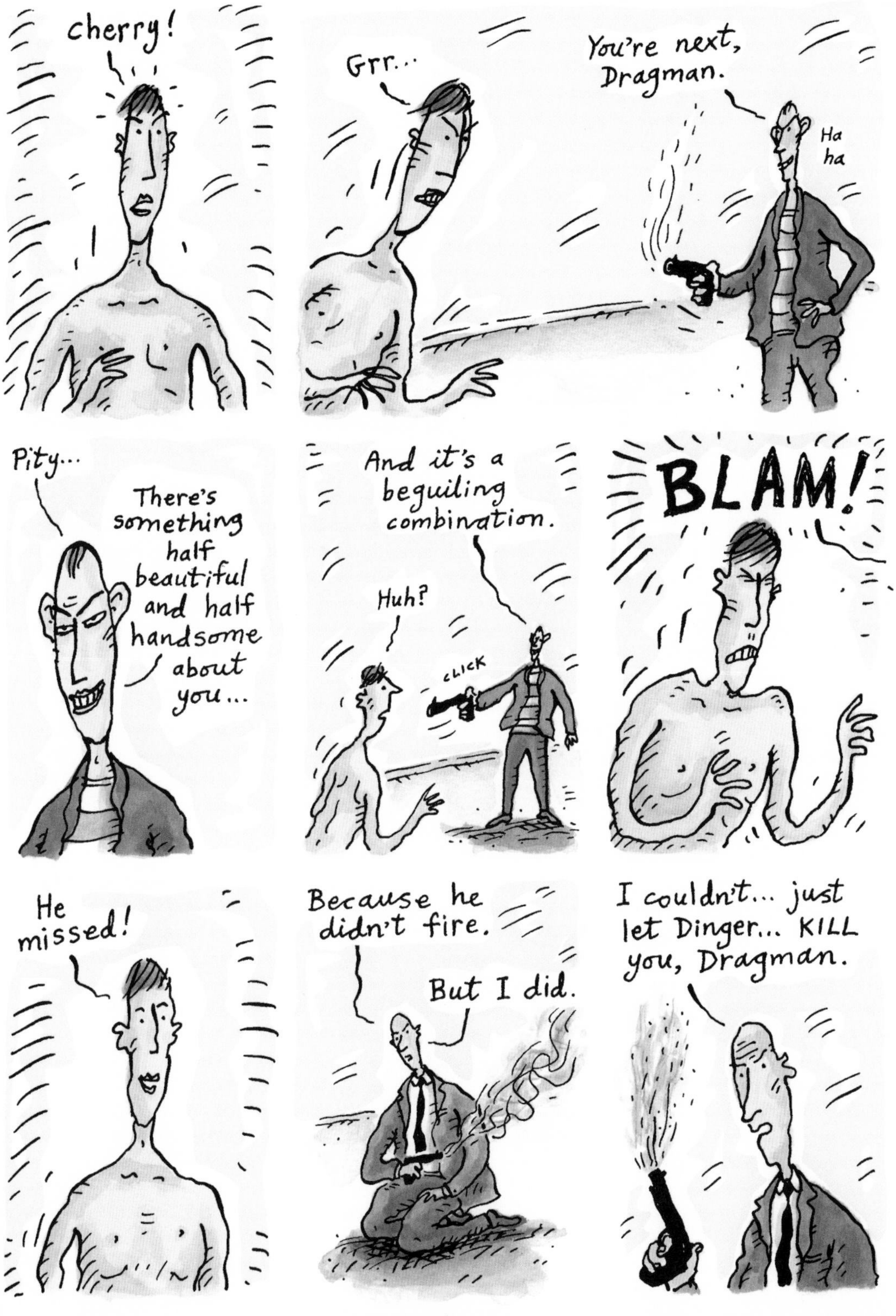
cherry!
Grr...
You're next, Dragman.
Ha ha
Pity...
There's something half beautiful and half handsome about you...
And it's a beguiling combination.
Huh?
CLICK
BLAM!
He missed!
Because he didn't fire.
But I did.
I couldn't... just let Dinger... KILL you, Dragman.

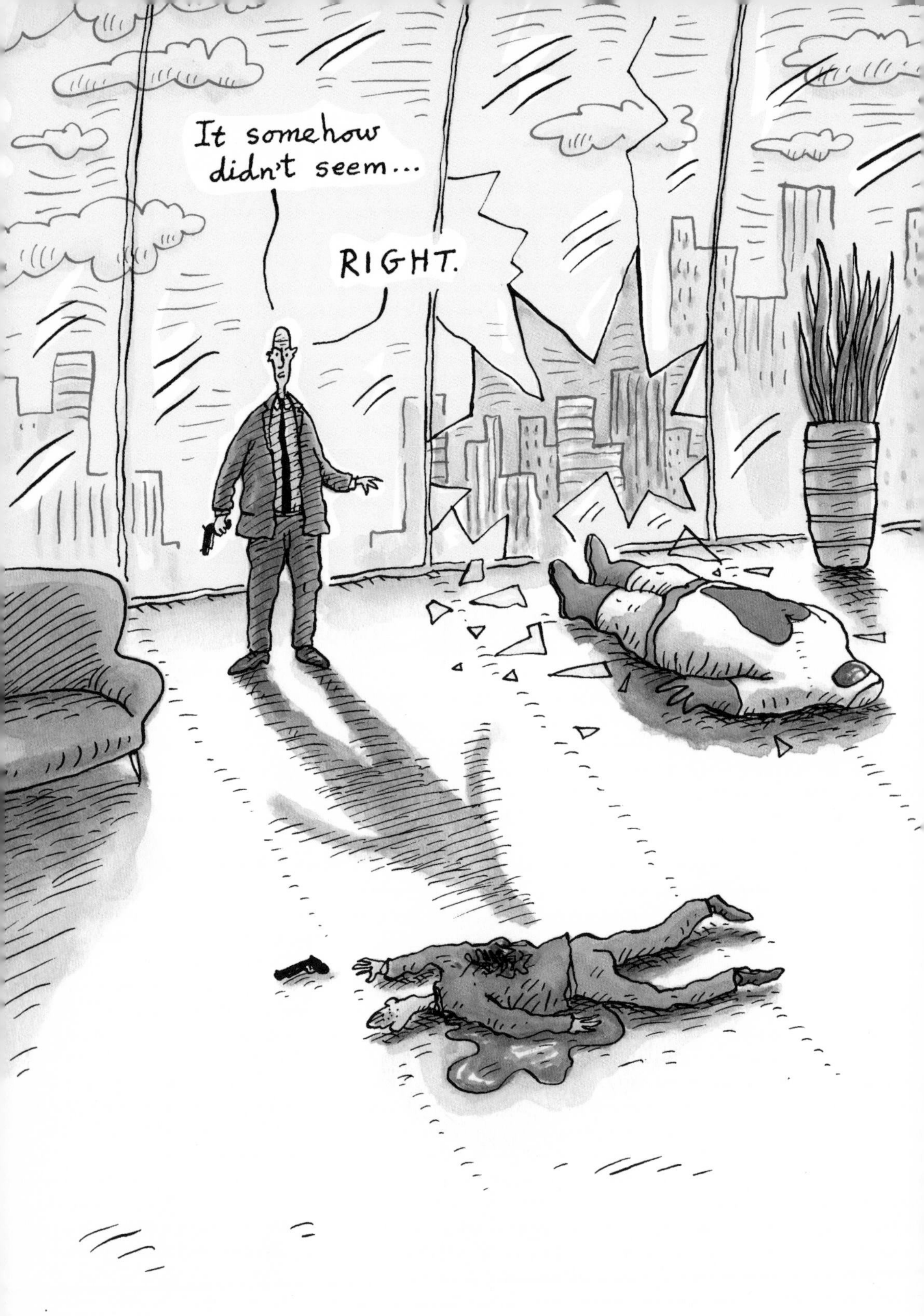
It somehow didn't seem...
RIGHT.

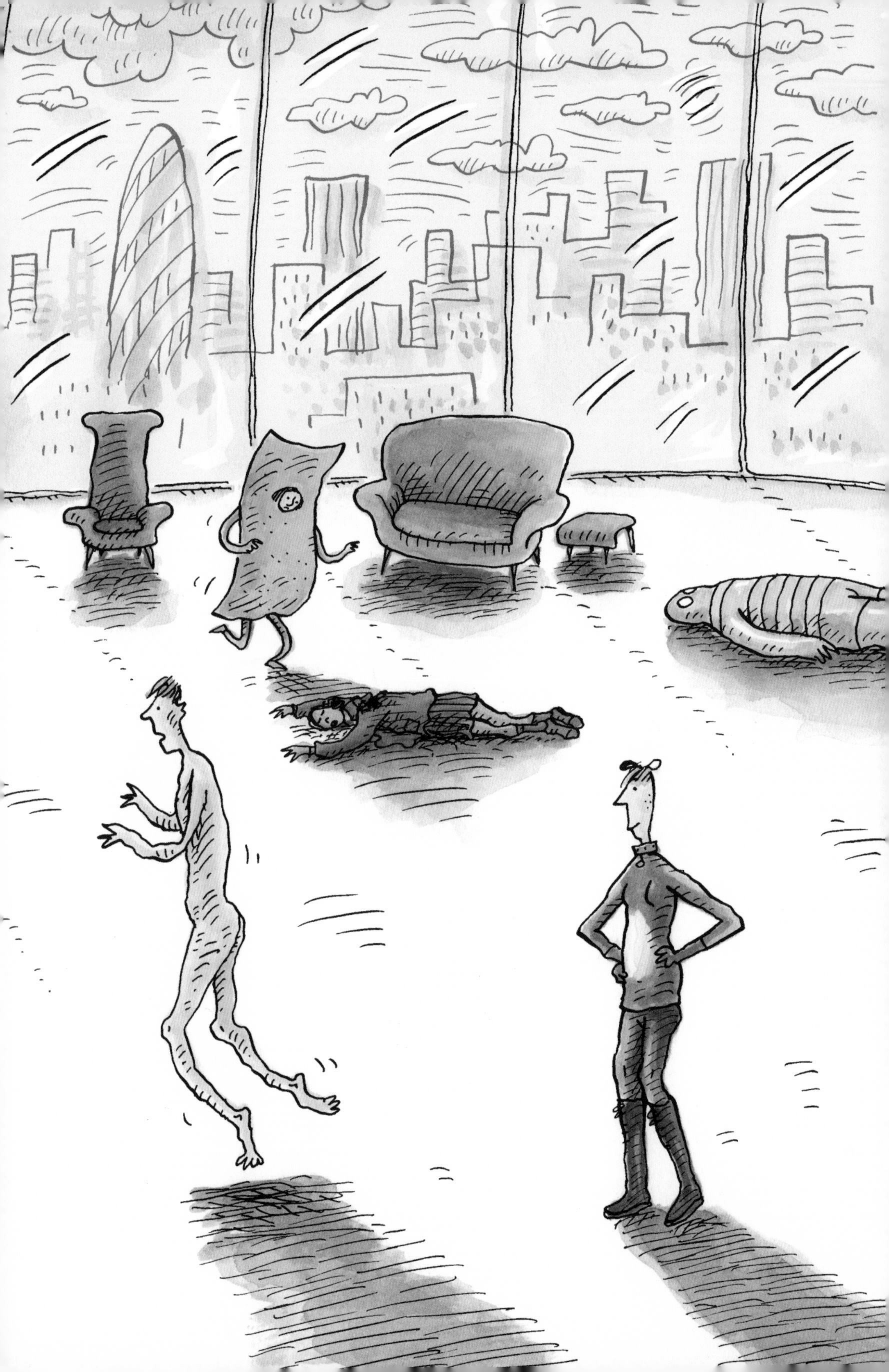

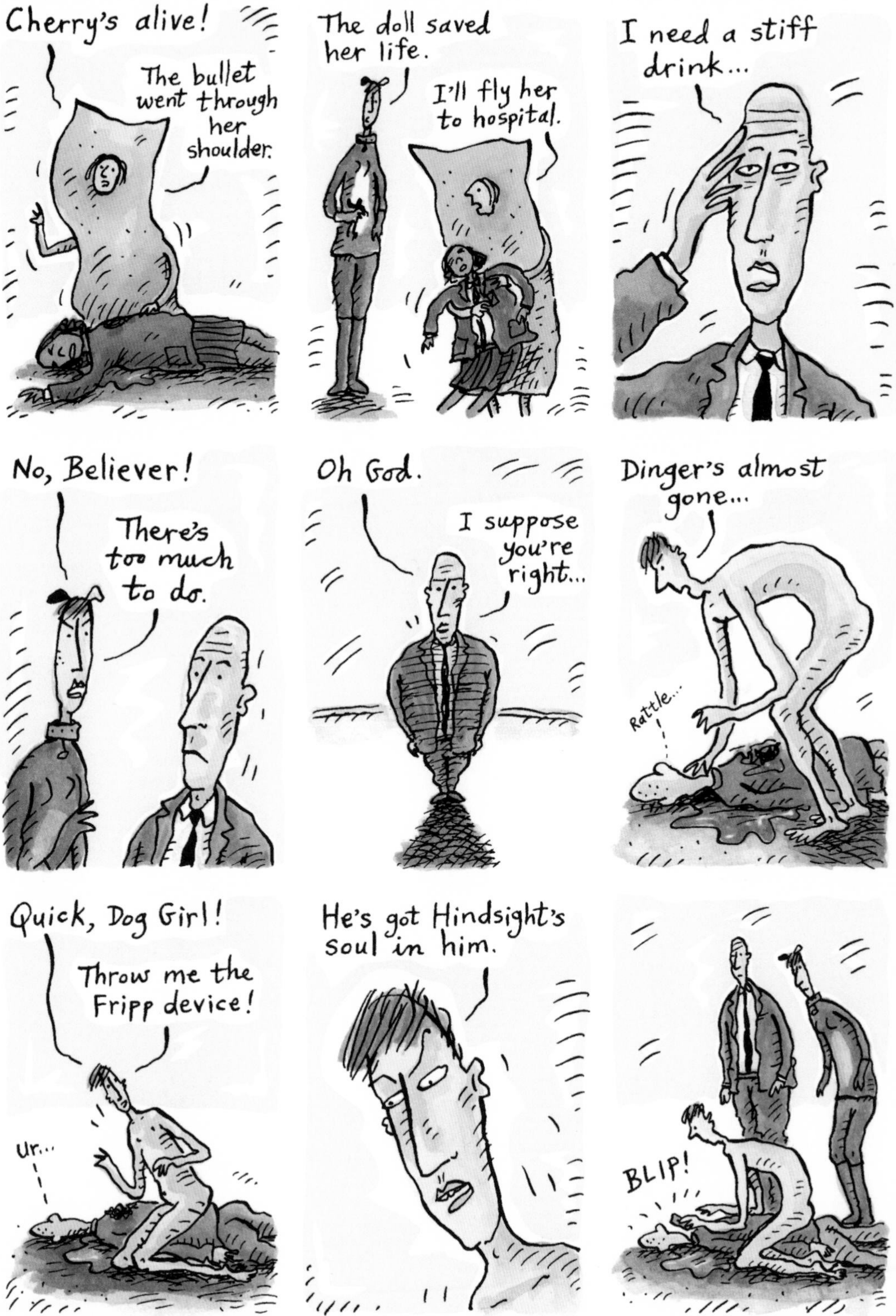
Cherry's alive!
The bullet went through her shoulder.
The doll saved her life.
I'll fly her to hospital.
I need a stiff drink...
No, Believer!
There's too much to do.
Oh God.
I suppose you're right...
Dinger's almost gone...
Rattle...
Quick, Dog Girl!
Throw me the Fripp device!
Ur...
He's got Hindsight's soul in him.
BLIP!

a few weeks later...

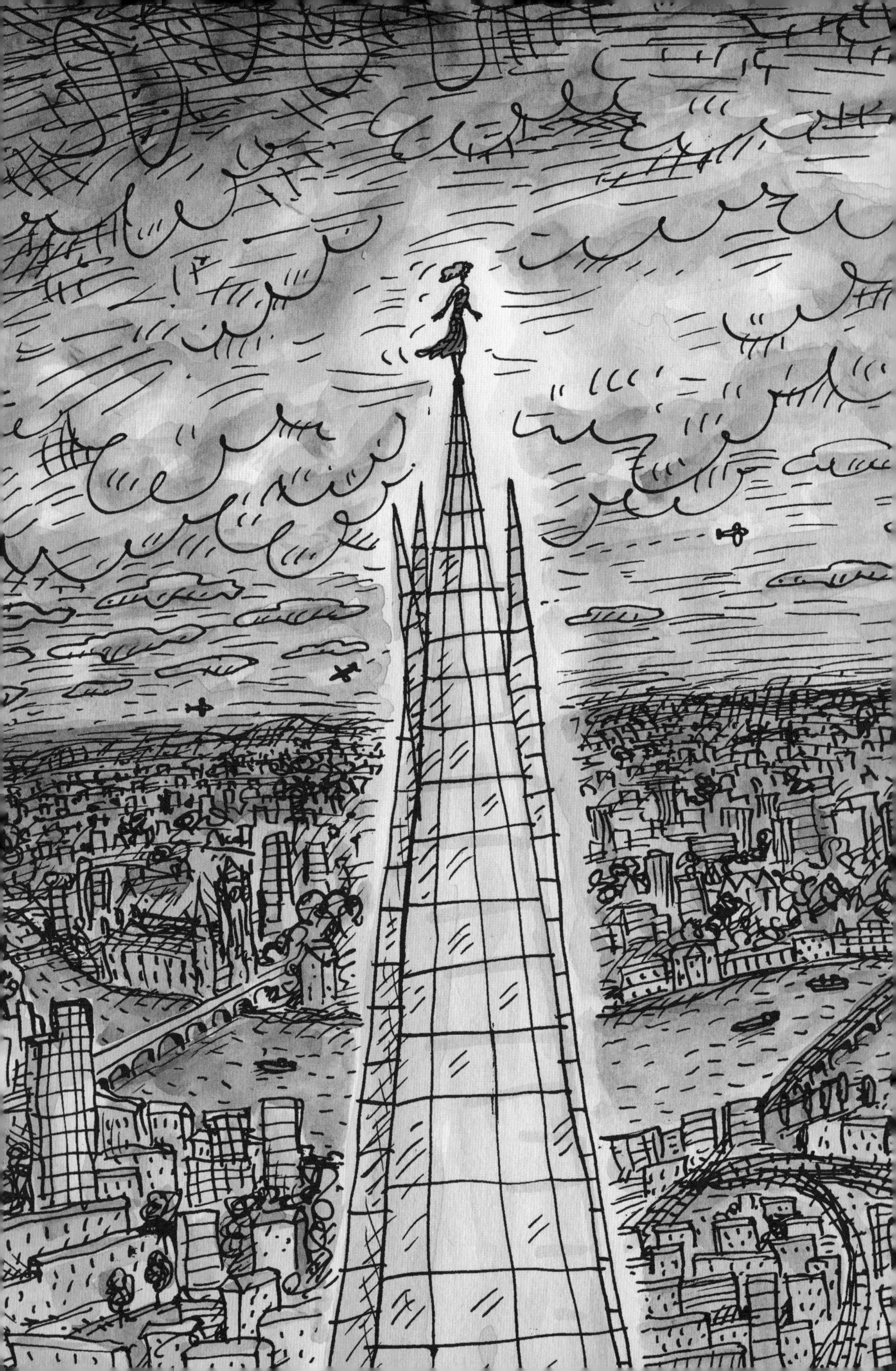

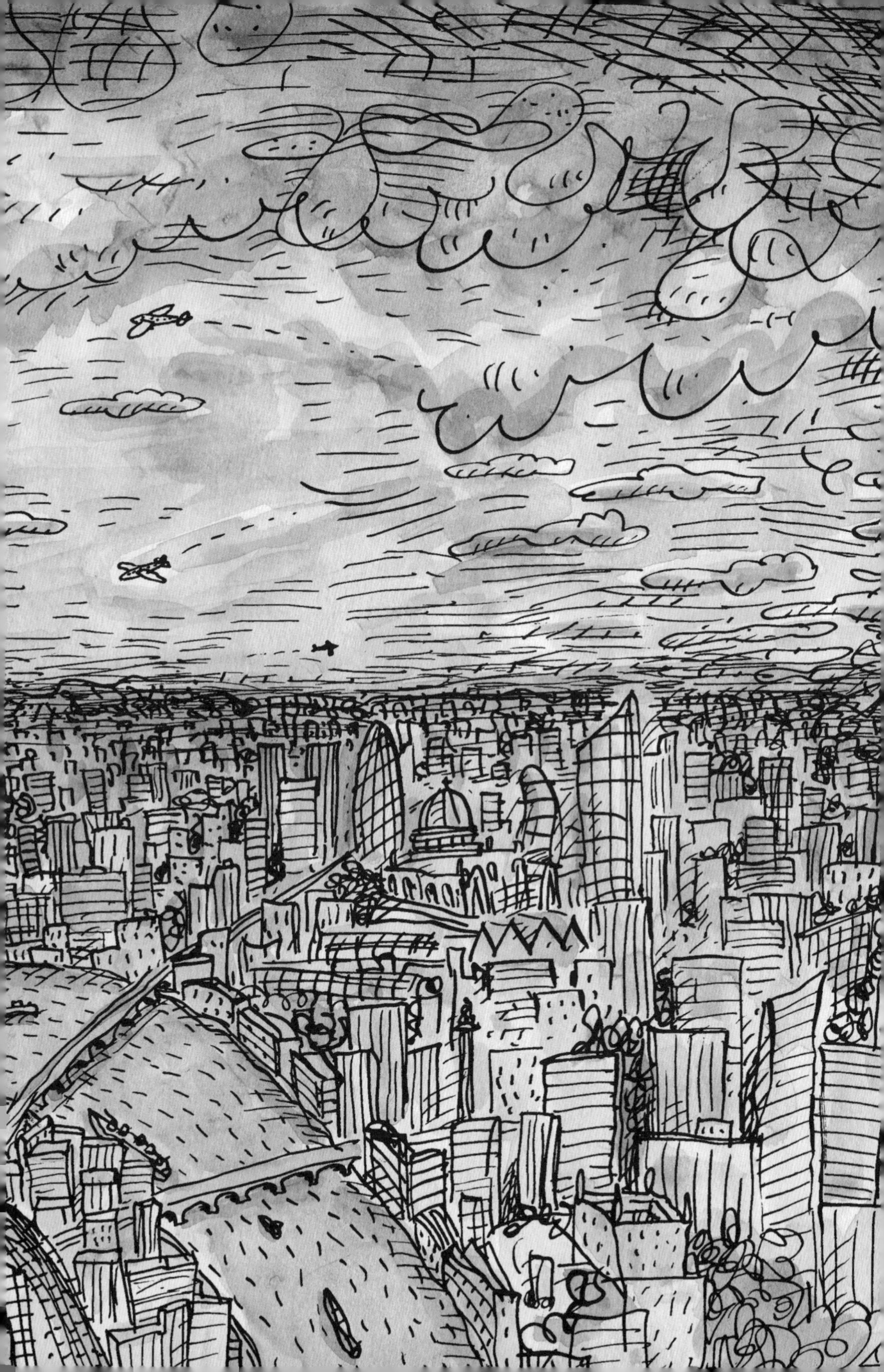

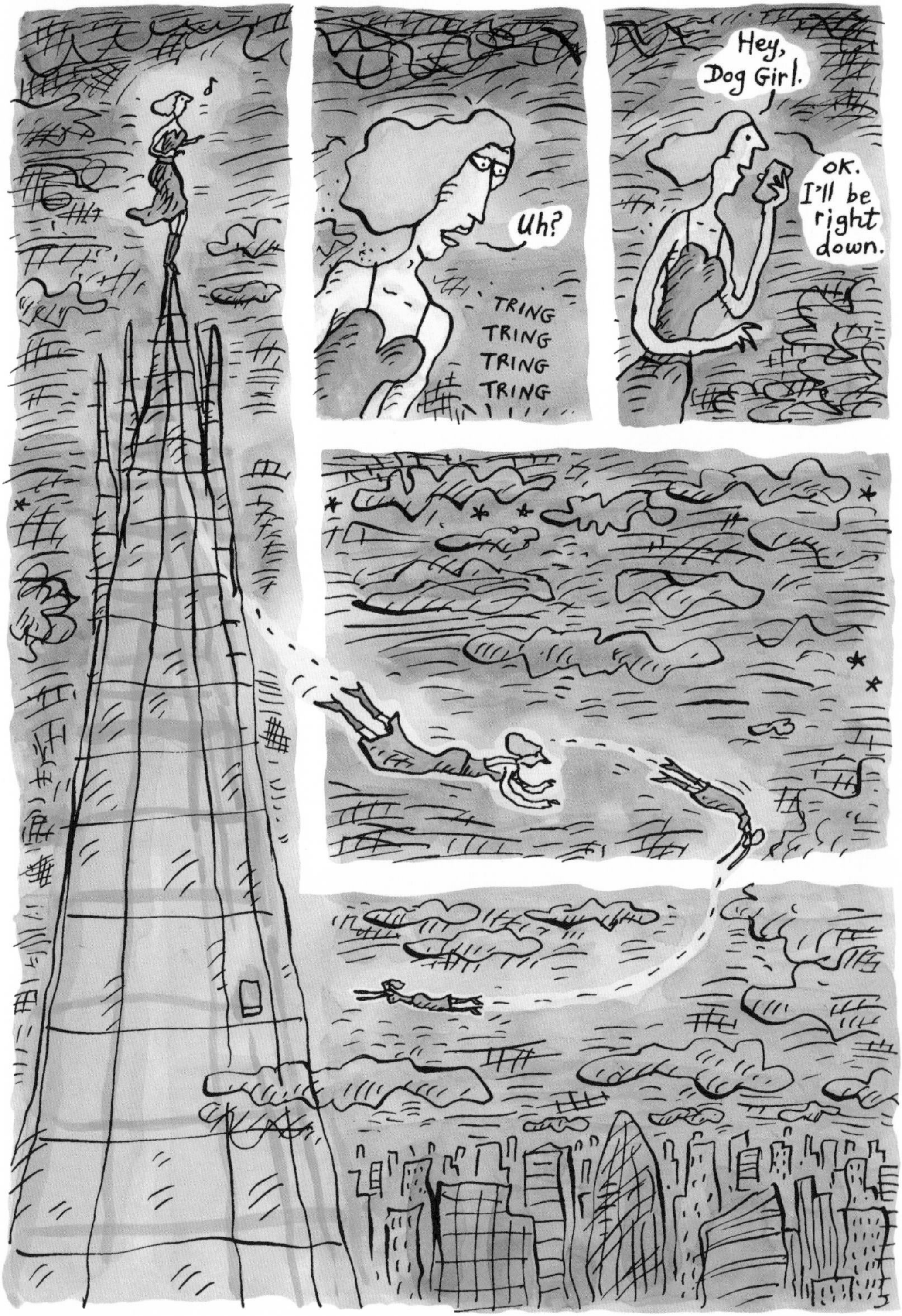
Uh?
TRING
TRING
TRING
TRING
Hey, Dog Girl.
OK. I'll be right down.

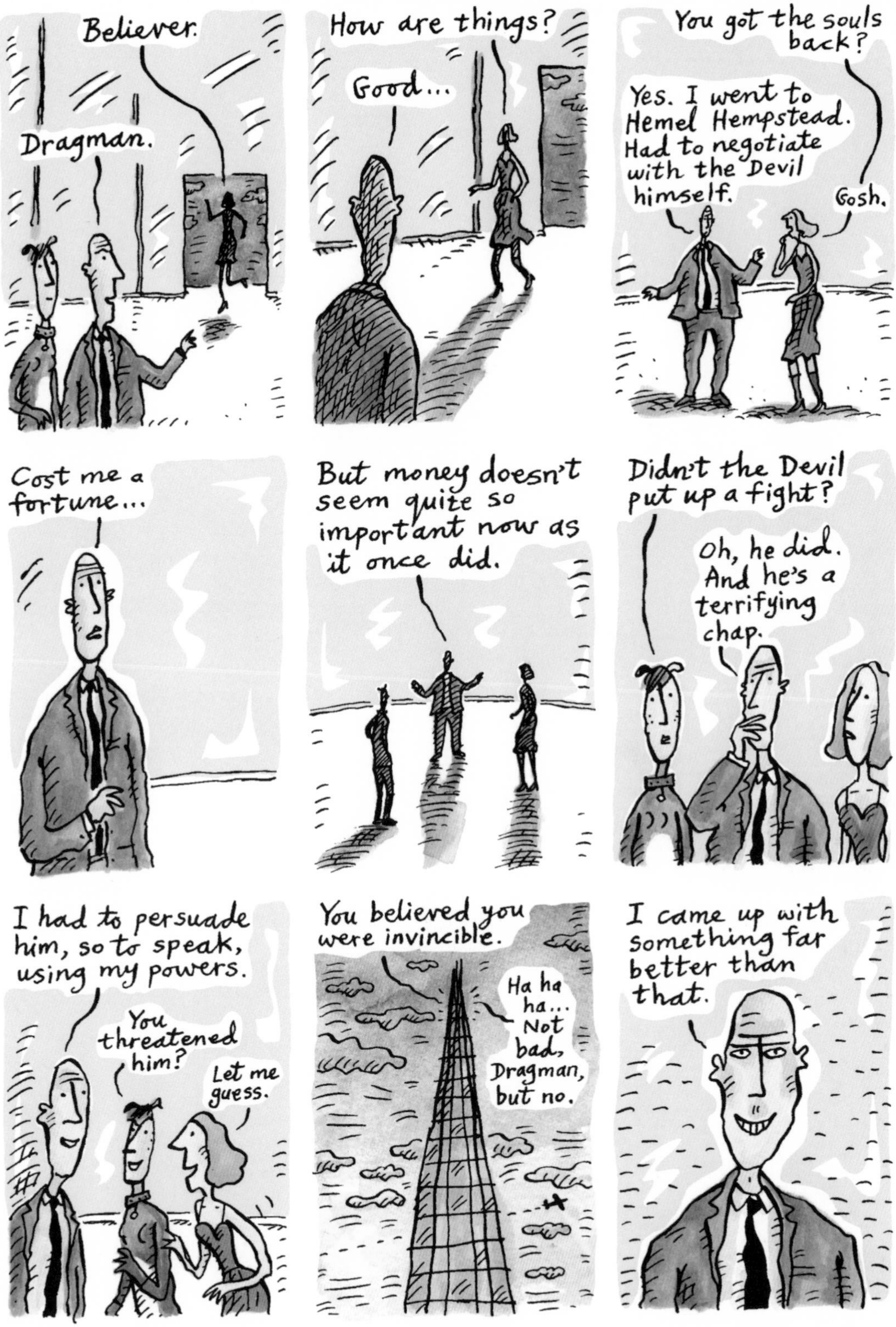
Believer.
Dragman.
How are things?
Good...
You got the souls back?
Yes. I went to Hemel Hempstead. Had to negotiate with the Devil himself.
Gosh.
Cost me a fortune...
But money doesn't seem quite so important now as it once did.
Didn't the Devil put up a fight?
Oh, he did. And he's a terrifying chap.
I had to persuade him, so to speak, using my powers.
You threatened him?
Let me guess.
You believed you were invincible.
Ha ha ha... Not bad, Dragman, but no.
I came up with something far better than that.

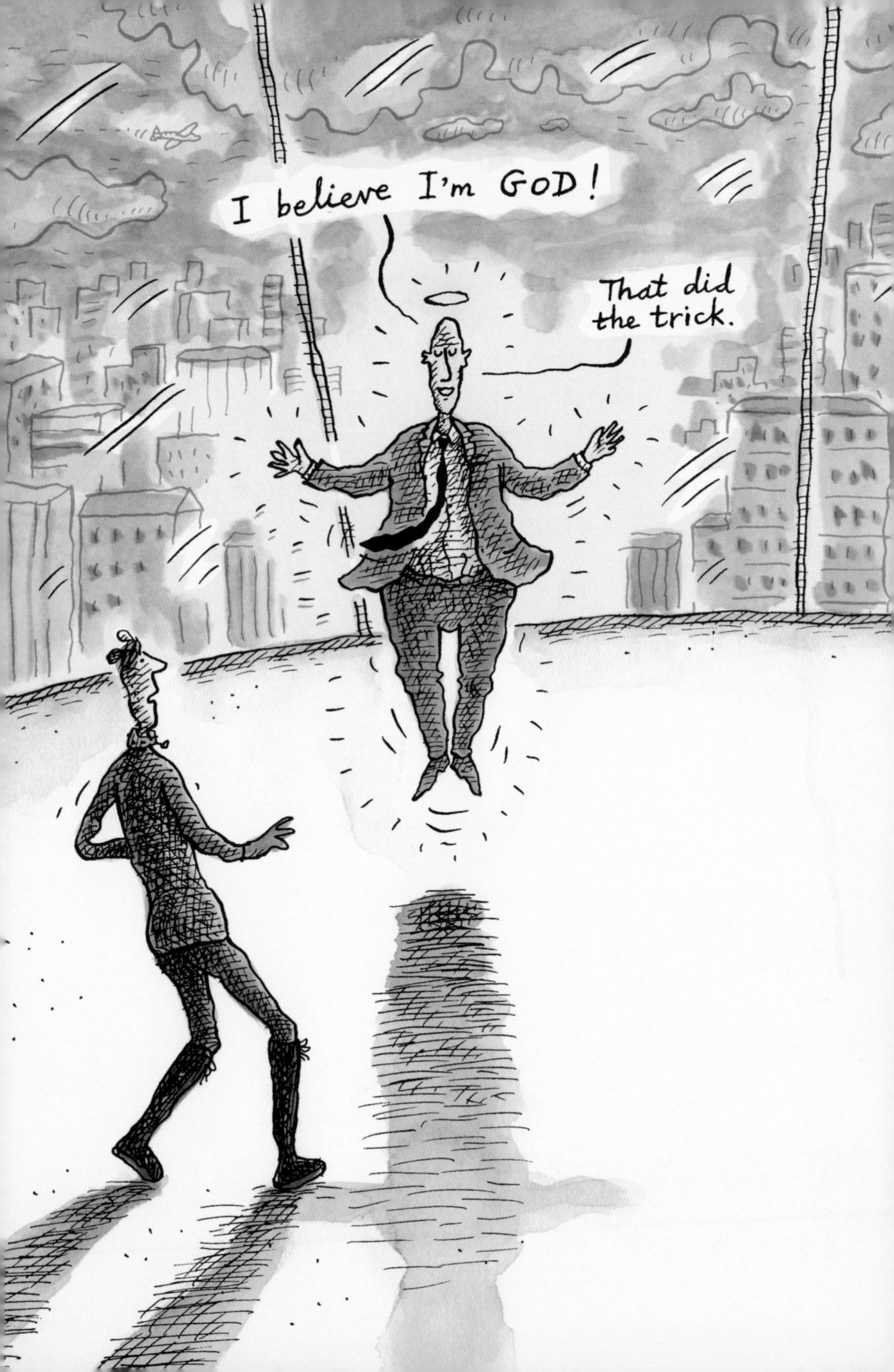
I believe I'm GOD!
That did the trick.

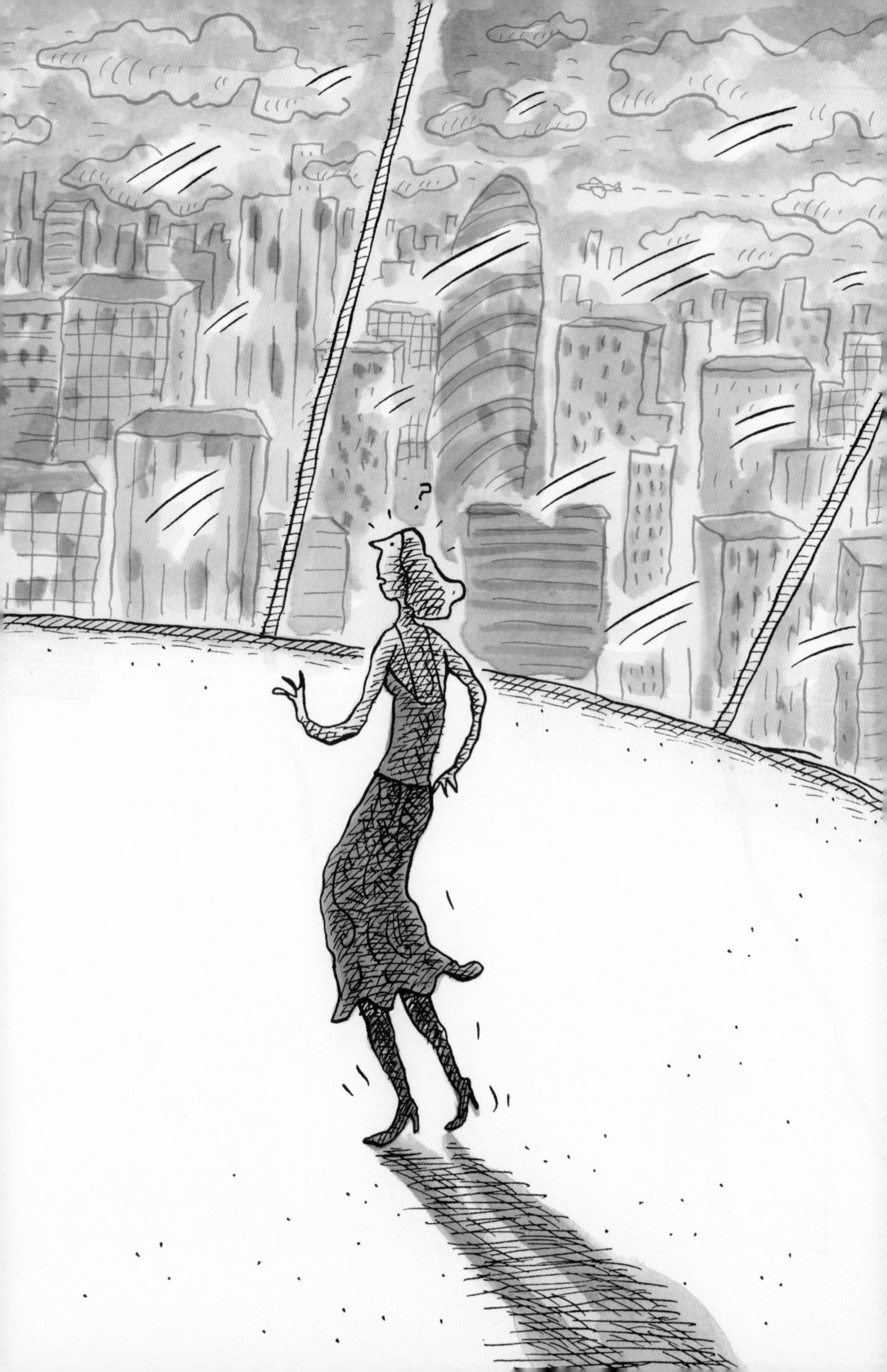

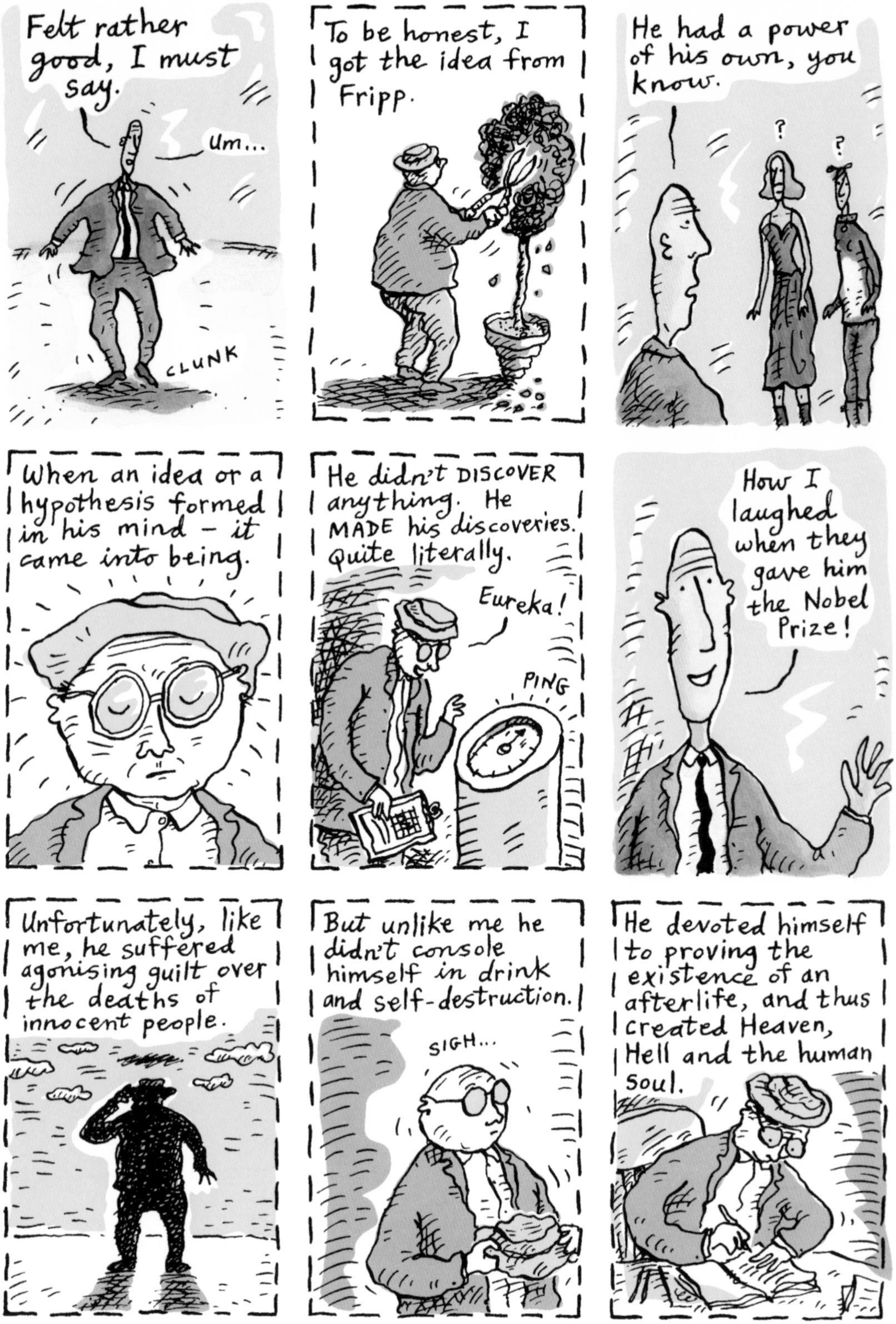
Felt rather good, I must say.
Um...
CLUNK
To be honest, I got the idea from Fripp.
He had a power of his own, you know.
?
?
When an idea or a hypothesis formed in his mind – it came into being.
He didn't DISCOVER anything. He MADE his discoveries. Quite literally.
Eureka!
PING
How I laughed when they gave him the Nobel Prize!
Unfortunately, like me, he suffered agonising guilt over the deaths of innocent people.
But unlike me he didn't console himself in drink and self-destruction.
SIGH...
He devoted himself to proving the existence of an afterlife, and thus created Heaven, Hell and the human soul.

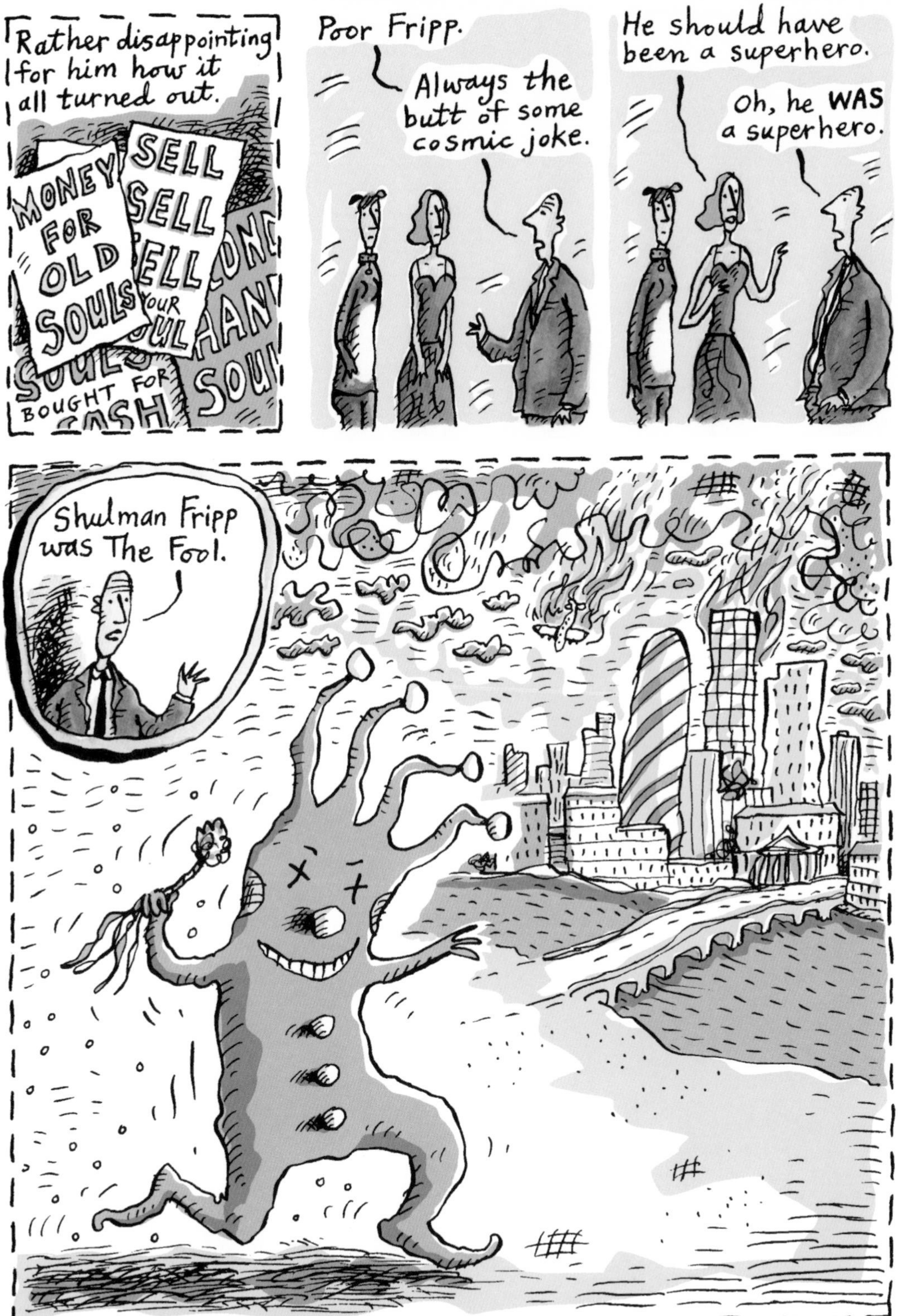

Rather disappointing for him how it all turned out.
MONEY FOR OLD SOULS
SELL SELL SELL SELL YOUR SOUL
SOULS BOUGHT FOR CASH
Poor Fripp.
Always the butt of some cosmic joke.
He should have been a superhero.
Oh, he WAS a superhero.
Shulman Fripp was The Fool.

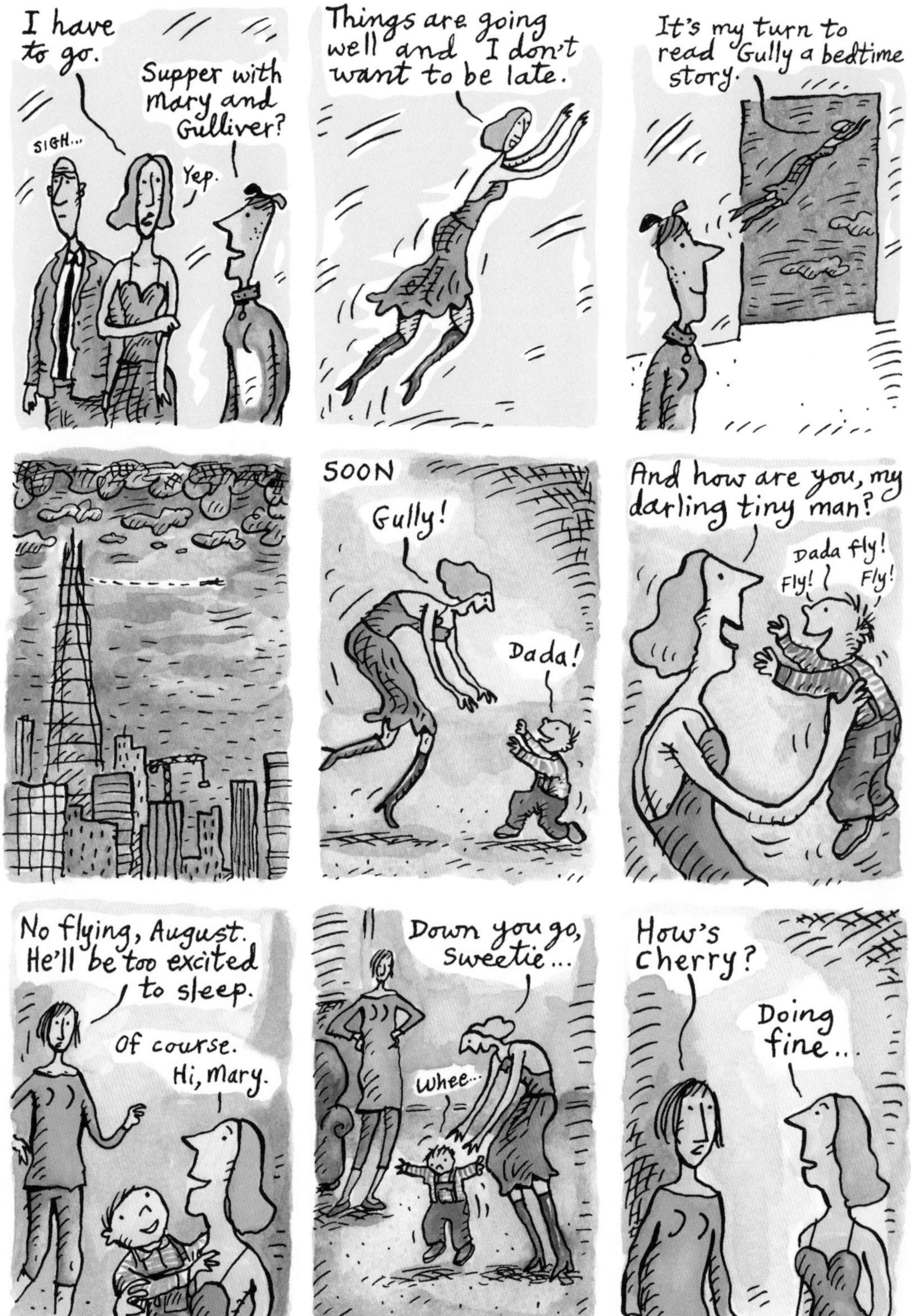
I have to go.
Supper with Mary and Gulliver?
SIGH...
Yep.
Things are going well and I don't want to be late.
It's my turn to read Gully a bedtime story.
SOON
Gully!
Dada!
And how are you, my darling tiny man?
Dada fly!
Fly!
Fly!
No flying, August. He'll be too excited to sleep.
Of course. Hi, Mary.
Down you go, Sweetie...
Whee...
How's Cherry?
Doing fine...

She'll be back at school soon.

Good.

Though there's a funny thing...

Her parents got their souls back... but they're changed.

more lemonade, darling?

Another cushion?

Thanks, Mum and Dad.

They've got new hobbies. New likes and dislikes.

I reckon there was a mix-up and they got the wrong souls.

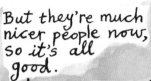

But they're much nicer people now, so it's all good.

Cool

Oh... Mary!

I've got something for you.

Well, for Gully, really.

The pipe should be dropping it off right about...

CRASH!!

ZAP! Now.

A pile of wood?

Not just wood. Screws, hinges, windows...

And a ladder.

The tree house!

317

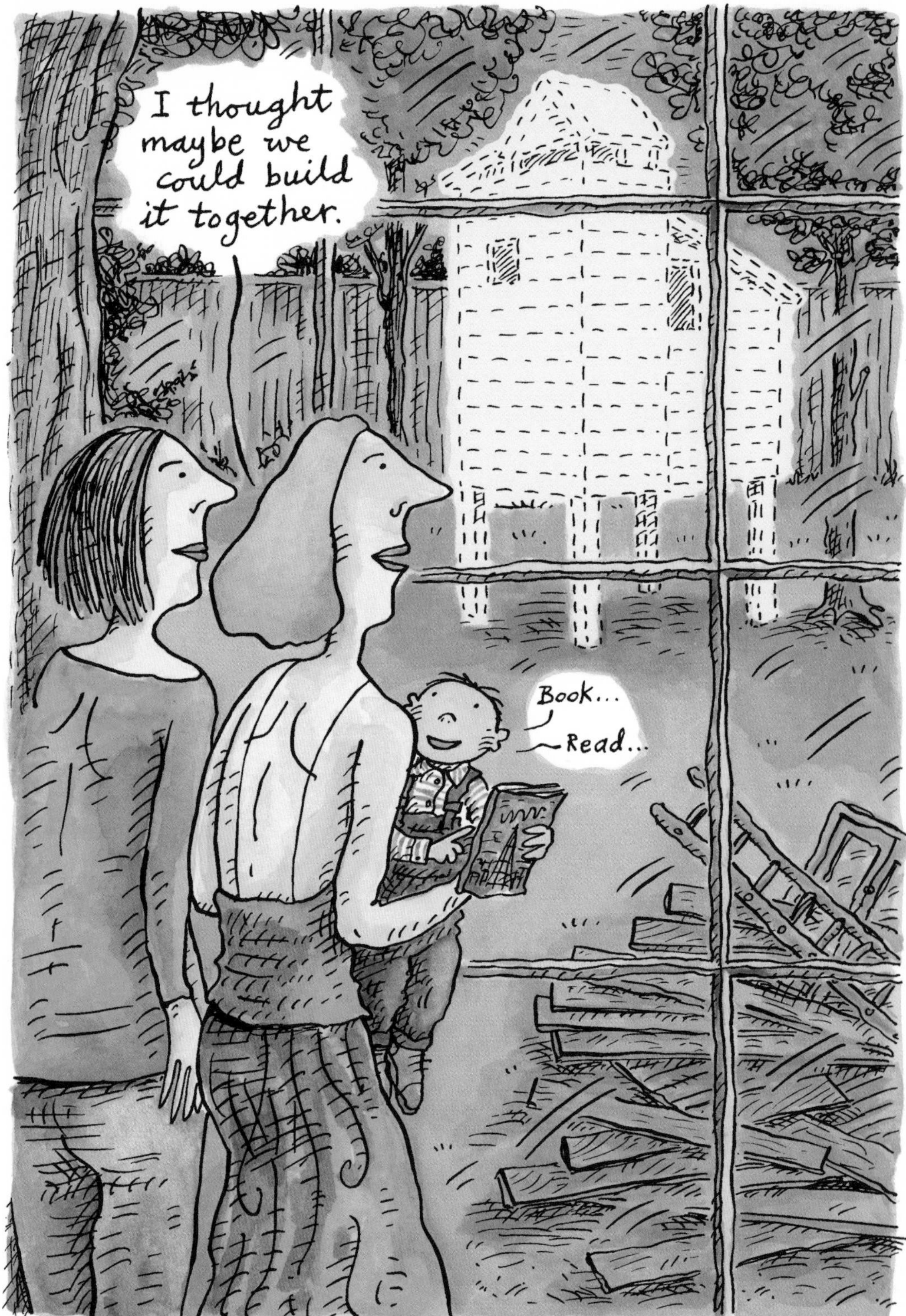
I thought maybe we could build it together.
Book...
Read...

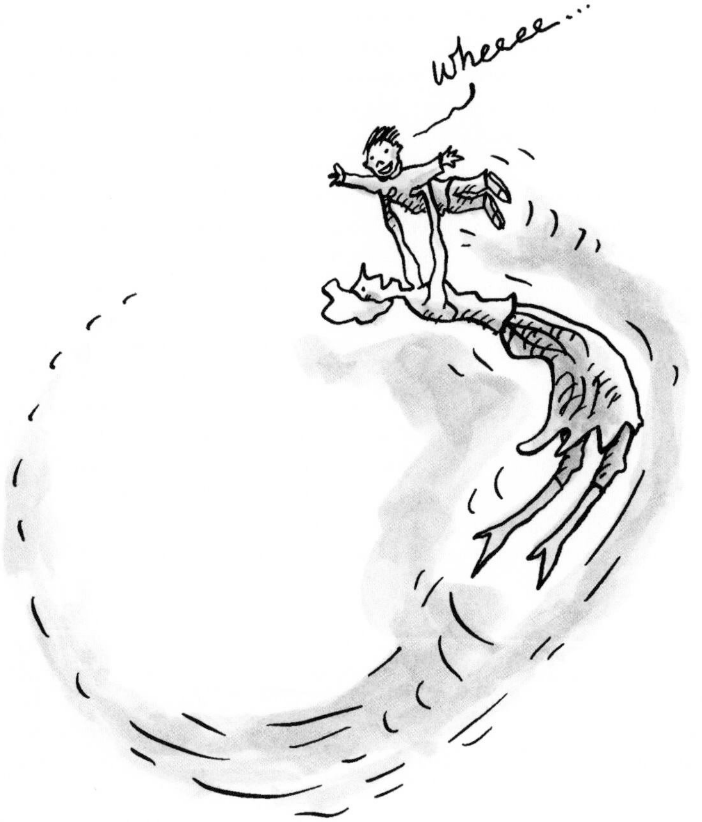
Wheeee…

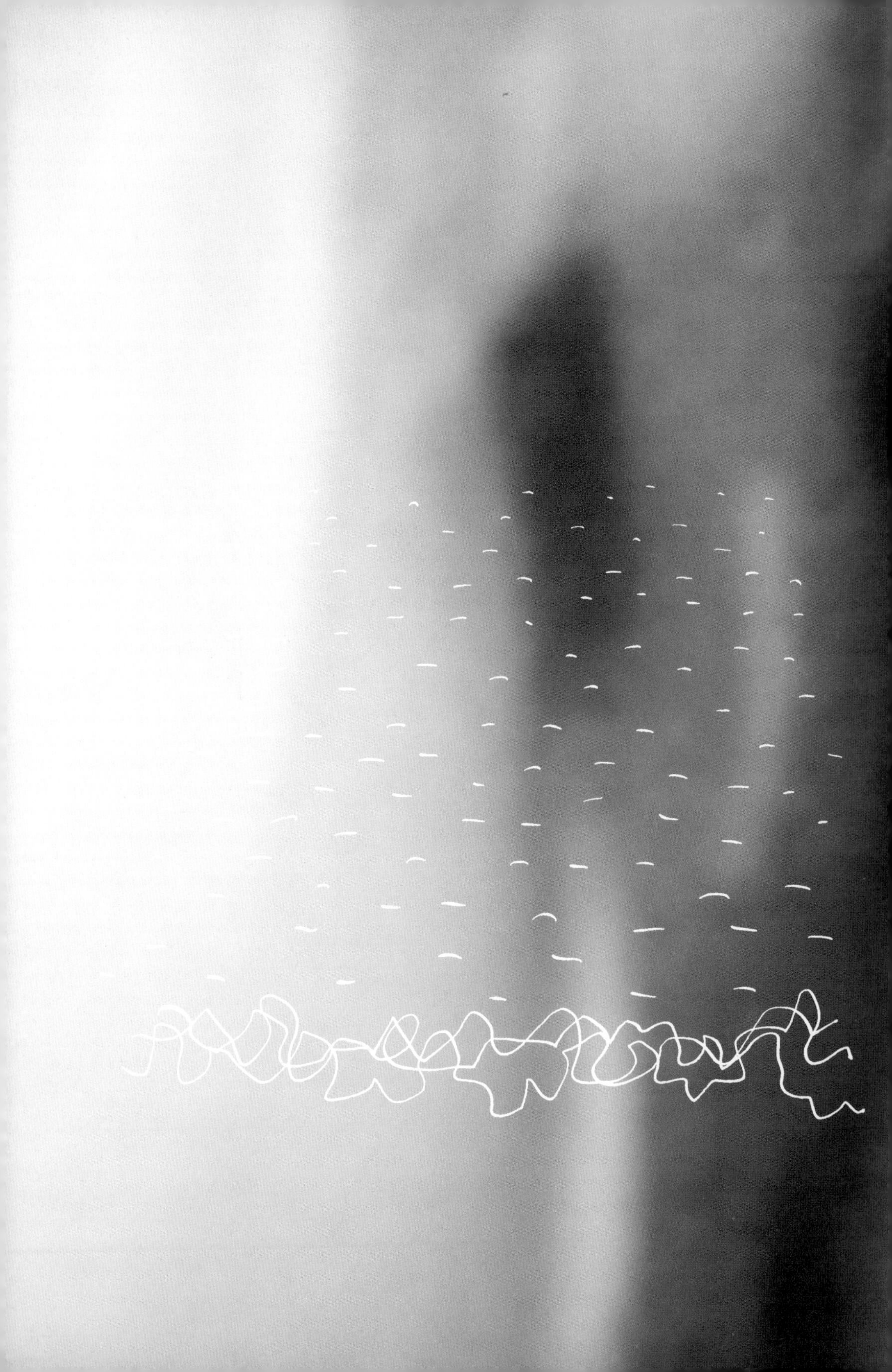

Epilogue

I walk with Mother along a beach and beside us the sea
writhes, reflecting the sky like bands of living light and
illuminating the black ruins of a few scattered wooden huts
that rise from the jagged seagrass and collapsed dunes
like burnt finger bones. As we get closer it becomes clear to me
where we are. This is the site of Hindsight's beach house,
now long gone, and I turn to Mother, watching her as she
stares at the remains.

'You're The Weathergirl, aren't you, Mother?'

'Ha, I used to be.'

'And this world that you and I share dreams about...'

'For you it's a dream. For me it's the world I live in.'

'The future?'

'Yes.'

'One of an infinite number of possible...'

'No, no. That's wrong. The future isn't like that. This is it.
One future.'

Mother picks up a shell – a long, flat, razor shell, wet from
the surf – and watches as it desiccates, starts to crumble into
sand, then solidifies back into a shell.

'The future isn't fixed, August. Events in the present continually change it until, for the briefest moment, it solidifies. Happens. Then it's gone, slipped away into memory.'

'So Hindsight was wrong. He said seeing the future was a useful skill.'

'He said that?' She casts the shell down, smashing it on a rock. 'Then yes, he was wrong. Seeing the future is like riding in a tiny boat, tossing and twisting as waves from the present hit it. It's a curse that, thankfully, I don't seem to have passed on to you. Except when you dream.'

She looks at me, making sure I'm paying attention.

'August, if it were possible to truly see the future, it would mean the loss of all hope.'

'Mother... perhaps you can help me out with something. I would have asked Hindsight but, well, he's not around any more.'

'What is it?'

'Years ago, someone told The Fist that my power came from wearing women's clothes. That's why I was thrown out of the club. I always thought it could only have been Hindsight, but...'

'It was me. I wanted you out of that superhero world

I knew what it was like and I never wanted you in it. But I was wrong. It turned out that the only way you could save yourself was to be yourself. To be Dragman.' She sighs. 'So much for seeing the future. Never trust it, August.'

I decide to bring up the subject that always hangs over us, unspoken, like twilight. Now or never.

'Mother...'

'No, August. I won't discuss your father.'

I stop walking and Mother recedes, a slight figure striding forward alone into the night. Some of the wooden houses stand upright now and, as I watch, their roofs reform, glass appears in the windows and yellow electric light glows out through the dark. Faint music from a radio passes me on the breeze and small children scatter among the dunes waving flashlights and shrieking as they play fox and chickens.

'Sorry...' I think I hear, blown back on the wind, then Mother is gone.

I finger the plastic and metal disc in my pocket – the disc that holds Hindsight's soul – and up ahead in the dunes I see Hindsight's beach house reconstructing itself. Then the lights come on.

Afterword...

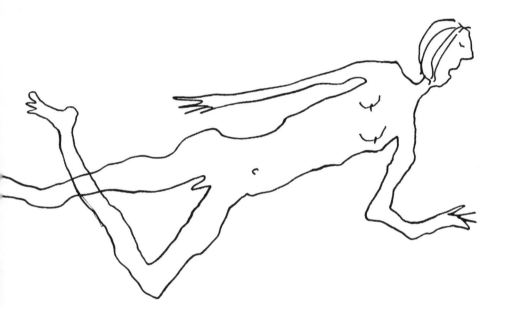

I am not August Crimp

I am not August Crimp... However, like August, I am
a man who wears women's clothes and, like August,
one day I found a stocking down the back of an old
sofa and instinctively put it on. Also, like August, I
agonised over why I wasn't content to be a boy. Maybe
there'd been a mess-up in my genes. Or something
had happened during my upbringing. Perhaps God
had made me like this. Or maybe I even, somehow
or other, decided it for myself. Whatever the reason
– and eventually I decided the reason didn't
matter – I found myself floating through
life wishing I'd been born a girl and, once
the idea occurred to me, dressing as one in
secret whenever the urge became too strong
to resist. Afterwards I would be filled with
feelings of sadness, fear and guilt. Sadness
at being back in the real world of my male
self. Fear of being discovered ... and guilt at
doing something I thought – no, I *knew* – was
perverted and abnormal. I was clearly sick in
the head.

Self-portrait polaroid,
c. 1986

Back then, in the late 1960s and 70s, transvestism
was on a very long, alphabetical list of sexual
deviations. There were certainly no role models for a
teenage boy obsessed with dressing as a girl.

The only cross-dressers I ever saw were men playing women for laughs in films or on television. Female impersonators like Danny La Rue or comedians in the *Carry On* films or *Monty Python's Flying Circus*. I was convinced that, dressed as a woman, I must look utterly ridiculous. A joke.

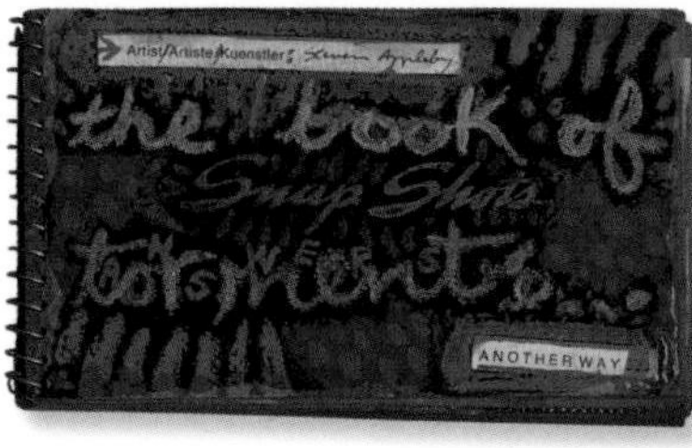
ANOTHER WAY

Art school, c. 1979

In the 1980s I moved to London where, in a remainder bookshop, I found a copy of *Dressing Up*, Peter Ackroyd's 1979 history of transvestism and drag, where I learnt that for centuries, in almost every country in the world, men and women had worn each other's clothes ever since clothes had been invented. It seemed I wasn't quite as weird and alone as I'd thought.

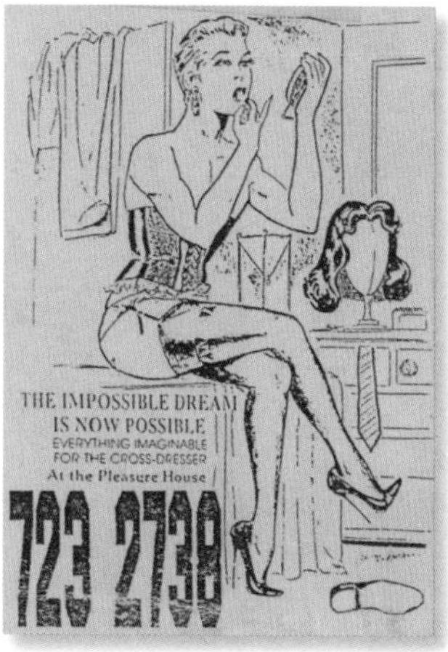
THE IMPOSSIBLE DREAM
IS NOW POSSIBLE
EVERYTHING IMAGINABLE
FOR THE CROSS-DRESSER
At the Pleasure House
723 2738

Flyer, London, 1980s

In the mid 1980s my work began to be published in newspapers and magazines and I couldn't resist slipping my dressing-up obsession into my comic strips – disguised, of course. Humans who feel compelled to dress as plants or fish; aliens who camouflage themselves as coat-hangers; dissatisfied items of furniture – chairs, for example – who yearn to be tables. In my cartoons, as in the real world, things were not always quite what they seemed.

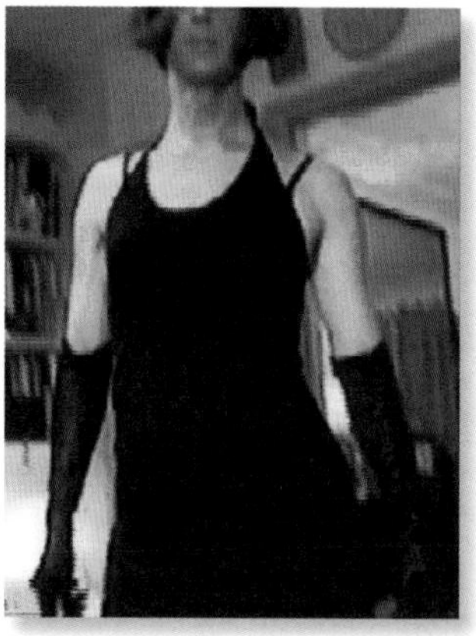

Steven, c. 1994

And then, in the 1990s, the internet arrived. One idle evening it occurred to me to type the word *transvestite* into an early search engine – and everything changed. Hundreds and thousands of pages of hits came down the wires and filled up my computer screen. Millions of men just like me were out there wearing women's clothes behind closed curtains and locked doors. Not only was I not alone, I was one of many. If I was a pervert, then I was in the company of countless numbers of other perverts. Slowly I started seeing cross-dressing as a positive, magical thing rather than a curse. I began thinking of myself as transforming from a man into an exotic, mythical creature, like a centaur, perhaps, only part-boy/part-girl, rather than part-boy/part-

aaaaaaagh!!

Mrs Plant-person finds out that her husband is really an alien life-form.

SATURDAY-SUNDAY APRIL 14-15 1990

Guardian, April 1990

goat. In my head, putting on the clothes of the opposite sex gradually shifted from being a sickness to feeling like a delightfully naughty blessing. Dressing up was a way of stepping through a wardrobe from one world into another. It was liberating – and FUN.

I always dress as a fish in the privacy of my own room...

Captain Star, Germany, late-1980s

Transvestites began making appearances in my books and comic strips. A female version of myself featured in an episode of my BBC Radio 4 series, *Steven Appleby's Normal Life*, and a musical play based on my work was titled *Crocs in Frocks*. But by the early 2000s I'd had enough of leading a double life. Cross-dressing in secret once or twice a week felt dishonest and stifling. I'd learnt to be comfortable with being a transvestite and now I was desperate to be open and live as one. Also, I had young children and wanted them to grow up knowing their father as a complete person, not someone with a huge

SEXUAL TABOOS ~ no 1

How do you do?

a man, dressed as a woman, dressed as a man.

Sexual Taboos, Punch c.1990

LET'S JOIN DRAGMAN AS HE SAVES SOME FASHION VICTIMS.
Oh no, that's tragic!!
Steven Appleby
I'm only just in time! You look a FRIGHT in that shirt!
DRAGMAN!
SOON.
Tut tut! Those overalls don't go with your eyes, Farmer Fred!
?
AND...
Someone with your skin colour should NEVER wear grey pinstripe!
LATER.
Hurrah!
Thank you, Dragman!
Another mission accomplished.
You've saved me from drab conformity at the bank!

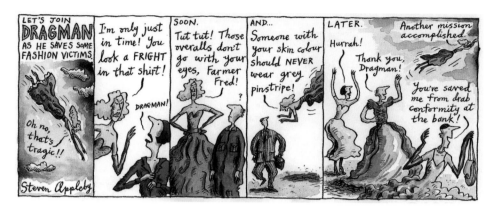

First 'Dragman' strip, Guardian, 2002

secret which would, inevitably, one day come out... And what effect might that have on our relationship? So I took to wearing androgynous clothes, jewellery, nail varnish and make-up and began opening up about my transvestism to family, friends and employers. Thankfully, I never had a bad response.

Finally, in 2007, I started dressing as a trans-woman all the time and for many years now haven't owned a single item of male clothing. I'm trying to be *me*, so am comfortable looking feminine but continuing to be called Steven. Surely there don't need to be any rules?

CROCS IN FROCKS
(or) THE KNITTING PATTERN ATROCITIES
FROM THE SECRET WORLD OF Steven Appleby
AN ENTERTAINMENT FOR ADULTS BY NPV AT MAGIC EYE THEATRE
BOX OFFICE: 020 7708 5401

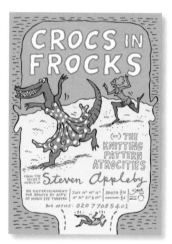

'Crocs in Frocks' poster, 2006

Incidentally, like August, I married a carpenter – but just as I'm not August, my wife isn't the model for Mary Mary.

Funny old world...

Steven Appleby, 2019

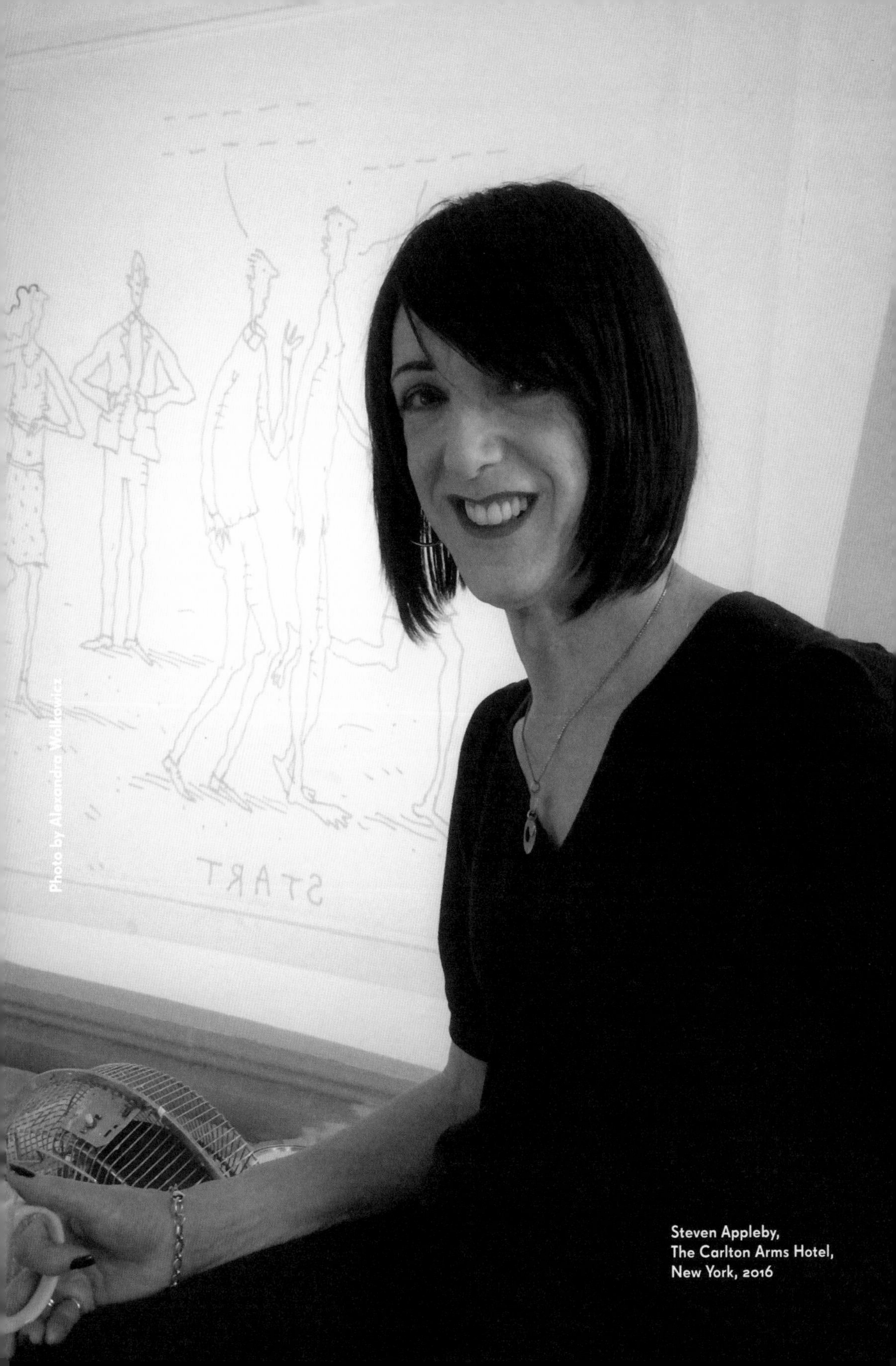

Photo by Alexandra Wolkowicz

Steven Appleby,
The Carlton Arms Hotel,
New York, 2016

Thank you...

...for buying and reading 'Dragman'. I hope you enjoyed it.

Creating this book has been a long and unusually difficult process for me, taking eighteen years from the initial appearance of a simple, humorous version of 'Dragman' in my Guardian comic strip, to the three hundred-odd pages you now hold in your hands. Perhaps I found it hard because 'Dragman' is my first long-form, narrative-driven graphic novel. Or perhaps because its central character, August Crimp, struggles with issues very close to my own. Whatever the reason, I set the book aside numerous times and would probably never have completed it were it not for the help, encouragement and bullying of the many people listed below. I hope I haven't forgotten anyone. If I have, I apologise very humbly and sincerely.

Thank you...
to **Nicola Sherring**, colourist extraordinaire and the mother of my children, without whose presence in my life most of my work would have been different and without whose constant support my trans-life couldn't have flourished as it has and this book would not be what it is; to my sons, **Jasper** and **Clem**, and stepsons, **Tom**, **Alfie** and **Stan**, for listening to my moaning, encouraging me and putting up with me shutting myself away for months on end to 'live in the world of the book'; to my dear, dear friend and collaborator **George Mole**, with whom I worked on numerous books and cartoon series and, for a while, on 'Dragman' – until it headed down a path that I felt was mine alone, and for which I apologise; to **Patrick Walsh**, my wonderful agent and friend who encouraged, cajoled, badgered, pushed, bribed, threatened and flattered this book out of me over many, many years and many, many lunches and suppers; to **Dan Franklin** at Jonathan Cape who was told, back in 2011, that he'd be seeing a first draft within a few months and who patiently hung in there and waited. And waited; to **Linda McCarthy**, my cousin and Small Birds Singing film maker, for a lifetime of love, support and meals as I worked in the thinking shed in the woods behind her house; to **Pete Bishop**, for his fizzing creative honesty and never-failing support in over thirty years of collaboration and friendship; to **Karen Brown**, for years of encouragement, the loan of her house to write in, and for tough words when only tough words would do; to **Art Lester**, for evenings given over to endlessly discussing ideas, patiently reading drafts, and putting up with years of moaning self-doubt; to trusted friend **Nick Battey**, for reading early versions and fragments

was invaluable and changed the course of the book; to dear **Kasper de Graaf** for reading drafts and always answering my cries for help; to **Cathy Huszar**, for running my studio and my life – as well as helping bring up my kids; to **Andrea Mason**, of Literary Kitchen, for the deadlines and wise advice of her creative writing course and for letting me chatter through endless dog walks and tea-drinking sessions; to **Jess Crimp**, for bringing August Crimp alive by allowing me to borrow her surname; to my friend **John Shirley**, who I wish could have read this book so we could chat about it but, sadly, that will never happen; to **Dr Nicola Streeten**, for invaluable help and advice with my Arts Council application and subsequent public engagements; to **Michelle Ross**, from trans-health organisation CliniQ, for reading and discussing drafts; to **Ruth Keen**, my German translator and friend, for years of unswerving positivity; to **Neil Bradford** and all at Jonathan Cape for taking this book from my head and helping it become the physical object you now hold in your hands; to **Altaimage** for the beautiful colour reproduction; to **Faith Penhale** and **Will Johnston** at Lookout Point TV for believing in me and 'Dragman'; to **Jean-Luc Fromental** at Denoel; to **Merijn Hollestelle** at Podium; and to **Riva Hocherman** at Metropolitan Books for her trust in me and her uplifting comments exactly when I needed them; to **Malcolm Garrett** and **Jane Plüer** for invaluable design advice and to anyone else who has helped, encouraged, read a draft, or just listened to me go on and on about it, including... **John Ash** and **Margaret Halton** at PEW Literary; **Luke Speed**, **Alexandra McNicoll**, **Alexander Cochran** and **Jake Smith-Bosanquet** in the rights departments of Conville & Walsh and Curtis Brown; to **Jo Unwin**, who many years ago said I should make 'Dragman' into a book; to **Julie Tait**, of LICAF; and to **my siblings, family, friends, neighbours, local shops, clients, work colleagues** and **everyone I come into contact with during day-to-day life**, including the real **Junction Jazz Bar**. I cannot express how much I appreciate that you took in your stride my decision to come out as a transvestite in the 1990s and, subsequently, to live 24/7 as a trans-person from summer 2007. I can honestly say that I haven't had a bad experience during these past twenty years. And finally: thank you to all the **cross-dressers, drag queens, t-girls, transwomen** and **transmen** I have met over the past twenty years whose friendship has informed and enriched my life immeasurably.

Metropolitan Books
Henry Holt and Company
Publishers since 1866
120 Broadway
New York, New York 10271

Metropolitan Books® and m® are registered trademarks of
Macmillan Publishing Group, LLC.

Watercolour colouring by Nicola Sherring
Digital colouring by Steven Appleby
Colour retouching by Steven Appleby and Clem Appleby
Cover by Steven Appleby
Typographical design by Jane Plüer
Distributed in Canada by Raincoast Book Distribution Limited

Library of Congress Cataloging-in-Publication Data

Names: Appleby, Steven, author, artist.
Title: Dragman : a novel / Steven Appleby.
Description: New York : Metropolitan Books/Henry Holt and Company, 2020. |
Identifiers: LCCN 2019036640 (print) | LCCN 2019036641 (ebook) | ISBN
  9781250172648 (hardcover) | ISBN 9781250172655 (ebook)
Subjects: LCSH: Graphic novels.
Classification: LCC PN6737.A67 D73 2020 (print) | LCC PN6737.A67 (ebook)
  | DDC 741.5/942—dc23
LC record available at https://lccn.loc.gov/2019036640
LC ebook record available at https://lccn.loc.gov/2019036641

Our books may be purchased in bulk for promotional, educational, or business use. Please
contact your local bookseller or the Macmillan Corporate and Premium Sales Department at
(800) 221-7945, extension 5442, or by e-mail at MacmillanSpecialMarkets@macmillan.com.

Printed in China

1 3 5 7 9 10 8 6 4 2

ABOUT THE AUTHOR

STEVEN APPLEBY is a cartoonist and illustrator who has created comic strips for the *Guardian*, the *Times*, and *New Musical Express*, among numerous other periodicals. He has also created and written a comedy series for BBC Radio 4 and a highly successful animated television series, *Captain Star*; he collaborated on a musical play, *Crocs in Frocks*; and he regularly exhibits paintings and drawings. He lives in London.

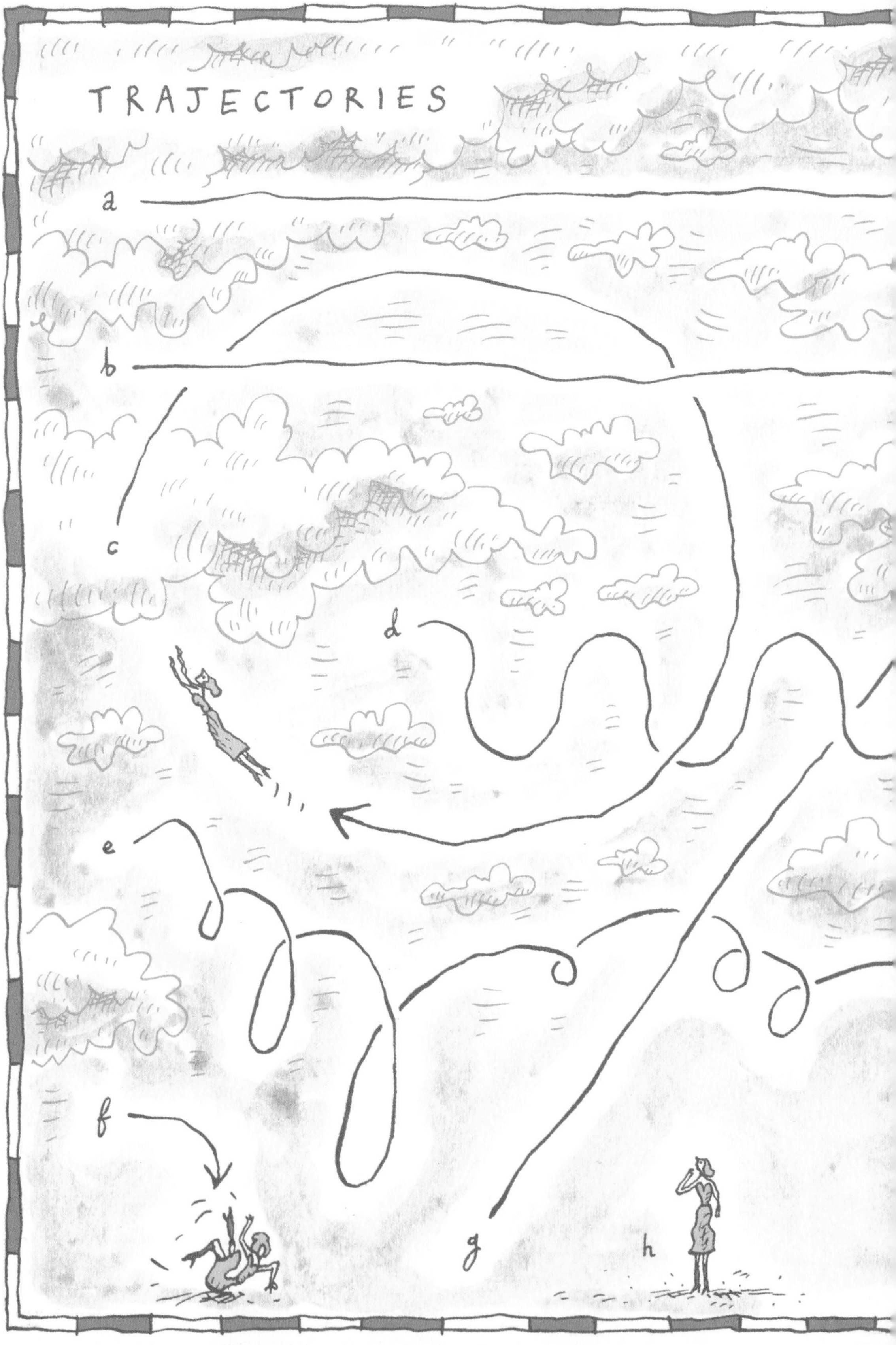
TRAJECTORIES
a
b
c
d
e
f
g
h